GREGORY ZILBOORG, M.D. (1890-1959) was born in Russia and attended the Psychoneurological Institute of St. Petersburg. Coming to the United States, he obtained a medical degree from the College of Physicians and Surgeons of Columbia University and from 1926 to 1931 he was on the staff of Bloomingdale Hospital, New York City. He studied in Berlin at the Psychoanalytic Institute and taught at the State University of New York, New York Medical College, Fordham University, St. John's University, and the University of Montreal. He translated important works from both Russian and German and was the author of many books and articles. His publications include: *The Medical Man and the Witch During the Renaissance* (1935); *The History of Medical Psychology* (1941); *Mind, Medicine and Man* (1943); *The Psychology of the Criminal Act and Punishment* (1954); *Sigmund Freud* (1951); and *Freud and Religion* (1958).

A History of

MEDICAL
PSYCHOLOGY

GREGORY ZILBOORG, *M.D.*

The Norton Library
W · W · NORTON & COMPANY · INC ·
NEW YORK

L'histoire rend manifestes nos erreurs.
L'histoire nous rend modestes et fait
entrer en nous la persuasion, que l'er-
reur est loin d'être une exception.

F. DEL GRECO

CONTENTS

7

FOREWORD

THESE pages owe their existence not only nor even primarily to those who wrote them. To a number of persons, some no longer living, gratitude is due for guidance, moral support, and inspiration. The first notes outlining the book were penned late in 1926; the first person to be consulted on the subject was Dr. Thomas W. Salmon, then professor of psychiatry at the College of Physicians and Surgeons in New York. Dr. Salmon's responsive encouragement did much to put into effect the plan of writing a history of medical psychology. He was an eager, serene enthusiast and tireless. To him psychiatry was a specialty dealing with the living psychology of living people; it was devoid of formalism or rigid classificatory bureaucracy. Psychiatric education, organization of research, and mental hygiene were to him dynamic forces. He saw clearly that the history of medical psychology is the rational foundation of psychiatry. Unfortunately, he died in 1927 before it was possible to submit to him any of these pages, but his moral and intellectual support proved invaluable. Also, it was through Dr. Salmon that it became possible to do a great part of the preliminary work on this book under the protective roof of Bloomingdale Hospital, now the Westchester Division of the New York Hospital. It was while there that I asked my colleague on the staff, Dr. George W. Henry, then Director of the Laboratory, to prepare some special chapters [excluded from this edition].

To Dr. Mortimer W. Raynor, then Medical Director of Bloomingdale Hospital, particularly grateful acknowledgment is due. Guide and friend, he was keenly interested in the progress of this book and he was the first to read some of its chapters; he followed the growth and the vicissitudes of the manuscript with enthusiasm and the fraternal pride so characteristic of his attitude toward any younger colleague who was engaged in a new study. More than anyone else, Dr. Raynor was helpful with advice and counsel. He was respectful of our psychiatric past and solicitous that its record be preserved. He collected many notes and uncovered valuable material for the history of Bloomingdale Hospital which he hoped to write some day. He always wished that this book might have been completed sooner; many of his plans and hopes for it were brought to naught by his untimely death in 1935.

One also feels deeply indebted to the many pioneers in the field who proved of invaluable assistance in the laborious and slow work of collecting the material for this book. Since no history of medical psychology was available as a guide, the task proved more complex than originally foreseen; the clinicians of the past century were more aware of the value of psychiatric history than our generation, and they broke the ground and laid the first stones in the foundation of a comprehensive history of psychiatry which was and still is to be written. Jelliffe's translation of Friedreich some twenty-five years ago offered valuable source material but no true historical perspective. Kannabich's history of psychiatry which appeared in Russian in 1928 presents a useful compilation, the first in several generations; it is, however, too condensed to serve as a source book. Research in this field has not yet been properly systematized. Friedreich, Calmeil, Lélut, Trélat, and particularly Armand Semelaigne and his son René were the pioneers of historical psychiatric research and they are still the exemplary representatives in the field. Nor can one pass over without a thought of gratitude the historical essays of D. H. Tuke and of Theodore Kirchhoff.

As to the plan of this book, a glance at the table of contents will make it clear. It is intended to serve as an introductory historical survey of medical psychology rather than of psychiatry. "Psychiatry" is a term hardly one hundred years old and it now designates more the specialty than the whole field of abnormal psychology and the contingent mass of practical and theoretical problems. Historically the term "medical psychology," or "psychological medicine," is older and more comprehensive.

Dr. Henry's two chapters are an important beginning of the historical evaluation of a very significant part of psychiatric history, the part marking the age-long effort which finally succeeded in establishing the specialty of psychiatry by differentiating organic mental disorders from neuroses and psychoses and by transforming asylums into hospitals. There are many more chapters to be written by the future historian—such as those on psychiatric education, on such modes of auxiliary treatment as occupational therapy, or on psychiatric nursing—which are outside the scope of this book. If these be omissions, they are deliberate omissions which, it is deemed, will add to the clarity of the historical perspective rather than detract from it. There are other omissions which were made with the same intention: for instance, mention of the great educational influence of Elmer E. Southard who brought up a whole generation of brilliant contemporary American psychiatrists. American psychiatry has of necessity to be viewed only as part of an immense whole and not as a separate unit. It not only deserves to but must be treated as a separate subject, and to do it justice a special history of American psychiatry should be written. Fortunately, plans for such a history are being considered now. The historical consciousness of American psychiatry is reflected in the recent appointment by the American Psychiatric Association of a special committee on the history of psychiatry. It is in a future historical survey of American psychiatry that the inception and the development of mental hygiene will find an honorable place. The mental hygiene movement is typically American in its pioneering spirit; it is a topic apart and can not therefore be included in a brief general history of medical psychology. Mental hygiene is, moreover, so recent and so vigorous a phenomenon that no proper historical evaluation of it is possible at this date. The dynamic and creative leadership of Clifford Beers, Thomas W. Salmon, and Frankwood E. Williams opened many new fields of activity such as child guidance and preventive psychiatry, which bid fair to be two of the chief instruments for combining sociological and psychiatric research. The history of this extension of psychiatry is being made under our own eyes and it must await its special student.

For the quality of the final manuscript I am deeply indebted to Miss Margaret Norton Stone and Miss Suzette Watson. The checking of names, dates, quotations, as well as the reading of proofs, they performed with painstaking and intelligent industry and an excellent sense of accuracy.

Gregory Zilboorg

New York
October, 1941

A History of

MEDICAL PSYCHOLOGY

1

PROLOGUE

I

A FEW days before his death, in 1776, David Hume wrote to the Comtesse de Boufflers, "My disorder is a diarrhoea, or disorder of my bowels, which has been gradually undermining me these two years; but within these six months, has been visibly hastening me to my end. I see death approaching gradually without anxiety or regret. I salute you with great affection and regard for the last time."

Traditionally one could not wish for greater detachment in a historian. Yet one wonders whether this attribute is to be found in the majority of historians or scientists; moreover, it is questionable whether it is even a desirable attribute. This ideal detachment denotes a certain lack of feeling—it is cerebration, pure, unadulterated. A historian can ill afford to review the events of the human past with the cold eye of an observer unconcerned and unaroused. Events are results of human drives, passions; they are charged with the intensity of human needs, of anxieties, loves, hatreds, ambitions, and failures. To look upon these events as if they were dots on a chart or figures on a statistical table means to miss the most essential aspect of man's business of living and, in the long run, means to miss the essence of history. More than that, detachment is frequently but a mask for narrowness of vision. Since it is almost impossible to divest one's self of one's habits of thought, complete detachment easily becomes indifference to everything that does not fit into the rut of conveniently invisible prejudice. The historian of this type is a one-sided chronicler or narrator who misses a great deal of the inner content, even if he does present all the available facts. He represents a species of dispassionate inflexibility. "How can one fail to miss a great deal if one persists in considering the world from one side or the other of the House of Commons?" (The question is posed by Lytton Strachey in his essay on Macaulay.) Narrow horizons and barrenness of perspective begin to encroach and impede the very understanding for which history is studied and written.

If proper enjoyment and enlightenment are to be derived from the reading and writing of history, one must mobilize, not anesthetize, one's feelings, revitalize all strivings, even weaknesses and passions; otherwise it will be totally impossible to put one's self in the place of Alexander the Great or Jesse James or Cromwell or Julius Caesar or the humblest slave of ancient Rome. Without pluralistic partiality, one is bound to become amorphously impartial and to miss the very thing that one has set out to learn—history.

This seemingly paradoxical suggestion may arouse opposition and an attempt on the part of the reader to reassert the traditional view that only a detached report of the facts of the past is true history. One would have then to recall once again the wisdom of Lytton Strachey: "Facts relating to the past, when they are collected without art, are compilations; and compilations, no doubt, may be useful, but they are no more history than butter, eggs, salt and herbs are an omelette." The art is not only intuition combined with enlightened intelligence and skill, but the ability to feel the fact relating to the past, to absorb and to reconstruct the inner atmosphere of an endless series of events. One must be particularly vigilant in this respect when dealing with medical history.

Man has always feared illness and has always admired healers; he is apt to look at the story of medicine with one-sided contempt or one-sided admiration. Because Ambroise Paré was a great physician, the father of modern surgery, we generally overlook his conviction that the devil caused women to become witches and that witches should be destroyed and not treated as sick people. We thus have two different presences of Ambroise Paré: one a scientific, benevolent court doctor of the sixteenth century and the other an obscurantist, an intolerant and heartless courtier who tried to poison the royal mind with the Levitical injunction, "Thou shalt not suffer a witch to live." If we recall that this state of affairs existed almost one hundred years after Agrippa and Weyer had proclaimed a humanistic and psychiatric point of view in the medical world, then to overlook the murmurings of Paré's prejudices means to ignore the tenor of an entire period of medical history and to misunderstand the whole spirit of medicine. Vital details and factors are frequently disregarded because of our singular psychology in relation to our past. Of this psychology we must take frank cognizance.

Before becoming a part of our past, a thing is a part of our present. After an initial thrust of opposition to anything that is new, we may accept and even admire it as a novelty and an accomplishment. For a time we delight in it, until the sense of newness is worn off and another fashion is born. At this point the former novelty becomes "old-fashioned"—an epithet which connotes benevolent and at times not so benevolent contempt. The hat we admired last year begins to look funny, then queer, then ridiculous. Finally, when it is quite unacceptable, it is cast into oblivion; it becomes part of the past. After a certain time has elapsed, if the hat happens to be unearthed, we find that we neither admire it as we once did, nor do we treat it with the various gradations of contempt which we had experienced during the period of transition. Instead we look upon it with a friendly smile; we call it "quaint," "delightful." It amuses us and captivates our fancy; it has become an antique. We wear it no more but we keep it. We become collectors. We like to look at the old hat every now and then and thus revive and relive a phase of our past. All this is equally true of a piece of furniture, an almost illegible book, a threadbare rug, an ancient legend, events of great or small magnitude which we collectively call history.

The business of collecting is of immense psychological value to us. Through it we gratify, among other things, one of our most potent strivings—the need to maintain our spontaneous conviction that we are right and good, that we are better than we have been, that we are getting on. True, we are inclined to idealize "the good old days," but in truth we do not want to see them return. We proclaim the merits of the past to emphasize the greater merits of the present. This trend is in a major degree responsible for our sustained interest in history, particularly in medical history. We give due credit to the great doctors of the centuries gone by. We erect monuments to them and write their biographies, but we never fail to state that they were products of their age and in many respects did not know any better; naturally they were ignorant of the things which have led us to make this or that discovery. The undercurrent of condescending admiration cannot help but blur our perspective, since it seems to be exerted only in order to gratify our self-inflationary propensities. If history is to serve its true purpose of enlightenment, more than a mere warning is needed before we become capable of discounting our trend toward self-aggrandizement, before we can understand the insight of Emile Littré who wrote one hundred years ago, "If the science of medicine is not to be lowered to the rank of a mere mechanical profession, it must preoccupy itself with its history. . . . The pursuit of the development of the human mind, this is the role of the historian." We may add that this type of historical preoccupation will make us more humble.

What is true of history in general and of medical history is even more incontrovertibly tenable in the history of medical psychology or psychiatry. Here the compilation or cataloguing of events and chronological data will serve scant if any purpose. Mere arrangement of the happenings of the past in the form of a backdrop for the pageant of a self-appreciatory present would produce little more than a heavy veil over the real meaning of the complex and unfinished task of solving the problems presented by mental disease. The task of the pages which follow is not to justify the present but to understand it, to apprehend its obscurities, pitfalls, and the multiplicity of contradictions which arrange themselves in a great variety of constellations—psychological, social, and cultural—and which still stand like an invincible army actively defending the secret that is mental disease. To bear this purpose in mind means to accept an important amendment to the tradition of medical historical pursuits and to make history not a boast but a contemplative critical confession.

II

ALL these considerations are imperative when we deal with medical psychology, for the history of this branch of our curative endeavors is different both in spirit and substance from the history of general medicine or surgery. No matter how far back into the remote past we delve, the sick man has never doubted that he was sick. Whether the ailment was headache or fever, a broken leg or an abscess, man has always been aware of his pain. The stars and the moon and the sun were of little avail to him no matter how much he revered and worshiped them, and almost before he learned to raise his head from the cradle of primitive civilization he learned to ask others to relieve his physical distress. Whether he sought help of his companion of the forest or the desert, or of the primitive priest, the shaman, the medicine man, whether it was magic he desired or infusions of herbs, he was making the history of medicine: his very demand for help caused the appearance of primitive doctors. It may be said with considerable certainty that it was not the doctor who by some miracle of spontaneous generation appeared first on the scene and, inspired by a lofty love for suffering humanity, sought to alleviate pain and began to make medical discoveries. Guided from the very beginning by the demands of the patients, the doctor had to respond and to serve; it was his business at all times and at all costs to supply what the patient wanted. This particular type of relationship between patient and doctor was and still is the most potent stimulus to the progress of medicine and surgery. The doctor had to learn the best way to cure a disease; he had to recognize a new disease at the very moment of its appearance; he had to find out instantaneously, as it were, the secret of the new disorder and how to control it. The patient had no independent theories to offer; he was not interested in the theories of disease. He knew but one thing: he was in pain. He wanted but one thing: to be relieved. He readily submitted to the inhuman agony of amputation or the removal of a stone without an anesthetic in order to be rid of prolonged illness and pain.

More often than not, the patient trusted and idealized his doctor. Even in later centuries, when the doctor abandoned his mystical medical communion with supernatural spirits and became a layman, he was still considered an individual apart. He had to be a good man, an honest, pious, self-sacrificing person, one with more than a tinge of pompous dignity and social sainthood whom the community appointed to minister to the health of its members. The idealized character and way of life which were demanded by the patient of his doctor constitute a major factor in the ethical tradition of the medical profession as we have known it in a documentary way for almost three thousand years. The Hippocratic oath is not merely a dignified formulation of the high ethical standards of one great physician, not so much his own original conception, but rather the expression of a tradition which ailing human beings had imposed upon their healers. Throughout the centuries the standard of this compulsive heritage has undergone little modification. In the ninth century the great physician from Bagdad, Rhazes, recapitulated the criteria for discerning a good doctor and, Oriental though he was, reflected clearly the spirit of the Greek father of our European medicine. Rhazes cautioned the patient against a physician who is interested in poetry or in music, for it was his opinion that a doctor's mind should be on medicine and on medicine alone. Today we are still inclined to be suspicious of a doctor's professional ability and integrity if he takes active part in politics or writes novels. The patient demands a single-minded, almost monastic and priestly devotion to the ministry of healing.

If we turn to mental diseases, the picture of the historical process changes completely. In the first place, the mentally ill patient was not even aware that he was ill. If he had "lost his mind," he truly had no mind to appreciate the fact that it was lost. He became a person of different mind and temper, different in the opinion of those about him but not from the point of view of the patient himself. A man afflicted with a mental illness did not know that he was a "patient" and more frequently than not he violently protested against being called sick. In so far as he had become gradually or suddenly unlike other members of the community and yet appeared sound of wind and limb, he was feared, not pitied, and, in conformity with the animistic propensities of primitive cultures, he was looked upon as a bearer of supernatural power. If it was a benign power or spirit that possessed him, he was naturally to be admired and revered. If it was an evil spirit that had taken up residence within him, he was indulged in order to mollify the evil one and to avoid its revengeful scourge. It is easy to see that, whatever the spirit, the epileptic or the pathologically depressed or exhilarated man was looked upon as a superior person, endowed with powers, base or lofty but greater than those of the merely normal mortal. His illness was a secret, a mystery to be revealed to no layman and only in part to the priest. Before humanity began to presume that the initiated, the priests or the saints, could cast out the devil, it was considered a matter of course that the mentally sick were in some way too sacred and good or too powerful for anyone to venture to reduce them to the unblessed state of normalcy. In other words, from the very outset it was taken for granted that medicine had no power, even had no right, over the mentally sick. This unwritten dictum was potent enough not only to retard the introduction of medicine into the field of mental disease but actually to exclude it. The mentally sick patient cared not to hear about doctors and the frightened community dared not seek the help of medicine, lest this gross and crass profession desecrate the integrity of their animistic faith. Things of the spirit, of the supernatural, might not be touched by the hand of the earthy, materialistic, herb-brewing and urine-smelling medicine man.

The deeper causes for this sharp separation of medicine from mental illness do not concern us here. As the story of medical psychology unfolds itself, we hope these causes will become clearer but, whatever they may be, the very existence of the cleavage indicates what potent, almost insurmountable forces have always militated against a scientific understanding of mental diseases.

We must also bear in mind the obvious but so frequently forgotten fact that doctors are also human, regardless of how much they are idealized by actual or potential patients. They are also children of their own era and followers of the beaten path of a given culture. No wonder that the great men who represented medicine were for a long time of the same mind as the rest of the community. Fearful, they too were more than willing to leave the meek and the poor in spirit to the priest, to the self-appointed spiritual adviser or to the primitive and, later, civilized quack. From a thing of many good and evil spirits mental disease gradually evolved into a thing of the spirit, of the soul, and became insulated against any possible invasion by the inquiring scientist. Greek and Roman medicine and its offspring in northern Africa and, later, in the Arabian Empire were but a partial scientific diversion from the established tradition. Whether permitted to lodge and dance in the churches of patristic Christianity, whether burned to death at the stake, in the eyes of the whole civilized world the mentally ill remained beyond the pale of medical endeavor. These "supernatural" human beings, confronted by a world that closed its mind to them, were slow to gain their rights of citizenship in the kingdom of medicine. Even a pioneer like Felix Plater could not penetrate the thick walls of the confirmed order of misunderstanding. Plater (1536–1614) went so far as to live in the dark dungeons in which idiots and psychotics were kept. He was a serious doctor, endowed with a true medical curiosity, and he wanted to know how these wretches fared and what their troubles were. He came out of the dungeons refreshed with new observations but carrying with him into the open not a little of the darkness in which he had lived. He produced an acceptable classification of mental diseases and came to the conclusion that this terrible affliction must be the handiwork of the devil and not of natural causes. Plater was not an exception among his medical contemporaries and not without partisans for almost two centuries after his death. Two generations earlier Johann Weyer had already dared to state and had proven to the satisfaction of a few enlightened spirits that mental illness was a natural disease, just as natural as a headache or a wound filled with pus; but his voice, though strong and persuasive, was drowned in the calumny of Dominican fanatics, frightened citizens, irascible judges, and indignant lawyers. His books were forbidden, his opinions derided.

Volcanic passions raging with such destructive intolerance could not and cannot be the result of mere lack of knowledge. They indicate that some elemental force, some basic and blind human instinct must be touched by the very emergence of the problem of mental disease. The specific nature of this force does not concern us here, in this opening chapter, but we must take cognizance of its dynamic impetuosity and persistence in order to understand why psychiatry did not develop along the same lines as medicine and surgery. While the latter were created, stimulated, forced into being as it were by the sick man himself, psychiatry was a discovery of the medical man. He faced danger to his reputation and person when he tried to convince the world that the "insane" were ill and to convert the neurotic and the "insane" to the singular belief that they were sick people and could be treated as such and cured. The patient suffering from appendicitis created the abdominal surgeon, the feverish and delirious man who had a sharp pain in his chest created the specialist in pneumonias, but it was the doctor who created the specialty of psychiatry. He did it uninvited and against terrible odds, against the will of the public, against the will of established legal authority, and against the will of a variety of established religious faiths. With the co-operation of the City Council and Cardinal of Metz, Cornelius Agrippa narrowly escaped joining his forefathers by way of the stake (1519); Reginald Scot's *The Discoverie of Witchcraft* (1584), which meant the scientific unmasking of it, was ordered destroyed by King James I who wrote a refutation of Scot which is a reassertion of traditional demonology.

The process of opposing psychiatry has not lost its impetus and the conquest of the field of mental disease by medicine is far from complete. Today we are still ashamed to confess to a neurosis or a more serious mental illness; we conceal the fact of suicide as if it were still a true crime against God and the State. As in the remote past, we think of suicide as an act of either great courage or great cowardice. We either revive in ourselves the emotional memory of our primitive ancestors who could enter Valhalla only if killed in battle or by their own hand and who were, therefore, heroes of great courage, or we sense the rumbling memories of later centuries, when to kill one's self meant to shirk one's duty as a citizen whose life belonged to the State and to be, therefore, a coward and a sinner and not a sick man. Scoffingly, and with not a little anxiety, we still admonish the neurotic or the psychotic to "pull himself together," as if he were physically falling apart and could prevent it. Or we tell him to use his will power to give up his "notions," as if mental sickness were not an affliction but a perversion freely chosen and willfully adopted by the patient. This irrational struggle against medicopsychological intervention may explain the fact that in no other field of disease is there so much avoidance of medicine in the form of widespread quackery, that is, nonmedical philosophizing on "re-education," "psychological or psychoanalytic guidance" by various nonmedical amateurs, lay and clerical. In many respects these amateurs are more readily accepted by patients and their relatives than are psychiatrists and mental hospitals.

A visualization of this problem as it unfolds itself through the ages will make it clear that the story of medical psychology and the birth and development of psychiatry necessitate an approach entirely different from that required by the history of medicine and surgery. The latter could be told in the story of doctors and their endeavors, but the former requires an investigation into the development of culture, into some aspects of jurisprudence, theology, and philosophy. For a period of numberless centuries these branches of thought, and not medicine, dealt with mental disease. They claimed it theirs by right of eminent domain and they refused to admit the medical man or permitted him only a limited right of way.

2

❋ ❋ ❋ ❋ ❋ ❋ ❋ ❋ ❋ ❋ ❋

PRIMITIVE AND ORIENTAL
MEDICAL PSYCHOLOGIES

I

THE title of this chapter is, strictly speaking, a misnomer, for the primitive races of the remotest past did not think in medical or psychological terms as we do now. "That diseases abounded even in the imaginary Golden Age of early man, ten thousands of years ago, yes, even in the Paleozoic Era, millions of years before, is demonstrated by the investigations of human and animal remains of primordial and prehistoric times." [1] Tuberculosis, for instance, existed as far back as in the Stone Age.[2] The attitude toward disease, based not on the intellectual synthesis of observations, as it is today, was rather a spontaneous emotional reaction to pain; it was fear. The frightened man was driven into the realm of fantastic thinking. He knew very little, and the little he knew was merely a knowledge of self. He was unable to think of or to feel the outer world in other terms than those of himself and he populated this world with imaginary beings—useful ones, even as were some of his friends, and injurious ones, like many of his own hatreds. This is the psychological origin of the fantasies about good and evil

[1] Karl Sudhoff: *Essays in the history of medicine.* New York
[2] *Ibid.*, pp. 186 *et seq.*

27

the mystical cosmogony which has always been anthropomorphic. There was apparently no division into physical and mental diseases; sickness was all mental in the sense that primitive man might have used the word—spiritual or, rather, spiritistic. There is reason to believe that sick or old people were simply killed off [3] as annoying encumbrances. The mentally ill were probably no exception, although in some parts of China, for instance, the tradition of being kind to the mentally ill would suggest that murder was not the only treatment employed. As the development of the primitive man progressed, he soon discovered that one might influence the sick by means of what we call today hypnotism. The shamans of certain Siberian tribes definitely practiced hypnotism and in Cochin China, as well as in the eastern part of the Malay Archipelago, priests indulged in a form of hypnotic treatment, using an assistant as a medium.

Our knowledge of the primitive psychiatries is, however, less than fragmentary, although it seems fairly certain that the primitive man a very frightened human being and that his world was populated irits which were but images of his own anxiety. His psycholog- es were dedicated more to the problem of getting rid of the d fear generated by illness than to realistic efforts to ess itself. The cosmogonies and traditional medicine people extant bear witness to this attitude. vident five thousand years B.C. in the days of vptian medicine, and among those nations ivilization many centuries later. There is que Nationale in Paris which relates h Dynasty of Pharaohs; she was oniacal possession. The Egyp- her.

ent medicopsychological he earliest monotheistic

rvölker. In Neuburger and ɔ2, vol. I. Also, John Koty: völkern. Stuttgart, 1934.

nations, again we find little change. What has been said of the incidence of mental illness among primitive people and the Egyptians is true of the Jews of the scriptural ages. There was no dearth of clinical material. Hannah, the mother of the prophet Samuel, was apparently afflicted with a severe neurosis. Saul suffered from recurrent depressions, both homicidal and suicidal. Ezekiel was coprophagic. The ecstatic states of some of the prophets are very suggestive of pathological mental states. There is the report of David, who escaped from the captivity in which he was held by the king of Gath by feigning madness: "He . . . let his spittle fall down upon his beard," and the king of Gath said to his servants, "The man is mad." [4]

Observations on mental illness, the knowledge of certain clinical pictures, apparently were not wanting and were rather correct. As far as the understanding of mental diseases was concerned, however, scriptural psychiatry did not depart from tradition. "The Lord shall smite thee with madness, and blindness, and astonishment of heart." [5] This was not a metaphorical phrase; it was meant literally. Again, in Leviticus, it is plainly stated that "a man also or woman that hath a familiar spirit, or that is a wizard, shall surely be put to death: they shall stone them with stones: their blood shall be upon them." [6] Saul was believed to have the power of "an evil spirit from God."

We ought to make careful note of these pronouncements, particularly of the one in Leviticus, for they were destined to serve in centuries to come as a text to justify the execution of many a person who was mentally ill. In addition, they reveal clearly the hostility which has always been felt, wittingly or unwittingly, toward people afflicted with neuroses or psychoses. Many centuries passed before humanity made some headway along the road toward a more enlightened relationship to the mentally ill and before the defenseless and fearful "wild people" or "werewolves" were at last designated by the seemingly more sympathetic, although still contemptuous, "nut" or "fool" of today.[7] Time and again we shall meet with this hostility as a determinant of our medicopsychological thought—not only in the later Dark Ages, but at

[4] I Samuel 21: 14–15.
[5] Deuteronomy 28: 28.
[6] Leviticus 20: 27.
[7] M. Höfler: *Altgermanische Heilkunde*. In Neuburger and Pagel: *op. cit.*, vol. I, pp. 456–480.

the time of the American and French Revolutions, in the nineteenth century, and even in our own day.

Since man sought safety from his uncertainty and anxiety rather than control of the causes of his psychological difficulty, the general trend of the very early attitudes could not be anything but animistic. "The Scriptures present only one side of human life, that which concerns the idea of salvation; for the rest the treatment of man is incidental." [8] Yet our historical perspective would be warped indeed, if we gave the impression that the beginnings of man's contact with mental disease presented merely sterile fantasies of magic and animistic imagery. True, our civilization from the primitive man to early Hebraic culture contributed almost nothing to our understanding of psychological difficulties. But other cultures, though animistic and mystic, began to sense that there was a comprehensible meaning in what we call today neuroses and psychoses, and the intuitive perception which these cultures reveal was far from idle and vain speculation. The whole course of the history of medical psychology would remain unintelligible, or at least misunderstood, if we were to pass over as unimportant such cultures, for instance, as those of the Hindu and the early Greek.

III

THE Hindu medical system was very elaborate and complete.[9] The standard of medical ethics was high and does not suffer from comparison with that of Hippocrates.[10] The literature was voluminous; Liétard counts two hundred and thirty authors and five hundred titles. Moreover, while it is difficult to establish the exact chronology of Hindu medical writings, there is good reason to believe that Hindu medicine was an original system which developed independently of the Greek. This is an important point to remember, for we are accustomed to think of our knowledge as deeply rooted and having its source almost

[8] George Sidney Brett: *A history of psychology*. London, 1912, vol. I, p. 231.

[9] L. Cerise: *Notice sur les doctrines psycho-philosophiques des anciens philosophes hindous*. Annales Medico-Psychologiques. Paris, 1843, vol. II; 1884, vol. III.

[10] G. A. Liétard: *Le médecin Charaka. Le serment des hippocratistes et le serment des médecins hindous*. Bulletin de l'Academie de Médecine. Paris, 1897, pp. 565–575.

exclusively in Greek thought. As far as psychiatry is concerned, it is worth while to ponder over the possibility that Hindu thought, original and potent, traveled westward in the early centuries of our Christian Era by way of Persia, Greece, Africa (Alexandria), and Rome. At some unknown point and in some unknown manner it deeply affected our own European culture. We find many similarities in Hindu and Greek writings, but "some coincidences would appear rather to be that of observers of the same facts, than of borrowers from the same books. The description of some diseases which seem to have been first known in India, as well as internal administration of metals, they could not have borrowed from the Greeks." [11] The Hindus practiced rhinoplasty; they operated on cataracts; they were acquainted with vaccination; [12] in the *druvyabhidhana,* or their *materia medica, datura stramonium* was advised for asthma and *nux vomica* for paralysis and dyspepsia.[13]

Between this advance in medical science dealing with physical diseases and the status of psychopathology there existed a salient discrepancy. In the Hindu system, mental disorders remained largely within the domain of priestly metaphysics, an attitude which is to us of paramount importance. Without a clear understanding of this fact, many points in the future development of our medicopsychological ideas are bound to remain obscure. It is interesting to note that the origin of the Hindu medicine is connected with a legend reminiscent of a similar tradition regarding the birth of Greek medicine. The two Asvins, sons of Surya (sun), are suggestive of the two sons of Aesculapius, the godlike originator of the Greek art of healing who was himself a descendant of Apollo (sun). Apparently the problem of illness awakens in man, wherever and whoever he may happen to be, a definite reaction which is responsible for many similarities in the folklore and primitive sciences of people widely separated by oceans and continents. This phenomenon is indicative of a certain universality in human psychology of which we should never cease to be aware: similar emotional states produce similar deeply seated psychological reactions and imagery, regardless of many cultural and historical differences. It is thus possible for us to use the

[11] J. F. Royle: *An essay on the antiquity of Hindoo medicine.* London, 1837, p. 62.
[12] H. H. Wilson: *Oriental Magazine.* Calcutta, February and March, 1823. Quoted by Royle: *op. cit.,* note p. 56.
[13] Royle: *op. cit.,* p. 60.

history of the ancient philosophical psychologies as a source for our understanding of the problems with which medicopsychological sciences of today find themselves confronted.

IV

MEDICOPSYCHOLOGICAL ideas are found in profusion in the literary monuments of ancient India: the Vedas, the Code of Manu, Mahabharata, Ramayana. More specifically, the contributions of the Hindus are connected with the name of Suśruta, who lived apparently a hundred years before Hippocrates, and with that of Charaka. The fourth part of Yajur-Veda, "Buthavidya," deals with mental diseases proper and follows the traditional belief in demoniacal possessions. Suśruta, on the other hand, seems to be further advanced and may be said to forecast the psychopathology of the nineteenth and twentieth centuries. He suggests that passions and strong emotions might cause not only mental diseases but might even be responsible for certain physical conditions which require the help of surgery.

In brief outline, the main trend of Hindu medical psychology in certain respects parallels the Greek. The soul inhabits the cavity of the heart. It uses the body or various parts of the body as its instruments, but in addition it possesses an essential faculty called *manas*, which we would call perception. The soul also possesses *boudhi*, intelligence, and *ahankara*, consciousness. The principal vital act, physical or psychological, is *prana*—respiration. This concept may well recall the *pneuma* of Hippocrates.

"The innate dispositions of man are three in number: (1) wise and enlightened goodness—the source of equanimity; its seat is in the brain; (2) impetuous passion—the source of pleasure and pain; its seat is in the chest; (3) blind crudity of ignorance—the source of bestial instincts; its seat is in the abdomen." [14] Combinations of these three dispositions produce a variety of individual temperaments which are, however, dependent chiefly on the quantitative distribution of the primary elements: fire, water, earth, and ether. Fire is considered the source of

[14] Cerise: *op. cit.*, vol. III, p. 13.

virtue and goodness—"flame goes upward"; air—the source of passions; earth and water—the sources of darkness and imbecility.

The Hindus believed in the transmigration of the soul. In part the process is pictured in this way: the *manas* (inner faculty) absorbs the faculty of speech and other motor functions; it then retires into *prana* (breath); *prana* in turn withdraws into the living soul which, accompanied by the envelope of vital energy, leaves the body with the last breath, ready to transmigrate. Cerise observes that the theories on temperaments of the Greek philosopher Empedocles are almost identical with those of the Hindus and that the three innate dispositions bring to mind the three souls of Plato. The vital energy of the Hindus is likewise akin to the Hippocratic vital force. The Platonic concept of primary ideas that live outside the body recalls the Hindu theory that the soul floating in the universe carries with it a number of "memories" which it contributes to the personality of the individual chosen later as its new abode or instrument.

The psychology of man as visualized by the Hindu, despite its apparent physical and physiological foundation, was a mystic philosophy as well as a psychology. This union of religion and psychology is a very old phenomenon and it was destined to play a critical and almost fatal role in the history of psychiatry. We may even anticipate some of the difficulties ahead if we recognize the fact that scientific phenomena can be studied only when they are viewed as phenomena of nature, having no conflict with traditional theological dogma. Even the question of the earth's revolving around the sun could not be settled until theology permitted the observations of Copernicus and Galileo to be recorded and studied. No conflict between science and theology was perceived by the Hindus of the days of Suśruta and Charaka; no separation between the two appeared to be needed and the Hindus derived their psychological theories from their theology, or, rather, they conceived of their psychology as a philosophy of life. Human life in all its forms was considered as a series of links in a long chain of natural functions; this attitude excluded any very clear concept of psychological abnormalities. The Hindus thought that the act of uniting body and soul was accomplished when a human being was born. The waking state of man was one of the manifestations of this unity. The dream was another form, as was deep sleep. Ecstasy was another. Finally there was death—the parting of the soul and the body. The various states covered by the words "ecstasy" and "stuporous conditions" must have been considered mere manifestations of the co-operation, or the loss of the living partnership, between the soul and its physical instrument—a phenomenon of spiritual migration.

The doctrine of transmigration of the soul affected not only the psychophilosophical theories of the Hindu. It also had profound sociological consequences which are of psychiatric import. It is incumbent upon man to propitiate the nature of his soul as he conceives it. Two modes of propitiation suggested themselves. One was to make fertility of the race the motive force for man's justification of his life: the more children born, the greater the number of accommodations offered to the multitude of roving souls. The other was contemplation, absorption into the infinite, abandon to the pantheistic ideals which would finally relieve the soul and set it free for its endless migration. The Brahman ideal of fertility was left to the demos,[15] whose proverbial fecundity is still one of the most distinguishing characteristics of India, populous despite centuries of pestilence. The Buddhistic ideal of contemplation and pantheistic deep absorption was left to the aristocracy, the privileged or ruling classes in general.

Again it should be noted that this psychological orientation is not confined to the Hindus alone. Every now and then, under the stress of cultural crises, the same mystical trends common to all men emerge from what appears to be the unknown and reassert themselves, disguised in the contemporary terminology and customs. Napoleon's mystic assumption of the crown from his own hand set forth the pantheistic ideal in the form of imperialism; the ideal of fertility appeared in his belief that the greatest woman is the one who bears the greatest number of children. The phenomenon which we now call Hitler or Mussolini presents the same picture, requiring that the demos resume its role of boundless fecundity, so that there be as many Germans or Italians as conceivable by mind and race, and leaving the contemplation and fulfillment of the ideal of racial being to the few privileged who are not as fertile, or are even celibates.

The psychiatric aspects of this attitude are of great interest. The

[15] The eighth part of Yajur-Veda bears the title "Bajikarana," which means the art of the indefinite propagation of mankind.

ideals of contemplative pantheism espoused by the privileged led to the contempt for death which is so poignantly clear in the folklore of the Teuton, the Hindu, and the Chinese. This contempt for death at times developed into a cult of death and individual, ritualistic suicides or mass suicides were the result; these are found in old Teutonic sagas, in India, China, and Japan. Since such practices were a part of the recognized philosophy of life, they did not appear abnormal to the peoples of these nations; but when emerging from the dead past into modern life, and in modern dress, systematically practiced suicide gives the decided impression of mental pathology. We find such outbreaks here and there in ancient Greece, in Paris during the French Revolution, and in the so-called suicide clubs in Germany, particularly Prussia, following the Franco-Prussian War. However, it would be inaccurate to assume that the philosophy of the Hindus and its overt or covert percolation into many parts of the East and the West were responsible for the mental abnormalities just cited. It is more correct to view the problem from a somewhat different angle. The primitive anxiety of the early races gradually found a certain amount of consolation in elaborated pantheistic philosophy, which was but a metaphysical expression of, and an adaptation to, individual helplessness. From the historical point of view, the value of the Hindu psychophysiological theories lies in the fact that they expressed in writing and in well-systematized formulations the fundamental attitude of the human mind, an attitude usually devoid of self-conscious formulatory clarity, rather an impulse, an uncontrollable drive.

Mental disease, however, whether viewed with the clouded vision of a very primitive man, through the mystic eyes of Mosaic law, or through the pantheistic glasses of the Hindu, remained a mystery, reprehensible or admirable, which did not seem to belong to medicine. It was the mission of Greek science to make the first serious attempt to place the consideration of mental diseases on a scientific medical basis.

assumes that it is one thing, set and definable. Is it truly disease?

3

THE GREEKS *and* THE ROMANS

G REEK medicine grew out of the same psychological soil as did the healing arts of other ancient peoples; its roots were man's uncertainty and his obscure speculations on his place in this world. The healer was at once the spiritual and the medical authority of the race.

Aesculapius is traditionally considered the god of medicine, and Hippocrates, who died in the early years of the fourth century B.C. (377), is considered the first layman to become a professional doctor and thus the Father of Greek Medicine. We must bear in mind in this connection that in those remote days, as is still the tendency in ours, medicine dealt with physical pains only; psychological troubles were not often suspected of being diseases and they were hardly ever considered the special concern of the physician.

Five hundred years before Hippocrates, in the days of Homer, the healing god Aesculapius had not yet been deified. In the *Iliad* Homer refers to him merely as a chieftain whose sons Machaon and Podalirius differed from other heroes in that they possessed a superior skill in healing wounds. Their skill, therefore, was mostly surgical. No reference to their possible interest in mental disease is made, but Greek mythology abounds in illustrations of madness. The Homeric tradition was theurgic: man becomes mentally ill because the gods take his mind away. Mental illness meant nothing more than flagrantly queer behavior. There was no curiosity for psychological detail. A mad man was someone who, like Ulysses when he simulated madness, would yoke a bull and a horse together, plowing the sands of the seashore and sowing salt instead of corn. Ajax was mad and slew a flock of sheep, thinking he was attacking his enemies; on regaining his senses he was so overcome with remorse that he threw himself on his sword and died. Orestes was mad and saw visitations of furies which his sister Electra could not see. The daughters of Proetus, the king of Argos, had taken vows never to marry. They were opposed to the worship of Dionysus and stole gold from the statue of Hera. As a result, divine power made them mad and they believed themselves to be cows; they would leave the royal palace to run wild, lowing in the forest. Melampus, the seer who lived about three centuries before Homer and who is supposed to have cured Hercules of his mental trouble, was summoned to minister to the royal cow-daughters. Melampus was an observant man, not only a seer; he had often noticed that goats who had eaten white hellebore purged themselves abundantly. He promptly mixed hellebore with milk and administered it to the daughters of Proetus; then he had robust youngsters chase them over the fields till they were nearly exhausted. Bathing in the fountains of Arcadia followed and the cure was successfully completed.

The Greek laity of later centuries was still under the influence of the traditional attitude toward mental diseases and viewed them with a mixture of crude medicinal empiricism and mystical prejudice. Euripides, who was a contemporary of Hippocrates, could still write that Lyssa, the goddess of night and madness, made Hercules lose his mind.

The medical centers of the pre-Hippocratic days were the Aesculapian temples. In these the Aesculapiadae, the priestly inheritors of the secrets of healing, would start the treatment with imposing religious ceremonies. The powers of the god of healing were recounted. The patient would sleep near the temple and dream of the god appearing and producing the miracles of cure; depending upon the nature of these dreams, various fomentations with decoctions of odiferous herbs were used. Even a little over a century before Hippocrates the Aescuiapian temples were still the centers of medicine and the oracles still the source of a great deal of medical, and especially medicopsychological, advice.

Many mentally ill were far from being recognized as sick people. Some of them were chosen to interpret and cure human ills, as shown by the fact that the Pythias of the Delphian oracle, to judge from the descriptions of their behavior, were afflicted with mental illnesses of considerable severity. The templar, theurgic medicine of the Greeks was unable to raise the question of what mental illness was; it was steeped in the tradition of primitive mysticism which is common to all lands and to all men. This mysticism caused man to fear and to hate the mentally ill more than to be puzzled by them; some of them were taken into the temple to be healed or even to do the healing, while others, as suggested by Aristophanes,[1] were forbidden entrance into the temple and were even chased away with stones. If an explanation of the cause of mental illness was ever attempted, it was always both simple and obscure, with an occasional glimpse of accidental reasonableness. Thus, when the Spartan king Cleomenes became mentally ill, his trouble according to some was due to his offending an oracle, while according to others it was caused by too much wine consumed with Scythian ambassadors.

II

THE Greek genius did not remain absorbed in and attached to its own mythology for very long. It was a rational genius, acutely sensible to problems of life and keenly curious about man as a human being. As early as the sixth century B.C. the Greek mind turned toward observations and a certain amount of experimentation. Alcmaeon, for instance, was not the mystical performer of the Aesculapian brotherhood. He wanted to see for himself, and it appears that he was the first to dissect a human body. He enucleated an eyeball and seems to have established the fact that our senses are connected with the brain. The puzzle that is human reason preoccupied him; he searched for the seat of reason and the soul and placed it in the brain. Pythagoras,

[1] Aristophanes: *Birds*, 524.

who was a contemporary of Alcmaeon, postulated the existence of a
world soul; he derived his philosophy from this belief. His was
the interest in abstract principles, but Alcmaeon was interested in
man directly and his name is a signpost on the road to a scientific
physiological psychology, thus marking the early abandonment of the
theurgic, templar attitude toward disease.

But at that early date it was still impossible to produce an empirical and rational medical psychology. The medical man's attention was
naturally drawn to the body and to its ills; like the average physician
of today, almost twenty-five centuries later, he took the existence of
mind and reason for granted and left to the speculative philosopher
the whole mass of problems connected with psychology. Even after
this philosopher did turn away from theurgic contemplations of the
cosmic and began to concentrate on man and living, he had only
his absorbing curiosity and penetrating intuition upon which to rely.
Heraclitus (535–475 B.C.), for instance, was critical of the physicians
of his day and accused them of indulging in poetic speculations. He
wanted them to study the phenomena of nature and he looked for
what he called "fixed measures," or laws of nature, in our present-
day language. But he had to fall back on speculations and assumptions
which could not be proved. To Heraclitus reason depended upon the
fire within man: the drier the fire, the wiser the soul, or reason, or
judgment; the more humid the soul, the closer it is to being ill—an
extreme excess of humidity will bring on imbecility or madness.[2]

Yet the same Heraclitus, whose psychopathology was traditionally
naïve, insisted with unique intuitive insight that, though reason is
common to most people, most people live as though they have an
understanding of their own. In other words, Heraclitus was probably the very first who called attention to the individual as such
and who implied the need of thorough individualization in psychology. This trend in Greek thought was neither fortuitous nor fleeting; it took firm hold. Protagoras, who was a youngster at the time
of Heraclitus' death, proclaimed that "man is the measure of all

[2] C. F. Michéa: *Des doctrines psycho-physiologiques considérées chez les anciens,
Annales Médico-Psychologiques*. Paris, 1843, vol. I, p. 210.
    Also, Jacob Bernays: *Heraclitische Briefe*. Berlin, 1869.
    Also, Houdard: *Histoire de la médecine greque dépuis Esculape jusqu'à Hippocrate
exclusivement*. Paris, 1856.

things," thus emphasizing both the importance of the individual and the humanistic attitude, which did not assert itself as a potent factor until almost two thousand years later. Empedocles, the slightly older contemporary of Protagoras, was deeply interested in the problems of change in man's behavior and thought, and it was he who was impressed with the importance of the emotions. He saw in the emotions of love and hate the fundamental source of change and living, a thought which Plato took over, in part, in his emphasis on the role of Eros in the individual and social life of man. The full significance of this orientation was not realized until the twentieth century, when the clinical studies of Freud revealed the profound import of these two affects, love and hate, of these two "passions" as they were called by writers of the seventeenth and eighteenth centuries. Seeking for an anatomical basis of psychology, Empedocles placed the seat of the soul in the heart, but the old tradition of placing the soul in the diaphragm was not entirely discarded. The word "phrenos," meaning the diaphragm, also acquired the meaning of mind, and an old Greek physician Aristo called the diaphragm "the temple of the body," just as Aristotle called the heart the *sensorium commune,* the "rendezvous of sensations" as the French medical historian Lélut aptly translated this term.

The problem of finding a suitable seat for the soul in the human body was one which engaged the speculative attention not only of physician and philosopher in pre-Hippocratic Greece. It remained a subject of discussion and an unsolved puzzle for many centuries to come; it still is a purely speculative problem in present-day psychology and physiology. The physiological truth apperceived by Alcmaeon twenty-five centuries ago has found many scientific corroborations through the research in brain physiology, but the puzzle of our psychological activity, of the life of feeling and thinking and its relation to one definite organ of the body, such as the brain, remains more a belief than a fact, more a tradition of thought than a demonstrable scientific truth.

Aside from this psychophysiological problem which Greek thought raised for future scientists to ponder over and work upon, Greek philosophy established a tradition which must be pointed out here with special emphasis: the tradition of considering the human mind exclusively the province of philosophy, religious or secular. For many centuries to come this was an attitude never questioned by the medical man; and whenever medicine did make an attempt to investigate the mind in the light of medical experience, the theologian and later the philosopher, rooted in and armed with perennial tradition, raised violent objections. Descartes was silently considered a much greater authority on the question of human psychology than any of his medical contemporaries in the seventeenth century. Immanuel Kant, toward the very close of the eighteenth century, violently opposed the medical man's intrusion into the field of psychopathology. The medical man had to wait many centuries, almost until our own day, before he was able to approach the human mind with any degree of certainty that neither the philosopher nor the theologian would look upon him as an intruder into a field he should not aspire to plow, still less consider his own.

Imagination is difficult to destroy

We thus see that the principal and constant obstacles to the development of a rational, scientific medical psychology—theurgic mysticism and abstract philosophy—were both present in Greek thought, and both were sufficiently potent so that medicine from the very beginning was forced to enter the field of psychopathology not as a welcome, benevolent brother in search of the truth, but as a belligerent who at once had to combat opposition and conquer the right to heal.

It was in the midst of these obstacles that Hippocrates boldly introduced psychiatric problems into medicine. It is only in the light of this singular constellation of scientific thought that the spirit and the verve of Hippocrates can be fully understood.

III

HIPPOCRATES lived in an age unique in history. Pericles, Anaxagoras, Thucydides, Phidias, Sophocles, Euripides, Aristophanes, and Socrates were all his contemporaries. It was the age of Hellenic enlightenment. Political science, philosophy, ethics, drama, sculpture, and architecture attained a height never before known among Europeans. The critical evaluation of life and the world, of man and the community, was developing in an atmosphere of inspired inquiry, of an eager yet sober curiosity. It was perhaps natural that medicine, too, should come into its own in the midst of this heightened spiritual activity. It stepped out of its templar captivity and asserted itself boldly, in a manner so earnest and so vigorous that, like Greek philosophy, it left an indelible influence on the centuries to come.

Hippocrates was the most important personage in this period of medical history and, strangely, almost the only one. While it is possible that a number of worthy predecessors of Hippocrates did exist but were forgotten, since a great many events and persons of Greek antiquity were lost to man's memory, the fact remains that Hippocrates seems to stand alone, marking a rather sharp turning point in the history of medicine. Neither his unknown predecessors nor his immediate pupils seem to have been equal to his genius or historical influence, and a number of his medical intuitions continue to influence the medical thought of today. He became almost a mythical figure and at times it may appear that he was not at all one person, but rather a composite synthesized on the basis of many writings and traditions.

Hippocrates and Hippocratic medicine were descendants, but not inheritors, of the templar medicine. The temples of healing, established near medicinal springs, had their Aesculapiadae; the membership in these medical brotherhoods was originally hereditary, but as time went on outsiders were admitted and various groups were formed which became known as schools. Thus arose the schools of Cos, Cnidus, and Rhodes. It was at the school of Cos that Hippocrates received his early training. It is evident that he emerged from the very source of ancient medicine while its tradition was still powerful, even though on the wane. The only authentic manifestations or descriptions of human ills by which Hippocrates might have been guided at the beginning of his career were probably little more than the complaints which had been written on the walls of Aesculapian temples. His earliest writings, the *Praenotiones* and the *Prophetica*, were apparently compilations of such complaints, and among these are to be found the earliest written records of the symptoms of depressions, known in those days, and in some parts of Europe even to-day, as melancholia.[8]

It is important not to overlook the fact that the glory of the Age of Pericles was somewhat dimmed by the popularity of many superstitions not at all conducive to clear scientific thinking, by Sophistic formalism, and by signs of social decay. Thucydides, the great historian of the time, caustically observed, "The common meaning of words was turned about at man's pleasure; the most reckless knave was deemed the most desirable friend; a man of prudence and moderation was styled a coward; a man who listened to reason was a good-for-nothing simpleton. People were trusted exactly in proportion to their violence and unscrupulousness, and no one was so popular as the successful conspirator, except perhaps one who had been clever enough to outwit him at his own trade; but anyone who honestly attempted to remove the causes of such treacheries was considered a traitor to his party. . . . As for oaths, no one imagined that they were to be kept a moment longer than occasion required; it was in fact an added pleasure to destroy your enemy, if your hand managed to catch him through his trusting to your words." [4]

The spirit of the Hippocratic oath as well as the social conscience of Socrates stand out in strong relief against the background of this efflorescence of Athenian culture which already bore the sores of its decadence. Hippocrates, the medical man studying and caring for the physically ill, was apparently a welcome contribution to contemporary Greek culture; but Hippocrates, the medical psychologist, must have at once felt the opposition which that culture presented to him. In his medical writings, as long as he deals with wounds, aches, and pains, he is composed and factual, but on clinical psychological matters he is provocative, sharp, even vehement at times. His emotions were apparently severely aroused by popular, self-contained, and self-contented ignorance. The opening sentences of his *Sacred Disease*, the popular name for epilepsy in those days, at once betray the almost angry concern of Hippocrates: "It thus appears to me to be in no way more divine, nor more sacred than other diseases, but has a

[8] Emil Isensee: *Geschichte der Medicin*. Berlin, 1845, Part II, Book 6, pp. 1216, 1217.
[4] Thucydides: *History of the Peloponnesian War*, III, 82.

natural cause from which it originates like other affections." And again, "They who first referred this disease to the gods appear to me to have been just such persons as the conjurors, purificators, mountebanks and charlatans now are, who claim great piety and superior knowledge. Such persons thus . . . use the divinity as a pretext and a screen for their own inability to afford any assistance." Or, "They use purifications and incantations and, it seems to me, make the divinity out to be most wicked and impious." "If you cut open the head, you will find the brain humid, full of sweat and smelling badly. And in this way you may see that it is not a god which injures the body, but disease."

Hippocrates was a true physician and, therefore, did not limit himself to protestations and vituperative theories. He was primarily a clinical observer. He gave the description of a case of so-called "puerperal insanity," [5] known today as "post-partum psychoses"; he gave an excellent description of what appears to have been a psychoneurosis with phobias; [6] he described in great clinical detail the deliria in tuberculous and malarial infections; he made note of the disturbance of memory in a case of dysentery,[7] and of an acute mental confusion following a severe hemorrhage.[8] The writings of Hippocrates are replete with such clinical observations; he held his keen eyes fixed on the course of each disease and its final outcome. Prognosis was the cornerstone of the school of Cos in contradistinction to that of Cnidus, which stressed the importance of diagnosis.

However, in the treatment of various mental diseases, and apparently he was consulted frequently in such cases, Hippocrates seems to have contributed little that was not traditional. He was once called to attend Democritus, the great contemporary philosopher, whom friends considered mentally sick. Democritus himself was interested in mental diseases and believed that severe emotional states might even induce convulsions. Hippocrates came to see him because of the

---

[5] Armand Semelaigne: *Etudes historiques sur l'aliénation mentale dans l'antiquité.* Paris, 1869, vol. I, p. 21. Also, *On epidemics,* III, sec. XVII, particularly cases II and XIV.

[6] *On epidemics,* V, sec. LXXXII.

[7] *Ibid.,* III, sec. XVII, case XIII.

[8] *Ibid.,* I, case VII.

philosopher's alleged state of madness and found him contemplating dissected animals. Democritus, by way of explanation, said to the Father of Medicine, "How could I otherwise write on the nature of madness, its causes and the mode of alleviating it? The animals which thou seest here opened—I opened them not because of hate of the work of the divinity, but because I am searching for the seat and the nature of bile; for thou knowest it is usually, when it is excessive, the cause of madness." [9] It is not known whether it was on the occasion of this consultation or at some other time when he saw Democritus that Hippocrates failed to rise above the wisdom of Melampus: he prescribed hellebore.

There were certain mental disturbances, obvious even to the layman of our day, which continued to remain unrecognized. Socrates, who was ultimately considered a dangerous criminal, never was considered mad. Yet it is related that Socrates was guided by singular inspirations and thoughts which on occasion took the form of audible voices (auditory hallucinations?) and, when he was about forty years old, he is supposed to have had trancelike states in which he would maintain a standing posture (stupor?) for hours. "He stood motionless from early morning on one day till sunrise on the next, through a whole night when there was a very hard frost." [10]

One may not pass this incident without a thought of the present day, twenty-odd centuries after Hippocrates, when many a criminal, less illustrious than the immortal Socrates, is executed, his severe mental disease, like the schizophrenia of which Socrates apparently suffered, overlooked until after the State has done its duty in taking his life. However, as even today, the laws dealing with the mentally ill were deficient or otherwise wanting in enlightenment only in cases of capital crimes; in matters of madness affecting civil problems, like handling money, or managing one's affairs in general, the law in Athens appears to have been as it is in the world today, more liberal and seemingly more enlightened. A son, if he could prove that his father was incompetent because of a mental disease called by Hippocrates "paranoia," would be granted the request to have a guardian ap-

[9] A. Semelaigne: *op. cit.*, p. 13.
[10] Theodor Gomperz: *Greek thinkers.* Translated by Laurie Magnus. London, 1901.

pointed. This law was considered important enough for Plato to re-
tain it in his ideal State.[11] Hippocrates seems to have been considered
an authoritative psychiatric expert witness, and his experience in forensic psychiatry must have been valued. He once appeared as expert
witness when a woman was brought to court on the indictment of
miscegenation and testified that there was nothing criminal or unnatural in the fact that the defendant, although fair skinned, gave birth
to a dark-skinned child. He claimed that the woman was deeply impressed by the sight of the Ethiopians, that this was sufficient to affect her imagination and thus to influence the color of the offspring,
and that she need not have borne her child by an Ethiopian.

It is clear that Hippocrates' views on mental diseases were rather
liberal and flexible. His psychological theory does not seem to have
been one sided. In speaking of epilepsy he called upon the uninitiated
to examine the brains of the epileptics; when he saw Democritus, the
latter expressed his agreement with Hippocrates that madness is due
to bile, and finally, as illustrated by his testimony in court in favor
of an accused woman, Hippocrates believed that profound emotional
states might even affect the color of skin of unborn children. In other
words, it would appear that Hippocrates, depending upon the case
and the occasion, favored a purely anatomical view represented even
in the twentieth century, which claims that a disease or injury to the
brain is the sole cause of mental illness. Yet he also believed in the
physiological theory, in our days represented by psychiatric endo-
crinology, which claims that certain body juices are responsible for
madness. Finally, he was occasionally of the opinion that purely mental, emotional states may produce deep changes, even physiological
changes, in an individual; this point of view, particularly when applied to such a case as that of the woman who gave birth to a dark-
skinned baby, would be considered very radical even today, although
the purely psychological theory of mental diseases appears to be playing a dominant role in the psychiatry of the twentieth century.

The inferential triple alliance between anatomy, physiology, and
psychology, which is reflected in various attitudes of Hippocrates, requires some elucidation, however, in order that the impression may

[11] Plato: *Laws*, 929.

not be gained that, great clinician though he was, Hippocrates was merely an eclectic or a clinical opportunist.

Hippocrates was not what the modern medical vernacular calls a "research man." He was a clinician and a busy one, and he contributed an untold number of extremely accurate observations which are still useful in present-day surgery and medicine. He offered a perfectly rational classification of mental diseases. The terms in which he designated them are still used in modern psychiatry, although in many respects they now have a different meaning. His classifications include epilepsy, mania (states of abnormal excitement), melancholia (states of abnormal depression), and paranoia (an illness we would call to-day mental deterioration). He also recognized hysteria, although this was not considered a mental disease, but rather a physical affliction limited to women and caused by the fact that the uterus, thought of apparently as a free, peregrinating organ, would wander about the woman's body. The sexual causation of hysteria almost universally accepted today was not consciously suspected by Hippocrates, but intuitively he must have sensed it, since he considered marriage the best remedy for this affliction in the case of girls.

Even though in matters of treatment the suggestions of Hippocrates do not bear the mark of that originality and scientific permanence which distinguish his clinical observations, they are characteristic in that they do not appear to have been born out of a routine-ridden mind. Rather, they are dictated by the contingencies of the clinical situation, even though limited by the spirit and misconceptions of his times. Bleeding, for instance, which was destined to become appallingly universal in the seventeenth and eighteenth centuries, was used not infrequently in Greece. Hippocrates, in *Of Diseases*, reveals a reasonableness and clinical sobriety unknown to his medical brethren of twenty centuries after his death: "When the head is gorged with blood, patients act sometimes as if they were intoxicated; it is then necessary to open a vein. But then we often make fruitless attempts to take away much blood, when there is but little in the affected organ." One can find in his *Aphorisms* a plethora of keen clinical remarks. He noticed, for instance, that a physical disease, when it occurs in madness, is apt to alleviate the mental illness.

He says, "Dysentery, or dropsy or ecstasy, coming in madness, is good"; [12] or, "In maniacal affections, if varices or hemorrhoids appear, they remove mania." [13] These observations reflect a clinical intuition which was utilized twenty-three centuries later when paresis, the mental disease due to syphilis, was first treated with malaria, and when other mental illnesses began to be treated with typhoid vaccines or electric apparatus to induce artificial high-degree fever.

Returning to the theoretical conceptions which Hippocrates introduced into his psychiatry, we find first of all that he was groping for a theoretical foundation for his medical psychology. But medical psychology to be rational and scientific must be based on the empirical understanding of the individual patient; such understanding is possible only when our knowledge is advanced enough to discern individual psychological details. The Age of Hippocrates had not yet risen to this level of individualization, which characterized European romanticism. Hence, even the genius of Hippocrates, despite his keen sense for clinical detail, was unable to go beyond semipostulative physiological aspects of mental diseases.

He followed Alcmaeon when he considered the brain the central organ of reason, but he did not press the point. On the other hand, he was certain, as we are fully convinced today on the basis of strict scientific evidence offered us by generations of experimental work on the central nervous system, that our sensations and motor activities are registered in and depend on the brain. He even observed that an anesthesia is a sign of brain injury: "Persons who have a painful affliction in any part of their bodies are in a great measure insensible of pain and disordered in intellect." [14] In his discourse on the *Sacred Disease* he comes to the emphatic conclusion that it is by means of the brain that we think, dream, and feel, that a number of complex processes go on in the brain when "we are mad, delirious or possessed of apprehension and terrors in the midst of the night or at the rise of the sun," and that "causeless restlessness and worry" also come from the brain.[15]

Yet Hippocrates, while holding the brain in high esteem, did not

[12] *Aphorisms*, VII, 5.
[13] *Ibid.*, VI, 21.
[14] *Ibid.*, II, 6.
[15] *The sacred disease*, XVII.

consider its role supreme and absolute. He seemed to be testing all avenues of approach and at times he was inclined to consider that purely psychological forces preside over all our organic functions, including those of the brain. He thought in terms of a *vital force*—something akin to Bergson's *élan vital*—a force bound in some way to the body through the sensory and motor systems (the spinal cord and the brain), but capable of acting on its own initiative through the agency of the body. When we are awake, argued Hippocrates, we are constantly exposed to the impacts of the outer world, and we take cognizance of these impacts in that we have sensations and respond to them; but when we are asleep, and shut off from the outside world and its proddings, our mind then goes on doing its job without interference—thus dreams are produced. In this respect Hippocrates may be considered the forerunner of Freud, as was Plato who followed Hippocrates' view on sleep and dreams; for here we find the germinal idea that dreams are expressions of our mind's desire when it is not impeded by the demands of outer reality. This purely psychological excursion of Hippocrates was left without elaboration. The Father of Medicine was more interested in practical matters than in speculations and paid greater attention to the clinical approach, which offered more tangible if not more conclusive observations.

It is clear, however, that despite his emphasis on the role of the brain, Hippocrates did not ascribe to it independent, inherent psychological qualities. He rather thought that breath (air, *pneuma*) is the source of intelligence and feeling. The *pneuma* reaches the brain through the mouth and is then distributed to all parts of the body.[16] Here Hippocrates apparently follows the tradition of the days of Homer as well as of the ancient Orient. Evidently the *pneuma* of Hippocrates and the *prana* of the Yajur-Veda are identical.

But, apart from these considerations, the medical psychology of Hippocrates is chiefly physiological. In addition to the *pneuma*, he considered phlegm a very important substance (hence phlegmatic temperament); and, particularly in mental diseases, bile (yellow and black) played a predominant role (hence choleric and melancholic

[16] Jules Soury: *Nature et localisation des fonctions psychiques chez l'autheur du traité de maladie sacrée, Annuaire de l'école pratique des hautes études.* 1907, pp. 5–35.

temperaments). A sudden flux of bile to the brain brings on unpleasant dreams and a feeling of anxiety; a superabundance of black bile causes melancholia. On the other hand, a state of exaltation is due to the predominance of warmth and dampness in the brain. Hippocrates considered that seasonal climatic conditions are of some importance; manias, melancholias, and epileptic disorders he thought of as diseases of spring.[17]

On the surface, the medical psychology of Hippocrates may appear fragmentary, but actually it represents a serious attempt on the part of an experienced physician to bring together whatever knowledge the philosophy, anatomy, and physiology of his day had put at his disposal; it was an effort to construct a more or less unitary system, no matter how speculative, of man as a whole rather than of man as a conglomerate of separate units. If Hippocrates strove toward the liberation of psychiatry from mystical prejudice and toward a unified, biological point of view on mental diseases, he did so without many established scientific facts at his disposal. He did it almost purely intuitively, but with immense clinical perspicacity and professional authority.

For centuries to come he remained the only true authority, yet his influence on his immediate contemporaries left a great deal to be desired. The historian Herodotus accepted many Hippocratic views; Xenophon the soldier, apologist of Socrates, followed the same trends of thought. But the poets and tragedians of Greece followed the traditional theurgic views. Plato held Hippocrates in high esteem and spoke of him in laudatory terms in the dialogues *Phaedrus* and *Protagoras*. However, the idea of elevating the brain to its great role in the psychophysiological economy of man was not fully shared by post-Hippocratic scholars and philosophers. Plato appears to have been only an exception in this respect. Aristotle, Epicurus, and Zeno considered the heart the center of our psychophysiological activity. One may say, and feel, that there is a considerable degree of accuracy in the saying that Hippocrates wrote the first page of the history of medical psychology and that this page remained open for many years without the addition of a single line.

Almost a century and a half elapsed before two other investigators,

[17] *Aphorisms*, III, 1, 20.

who were also Greeks, Herophilus and Erasistratus, discovered the venous sinuses in the skull and the actual nerve trunks leading to or coming from the brain. This retardation in neurological research was undoubtedly due to the fact that the great influence of Aristotle and the Epicurean and Stoic philosophies diverted medicine from the observational and experimental path which Hippocrates would have wished it to follow. This is a point not to be passed over lightly, for it denotes an almost permanent characteristic of the history of psychiatry—a tendency in medicine to make an earnest beginning in psychiatry and then to shy away, as it were, and to recede in favor of the speculative philosopher. This explains why the efforts made by Hippocrates did not escape the usual fate of most psychiatric beginnings. While it is true that Hippocrates was not forgotten even after his writings, like those of others of the Greco-Roman world, were lost, the human mind soon became again less a medical problem than a philosophical one. *Is this so good?*

It will be necessary for us now and for a certain period of time to come to take into serious consideration the thoughts of Plato and especially the system of Aristotle, and the speculations of their followers, lay and cleric. For to understand the whole historical process of medical psychology, the vicissitudes of the past and the pitfalls of the present day, we must for a time pay heed not to what the doctor had to say, but to what the contemplative thinker thought.

IV

PLATO (427–347 B.C.), although he always spoke of Hippocrates in terms of high esteem, presents nevertheless a step backward in the history of psychology. Keen analysis, penetrating intuition, and great learning are combined in Plato with a mysticism highly reminiscent of Oriental philosophies. Plato's man is but a physiological instrument for the expression of the universal; his man is also but an atom serving to make up and to maintain the body politic. Man is fundamentally so distant from his own mind-soul that his whole life, personal and social, must apparently be spent on keeping mind and body together. "There are two principles," says Plato, "mind and matter, of which mind is the true reality, the thing of most worth, that to which everything owes its form and essence and the principle of law and order in the universe; the other element, matter, is secondary, a dull, irrational, recalcitrant force, the unwilling slave of the mind, which somehow but imperfectly takes on the impress of the mind." [18] This being the case, Plato considers ideas true realities which live outside ourselves. When we have a sensation which in turn generates an idea, this idea is not new at all, but a remembrance of the past—all knowledge is reminiscent, as if knowledge were pre-existent.

Plato's psychopathology is correspondingly idealistic and mystical. The soul consists of two parts, the rational and the irrational. The rational soul presides over the other; its seat is in the brain; it is immortal and divine. The irrational, or animal, soul is mortal; it is the source of pleasure, pain, audacity, anger, fear, hope, and love. It will be noted that Plato relegates the whole field of human affects, all the instincts and their emotional derivatives, to a lower plane; he is not able to recognize in them their true, biological rationale. Plato distributes the affects all over the body in an orderly if arbitrary and naïve manner. The seat of the irrational soul is the chest. Anger and audacity reside in the heart. Hunger and other appetites and passions are placed between the diaphragm and the navel. The cerebrospinal system is given recognition as a carrier of sensorimotor activities.[19] To use the words of Brett,[20] "Plato's psychology in the 'Republic' is a kind of phrenology on a large scale. In a manner more characteristic of the primitive man than of a Greek philosopher, Plato conceives of man as an inverted plant: for Divine power suspended the head and root of us from that place where the generation of the soul first began." [21]

On the basis of these premises it is not difficult to derive the Platonic views on mental disease. The irrational soul may become ill, that is, it may sever its ephemeral union with the rational soul. Man under these circumstances becomes mad. There are three kinds

[18] Frank Thilly: *A history of philosophy*. New York, 1914, pp. 65, 66.
[19] *Timaeus*, and also Michéa: *op. cit.*, p. 125.
[20] Brett: *A history of psychology*, vol. I, p. 68.
[21] *Timaeus*.

of madness—melancholia, mania, and dementia.[22] When a man appears too happy or too sad, when he is bent too much on the pursuit of pleasure or the avoidance of pain, he is devoid of reason—he is mad. As to the causes of this madness, Plato follows Hippocrates: morbid humors reaching the three seats of the irrational soul produce sadness, chagrin, audacity, cowardice, defects of memory, or stupidity.[23] However, not all abnormal conditions are due necessarily to the disturbance of body juices. When the soul, pure reason, enters the body, it may prove too strong and it may then not only produce mental changes but also affect the body. "Where the action of the soul is too powerful, it attracts the body so powerfully, that it throws it into a consuming state." [24]

At this point Plato definitely deviates from the empirical attitude of Hippocrates and turns to the inspired views of the past. There are two kinds of folly, he says in his Socratic *Apology:* madness and ignorance. But there are also two kinds of madness, two kinds of manias; one is a result of disease, but the other is a gift of the gods. The latter needs no intermediary in the form of the irrational soul; it is celestial; it is a higher form of madness and it possesses prophetic qualities. The delirium of the prophets is due to Apollo, that of the "initiated" to Dionysus, that of the poets to the Muses, that of lovers to Aphrodite and Eros. Apparently it was difficult for Plato to bring the multiplicity of human psychological reactions into one system; it was impossible for him to view them objectively, without moralistic criteria. As a result, the great effort made by Hippocrates seemed not a little in vain: by reintroducing the concept of divine, revelatory madness, Plato reasserted the "low" nature of ordinary madness—a conception which Hippocrates opposed as much as the conception of sacred madness. The medical point of view was thus considerably weakened by Plato; this is particularly true in view of the fact that Platonic thought exercised an enormous influence for several centuries, including the early part of the Christian Era. The worth of Plato's great pupil, a greater philosopher, was not actually realized

[22] Michéa: *op. cit.,* pp. 213 *et seq.*
[23] *Ibid.,* p. 213.
[24] Quoted by Forbes Winslow in *On the preservation of the health of body and mind.* London, 1842.

until he was rediscovered and then restored by Thomas Aquinas in the thirteenth century. In the meantime, through Plato, Athenian culture spoke as if for the last time to the coming European culture, and its voice, which was at least inferentially derogatory to the mentally ill, invited the medical psychologist to look back rather than forward.

v

ARISTOTLE (384–322 B.C.) was a pupil of Plato but not his disciple. The son of a physician, he preferred the world of natural phenomena to mystic speculations. He may be said to have been the first and only Greek philosopher who in his studies and teaching embraced all the knowledge in the possession of the ancient world, and it was he who strove to systematize and unify this knowledge. He formulated the laws governing rational thinking; he studied mathematics and physics, zoology, botany, and biology in the broadest sense of the term; and it was he who laid the foundation of the science of psychology. Knowledge to Aristotle was not conceptual, not "reminiscent" as it was to Plato; the material world was to him a world of phenomena worthy of study. We must perceive and understand this material world through the use of our sense organs. Hence our perceptions play a decisive role in the acquisition of knowledge. The soul is that which moves the body and determines its structure; man has hands because he has a mind. Here we see the first forecast of the eighteenth-century Lamarckian biological ideas. Nutrition, growth, and reproduction are functions of the soul. Hence plants, too, have a soul. So do animals, whose soul, as well as having the functions characteristic of plants, is the source of pleasure, pain, desire, and aversion. While man alone possesses reason, he also performs the functions of the plant and the animal and therefore also possesses the souls of the plant and animal. Aristotle thus had an evolutionary point of view.

He, too, divides the human soul into two parts: the rational, which is the source of prudence, wisdom, cleverness, memory; and the irrational, which is the source of temperance, justice, and courage. But, unlike Plato, Aristotle does not consider the soul or the various souls of man separable from each other; all souls of man, the nutritive, the motor, the sensitive, and the rational, act as a unit; they are functions of which the body is a corollary. Except for the terminology, it would seem that Aristotle was formulating the concept of total reactions as we understand them today. Psychological reactions are all total reactions and Aristotle seems to have known this well. These views, as well as the detachment of a truly scientific mind, would not allow him to feel shocked when he found animal traits in man. In his *Ethics*, for instance, he speaks of the animal, cannibalistic tendencies found among savages and the mentally ill; he even cites a case of a man who killed his mother and ate her body. He goes down the scale of living things and speaks of the behavior of plants and sponges.

It is very interesting that Aristotle ascribed no role to the brain and spinal cord in the functions of sensations and perceptions.[25] The center, the meeting place of all sensations, the *sensorium commune*, is the heart; it is in the heart that images and memory combine into thinking.

Aristotle's psychology of affects is ingenious and extremely keen. If certain sensations propitiate the activity of a function, we experience pleasure; if a function is impeded, we experience pain. Reason is creative and is independent of man or matter; it is immortal. It cannot be attacked by any illness, because of its immaterial and immortal nature. This orientation should be carefully noted; it was destined to play, overtly or covertly, a decisive role in the whole history of psychiatry, for it definitely leads, as it actually did lead Aristotle, to the conclusion that only man and his so-called lower souls can become ill. This point of view naturally must reject the very existence of purely psychological troubles. It must insist that every mental illness is a physical, organic illness. Aristotle thought of mental defectives and of illnesses leading to mental deterioration; he said that there are those who are reduced to this state by an illness.[26] Aristotle did not look upon psychological reactions as definitely separable into healthy or morbid phenomena, but he apparently considered them, as we do today, numerous links in an endless chain of events. This

[25] *De anima*, II, 2.
[26] J. L. Heiberg: *Geisteskrankheiten im klassischen Alterum, Allegemeinen Zeitschrift für Psychiatrie.* Berlin, 1927, vol. 86, p. 14.

attitude enabled him to watch and observe various transitional psychological states. He mentioned the hypnagogic hallucinations which are so common among normal people. He was also interested in constitutional mental characteristics, and he saw that all great thinkers, poets, artists, and statesmen were of "melancholic temperament." He mentions in this connection Empedocles, his own teacher Plato, and Socrates.[27] He also thought that mental illness may add to, rather than substract from, the functions of a given personality. He cites the case of a poet by the name of Marascos who, when well, was a rather poor or mediocre poet; whenever Marascos had an attack of mania, he wrote excellent poetry.[28]

As for Aristotle's psychological physiology, as has been said, he ascribed to the heart the role which Plato ascribed to the brain. He had to find a function for the cerebrum, however, and, while his speculation is sufficiently fantastic to evoke amusement in a contemporary reader, it is extremely interesting, because it demonstrates the ease with which psychophysiological hypotheses are constructed. This ease never left the student of mental diseases; throughout the history of psychiatry psychologists and psychiatrists have clung to the conviction that various bodily changes, fortuitous or not, are the only agencies responsible for our emotional life, normal and abnormal. This trend has hardly changed in twenty-five centuries. Even those who today seem to have abandoned this trend in favor of purely sociological and cultural explanations of mental disease, only seem to have deviated from the Hippocratic and Aristotelian hypotheses. They still view man's psychology in the light of the unassailability of his mind and are inclined to produce an extrapsychological psychology, a psychology in which pure reason, the superior soul of man, remains always independent and supreme, never impeded or marred by illness. If we bear these general considerations in mind, the Aristotelian hypothesis loses much of its apparent naïvité and serves as an excellent prototype of the chronic prejudice which has come down to us through the ages, almost unchanged in substance even if modified as to terms and structure.

Aristotle thought that the soul, while its superior part is immate-

[27] *Problems*, XXX, 1.
[28] Isensee: *op. cit.*, p. 1226.

rial, is yet material in its other parts consisting of a fifth element, ether. But the soul is unable to function without warmth. The Hippocratic theory of the bile he therefore considered only partially correct. It is not the black bile which by and in itself carries the cause of mental disease, or of even normal psychological reactions, but warmth or cold. The black bile is merely a carrier of heat and cold. If it is moderately cold it produces vertigo, apprehensiveness, or a state of being stunned; if it is warm, gaiety and carefree joy appear. Very cold bile makes man cowardly and stupid; very hot bile generates amorous desires, cleverness, and loquacity. The same heat in the bile is also responsible for the enthusiastic fury of the sibyls and the suicidal impulses of man.[29] This psychophysiological system seems to leave the brain totally out of consideration, but Aristotle would not overlook such a large organ even if he had little respect for it. He therefore assigned to the brain a special, passive but important, task. "To him the brain, an excremental and almost inorganic part of the body, devoid of blood, warmth and sensibility, in its position at the top of the body presided over only one function—that of condensing, by means of its cold consistency, the hot vapors which arise from the heart." [30] These vapors, when cooled by the brain, are condensed in the form of dew, and thus refresh the heart and make it more temperate to human activity.

We find here the first suggestions that so-called nervous states are due to vapors. After Harvey's discovery of the circulation of blood in 1628, almost nineteen centuries after Aristotle, the idea that mental troubles were due to vapors was revived and various neurotic states began to be called by the English "vapors" and by the French *maladies vaporeuses*. The Aristotelian system could stand on its own merits even after scientific investigation in later years led the physician and the biologist to move the *sensorium commune* from the heart to the brain. Aristotle's pupil Strato disagreed with his great teacher and paid much more respect to the brain, but he was rather an exception. As has been stated before, the Aristotelian trend prevailed among the leading schools of thought in Greece and Rome.

This brings us to a very interesting and seemingly paradoxical sit-

[29] *Problems*, XXX.
[30] Michéa: *op. cit.*, p. 52.

uation, the psychological and historical meaning of which will become clear as we come to study the medical psychologies of modern times, and particularly those of the late nineteenth and twentieth centuries. To state it briefly, the paradox is this: Plato the idealist, the mystic, the deductive philosopher, was a proponent of studies of organic cerebral pathology; Aristotle the pure biologist, the inductive scientist, stimulated the study of psychology proper. The reverse would have been more logical.

VI

ARISTOTLE's system of thought was born at a time when the greatness that was Athens had passed its peak and turned toward its decline. The scientific curiosity of the Greek had not declined, but the political influence of Greece on the ancient world had begun to wane rather rapidly. The Peloponnesian War, culminating in the fall of Athens (404 B.C.), was a factor in this decline and by the time of the death of Alexander the Great, in 323, the cultural center had shifted east from Athens to Alexandria, which flourished particularly under Alexander's General Ptolemy (323–285 B.C.). The significance of this shift cannot be overestimated, and we shall return to this question presently. In the meantime we must review briefly a few important influences which were inherited from Greece by the new masters of the ancient world, the Romans.

The Romans were practical people and their interest in philosophy and science had always been much smaller than their interest in the political, social, and judicial structure of their empire. In matters of speculative thought, of science, and particularly of medicine, they were borrowers rather than contributors; they were always to remain under the influence of Greek science. There were few great physicians in Rome who were real Romans. For centuries the Greeks held the monopoly of learning, while Rome developed its far-flung empire with its characteristic institutions. Thus the inheritance of Greece acquires a particular importance, for it appears to have used the Roman

Empire as a vehicle by means of which its undying influence could be carried into medieval Europe and the modern world.

And great, indeed, was the inheritance that was Greece. The two hundred years which followed the death of Aristotle were productive in many scientific fields. Euclid formulated his geometry; Eratosthenes calculated the size of the earth; Archimedes made his permanent contribution to physics; and Hipparchus laid the foundation for the development of astronomy. Nor were the humanities forgotten or neglected. True, the medicine of Hippocrates remained more or less at a standstill and even began to show signs of decline, in that the followers of Hippocrates were not equal to their teacher; their attitude was dogmatic and more literal than creative. From the standpoint of psychology one might safely say that Hippocratic medicine, having shown so keen a sense of detail for manifestations of physical diseases, abandoned or lost even the little sense for psychological detail which it had at the outset.

That the interest in man, in his mind and his behavior, became the domain of the philosopher, even in the days of or soon after Hippocrates, has already been stated. As time went on, this feature of the history of psychology became even more accentuated. When Aristippus founded his school in Cyrene (466 B.C.), and Antisthenes his Cynic school (366 B.C.) at the Gymnasium of Cynosarges near Athens, the foundation was laid for the development of Stoicism and Epicureanism. The Cyrenaic school and the Cynics, their offshoot Epicureanism, founded by Epicurus (342–270 B.C.), and Stoicism, founded by Zeno (336 264 B.C.), were all dependent on Democritus, the originator of the atomic point of view. Each in a different way stressed the importance of the sensations and feelings of man, and each was preoccupied directly with problems of human behavior and problems of the individual's relationship to his fellow men, rather than with man's position in the cosmos. Man was born untouched, unlearned, a *tabula rasa*, they claimed. The experiences of the individual in his environment are the only things which engrave their results on this smooth, unscratched tablet that is man at his birth. Thus man becomes an individual aware of what people, life, duty, and living are. In other words, the environment, as we would say today, became a matter of major importance and man the individual, in relation to his environment, became the mere instrument of personal and public existence. Both the Stoics and the Epicureans denied the existence of a hereafter, leaving man to manage the affairs of this earth on his own responsibility, and only on his own. It is quite natural that this mental attitude should have increased the interest in social and psychological details and should have led to practical, or rather pragmatic, ethics, to introspection and to contemplation, factors which are all prerequisites for the true development of the psychology of man. But the work of development was left to future ages. Greece could do no more than build the foundation and lay the possible plans. This was an enormous task, a task discharged with brilliance and depth; but it was no more than a beginning.

Another series of factors should be borne in mind in this connection. Hippocrates, Socrates, Plato, and to a great extent Aristotle, studied and taught in a more or less homogeneous Greek atmosphere. However, the Macedonian victories created an empire which linked Greece very closely with the Orient. After the death of Alexander and the shift of the center of learning to Alexandria and Egypt, Greece became but a province of the Roman Empire and contact with the Orient increased. The mysticism of Egypt, India, and Persia began to leave its mark on successive generations. At the same time the influence of Stoic philosophy and ethics led to the gradual approach of the concept of a single God. This ethicophilosophical growth, therefore, was essentially a form of monotheistic idealism before the advent of the Christian Era. Soon the early Christian trends began to make themselves felt, and yet the sum total of the scientific equipment which was at the disposal of the world came from polytheistic, pagan sources. A tricornered, inner conflict ensued: mystical monotheism of early Christianity, Oriental mysticism of a pantheistic nature, and pagan scientific, somewhat eclectic, realism—all fought and strove for a new synthesis.

Whatever divergences these cultural and philosophical trends might have represented while they were developing, they all included an emphatic interest in man and his nature: not only ethics but everything pertaining to man became of vital interest. The mysticism which overwhelmed the minds of the early centuries of our era had not yet come to assert itself, and, therefore, man as an individual had not yet been lost in the great wave of expiatory seeking of salvation.

Anatomy was studied rather diligently, particularly by the school of so-called "solidists"; Herophilus and Erasistratus stand out as the very great of the closing centuries of antiquity. They studied the human brain with great care, and Erasistratus pondered the possible relationship between the number of cerebral convolutions and intelligence. He was a physician and is said to have diagnosed the nervous condition of Antiochus as "amorous melancholy." The Greco-Roman physicians apparently thought seriously that love, that is, the emotional characteristics of love, was a form of mental disease, a belief which was carried over into the psychiatry of the Arabs. On the other hand, more sober speculations began to percolate into medical thoughts. The old problem as to the role of the *pneuma* and heat continued to hold the interest of the medical student. Erasistratus took issue with Aristotle and denied the existence of innate heat. "Man cannot live, if he does not constantly take in air; air is life, or at any rate the condition for the maintenance of life; it produces and sustains the warmth of the body; there is no innate heat." [31] It is very striking that an intuition which sounds like pure speculation will prove at times to be a sound, scientific fact. The contention of Erasistratus was proved almost twenty centuries later by the discoveries of Lavoisier and Laplace.

VII

THE scholars of Alexandria depended mostly on the subvention of the government. About 150 B.C. the various representatives of the dynasty of the Lagides, under Ptolemy-Euergetes II, were indulging in a characteristic series of quarrels, and the status of scholars became more uncertain. A number of them began to migrate to Rome, and for a while Rome became the center of scientific productivity. Nothing original was contributed to mental science, however, until the appearance of Asclepiades toward the middle of the first century B.C. Cicero quoted Crassus as saying, "When Asclepiades, who was my

[31] A. Semelaigne: *op. cit.*, p. 83.

physician and my friend, smothered his professional colleagues with his eloquence, he did this not only by virtue of his eloquence but also by virtue of his science." [32] The years of the birth and death of Asclepiades are unknown. His writings were lost. He started as a rhetorician and later espoused a medical career. He was as skillful as he was vociferous. He was despised by many and admired by a number of the notables of his day.

Asclepiades broke with the past very sharply. He proclaimed the whole of Hippocratic teaching to be "a meditation of death." He followed Democritus and Heraclitus and thought of the human body as a multitude of atoms which are in constant motion. If the spaces between the atoms (pores) became too small or too large, an illness ensued. This constant constriction and relaxation of the pores became known as the theory of *strictum et laxum*. The medical tradition which followed this theory became known as methodist. The great pupil of Asclepiades, Themison (123–43 B.C.), developed this theory more thoroughly.

What knowledge we have of the work of Asclepiades we owe to Caelius Aurelianus. In accordance with his philosophical methodism and particularly with Epicureanism, Asclepiades did not believe that the soul had any special seat in the body; he thought of it in terms of a convergence of all perceptions. He added nothing new to the traditional views on mental diseases, but because of the greater interest in man as an individual, which was inherent in the predominating philosophic orientation, we find in Asclepiades a keen awareness of psychological detail. A new breadth as well as depth characterizes his clinical psychology. He was the first to divide diseases into acute and chronic. [33] Mental diseases proper had for centuries been differentiated from delirious states (phrenitis) due to fever. Asclepiades studied the febrile reactions and shrewdly differentiated them from mental disease, not only on the basis of the presence of fever but also on the basis of psychological characteristics. He pointed out the lethargic, semicomatose states to be found in certain deliria (*cum corporis atque mentis oppressione*). He preferred the term *furor* when describing

[32] *Ibid.*, p. 88, footnote.
[33] Kurt Sprengel: *Histoire de la médecine depuis son origine jusqu'au dix-neuvième siècle.* Translated by A. J. L. Jourdan. Paris, 1815, vol. II, p. 13.

an excitement, and it was he, or Caelius Aurelianus in writing about him, who objected even at that early date to the term "insanity," which was apparently as much in use then as it is now, but which he rightly considered a popular rather than a clinical term (*furor quem vulgo insaniam dicunt*). A mental disease, Asclepiades sensed, was due to emotional disturbances, which he called "passions of sensations" (*alienatio est passio in sensibus*)—a point of view almost identical with present-day trends in psychopathology. How surprisingly keen the observations of Asclepiades were can be judged from the fact that he was able to differentiate between delusions and hallucinations; such a differentiation was not established in psychiatry until the first quarter of the nineteenth century, when the French psychiatrist Esquirol brought the matter to the articulate attention of the profession.

The Greeks considered both delusions and hallucinations under one heading, *phantasia;* this was rendered into Latin as *visum.* Asclepiades considered two varieties: one in which the patient sees an object but perceives it as something else (*ex visis veris ducentes, quidam mentis errorem*), which is known today as a delusion; and the other in which the patient hears or feels things although there is nothing near to hear or feel, *silentibus sensibus,*[34] the phenomenon designated by Esquirol as hallucination.

Semelaigne, who could not forget the characteriological peculiarities of Asclepiades, sums up his view rather tersely: "Despite his exaggerations and somewhat charlatanesque tendencies, Asclepiades possessed a marvelous sagacity."

The originality of Asclepiades was not limited to his clinical observations; he was as original in the problem of the treatment of mental disease and as consistently interested in the individual patient. He, therefore, was radically different from his predecessors. He invented ingenious devices to make things more comfortable for the patients: a suspended bed, for example, the swaying of which was supposed to have a sedative effect on disturbed patients. He is said to have invented "a hundred kinds of baths." [35] He considered "musical harmony and a concert of voices" very valuable therapeutic measures.

[34] A. Semelaigne: *op. cit.*, p. 92.
[35] Pliny: L, XXVI. Cited by Casimir Pinel in: *Du traitement de l'aliénation mentale aiguë en général et principalement par les bains tièdes prolongés etc.* Paris, 1856, p. 3.

He objected violently to bleeding, considering it equivalent to stran-
gling. Bleeding, he said with characteristic emphasis, might be successful in Athens, but it was more likely to be injurious in Rome,
because the Romans were already worn out with debauchery. He objected with the same vigor to the cells and dungeons in which the
mentally ill were kept. Darkness, insisted Asclepiades, excites terror;
patients should be kept in well-lighted places.[86]

VIII

EVEN the above brief review of the psychiatric contribution of Asclepiades should bring into relief the fact that Rome toward the close of
the pre-Christian Era was passing through a period of humanism in
medical psychology. Problems of individual management of the mentally ill, problems of their manifold psychological reactions, problems
of environmental modifications were no more merely theoretical,
academic considerations, but tasks which the physician as well as the
community began to look upon both with great interest and a growing
sense of responsibility. Medical psychology broke through the confines of the limited medical or semipriestly groups and became a subject of interest to every thinking man. The cultivated layman awoke
to the issues raised by mental illness—philosophical, psychological,
sociological, judicial. For the first time in the history of medicine we
find this awakening, and an elaboration of the issues involved occupied the minds of Imperial Rome, of Cicero, Plutarch, and Celsus.

Cicero (106–43 B.C.) was not a blind follower of the Epicurean
Asclepiades. He was a Stoic and he was devoted to Greek learning,
which he said came not as a weak stream gliding from Greece, but
as a mighty and rapid flood to within the walls of Rome.[37] He opens
his third book of *Tusculanes* with the following words: "Man being
composed of body and soul, why is it that so much attention has been
paid to the art of the preservation of the body and the curing of
bodily ills; why is it that this art, which because of its usefulness was

[86] Le Clerc: *Histoire de la médecine*, 1796. Chapters on Celsus and Caelius Aurelianus. Also, Kurt Sprengel: *op. cit.*, vol. II.
[37] *De Republica*, II, 19.

attributed to the power of the gods, has so badly neglected the development of the art of healing the soul?"

Cicero even shows insight into what we call today psychopathic personalities, or neurotic characters, and he continues, "Where men are carried away by desire of gain, lust of pleasure, and where men's souls are so disordered that they are not far off unsoundness of mind (the natural consequence for all who are without wisdom), is there no treatment which should be applied to them? Is it that the ailments of the soul are less injurious than physical ailments, or is it that physical ailments admit of treatment while there is no means of curing souls? But diseases of the soul are both more dangerous and more numerous than those of the body. For the very fact that their attacks are directed at the soul makes them hateful, 'and a sick soul,' as Ennius says, 'is always astray and cannot either attain or endure: never does it cease to desire'; and to say nothing of others, what bodily diseases can be more serious, pray, than these two diseases of distress and desire? And then how can we accept the notion that the soul cannot heal itself, seeing that the soul has discovered the actual art of healing the body, and seeing that men's constitutions of themselves, as well as nature, contribute a good deal to the cure of the body, and not all of those who have submitted to treatment succeed at once in making recovery as well, whereas we see, on the contrary, that souls which have been ready to be cured and have obeyed the instructions of wise men, are undoubtedly cured?" [38]

True to his convictions, which have survived to our own day, Cicero momentarily forgets or overlooks the physician and exclaims, "Assuredly there is an art of healing the soul—I mean philosophy. . . . We must use our utmost endeavor, with all our resources and strength, to have the power to be ourselves our own physicians." [39] But Cicero raises his voice against general superstition and the confidence placed in oracles and sharply enjoins: *Jam et nihil possit esse contemtius!* ("Indeed, nothing could ever be more reprehensible.")

It is truly remarkable to what extent Cicero not only seems to have familiarized himself with the subject of psychiatry, but also how advanced and both critical and creative his conception of mental dis-

[38] *Tusculanes*, III, 2, 3.
[39] *Ibid.*, III, 3.

ease was. He questioned the validity of the old views, which maintained that mental disease is due to a disturbance of our sensori-perceptive apparatus. Hercules, he argued, pierced his own sons with arrows, mistaking them for the sons of his enemies not because his eyes failed him but because, despite his good vision, he suffered from an illusion (*visum*). It was the mind of Hercules, his soul, which made the mistake. When we concentrate on a certain thought and become abstracted, there are a number of things which reach our sense organs, and yet we fail to see or hear these things; they fail to impress themselves upon us because the soul is diverted and shuts itself out, as it were, from the intrusion of sensory impressions, which constantly knock at its door. Cicero concludes that the mind is of fundamental importance, and not perceptions, true or false. "One proves nothing when illusions in madness or dreams are refuted later in retrospect" after the patient has recovered,[40] for while mad or dreaming we do not doubt the truth of our alleged "false" perceptions. A mental disorder is a disease by itself, a disease of the mind. Therefore, Cicero objected to the term "melancholia" on the ground that it suggested black bile as a causative agent.

Cicero goes further than Asclepiades, who admitted the role of emotions when he spoke of the "passions of sensations." Anger, says Cicero, and fear and pain might also produce a mental disorder. Of course, milder forms of emotions do not cause such disorders; such feelings as envy and pity, he says in *Tusculanes*, do produce psychological changes, but these are mere perturbations (*perturbationes*) and not diseases. Cicero would also reject the Greek term *mania* in favor of *furor*. He distinguishes *insania* from *furor*; *insania* is an absence of calm and poise, but *furor* denotes a complete breakdown of intellectual capacity, which makes the afflicted individual legally irresponsible. That is why, says Cicero, the twelve Tables specified not *si insanus*, but *si furiosus essit*. This is one of the earliest references to the problem of legal responsibility of the mentally ill.

The emphasis on details and the deep humanitarian interest in the mentally ill, so prominent in Cicero, are particularly well illustrated by Plutarch (46–120 A.D.). Not being a physician, he must have borrowed knowledge from medical friends, or perhaps a personal ex-

[40] *Acad.*, II, 27.

perience brought him in close touch with some mentally ill. Whatever the case, Plutarch left to us a description of a depressed person which is both realistic, that is, clinically true, and pervaded with a sense of profound compassion for the mentally sick. The description throws light not only on the mental attitude of some of the cultivated men of the time, but also on certain characteristics of psychopathological reactions, which are hardly different from those of certain psychotics whom we could observe in our contemporary hospitals. When a man is depressed, says Plutarch, "every little evil is magnified by the scaring spectres of his anxiety. He looks on himself as a man whom the gods hate and pursue with their anger. A far worse lot is before him; he dares not employ any means of averting or of remedying the evil, lest he be found fighting against the gods. The physician, the consoling friend, are driven away. 'Leave me,' says the wretched man, 'me the impious, the accursed, hated of the gods, to suffer my punishment.' He sits out of doors, wrapped in sackcloth or in filthy rags. Ever and anon he rolls himself, naked, in the dirt confessing about this and that sin. He has eaten or drunk something wrong; he has gone some way or other which the Divine Being did not approve of. The festivals in honor of the gods give no pleasure to him, but fill him rather with fear and affright. He proves in his own case the saying of Pythagoras to be false, that we are happiest when we approach the gods, for it is just then that he is most wretched. Temples and altars are places of refuge for the persecuted; but where all others find deliverance from their fears, there this wretched man most fears and trembles. Asleep or awake, he is haunted alike by the spectres of his anxiety. Awake, he makes no use of his reason; and asleep, he enjoys no respite from his alarms. His reason always slumbers; his fears are always awake. Nowhere can he find an escape from his imaginary terrors." [41]

IX

In addition to the testimony of such illustrious laymen as Cicero and Plutarch, another nonmedical witness, Cornelius Celsus, left us a

[41] Quoted by J. C. Bucknill and D. H. Tuke in *A manual of psychological medicine,* Philadelphia, 1879, p. 230.

valuable document concerning the state of medicine of that period. Celsus was apparently a highly cultivated person of encyclopedic medical knowledge; his medical compilations so impressed certain of his readers that some of the commentators even called him the Latin Hippocrates, the Cicero of Medicine, or even *Medicorum deus*, the god of the medical men.[42] There is no doubt that his compilation, *De re medica*, is one of the most important historical sources for the understanding of Roman medicine, but it is doubtful whether Celsus himself contributed anything original either to the art of healing or to medical theory.

His treatise was the first medical work written in Latin instead of in Greek, as was the tradition. The years of his birth and death are uncertain. He was probably born under Emperor Augustus (27 B.C.–14 A.D.) and he wrote under Tiberius (14 A.D.–37 A.D.).

The eighth chapter of the third book of *De re medica* is devoted to mental diseases. Celsus propounds no theories of his own, nor does he adopt exclusively those of anyone else. He follows partly Hippocrates, partly Asclepiades; he dislikes speculations. If philosophy could make good medical men, he avers, the philosopher would always be a better healer than the physician. The philosopher possesses only the knowledge of words, not the knowledge of how to treat sick people.[43] Celsus divides diseases into local and general (*totius corporis*); madness belongs to the affections of *totius corporis*. This is a point of great significance, for, although the thought is probably not original with Celsus, it is apparently the earliest expression of a point of view which had been already partly expressed by Cicero, and which did not reach its full scientific development till the twentieth century. The fundamental significance of this view is the conception that in a mental disease the whole personality, and not some single bodily organ, is affected. This type of orientation toward psychological problems denotes a well-advanced individualization of attitude which obviously excludes the old superstitious views on mental diseases. We must bear in mind that, at the time in which Celsus was writing his treatise, superstition and mystical trends were already widespread in Rome. Celsus makes no reference to supernatural causes of mental

[42] A. Semelaigne: *op. cit.*, p. 102.
[43] *Ibid.*, p. 108.

disease, but he calls epilepsy *morbus comitialis;* this name is derived from the fact that the Romans still viewed an attack of epilepsy as of such bad omen that it would arouse the citizens of the community to a special assembly—*Comitia.*

Celsus follows Asclepiades in dividing diseases into acute and chronic; he does not favor the use of the terms "mania" and "melancholia." In accordance with the custom established since Hippocrates, Celsus separates febrile diseases which cause deliria from other mental disturbances which are not accompanied by fever and which are mental diseases proper. The latter Celsus groups under the general name of insanity. Some of these diseases correspond to what was traditionally called melancholia; others are characterized by hallucinatory states. "Some," says Celsus, "err in having false images, and not in their whole mind, as Ajax and Orestes are represented in poetic fables; in others the whole mind . . . is affected." [44] He describes in some detail optic, or visual, hallucinations. It is obvious that in the time of Celsus the description of individual mental diseases had reached a considerable degree of refinement. Evidently the greater observational knowledge of mental diseases was due not only to the greater curiosity and industry of the physician, but also to an increase in the number of the mentally ill, a problem which imposed itself on the physician and taxed his ingenuity. As a result, the question and the manner of treatment of the mentally ill began to be considered in greater detail. The incidental information derived from the discussion of treatment throws more than one telling highlight on the type of diseases with which the contemporaries of Celsus had to deal, on the mental attitude toward difficult cases, and on the modes of treatment, which made up in speculative ingenuity what they lacked in rational, scientific foundation.

"It is necessary to oppress with very harsh, corrective measures all those whose malady does not exceed words or even trifling assaults with the hands; but it is proper to confine those who conduct themselves violently, lest they injure themselves or other persons." [45] Celsus speaks of the application of fetters, a practice of "restraint" not entirely abolished even today in some parts of Europe or

[44] Bucknill and Tuke: *op. cit.,* p. 30.
[45] *De re medica,* III, 18.

America. The problem of restraint has for centuries followed the line of least resistance and, as we see, it is a very old problem. Speaking of certain types of abnormal behavior, the prototype of which was that of Ajax, Celsus says, "When he has said or done anything wrong, he must be chastised by hunger, chains and fetters. He must be made to attend and to learn something that he may remember, for thus it will happen that by degrees he will be led to consider what he is doing. It is also beneficial, in this malady, to make use of sudden fright, for a change may be effected by withdrawing the mind from that state in which it has been." [46] These lines of Celsus are discouragingly telling of the slow pace which is characteristic even of the most curious and scientific minds.

It would be unwise and historically unsound to dispose of these remarks of Celsus merely by setting them down and implicitly or explicitly charging them up to the lack of knowledge or lack of understanding of the times. In expressing these views, Celsus demonstrated not only that he was the child of his age but, and this is more important, that he was the child of man. He betrays an almost eternal inclination to view the disturbances of mind as almost exclusively disturbances of intelligence, of understanding, and he naïvely insists that a certain amount of crude cruelty like physical coercion, and more refined torture like fright, might bring a mentally sick man to his senses. This, as has been repeatedly hinted here, is not the fault of the ancients alone, nor the personal sin of Celsus or his teachers. Almost nineteen centuries later the great psychiatric reformer Philippe Pinel, who took the chains off the mentally ill in Paris, still believed in fright as an effective remedy, and Benjamin Rush, working in Philadelphia during the American Revolution and like Pinel at the turn of the eighteenth century, still recommended ingenious intimidation as a good remedy. In the middle of the nineteenth century superintendents of the state hospitals in a meeting assembled (later to become the American Psychiatric Association) voiced many arguments in favor of physical restraint of the mentally ill. The very persistence of this trend would suggest that we are dealing here with a fundamental mistake, with a fundamental blind spot about mental diseases, of which we are not fully free even today.

[46] *Ibid.*

This mistake can only be discussed in greater detail when we come to consider the revolutionary changes in medical psychology, which did not begin until early in the twentieth century. The physical management of the mentally ill could not become rational if the psychological problems involved remained a mystery. Nor should one expect to find under these circumstances that the medical treatment of these maladies was any more rational or efficacious. Despite Asclepiades, and apparently in accordance with prevailing trends, Celsus would keep certain mental patients in total darkness. Also despite Asclepiades, who thought that bloodletting was tantamount to murder, Celsus was not averse to this practice. He recommended enemas and clysters even as in some quarters today we recommend the administration of colonic irrigations in a number of mental diseases. The age-old use of hellebore was to be continued. If patients could not sleep, Celsus recommended giving them a decoction of poppies or henbane to drink. This decoction, known centuries later as opium or morphine, has been used extensively in hospitals for mental diseases until our own day, when pharmaceutical preparations like hyoscyamine and other somniferous chemicals came into vogue. Again it must be noted that it is the chemical agent, not the principle or attitude, which has changed or "made progress." Emetics, too, were recommended by Celsus, almost as much as by Benjamin Rush. It was also advised in certain cases that patients' heads be shaved and anointed with rose oil or other aromatic substances.

As one ponders over this variety of remedies, one should not try too strenuously to fit their use into the prevailing views on the physiology or psychology of mental diseases. As a matter of fact, it appears rather that certain traditions carried the physician along with them, regardless of his theoretical views. Bloodletting, for instance, had been in use for a long time before the theory was propounded that the flow of blood would remove enough black bile to relieve the patient from the feeling of sadness and oppression. Another example is the use of white hellebore, or, later on, of other purgatives. Melampus used hellebore first because he happened to think it would do the royal daughters as much good as it did the goats in the herd. The Hippocratic dogmatists used it because it was supposed to eliminate the black bile from the intestines. Asclepiades used it too, but for still other reasons. As an atomist he thought that hellebore would relax the atoms so that the spaces between them would increase; he also thought that if enough fluid were removed the spaces between the atoms, the pores, would become correspondingly constricted. All these considerations re-enforce one's impression that despite the various medicopsychological or psychophysiological theories, many remedies remained in use as a matter of habit or, to say it more euphemistically, as a result of tradition. Consequently, the true contribution of the period under consideration is to be looked for not in the remedies applied, but in the psychological observations made.

x

In the absence of an empirical and systematic understanding of mental diseases, this question of clinical observations becomes one of paramount importance. In matters medical and particularly medicopsychological, Imperial Rome was already oscillating between charlatanism and superstition. Even Archigenes, whom Heiberg is inclined to consider the greatest psychiatrist of ancient Rome and whom Alexander of Tralles called divine, used to prescribe amulets as remedies for mental trouble. The ability to detach one's self from the weaknesses of one's age and to proceed with cool and objective observations is a merit of high order. Many physicians of that time were capable of this detachment, which is one of the paradoxical characteristics of the declining rationalism and positivism of the ancient world.

Among such physicians the most outstanding is probably Aretaeus of Cappadocia. Aretaeus was an adherent of the pneumatic school in medicine. We mention here his biophilosophical allegiance only to disregard it. For when the good clinician is confronted with a patient whom he must observe and study as a human being, and not as a phenomenon to corroborate or confute a philosophical or religious principle, he seems to discard, as he always should, his philosophical bias. Therefore, whether we study the pneumatist Aretaeus or the most illustrious of the methodists, Soranus, the keen, simple, and at once humble descriptions of what these men were able to see prove a most important and most permanent contribution to the knowledge of mental diseases, as if this knowledge were not marred at all by any theoretical divagations. These clinicians appear to have been truly humble in the face of clinical phenomena—a fact rather exceptional in those days; for at all times, and particularly in times of superstition, man is inclined to indulge in that variety of megalomania which makes the doctor think of himself as a know-all and of his remedies as cure-alls. This was the tendency which was becoming more and more conspicuous in the first century of our era, and this is the tendency which was so laudably overcome by Aretaeus of Cappadocia. Relating a case of a man whom physicians considered incurably affected by melancholia, Aretaeus reports that that man surprised the pessimistic medical men by recovering fully from his illness after he had fallen in love. Aretaeus concluded: "It is impossible, indeed, to make well all who are ill; for then would a physician be superior to a god." [47]

Aretaeus lived toward the end of the first century A.D. Cumston [48] thinks that he lived between 30 and 90 A.D., which is probably more correct than the view of those who would place him in the second century A.D.,[49] or between the first and the fourth,[50] or definitely even after Galen.[51]

Aretaeus looked for the seat of mental disease in the head and the abdomen. When the disease comes from the abdomen, the head becomes affected secondarily. This is a far-reaching thought, for it deviates from the old idea that each disease has its own place and affects only its own place. It foreshadows the Galenic view that a great many parts of a person may be affected by *consensus*, as Galen put it, even though these parts are not the direct bearers of the malady. The increasing tendency to consider the individual a unitary, biological system, rather than a mechanical collection of so many parts, is here reflected with added strength.

At the time of Aretaeus, physicians began to become more and more

[47] C. B. Farrar: "Some origins in psychiatry." *American Journal of Insanity*, vol. 64, p. 552.
[48] C. G. Cumston: *An introduction to the history of medicine*. New York, 1926, p. 108.
[49] A. Semelaigne: *op. cit.*
[50] Robert Fuchs: *Geschichte der heilkunde bei den griechen*. In Neuburger and Pagel: *op. cit.*, vol. I, p. 286.
[51] F. Del Greco: in Marie's *Traité international de psychologie pathologique*. Paris, 1910, vol. I, p. 42.

aware that certain states of abnormal exhilaration, the so-called "mania," are related to certain states of abnormal depressions, the so-called "melancholia." Aretaeus was inclined to consider these two pathological states as expressions of one illness; this view was ultimately developed in the history of psychiatry into the conception of what we call today manic-depressive psychosis—a series of alternations of manic and depressive attacks. Aretaeus, while inclined to adopt this view, yet states, and quite rightly, that "mania . . . is not always . . . the off-spring of melancholia;—since it often begins originally without any preceding melancholy." [52] Younger people, Aretaeus thought, are more apt to develop mania, while older people are more predisposed to melancholia. This he explains on the basis of the variations of the amount of heat in the blood. Aretaeus was the first to consider the mental disorders of senescence as a separate entity. He also considered wine and love as producing separate types of mental diseases. If we recall the spirit of hedonism in the Rome of the time, its debauchery and recklessness of living, it will become clear that the psychiatrist could not overlook the appearance of alcoholic mental disorders and other toxic pathological states.

Aretaeus was the first, or at any rate the first known, to become interested as we are today in the personalities of the people who later develop severe mental diseases, the so-called prepsychotic personalities. In doing this Aretaeus characteristically abandoned the humoralistic terminology ("phlegmatic," "choleric" temperaments) and limited himself to clear description. Persons who are subject to furor or mania, says Aretaeus, are "naturally irritable, violent, easily given to joy, have a facile spirit for pleasantry or childish things." [53] Those who are prone to be of depressive proclivities are apt to develop melancholia. There is here the first hint that certain mental diseases are but a psychological extension of the so-called normal personality traits of the given individual.

In the days of Aretaeus there must have been a more or less general return to the mystic, pre-Hippocratic views that some mental diseases are of "inspired" nature, and Aretaeus devotes some time to refuting

---

[52] Thomas Arnold: *Observations on the nature, kinds, causes and prevention of insanity.* London, 1806, vol. I, p. 45.
[53] Ulysse Trélat: *Recherches historiques sur la folie.* Paris, 1839, p. 12.

this view in a manner which is both objective and fully consistent with his trend toward considering the prepsychotic characteristics of the patient. If manics do compose poetry or orate on astronomy and philosophy, they do so not because of divine inspiration but because of their previous education.[54] Yet Aretaeus thought that heart disease might make one clairvoyant at times.[55] In describing various mental states he, more than any of his predecessors, seems to have paid particular attention to what the patients thought and felt, to their ideational content as we would say today. In this respect he was almost two thousand years ahead of his time.

In addition to his attention to the ideational content Aretaeus, like Archigenes, excelled in the art of prognosis. He was inclined to consider mental diseases from the point of view of what the final outcome of the given disease would be. This inclination to estimate a mental disease by its ultimate outcome was destined to become one of the most potent, at times useful, and on the whole rather dangerous if not sterile, methods of studying clinical psychiatry. Toward the close of the nineteenth century this prognostic point of view culminated in the Kraepelinian system, which would determine the nature of a given mental disease by its final outcome. To predict an outcome is quite obviously a different thing from determining the meaning of the disease. Aretaeus, on the basis of his rich clinical experience, could predict the general outcome of a number of mental conditions. This merely testifies to the fact that apparently he followed many of his patients to the very end, but, as a result of circumstances to be considered when we discuss the psychiatry of the latter part of the nineteenth century, this natural trend to predict has become almost the foundation of clinical psychopathology.

Aretaeus could not, of course, predict the future of his own trend toward prognostication, but he used it to great advantage in combination with his clinical descriptions. There are characteristic illustrations of Aretaeus' sense of psychological detail. The manic patients abandon themselves to "gaiety, laughing, playing, dancing day and night"; they are irritated by any restraint. Some are not violent while others "destroy their clothing and are inclined to maltreat or kill" those about them. Some of them have "their memories reawakened with

[54] A. Semelaigne: *op. cit.*, p. 129.
[55] *Ibid.*, p. 155.

the greatest lucidity," so that "they know astronomy, philosophy and poetry as if they had been en rapport with the muses." [56]

"Mania," says Aretaeus, "is distinct from senile disorders, which are a calamity of old age and progressive and incurable." "Mania, on the contrary, is intermittent and can be entirely cured by good treatment." "Mania terminates in two ways, either by remission or by total cure. The remission is not salutary, if it occurs spontaneously." This is a very keen observation. It is still true today, because remissions without treatment almost invariably lead to future manic attacks. Aretaeus observed and described a number of mental states, the nature of which we did not learn to understand till we had before us the contributions of Kraepelin, Bleuler, and Freud. But Aretaeus noticed them and attempted to differentiate these apparently schizophrenic states from mania, a word which seems to have been for centuries the terminological wastebasket for a number of mental diseases. Some persons, he said, suffered in such a manner that they appeared "stupid, absent and musing." This illness, stated Aretaeus, had no resemblance to mania, being a stupefaction of the sense of reason and other faculties of mind" (caused by refrigeration, whereas the cause of mania is of a hot and dry nature, and its symptoms are turbulent).

As to melancholia, which to Aretaeus already appeared to be a "modification of mania," "it does not affect the intellectual faculties." Aretaeus seems here almost fully ready to accept the fact that one's intellectual faculties may remain unaffected and yet one may be severely ill mentally, and to foreshadow the French view of *folie raisonnante*—reasoning insanity. The melancholic patients, he continues, are "restless, sad, dismayed, sleepless"; they are "seized with terror, if the affection makes progress." "They become thin by their agitation and loss of refreshing sleep." "At a more advanced stage, they complain of a thousand futilities and they desire death." They "tear their own members in a religious spirit and to make a sort of homage to the gods, who demand this sacrifice." All this "is a consequence of a profound conviction and sometimes leaves those whom it torments gay in spite of their sadness, and free from all care as if affiliated with the divinities."

Aretaeus may have had the opportunity to see some of the mass trends toward martyrdom, which were prominent at the time, but there

[56] Trélat: *op. cit.*, p. 13.

is no doubt that his keen clinical eye did not fail to notice the many almost ecstatic, self-destructive, masochistic states which are found among agitated depressions without religious trends. His descriptions of these states have stood the test of time and they are as valid today as they were when he was practicing and writing. Unlike the mass convulsive and self-flagellating psychopathic states of later centuries, which finally disappeared from the psychiatric scene, never to be seen again, the melancholics of Aretaeus are still observed in our time, although under different psychiatric labels. Evidently the melancholia of that time included not only the depressed but also a number of people whom we would now call paranoias or schizophrenias. Aretaeus also saw patients who "fear that people wish to give them poison and who develop hatred for mankind, flee into solitude or become surreptitiously addicted to religious practices."

"Generally speaking," says Aretaeus, "melancholia tends to recur but it cannot be doubted that the disease has either been cured, or it had intervals for years." This thought of Aretaeus was soon fully forgotten. That this type of melancholia can be cured was not brought into the orbit of psychiatry until 1911, when E. Bleuler rather startled the profession with his new understanding of the disease.

What we call today mental deterioration did not escape Aretaeus either. This is frequently the terminal stage of certain types of schizophrenias. He observed it in the advanced stages of some of his melancholics. "It is not rare to see their sensibility and intelligence fall into such a degree of degradation that, plunged into an absolute fatuousness, they forget themselves, pass the remainder of their lives as brute beasts, and the habits of their bodies lose all human dignity."

Aretaeus not only knew well how to describe individual psychological conditions or states, but in an almost modern spirit of scientific discernment he compared the various clinical pictures and pointed the way toward differentiating one from another. In other words, he had a good sense for and of the value of differential diagnosis—the most important and difficult work in medicine, and particularly in psychiatry. He was especially careful to differentiate the manias and melancholias from states of inebriation, from alcoholic hallucinoses, and from common febrile deliria.

As far as treatment is concerned, Aretaeus differed in no way from

Celsus and his other contemporaries, except that he does not seem to have favored the coercive measures which were so popular with his colleagues.

Separate mention is to be made of his views on hysteria. They were in no way different from the traditional views, but hysteria was destined to play an extraordinary role in the history of psychiatry, and whenever the problem of this illness is raised or even mentioned by a great physician, it is worth while to set down the statement for purposes of record and future consideration. Aretaeus believed that hysteria is a disease limited to women. It is due to the migration of the uterus upward, which produces "hysterical suffocation." The uterus "is suddenly carried upward, remains above for a considerable time, violently compresses the intestines, and the woman experiences a choking sensation, after the form of epilepsy, but without convulsion . . . and, moreover, the carotids [arteries?] are compressed from sympathy with the heart, and hence there is heaviness of head, loss of sensibility and deep sleep." [57]

XI

IF the writings of Aretaeus of Cappadocia permit us a fairly good insight into the types of mental diseases prevalent toward the end of the first century A.D. in Imperial Rome, the works of Caelius Aurelianus present a valuable adjunct in that they offer a critical review of the prevalent methods of treatment. Caelius writes on his own account but also, if not primarily, in order to present the works of Soranus, his great predecessor and probably the greatest physician of the time in matters of therapeutic intent and in the critical evaluation of what should be done for patients. Caelius Aurelianus was a product of Carthage, the new scientific center and the rival of Alexandria. An African, a Numidian from the town of Sicca, he practiced and wrote some time during the periods covering the reigns of Trajan (98–117 A.D.) and Hadrian (117–138). He wrote in a Latin which was

---

[57] In addition to references given, cf. Aretaeus: *On the causes and symptoms of acute diseases.* Translated by Francis Adams. London, 1856, Bk. II, ch. xi; Bk. I, chs. v and vi. Also, Trélat: *op. cit.*, and Pinel: *op. cit.*, p. 7.

rather labored and obscure, since his mother tongue was neither Greek nor Latin. He followed the principle of the methodist school and it is to him that we owe the rendition of the works of Soranus into Latin. As a matter of fact, the writings of Soranus were lost and all we know about him we owe to Caelius.

Soranus, of whose life we know almost nothing, seems to have been interested primarily in obstetrics and gynecology, but he paid more than passing attention to mental diseases. He described these with a great clarity reminiscent of the skill of Aretaeus. His theoretical views, while in the main methodist, did not seem to be of great import to himself; it was the methods of treatment which preoccupied him. Soranus, even more than Aretaeus, seems to have been interested in the ideational content of the mental disturbance, as exemplified by the following description of some of his maniacs. "The attacks are either continuous or separated by intervals during which the patients are sometimes in complete ignorance of the agitation which they had abandoned, and sometimes they preserve a vague knowledge of what has happened; . . . the patient may imagine he has taken another form than his own; one believes himself a sparrow, a cock, or an earthen vase; another, a god, orator or actor, carrying gravely a stalk of straw and imagining himself holding a sceptre of the world; some utter the cries of an infant and demand to be carried in arms, or they believe themselves a grain of mustard and tremble continually for fear of being eaten by a hen; some even refuse to urinate for fear of causing a new deluge." [58]

Soranus describes stupors very carefully. But it is in discussing the treatment that he reveals great concern and even eager and scornful combativeness in relation to the practices of his day. If he considers a given procedure wrong, he respects no authority in his suggestions, and, methodist though he was, he protests with vigor against the very masters of the school, Asclepiades and Themison. Soranus objects to hard and fast rules. Methodism insisted on stressing the points which various diseases have in common rather than their differences. He insists on constant individualization of the cases to be treated. He objects to the indiscriminate use of such violent medications as emetics and purgatives, and he voices unstinted criticism of those followers of Asclepiades who prescribed large doses of alcohol. "Inflammation of an

[58] Caelius Aurelianus: *Cronic*, I, V. Also, Trélat: *op. cit.*, pp. 24, 25.

organ as delicate and sensitive as the brain and its membranes is increased by the slightest excitation. . . . How can it occur to the mind of any man to dispel intoxication by intoxication?" [59] Moreover, Soranus thought that mania is frequently caused by alcoholic excesses, and he inveighs against Themison for overlooking this point. Speaking of Themison, Titus, and other devotees of Asclepiades, Soranus continues, " 'They prescribe placing all patients in darkness without ascertaining whether the absence of light is in some cases irritating, without ascertaining whether or not this measure adds another burden to the affected head. . . . Rather than being themselves disposed to cure their patients, they seem to be in a state of delirium; they compare their patients to ferocious beasts whom they would subdue by the deprivation of food and by the torments of thirst. Misled without doubt by this error, they advise that patients be cruelly chained, forgetting that their limbs might be injured or broken and that it is more suitable and much easier to restrain the sick by the hands of men than by the weights of often harmful iron. They even advise bodily violence, like the use of the whip, as if such measures could force a return to reason; such treatment is deplorable and only aggravates the patient's condition; it stains the body and limbs with blood—a sad spectacle indeed for the patient to contemplate when he regains his senses.' " [60]

This vigorous humanitarian tone of practical justice, sensitive compassion, and psychological sobriety is not to be found frequently among the medical psychologists of the ancient world. Soranus is in this respect a worthy forerunner and almost a spiritual contemporary of Chiarugi, Pinel, Tuke, and the great reformers of our state hospital systems of the nineteenth century.

Soranus continues with his critical survey. " 'They have the patients fall asleep by the use of the poppy; but this provokes a drowsiness or morbid torpor instead of good sleep; they rub the patient's head with oil of rose, wild thyme or castor oil, thus exciting the very organ which they are trying to quiet down; they use cold applications, ignorant of how often this acts as an exciting agent; often and with so little measure they use irritant clysters and by means of these more or less acid injections they produce no other results than dysentery.' " [61] While music

[59] Caelius Aurelianus: *De morb. acut.*, I, XI.
[60] Trélat: *op. cit.*, pp. 34, 35.
[61] *Ibid.*, p. 36.

may occasionally do some good, " 'they have recommended Phrygian rhythm, full of sweetness and vivacity . . . and the bellicose Dorian rhythm; but it often happens that the harmony of musical accords produces a furious agitation which makes the patient say that he is possessed of a divine spirit. They have advised also that the insane be permitted to indulge in the pleasures of love; but this passion is often the very cause of the malady. Thus some have imagined themselves descending into Hades for the love of Proserpine; some have believed they were favored by a promise of marriage to a goddess, although she was the wife of another. One man enamored of the nymph Amphitrite cast himself into the sea. . . . It is absurd to believe that love, which itself is so often a fury, can suppress furious agitation. It is difficult to say whether the mad should be permitted to have sexual relations; the suppression of the desire for love sometimes agitates them, but more often they are found in a more grievous state after the venereal act.' " [62]

Evidently the abuses in the treatment of the mentally ill aroused Soranus to a state of great discontent. He seems to have had always before his mind's eye the human being who was ill, and not a disagreeable, psychological phenomenon which offends the exalted picture man has of himself and which slights the pride of the doctor who is called upon to deal with the so-called insane. Soranus goes into infinite details of the treatment and management of the mentally ill. No effort seems too great to minister to their comfort. No one called to this ministry, doctor or attendant, may spare his vigilance, ingenuity, and labor; he should strive to be of service to the patient rather than to assert control over him.

The principles which Soranus wished everyone to follow are well reflected in his prescription for dealing with maniacs. "Maniacs must be placed in a moderately lighted room, which is of moderate temperature and where the tranquillity is not disturbed by any noise. No paintings should adorn the walls of their habitation; the air should enter through elevated openings. The patients should be placed preferably on the ground floor, for the majority of them are not infrequently disposed to jump out. Their beds should be solidly fastened and placed in such a manner that they do not see persons who enter; a variety of

[62] *Ibid.*, pp. 36, 37.

irritations is thus avoided. If they are in a state of agitation such that they cannot be given any bed other than straw, the latter should be carefully chosen, prepared and stripped of all hard substance. . . .

"If any part of the body has suffered from the patient's restlessness, warm applications, held by soft and very clean material to the head, shoulders and chest, are useful. It is necessary to employ fomentations of mixed warm oil, a light decoction of tallow or of linseed oil being preferred because of its softening qualities. Frequent comings and goings, especially on the part of strangers, should be forbidden, and the attendants should be rigorously advised to limit the excursions of the patients so that they will never be exasperated by too much vivacity. Nevertheless, it is equally necessary to avoid increasing their unreasonableness by too much inactivity and resulting feebleness.

"Much tact and discretion should be employed in directing attention to their faults; sometimes misbehavior should be overlooked or met with indulgence; at other times it requires a slightly bitter reprimand and an explanation of the advantages derived from proper conduct.

"If patients are agitated or struggle against restraint, or if they are exasperated by seclusion, they should be controlled by a number of attendants, who should take care that their purpose is disclosed as little as possible. Thus, patients may be approached as if frictions were to be given, and thereby unnecessary resistance will be avoided. If the sight of men irritates them, restraining bands may be employed, a measure which is seldom required. These bands must be of soft and delicate texture and all joints must be carefully protected. The greatest precautions must be taken in order to avoid shock, for the careless application of restraining bands increases or even produces fury instead of appeasing it." [63]

In addition to these very carefully thought-out details of management and care, Soranus gives detailed descriptions of when and how to apply cupping or enemas during the illness and convalescence, and of the aftercare during the period immediately following recovery from the illness.[64] Whenever possible, he avoids the use of drugs. " 'In cases of fatiguing wakefulness it may be beneficial to carry the patients in a litter or sedan chair, or even upon the entwined hands.

[63] Caelius Aurelianus: *De morb. acut.*, I, IX.
[64] *Ibid.*, I, XI; I, V.

The monotonous sound of falling water often induces sleep. The application of warm sponges to the eyelids relieves the distress arising from long privation from sleep, and its soothing action may extend even to the cerebral membranes.' " [65] These suggestions are offered as substitutes for the decoctions of poppy seeds.

Soranus was apparently the first who took into consideration the cultural factors in the treatment of mental patients. He described in detail how and what to read to patients during their convalescence. A laborer should be engaged in conversation about the cultivation of the fields, and a sailor, in a discussion of navigation. If the patient is grossly ignorant, he should be approached with only very general topics, or with simple calculations. " 'It is possible, in fact, to arouse the interest of all kinds of persons, but care should be taken to encourage the patients by complimenting them when possible.' " [66]

" 'Those patients who have nearly recovered may be permitted to listen to the disputations of philosophers. Sadness, fear and rage have often been dispelled in this way, and philosophers have thus contributed much to the re-establishment of health.' " [67]

These few excerpts dealing with the psychotherapeutic principles of Soranus, as they were related to us by Caelius Aurelianus, reveal not only a good clinician but a humanitarian personality who approached the clinical problem before him with a thoughtful thoroughness and apparently with a sympathetic understanding of the person he was called upon to treat. Natural and self-understood as such an attitude appears today, Soranus seems to have voiced a new note in Roman psychiatry. Many of his predecessors whose names have come down to us appear to have been preoccupied with the intellectual problem at hand—as if it were a curious puzzle to solve (Celsus), or an opportunity to be clever (Asclepiades), or an additional occasion to test or to display one's speculative propensities (the Hippocratic dogmatist). The turn of the first century of our era marks the appearance of a true humanism in psychopathology, and both Aretaeus of Cappadocia and Soranus, supplementing one another, present the very essence of this humanism: a keen interest in man and in the minutest aspects of his

[65] Trélat: *op. cit.*, p. 30.
[66] *Ibid.*, p. 32.
[67] *Ibid.*, p. 33.

behavior, a flair for characteriological differentiations, and a deeply seated and live therapeutic intent. Aretaeus proved himself worthy of his task by the mastery of description and detail, while Soranus rose to heights of therapeutic acumen theretofore unsurpassed. Neither Aretaeus nor Soranus was hampered in his professional growth by strict allegiance to the physiological philosophies he espoused. Both plainly stated their respective theoretical positions and both preferred to be led by their clinical experience rather than by loyalty to the theories to which they officially adhered. This is probably why the pages of Aretaeus and those of Soranus give one such a sense of freshness and conviction, and why the fervor of criticism which Soranus voiced against the therapeutic routinism of his predecessors compares only with the ardor of Hippocrates in his discourse on the *Sacred Disease*. An old fire seems to have been rekindled in the psychiatrist, a fire which unfortunately was not destined for very long to give its salubrious glow to the medical profession or to the community. The spirit of superstition was beginning to infiltrate the science of medicine and man's attitude toward his own mind.

Caelius Aurelianus, the man who admired Soranus so much and who followed his principles, is perhaps one of the earliest examples of this transition from the all too brief medicopsychological humanism to moralistic superstition. In this attitude he reflects, of course, the spirit of the time, and the problems he deals with demonstrate how much the field of psychological medicine had become extended and how many more and new psychopathological phenomena had been included in the field of medical work. Caelius, like Celsus, warned against setting store in the philosopher's ability to cure madness; evidently the philosopher continued then, as he continued for centuries, to claim the field of psychiatry as his own. Caelius adds, perhaps not without some irony, that philosophy may itself be a cause of madness. In enumerating some of the causes of mental disease, he speaks of head injury, suppression of menses, exposure to strong sunlight, abuse of wine, digestive disturbances, superstition, and too much love for philosophy, glory, or money.

As a methodist, he would not separate soul and body too sharply. What is truly remarkable, he disparaged those who would make a diagnosis on the basis of a single sign or of a very few. Like a twentieth-century scientific psychiatrist, he insisted that diagnostic conclusions be drawn only on the basis of the total picture—*ex toto signorum consensus*. His description of phrenitis is clear and abounds in detail. His rendition of the clinical manifestation of mania and melancholia is worthy of the pens of Aretaeus and Soranus. His *De morbis chronicis*, particularly Chapters V and VI, reveal a humanistic and experienced clinician.

In Caelius we find for the first time a sharp deviation from the rational hedonism which characterized the Age of Pericles, particularly in matters sexual. The ascetic trends of the early Christians had evidently made themselves felt more definitely, and perhaps, too, the debauchery which characterized Imperial Rome had brought the erotic components of psychopathological states more clearly into evidence. Consequently, Caelius must have observed a number of erotic trends and deviations. Humane and kind though he was toward his mental patients, he left no doubt that he was repelled by what we would call today compulsive erotic behavior or otherwise strong erotic trends. *Nostra corporis*, states Caelius, *loca divinia providentia certis destinavit officiis*—each organ has its own function in accordance with the will of Divine Providence. The sexual perversions apparently prevalent in the days of Caelius aroused him to protest and disgust; the tolerance and even glorification of certain sexual gratifications by a Plato or a Socrates had fully disappeared. The tide seems to have turned away and against the widespread sensuality of the day, and Caelius considered it "the most malignant and fetid passion of the mind (*mentis passio*)." Yet, his medical habits of thought were not entirely overshadowed by his disgust, and he considered sexual perversions and extreme sexual indulgence illnesses which at times were epidemic in character (*coacervatim*). The treatment of epileptics in the days of Caelius Aurelianus was apparently not unlike the treatment of certain mental conditions in various countries, including the United States, today. The knife of the surgeon and not the skill of the psychiatrist was resorted to; epileptics were castrated. Caelius emphatically reminds us that eunuchism does not relieve one of epilepsy.[68]

Despite his realistic attitude toward surgery in psychiatry and his brilliant clinical positivism as expressed in his principles of diagnosing

[68] A. Semelaigne: *op. cit.*, p. 169: *Eunuchismus vires amputat, non epilepsiam solvit.*

ex toto signorum consensus, Caelius could not escape the spirit of growing superstition. He believed that certain cases of furor are definitely
clairvoyant, and in his *De incubone* he accepted and reformulated the
increasingly popular ancient belief that there exists a special type of
demon who appears under the guise of a man and whose business it
is to tempt and seduce women sexually.[69] It was this belief which crept
into psychopathology almost imperceptibly, only to take possession of
the field and play a most prominent and gruesome part in medieval
psychiatry, remaining a potent element until almost the close of the
seventeenth century.

XII

THE period under consideration culminated in the contribution of
Galen (130–200). Seven centuries intervene between Hippocrates and
Galen. These years saw a series of radical political and cultural changes
in the Greco-Roman world. A variety of scientific theories was evolved.
The stream of Oriental mysticism, which for almost five hundred years
had been diluting the substance of classical science, asserted itself more
and more forcibly, so that at the time of Galen the breakdown of intellectual, classical culture was considerably advanced and it began to
be submerged by emotional speculation. Those few who still followed
the best that was in Greek scientific tradition sought to cull out, to com-
pile, and to reformulate all that was found useful in the various contemporary and ancient schools of thought. Eclecticism was born. It
was, as we see, a conservative movement which sought to preserve the
best of classical learning and tradition. In Galen eclecticism found
not only its leading medical exponent but also its scientific and historical justification. An old historian characterized Galen in the words:
*Galenus, medicorum post Hippocratem princeps, philosophus, gram-
maticus.*[70] "Like Hippocrates, who brought together the medical
knowledge of his day and gave it an independent existence both as
a science and as an art, Galen collected and co-ordinated all the medi-

---

[69] *Ibid.* Also, A. Brierre de Boismont, *Hallucinations or the rational history of apparitions, etc.* 1853, p. 319.
[70] Ch. Daremberg: *La médecine, histoire et doctrines.* Paris, 1865, p. 59.

cal knowledge which had been accumulated by his predecessors. He then enriched it with his own observations, and he created a medical system which, under the name of Galenism, continued to dominate the medical world almost till the middle of the eighteenth century, despite the circulation of the blood and many other discoveries." [71]

Galen has this to say about himself. "In my youth, I studied the doctrines of all the sects and I absorbed all their principles. I condemn or hate none of them; I understand them all. My mind was nursed on the teachings of the empiricists as well as on the lessons taught by the dogmatic scholars; having partaken from both these sources, why should I nurse hatred for either? Be it therefore understood that I do not condemn any of the schools, but I came to understand that true science consists in correlation of the various principles of the various doctrines. Free from any sectarian spirit, I felt capable of stating courageously what I thought." [72] Galen was in actuality much less courageous than he wishes to present himself,[73] and much less modest; he was impetuous, polemic to the point of being querulous, a man of tremendous drive for literary production and rhetorical verbiage. Temperamentally, too, he would seem to have been well suited to adopt an eclectic attitude. He attempted to reconcile or rather to juxtapose Hippocrates and Plato, Aristotle and Epicurus, Zeno and Erasistratus.

At times Galen's scientific positivism was unequivocal. "Do not go to the gods," he cried, "to make inquiries and thus attempt by soothsaying to discover the nature of the directing soul . . . or the principle of action of nerves; but go and take instruction on the subject from an anatomist." [74] On the other hand, Galen was a confirmed teleologist. He was not satisfied by observations alone. He felt the need to establish the reason for the fact that this or that organ was put together as it was. He carefully traced the sixth pair (now the tenth) of cranial nerves to the viscera; he pondered over the loop- and basket-like arrangement of the twigs of these nerves around the stomach, and, following a bit too literally the principle of Aristotle that nature does nothing in vain, Galen decided that the loops are arranged as they are in order to serve as protection against undue distention of

[71] *Ibid.*, p. 59.
[72] *De locis affectis*, III, 3.
[73] Daremberg: *Histoire des sciences médicales.* Paris, 1870, vol. I, p. 208.
[74] *De locis affectis*, III, 7.

the viscus when it is full of food.[75] He thought the human hand was perfectly conceived by the Creator. He described in detail its muscles and tendons and was led to the conclusion that the hand is a testimony to the Supreme Wisdom. How much keener the teleological drive of Galen was than some of his observations can be judged from the fact that the hand he described proved to be that of an ape, a fact which led a student of Galen to remark, "Here one sees the wisdom of the Creator singularly compromised by the presumptuous ignorance of Galen." [76] Galen also noticed quite correctly that the phrenic nerve pierces the diaphragm and spreads into branches on its undersurface; he expressed the opinion that all this was in order to lift the diaphragm periodically, the movement making possible the up-and-down motions of breathing.

These teleological excursions of Galen, his occasional mystical trends, and not infrequent obscurity should be viewed as his tribute to the times as much as to his rhetoric, polemics, and an expression of temperament. Despite these and despite his eclecticism, his mind was far from sterile. While many of his ideas were discarded by history or refuted by better knowledge, his contribution must be considered with care and detail, for no other medical figure in history was destined to exercise such great, or at least such prolonged, influence on medicine.

One of the most important thoughts which Galen developed was that alluded to by Aretaeus. Symptoms do not always indicate that the organ, or the part which shows the symptom, is actually affected by disease. Another part may be primarily affected and the symptom may appear by *consensus*, by "sympathy," in a different, essentially sound part. In a delirium due to pneumonia, for instance, the soul is affected not because the seat of the disease is in the head, but because "the principle of the soul has become affected by *consensus*, in sympathy, as it were, with the affected lungs. On the other hand, in phrenitis [present-day meningitis, apparently] or in lethargy the soul, which is the head, is affected primarily and not by *consensus*." [77] This is not merely a point of theoretical, academic value; it has a direct bearing on treatment. It is obviously useless to apply remedies to the

[75] *De usu partium*, IX, 11; V, 9.
[76] Daremberg: *Histoire des sciences médicales*, vol. I, p. 218.
[77] *De locis affectis*, II, 10.

head in cases of deliria, as it is of no avail to apply remedies to any place but the head in cases of phrenitis.

A student of anatomy, Galen pays particular attention to the central nervous system. Apparently following Plato's views that man is an "inverted plant," he considers the spinal cord an outgrowth of the brain, as the trunk of a tree is an outgrowth of its root.[78]

The brain is the center of all sensation and motion. But Galen abandons both Plato and Aristotle when he considers the principle which is responsible for the function of the brain. It is not pneuma, or spirit, but rather the "temperament," the degree of dryness or softness of the nerve tissue, an idea apparently of Aristotelian origin. Impressions (stimuli) appear to Galen as material things, like little hammers, one could say. If impressions strike a soft part of the brain, one *feels;* if they strike a harder part of the brain, one *moves.* He identified several pairs of cranial nerves and described their physiological functions correctly.

Psychic functions are centered in the brain. Galen does not think that these can be localized more specifically. The brain must have eyes and ears in order to see and hear, but it needs no intermediary organs in order to think, reason, recall, or make a choice of what to do.[79] Yet one finds in Galen no clarity on the subject. As a matter of fact, he remains fully confused on this point. On the basis of the above, it would seem that Galen does ascribe to the soul, the mind, an independent and almost immaterial existence; yet in his criticism of the Stoics he states, "Truly, if there were no pleasure nor pain, nor even sensation in the elements devoid of passion, there would be no memory, no reminiscence, no perception; for sensation is the root, the very source, as it were, of all these faculties. If there is no pleasure, nor pain, nor even sensation, then there are no psychic functions, and therefore one would be forced to say that there is also no soul." [80]

This statement would place Galen among the earliest representatives of sensualist psychology, which was particularly influential in the England of the seventeenth century. But Galen was not consistent in his theoretical psychology; his chief interest was physiology and

---

[78] *De locis affectis*, III, 8. *Cf.* also, Jules Soury: *Le systeme nerveux central.* Paris, 1899, pp. 259–309.
[79] *Ibid.*, II, 10. Also, A. Semelaigne: *op. cit.*, p. 194.
[80] Daremberg: *La médecine, histoire et doctrines*, pp. 83, 84.

the correlation of his physiological views with mental disease. Strictly speaking, his physiological psychology contributed very little that was new and he added little to the clarification of the problem of mental disease. But his influence on medical thought was for centuries so great and so continuous that it is necessary to have a clear view of Galen's system, which can be briefly summarized.

Food passes from the stomach to the liver, which is the source of heat; here it is transformed into chyle and then permeated with spirits innate in every living substance, the so-called *natural spirits*. The substance then is carried through the veins to the heart. In the meantime, the air coming through the windpipe and lungs, the pneuma, which carries the vital principle, combines with the *natural spirits;* thus, the *vital spirits* are produced. These rise toward and into the brain and there become converted into *animal spirits*. Galen's principle was *Ubi nervorum principium ibi etiam animae principatus*,[81] the seat of the soul is inseparable from the nerve centers. The *animal soul* is the rational soul; its seat is in the brain, which is the seat of reason.[82] Galen proceeds to derive a descriptive psychology and divides the rational soul into two parts, the external and the internal. The external parts or functions are those of the five senses; the internal functions are imagination, judgment, memory, apperception, and movement. Galen followed a rather scientific procedure, for he demonstrated his conclusions by animal experiments. He would expose the brain and the heart of a living animal, usually a pig, and show that the compression of the brain would bring about the loss of sensory and motor functions, while the compression of the heart would affect only the arteries. He would then conclude that it was the brain (as Plato thought) and not the heart (Aristotle) which was the seat of the soul. That the arteries were affected by the manipulation of the heart Galen observed clearly, but that the heart might therefore have something to do with the flow of blood in the arteries he was unable to conclude. In other words, he actually observed and manipulated the circulation of blood but failed to discover it.[83] History was not ready, and there-

[81] *De placitis Hippocratis et Platonis.*
[82] The word "animal" as used here does not have the connotation it has in modern English. It is related to the word *anima*, soul.
[83] A. Semelaigne: *op. cit.*, p. 188.

fore the keenest observer was blind to what he saw with his own eyes and would not comprehend what he described with his own pen.

Galen relegated to the heart the role of the seat of one of the two irrational souls. The seat of the other was in the liver. The word "irrational" apparently meant in those days what we mean today by emotional. The heart is the center of the irascible, energetic, or male soul; the liver, the seat of the sensual, concupiscent, female soul.

While refusing to speculate on the immortality of the soul, a pastime he left to the philosopher,[84] Galen took issue with Plato. "The soul is the slave of the body and is consequently dominated by the body. Plato himself recognizes the fact when he mentions the stupidity of children, the loss of memory and the deliria of old age, and mania and melancholia as resulting from morbid humors."[85] On the other hand, "those who concede that the soul is a material substance will also be forced to concede that it is the slave of the temperaments of the body, since these temperaments may drive the soul out of the body, make it delirious, deprive it of memory and judgment and make it sad, timid and downcast, as we see it in melancholia."[86] Not only the quantity of brain substance but also its quality is important. "The keenness of the mind depends upon the fineness of the brain substance. Slow thinking is due to its heaviness. . . . Its firmness and stability produce the faculty of memory. The shifting of opinions is produced by the mobility of the brain."[87] Climate has a great deal to do with the psychological characteristics of people.[88] The Athenians, for instance, were clever and gracious because of the light air they breathed; while the heavy atmosphere of Theban villages made the citizens of Thebes slow thinkers.[89]

As to mental diseases, that is, disturbances in the functions of the animal spirits, they may be due to the direct affection of the brain or to its affection by *consensus*. Dementia (*amentia*) and imbecility (*stultitia, fatuitas*) result from the rarefaction and diminution in quantity

[84] *De plac. Hip. et Plat.*
[85] A. Semelaigne: *op. cit.*, pp. 189, 190.
[86] *De plac. Hip. et Plat.*
[87] *De usu partium.*
[88] This thought was not foreign to Hippocrates, Plato, and Aristotle.
[89] Michéa: *op. cit.*, p. 266.

of the animal spirits and from the coldness and humidity of the brain.[90]
Mania and melancholia are due to direct brain disease, while as an example of mental disease developing by *consensus* Galen cites drunken-
ness. The wine fills the whole body with warm vapors, which cause a
disorder of the irascible soul (heart) and the sensual soul (liver); in
this way judgment (brain) becomes secondarily impaired.

Galen's eclecticism produced a considerable confusion in his view
on the humoral theories of Hippocrates. He accepted them but frequently failed to apply them. He spoke of the febrile delirium (phrenitis) as caused by yellow bile and also considered yellow bile responsible for the irritability and outbursts of anger seen in mania. His
views on melancholia are even more confusing. They came to us second-
hand, through the work of Aetius (sixth century A.D.).[91] Occasional
references to melancholia are found in *De locis affectis*.[92] Galen thought
of a melancholic humor (*succus melancholicus*) as a waste product of
the liver and spleen. The brain is affected by *consensus*. The melancholic is sad, because his sensual soul is affected and he is thereby
deprived of love and joy, the two chief characteristics of the sensual
soul, the seat of which is in the heart.

Galen rejected the idea that in hysteria the uterus wanders in the
body like an animal, and yet he thought hysteria was caused by a local
"suffocation," engorgement of the uterus. He found medication of no
avail in hysteria. On occasion, he advised stimulation of the clitoris and
of the neck of the uterus.[93]

Galen contributed nothing new, either to the therapy or to the
clinical description of mental diseases. But his total contribution was
monumental. It was a kind of summary of, as well as epilogue to, the
classic Greco-Roman period in medicine. Political historians divide
ancient history from medieval by emphasizing the decisive invasion
of Rome by the Barbarians in the latter part of the fifth century. We
must note, however, that the Dark Ages in medical history began with
the death of Galen in 200 A.D.

[90] *De sympt. causis.*
[91] Aetius: *De melancholia, ex Galeno & Rufo* in *Contractae medicinae*, III, 2, ix.
[92] Particularly in III, 4 and 6.
[93] E. Frederick Dubois: *Histoire philosophique de l'hypochondrie et de l'hystérie.*
Paris, 1837, p. 458.

4

THE GREAT DECLINE

I

AS THE chapter of Galen's life came to a close, so came to a
close a chapter of medical history the meaning of which cannot
be overestimated. "Medical wisdom came to an end with the
passing of Galen," states the medical historian Paul Diepgen. The
medical world entered that twilight which is commonly called the
Dark Ages. This transition was neither abrupt nor accidental, and it
must be properly assessed by one to whom the history of medical
psychology, like any history, is a process without gaps. One may not
lay the responsibility for this retrogressive change at the portals of
the Christian Church. "The Church contributed to but was not responsible for medievalism. . . . Just as the Christian recognized no
truth above Christ, so the Saracens recognized no one above Mohammed, or the Jew no truth above that of Moses." [1] Yet a number of
writers are inclined to see the problems in a different light. "It may
occur to one to wonder," says Bury, "how history might have been
altered—altered it surely would have been—if the Christians had cut
Jehovah out of their programme and, content with the New Testament, had rejected the inspiration of the Old." [2]

[1] Paul Diepgen: *Geschichte der Medizin.* Berlin, 1914, vol. II, p. 9.
[2] J. B. Bury: *A history of freedom of thought.* New York, 1913, p. 54.

A similar thought appears to have been in the mind of Calmeil, who emphasized the impossibility of developing a scientific medical psychology. "Abraham and Lot not only heard voices of supernatural beings, who predicted to the first the birth of Isaac and to the second the perdition of the corrupted cities, but at their leisure they observed the features of the emissaries of the Lord: they even spent several hours with them; they saw them walk, act and even satisfy their human-like needs of food. . . . Almost all hallucinations were assigned to exterior, positive agents . . . [hence] monomaniacs were classed as heretics, as disciples of the devil and apostates." [3] Still other interpreters of medical history remind us that not only the Old Testament contributed considerably to the mystic and demonological psychiatry of the Middle Ages, but also the New Testament. For did not Christ also cast out devils, and did not the principles of the persecution of the mentally ill as "heretics" evolve on the stress which St. Augustine laid upon the words used by Christ in one of his parables: "Compel them to come in"?

These quasi-explanatory contentions bear the imprint of plausibility, but unless carefully tested they may prove speculative and rather fragmentary and may blur the outlook on the actual course of historical development. Medical psychology bears a much more intimate relationship to cultural changes than does any other branch of medicine, and it is also more closely woven together with and more directly an outgrowth of the deeply seated human instincts. The scientific approach to medical psychology to a very great extent depends on and varies with man's attitude toward himself and the outside world. This attitude has never been fully objective; as we have seen in the writings of the Greeks, even their greatest philosophers were either hesitant to admit that the soul might become ill, or they definitely denied such a possibility. Man, whether primitive or civilized, always feels too anxious about the very thing he considers his highest endowment —his mind, his soul. In his anxiety, particularly in times of considerable stress, he always falls into the ambiguous and self-contradictory state in which he views the world in a manner of mystic humility and his own mind in a light of inalienable perfection. This double view-

[3] L. J. Calmeil: *De la folie considérée sous le point de vue pathologique, philosophique, historique et judiciaire.* Paris, 1845, pp. 94, 95.

point in all its multifarious manifestations has always interfered with
the establishment of a sound medical approach to our human psychology.

As Greco-Roman medicine was on its way to temporary retreat, the
process of retrogressive change in man's attitude toward himself reached
a considerable degree of intensity throughout the Roman Empire.
Greek medicine and Greek culture, transplanted to Alexandria, had
endured a protected existence, and classical learning had even flourished
for a century and a half with the benevolent support of the dynasty.
Then the lure of Rome began to be felt. Rome was a practical, administrative nation, never greatly interested in original scientific research, and content with what the Greeks had to offer. In medicine
particularly, the Greeks were considered the sole authorities: Greek
or Greek origin was taken as a guaranty of authenticity for a book.

Unfortunately, it was not the homogenous ancient Athens but Alexandria which was the source of classical knowledge. Alexandria represented a peculiar conglomeration of Jewish, Egyptian, and Persian
trends, and not everyone who came to Rome was really Greek by
culture or learning. Even in the days of Asclepiades, Roman medicine
was under the influence of the Oriental predilection for the excessive
use of drugs. Charlatanism and Oriental superstitions crept in and
established themselves as an integral part of medical practice. Archigenes, excellent clinician though he was, had to rely occasionally on
talismans. "Such of the disciples of Themison as Scribonius Largus
and Vectius Valens . . . sought the popular remedies of peasants and
huntsmen, whose superstitious notions they readily engrafted upon the
body of their systems. . . . The liver of a dead athlete was a sovereign
talisman against epilepsy." [4] "Greek" practices became so compromised
in the eyes of cultivated Romans that a reaction set in against the
Greek. Thus the great Cato explicitly warned his son against any
contact with the degeneracy of Greek physicians.[5] "For a prolonged
period it was impracticable to distinguish between the knavish empiric
who prostituted the slight knowledge of surgery and medicine obtained
in the bathing establishments or barber shops, to trafficking in the credulity of the sick and the infirm, from the earnest and dignified profes-

[4] George F. Fort: *Medical economy during the Middle Ages*. New York, 1883, p. 9.
[5] Plutarch: *Vita Catonis*, 22, 23

sor who identified his practice with the system of Aesculapius or Hippocrates." [6] Pliny in his *Natural History* gives a graphic picture of the conglomeration of popular superstitions and Oriental practices of magic under the flag of medicine. Galen, telling us how he came to write his books, painted an extremely unfavorable picture of the medical profession of his day.[7]

This state of affairs was, of course, a part of the general cultural atmosphere of the times. Rome was leading an extremely tense, emotional life. Hedonistic Epicureanism rivaled semiascetic Stoicism. Seneca, Epictetus, and Marcus Aurelius were very close to a contemplative passivity in relation to the world; they were close to the ideal of inactive and mystic, inner life. While Marcus Aurelius had to spend a great deal of his time in the fields of the Moravian Campaign, he was what we would call today a pacifist; he was submerged in the meditative awareness of man's smallness and insignificance. " 'It is he,' " we read in his *Meditations*, " 'he who decreed thy fashioning that now decrees thy dissolution; thou art accountable neither for the one nor for the other; therefore depart in peace, as he that bids thee depart is at peace with thee.' " [8]

Barbarians were moving in from the North and the East. The world was both changing and closing in on man. The sense of doom and the sense of the eternal were combined. A yearning for deeper, purely personal experiences and the groping for the ideal of and communion with a single God were clearly coming to the surface, to become factors in the new culture, or at any rate important factors in the complete decline of the culture that was the classical world. From this point of view, the appearance of Christ about a century before Galen seems historically natural and inevitable.

The consciousness of our human, spiritual infirmity grew deeper and deeper so that by the time Christ was teaching in Judea, Philo, a Jewish philosopher in Alexandria, was engaged in combining the Hebrew, philosophic tradition with parts of Plato and Stoicism. He attempted to establish a cult which claimed that human life was the restoration of the fallen soul, that every element in the universe has

---

[6] Fort: *op. cit.*, p. 19.
[7] *De libr. propr.*, I, 11.
[8] Quoted by C. F. Webb· *A history of philosophy*. New York, n.d., p. 87.

its occupant, and, hence, that the atmosphere is populated with spirits. Everything purely human was to be depreciated. The old Greek tradition of looking at every manifestation of human activity as worthy of scientific inquiry was definitely disappearing. The very existence of man as man was thought to be due to an original moral fall, an original sin. One hears in this cult reverberations of ancient Hindu mysticism, of the Oriental conception of communion with the Divine World Spirit as taught in the Sacred Book, the Bhagavad-Gita. This had a particular appeal in the atmosphere of dying classicism, and the deeply subjective states of faith and ecstasy became the criteria of truth. "The center of the attention became the beyond. Under these circumstances conditions were naturally not favorable for the development of such earthly matters as the healing art." [9] The goal became salvation—personal, mystic salvation. There was no place for such a crudely sacrilegious matter as medicine of the mind. The whole field of psychology was transferred to fields other than medicine, and it is to mystical philosophy and to religious experiences that one turns from now on to learn about man. It is this stream of experiences which continued for centuries to serve as the very foundation for the principles of dealing with the mental frailties and psychological troubles of human beings.

Toward the beginning of the second century the schism from classical sciences deepened to the point of almost complete cleavage. The cabalistic teachings of the followers of Akiba, the theosophic flights of the Gnostics, the emotional intensity and the mysticism of the Christian Fathers, the deepening abstractions of the Neoplatonists—all presented a united front against the weakened, pagan, polytheistic science. To be sure, "the medical school of Alexandria . . . maintained its ranking pre-eminence—so much so, indeed, that down to the time of the Christian Emperors, the fourth century, it was sufficient for an adventuring physician at Rome to announce himself as an Alexandrian student in order to acquire instant favor." [10] But original work and original thinking had almost ceased. Medical science was making its inventory, in order eclectically to bequeath itself to posterity. Another world was being born.

As has been pointed out, Philo and his followers, Akiba and his

[9] Diepgen: *op. cit.*, vol. II, p. 8.
[10] Fort: *op. cit.*, p. 54.

cabalistic cult were already teaching that the world was populated with spirits. "On the other hand, if we turn to the contemporary systems of partially Christianized theosophy or religious speculation—which are usually grouped under the common name of Gnosticism, because their adherents claimed for an inner ring of initiates the exclusive possession of a secret *gnosis*, that is, knowledge or wisdom—we find them indulging a mythological fancy in the invention of long chains of mediators between God and man." [11] These Gnostics can serve as the most telling expression of the age in so far as they were "an amalgamation of elements purely Grecian and Christian, united with the theogony of Ancient Egypt and the strange cult of the Orient." [12] Thus one more and very important stone was laid in the foundation of the formidable structure which became known as demonology and which was to rule medical psychology for sixteen hundred years.

It must be emphasized that these trends were the result of a general amalgamation of the various streams of thought prevalent at the time, rather than an exclusive outgrowth of the early Christian theology. As a matter of fact, the early Christians appear to have been strict monotheists, and they accepted no mediators between God and man, except Christ. St. Paul warned against the fusion of Christian and theosophic thought.[13] "The tendency to multiply mediators reacted on Christianity itself, practically in the development of saint-worship, and theoretically in the interpolation of a hierarchy of angels between a Christian and his Saviour, similar to the hierarchies of gods in the latest Platonists, by a writer who took the name of St. Paul's Athenian convert, Dionysius the Areopagite. In an uncritical age he acquired a high authority as a companion of the Apostle." [14] An anxious, spiritistic polytheism was engrafted on the expanding monotheism, and it not only interfered with medicine but conquered and subjugated it.

The Christian Father Origen, who was not an exception in this general opposition to objective knowledge, is a case in point. Origen (185–254) was a pupil of the great eclectic scholar Clement of Alexandria. Emotional, tumultuous, impetuous, he lived and acted out his great, ecstatic faith. He was converted at eighteen and soon mutilated

[11] Webb: *op. cit.*, p. 96.
[12] Fort: *op. cit.*, p. 57.
[13] *Colossians*, II, 8–22.
[14] Webb: *op. cit.*, p. 97.

himself in order to kill the carnal part of his life. A preacher and restless proselyte of the new faith, he felt that the scientific traditions of Alexandria were the greatest enemies of his spiritual mission. He wrote a treatise against Celsus. He stated that "the splendid being Raphael had special care of the sick and infirm." [15] Origen "divided the human body into thirty-six diverse parts . . . each . . . under the supervision of a particular *Gnome* or Divinity." [16] He claimed that certain names or words, such as "Adonai" or "Sabbath," were endowed with great and vital virtues; he thought that famine and the sterility of women were caused by evil spirits.[17] The mind of Cyprian (d. 258), the Bishop of Carthage, turned in the same direction; he thought that luxations and fractures of the limbs were caused by demons. Lactantius, in his *Divine Institutions,* described how demons work to injure human viscera and thus affect the human mind.[18]

II

EXPOSED to this restless flood of emotional assumptions, the schools of higher learning also soon began to show the wear and tear of premature age. Schools were established for the sole purpose of wearing down the remnants of classicism and "the direct consequence of this abnormal condition, so foreign to the splendid system established by the Lagides, revealed itself in the diminishing number of mathematicians, historians and medical professors, and attested the profound alteration in scholastic affairs superinduced by the vicinity of their increasing rivals." [19] Religious debates and metaphysical contentions took precedence over the empirical traditions in medicine. Exceptions, Christian or pagan, became fewer and fewer.

Galen was acutely aware of the situation, and he ridiculed the Hebrew and Christian sects.[20] He said that the followers of Moses and

[15] Fort: *op. cit.,* p. 66.
[16] *Ibid.,* p. 85.
[17] Sprengel: *Histoire de la médecine, etc.,* vol. II, p. 150.
[18] *Divine Inst.,* II, 15. *Et occulte in visceribus operati, valetudinem vitiant, morbos citant, somniis animos terrent, mentes furoribus quatiunt.*
[19] Fort: *op. cit.,* p. 61.
[20] *De differentia pulsum,* II, 4.

Christ were so rigidly sectarian as to be unworthy of the name of physicians and philosophers.[21] He discredited the belief that certain Oriental names had a special power and, therefore, he disapproved of calling certain medicaments by their Babylonian names. He attached no importance to the unintelligible sounds produced by little children,[22] which were supposed to have curative power. Galen also denied any significance in the meaning of numbers in their relation to so-called critical days. Yet, while one is inclined to doubt the assertion of Alexander of Tralles that Galen approved of incantation,[23] even Galen was not entirely free from a certain degree of superstition. He decided to become a physician because his father had had a dream which appeared to be an omen. It was also on the strength of a dream that he refused to follow Marcus Aurelius in a military campaign. He even criticized Epicurean physicians for paying little attention to dreams in evaluating the diagnosis and prognosis of diseases.[24] Even in Galen's time, many people seem to have ceased to examine and discuss matters in order to find truth; they rather felt that they must be partisan because they belonged to a given sect or because through family ties or ties of friendships they were bound to a given school of philosophy.[25] And so it happened that "to resist [the] downfall of a progressive science, the Alexandrine polytheistic schools, borne along by the force of religious debates, were utterly impotent; and indeed it would appear that towards the conclusion of the third century the serious study of the curative art was in a measure abandoned by its professors, in order that they might confront increasing sectarians upon the identical plane of supernatural efficacy in the treatment of maladies." [26]

The final deterioration of scientific knowledge thus became inevitable. "Suspended between a metaphysical idealism and a delirious, theurgic world view, the school of Alexandria became lost in the wilds of a new polytheism, wilds populated by a number of subaltern powers, which could be brought to serve man by means of magic." [27] Rome, which ever since Asclepiades had drawn from Alexandria some of its

[21] Ibid., II, 3.
[22] Sprengel: op. cit., vol. II, p. 141.
[23] Daremberg: La médecine, histoire et doctrines, p. 96.
[24] Ibid., pp. 95–96.
[25] Ibid., p. 97.
[26] Fort: op. cit., p. 63.
[27] A. Semelaigne: Etudes historiques, etc., p. 85.

best scholars, could summon no stamina to resist the influx of the trends of cultural deterioration. As early as the second century, during the reign of "Hadrian and the Antoninii, a public proffer was made by the Jews and Pagans at Rome of initiation into . . . occult sciences, formerly the exclusive property of the Egyptian priesthood, whose possession it was asserted gave an undisputed control over the world of demons and by the potential efficacy of amulets, talismans, and uttered spells, procured for the possessor a mastery over nature." [28] In this atmosphere the criminal expansiveness and almost insane intolerance of some of the emperors helped to deal the mortal blow which the whim of history had prepared for science with such relentless inevitability.

When a man abandons himself to his emotions, these emotions, no matter how lofty and inspired, naturally divert him from that calm curiosity about himself and others which is the very keystone of medical psychology. But when men, individually and jointly as a culture, abandon themselves to emotions, that curiosity which would lead them to the tolerant understanding of themselves and others becomes transformed into suspicious dislike of dissenters and into arid intolerance. In ancient Greece this type of intolerance had appeared in times of cultural crises. Anaxagoras was accused of blasphemy because he considered the sun a mass of flaming matter and the gods but inventions of the human mind. While Pericles saved him from death, Anaxagoras was heavily fined and was expelled from Athens. Protagoras, too, was forced to flee Athens, because he would not recognize the existence of the gods. The execution of Socrates in 399 B.C. was an act of intolerance. Aristotle was suspected of impiety and left Athens "lest he should sin against philosophy." On the whole, however, acts of intolerance were not many in Greece and they were more or less isolated.

As to Rome, that empire began in the spirit of a practical, utilitarian state, and it had little interest in the divergence of people's opinions. Rome was not a battleground but a market place of ideas. Neither scientific thought nor superstition was combated. The Roman policy was to tolerate and, if possible, to exploit all opinions and beliefs. Cicero considered superstition of the masses very useful. The maxim of Emperor Tiberius (14–37) is typical: "If the Gods are insulted, let them

[28] Fort: *op. cit.*, p. 78.

see to it themselves." But an attitude of superstition and suspicion soon came to replace the short-lived tolerance of Rome. Vespasian (69–79), although he sent scribes to Alexandria to copy books, ordered the death of a number of people merely because they were philosophers. Trajan (98–117) issued an edict making the adoption of Christianity an offense punishable by death. Hadrian (117–138) tried to import foreign gods to Rome.

Under Antoninus the Pius (138–161) and his successor Marcus Aurelius, sciences were allowed a breathing spell; yet the waning powers of the sciences themselves could not rise in strength enough to prevent Antoninus from holding frequent counsel with the Chaldeans, nor could they prevent the outcropping of Gnostic and other magic schools in Rome under Aurelius. Caracalla (211–217) destroyed the books of Aristotle and ordered the Peripatetics exterminated. Alexander Severus (222–235) worshiped simultaneously Moses, Christ, and Orpheus, and he ordered a statue of Apollonius of Tyana, a prominent magician of his time, to be placed in his "chapel" beside that of Christ. Plotinus (204–270) taught that ecstasy and absolute unity are inaccessible to reason and that the latter is an uncertain source of knowledge. Claudius II (268–270) erected a statue in honor of the magician Simon. Alchemy began to come into vogue. Diocletian ordered all books on the chemistry of silver and gold to be burned; he was also responsible for the terrific slaughter of scholars and prominent men in Alexandria in 296. Julian the Apostate (361–363) protected the magic arts, and Constantine, whose Edict of Milan in 313 established Christianity as the religion of the State, forbade the study of Plato and Aristotle.

Thus it was that the first three centuries of our era, even before the establishment of Christianity as a political and a spiritual instrument, culminated in the development of superstition, obscurantism, and crass intolerance. Although official Christianity made several attempts to combat the practice of magic, it was helpless in the face of its own "delirious theurgy." For it must be borne in mind that the Christian Fathers, even those who were medical minded like Tertullian (d. circa 222), would not deny the existence of the supernatural beings which were postulated by the magicians. It would seem that the Fathers shrank from magic, not so much because it represented an unscientific attitude and a bow to untruth, but because they saw in magic a religious impurity. Soon even the remnants of classical science were to be pushed into obscurity because of their pagan impurity.

To combat superstition and magic by means of authority and belief is at best a spurious undertaking; the only weapon left under those circumstances is intimidation and physical coercion—the most common, most painful, and most unsuccessful tools of political history.

It is not surprising, therefore, that Christianity was well-nigh powerless in its efforts to suppress superstition and occult practices. A synod in Spain in 305 condemned magic, but magic continued to flourish. An order of Constantine in 319 proved no more efficacious. The synod of Laodicea in 343 pronounced the exercise of magic arts evidence of intercourse with demons. Thus, under the guise of combating the ignorance of the masses, man finally came to the official recognition of the efficacy of magic. It did seem to bring about communion with the unknown and the powerful, but it was a bad communion and a bad power. Contact, congress, and communion with good spirits were allowed; the differentiation between the good and the evil became a matter of emotional conviction sanctified by the formality of ceremony and authority, at first purely religious and later also juridical. In the year 429 the *Codex Theodosianus* officially prohibited magic and gave formal recognition to the view that magic was bad and criminal. A united legal front of the temporal and spiritual powers was formed for the future prosecution of the "possessed" and the witches. Soon a heretic by the name of Priscillian was executed in Spain. The principle of punishing the sorcerer and the witch by death became a reality of the culture which supplanted classicism.

The whole field of mental diseases was thus torn away from medicine. Medicine at first did not seem to relinquish this territory unwillingly. Medical psychology as a legitimate branch of the healing art practically ceased to exist. It was recaptured by the priest and incorporated into his theurgic system. Seven hundred years of effort seemed for a long while to have spent themselves in vain. The ardent voice heard in Hippocrates' discourse on the *Sacred Disease* was lost in the wilderness; it was silent for nearly twelve centuries.

Imagination becomes stronger than fact, and destroys reality.

III

As ONE reviews the various stages of the decline of classical science, one might drift to the erroneous conclusion that the theurgic and barbaric philosophies, combined with the military vicissitudes of the time, had catapulted rational curiosity and science to their ultimate deaths. But as long as the process called history has not come to a standstill, human life continues; and as long as human life exists there is wonderment, there is curiosity, and there are endless attempts to answer the ever-growing number of questions which life imposes upon man. The so-called Dark Ages are not ages of death and decomposition; they are restless, disturbed, and disturbing ages, fertile with anxious gropings and the keen, if at times bewildered, exercise of imagination. The medical psychologist may not pass over these centuries without serious contemplation, for they brought to expression a remarkable variety of psychological reactions which, right or wrong, reflect the very essence of man's struggle with himself and with the knowledge of himself which science had so slowly and so painfully acquired. The mystic trends of primitive people represent original outcroppings of man's anxiety in the absence of science; the trends of the peoples of Greece, Rome, Alexandria, or Carthage, in their spiritual and political misfortunes, indicate a militant, theurgic philosophy which rose in revolt against science. This militant anxiety and hostility to knowledge was a cultural combination new in the history of man. The cultivated man began to feel out of place; he felt his interests were being trodden upon with a vigor and fanaticism which he was unable to overcome. The lover of books, the seeker after knowledge, yearned to and did retire from life. "The sword and not the pen reigned and so knowledge, and with it medicine, took refuge behind the walls of monasteries." [29]

The monasteries were far from safe at the beginning. Originally "the word monk [*monachus*] was synonymous with ignominious infamy in vulgar prejudice," [30] so much so that in the year 390, by a rescript of Valentinian II, the associated hermits were subjected to

[29] Diepgen: *op. cit.*, vol. II, p. 21.
[30] Fort: *op. cit.*, p. 148.

persecution. There was one monastery destined to play a great role as the source of medical knowledge; founded by St. Benedict, it stood on Monte Cassino, on the ground previously occupied by a temple of Apollo. Seventeen years before the passing of St. Benedict the monastery became the place of refuge for Cassiodorus, the medical scholar who had been secretary to Theodoric, the illiterate king of the Ostrogoths. In the quiet monastic life Cassiodorus taught the brethren the knowledge of medicine. On his deathbed St. Benedict counseled his brethren to maintain their interest in the healing art. Medical science in Western Europe became primarily monastic. The very Church, whose theurgy militated against medicine in many respects, was the asylum for the fugitive disciples of Hippocrates and Galen. For a while, too, a number of people whom we might call medical intellectuals rather than physicians—Daremberg aptly dubs them *philiatres*—maintained the tradition of reading Greek medical books, and they saved small parts of the Greek psychological contributions. Theirs was merely book knowledge, of course, and their writings were but artless compilations. On reading them "one does no longer ask what a writer has done or what contribution he has made to medicine; one merely tries to recognize which other writer he is translating, or copying or abstracting; medical science began to live on what it was able to borrow from the past." [31]

These compilers did, however, render a great service to the history of medicine. Without them we might never have known of Marcellus, a physician of the third century who contributed to the clinical picture of lycanthropy, a mental disease now extinct. Persons affected by it would wander about at night in deserted places—preferably cemeteries—and howl like wolves. We owe the data on Marcellus to Oribasius (323–400) who was termed "the ape of Galen." Oribasius himself made no pretense at originality, stating in the preface to his *Collecta Medicinalia*, "I shall be careful to omit nothing of what Galen has said." [32]

There were also occasional but very rare sparkles of speculations in terms of cerebral localizations. Posidonius, in the fourth century, considered the seat of the imagination in the forepart, understanding

[31] Daremberg: *Histoire des sciences médicales*, vol. I, p. 248.
[32] Quoted by P. V. Renouard: *History of medicine*. Cincinnati, 1856, p. 239.

in the middle cavity, memory in the posterior section of the brain.[33] Nemesius, the first Bishop of Emesa, placed memory in the middle cavity and judgment in the posterior. Aetius in the sixth century re-peated the same speculations. These opinions were not based, of course, on direct observations. Human bodies were not to be dissected for many centuries. Galen had to limit himself to the dissection of pigs. He could not dissect even apes, because of their similarity to man.

But the majority of those who were interested in medicine kept but a tenuous contact with the past, and about the fourth century an interest in astrology awoke to play an important part in the history of medicine; mental diseases, which apparently were increasing in num-ber, had been almost completely excluded from medicine and had be-come a part of general superstition. A gradual systematization of the superstitious attitude began to be defined. Superstition with regard to mental disorders had always existed, even, of course, in pre-Christian Rome. The spirits of the woods, the *silvani* and the *fauni*, were supposed to cause mental illness. Pliny calls some of the mental diseases *ludibria faunorum;* the popular name for a mentally ill person was *larvarum plenus* or *larvatus,* that is, full of *larvae,* or phantoms. Occasionally the designation *cerritus* was used, meaning one upon whom the goddess Ceres took vengeance. The poet Vergil spoke of *incubi,* the beings who were given a uniquely active part in the demonology of later centuries. The Stoics believed in the clairvoyant powers of the so-called insane.[34] It will be recalled that Caelius Aurelianus devoted many pages to *incubi;* he also spoke of supernatural beings, *subacti* and *molles,* which were supposed to cause insomnia and night terrors. Silimachus even described epidemics caused by *incubi* in Rome.[35]

The early Christian authorities were puzzled and frightened by the whole phenomenon of mental illness. It was difficult for them to assign all mental disorders to the work of the devil, since some of the mentally sick were preoccupied with religious problems which they wove into the meshwork of their pathological ideas. The question frequently arose—were the authorities dealing with a saint or a disciple of the devil? Thus the Christian Father Tertullian, well versed in

[33] Diepgen: *op. cit.,* vol. II, p. 6.
[34] Cicero: *De divinatione,* I, 50, 54.
[35] A. Semelaigne: *op. cit.,* pp. 106, 107.

medical learning, devoted the twenty-sixth chapter of his treatise on the soul to a characteristic illustration. He wrote of a certain Montanus, who, although a heretic, claimed to be the instrument of the Holy Spirit, appointed to bring a new light to the Christian world. Montanus knew two women, Prisca and Maximilla, and all three were apparently somnambulistic and suffered from attacks of *grande hystérie*. Two bishops in succession, St. Zephyrinus and St. Victor, were convinced of the prophetic powers of these three sick people, and they were accorded "letters of peace." Tertullian at first thought that Montanus and his two friends were "in error," but he soon felt convinced that when in ecstasy they really possessed prophetic powers.[36] There were some who disagreed with Tertullian, but many more agreed. "There is now among us," he relates, "a sister who is favored with the gift of revelations. These come to her in church in the midst of the consecration of sacraments, when she enters the state of ecstasy. While in this state, she converses with angels and at times even with our Lord Jesus Christ. In her rapture she sees and hears the celestial secrets, she knows what is concealed in the hearts of some people and she gives information about salutary remedies. . . . After the people, the mass over, leave the church, this sister tells us of all she has seen in order that we may examine her and judge her revelations." [37] These lines were written in the third century of our era, even before all pagan temples of Aesculapius had disappeared, and they already show a tendency to return to templar, ecstatic mysticism. The sick woman described by Tertullian is reminiscent of "Isis who used to advise the Egyptians about remedies, or of the Pythia who divined the murderous plans of Procles." [38]

On the other hand, St. Cyprian seems to have been less inclined to consider mental diseases with religious ecstatic trends as coming from the Lord and the angels. In his seventy-fourth Epistle he relates, "At the time when the believers fled from persecution a woman suddenly appeared; she fell into a state of ecstasy and claimed she was a prophetess. Moved by impulses which came from the principal demons, she performed wonderful things—real miracles. She boasted of even being

---

[36] Aubin Gauthier: *Histoire de somnambulisme*. Paris, 1842, vol. II, p. 119.

[37] *Ibid.*, pp. 119, 120.

[38] *Ibid.*, p. 120. The author here quoted was a pious Catholic who concluded his *Histoire de somnambulisme* with a humble and devout letter to Pope Gregory XVI.

able to produce earthquakes. By means of shouts and lies she succeeded in subjugating all the spirits so that people began to follow her orders and do anything she wished. The evil spirit which possessed her made her walk barefooted over snow and ice throughout a severe winter, and she experienced no harm. She seduced one of the priests, Rusticus, and also a deacon. It was soon discovered that she had evil relations with the two men. A man highly commendable, an exorcist, was sent to see her and say his exorcisms, but strangely enough the woman got it into her head, just before the exorcist arrived, to announce that a hostile man, a seducer and unbeliever, was coming to fight her. The woman was so impertinent that she had no fear of profaning the Holy Sacraments, since she herself said mass and administered baptism.

"Hence a great question arises: is baptism, when administered by the devil in the name of the Father and the Son and the Holy Ghost, at all valid?" [39] This question troubled the theologians for many centuries and the authorities continued to raise it as late as the fifteenth century. Whatever the answer, it was based on considerations of ceremonial observance only.

Credo ut intelligam was the motto of the age, and hostility to science grew more intense and more open. St. Basil (330–379) regretted the youth in which he had studied classical literature. St. Jerome (d. 420) made a vow never to read pagan books. Toward the end of the sixth century Pope Gregory the Great (d. 604) declared "a knowledge of grammar even for a layman to be indelicate, while for a bishop such familiarity was disgusting." [40]

At the beginning of the seventh century this attitude became thoroughly crystallized. Psychiatry finally became a study of the ways and means of the devil and his cohorts. St. Gregory of Tours (d. 594), as he was cupping for a headache, "touched the disordered spot with the sombre pall of St. Martin's sepulchre and petitioned forgiveness of the holy martyr for applying profane medication." [41] The same bishop proclaimed that he who rendered himself worthy of celestial cures needed no help of terrestrial doctors for the treatment of the mentally ill; he considered the application of sainted relics the most valuable

[39] St. Cyprian: Abbreviated from Epistle 74, translated by the Rev. Ernest Wallis in *The ante-nicene fathers*. Buffalo, 1885–1887, p. 393.
[40] Gregorius Maximus: *Epistolae*, IX, 48. Cited by Fort: *op. cit.*, p. 103.
[41] Fort: *op. cit.*, p. 136.

medication to dispel the devil and his agents. At approximately the same time the Greek physician Alexander of Tralles treated colic by the application of a stone on which an image of Hercules overcoming the lion was carved. Exorcism, as can be inferred from St. Cyprian, began to be considered imperative, and, correspondingly, incantations became an indispensable adjunct of even legitimate medicine. Aetius recommends the use of the following words, when administering certain ointments: "May the God of Abraham, the God of Isaac and the God of Jacob, deign to bestow upon this medicament such and such virtues." [42] The extraction of a fishbone from the throat was accompanied by the words: "Bone, as Jonah came out of the whale's belly, come out of the throat." [43] Over a thousand years before Gregory of Tours and Aetius, Mazdejesnan, the Persian who bore the title "victor of sickness," practiced methods of healing by means of magic words.[44] The Egyptians used the same methods; the administration of an emetic, for instance, had to be accompanied by the formula: "Oh, reappearing Demon, who resides in the belly of so and so, son of so and so [mother]. Oh, thou whose father is named 'he who destroyed heads' and whose name is cursed forever. . . ." [45]

The animistic past of prehistoric life, the mysticism of the early races, and the theurgic ceremonialism of an expiring empire became fused to bury the fragments of what positive knowledge was left.

IV

To DENY that mental diseases are diseases, or to insist that they are forms of demoniacal manipulations, does not, of course, diminish the number of the mentally sick. Psychoses and neuroses were, if anything, increasing in number and variety. The clergy excluded psychiatry from medicine but was unable to abolish it. It merely reappeared under the name of demonology. Moreover, in order to combat the devil, it was necessary to study his ways, and in order to relieve one of the devil,

[42] Renouard: op. cit., p. 240.
[43] Ibid.
[44] H. Bernheim: "Historical Introduction," Hypnotisme, suggestion, psychothérapie. Paris, 1891, p. 7. Also, Henri Cesbron: Histoire critique de l'hystérie. Paris, 1909, p. 12.
[45] The Leiden papyrus, quoted by Cesbron: op. cit., p. 13.

it was necessary to study the signs of the devil's influence. In other words, the study of the symptoms and of the ideational content of mental diseases continued, under names different from those established by medical psychology. Empirical, psychopathological data not only remained at the disposal of the clergy, but they had to be properly assessed. The clergy were compelled by virtue of their interest and preoccupation to observe and to classify the symptoms of mental disorders.

In the records of those days the historian of medical psychology finds a number of interesting details which have a bearing on the diagnosis of mental diseases. The demonologist began very early to study signs of diabolic possession. Each sorcerer or bewitched person possessed by a demon must bear some mark of such possession. According to Tertullian, the corrupter of mankind marked his human collaborators so as to recognize them. "St. Hippolytus, the martyr, saw: *adducit eos ad adorandum ipsum, ac sibi obtemperantes sigillo suo notat.* He described among these so-called stigmata, various *naevi,* pigmented spots and particularly those of anesthesia. Later on the nature of these various signs was worked out in detail and particular stress was laid on skin anesthesias, or the anesthesias of mucous membranes, anal, pharyngeal, and corneal." [46] Here we deal with a series of signs which from the third century on were called *stigmata diaboli* and which were incorporated in the latter part of the nineteenth century almost without change into Charcot's clinical picture of major hysteria. The facts observed were the same; their interpretation was different. The methods of discovering or eliciting them were also different; the methods were certain but they naturally lacked the delicacy which is provided by modern bedside traditions and instruments. When the inquisitors took charge of hunting out the possessed, they would enter a village accompanied by "special assistants known as prickers, whose function it was to prick the suspected person in various parts of the body until an insensitive zone was discovered." [47]

Man was thus lost as an individual, and lost he was despite the fact that traditional theology endowed him with an absolutely free will. Suspended between the devil and eternity, man seemed to have noth-

[46] Cesbron: *op. cit.,* p. 122.
[47] *Ibid.,* pp. 123, 124.

ing left to him but to struggle constantly against temptation and as constantly to rap at the door of the beyond. The ancient pantheistic emotions and philosophy, within the frame of theology guided by a personal God, were submerging all other human interests. Perhaps no one has ever expressed this state of mind, its longings and yearnings, as well as did St. Augustine in these words of ecstasy: "And our discourse was brought to the point where the very highest delights of the carnal senses, in the very purest material light, were, in respect to the sweetness of the life to come, not only not worthy of comparison, but not even worthy of mention. Elevating ourselves still further and attaining a more ardent affection for the Supreme Being, we passed through all bodily things, in order to reach to the very heaven, where the sun, the moon and the stars which hang above the earth are suspended. By meditation and discourse, and through admiring Thy works, we soared still higher; we entered our own minds and went beyond them, that we might arrive at that region of never-failing plenty where Thou feedest Israel forever with the food of truth." [48]

Life, actual living, had become an intermediate, ephemeral episode between two great unknowns—a past of no interest to the thinker of the day and an ultimate future which demanded sacrifices. Psychological questions took on a distinct coloring of anxiety. The whole problem of man's functioning, physical and psychological, had to be reconciled with the all-abiding and all-pervading faith. The human soul remained a baffling puzzle, and it had to be solved in order that the temptation of man to ask questions and to demand rational answers might be allayed. What is this soul, which is everything and yet resides in so lowly an abode as the human body? Is a new soul created every time a human being is born? "Yes," answered some, who were therefore called "creationists." "No," others, "traducionists," insisted: the soul is transmitted from parent to offspring.

The Christian dogma had not yet been fully crystallized, and these questions and answers were foremost in the minds of those who were thinking, reading, and writing. What was the relation of knowledge (*logos*) to God, or Son to Father? Was Christ created or begotten? These were burning questions. The words "begotten, not made, being of one substance with the Father" were inserted into the Creed by the

[48] *Confessions*, IX, 10.

Council of Nicaea in 325. This attitude proved of paramount importance to theoretical psychology. It reflected the old Platonic theory of primary ideas. Subjectivism became the cornerstone of medieval psychology. Aristotle was forgotten for almost one thousand years, and it is very interesting in this connection to take note of the fact that present-day dogma is not only predominantly Aristotelian but explicitly hostile to Plato, while the leaders of Christianity during the first several centuries were almost entirely Platonist. St. Augustine saw that he had learned from Platonists the same doctrine as was taught in the opening verses of the Fourth Gospel.[49] "With increased subjectivism . . . interaction of religion and psychology becomes so marked that religion becomes psychological, and the psychology utilizes religion as a regulative standard." [50]

It was St. Augustine who formulated and systematized the medieval principles of human psychology: "Man is a union of soul and body. The soul is the directing and forming principle, but how it acts on the body is a mystery. Sensation is a mental not a physical process. Sense perception, imagination, and sensuous desires are functions of the sensitive, inferior soul; memory, intellect, and will, of the intellectual or superior soul or spirit, which is in no wise dependent on the body. All those functions are functions of one soul. . . . Since the will is present in all modifications of the soul, we may say that these are nothing but wishes. . . . The eternal blessedness of the soul in God cannot be demonstrated: our hope in it is an act of faith." [51]

"It seemed as though the will could be regarded as equal in all men, so that, if there were differences in the intellectual endowments of individuals, there would yet be a common denominator in the will." [52]

"When Augustine said: 'I desire to know God and the soul,' he was directly formulating the scope of psychology for many succeeding centuries. Though he may not have been fully aware of the fact, his own treatment both of God and the soul was a complete fusion of theology and psychology." [53]

[49] *Ibid.*, VII, 9.
[50] Brett: *A history of psychology*, vol. II, p. 17.
[51] Thilly: *A history of philosophy*, pp. 150–151.
[52] Brett: *op. cit.*, vol. II, p. 20.
[53] *Ibid.*, p. 19.

This complete fusion was effected earlier in the West than in the East. The East maintained for a while longer its cultural contact with the vanishing Alexandrian tradition. Before Alexandria finally fell into the hands of the Arabs, it yielded two students who stand out as the last monument of the past—for Byzantine medicine, too, was dying. The first was Alexander of Tralles (525–604); the second, Paul of Aegina (625–690).

Alexander of Tralles had traveled extensively and gained considerable personal influence both in Rome and Constantinople during the reign of Emperor Justinian. His brother was the architect of the Cathedral of St. Sophia in Constantinople. Alexander's writings were translated into Latin, Hebrew, and Arabic and thus were made available to a number of future generations and influenced medical thought. But his place in the history of medical psychology is infinitesimal despite the fact that his is one of the greatest names in the chronicles of medicine. He deserves mention merely because he was so widely read through the centuries when original thought on mental diseases was nonexistent, and when the old classics were not yet exhumed from their temporary graves.

Alexander of Tralles is also interesting in that he is a typical transitional figure. He was a follower of Galen and Hippocrates but was already a superstitious semi-Oriental. Byzantine physicians were closer to the East, and they vied in the application of numerous remedies found in all sorts of *receptarii,* the original source of the medieval "Dreckapotheke." Alexander is known to have prescribed a course of treatment which was to last two years, with a different potion to be taken every day during the period. He believed that the burned, bloody cloak of a gladiator, reduced to ashes and mixed with wine, was an efficacious remedy, as were the testicles of a young cock if taken with milk for five days before breakfast, or the excrement of a dog who had been starved for fifteen days.[54] Nor was Alexander of Tralles free from the sophistry of his age which made Daremberg call him an *iatrosophiste.* His medical psychology, theoretical and practical, followed Celsus, Aretaeus, Soranus, Caelius, and Galen. Illusions and hallucinations he would treat with various "artifices"—a form of

[54] Ulysse Trélat: *Recherches historiques, etc.,* p. 51.

naïve psychotherapy in which he tried to outwit the patients' "false ideas." He was a great believer in purgation and used it frequently and thoroughly. "We know," he says, "that the pioneers among the ancient physicians resorted to the use of white hellebore when they observed that other purgatives failed to alleviate the illness, but I prefer to use the Armenian stone," [55]—a compact, calcareous stone containing quartz, mica, and copper ore. He was opposed to bleeding. He was a rather thoughtful eclectic and moderate mystic, but he was one of the last who studied Greco-Roman medicine thoroughly and who left a medical text that was used by following generations.

If Alexander of Tralles still made occasional attempts to assert and to use his own judgment, Paul of Aegina, said to have been the last Byzantine physician, assumes more definitely the role of a humble servant of the past. "Twice he states, in the preface to his surgical compendium, that he claims no originality; he composed his compendium merely by following the ancient sources . . . for he was not audacious enough to believe that the ancients could have omitted anything of importance to the art of healing. He said that he drew from the writings of Galen and Oribasius and from other best authors, but these authors were definitely the ones from whom Oribasius himself had borrowed various chapters for his books." [56] In expressing this attitude, Paul of Aegina marks more definitely than any of his predecessors the turning point of medical history; he accepted the supposed omniscience of the ancients without doubt or criticism. He may therefore be justly considered the first medical medievalist. Paul's interests were mainly surgery and obstetrics; the Arabs frequently called him "the Obstetrician." His interest in mental diseases was more or less routinely formal; his theoretical views were eclectic, a condensation of Galen's ideas. Medical books based on original observations had disappeared. Only medical synopses were valued. "People no longer remembered the great masters; all they wanted were brief descriptions. They contented themselves with the mere statement of recipes for the treatment of diseases, without even stopping to consider the differences which certain diseases might present. A name, a formula, that is all a physician of that day cared to know. . . . Hippocrates and Galen sur-

---

[55] Alexander of Tralles: *De arte medica*, Book I, xvii. Also, C. Pinel: *op. cit.*, p. 22.
[56] Daremberg: *La médecine, histoire et doctrines*, p. 113.

vived, not because they had been read by the medical profession of the Empire, but because of their reputation." [57]

Paul of Aegina approved of this trend in medicine; he felt that the physician must be given terse, simple directions of what to do on various occasions, that he should be assisted almost in a manner of spoonfeeding. The tenor of medical life adjusted itself to the general cultural tenor of the times. The mainsprings of intellectual activity were no longer curiosity and research, but a certain elastic, logical ingenuity which proved by means of intellectual constructions that the past contained everything, and that the human mind could best be used to reaffirm the authority of the past rather than to reconsider it. This was the spirit which later came to be known as scholasticism.

v

The Arabs took Alexandria in 640. The great library was destroyed. Western medicine had been in historical hibernation for some time; now Eastern medicine entered its scientific twilight. The study of the human mind suffered most of all. In the year 800 *De natura hominis* appeared from the pen of Meletios of Tiberiopolis; it was but a "theologico-sophistic anthropology." [58] In 950 the work of Theophanes, *Compendium totius artis medicinae*, was written at the order of Constantine VII. It betrays no original thought. It is a document testifying to the stagnancy and uninspired repetitiveness on which medical thought had come to exist.

In psychopathology demonological theories established themselves to the fullest extent; in medicine in general, Arabian pharmacological influences began to replace the Greek. The Oriental became the authority. In the latter part of the sixth century the Persian king, then at war with Emperor Justinian, offered the Emperor an armistice, in order to obtain the services of the Roman physician Tribunus. In the middle of the fourteenth century Emperor Andronicus III suffered from a rat bite; a Persian physician was summoned to treat him. The fascination

[57] *Ibid.*, pp. 111, 112.
[58] M. S. Krüger: *Synchronistische Tabellen zur Geschichte der Medizin*. Berlin, 1840, p. 15.

of everything that was Greek and the solidity of Greek science were gone; the Persian and the Arab were the possessors of scientific authority. The medical literature became an assemblage of corrupted texts. It was not rare for a medical treatise, before being used extensively, to be translated from the original Greek into Syrian, from Syrian into Arabic, and from Arabic into Latin; it thus ultimately suffered from many defects of judgment which were multiplied by rather lax literary ethics and disrespect for originality of thought.

Simeon Seth in 1060 compiled a number of lists of Arabian medicaments. Synesius in 1150 translated an Arabian treatise on fevers, and in 1250 Nicholas Myrepsos composed his *Antidotarium*, a more complete compilation of the pharmacological views of the Arabs. Pharmacology became the cornerstone of treatment.

As to psychopathology, the time seems to have become fully ripe for the monk to replace the doctor. Michael Psellus (1020–1105) writes an encyclopedic work, the medical part of which is reminiscent of Celsus, in method rather than in content. No trace is found of the views of the Greeks on medicopsychological matters. Instead, there is a detailed account of the hierarchy of demons who are troubling and vitiating the functioning of the human soul. Psellus himself was subject to hallucinatory experiences. To him belongs the singular honor of having been the first to "codify" and systematize the demonology which became for a long while the unshakable foundation of medieval psychiatry. Thus, we may see that by the beginning of the twelfth century Byzantine medicine, too, had ceased to exist as an offspring of the Greco-Roman medical tradition.

Unusually rare exceptions like John Actuarius were unable to disperse the heavy clouds which enveloped psychiatry. Actuarius, the first to describe the intestinal worm *trichocephalus dispar*, was read by medical men till the middle of the nineteenth century. He was opposed to demonological psychiatry and followed the Galeno-Hippocratic humoralism.[59] He added nothing new, but to be able to separate himself from the superstitions of his day and walk the trodden path of Galen was in itself an intellectual feat of no mean importance.

---

[59] Renouard: *op. cit.*, p. 268. Also, Th. Kirchhoff: *Geschichte der Psychiatrie*, in Aschaffenburg's *Handbuch der psychiatrie*. Leipzig and Vienna, 1912. *Allegem. teil*, 4 *Abt.*

The decline was complete and to many it appeared final and irrevocable. The center of what was left of learning moved west again. The bellicose Arabs swept over a part of Western Europe carrying on the blades of their swords the streaks of classical knowledge which had been saved in the midst of wars, barbaric invasions, mystical prostration, and disconsolate trepidation before the devil and his work.

5

⁂ ⁂

THE RESTLESS SURRENDER
TO DEMONOLOGY

I

TRADITION, particularly in times of cultural crises, performs a useful conservative function. It preserves from total destruction those values which seem overwhelmed by the onslaught of abrupt and catastrophic changes. But tradition, when it becomes a persistent belief, degenerates into an uncritical habit of thought and becomes a stubborn obstacle to the further growth of the values it tends to preserve. Tradition has contributed a great deal to our misunderstanding, if not ignorance, of those centuries which intervene between the decline of classical knowledge and the revival of scientific curiosity during the Renaissance. These centuries seemingly have nothing dazzling or dramatic to commend themselves to the student of thought. Yet these thousand-odd years of alleged cultural mist and spiritual night represent a period of endless struggle and anxious search. Most of the great names of the time have been forgotten, or were never remembered. Many daring thoughts and tormented gropings have been passed over unnoticed. Consequently the long centuries preceding the Renaissance are almost unknown. The historian of medical psychology is no exception among those who attempt to tell the story of human history, and yet it is incumbent upon him more than upon any other historian to take cognizance and stock of this millennium of twilight, for it is during this period that the little we possess of the previous centuries' knowledge of human psychology was preserved. Moreover, medical psychology, under different names and various guises, was actually broadened and elaborated. Since our knowledge of these centuries is scanty, and our perspective incomplete and distorted, an attempt, no matter how awkward and modest, must be made to stop and to look into the mist, to try to perceive the shadowy outlines of man's attempts to understand himself.

Tradition in some quarters credits the Arabs with the preservation of medical knowledge; in others the Arabs are treated with a certain degree of mockery and ill-concealed, self-satisfied contempt. There are those who insist that "the Jew and the Syrian, whose home lands had been wasted by the Mongols, were almost exclusively responsible for the intellectul pre-eminence with which the Arabs have been credited," [1] and others maintain that "with the not striking exception of the advance in pharmacology, in five hundred years little or no advance in medicine proper was made, while it became contaminated with all sorts of nonsense and fatuity." [2]

These statements might be quite true if we were to stand before a period of history and demand that it satisfy our wish for progress as we understand it today. They will become much less true if we try to understand the historical process itself.

Toward the end of the sixth century the Bedouins, seminomadic inhabitants of the Arabian desert, were a barbarian people who but occasionally came in contact with the higher culture of their neighbors. In less than fifty years these nomads were transformed by their prophet Mohammed into a unified whole. Mohammed died in 632. The uncompromising proselytism with which he inspired his followers burst into aggressive flame and within less than eighty years (711) the Arabs were masters of Babylonia, Persia, Syria, Egypt, and Spain. Twenty-one years later their successful march into the heart of Europe was

---

[1] Jonathan Wright: *Arab Science*, I, "Methods in medical history," *Medical Journal and Record.* New York, February, 1928, vol. 127, p. 155. Wright reflects the views of Miguel y Palacios (*Islam and the Divine Comedy*, London, 1926) and of E. G. Browne (*Arabian medicine*, Cambridge, 1921). *Cf.* also, Daremberg: *Histoire des sciences médicales*, vol. I, pp. 279 *et seq.*

[2] Wright: *op. cit.*, p. 155.

stopped by Charles Martel at Tours and Poitiers. Their meteoric political expansion was accompanied by a no less phenomenal acquisition of scientific knowledge. The Arabs showed an extraordinary capacity for learning—their spectacular assimilation of newly acquired knowledge is suggestive of a similar ability shown by the Japanese at the end of the nineteenth century [3]—but almost at the very heels of the development of Arabian learning came its decline.

At the time the Western Caliphate (756–1031) reached its height, the sources from which Arabian learning emanated were cut off by the Mongols. Pressed by the Europeans in the West and dispossessed by the Mongols in the East, the Arabs were caught in a vice of two crushing forces. For a period of six hundred years they had played the role of carriers of knowledge. They were little interested in changing the social and cultural habits of the people they conquered; they were satisfied with the imposition of taxes. At least at first the moral atmosphere was free and favored the further development of science. The Arabs borrowed freely and eagerly from the scientific equipment which they found among the conquered. They treated the monotheists, the Jews, and the Christians with tolerance and, at first, even with friendliness. "More tolerant in matters of religion than the Christian Princes of their times, they received, without distinction of country or religion, all the men of merit who took refuge in their States, gave them employment, and recompensed them for their services. On this account, the philosophers and persecuted heretics often sought an asylum among the Infidels and carried to them, in return, the light of Greek civilization." [4]

By the middle of the eighth century some Nestorian physicians who had been forced to flee their homeland had settled in Bagdad. The best known among these was the medical family of Bakthishua ("The Servants of Christ"), whose services were greatly valued at the court of the Caliph. One of them is said to have cured the wife of Harun-al-Rashid (786–809) of a mental disease. The method of treatment was a rather crude psychotherapy of intimidation and reproach. Another Christian, Honain (800–850), later known to writers in Latin as

[3] Erik Nordenskiöld: *Die Geschichte der Biologie*. Jena, 1926, p. 69.
[4] Renouard: *op. cit.*, p. 256. Moslem and Christian were at the beginning friendly with one another. The Catholic Prelacy not infrequently sought medical advice from the Arabs. *Cf.* Conde: *Historia de los Arabes*. Also referred to by Fort: *op. cit.*, p. 258.

Johannitius, was paid in gold of equal weight for each book translated for Harun-al-Rashid. "Honain gave the Arabs access to Aristotle, Hippocrates and Galen, whom he translated into Syrian. It is through his translation that the Arabs were enabled to continue the tradition of Greek medicine, the clarity of which they obscured to a great extent; this clarity was not re-established till the sixteenth century, when the great classics were rediscovered and published. Galen was Honain's favorite writer. . . . Honain's son Isaac was better known than his father in medieval Europe, and he was considered the authorized translator of Greek medical writers; he became the teacher of a number of French and Parisian physicians; his texts were highly valued in the twelfth and thirteenth centuries." [5]

The necessity of dealing with epidemic diseases soon called upon the Arabs to pay even closer attention to the healing art. In 572 an epidemic of the "pustular plague" raged in Arabia. Eight years later it spread all over Europe, and a year before Spain became an Arabian possession it devastated that country. In 670 a medical work, *Pandects*, was written in the Syrian language by Ahron. This was translated into Arabian by the Jewish writer Masardjaweih. It gives the first clinical description of smallpox.

Within a little over two hundred and fifty years Arabian medicine reached a height reminiscent of the best days of Greek medicine. The dignity of the medical profession was restored. The ethical Hippocratic spirit was reawakened and rose in opposition to the medical charlatanism which was so widespread. In this reawakening the great physician Rhazes (860–930) played an important role. Rhazes was the chief physician of a large hospital in Bagdad which at that early date was sufficiently progressive to have a division for the mentally ill. He was an indefatigable worker, an assiduous student, and a prolific writer; he wrote two hundred and twenty-six books in which he followed Galen, Paul of Aegina, Aetius, and Pliny. He was called "the Galen of the Arabs." His *Liber medicinalis ad Almansorem* served as a reference book even in the seventeenth century.[6] He pleaded always for serious study, " 'for it is impossible to see and try everything in one's own

[5] L. Meunier: *Histoire de la médecine depuis ses origines jusqu'à nos jours.* Paris, 1924, p. 159.
[6] Diepgen: *Geschichte der Medizin*, vol. II, p. 16.

practice; the knowledge and experience of a single individual, compared to the knowledge and skill of all men, of all ages, resembles a slender brook of water that flows by the side of a great river.' " [7] To Rhazes, as to Hippocrates, the individual was the center of medical attention. Rhazes insisted that the patient study his physician and demand from him a high standard of integrity. " 'Study, carefully, the antecedents of the man to whose care you propose confiding all you have most dear in the world; that is to say, your health, your life, and the health and lives of your wife and children. If the man is dissipating his time in frivolous pleasures, if he cultivates with too much zeal the arts that are foreign to his profession, such as music and poetry; still more, if he is addicted to wine and debauchery, refrain from committing into such hands a trust so precious. He merits your confidence, who, having early applied himself to the study of medicine, has sought skillful instructors and seen much disease; who has united to the assiduous reading of good authors, his personal observations.' " [8]

Despite the inspired earnestness of Rhazes and Arabian medicine as a whole, however, the theocratic basis of the Arabian empire and the theurgic foundation of its culture stood in the way of truly original works. The Arabian physician shared the handicaps of his Christian colleague in that the Koran for the Arab, like the Scriptures for the Christian, was considered the source and authority for all knowledge. There were no schools of higher learning outside the official schools where the Koran was taught, and there were no teaching opportunities for the philosophers, the great majority of whom were physicians. [9] Anatomical dissections were forbidden by the Koran and men were not permitted to look at naked women. Consequently little if any progress was made in anatomy, obstetrics, or gynecology. Mathematics, astronomy, and especially pharmacology made some forward steps; there were some original contributions to the problems of measles and smallpox. For the rest, the Arab had to rely on his own ingenuity and on the distorted and not fully authentic Greek past. One therefore searches in vain for new ideas about normal and abnormal psychology among the Arabs. They followed the psychophysiological theories of

[7] Renouard: *op. cit.*, p. 258.
[8] *Ibid.*, p. 257.
[9] Nordenskiöld: *op. cit.*, p. 71.

Galen and Hippocrates, particularly of the former, and contributed little that was new to the treatment of mental diseases. They extended the use of medicaments, particularly that of poppy seed (opium). Nevertheless, they brought a refreshing spirit of dispassionate clarity into psychiatry. The Arabs were free from the demonological theories which swept over the Christian world and were therefore able to make clear-cut clinical observations on the mentally ill.

Najab ud din Unhammad, a writer who was apparently a contemporary of Rhazes, left many excellent descriptions of various mental diseases. His carefully compiled observations on actual patients made up the most complete classification of mental diseases theretofore known. The original treatise of Najab was lost. His views come to us through Muham mad Akbar, who wrote a medical work in Persian in the seventeenth century entitled *Tibb-i-Akbari*. Akbar used an Arabian commentary on Najab written in 1450.[10]

Najab describes *Souda a Tabee*, apparently a febrile delirium accompanied by bizarre behavior, in which "the patient shows great carelessness as regards clothing, attention to the bodily requirements and the calls of nature . . . childish merriness of heart, and unprovoked laughter. . . ." The same disease in the young (apparently chorea) shows us a patient who "manifests intense anxiety, and suffers from a constant dread of something unknown, these symptoms being associated with extraordinary movements of the hands and feet, leaping, beating the ground, etc."

This disease, if it becomes chronic, ends in *Janoon*, in which "the patient is extremely restless, sleepless, taciturn, shows great antipathy to mankind, is violent"—a clinical picture suggestive of our present-day agitated depressions. The word *Janoon* originally signified fighting and beating the earth with the hands and feet. Najab considers this disease of unfavorable prognosis—that is, that patients afflicted with it do not recover.

There is also a very good description of those ruminative, anxious states of doubt which are today associated with the compulsion and obsessional types of neurosis, and which the Arab physician ascribes to too much love for philosophy and law. He calls it *Murrae Souda*. He

[10] J. G. Balfour: "An Arab physician on insanity," *Journal of Mental Science*. London, 1878, vol. XXII.

speaks of a type of mental disease which is apparently degenerative in nature and associated with the involutional period of man's life; he calls it *Malikholia a Maraki*, or *Nafkhae Malikholia*, or *Nafkhae Maraki*. It is ascribed to a special heat ascending to the brain; it is accompanied by combined priapism and sexual impotence. "*Nafkhae* is the name of that particular form of air or vapor which the angel Gabriel is said to have blown or caused to pass from his coat sleeve into the windpipe of Mary, the Mother of Jesus, for the purpose of impregnation." [11] A form of persecutory psychosis is very well described under the name of *Kutrib*. The Greek term *mania* is also used, to describe states of abnormal excitement. A variety of mania in which states of destructiveness are quickly alternated with those of gentleness and fawning is called *Daul-Kulb*.

There is a group of disorders of judgment which is called *Haziyan*. One of the forms belonging to the group is *Mibda a illut dimagh*, and it manifests itself "by the mind magnifying whatever is presented to it, and leading to actions that are outrages of society . . . to displays of opposition, to absurd conduct." Evidently we have here the earliest description of the type of antisocial behavior now commonly called psychopathic or criminal.

Ishk designates a depressive state which is combined with deep anxiety. The term is taken from the word *ishka*, meaning a creeper which twines around a tree and gradually causes its death. *Ishk* is caused in some unknown manner by love: *Haram* is caused by impure love and *Pak* by pure love carried to excess.

In all, Najab described nine classes of mental illness covering approximately thirty individual diseases. As has been said, the treatment was traditional: good diet, baths, liniments, changes of climate, soft music, pleasant surroundings, in some cases bloodletting.

Rhazes, too, was a master of clinical description, and in matters of therapy he followed more or less the beaten path. He used purgatives and, like Alexander of Tralles, preferred the Armenian stone. [12] The few direct psychotherapeutic measures used seldom went beyond altercation with patients; "such altercation is like stirring of a dead fire to make it burn afresh; it whets a dull spirit, and will not suffer the mind

[11] All quotations from J. G. Balfour: *op. cit.*
[12] See p. 114.

to be drowned in those profound cogitations which melancholy men are commonly troubled with." [13]

Paradoxical as it may seem, the more learned an Arabian physician, the smaller was his contribution to the study of mental diseases. Such a remarkable personality as Avicenna (980–1037) followed a form of neoplatonism, although adhering to Aristotle. "Strictly speaking, his scientific contributions were mostly of a formal nature; his great reputation in the Orient and later his still greater renown in Western Europe were due more to his brilliant style and excellent arrangement of subject matter than to any originality of thought." [14] Avicenna's was an eclectic medical psychology seeking the seat of melancholia in the stomach, liver, and spleen,[15] but he was explicit in his sober empiricism: "Some ascribe melancholia to the influence of demons, but I do not share their views." [16] Nor did Avenzoar (d. 1161), the teacher of Averrhoes, rise above the eclecticism of confused Galenic speculations, although he did object definitely to the use of the cautery,[17] which apparently had become a legitimate instrument for the treatment of mental diseases. The need for a new psychology was felt, and as long as this need was not satisfied no new approach to mental diseases was possible. Every now and then speculation would attempt to liberate the thinker from the confinement of his ideological prison, but mere speculation could lead to nothing more than the amusement of future students of history. Avicenna, for instance, was unable to broaden his biological horizon by the conviction that if a hen fights a rooster and overcomes him, she may, in her ecstatic pride of victory, actually develop male spurs.[18]

The search for a new orientation seems to have gradually brought the scientific mind to the realization that the eclectic outgrowth of Greek medicine was intellectually sterile; this realization stimulated a mind which turned to the most important and most fertile source of Greek science, to Aristotle. Avicenna studied Aristotle but his commentary on the peripatetic philosopher was tinged with speculative

---

[13] Robert Burton: *Anatomy of melancholy.* London, 1837, p. 548.
[14] Nordenskiöld: *op. cit.,* p. 72.
[15] Trélat: *Recherches historiques sur la folie,* p. 56.
[16] Quoted by Sprengel: *Histoire de la médecine, etc.,* vol. II, p. 315.
[17] Sprengel: *op. cit.,* vol. II, pp. 332 *et seq.* Also, Meunier: *op. cit.,* pp. 168, 169.
[18] Diepgen: *op. cit.,* vol. II, p. 78.

divagations. It was the lot of Averrhoes to introduce the Aristotelian views in a manner different from that of speculative and compilatory tradition.[19] Averrhoes, or, in Arabian, Ibn Rosch, was born in Cordova, Spain, in 1120. His father was a prominent judge. Averrhoes studied philosophy, medicine, and jurisprudence in Cordova, which for a period of several centuries was the center of Arabian learning in Spain. Upon the completion of his studies he held the office of judge of Seville for several years; he later became governor of a province. Once, however, he too had to experience the difficulties resulting from the religious fanaticism which became so strong in Mohammedan Spain toward the middle of the twelfth century. He was arrested for freethinking and as a heretic he was banished to live in a Jewish village near Cordova. Fortunately a few years later death claimed the ruler who was responsible for this act of injustice, and his successor brought Averrhoes back to Cordova. The great scholar was reinstated in his civil rights and honors and lived at the court. He died within a few years, in 1198. Soon after his death Arabian science fell victim to religious intolerance.

Averrhoes may be considered the last Arabian contributor to Western European thought. He was considered the most authoritative commentator on Aristotle. He deepened and expanded many an aspect of Aristotle's biological philosophy and, caught as he was by the wave of religious intolerance, he came to the ingenious conclusion that there is a "double truth," truth begotten by faith and truth derived from rational philosophy. What is true in theology may not be true in philosophy, and vice versa; yet the two truths are not mutually exclusive. This was a philosophic construction of paramount importance, for it made it possible and legitimate, at least in principle, to study many a phenomenon which seemed to contradict the scriptural dogma. Following this principle, many generations of theologians were able to espouse science without having their consciences troubled, but it was many years before this approach could be fully utilized in the study of mental phenomena. A welter of prejudices and misconceptions had to be overcome in this twilight of Western European thought. In the meantime, the rediscovery of Aristotle and the principle of double

---

[19] What follows is a condensation of Nordenskiöld's (*op. cit.*, pp. 72 *et seq.*) concise and most succinct statement on Averrhoes.

truth made it at least permissible to study Aristotle and to reassert a scientific attitude. The revival of Aristotle was the first glimmer of a new dawn. The glimmer was very faint, for Western Europe was still groping among the ruins of the classical world and had not yet found itself. The day which followed was slow to arrive.

II

In Western Europe medicine was not entirely disinherited, but it became an art for the healing of bodily ills only. As Alcuin, the chief adviser of Charlemagne, stated, medicine was *scientia curationum ad salutem corporis inventa*. Public lessons on Hippocrates and Galen were given in Ravenna toward the end of the eighth century.[20] The Merovingian and Carolingian kings had their archiaters; they were all clerics. But even the field of physical medicine was deeply marred by unscientific beliefs and ceremonies. Thus, in the days of Charlemagne "headache was frequently cured by saintly recommendations to a figure of the sick head and by the placing of a cross on it."[21] Lay schools and lay physicians were still active in the eleventh and twelfth centuries, but by the thirteenth almost all medical writers and physicians were clerics. What is really interesting from the standpoint of psychopathology is not what we find on mental diseases in the medical writings of the time, but the fact that we find no discussion of them, either by those who were interested in medicine or by those who were physicians. The general attitude was that of a man inspired by the unusual and looking upon it as a miraculous phenomenon. When lightning struck a church in Liège in 1182, Renier wrote a treatise on lightning without referring to any natural causes.[22]

In the confusion of naïve, authoritarian beliefs medicine as a science of the body seems to have divorced itself completely from the consideration of mental phenomena. The chief topics of interest were dietetics, herbs, and drugs. Trotula, one of the famous group of *mulieres salernitanae* (women of Salerno), did mention the black bile,

[20] Daremberg: *Histoire des sciences médicales,* vol. I, p. 257.
[21] Fort: *op. cit.*
[22] Sprengel: *op. cit.,* vol. II, p. 385.

but the *Flos Medicinae*, written in verse, deals with dietetics and general physical hygiene only. Didier, who later became Pope Victor III, wrote on pharmacological and "astronomical" topics, adding mystical confusion to medicine. The Abbess Hildegard in the twelfth century was an influential medical writer; she was dominated by astrology and pharmacological magic. St. Hildegard thought that Eve's first menstrual period was due to her moral fall. Constantinus Africanus (d. 1087) and Gerhard of Cremona occupied themselves with translations of Arabian writing. In the twelfth century the reading of Arabian literature was still considered proper enough so that an archbishop could present a treatise by Avicenna to the Abbey of Terterbon. The Universities of Bologna and Paris undertook a detailed study of Arabian writers. Scholars were students of books and not investigators. Even Albertus Magnus, the teacher of St. Thomas and a thinker of the first order, resorted to quotations from the early fathers to prove his biological views.[23] Man, it was insisted, had eleven ribs and as a proof of this contention the story of Eve's creation was cited. Psychiatric interests were surrendered to the professional hunter of heretics or to the lonely contemplator of the world who still dared to puzzle about the nature of the human mind. Psychology and psychiatry became completely isolated toward the close of the twelfth century and actually disappeared as subjects of scientific consideration.

III

By the ninth or tenth century psychological problems had become definitely confused with those of theology and theosophy. The human side of psychology was either avoided or overlooked. Other more general problems held one's attention. People "wanted to know exactly what such a term as 'transubstantiation' means when an animal and not a man eats the consecrated host. Does the mouse that eats the consecrated host eat the body of the Lord?"[24] The contemplative student was groping in the midst of such preoccupations with no tool for investigation but his own imaginative ingenuity.

[23] Diepgen: *op. cit.*, vol. II, pp. 37 *et seq.*
[24] Brett: *A history of psychology*, vol. II, p. 89.

The Augustinian psychology, idealistic and mystic, offered little to the scientific inquirer. Dialectic subtleties, so varied, keen, and numerous at the time, left little that was tangible to one who wished to touch the riddle of the human mind. Every now and then a spark would arise from the darkness and cast a fleeting light which would remain unobserved by scholars. Toward the end of the ninth century John Scotus Erigena made an attempt to probe a little deeper into some functions of the human mind and formulated the concept of *intellectualis visio*, designating a faculty of the mind akin to introspection. William of Conches (1080–1154) made an attempt to digress from orthodoxy, but he was soon reprimanded and he turned to sciences. This is a very important fact. It would seem that the development of many sciences was propitiated by the very prejudices of the theological age. Anyone who felt unsafe in theology or psychology, for fear of stumbling into heterodoxy, sought intellectual refuge in the study of nonpsychological phenomena, of sciences in general. William of Conches had to turn to the study of Galen and the Arabs. Hugh of St. Victor had to turn in the same direction. Yet toward the end of the twelfth century there was apparently considerable preoccupation with psychological matters and the preoccupation began to assert itself. It was naturally handicapped not only by ignorance but even by the absence of a proper psychological vocabulary, which made matters more recondite and difficult.

Alcher, a pious man and a friend of Isaac the Abbot of Stella, "appears to have studied the body and so arrived at the point of asking the Abbot of Stella to give him some account of the soul." The interlocutors sensed that somehow they must set theology aside and, to use a modern philosophic term, consider the soul "as such." So they agreed beforehand that the Abbot need not say what the soul " 'was before sin, or is in the state of sin, or will be after sin'; this probably saved much time and induced the Abbot to begin at once on the main points of psychology." [25] The Abbot defined imagination to his medical friend. Imagination, he averred, was intelligence clothed in sensation. A daring thought and a profound one! The Abbot's definition is both brief and turgid, but it contains the implication that imagination is somehow connected with inner sensation, an idea tenable even today.

[25] Brett: *op. cit.*, vol. II, p. 101.

Unfortunately, the mind of the twelfth century was unable to plow any deeper or to harrow any smoother the paths of psychological insight. It possessed on occasion an intuitive grasp but not enough intellectual elasticity to follow it through.

The Abbot continued, "Reason is applied to things present and, as it were in the mouth of the heart, masticates what the teeth of *ingenium* are grasping, or chews the cud which the belly of memory presents a second time." [26] Finally, the Abbot comes to the very edge of asserting the existence of the unconscious, the recognition of which is not fully granted by a number of medical men even today: *nec versatur semper in intuitu scientis omne quod scitur,*[27] that is, not everything known is continually present, nor does all that a man knows remain always directly present to the eye of the mind. We may note as a characteristic of the time that when Alcher, the medical man, did conceive the daring question of what the soul is, regardless of what it "was before sin, or is in the state of sin, or will be after sin," he found it necessary to consult a clerical authority.

The medical man dared not look independently into normal or abnormal psychology. Those suffering from psychological difficulties were treated as heretics, but the few who were fortunate enough to be considered "naturally" ill were for centuries treated with exorcisms. An old manuscript of the tenth century [28] illustrates rather clearly the

---

[26] *Ibid.*, p. 102.

[27] *Ibid.*

[28] *Kyklos (Jahrbuch des Instituts für Geschichte der Medizin an der Universität Leipzig),* vol. II, pp. 274, 272. (I am indebted to Dr. Henry Sigerist for first calling my attention to this manuscript.)

"*Ad matris dolorem. In nomine patris et filii et spiritus sancti. Domine deus miliciae angelorum, ante quem stant angeli cum magno tremore. Amen, amen, amen. Matrix, matrix, matrix, scrinia matrix, rufa matrix, alba matrix, pulposa matrix, sanguinaria matrix, capitanea matrix, neufredica matrix, explenetica matrix, demoniaca.*"

"*In nomine dei patris et filii et spiritus sancti. Domine deus militiae angelorum, cui adstant archangeli cum magno tremore dicentes: Sanctus, Sanctus, Sanctus. Dominus deus sabaoth, vide infirmitatem fragilitatis nostrae, attende facturam naturae nostrae et opus manuum tuarum, ne despicias; tu enim fecisti nos et non ipsi nos. Compesce matricem famulae tuae N. et sana contritiones eius, quia commota est.*

"*Coniuro te, matrix, per sanctam trinitatem, ut sine aliqua molestia redeas ad locum tuum et inde te non moveas neque declines, sed sine iracundia revertaris ad locum, ubi deus te condidit.*

"*Coniuro te, matrix, per novem ordines angelorum et per omnes virtutes caelorum, ut cum omni mansuetudine et tranquillitate revertaris in locum tuum et non inde te moveas neque aliquam molestiam huic famulae dei N. inferas.*

"*Coniuro te, matrix, per patriarchas et prophetas et per omnes apostolos Christi,*

attitude toward the problem of hysteria which, as will be remembered, was thought due to the wandering of the uterus over the body. The quotation in Latin is given in the footnote. Following is an English translation: "To the pain in the womb. In the name of God the Father, God the Son and God the Holy Spirit. Lord, our God, who commands the host of angels that are standing before Him in trembling awe. Amen, amen, amen. O womb, womb, womb, cylindrical womb, red womb, white womb, fleshy womb, bleeding womb, large womb, neu-fredic womb, bloated womb, O demoniacal one!"

The invocation which follows illustrates that the old theory of the wandering uterus became welded with the demonological concepts.

"In the name of God the Father, God the Son and God the Holy Spirit. O Lord of Hosts, surrounded by the archangels who in trem-bling awe say: Holy, holy, holy. O Lord Zebaoth, look at our infirmity, at our weakness, direct Thy attention toward the form of our nature and do not despise us, the work of Thy hands! For Thou hast made us and not we ourselves. Stop the womb of Thy maid N. and heal its affliction, for it is moving violently.

"I conjure thee, O womb, in the name of the Holy Trinity, to come back to the place from which thou shouldst neither move nor turn away, without further molestation, and to return, without anger, to the place where the Lord has put thee originally.

"I conjure thee, O womb, by the nine choirs of angels and by all the virtues of heaven to return to thy place with every possible gentle-ness and calm, and not to move or to inflict any molestation on that servant of God, N.

"I conjure thee, O womb, by the patriarchs and prophets, and by all

---

per martires et confessores atque virgines et omnes sanctos dei, ut non noceas huic famulae dei N.

"*Coniuro te, matrix, per dominum nostrum Jesum Christum, qui siccis pedibus super mare ambulavit, infirmos curavit, demones effugavit, mortuos suscitavit, cuius sanguine redempti, cuius vulnere curati, cuius livore sumus sanati, per ipsum te coniuro, ut non noceas huic famulae dei N., ut non caput eius teneas, non collum, non guttur, non pec-tus, non aures, non dentes, non oculos, non nares, non scapulas, non brachia, non manus, non cor, non stomachum, non epar, non splen, non renes, non dorsum, non latus, non artus, non umbilicum, non viscera, non vessicam, non femora, non tibias, non talones, non pedes, non ungues teneas, sed quieta pauses in loco, quem tibi deus delegit, ut sana sit haec ancilla dei N.*

"*Quod ipse praestare dignetur, qui unus in trinitate et trinus in unitate vivit et regnat deus per omnia saecula saeculorum. Amen.*"

the disciples of Christ, by the martyrs and confessors and the virgins and all the saints of the Lord, not to harm that maid of God, N.

"I conjure thee, O womb, by our Lord Jesus Christ, who walked over the sea with dry feet, who cured the sick, who expelled demons, who brought the dead back to life, by whose blood we were redeemed, by whose wound we were cured, by whose plight we were healed, by Him, I conjure thee not to harm that maid of God, N., not to occupy her head, throat, neck, chest, ears, teeth, eyes, nostrils, shoulderblades, arms, hands, heart, stomach, spleen, kidneys, back, sides, joints, navel, intestines, bladder, thighs, shins, heels, nails, but to lie down quietly in the place which God chose for thee, so that this maid of God N. be restored to health.

"May He, who lives as one in Trinity and as three in unity, the Lord who rules through all the centuries, consider this as worthy of his mercy. Amen."

It will be noted how carefully all external and internal parts of the body are here enumerated, even the heels and the nails. Apparently it was feared that failure to mention even a minor part of the body might expose the patient to the danger of having the wandering uterus settle in just that part and thus make the exorcism ineffective.

Despite the fact that the mentally sick were considered possessed by the devil and therefore impure, torture and mass execution of "witches" and "sorcerers" did not come into vogue until some time later. At first the attitude toward the possessed was considerate and kind. The miraculous powers of the tombs of the saints were invoked for their relief.[29] Conjurations were used: "Godehard . . . one day journeyed along the municipal streets on cloister business, and met a personage so afflicted. Close scrutiny and peremptory interrogatories revealed to the saint the foul presence of a demon, whom, by the irresistible power of divinity, he ejected from the enchantress' body, which restored her health to its former sanity." [30]

In the eleventh century we find the earliest representations of the possessed in painting. "In the manuscripts of Emperor Otto, which are preserved in the cathedral in Aix, one can see a miniature inscribed 'The Possessed Son,' where a young man is presented in the midst of a

[29] Sprengel: *op. cit.*, vol. II, p. 345.
[30] Fort: *op. cit.*, p. 276.

convulsive attack, his body turned backward forming an arch." [81] Similar paintings portray saints in the process of exorcising the possessed. The treatment was usually given in the name of a definite saint. "In aggravated cases actual presence of the medicinal saint was necessary; in less vexatious maladies the bare imposition of hands, accompanied by plaintive prayer, quickly healed the diseased." [82] "Wine washing [wine which had washed] . . . sacred objects, given to an imbecile, forcibly ejected an evil spirit from his mouth; while another tainted with idiocy was restored to instant health by simply transporting the fragments of St. Anastasius." [83]

Occasionally one heard voices denying the devil's power to produce mental disease—John of Salisbury, the Archbishop of Lyons, Agobard, and Abelard were among these—but apparently the issue was not yet acute. More detailed discussions of the problem had not become the order of the day.

Mental diseases spread. Epidemics of psychopathies began to appear and within less than two centuries the placid and faithful ignorance of psychopathology was subjected to a hard test. As the number of the mentally ill reached alarming proportions, the anxiety of the population and with it the anxiety of the clergy was enhanced. Passions were aroused and soon instruments of torture and burning fagots became the recognized tools of psychiatry.

IV

Toward the latter part of the thirteenth century there were signs indicating that the purely book scholarship which had ruled Europe for so long was coming to an end. The human intellect was awakening and curiosity was heaving to the surface. A period of contrasts set in; on one hand the old tradition of logistic subtleties held fast, and on the other the spirit of inquiry turned to observation, experience, and critical thinking. Philosophy reached its crowning achievement in the *Summa* of St. Thomas and the dogma became omnipotent. Institutions

---

[81] Cesbron: *Histoire critique de l'hystérie*, p. 131.
[82] Fort: *op. cit.*, p. 276.
[83] *Ibid.*, p. 277.

of higher learning were opened and the Inquisition was established. Human cadavers were again used for the study of anatomy and Roger Bacon was imprisoned for sixteen years. Hospitals were established, some even for the mentally ill, and others of the "possessed" were treated as heretics. It was in the thirteenth century that the medical man was first called doctor, that is, a learned man skilled in a profession or branch of knowledge. In a period of about one hundred and fifty years not less than fifteen universities were opened: the University of Paris (1205), the Collegium Chirurgicum in Paris (1260), the medical schools in Padua (1222), Naples (1224), Vienna (1364), Oxford (1249), Cambridge (1284), Lisbon (1290), Montpellier (1289), Lyons (1223), Avignon (1303), Pisa (1339), Cracow (1364), Heidelberg (1346), and Prague (1348).

Scientific controversy began to enliven the student's mind. Thaddeus of Florence voiced his disagreement with Galen and the Arabs. Albertus Magnus (1193–1280) became interested in biology. His pupil, Thomas Aquinas (1225–1274), created his system of thought based on Aristotle. Peter of Abano (1250–1315) wrote his *Conciliator Differentiarum;* the very title of the treatise is significant, since theretofore even the existence of differences had not easily been conceived. Yet Roger Bacon was unable to rid himself of the belief in the magic power of the voice. Guy de Chauliac, the great surgeon of the fourteenth century, warned against performing trephining operations at the time of the full moon. Arnauld of Villanova (1240?–1311?), the great clinician, considered the practice of medicine without astrology impossible. Mondino, the first in many centuries to open a human cadaver (1315), consulted the Salernitan descriptions of Copho instead of looking directly at what was before his eyes; Copho's descriptions were based on dissections of pigs! The need for authority rather than evidence was dying hard. The fear of the new was difficult to disperse.

The views of Aristotle and his Arabian commentators began to be regarded with apprehension and hostility; interest in Averrhoes was treated with active opposition. In the beginning of the thirteenth century the writings of Aristotle were publicly burned. His physics and metaphysics were forbidden; only his dialectics were later considered worthy of the attention of a Christian. Averrhoes was considered so dangerous that the remains of Peter of Abano, whose teaching had shown the influence of the Arabian philosopher, were burned in accordance with the rules and regulations of the Inquisition.

This institution was also a product of the thirteenth century. It was inaugurated in 1233 by Pope Gregory IX (the Pope who ordered the professors to refute Aristotle) and was fully established some twenty years later by Pope Innocent IV. By means of the Inquisition both the spiritual and temporal powers struggled for nearly four hundred years in a desperate but vain effort to smother the growing heresy. Free and independent thinking was thus authoritatively and forcefully interfered with at the very time when it made an attempt to rise from its secular dormancy.

It was an age of contrasts and inconsistencies. If we recall Thiers, who said that history is the scale of the Lord in the hands of man, and if we take into account the fact that man is not distinguished by consistency, we shall accept it as a natural and inevitable result that history cannot claim the distinction of being either consistent or kind. The thirteenth century is therefore a perfect example of the historicocultural growth of man. Frederick II, for instance, mirrored the self-contradictory spirit of the times and its singular amalgamation of enlightenment and cruel disregard of freedom. It was Frederick II who introduced the standards of medical education which have been essentially preserved until today. He promulgated the regulations which required that one study medicine for five years and then spend one year with an experienced physician or in a hospital (our present-day internship). The student would then be permitted to submit to a state examination which, if successfully passed, entitled him to the practice of medicine. In 1238 Frederick II permitted that a cadaver be opened every five years in the presence of the faculty and all medical students. This Hohenstaufen was interested in the writings of the Arabs. He was considered a freethinker. Tradition credits him with the statement that three impostors, Moses, Christ, and Mohammed, did a great deal of harm to this world. Yet between the years of 1220 and 1235 Frederick outlawed all heretics. He demanded that "those who did not recant should be burned, those who recanted should be imprisoned, but if they relapsed should be executed; that their property should be confiscated, their houses destroyed, and their children, to the second generation, ineligible to positions of emolument unless they had betrayed their father or some other heretic." [34]

The contrasts with which this period was so replete among those who may be called the rightful representatives of culture were not absent in the medical profession. The period under consideration boasted of such true luminaries in medical history as Actuarius, Arnauld of Villanova, Guy de Chauliac, Peter of Abano, and particularly Thaddeus of Florence; yet the general status of the medical profession was extremely low. A respectable citizen from the town of Senlis reported the following upon his return from a trip to Paris in the early part of the fourteenth century: "Dressed in very expensive habits, the physicians hunt out patients in the streets; the slaves of philosophy, they let it guide them in their treatment of sick people; obtaining health and happiness only for themselves they can boast of and enjoy being the ministers of the Lord." [35] Astrology and alchemy were becoming more and more popular. In 1317 the Pope showed great concern about this preoccupation and forbade the study of alchemy, but the mixture of superstition and inspiration which alchemy represented was not dispersed nor was its influence otherwise attenuated. The status of the alchemist gradually became that of a magician, and within a little over one hundred years it was transformed into that of a sorcerer who was subject to apprehension, torture, excommunication, and fire at the stake.

In an age of intellectual restlessness and perplexity the student who was curious about natural phenomena and who found but little satisfaction in dialectics and ecstasy turned to the field of direct, if superficial, perception. The medical man, helped by the influence of the Arabs, turned to the universe he could at least see with his own eyes, to the sun, the moon, the stars, and the elements, in the hope of finding some answer to the questions which puzzled him. Astrology became a subject of serious study. Belief in the powers of the celestial bodies became so strong that during the war of 1326 the Florentines were guided in their strategy by astrologists.[36] Medicine had not been free of

[34] Bury: *A history of freedom of thought*, p. 58.
[35] Daremberg: *Histoire des sciences médicales*, vol. I, p. 291.
[36] Diepgen: *op. cit.*, vol. II, p. 84.

certain astrological trends since the Pythagorean days. Numbers seem to have had some significance in relation to disease. The Hippocratic theory of crisis paid special attention to numbers and days; the Galenic tradition followed a lunar month of twenty-six days and had a special medical week and month (*mensis medicalis, septimana medicalis*). By the thirteenth century astrology had become a sort of method of approach to medical problems. It appears to have been a singularly confused but broadly conceived expression of an intuitive need to correlate the problems of human illness with the whole system of nature.

Arnauld of Villanova was a thorough student of Galen. He believed also in the devil and his satellites, of course. He had first to reconcile the Galenic humoralism with demonology; he claimed that if certain warm humors developed in the body, the devil and particularly the *incubi* might seize the victim, because the devil likes warmth. Next Galen had to be brought into the orbit of astrology; epilepsy is caused by the phlegm if its appearance is coincident with that of the first quarter of the moon; it is in the blood if it occurs in the second and third quarters, and in black bile if in the last.[37] Mars is responsible for melancholia; the color and the supposed heat of the planet have something to do with the color and the heat of the bile. Bleeding is still recommended, but the phases of the moon and the constellations are to be watched; the sign of the Cancer is most favorable for bloodletting. Ceremonial practices as therapeutics naturally could not be left out. A paternoster, modified in a certain way, would cure warts; the reading of the Gospel of St. John 1:1 and the recitation of the names of the Seven Sleepers were beneficial in cases of insomnia.[38] Arnauld also claimed that a hemorrhage in a certain woman which did not respond to medical treatment was stopped by a magic formula.[39]

The general attitude toward mental diseases in the thirteenth and early fourteenth century lacked clarity. The physician confronted with a psychopathological problem sought to put together as best he could the traditional and somewhat garbled physiologies of old Greece and Alexandria and the astrology, alchemy, demonology, and simple prayers of his own day. He was a product of a transitional age. It was a

---

[37] Karl Matthias: *Die Behandlung der Geisteskranken*. Marburg, 1887.
[38] Diepgen: *op. cit.*, vol. II, p. 77.
[39] *Ibid.*, p. 79.

prerenaissance of the arts and sciences. Duccio, Lorenzetti, the great painters of Siena, were the forerunners of the true renaissance in art as were Roger Bacon and Peter of Abano of the renaissance in sciences. But there seemed to be no forerunners of scientific psychiatry. Psychiatry now trailed behind more definitely. True, Roger Bacon wished to consider mental diseases as *natural* diseases, but his was a speculative protest and carried no medical authority. Moreover, his was the voice of an imprisoned monk and it therefore carried no spiritual authority. It was true, too, that the Salernitan Bartholomaeus advised that the mentally sick be "refreshed and comforted and withdrawn from any source of dread and busy thoughts. They must be gladdened with instruments of music and some must be given occupation." [40] Bartholomaeus does not mention diabolic possessions, nor does he deny them; but he sounds classical, reasonable, and extremely advanced for his age. " 'Madness cometh sometime of passions of the soul, as of business and of great thoughts, of sorrow and of too great study, and of dread; sometime of the biting of a wood-hound [mad dog], or some other venomous beast; sometime of melancholy meats, and sometime of drinking strong wine. And as the causes be diverse, the tokens and signs be diverse. Some cry and leap and hurt and wound themselves and other men, and darken and hide themselves in privy and secret places.' " [41]

But Bartholomaeus appears to have been an unusual exception, a voice from a very remote, healthy past or from just as remote a future. Popular medicopsychological beliefs were more influential in the consideration of the problems concerned. Witches were thought to be the cause of impotence and of loss of memory. Epilepsy was treated by means of a priest's writing out the text from the Gospel of St. Matthew, 17 and 20. Impotence was treated by putting together the halves of a nutshell, an old remedy recommended by Constantinus Africanus. Sterility in women was to be relieved by fumigating their genitalia with aromatic woods; the same treatment was found to be beneficial in cases of hysteria. The carrying of a smaragd was supposed to reduce sexual desire which was too strong and discomforting. The sapphire was supposed to add to one's intellect and wisdom and increase "the power

---

[40] Bartholomaeus: *Encyclopaedie*. Quoted by James J. Walsh: *Medieval medicine*. London, 1920, p. 192.
[41] *Ibid.*, p. 193.

of the eye." In Salerno mercury was used in the treatment of impotence, and the peony was employed against demons, sorcerers, and epilepsy. Gold and silver were considered beneficial when used against melancholia.

The idea that physical illnesses were natural and that mental illnesses were mostly supernatural became more crystallized. People felt the need to differentiate between a natural mental illness and a supernatural one. It was declared that if the shouting of a passage from the Bible into the ear of a patient having convulsions elicited a response, such a response was proof that the illness was a demoniacal possession, because the holy words had frightened the demon; if, however, the stuporous patient remained unaffected, the illness was natural.[42] The terms "devil sickness" and "witch disease" gained more and more frequent use. As to the remedies to be applied, they grew in a variety and originality increasingly devoid of rational foundation. In an old book of a somewhat earlier period [43] we find in another reference to the peony that it was useful in dispelling "devil sickness." For a "fiend-sick" man we read that one should "take a spew-drink, namely lupin, bishopwort, henbane, cropleek. Pound them together; add ale for a liquid, let it stand for a night, and add fifty libcorns [the seed to cure bewitching] or cathartic grains and holy water," or, "take clove wort and wreathe it with a red thread about the man's swere [neck] when the moon is on the wane, in the month which is called April, in the early part of October; soon he [the lunatic] will be healed." [44] If wolf's flesh, well dressed and sodden, be eaten by a man troubled with visions, "the apparitions which ere appeared to him shall not disquiet him." [45] Herbs mixed with ale and holy water were administered while masses were sung. A certain type of medicated bath was recommended for a "wit-sick" man: "Put a pail full of cold water, drop thrice into it some of the drink, bathe the man in the water, and let him eat hallowed bread and cheese and garlic and cropleek, and

[42] Diepgen: *op. cit.*, vol. II, p. 75.

[43] *Leechdoms, wortcunning, and starcraft of early England.* Collected and edited by the Rev. Oswald Cockayne, 1865. See Daniel Tuke: *Chapters in the history of the insane in the British Isles.* London, 1882.

[44] Quoted by Tuke: *op. cit.*, pp. 2, 3. Also, *Leechdoms, etc.*, vol. II, p. 137; vol. I, p. 161.

[45] Quoted by Tuke: *op. cit.*, p. 4. Also, *Leechdoms, etc.*, p. 361.

drink a cup full of the drink," or, "in case a man be lunatic, take a skin of a mere-swine [porpoise], work it into a whip, and swinge the man therewith; soon he will be well. Amen." [46] The means against which Aretaeus of Cappadocia had protested many centuries before began to be considered efficacious and even pious remedies.

The general status of psychological medicine is well reflected in this invocation of the time: "Bind me with chains and fetters as a lunatic who has lost his wits, and keep me in close custody until I repent and recover my senses." [47] And again: "A strong fellowe, provided for the nonce, tooke him and tossed him up and downe alongst and athwart the water, untill the patient by forgoing his strength had somewhat forgot his fury. Then he was conveyed to the church, and certain masses sung over him, upon which handling, if his right wits returned, St. Nunne had the thanks; but if there appeared small amendment, he was bowssened [ducked] againe and againe while there remayned in him any hope of life, for recovery." [48]

Miraculous cures, similar to those observed occasionally at Lourdes today, began to appear with increasing frequency in the thirteenth century. They took place at the tombs of saints. A woman by the name of Emmelot of Chaumont was suddenly stricken with flaccid paralysis. "They took her to the tomb [of St. Louis in St. Denis], a pole under each arm; her leg dragged along turned outward. After a few visits to the tomb, she was suddenly cured." "A Jehanne de Sarris whose 'legs were stiff and motionless,' was similarly cured." [49]

The ecstatic religious tradition, the faith in the miraculous, and the cultural monotony of medieval life must have contributed a great deal toward the spreading of mental illness. The riddle grew more puzzling and more frightening to what we would call today the man in the street. Medicine as a part of the total culture of necessity reflected the general fear which mental disease aroused, and it seemed to be willing to leave psychiatry, a specialty as yet unborn but a problem already complex, to those who claimed omniscience about the spirit of men. The mentally sick person began more to be feared and less to be pitied. As

[46] Quoted by Tuke: *op. cit.*, pp. 6, 7. Also, *Leechdoms, etc.*, vol. II, p. 335.
[47] Tuke: *op. cit.*, p. 9.
[48] *Ibid.*, p. 12.
[49] Littré: *Un fragment de médecine rétrospective, Revue de philosophie positive,* 1869. Quoted by Cesbron: *op. cit.*, pp. 131, 132.

a Frenchman said about those times, people loved God but were afraid of the devil. After the Inquisition had been established it often happened that the patient's own family would disavow him. Such mentally sick people, most frequently women, were literally thrown out into the streets. Unable to care for themselves, they wandered along the roads and through the woods. They lived in the stable with horses and cattle and would frequently lose all vestiges of their former human appearance. The very sight of them fed popular superstition and religious anxiety.

Man in his apprehension frequently took it upon himself to mete out to his own body the punishment which he thought the Lord wished him to endure. Epidemic, self-induced, ecstatic deliria appeared, transgressing the usual confines of self-punitive fasting and other ascetic self-denials. Self-torturing sects known as the Flagellants made their first appearance in the thirteenth century, and within less than twenty years a variety of self-scourging religious groups spread over Bohemia, Moravia, Poland, and Italy. Such groups were still to be found in Russia as late as the seventeenth century, under the name of "the Self-burners." Remnants of these self-punishing religious groups persisted in the old and the new world until even later.[50] Similar epidemics spread all over Europe, but they were not recognized as mental diseases, of course.

History knows of many examples of mass ecstasy in the Orient, in Ancient Greece, and in Rome. These were in many respects similar to the epidemics of the Middle Ages. The Dionysian festivities, the Roman Bacchanalias, and the occasional outbreaks of mass suicide in ancient Greece were apparently not different from many of the epidemics which raged all over the European continent from the thirteenth to the eighteenth century. The Church never condoned these outbreaks but looked upon them with suspicion; as early as the fifth century St. Augustine observed with disapproval the dancing epidemics among the Christians.

These epidemics, while definitely of a pathological order, are certainly psychosociological phenomena rather than manifestations of

[50] I am indebted to W. W. Norton for calling my attention to the self-torturing groups in New Mexico who even today inflict wounds upon themselves and others during their religious Christian ceremonies.

individual mental illness. The inaccurate terms applied to these phenomena, such as "mass hysteria" or "mass psychoses," are merely descriptive literary phrases and not diagnostic terms, for the individuals who form a part of these mass reactions need not be and are not always mentally sick. Under certain cultural circumstances a mass, a crowd of people, undergoes en masse a number of abnormal changes. To put it in the somewhat quaint language of an older writer, "There are epidemics of insanity which are met with among healthy people. The cause which produces these epidemics is moral contagion. The neuropathic, hysterical state which frequently manifests itself in such epidemics is not at all the cause of these epidemics; it is an epiphenomenon which is neither necessary nor always present. This hysterical state is the result of the influence which the mind or the emotions exercise on the nervous system." [51]

The number of mentally sick individuals, as well as the severity of psychopathological epidemics, became so imposing that toward the close of the fourteenth and at the beginning of the fifteenth century the State not only had to take swift and drastic cognizance of the danger, but it had to formulate its stand toward these frightful happenings. Moreover, the brewing spirit of critical opposition to traditional thinking, the grumbling of protest against constituted knowledge, and the deepening eagerness to search for new truths began to make themselves felt; these were pronounced heresy. Heterodoxy and many a mental illness were fused, or rather confused, in the minds of the constituted authorities. Arnauld of Villanova was excommunicated for his great interest in alchemy, but in less than a century and a half astrology and alchemy began to be called *scientiae*. These sciences were suspected of being of the devil. The magician, the sorcerer, the heretic, and the psychotic began to be perceived as one and the same the servants of Lucifer. A sense of doom seemed to be hovering over Europe. The awakening spirit which marked the thirteenth century became temporarily dormant. During the century and a half that followed, it was subjected to that invisible but patent cultural assimilation and gestation which finally brought about the rebirth known as the Renaissance. In the meantime tradition suffused with anxiety armed itself with both the

[51] Despine: *De la folie au point de vue philosophique ou plus spécialement psychologique.* Paris, 1875.

spiritual and secular sword to combat the invading cohorts of Lucifer which threatened to overrun the Christian world. Both the spiritual and temporal powers had to consolidate their strength. Theology had to produce a codified working dogma and jurisprudence a legal technique.

By the middle of the fifteenth century this process of consolidation of the instruments of canonic and temporal legality was well-nigh completed and in this atmosphere of anxious intensity and combative religious fervor medical psychology became a part of codified demonology, and the treatment of the mentally ill became for the most part a problem of legal procedure. The darkest ages of psychiatry set in. Thus on the very eve of the Renaissance—at the time when Ghirlandaio began to paint, when Michelangelo Buonarroti opened his eyes to the world, when Florence began to glow with the spirit and light of a new world, when Columbus began to yearn to set sail into an unknown world—medical psychology was plunged into a singular darkness even greater than the darkness which followed the breakdown of classical culture. It was a darkness full of turmoil and restless cruelty and yet, as we shall presently see, it was full of determined struggle for the recognition of new truth, new knowledge, and new freedom.

6

❖ ❖

THE BLOWS OF THE WITCHES'
HAMMER

I

N OT until we reach the first quarter of the twentieth century
will it be possible even partially to understand why it is that,
ever since the first efflorescence of scientific medical psychology in Athens, the science of the human mind trailed further and further behind other sciences, or why it appears to be the inevitable lot of
psychiatry always to make slower progress than other fields of knowledge. The puzzling but undeniable fact remains that medical psychology toward the end of the fifteenth century became welded with so
many abstract theological and legal questions that it seemed for a while
to be beyond redemption. Galen and Hippocrates were paid lip service
only, and their clinical theories were ingeniously interwoven with
considerations of sin and of the Author of all Evil. The physician of
the time reasoned in a manner betraying deep apprehension that his
preoccupation with clinical matters might be mistaken for indifference
to the questions of sin and virtue.

In the year 1496 a physician, Pollich von Mellerstadt, wrote a thesis
on syphilis, a disease very new at the time. He felt it necessary first to
raise the question of whether diseases sent by God may be treated by
natural methods. He had therefore to correlate disease and sin; he

had to preserve his manifest opposition to sin and yet justify his desire to treat a disease in a manner compatible with his medical judgment. Von Mellerstadt came to the conclusion that sinful strivings might very well originate in the brain but thought that the soul might be turned toward virtue by means of good nutrition.[1] The trend indicated in this careful conclusion persisted for centuries. Four hundred years after Villanova, in the seventeenth century, we find Zacchias, the personal physician of Pope Innocent X, saying quite earnestly: *Gaudet humore melancholico daemon;* [2] the devil rejoices in a bath of the melancholy humor. Galen's humoral theory is pushed into the background and the devil is elevated to the role of causative agent of melancholy. Sin and mental disease have become equated in the mind of man; the major sin of man and woman and the major preoccupation of the devil is sex. The accusation of pansexualism which was raised against Freud by his misunderstanding opponents early in the twentieth century was a psychologically unsound and scientifically untenable accusation, but it could have been raised with good reason against those of the fifteenth century who fancied devils, *incubi* and *succubi*, indulging in the perennial seduction of women and men respectively. Michael Psellus' *Demonology* of the eleventh century was but an innocent statement as compared with the similar and by far more influential contributions of the fifteenth century. Nider's *Formicarium*, which appeared in the beginning of the century, and the famous *Malleus Maleficarum* at the end of the same century were milestones of indomitable conviction and burning horror.

One must stop and ponder time and again the fact that in the days "in which science and art were reborn, when people were painting and sculpting anew and once more had turned towards investigation and writing, the making of new discoveries and new inventions, when the old classical world and bookprinting seemed to recast the face of Western civilization—in those very days humanity stood [in respect to belief in witches] on a lower level [of mental development] than do some of the primitive races of today." [3]

It need hardly be repeated that the horror which the thought of a

---

[1] Diepgen: *Geschichte der Medizin,* vol. II, p. 74.
[2] Isensee: *Geschichte der Medizin,* p. 1235.
[3] Carl Binz: *Doktor Johann Weyer.* Bonn, 1885, p. 3.

witch inspired and the hatred of such a woman as the source of evil—a hatred underlying the psychology of witch-hunting—were very old phenomena. They did not suddenly appear in the fifteenth century. The "witch's knot," or the "witch's ladder," had been almost universally feared for a very long time. The witch's ladder was feared in Scotland and its equivalent, *la ghirlanda delle streghe*, in Italy. The old Frankish law known as *Lex Salica* was very strict about witches, as was the *Codex Theodosianus*. The Council of Paris (829) enjoined the secular courts to uphold the sentences pronounced by the bishops. As early as the beginning of the seventh century Pope Gregory I took official action against sorcerers. By the end of the fifteenth the Christian world was suffering from the cumulative effects of centuries of superstition. These effects found expression in the writings and activities of the men who took close to their heart the conviction that the world was going to its final doom unless saved by some radical measures. As a physician the medical man was considered of no consequence in these measures; he could help only as a citizen and as a Christian, since the problems involved were those of salvation, of suppressing sedition, of saving the faith, of the total destruction of the devil's servants and their machinations.

The general state of mind may be inferred from remarks of the Benedictine abbot Johannes Trithemius, a great scholar and a very gentle person. Trithemius was a man whose friendship was sought by all important princes and scholars of his day. He was a man of whom a contemporary states that a goodness that could not be expressed in words rested upon his sturdy, manly brow and that his pure and luminous eyes appeared to reflect a celestial light. It was Trithemius who composed a book, at the request of Joachim of Brandenburg, entitled *Antipalus Maleficiorum*. We read in this book, "There is no part in our body that the witches would not injure. Most of the time they make human beings possessed and thus they are left to the devils to be tortured with unheard-of pains. They even get into carnal relations with them. Unfortunately, the number of such witches is very great in every province; more than that, there is no locality too small for a witch to find. Yet Inquisitors and judges who could avenge these open offenses against God and nature are few and far between. Man and beast die as a result of the evil of these women and no one thinks of the fact that these things are perpetrated by witches. Many suffer constantly from the most severe diseases and are not even aware that they are bewitched." [4]

Trithemius, of course, was not alone in his regret that there were not enough Inquisitors and judges to mete out the necessary punishment of witches. It fell to the lot of two Dominican Brothers to become the efficient and aggressive carriers of the universal anxiety which possessed the world of their day. These two, Johann Sprenger and Heinrich Kraemer, *Institoris*, were inspired with their great mission. Methodical and persistent Germans, they set out to become the leaders of a movement for the extermination of witches. It was to them a religious mission which had to be not only upheld by the Church, but sufficiently supported by the science and political structure of the day. They first obtained the authority of Pope Innocent VIII. On December 9, 1484, the Pope issued a bull, *Summis desiderantes affectibus*, which read as follows:

"Innocent, Bishop, Servant of the servants of God, for an eternal remembrance.

"Desiring with the most heartfelt anxiety, even as Our Apostleship requires, that the Catholic Faith should especially in this Our day increase and flourish everywhere, and that all heretical depravity should be driven far from the frontiers and bournes of the Faithful, We very gladly proclaim and even restate those particular means and methods whereby Our pious desire may obtain its wished effect, since when all errors are uprooted by Our diligent avocation as by the hoe of a provident husbandman, a zeal for, and the regular observance of, Our holy Faith will be all the more strongly impressed upon the hearts of the faithful.

"It has indeed lately come to Our ears, not without afflicting Us with bitter sorrow, that in some parts of Northern Germany, as well as in the provinces, townships, territories, districts, and dioceses of Mainz, Cologne, Trèves, Salzburg, and Bremen, many persons of both sexes, unmindful of their own salvation and straying from the Catholic Faith, have abandoned themselves to devils, incubi and succubi, and by their incantations, spells, conjurations, and other accursed charms and crafts, enormities and horrid offences, have slain infants yet

---

[4] Binz: *op. cit.*, pp. 6, 7.

in the mother's womb, as also the offspring of cattle, have blasted the produce of the earth, the grapes of the vine, the fruits of trees, nay, men and women, beasts of burthen, herd-beasts, as well as animals of other kinds, vineyards, orchards, meadows, pasture-land, corn, wheat, and all other cereals; these wretches furthermore afflict and torment men and women, beasts of burthen, herd-beasts, as well as animals of other kinds, with terrible and piteous pains and sore diseases, both internal and external; they hinder men from performing the sexual act and women from conceiving, whence husbands cannot know their wives nor wives receive their husbands; over and above this, they blasphemously renounce that Faith which is theirs by the Sacrament of Baptism, and at the instigation of the Enemy of Mankind they do not shrink from committing and perpetrating the foulest abominations and filthiest excesses to the deadly peril of their own souls, whereby they outrage the Divine Majesty and are a cause of scandal and danger to very many. And although Our dear sons Henry Kramer and James Sprenger, Professors of Theology, of the Order of Friars Preachers, have been by Letters Apostolic delegated as Inquisitors of these heretical pravities, and still are Inquisitors, the first in the aforesaid parts of Northern Germany, wherein are included those aforesaid townships, districts, dioceses, and other specified localities, and the second in certain territories which lie along the borders of the Rhine, nevertheless not a few clerics and lay folk of those countries, seeking too curiously to know more than concerns them, since in the aforesaid delegatory letters there is no express and specific mention by name of these provinces, townships, dioceses, and districts, and further since the two delegates themselves and the abominations they are to encounter are not designated in detailed and particular fashion, these persons are not ashamed to contend with the most unblushing effrontery that these enormities are not practised in those provinces, and consequently the aforesaid Inquisitors have no legal right to exercise their powers of inquisition in the provinces, townships, dioceses, districts, and territories, which have been rehearsed, and that the Inquisitors may not proceed to punish, imprison, and penalize criminals convicted of the heinous offences and many wickednesses which have been set forth. Accordingly in the aforesaid provinces, townships, dioceses, and districts, the abominations and enormities in question remain unpunished not without open danger to the souls of many and peril of eternal damnation.

"Wherefore We, as is Our duty, being wholly desirous of removing all hindrances and obstacles by which the good work of the Inquisitors may be let and tarded, as also of applying potent remedies to prevent the disease of heresy and other turpitudes diffusing their poison to the destruction of many innocent souls, since Our zeal for the Faith especially incites us, lest that the provinces, townships, dioceses, districts, and territories of Germany, which We have specified, be deprived of the benefits of the Holy Office thereto assigned, by the tenor of these presents in virtue of Our Apostolic authority We decree and enjoin that the aforesaid Inquisitors be empowered to proceed to the just correction, imprisonment, and punishment of any persons, without let or hindrance, in every way as if the provinces, townships, dioceses, districts, territories, yea, even the persons and their crimes in this kind were named and particularly designated in Our letters. Moreover, for greater surety We extend these letters deputing this authority to cover all the aforesaid provinces, townships, dioceses, districts, and territories, persons, and crimes newly rehearsed, and We grant permission to the aforesaid Inquisitors, to one separately or to both, as also to Our dear son John Gremper, priest of the diocese of Constance, Master of Arts, their notary, or to any other public notary, who shall be by them or by one of them, temporarily delegated to those provinces, townships, dioceses, districts, and aforesaid territories, to proceed, according to the regulations of the Inquisition, against any persons of whatsoever rank and high estate, correcting, mulcting, imprisoning, punishing, as their crimes merit, those whom they have found guilty, the penalty being adapted to the offence. Moreover, they shall enjoy a full and perfect faculty of expounding and preaching the word of God to the faithful, as often as opportunity may offer and it may seem good to them, in each and every parish church of the said provinces, and they shall freely and lawfully perform any rites or execute any business which may appear advisable in the aforesaid cases. By Our supreme authority We grant them anew full and complete faculties.

"At the same time by Letters Apostolic We require Our venerable Brother, the Bishop of Strasburg, that he himself shall announce, or by some other or others cause to be announced, the burthen of Our

Bull, which he shall solemnly publish when and so often as he deems it necessary, or when he shall be requested so to do by the Inquisitors or by one of them. Nor shall he suffer them in disobedience to the tenor of these presents to be molested or hindered by any authority whatsoever, but he shall threaten all who endeavour to hinder or harass the Inquisitors, all who oppose them, all rebels, of whatsoever rank, estate, position, pre-eminence, dignity, or any condition they may be, or whatsoever privilege of exemption they may claim, with excommunication, suspension, interdict, and yet more terrible penalties, censures, and punishment, as may seem good to him, and that without any right of appeal, and if he will he may by Our authority aggravate and renew these penalties as often as he list, calling in, if so please him, the help of the secular arm.

"Non obstantibus . . . Let no man therefore . . . But if any dare to do so, which God forbid, let him know that upon him will fall the wrath of Almighty God, and of the Blessed Apostles Peter and Paul.

"Given at Rome, at S. Peter's, on the 9 December of the Year of the Incarnation of Our Lord one thousand four hundred and eighty-four, in the first Year of Our Pontificate." [5]

Sprenger and Kraemer, despite the authority vested in them by this papal bull, found it difficult at first to gain the confidence of the communities in which they started their work; a bishop once closed the door on Kraemer, and the people of the towns to which the two friars came to do their duty would frequently meet them with curses and threats. Sprenger and Kraemer were not men who gave up in battle and they decided to call upon their literary propensities and scholarship—qualities not frequently found among the Dominicans, whose powers were supposed to be in preaching rather than in learning. True dogs of the Lord, *Domini canes* as they dubbed themselves in those days, their duty was to wander over the Christian world and bark against rising heresy and sin for the greater glory of Christendom. The two theologians, Sprenger and Kraemer, wrote a book which was to become the most authoritative and the most horrible document of that age. It was entitled *Malleus Maleficarum*—the Witches' Hammer.

[5] Quoted by the Reverend Montague Summers in his translation of the *Malleus Maleficarum*. 1928, pp. xliii–xlv.

The authors, apparently chastened a little by their experience with some inhospitable communities and a few unreceptive clergymen, decided to proceed cautiously in order to secure unchallengeable authority. Consequently, almost two and a half years after the issuance of the papal bull, they submitted the *Malleus* to the Faculty of Theology at the University of Cologne. On the nineteenth of May, 1487, Dean Lambertus de Monte called a faculty meeting. The Dean affixed his signature to the indorsement of the *Malleus;* four out of seven professors concurred in similar manner. The lack of unanimity was not acceptable to the Inquisitors. They persisted; they prepared a new letter of indorsement and, whatever their powers of persuasion, these powers must have proved sufficiently intimidating, for the remaining members of the faculty finally signed the document. The two Inquisitors were now in possession of both spiritual and academic authorization. This was comforting but perhaps not sufficiently practical as an instrument for real action.

It soon became evident that this difficulty had already been overcome, at least in part, for the two friars were evidently keen, practical men. Before coming to the University of Cologne they had secured a special document from Maximilian, the King of Rome; this was issued from Brussels, dated November 6, 1486, with royal signature and seal duly affixed and in perfect order. In the document the King took official notice of the *Summis desiderantes affectibus* and gave official support to Sprenger and Kraemer in the discharge of their sacred duty. Confronted with this royal decree, the Faculty of Theology could not but agree to the last request of the Dominicans, which in view of the royal command was more a demand than a request; a number of certified copies of the Faculty's letter of indorsement and approbation were prepared and handed to the humble friars. These letters they were to use at their discretion, whenever and wherever they might be met with distrust or other forms of difficulty.

The two men could now proceed without stint or concern; the Holy See, the professors, and the Royal Throne were behind them. Printing, the great instrument of civilization and itself a product of the Renaissance, served them in good stead. The publication of the *Malleus Maleficarum* was launched sometime between 1487 and 1489; the practical application of its thesis was begun with great fervor. The

Malleus became the textbook of the Inquisition. It went through ten editions before 1669 and through nine more before another century had passed. Bookmaking was not as efficient in those days as it is in ours, nor was literacy a characteristic of the age; thus, nineteen editions stand out as imposing and incontestable testimony not only to the popularity of the book but to the great need of the time which it undoubtedly filled. It was not translated into a modern language until the twentieth century. A German translation by J. W. R. Schmidt appeared in 1906 and an English one by the Reverend Montague Summers in 1928.

A German university professor of the latter part of the nineteenth century, mindful of the nature of the *Malleus* and also of the fact that it was the conception and the creation of two German monks, has this to say about the book: It is "a heavy volume in quarto, so insane, so raw and cruel, and it leads to such terrible conclusions, that never before or since did such a unified combination of horrible characteristics flow from a human pen. Many feelings well up in the [present-day] reader who is forced to work through its text; feelings of oppression, disgust, mournful sadness, and national shame. Which [of these feelings] predominates, it is difficult to say." [6]

"The thesis of the *Malleus* is as simple as it seems to us horrible. It is divided into three parts. The first part represents an argument which attempts to prove the existence of witchcraft and witches, or to be more correct, to prove by argumentation rather than by factual demonstration that he who does not believe in the existence of witches is either in honest error or polluted with heresy. The second part is devoted to what we would call today clinical reports. It tells of various types of witches and of the different methods one should use to identify a witch. To use modern terminology, it describes the clinical pictures and the various ways of arriving at a diagnosis. The third part deals with the legal forms of examining and sentencing a witch. It goes into the details of legal technicalities and the technique of delivering a witch from the devil or to the secular arm of justice for execution, in most cases by burning. It is not a dispassionate, cold, legalistic treatise; it is, rather, polemical, argumentative, scornful or threatening in tone, and uncompromising. It is written with firm conviction and a fervent zeal which

[6] Binz: *op. cit.*, p. 10.

made the authors totally anesthetic to the smell of burning human flesh." [7]

We must not forget, of course, that the whole problem of witchcraft, and the structure of clerical and temporal jurisprudence which it erected, was not the exclusive result of a miscarried psychopathology or of a psychopathological bent in theology. There was a restlessness in the body social and politic of Christian Europe; the *Malleus* was a reaction against the disquieting signs of growing instability of the established order, and hundreds of thousands of mentally sick fell victim to this violent reaction. Not all accused of being witches and sorcerers were mentally sick, but almost all mentally sick were considered witches, or sorcerers, or bewitched. The sort of "persecutory mania" which was displayed by the Church and the State during the period under consideration was undoubtedly due to the sense of insecurity and the growing awareness that new social forces and new spiritual ideals were about to rise and to threaten the very heart of the regime which ruled medieval Europe. That all these forces were opposed and cursed as being of the devil there is no doubt. This was the tradition of the day. When Henry VIII wearied of Anne Boleyn, he found no more respectable argument than that he had been seduced by witchcraft into the marriage; he cited as proof that the Lord had not allowed them to have any male issue. Witchcraft was a well-adapted and most pious-sounding rationalization for anything which anyone opposed or wanted to destroy.

Even today there are still some who know this period so well and who are so imbued with its spirit that they frankly admit the presence of acute sociological issues in the problem of witchcraft. One of these, the Reverend Montague Summers, speaks in a voice dramatically reminiscent of the heyday of Sprenger and Kraemer. Though one should make due allowance for the element of unconscious caricature and conscious but misplaced pious enthusiasm, the Reverend Summers' words are both revealing and picturesque. In his foreword to the English edition of the *Malleus* he speaks of witches—in whose existence he continues to believe—and says, "Their objects may be summed up as the abolition of monarchy, the abolition of private property and of in-

[7] Gregory Zilboorg: *The medical man and the witch during the Renaissance*. Baltimore, 1935, pp. 8, 9.

heritance, the abolition of marriage, the abolition of order, the total abolition of all religion. It was against this that the Inquisition had to fight and who can be surprised if, when faced with so vast a conspiracy, the methods employed by the Holy Office may not seem—if the terrible conditions are conveniently forgotten—a little drastic, a little severe? There can be no doubt that had this most excellent tribunal continued to enjoy its full prerogative and the full exercise of its salutary powers, the world at large would be in a far happier and far more orderly position to-day. Historians may point out diversities and dissimilarities between the teachings of the Waldenses, the Albigenses, the Henricians, the Poor Men of Lyons, the Cathari, the Vaudois, the Bogomiles and Manichees, but they were in reality branches and variants of the same dark fraternity, just as the Third International, the Anarchists, the Nihilists and the Bolsheviks are in every sense, save the mere label, entirely identical." [8]

The overwhelming fear which the old medieval order experienced toward the close of the fifteenth century was so real and so pervading that its force communicated itself almost unaltered by four and a half centuries to this sympathetic student of witchcraft.

In this atmosphere no one was safe—man, woman, or child. Boys of ten and eleven, girls of nine and ten did not escape prosecution and conviction. [9] The contentions which were undoubtedly heard from many quarters, that at least some of those prosecuted were sick people who suffered from delusions and hallucinations, were ineffective. The *Malleus* dismissed these contentions with arguments of ardent conviction and with a cold security of being right. The *Malleus* overlooked no single detail; it left no loophole through which doubt and uncertainty might creep.

II

THE *Malleus* is terrifyingly simple in dealing with its problem. "Those err who say that there is no such thing as witchcraft, but that it is purely imaginary, even although they do not believe that devils exist

---

[8] Rev. Montague Summers: *op. cit.*, p. xviii.
[9] *Ibid.*, p. xix.

except in the imagination of the ignorant and vulgar, and the natural accidents which happen to a man he wrongly attributes to some supposed devil. For the imagination of some men is so vivid that they think they see actual figures and appearances which are but the reflections of their thoughts, and then these are believed to be apparitions of evil spirits or even the spectres of witches. But this is contrary to true faith which teaches us that certain angels fell from heaven and are now devils, and we are bound to acknowledge that by their very nature they can do many wonderful things which we cannot do. And those who try to induce others to perform such evil wonders are called witches. And because infidelity in a person who has been baptized is technically called heresy, therefore such persons are plainly heretics." [10]

This passage from the *Malleus* is perhaps the most significant statement to come out of the fifteenth century. Here, in a concise and succinct paragraph, two monks brush aside the whole mass of psychiatric knowledge which had been so carefully collected and preserved by almost two thousand years of medical and philosophic investigation; they brush it aside almost casually and with such stunning simplicity that no room is left for argument. How can one raise objections to the assertion, "but this is contrary to true faith"? The fusion of insanity, witchcraft, and heresy into one concept and the exclusion of even the suspicion that the problem is a medical one are now complete. It is no longer a matter of popular superstition; it is an authoritative principle of faith and law. Nothing may shake this dogma. No fact may be brought forth to cast a shadow on this principle. Yes, assert Sprenger and Kraemer, it may even be true that in certain cases witches suffer from delusions. Some witches are actually transferred from one place to another by the devil's power; this is the phenomenon of transvection. Other witches only believe that they were transvected, that is, they imagine something which did not really take place. They have an illusion, but this really has no bearing on the matter, for "although these women imagine they are riding (as they think and say) with Diana or with Herodias, in truth they are riding with the devil, who

---

[10] *Malleus Maleficarum* (English edition), pp. 2, 3. For a detailed study of this text from the standpoint of clinical psychopathology, the reader is referred to *The medical man and the witch during the Renaissance*.

calls himself by some such heathen name and throws a glamour before their eyes. . . . The act of riding abroad may be merely illusory, since the devil has extraordinary power over the minds of those who have given themselves up to him, so that what they do in pure imagination, they believe they have actually and really done in the body." [11] Thus even illusions acknowledged as such by the *Malleus* do not excuse a woman from the crime of being a witch.

The belief in the free will of man is here brought to its most terrifying, although most preposterous, conclusion. Man, whatever he does, even if he succumbs to an illness which perverts his perceptions, imagination, and intellectual functions, does it of his own free will; he voluntarily bows to the wishes of the Evil One. The devil does not lure and trap man; man chooses to succumb to the devil and he must be held responsible for this free choice. He must be punished; he must be eliminated from the community. More than that, his soul, held in such sinful captivity by the corrupted, criminal will within the body, must be set free again; it *must* be delivered. The body must be burned.

The auto-da-fé, which appears to the modern man so gruesome and so horrifying, thus appeared to the man of those days an act of mercy, a solemn and invigorating salvage of something pure and immortal from the clutches of evil and darkness. It was an act of lofty devotion and pious genuflection before the great wisdom and glory of the Lord. Despite all the legal subtleties of the procedure and despite the cold, heartless tortures of so many human beings, this imposing of the supreme purification by fire was an act of ecstasy and devout communion with the will of God.

Unless one keeps this attitude of profound devotion in mind, one is apt to misunderstand the fundamental reaction of many generations toward the mentally ill. It is a reaction of fear and of endless anxiety which arouses to utmost intensity the drive to self-defense, a drive which is capable of utter cruelty and revengefulness. But civilized man —and even the man of the fifteenth century was sufficiently civilized— is not capable of giving vent to his great reservoir of bitter hatred and relentless cruelty unless he finds a good, lofty, and noble reason which will allow him to justify in his own eyes his need to hate, to destroy, and to kill. The *Malleus* is the culminating point of such a rationaliza-

[11] *Malleus*, p. 7.

tion; that is what made it so authoritative, so relentless, so very right-eous, and so incontrovertible in the eyes of its authors, its readers, and the judges who used it as a textbook.

The psychopathological theory adopted by the *Malleus* does not fully discard the remnants of the Galenic tradition, but its authors are careful to avoid any undue emphasis on medical authority, for "no witchcraft can be removed by any natural power, although it may be assuaged." [12] Even the Biblical reports of cure by "natural" means had to be meticulously, although reverently, refuted so that they might be brought into harmony with the spirit of the *Malleus*. "And as for that concerning I Kings xvi: that Saul, who was vexed by a devil, was al-leviated when David played his harp before him, and that the devil departed, etc. It must be known that it is quite true that by playing of the harp, and the natural virtue of that harmony, the affliction of Saul was to some extent relieved, inasmuch as that music did somewhat calm his senses through hearing; through which calming he was made less prone to that vexation. But the reason why the devil spirit de-parted when David played the harp was because of the might of the Cross, which is clearly enough shown by the gloss, where it says: David was learned in music, skillful in the different notes and har-monious modulations. He shows the essential unity by playing each day in various modes. David repressed the evil spirit by the harp, not because there was so much virtue in the harp, but it was made in the sign of a cross, being a cross of wood with the strings stretched across. And even at that time the devils fled from this." [13] "Even at that time" means a thousand years before the advent of Christ.

Having firmly established its theoretical and legal position, the *Malleus* proceeds to review actual cases. These cases are of particular interest to the historian of medical psychology, for they demonstrate not only that mental diseases were numerous, but that the manifesta-tions of these diseases were accurately recorded by both Inquisitor and judge, although consistently misinterpreted in accordance with the tenets of prevailing demonology. The ideational content of the given mental illness—the abnormal thoughts of the patient without examina-tions of which no scientific psychiatry is possible—was considered not

[12] *Ibid.*, p. 161.
[13] *Ibid.*, p. 41.

only important but evidential corroboration of the principles of demonological philosophy. What the patient thought and imagined was considered a true rendition of actual happenings. If a woman insisted she had seen the devil and had heard a voice admonishing her to kill someone, and if she insisted that she obeyed and did kill, her statements were taken for truth. It was not even necessary to establish the corpus delicti; in the eyes of the judges she was a self-confessed ally of the devil, and a murderess.

It is as if today we listened to a person afflicted with a paranoid schizophrenia and heard him say that detectives were after him, that he had killed a good man, and that he heard voices coming to him by radio waves from the next building, and we then set out to look for the transmitter and at the same time instituted proceedings charging the patient with murder in the first degree. Even as today we take the necktie and shoelaces from a condemned man, for fear that he may kill himself before the law can kill him in due course, so the apprehended witches and sorcerers were deprived of their shoestrings, because on occasion some of them would add the crime of suicide to their other mortal sins. Just as today the ideational content of many of the mentally ill deals with sexual matters, so in the days of the *Malleus* the witches and sorcerers were preoccupied with these matters. Centuries of asceticism and rigorous self-restraint only accentuated the erotic trends which were set free in the thoughts of the mentally sick. The misogynous age of the *Malleus* saw in all this, as in many other things, the intricate deviltry of Lucifer.

The devils "have six ways of injuring humanity. And one is, to induce an evil love in a man for a woman, or in a woman for a man. The second is to plant hatred or jealousy in anyone. The third is to bewitch them so that a man cannot perform the genital act with a woman, or conversely a woman with a man; or by various means to procure an abortion, as has been said before. The fourth is to cause some disease in any of the human organs. The fifth, to take away life. The sixth, to deprive them of reason." [14] The whole field of sexology, psychopathology, and criminology is condensed in this simple statement which leaves no doubt as to its righteous serenity. There is little doubt about anything; everything is simple, clear, and direct. In the diocese

[14] *Ibid.*, p. 115.

of Basel, in the district of Alsace and Lorraine, a laborer spoke roughly to a certain querulous woman and she threatened him with revenge. The laborer at first paid little attention to her threat, but that evening he felt a pimple on his neck. He rubbed it and soon his face and neck appeared swollen. Some sort of rash which was thought to be "a horrible leprosy" appeared all over his body. The laborer went to his friends and reported his encounter with the woman. The woman was soon apprehended by the authorities and made to confess to her crime. When the judge asked her the motive of her crime, she said, " 'When that man used abusive words to me, I was angry and went home; and my familiar began to ask the reason for my ill humor. I told him, and begged him to avenge me on the man. And he asked what I wanted him to do to him; and I answered that I wished he would always have a swollen face. And the devil went away and afflicted the man even beyond my asking; for I had not hoped that he would infect him with such sore leprosy.' And so the woman was burned." [15]

Wizards and sorcerers are also cited by the *Malleus*, but rather briefly, since next to the devil the ascetic mind saw in woman the source of all evil. Conscious unwillingness to work with the devil was not considered an extenuating circumstance. The authors of the *Malleus* frankly admit, "We have often learned from the confessions of those whom we have caused to be burned, that they have not been willing agents of witchcraft." [16]

The question of differential diagnosis, that is, of distinguishing between witchcraft (a supernatural phenomenon) and natural disease, is raised by the authors of the *Malleus* and due respect is paid to the skill of doctors, but the criteria are as indefinite as they are tenuous. Sprenger and Kraemer speak of extrinsic causes accompanied by bad humors in the blood and the stomach, as if these could be easily seen. If the presence of these is not established, then the trouble is due to witchcraft. If the disease is incurable, it is due to witchcraft; if it sets in with great suddenness, it is due to witchcraft. "All witchcraft comes from carnal lust, which is in women insatiable. See Proverbs XXX: There are three things that are never satisfied, yea, a fourth thing which says not, It is enough; that is, the mouth of the womb. Wherefore for the

[15] *Ibid.*, p. 137.
[16] *Ibid.*, p. 102.

sake of fulfilling their lusts they consort even with devils." [17] Certain chapters of the *Malleus* are so replete with sexual details that the book at times might well be considered a handbook of sexual psychopathies.

The hallucinatory experiences, sexual or not, of the psychotic women of the time are well described by Sprenger and Kraemer, and one or two of them may well be cited here as excellent clinical illustrations of the psychopathological aberrations of both patient and investigator, and as testimony to the sadism which filled the minds and the hearts of the sinful and the pious of that cruel age.

"We Inquisitors had credible experience of this method in the town of Breisach in the diocese of Basel, receiving full information from a young girl witch who had been converted, whose aunt also had been burned in the diocese of Strasbourg. And she added that she had become a witch by the method in which her aunt had first tried to seduce her.

"For one day her aunt ordered her to go upstairs with her, and at her command to go into a room where she found fifteen young men clothed in green garments after the manner of German knights. And her aunt said to her: Choose whom you wish from these young men, and I will give him to you, and he will take you for his wife. And when she said she did not wish for any of them, she was sorely beaten and at last consented, and was initiated according to the aforesaid ceremony. She said also that she was often transported by night with her aunt over vast distances, even from Strasbourg to Cologne. . . ."[18]

"Here is another example from the same source. There was lately a general report, brought to the notice of Peter the Judge in Boltingen, that thirteen infants had been devoured in the State of Berne; and public justice exacted full vengeance on the murderers. And when Peter asked one of the captive witches in what manner they ate children, she replied: 'This is the manner of it. We set our snares chiefly for unbaptized children, and even for those that have been baptized, especially when they have not been protected by the sign of the Cross and prayers' (Reader, notice that, at the devil's command, they take the unbaptized chiefly, in order that they may not be baptized), 'and with our spells we kill them in their cradles or even when they are

[17] *Ibid.*, p. 47.
[18] *Ibid.*, p. 100.

sleeping by their parents' side, in such a way that they afterwards are thought to have been overlain or to have died some other natural death. Then we secretly take them from their graves, and cook them in a cauldron, until the whole flesh comes away from the bones to make a soup which may easily be drunk. Of the more solid matter we make an unguent which is of virtue to help us in our arts and pleasures and our transportations; and with the liquid we fill a flask or skin, whoever drinks from which, with the addition of a few other ceremonies, immediately acquires much knowledge and becomes a leader in our sect.' " [19]

It is unnecessary to go into the unsavory details of the actual examination of the witches. These would bring only added testimony to the ingenious cruelty of those who, once they sense the strength of their power and are convinced that they are right, know no bounds. The history of medical psychology will not be enriched by these details, and the history of man's own madness need not here be recapitulated.

Despite all the horror and darkness of the *Malleus Maleficarum*, it is an instructive book. It is enlightening and the student of social changes may well find in it more than one hint of the causes of the cultural breakdowns which appear every now and then in the course of history.

As a final impression, one may carry away from the perusal of the *Malleus* the antierotic, misogynous nature of the book. The role of sex in the whole history of our civilization and man's attitude toward woman's part in social life as one of the factors of social problems are thrown into painful relief in this piece of legalistic and theological literature of the early Renaissance. The Old World seems to have risen against woman and written this gruesome testimonial to its own madness. Even after she had been tortured and broken in body and spirit, woman was not granted the privilege of facing the world in a direct way. The witch, stripped of her clothes, her wounds and marks of torture exposed, her head and genitals shaven so that no devil could conceal himself in her hair, would be led into court backwards so that her evil eyes might not rest on the judge and bewitch him.

Never in the history of humanity was woman more systematically

[19] *Ibid.*, pp. 100–101.

degraded. She paid for the fall of Eve sevenfold, and the Law bore a countenance of pride and self-satisfaction, and the delusional certainty that the will of the Lord had been done.

The spirit expressed and fostered by the *Malleus* continued to remain the keynote of the Law for over two centuries. Europe was in the throes of its imaginary horrors and the veritable terror with which it responded to its own delusions. This spirit is well reflected in the fervent words of the Burgundian Judge Boguet, who lived in the days of Henry IV, almost a century after the publication of the *Malleus*.

"I believe that the sorcerers could form an army equal to that of Xerxes, who had one million, eight hundred thousand men. Trois-Echelles, one of those best acquainted with the art of sorcerers, states that under King Charles IX France alone had three hundred thousand sorcerers (some read it as thirty thousand). This being the case, what are we to estimate the total number to be if we are to include other countries and regions of the world? Are we not justified in believing that since those days the number has increased at least by half? As to myself, I have no doubt, since a mere glance at our neighbors will convince us that the land is infested with this unfortunate and damnable vermin. Germany cannot do anything but raise fires against them; Switzerland is compelled to do likewise, thus depopulating many of its villages; Lorraine reveals to a visitor thousands and thousands of poles to which the sorcerers are tied; and as to ourselves, who are not exempt from this trouble any more than others are, we are having a number of executions in various parts of the land. Now to return to our neighbors; Savoie is not yet emptied, since she sends us daily an infinite number of people possessed by devils who, when conjured up, tell us that they were put into the bodies of those poor people by sorcerers. Adding to this the fact that the principal ones whom we have burned here in Burgundy came originally from there, what judgment are we to form of France? It is difficult to believe that she will ever be purged, given the great number that she had in the days of Trois-Echelles, let alone other outlying regions. No, no, the sorcerers reach everywhere by the thousands; they multiply on the earth like the caterpillars in our gardens. . . . I want them to know that if the results were to correspond to my wishes, the earth would be quickly purged, because I wish they could all be united in one body so that all could be burned on one fire." [20]

The devil was everywhere and the earth was his empire. Weyer, the true founder of modern psychiatry, with characteristic sarcasm counted seventy-two "Princes of Darkness" under Lucifer and 7,405,926 devils administering the affairs of the empire.[21] Man was not safe anywhere. Even the thousands of good Boguets of Burgundy and the tens of thousands of bonfires did not seem to be sufficient. At times the chasing of one devil from a body was not enough. St. Fortunatus labored over a possessed man until he cast the very last devil out of him, bringing the total for one unfortunate person to 6,670.[22]

To use the words of Daremberg, the fifteenth century was a summary of the past and a preface to the future. Its spirit died hard. It conceded defeat with stubborn slowness and systematic horror, but it was unable ultimately to survive against the laws of nature. Montaigne's keen irony comes to mind: "Through presumptions they make laws for nature and marvel at the way nature ignores those laws."

III

"THE presumptions which made laws for nature" continued to rule the world as the sixteenth century was ushered in. The fifteenth more than any other previous century had made one thing very clear: Europe had lost the value and even the conception of the individual. In its fervent striving for salvation it lost the man whose soul it wished to save. While the abysmal drive to save the soul of man by bringing man to his perdition reached even greater intensity during the sixteenth century, a new phenomenon appeared on the horizon of the Christian world: the individual was born—a creature restless, self-assertive, self-

[20] Henri Boguet: *Discours des sorciers*, "Dedication" to the Abbot of Acey. Lyon, 1603.
[21] Johann Weyer: *Pseudomonarchia Daemonum* (according to Binz not added to the *De praestigiis et incantationibus* until 1583). Bodin refers to this conclusion (*De la demonomanie des sorciers*. Anvers, 1586, p. 375), which he found in the edition of 1578.
[22] B. de Moray: "Preface" to *Procès verbal fait pour délivrer une fille possédée*. Paris, 1883, note p. lix.

contradictory, independent, fearless, quixotic, and reckless. The sixteenth century suddenly revealed an efflorescence of turbulent spirit never before known. Man as a person acquired as if suddenly a special interest and meaning. As if symbolic of this interest, in 1501 there appeared a book by Magnus Hundt, *On the Nature of Man*. The word *anthropologia*, the knowledge of man, was here used for the first time.

The magnificent depth of Leonardo, the tortured greatness of Michelangelo, the flashy carelessness of Raphael, the recklessness of Cellini, the fiery heart and voice and burning eyes of Savonarola hovered over the century. These men were not ghosts, nor memories of the past, nor glimpses of the future; they were present in the flesh. This was the age of destruction and achievement. Luther raged against the old order in Rome, clinging to the same old order in Germany. The heretofore almost unknown peasantry began to rise as real human beings. The Papacy, already not a little unconventional in the fifteenth century, particularly since the adventuresome Cibo was elevated to the throne as Innocent VIII, reflected the nervous, multicolored and multitempered spirit of the age: Julius II, patron of the arts and tempestuous, gifted soldier; Leo X, man of this world and connoisseur of good living; the Borgia Alexander VI, who combined acumen with recklessness, pleasures with piety, and paternal devotion and loyalty with carefree disregard of friend and enemy alike.

It was the age of the cruel and revengeful Pietro Aretino, rascal and blackmailer, poet and lecher, the great art critic and roué to whom honesty was but a word, piety but a ceremony and goodness but a mask, who was nevertheless popular, powerful, and effective.

It was the age of the perverse and magnificent Medici; of Ignatius Loyola, who fought stubbornly and ruthlessly and yet obediently, and in whom there burned an inexorable fire of proselytism always under the control of harsh, keen, straight thinking; of Francisco Xavier, whose wings of spiritual fire took him to China and Japan more than four hundred years before Japan was opened to Western civilization, and who died physically depleted but inspired with burning faith and undying hope for the conversion of the whole world to the Church.

It was the age of the Humanists, whose interest was man and his character, his personality in action. This century gave us Tycho Brahe, Regiomontanus, Copernicus, Telesius, Cardanus, Giordano Bruno,

Nicolaus Cusanus—scientists of the first order. It gave us Erasmus, Melanchthon, Vives, Cornelius Agrippa. It brought forth Vesalius, whose revolutionary anatomy appeared in 1543; the anatomist Fallopius (d. 1562), who described the tubes of the female adnexa; Eustachius (d. 1574), who described the tubes connecting the mouth with the middle ear; Miguel Servetus, who discovered the pulmonary circulation of blood and who was burned in 1553; Girolamo Fracastorius, who described certain infectious diseases and particularly syphilis. There were such clinicians as Jean Fernel, who at his leisure calculated the size of the earth, and Felix Plater, and the colorful, tragic, and almost monstrous genius of Paracelsus. There were Ambroise Paré, the father of modern surgery; the plastic surgeon from Bologna, Gasparo Tagliacozzi; the founder of modern psychiatry, Johann Weyer. It was the time of Francis Bacon, of Rabelais with his destructive banter, and of Montaigne with his searching irony. It was the century in which Machiavelli wrote his *Discorsi* and *Il Principe*.

One may say without risking exaggeration that it is the sixteenth century which contributed most to our European civilization. It laid down the principles of the individual's striving for freedom and of his self-assertive, creative role in the making of history. It tore down the secular dominance of Rome, which was sacked so bloodily and so ruthlessly in 1527, and it brought forth a rascal and roué who braved danger and risked the good will of friends and enemies, spiritual and temporal, in the personality of Henry VIII.

It was a period that played, ate, prayed, and died hard; it killed and stole well. It was a century of progress and inspiration, of creative thought and inventive genius. Yet it was a century of darkness. It changed the human mind and it changed the map of Europe; it turned science into daring channels of unimpeded growth. But it did not change its attitude toward witches until it had almost reached its close. The twenty-seventh verse of the twentieth chapter of Leviticus continued to rule psychiatry: "A man also, or woman that hath a familiar spirit, or that is a wizard, shall surely be put to death: they shall stone them with stones: their blood shall be upon them."

IV

THE attitude of the medical profession and of some of the leaders of thought remained conservative on the question of witchcraft; Catholic or Protestant, these men continued "to love God and be afraid of the devil." In matters medical they clung to the authority of Galen in almost the same manner that they clung to the dogma of the Church. When Vesalius published his monumental work of anatomy, the traditional medical men were shocked; Vesalius' own teacher, Jacques Dubois (*Sylvius*), thought that Vesalius must be mad [23] to diverge so widely from Galen. Those who did see that Vesalius was right had to justify Galen and prove that the physician from Pergamon could not be wrong; consequently they were ready to argue that humanity must have degenerated considerably since the days of Galen, and that man's anatomy must have changed.

Melanchthon, the enlightened humanist, sent a congratulatory letter to Calvin soon after he learned that Servetus had been burned at the stake. The discoverer of the pulmonary circulation of blood had traveled in the Holy Land, and when he came back he described the barren physical geography of the country; this contradiction of the Biblical assertion that it was a land of milk and honey made an excellent pretext to deliver the soul of Servetus by fire.

John Lange (1485–1565), one of the distinguished clinicians of his day, describes a case of suicide on whom an autopsy was performed and in whose stomach were found a piece of wood, four knives, two pieces of iron, and a bunch of hair. He also cites a woman whom he had seen vomit two iron nails, two needles, and a bunch of hair. All these objects Lange believes were deposited there by some diabolical trick and were confirmations of the existence of supernatural diseases. That these objects might have been swallowed by a psychotic with suicidal intent does not occur to him. [24]

The surgeon Ambroise Paré believed that the devil could assume

[23] Diepgen: *op. cit.*, vol. III, p. 14.
[24] Cited by Calmeil: *op. cit.*, vol. I, p. 174; from Lange's *Medicinalium epistolarum miscellanea*, etc., published in 1554.

any guise from serpent to raven, turn pages in the dark, and throw things about the room at night. He reports the case of a nobleman who was apparently mentally sick. No medical remedies were of any avail, because a devil had entered into him. "The patient would become restless whenever anyone attempted to read to him a passage from the Holy Scriptures. . . . I want to assure you," continues Paré, "that I am not reporting all this merely to play it up as something new, but in order to make people recognize that the devil does enter at times into our bodies and tortures us with unheard-of torments. Occasionally he does not enter the body at all, but just agitates the good humors within us, or sends bad humors into the different parts of our bodies." [25]

Ambroise Paré was a great surgeon but consistently a die-hard thinker. Attending court one day, he found himself unable to countenance Charles IX's amusement with the tricks of a magician, and he cautioned His Majesty by whispering in his ear the Biblical injunction: "Thou shalt not suffer a witch to live."

Paré's illustrious contemporary, the clinician Jean Fernel, believed in the existence of werewolves—human beings actually transformed into animals by the devil. The affliction was called lycanthropy; it was considered a separate clinical entity. Pomponazzi and Theophrastus agree with Fernel and never doubt the existence of true lycanthropy. Fernel in his *Opera Universa Medicina* describes the various ways in which the devil affects man; he uses the ancient method of differential diagnosis, that of whispering a few words laudatory to God and watching the trembling of the patient. So strong was the tradition that even the earnest clinician who in accordance with the trend of the age wished to investigate and to see things for himself found it difficult at times to be disabused. We shall recall Felix Plater (1536–1614) who went to the dungeons where the maniacs and idiots of the town were interned and kept company with the insane. He came out of the dungeons sufficiently enlightened to offer a very good classification of mental diseases, but still firmly convinced that these diseases were caused by the devil.

[25] Ambroise Paré: *Œuvres*. Lyon, 1633, p. 784. Cited also by Calmeil: *op. cit.*, pp. 176–178. Weyer cites the same case in *De praestigiis daemonum*, Bk. IV, ch. XVI. Weyer credits the case to Jean Fernel; he is probably correct. Paré must have copied it from Fernel.

v

THESE beliefs were shared by the majority of the physicians of the time, but voices, self-contradictory at times to be sure, began to be heard questioning the popular beliefs, or taking them with a grain of salt, or even refusing to accept them. Skepticism was rising. The interest in true human experiences was awakened and from about the middle of the century on one may discern a growing protest against demonological psychiatry. But for a long while no one seemed ready to recall the canons of Timothy, which enjoined a man whose wife was disturbed by an evil spirit to take her to a doctor to be treated for her craze.[26] Timothy's advice was undoubtedly sound, but the doctor who would and could treat that craze rationally had not been born.

The whole problem was still in its theoretical stage. The Inquisition and its bonfires were raging, and the voices of protest were more or less cautious and general. Ponzinibius, for instance, ventured to remark that the ecclesiastic judges were in fact opposed to the Council of Ancyra, which proclaimed that the abominations attributed to sorcerers could never actually have been committed.[27] Levinus Lemnius (1505–1568) followed the humoral theory and emphasized that mental diseases, including epilepsy, are not supernatural diseases.[28] Nicolaus Pisonis, who was the personal physician of Prince Charles, felt that physicians might not disregard the existence of demoniacal madness. He followed Plato, who believed in the existence of inspired mania; yet he insisted upon following the tradition of Hippocrates, Galen, and Celsus and wrote a medical treatise devoid of the general superstition and demonological intolerance. He cautioned against the trend in medical practice of attributing mania too hastily to the influence of evil spirits.[29] Hieronymus Cardanus, although apparently believing in the existence of devils and even relating that seven such devils appeared before his father one evening, yet raised his voice against the general mistreatment of the so-called possessed.[30]

[26] B. de Moray: *op. cit.*, p. xxxvi.
[27] Calmeil: *op. cit.*, vol. I, p. 187.
[28] Levinus Lemnius: *Occulta naturae miracula.* 1561, Bk. II, chs. 2, 3.
[29] Nicolaus Pisonis: *De cognoscendis et curandis praecipuē internis humani corporis morbis, etc.* Cited by Calmeil: *op. cit.*, vol. I, pp. 211, 212.
[30] H. Cardanus: *De vita propria liber*, ch. 47.

Pierre Leloyer published in 1588 four books on *Spectres*, in which he described a number of exalted abnormal states which he had observed in Italy, France, and Morocco. He saw the patients chained to the walls and he studied them as sick human beings. In a special chapter, "On corrupted senses," he describes a number of auditory and visual illusions and hallucinations. Yet in the fourth book he ascribes psychopathological mutism to the devil, who occupies the body of man and remains silent; the devil enters a body only through that part or organ which is defective. As to lycanthropy, a human being cannot be transformed into an animal, but Satan with his inimitable art can merely deceive the afflicted individual and make him believe that he is an animal, so that he behaves like one and lives at times on carnage and blood. There were a few—Montanus, Schenk, Houlier, Erastus—who refused to believe that the devil had anything to do with mental diseases.[31]

Montaigne raised his ironic voice against demonology. In his essays, which appeared in 1580, he says, "The lives of the witches in my neighborhood are in danger whenever a new writer appears who takes their dreams for fact. Other tools than we have are needed to digest the examples offered us by the Divine Word. . . .

"I am a ponderous man and I tend toward the substantial and the probable. . . . I can see how people become agitated and wish to forbid my doubts and threaten me with terrible punishment. Indeed, this is a new mode of persuading. For Heaven's sake, my beliefs cannot be managed by blows! These people had better chide those who accuse them of holding false opinions; I merely state that they are impudent and narrow-minded. . . . A brilliant and sharp clarity is needed to be able to kill people; our life is too real and substantial for supernatural, fantastic incidents. . . . One should not always respect the confessions of persons involved in a crime, for there have been too many cases in which people accused themselves of having killed others who were afterwards found alive and in good health. Those extravagant accusations! I think it suffices to deem an individual, whatever his reputation, capable of what is human. In matters beyond his ken and of supernatural effect, one should trust only those authorized by supernatural permission. This privilege, which it has pleased the Lord to

[31] Calmeil: *op. cit.*, vol. I, p. 194.

bestow upon some of our testimonies, should not be debased and spread in a thoughtless manner. I have thousands of accounts such as: Three people saw him one day in the East, three others saw him the next day in the West—at such and such an hour, in such and such an attire. Certainly, I would not believe my own self. Is it not much more natural and more probable to assume that these people lie than to believe that a man can within twelve hours be transported from East to West? Is it not far more natural to think that our mind is deranged by the volubility of our crazed spirits than to believe that a mere mortal with the help of strange spirits could in person fly out through the chimney on a broomstick? Don't let us seek for illusions of unknown nature and of external origin, we who are continually haunted by our own private illusions. . . . I agree with St. Augustine that it is better to tend toward doubt than toward certainty in things which are difficult to prove and dangerous to believe. Some years ago I happened to visit the territory of a sovereign prince who, for my benefit and in order to dispel my incredulity, was gracious enough to let me see in his presence ten or a dozen prisoners of such kind, in a special quarter. Among them there was an old woman who was a witch indeed as far as ugliness and deformity are concerned, and who had been notorious in this profession for many years. I saw proofs and spontaneous confessions, and I looked at insensible spots on this miserable creature; I asked questions and spoke to her as long as I wished and I gave her my soundest attention. After all, I would prescribe for them hellebore rather than hemlock, for they appeared more demented than guilty. . . . As far as the opposition and the arguments of honest people against me are concerned, both here and elsewhere, I have not yet heard any arguments which refuted me or which could not have been resolved far more plausibly. . . . I often cut these [arguments] as Alexander did the knot. After all, it is setting a high value on one's conjectures, if for their sake one is willing to burn a human being alive." [32]

These lines appeared twenty years before the close of the sixteenth century. They betray a well-formed, self-conscious individuality, a sense of the dignity of man. If we recall in addition that Rabelais is pitiless in his mockery of the old-fashioned schoolman and of the whole tradition of medieval society, we shall hardly fail to feel that a new era

[32] Montaigne: *Essais*. London, 1754, vol. IX, pp. 17–22 (Bk. III, ch. XI).

has opened in the history of thought. Yet our perspective would be warped, indeed, if we overlooked the fact that the growing spirit of self-conscious dignity was too new to have the strength to overcome at once certain of the more shadowy aspects of a past which lingered on and fought for its maintenance with all the rancor and violence which human history has in its stores. The principles proclaimed in the *Malleus Maleficarum* continued to remain the basis of the administrative apparatus of the Church and State.

The Counter Reformation accentuated the sharp teeth of this apparatus. "One day a brigand accused of being a heretic would officially repent and reject his error and he would be set free; another day an innocent man would be condemned for having thrust a devil into the body of an epileptic, or for having attracted a number of evil spirits to a certain religious community. Everywhere theologians, provosts, criminal administrators, bailiffs, parliaments—were occupied with the prosecution and trial of lycanthropes and sorcerers. Monks took over the place of physicians and attempted to stop the convulsions of the energumens by actively conjuring the spirits. The possessed were condemned in groups of ten, fifteen, and bands of one hundred and fifty." [33] Under the reign of Francis I the justice of the time was dealt out to one hundred thousand persons.

Even the enlightened, those who were seemingly true children of the Renaissance and who strove to raise man to a sense of dignity, were unable to rid themselves of the prejudices which were elevated almost to dogma by the *Malleus*. Pico della Mirandola (1463–1494), who was so advanced in his philosophical conceptions that he could say that man himself chooses his own fate, says in his *Praenotiones* that he knew a priest who was seventy-five years old and who for a period of forty years had had relations with a *succubus* whom the priest called Hermeline. The devil followed the priest wherever he went, even in public places, always appearing in the guise of a woman. The priest thought he was able to exchange strange words with this woman while no one was able to notice. Some people thought him mad. Pico della Mirandola believes that the cleric had carnal relations with this phantom, and he assures us that another *succubus*, Fiorina, carried on a similar relationship of thirty years' duration with another priest he

[33] Calmeil: *op. cit.*, vol. I, pp. 215, 216.

knew.[34] Bodin, a great lawyer, refers to the case of Hermeline (Hermione) and records that her old lover-priest confessed also that he had sucked the blood of several babies. Bodin says the priest was finally burned alive.[35]

The question of the credibility of these self-confessed sinners was no longer a question at all; it was not even a medicolegal problem. It was treated as a matter of course; the lawyer and not the doctor was accepted as the sole authority in such matters. The formulations of the *Malleus* were refined and clarified and fully accepted by the penal codes. Bartholomeus, the professor of theology and a brother of the congregation of Saint Dominic, a man of "sane orthodoxy" whom the ecclesiastic judges considered an authority for several centuries, published a dissertation on the subject. In this he maintained that the possessed had full power of reason and that their statements, whether dealing with their own misdeeds or with those of their alleged accomplices, deserved the complete confidence of the court of law. There was no doubt that these people actually consorted with the devils in their nocturnal assemblies, where infamous deeds and abominable crimes were committed. There was no doubt that they practiced the act of fornication among themselves or with the spirits and that they were frightfully disposed (*acharnés*) toward little children.[36]

Bodin cites specific cases. A man of thirty-seven, absorbed in reading the Scriptures, was overcome with joy when a supernatural being appearing in the guise of a luminous ray of light touched his book, pulled his ears, and talked to him. Bodin considers this an illustration of how an angel came to protect the humble servant of God.[37]

A young girl, while praying at the tomb of her father, saw a black man appear who promptly admitted that he was Satan. He wanted to violate her; she struggled with him. Satan suggested to her that she scream and jump into a well or strangle herself. This, according to Bodin, is an example of possession by an evil spirit.[38]

A number of girls were deflorated under such circumstances. A girl of eighteen who was promiscuous with a spirit, an *incubus*, was burned

[34] *Ibid.*, vol. I, pp. 170, 171.
[35] Bodin: *op. cit.*, p. 183.
[36] Calmeil: *op. cit.*, p. 168.
[37] Bodin: *op. cit.*, pp. 17–22.
[38] Calmeil: *op. cit.*, p. 181. *Cf.* Bodin: *op. cit.*, p. 270.

at Cerdene. A witch who was burned in 1556 in the neighborhood of Laon had shared her bed with Satan.[39] Relations of men with *succubi*, while they did occur, were rare.

We see here the old misogynous tradition and the old trend toward lurid, erotic expatiations at the expense of the alleged witches. If we took the whole population of our present-day state hospitals for mental diseases, and if we sorted out the cases of dementia praecox, some of the senile psychoses, some of those afflicted with general paralysis, and some of the so-called involution melancholias, we would see that Bodin would not have hesitated to plead for their death at the stake, so similar and characteristic are their trends to those he describes. It is truly striking that the ideational content of the mental diseases of four hundred years ago is so similar to those of today. Young women, particularly virgins, suffering from dementia praecox (schizophrenia) today also speak of imaginary black men, but they call them Negroes. They also suffer from ideas of persecution and from fear of defloration. They have suicidal trends which at times appear in the form of hearing voices tell them that they should lay their hands on themselves. The hallucinatory voice of today is more apt to suggest that the afflicted person jump off the roof of a building instead of into the pit of a well, and the imaginary seducer of today appears to her more frequently as her doctor than as Satan, but the psychological substance of this pathological reaction is identical with that of the witch who was burned near Laon in 1556, and with that of many thousands who were burned elsewhere or who died as a result of torture.

This was the psychiatric atmosphere of the sixteenth century. This was the atmosphere of a good part of the seventeenth. It is to be emphasized here that this demoniacal and "devil" psychology, which ruled the minds of the man in the street, the doctor and philosopher, the priest and lawyer, was not confined to the Catholic world. Through its administrative apparatus the Catholic Church, as the one and only spiritual authority, was the first to formulate and systematize the demonological tradition which engulfed the world; but the tradition was not rejected by the Reformation. It was followed by Luther in Germany, Calvin in Switzerland, King James I in England, and the Puritans in the Commonwealth of Massachusetts long after the re-

[39] Bodin: *op. cit.*, p. 185.

mains of Sprenger and Kraemer were committed to the dust from which they came in full fury of misguided faith and misplaced inspiration. The spirit of the two friars lingered on for many long years. The last witch to be killed in Germany was Anna Maria Schwägelin. She was decapitated in Memmingen, Bavaria, on March 30, 1775. It was on June 18, 1782, that the last witch was decapitated in Switzerland in the town of Glarus, almost three hundred years after the meeting of the Theological Faculty of Cologne from which Sprenger and Kraemer had wrested an indorsement of their magnum opus.

THE FIRST PSYCHIATRIC
REVOLUTION

I

HISTORY is most often remembered by its brilliant and spectacular moments; it is impressive for the display of action and strife which appeals so much to student and amateur alike. Therefore, when history is brought to mind one usually thinks of political history, for it is the latter which is fraught with the most conspicuous deeds and the most rapid changes. Wars and revolutions come and go quickly, but their meteoric speed and bloodstreaked excitement make them appear as landmarks of endless human activity. The history of thought moves slowly, imperceptibly; its expression is quiet, almost inaudible, and it is always drowned out by the hurly-burly of self-approbatory political trumpeting. The bonfires of the Inquisition are apt to stand out most clearly in the memory of those who glance into the multicolored sixteenth century; the course of the little streams of thought which slowly gathered their waters in the subsoil of history may hardly be noticed, yet they were constantly swelling, to rise someday to the surface not only as newborn thoughts but as mighty, spiritual forces come to awaken man from his very long slumber.

In that same sixteenth century in which the witches' hammer seemed to provide the loudest noise, a certain process was, with gathering momentum, gradually leading man's conception of nature and of himself into more open, more fertile fields—fields which were fertilized with human blood or with the ashes of fagots and human bones, as the fields of man's history usually are.

We have alluded to this process on several occasions, particularly with reference to Montaigne and to his insistence on the dignity of man and on the self-conscious integrity of the individual. If we recall the first attempts at liberation of thought in the thirteenth century, we shall also recall the struggle of the then timid human intellect: furtively it tried to assert its freedom and as furtively it attempted to separate science from theology in order to acquire the right to study nature and man as they are, and not as they seem to be to the ecstatic mind which has its eye fixed on eternity and spiritual salvation. In those early days of a temporary dawn Albertus Magnus, interested in nature, was eager to make clear that his interests were not turning him away from tradition; nothing, he said, comes from nothing only in physics, not in theology. St. Thomas emphasized that philosophy leads from facts to God, and theology from God to facts. However, the sense of freedom once aroused could not remain static. Boccaccio (1313–1375) plunged into the very midst of life with all its mirthful perfidy and sensual laughter. The Black Plague, which devastated so many communities in the middle of the fourteenth century, was a contributing factor to the growing awareness that man alone is even more frail than the mystic painted him. The as yet not fully awakened social consciousness began to stir. The individual acquired an interest which before had been almost nonexistent. Dante wrote in the vernacular. Even the Bible was brought to the direct perception of those who were not necessarily scholars; Wycliffe (1320–1384) translated it into English.

The intellectual subtleties which dominated the thought of the schoolman began to lose or at least to loosen their centuries-old hold. Duns Scotus (1265?–1308) and William of Ockham (d. 1349) became interested in feelings, in true human, individual experiences. The same interests in a much more marked degree dominated the thought of Meister Eckhart (1260?–1327), to whom the value of the individual appeared so definite and important that he asserted: "If I

[man] would not exist, God would not exist." [1] What went on in man and what his emotions were became matters of keen preoccupation and fascinated puzzlement. How does man's conscience act and what is it? What does it make him do? Alexander of Hales (d. 1245), using the old term *synteresis* instead of the Ciceronian *conscientia*, attempted to make new observations on the feelings of remorse and on scruples. It was a long time before this curiosity percolated further into the ever-maturing human thought. Over three hundred years had to pass from the days of Alexander of Hales till the time of Levinus Lemnius, who published his *De Occultae Naturae Miraculis* in 1574 and who again brought into focus the problem of conscience. It took almost three hundred years before the scientific problems raised by another Englishman and Franciscan, Roger Bacon, became the legitimate problems of true scientific attention. But these three centuries were not a barren desert in the history of thought, although the sands may appear smooth and devoid of any trace of man's intellectual growth. For generations thinkers kept repeating with an almost monotonous regularity and insistence that man should be studied, not the soul. It seems as if the scholars had to convince themselves by hearing their own voices. Pietro Pomponazzi, like almost every scholar who taught or wrote in those days, says in his *De Immortalitate Animae* (1516) that the soul, the immortal spirit, does not concern him. He knows nothing about it; he can know nothing about it from personal experience. It is personal experience, understanding, the sensory apparatus which interest him.

It should be carefully noted that such scholars were not physicians. The medical man retired from the open fields of natural philosophy and seemed for a while to have retired also from the domain of the living, human mind. Responding to the general trend to restudy nature and to shake off the cobwebs of the mistakes of ancient science, physicians, too, studied and discovered new things; but they were more interested in anatomy than in psychology, and they studied cadavers rather than living human beings. Great contributions were made, of course, but those contributions added nothing to the knowledge of medical psychology. Rondeletius discovered (about 1550) that

[1] Max Dessoir: *Abriss einer Geschichte der Psychologie*. Heidelberg, 1911.

the nerves are separate strands, each having its separate structure. We have mentioned Vesalius, who revolutionized the whole field of anatomy, parting definitely with Galen and his incongruities. But it was the scholar and not the medical man who continued the almost passionate study of the living individual and his behavior. Since the immortal soul was excluded from consideration, the problems of perception, sensation, memory, and intellect acquired an exceptional value. Scaliger emphasized the importance of muscular sense and the relation of this sense to emotions. Some of the formulations of the time may seem to us naïve, but they were full of meaning; Scaliger asserted "that brave men feel the force of an insult in those muscles which serve for striking, while the less pugnacious type are affected in the organs of speech." [2]

For the first time the word *psychologia* is used. No doubt was left that man had come to the forefront of scientific attention and that a science of man's behavior was being born and christened. In 1590 Rudolf Goeckel published his *Psychologia—Hoc Est de Hominis Perfectione:* "Psychology, or on the improvement of man." The moralistic inference in the title was unavoidable, of course, since man's behavior was—as it still is—of interest only from the practical standpoint of leading the individual into the path of righteousness, or, as we would put it today, to social adjustment. Four years after Goeckel's *Psychologia,* his pupil Otto Casmann expressed the interest in man with even greater emphasis by writing a book entitled *Psychologia Anthropologica.*

It was quite natural that this trend should lead to problems of education, which were the subject of greatest interest to such humanists as Erasmus and Melanchthon and a great many others. They led directly to the problems of scientific method and learning of which Francis Bacon and John Locke were such illustrious exponents. It was not only the scholarly thinker, however, who expounded the idea and the ideals of individuality; men in increasing numbers *lived* these ideas and ideals. Restless and inspired, their penetrating minds determined not to yield any more ground to dogmatically revealed assertions at the expense of factual truth, they stood ready to die to preserve their intellectual integrity, and they frequently did die.

[2] Brett: *op. cit.,* vol. II, p. 172.

At the very close of the sixteenth century, as if symbolizing the new struggle and the coming of a new era of science, Giordano Bruno, once a Dominican monk, a brother of the same religious fraternity from which Sprenger and Kraemer had come, spoke loudly in defense of science; he was burned. Less tragic was the fate but not less emphatic the intellectual and spiritual aggressiveness of François Rabelais, who was able to remain both a clergyman and a physician and at the same time ruthlessly tarred and feathered with his mockery pope and king, monk and layman, judge and burgher. Rabelais, too, *lived* his protest and his inner freedom.

Questions concerning man's psychology continued to be raised, and solutions were sought by means of gallant introspection and observation. Telesius considered the problems of pleasure and pain and fathomed the developmental nature of the sense of touch. Campanella studied sensations. Both thought that various psychological reactions are connected by a causal chain of relationships. Erasmus, Thomas More, and particularly Vives were the first to turn their humanistic ideas toward the social and cultural issues of the day. Man was born. He was born as a self-contained unit and as a social atom, an integral, responsive, and responsible part of society.

The two chief orientations in psychology, particularly medical psychology, were thus imperceptibly arrived at but forcefully sketched during the course of the sixteenth century. The one deals with the characteristics and properties of the human mind as distinct from those of the soul and therefore looks for the cause of these properties and their functions in the activities of the human body and not the soul. This orientation is chiefly physiological, descriptive, empirical, and ultimately experimental. Francis Bacon (1561–1626) authoritatively contributed to this orientation. According to Bacon three main forces are responsible for all our psychological reactions: memory, imagination, and understanding. He emphasizes that these three forces are to be distinguished from the activities of the body, but his ultimate goal seems to be the establishment of a mechanics of psychology, that is, a measurable, physiological psychology. The trend was definitely away from metaphysics and foreshadowed the coupling of psychology with physics; the words *anima* and *spiritus*, so monotonously popular theretofore, began to be supplanted by a more modern terminology. It is interesting in this respect to recall how, despite the increasing separation of science from theology, the scientific vocabulary remained handicapped by old conceptions. Young Kepler, considering the properties of the loadstone, thought it had an *anima* attracting iron; but later on, when considering the movements of planets, he spoke not of an *anima*—a soul or a spirit —but of *vis*—a force.

The second orientation in psychology, which became rather well defined quite early in the century, dealt with human impulses, drives, emotions, affects; it led directly to the problem of the psychological motivation determining man's individual and social behavior. This interest in the purely empirical observations of what man does, feels, and thinks could never bear any scientific fruit unless the observer, regardless of his religious and ethical faith, had the detachment and the courage to see within himself and others the very nature of man. In other words, the psychologist who chooses to study the very dynamics of human emotions must be of sound biological views; he must have the daring to be able to see man as he is. The psychologist did not reach this scientific maturity until the last years of the nineteenth century, when Sigmund Freud published his first formulations. Thus it is even more impressive to find that the first true forerunner of Freud was a deeply religious man who lived three hundred and fifty years before Freud and whose background of religious tradition was combined with a truly devotional personality. The man was a Spaniard from Valencia, Juan Luis Vives, and his contributions to psychology surpass those of any of his contemporaries and of many of his scientific descendants for over three centuries.

II

Juan Luis Vives was born in Valencia in 1492 and died in Bruges in 1540. These forty-eight years comprised a rather uneventful life of scholarship and profound concern for reform, education, and deepening of social consciousness. Vives, too, was one of those men of the Renaissance who lived their new outlook on life, but his was not a life of tempestuous action and restless, combative peregrination. Rather it was a life of what he himself called in another connection "the internal agitation of thought." He used this expression in the most modern sense; it did not denote sterile preoccupation with the subtle, logistic niceties of the scholastics. At an early age he abandoned scholasticism self-consciously, deliberately, but not without great effort of will, for his early schooling was in the spirit of tradition and, judging from his preliminary education in Valencia, one would not have expected the development of a personality so succinct, so courageous, and so very modern. Vives' early education and the religious atmosphere of his upbringing awakened in him a devotional spirit which was his until the end. At his death, after years of creative intellectual effort in so many new fields of thought, he left an unpublished work entitled *De Veritate Fidei Christianae*, which was a spiritual continuation of the collection of his private prayers and devotional contemplations published in Antwerp in 1535 under the heading *Ad Animi Exercitationem in Deum Commentatiunculae.* "It is an outstanding tribute to his [Vives'] spiritual sincerity that when John Bradford put together his collection of 'Private Prayers and Meditations' in 1559, this great Protestant champion included a large number of Vives' prayers and meditations, for Luis Vives, like Erasmus and Thomas More, never left the Roman Catholic Church. The same prayers, though with variations of rendering, are repeated in the English Church Book of Private Prayers put forth by Authority in 1578. It is curious and interesting to find that the Spaniard Vives, of the Roman Catholic Church, though not in holy orders in it, is one of the chief sources of the official Book of Private Prayers, chosen for the Church of England, in Queen Elizabeth's reign." [3]

Vives' deep religious sincerity is emphasized, not because it has any special bearing on his contributions to psychology, but primarily because it is important to bear in mind that, unlike many of his contemporaries who broke with the old modes of thinking but also with the Church and the Faith, unlike Rabelais who even while saying mass would deliberately mispronounce words to ridicule, Vives, like Thomas More, found in his very faith the source and inspiration for newer

[3] Foster Watson: *Luis Vives, el gran Valenciano* (*1492–1540*). Oxford University Press, 1922, pp. 101, 102.

views and newer practical beginnings. The story of Vives' intellectual growth is the story of what was best and most productive and most enduring in the sixteenth century.

At the age of seventeen he went to Paris to pursue his studies. The scholastic tradition prevailed there as it did in Valencia. Vives soon found himself in a state of profound inner conflict. By training he was of a scholastic bent of mind; he knew the field and he was keen enough to master the tricky abstractions and subtle intricacies of the prevailing thought, but he felt that all these really had nothing to do with life and living. "The arts" appeared to him devoid of substance. Thus on one hand he admittedly enjoyed the scholastic exercises of intellectual neatness, while on the other he felt an anxious concern for the world of people—not for the world of notions—and he yearned to understand nature as it is and man's place in this nature as a living, working, struggling being, not merely as a carrier of sin and a seeker of potential salvation. The scholarly tutors and friends whom Vives left in Valencia he left behind not only spacially but spiritually. The one exception was Juan Población, a physician who apparently appealed to him for his advanced scientific views and whom he therefore always admired. The teachers whom Vives found in Paris became to him spiritual strangers who were "like a band of unconquered men defending the citadel of ignorance." He felt regret and painful contempt for those who were satisfied "to know nothing and yet to rave with a mad fury of words." He asserted that "whatever is in the arts was in nature first, just as pearls are in shells and gems in the sands." As someone has said, Vives was Baconian two generations before Bacon wrote. Vives gathered around him a group of young men, mostly Spaniards, and they discussed the true meaning of learning and the living faith. These discussions Vives summarized in 1514 in his *Christi Jesu Triumphus*.

In the same year he left for Bruges and Louvain. Here he spent almost eleven years; here he married; here he returned after a five years' sojourn in England to study and to commune with the scholars to whom he was spiritually closer than those of any other country, except perhaps England. He was always close to Erasmus, but the latter, a man of colder temperament, did not appear fully to reciprocate Vives' attitude. On the other hand, Erasmus recognized the worth of Vives and did not fail to acknowledge openly his admiration for the man who was "Spanish with a fine strain of French in him." He recommended Vives to Charles V. He wrote Thomas More, "Vives is one who will overshadow the name of Erasmus." Vives was then twenty-seven years old; Erasmus, twice as old, fifty-five.

At that time, in 1519, Vives published his *In Pseudo-Dialecticos*, which was fundamentally the expression of his bitter disappointment in the world of learning as he found it in Valencia and Paris. About the things he had learned he says, "I received them into my mind when I was impressionable. I applied myself to them with the highest zeal. They stick tenaciously. They came into my mind against my will. They stupefy my mind just as I am reaching forward to better things." Vives was eager to "un-teach them from [his] mind" at any practicable sacrifice. Even at that early period of his development he had a deep feeling for the common people, their needs and their wisdom, their social value. With melancholy scorn he wondered what would happen if the subtle words of the scholars were translated into the vernacular; he thought the mass of common laborers would "with hissing and clamor and clanging of their tools hoot the dialecticians out of Paris."

The thought that the scholar would learn more from nature and from the common working people than from wise princes and pompous professors stayed with Vives to the last. The gathering described by him in *Christi Jesu Triumphus* was not one of princes but of commoners who were interested in learning. In his treatise on ways and means of imparting knowledge, *De Tradendis Disciplinis* (1531), he says, "The student should not be ashamed to enter into shops and factories, and to ask questions from craftsmen, and to get to know about the details of their work. Formerly, learned men disdained to inquire into those things which it is of such great import to life to know and remember. This ignorance grew in succeeding centuries up to the present . . . so that we know far more of the age of Cicero or of Pliny than of that of our grandfathers." [4]

Vives, inspired with the vision of a new cultural world, exclaimed in his *In Pseudo-Dialecticos*, "I see from the depths a change coming. Amongst all nations men are springing up, of clear, excellent, free intellects, impatient of servitude, determined to throw off the yoke of

---

[4] *De tradendis disciplinis*, IV, 6. Quoted by Foster Watson: "The father of modern psychology," *Psychological Review*, 1915, p. 352.

tyranny from their necks. They are calling their fellow citizens to liberty." Later on, exposed more closely to the influence of Thomas More—a saintly personality and profound humanist—Vives formulated his hopes even more trenchantly, for his was the inspired ideal of a universal education which would fill the workingman's leisure with joy and lead to broader intellectual vistas and greater social cohesion. As his modern biographer Foster Watson puts it, "It was during Vives' connexion with the English Court [5] that he came forward from this progressive mediaevalism and struck the modern note, with a clearness and an emphasis such as had never been reached in England. . . . Catalan-Spaniard of Valencia by birth, while living in England, he sent forth a clarion cry in a letter to Henry VIII . . . 'Nothing is more vital than that due care should be taken in the formation by the young of right and sane opinions. They should know the aim and advantage of each element of welfare, its essential proportion, and how to estimate it. Youth will then become like tried goldsmiths, with a Lydian stone, which serves as an indication of values (positive and negative). . . . They will thus learn not to confuse small things with great. . . . Thus, provided with standards [social?], their religion will not yield precedence to outward form and ceremonies, and their conception of literature will not allow them to devote their energies to topics provocative of struggle and contention, which render men stubborn rather than wise. They will be drawn rather to those studies which lead to the consolidation of morals and the building up of life. . . . No one is outside of the scope of religion, and the mass of people (*vulgus*) will be helped in literature, partly by addresses (*concionibus*), partly by books, written in the mother tongue, advising them as to the subjects worthy of study, by which their good hours may not be passed in reciting old women's fables, nor in actions indifferent to good conduct.' " [6]

In 1522 Vives finished his detailed commentaries on St. Augustine's *Civitas Dei*. He addressed a dedicatory letter to Henry VIII. The king, at that time still happily married to Catherine of Aragon, replied with profuse praise and gratitude. Henry's letter was written from Greenwich on January 24, 1523. Its concluding sentence was: "We

[5] Between 1523–1528.
[6] Watson: *Luis Vives, etc.*, pp. 78, 79.

can assure you that our favor and good-will shall never fail in your affairs whenever opportunity shall offer itself on our part to be of helpfulness to you." When, shortly afterward, Vives set foot in England, he could not know that only five years later the same Henry VIII would refer to him very coldly as "a Spaniard named Ludovicus Vives, whom she herself nominates [as an advocate for her trial], who formerly read history in Oxford." "She herself" was Queen Catherine, whom Henry was about to divorce and who, heartbroken and despairing, saw her royal position and her humanistic leadership crumbling and the cultivated friend and counselor that was Vives turn his eyes back to Flanders.

There were many things which attracted Vives to England. There was Thomas More and his unusual family. There was the queen, an ardent humanist and a uniquely cultivated woman, versed in philosophy. There were a number of others, like Cardinal Wolsey and the many learned Spaniards of the queen's household. About one year after his arrival in England, Vives reached almost the highest point of his productive intellectual activity. In 1524 appeared the *De Institutione Foeminae Christianae*, the *Satellitium*, a series of over two hundred principles and elaborated slogans written for little Princess Mary, the daughter of Catherine, and *Introduction ad Sapientiam*. One should recall that those were the days when the *Malleus Maleficarum* was the textbook of a misogynous age, when woman was granted the sorry privilege of being a witch fifty times more frequently than man a sorcerer. In the dim light of this hatred of woman the attitude of Vives in England stands out as a beacon signaling the shores of a new world.

England was apparently going through a period of unusual respect for the intellectual achievements of women. The queen herself was remarkably well informed, and the atmosphere of the Thomas More household was symbolic of this respect and cultural freedom. More had three daughters, all of whom were keenly interested in letters. One of them, Margaret Roper, translated Erasmus' commentary on the Lord's Prayer into English. Erasmus described the household as follows: "More converses affably with his family, his wife, his son and daughter-in-law, his three daughters and their husbands with eleven grandchildren. . . . You would say his house was Plato's

Academy. I should rather call it a school, or University, of Christian Religion. There is none therein who does not study the branches of a liberal education." [7] More's *Utopia* appeared about seven years before Vives came to England; its spirit of "enthusiasm for humanity as distinct from the passion for scholarship" was not only something to which Vives was responsive, but the very essence of his philosophy of life. He always felt and thought, as he later said in his *De Tradendis Disciplinis*, that "we must transfer our solicitudes [from princes]to the people." "Having acquired knowledge, we must turn it to usefulness and employ it for the common good."

It was in this spirit that Vives, as if sensing that the horrible attitude toward woman in Germany, Italy, and France must be and could be rejected in the England of Thomas More, turned to the question of woman's education. He admired the enlightened, scholarly queen. He recalled the court of Isabella in Spain: "There hath been seen in our time the four daughters of Queen Isabel, that were well learned all. It is told me, in many places, that dame Joan, the wife of King Philip, mother of Charles, was wont to make answer in Latin, and that without any study, to the orations that were made after the custom in towns, to new princes. And likewise the Englishmen say by their queen, sister of Joan." [8] About Thomas More's daughters he remarked, "Now if a man may be suffered among queens to speak of more mean folks I would reckon the daughters of Sir Thomas More, Margaret, Elizabeth, Cecilia (and with them their kinswoman, Margaret Giggs), whom their father, not content only to have them good and very chaste, would also that they should be well learned. . . . For the study of learning occupieth one's mind wholly and lifteth it up into the knowledge of most goodly matters." [9]

Thus defending and asserting the intellectual and general cultural value of woman in our civilization, Vives continued step by step to formulate a systematic, practical social philosophy. For a while he taught history in Corpus Christi College at Oxford, then wrote his treatise *De Subventione Pauperum*. Not only does he preach that scholars should transfer their solicitudes to the common poor people,

[7] Quoted by Watson: *Luis Vives, etc.*, p. 52.
[8] *Ibid.*, p. 57.
[9] *Ibid.*, pp. 57, 58.

but he steadfastly does so himself. He is not interested in sentimental philanthropy but in real, organized public aid to the poor. He is critical of the ecclesiastic tradition of almsgiving, for this helps but little and solves the social problem even less. Relief to the poor should be organized not by philanthropic private citizens but by the municipalities, that is, by the State through civic, lay authorities. He recommends that the community seek out the needy, thus forecasting what is known today as social, or social welfare, work. The children of the poor should be given an adequate education. "As it is disgraceful," he says, "for the father of a family in his comfortable home to permit anyone in it to suffer the disgrace of being unclothed or in rags, it is similarly unfitting that the magistrates of a city should tolerate a condition in which citizens are hard pressed by hunger and distress." [10]

Vives thus completes the circle of his sociological ethics. He started with a keen sense of the responsibility of the scholar toward the community and the common people and correlated this feeling with the deep sense of responsibility which the community should have toward its less fortunate members. The poor are, of course, not the only ones among these unfortunates; Vives thinks of the sick in body and mind. The third chapter of *De Subventione Pauperum* deals with the ways and means of providing the necessities of life for all these people. He recommends that the sick among them be sent to proper hospitals. He enjoins that "the food shall not be scanty that their hunger is only half satisfied. This is one of the essentials in the care of those who are sick either in body or mind, for invalids often grow worse for lack of food. . . . Since there is nothing in the world more excellent than man, nor in man than his mind, particular attention should be given to the welfare of the mind; and it should be considered a highest service if we either restore the minds of others to sanity or keep them sane and rational. Hence, when a man of unsettled mind is brought to a hospital, it must be determined, first of all, whether his illness is congenital or has resulted from some misfortune, whether there is hope for his recovery or not. One ought to feel compassion for so great a disaster to the health of the human mind, and it is of utmost importance that the treatment be such that the insanity be not nourished and increased, as may result from mocking, exciting or irritating madmen,

[10] *Ibid.*, p. 62.

approving and applauding the foolish things which they say or do, inciting them to act more ridiculously, applying fomentations as if it were to their stupidity and silliness. What could be more inhuman than to drive a man insane just for the sake of laughing at him and amusing one's self at such a misfortune."

Under these circumstances a great responsibility rests on the physician. Vives paid serious thought to this question and in *De Anima et Vita,* his most important work from the standpoint of psychology, he emphasizes that a physician should know both nature and mind. This reminds one of the view of Galen, who expected a universal education from a physician and said that a good physician is bound also to excel in philosophy (the ancient term for science). Vives' remarks about the treatment of the mentally sick reveal that a rather supercilious and cruel attitude toward such patients was characteristic of his day. His own humanistic and humanitarian attitude, which made the individual the most important component of civilized life, was naturally carried over into his considerations of the problem of mental illness. The mentally sick are first and last men, human beings, individuals to be saved and to be treated with utmost humaneness. "Remedies suited to the individual patients should be used. Some need medical care and attention to their mode of life; others need gentle and friendly treatment, so that like wild animals they may gradually grow gentle; still others need instructions. There will be some who will require force and chains, but these must be so used that the patients are not made more violent. Above all, as far as possible, tranquillity must be introduced in their minds, for it is through this that reason and sanity return."

The passing shadow of Celsus momentarily obscures these enlightened lines. Chains and force were still in approved use and were to remain so for another two hundred and seventy-five years, until Pinel unchained the mentally ill in the midst of the French Revolution. On the other hand, the stress on the purely psychological, humanitarian approach to the patient is not only modern in the historical sense; it is contemporary. Present-day psychiatry, particularly hospital (intramural) psychiatry, would find nothing to add to or subtract from Vives' statement, except, of course, the chains.

The lines cited above were written only forty-odd years after the appearance of the *Malleus Maleficarum*. This would indicate beyond any doubt that the voice of true scientific development of medical psychology was strong and full at the very time when Sprenger and Kraemer held forth. But it would also emphasize once more the tragic cultural conditions of the time, in which the thunderous voices of two celebrated Dominicans could drown out the enlightened entreaties of Vives and his predecessors and a number of his followers.

Having stated his views on the care of the poor and the mentally ill, Vives turned to further and deeper contemplation of the problems of the human mind and of the relation between peoples and nations. Soon, however, he was faced with the break between Henry VIII and Catherine of Aragon. This situation was doubly tragic to Vives. In addition to the respect in which he held Henry, he was profoundly devoted and loyal to Catherine and suffered with her in her sorrow, and he felt that his stay in England had to come to an end, forcing him to break off his very satisfying contacts with intellectual companions and such spiritual friends as Thomas More and his family.

Vives left England to live for twelve years in Flanders, where he had started his creative, humanistic work. In these twelve years before his death he completed several books: *De Officio Mariti* appeared in 1528, as if it were a literary, philosophic response to Henry's divorce; in 1529, *De Concordia et Discordia in Humano Genere;* in 1531, *De Disciplinis;* in 1538, *De Anima et Vita* and a short study on the teaching of the Latin language. The purely religious work *De Veritate Fidei Christianae* was published in 1543, three years after his death.

As one reviews Vives' life and work as a whole, one is impressed with the sequential unity of his performance. His thoughts were a direct outgrowth and an integral part of his actual life, and vice versa. It was not only a new philosophic orientation that the man was seeking; it was a new mode of life. The maxims of his philosophy sprang from the actual happenings of life and from his own nature. They were constructive maxims derived from empirical data gathered by a mind of unique earnestness and responsiveness to the quickened pulse of the new era—an era in which he was living and to which he was one of the most fervent, creative, and instructive contributors. While this era is traditionally designated as that of the Renaissance, and while it foreshadowed the coming rationalism, it also contained more than the mere germ of the romanticism which was so characteristic of the latter part of the nineteenth century and which revolutionized modern European philosophy (Bergson), science (Einstein), and psychology (Freud). The romantic trend, which put the accent on self-observation, introspection, and understanding of feelings and emotions and their role in human behavior, was well defined in all the writings of Vives. It was this trend which made him stand out among all the humanists of his own and later days, and it was this trend which brought forth a social consciousness, a sense of the emotional, interdependent unity of all people and all nations. In this Vives was the forerunner of the political philosophers and sociologists of the nineteenth and early twentieth centuries: Durkheim, Tarde, Giddings. What Giddings designated as consciousness of the kind, what the French sociologists called the solidarization of social trends, Vives not only sensed but also attempted to formulate in his outlines of the principles of education (*De Disciplinis*) and in his precepts for international relations (*De Concordia et Discordia in Humano Genere*).

Thus oriented and preoccupied, Vives, as has been repeatedly stressed, felt that the mind—and by this he did not mean mere intellect —must be well understood and that a deeper understanding of the mind as it works and as it makes man act was the paramount prerequisite of all theoretical and practical learning, of philosophy, education, politics, and science. These ideas he felt; he observed their efflorescence in himself and he expressed them by allusions or by more or less general consideration in every book he wrote.

He did not, however, belong to that type of mind which remains satisfied with mere allusions and hints. Ten years after his return from England he had completed and published his most significant book, *De Anima et Vita* (Basel, 1538), in which he attempted to formulate his principles of human psychology. Here again, but more emphatically and succinctly than in his previous writings, he makes it clear that the essence of the soul, the subject of preoccupation of scores of generations, he would leave to the theologian and to the subtle dialecticians of the past. *Anima quid sit, nihil interest nostra scire, qualis autem, et quae eius opera, premultum.* ("What the soul is, is of no concern for us to know; what it is like, what its manifestations are, is of very great importance.") He touches but little on the false opinions of the thinkers of the past. He is not interested in refuting the old; it is the assertion of the new which prompts him to write. The human mind should be studied by careful exploration of one's own mental life. "On this account, it seems good to me to ponder deeply on some points of this great subject. . . . Recent philosophers have brought but little industry to the study, content with what had been left behind by the ancients. They have added nothing at all except problems almost impossible of solution. . . . Formerly the ancients involved themselves in great absurdities on this subject, for they thought wrongly of the mind, *which is not perceived by our bodily senses* [11]—and even their opinions on the very matters which we do perceive by the senses were most inept." [12] One must therefore start anew, but a further obstacle must be overcome: one must establish a proper vocabulary of words not only comprehensible but simple and in common usage. Vives was aware that the scholars of the time obscured the true meaning of words by their verbosity. He apparently looked forward to the day when the vernacular would become the source of a well-established and succinct scientific terminology. "We have employed not only words invented and accepted by common people, but also those which have become detrited through their use by learned persons. Although the congruity is small [between the accepted meanings and ours in using these words] we have tried to fit them into our structure. For there is nothing more recondite, obscure and unknown to all than the human mind, and until now the things belonging within its range could, least of all, be expressed and demonstrated by appropriate words. We have, however, tolerated some words and brushed up others; some we have kept, for such a procedure seemed most helpful to those who wish to learn." [13]

Vives then offers us the text of his treatise, comprising three chapters—two hundred and sixty-four pages altogether, excluding the index. It would require a great deal of time and space to give the full critical outline which this book deserves. It represents an interesting mixture of traditional and revolutionary thought, and it still awaits the historian who will do it full justice. For our purposes the psychological

[11] Italics ours.
[12] Vives: preface to *De anima et vita*. Basel, 1538, p. ii.
[13] *Ibid.*, p. iii.

evolution of Vives and the evolution of psychology in the sixteenth century are of primary interest, and only the highlights of this problem will be considered.

Since Vives had no independent knowledge of anatomy and physiology, he had to utilize whatever information there was at his disposal. His treatise is therefore influenced to a great extent by Aristotle; he places the *sensorium commune* in the heart. His psychological premises are traditional but he soon abandons tradition; his empirical mind turns to factual, descriptive considerations. He discards the belief which was popular in his day, that the motion of the stars and the planets affects the human mind. The mind functions in accordance with certain principles—in accordance with definite laws as we would say today—and it is the unique distinction of Vives to have been the first to point out and to describe the importance of psychological *associations*. He studies the various connections between thoughts and fragments of thought and, with a truly marvelous clarity, he cites example after example of associations through similarity, contiguity, and opposites. The first in the history of psychology, he recognizes the emotional origin of certain associations, their ability to revive long-forgotten thoughts, sensations, and emotions. "When I was a boy at Valencia, I was ill of a fever; while my taste was deranged I ate cherries; for many years afterwards, whenever I tasted the fruit I not only recalled the fever, but also seemed to experience it again."

The true importance of Vives has not yet been properly appreciated. It is always Hartley and Hobbes who are credited with the discovery of associations, but a perusal of *De Anima et Vita* leaves no doubt that Vives, almost a century before Hobbes, not only had a clear conception of associations but fully understood their relation to remembering and forgetting and fully understood as well the intimate relationship between emotions and the process of remembering and forgetting. He does not use the word "unconscious"—the introduction of this term was left to some writers of the nineteenth century and the formulation of the concept itself to Freud at the threshold of the twentieth—but Vives does describe how we at times register certain things without knowing that we do and how later on we may through a chain of associations recall what we knew, though we were unaware that we knew it. Vives is led to conclude that certain emotions enhance one's

memory, and from this conclusion he is naturally led to the consideration of emotions, to which he devotes the third chapter of the treatise—
one hundred and twenty-one pages, almost half of the whole book.

The courage and incisive greatness of Vives' mind never come to
light with such impressive clarity as in this chapter on emotions.[14] Vives
—the very religious, almost mystical, thinker, the profoundly conventional and inspired ethical mind, to whom man is the very acme of
creation and perfection—unflinchingly looks into the mind, unafraid of
seeing the very lowly and selfish drives of man. *Affectus omnes ex
amore*, he proclaims. But love generating affects is not always lofty.
Vives describes the egoistic drives of man, his appetites, his trends
of self-approbation, active love, and passive love—terms almost ultra-
modern, almost Freudian. Passive love, that is, the tendency to be the
recipient of love, produces gratitude; and gratitude is always mixed
with shame. Shame would naturally interfere with the sense of gratitude. Anything which gives one a feeling of being thwarted produces a
sense of anger. Love is mixed with hate. Here we have a definite statement of that puzzle of double feelings, of the clash of two mutually
contradictory affects, a phenomenon which was considered "illogical"
and therefore impossible before Vives and after him until the opening
years of the twentieth century, when Eugen Bleuler, following Freud
at the time, introduced the term "ambivalence." Vives even gains insight into the true nature of jealousy, which was and still is in many
quarters considered an expression of love. The element of hate, not as
a result but as a cause of jealousy, was revealed in the analysis of this
emotional reaction by Freud. Vives solves the problem almost in the
same manner. Jealousy, he believes, is fear that good will come to
someone whom we hate. He gauges the quality of various affects which
appear similar or identical. Resentment of a blow, he said, is less
violent than that following an insult. In other words, an affective im-
pact may elicit a stronger reaction than a physical one. Vives attempts
to describe how the natural egoistic trends of man are gradually transformed into emotions of higher social values. He thus foreshadows
the formulation of the modern concept of domestication or socialization
of human instincts.

In brief, two years before his death Vives, at the age of forty-six,

[14] *De anima*, Book III.

had reached a depth of human understanding surpassing that of any of his predecessors. His intuitive understanding of the dynamic role of emotions was not attained by the great psychologists of ensuing centuries until the psychological discoveries of our own generation. Sir William Hamilton remarked, in 1872: "Vives' observations comprise in brief nearly all of principal moment that has been said upon the subject either before or since." [15] These words could in many respects still be accepted without qualification. Vives was not only the father of modern, empirical psychology, but the true forerunner of the dynamic psychology of the twentieth century. It should be noted again that he was not a physician and was not exposed to any definite medical influences, except those with Juan Población, which were early and apparently not far reaching. As has been pointed out before, the medical profession, steeped in the tradition which Rabelais derided so pungently and which Molière over a century later lashed with his destructive caricature, was behind the times. Vives' revolutionary insight stands out almost alone, and yet he was the son of his age; he was one of the few, to be sure, but one of those whose effectiveness proved strong and lasting in the course of the evolution of thought.

In 1529, one year after he left England, Vives published his *De Concordia et Discordia in Humano Genere.* As if to round out and give full body to his life's philosophy, Vives contemplates the political vicissitudes of international relations as an integral part of human living. He seems melancholy and as nearly bitter as his temperament would allow. Among the two hundred and thirty-nine *symbola* which he had written for little Princess Mary five years before, he had included the motto *Sine querela;* he had told her that this was his own motto. He never complained, but this treatise on human relations in the field of international activity does appear to contain a note of disappointment and scorn. Wars, changes of frontiers he called "cases of theft." The political contentions and military campaigns which people study as history Vives considered unworthy of study, as they are but achievements of passion and not of rational judgment. He sought to visualize a group of nations living in awareness of their community of interest and in peace. His desire to cultivate humanitarian, ethico-rational standards in man as an individual recalls Bacon's "cultivation

[15] Quoted in Watson: *The father of modern psychology,* p. 339.

of the mind." Vives wished and hoped to extend the influence of these standards to the life of the community on a national and international scale. Such considerations are what make his contribution to medical psychology so invaluable, for modern psychology, like that of Vives, has deepened the recognition of the great value of the individual and yet extended psychology's scope of interest and horizon of activity to include history and sociology.

III

VIVES looked to the future. In his *In Pseudo-Dialecticos* he stated his quarrels with the old world, refused to compose his differences with the old traditions, and then proceeded to live the life of *pietas literata*, the life of an intellectual and idealist who called for the liberation of the human mind and the building of a better future life. This task he accomplished with brilliant consistency and with the magnificent dignity which was his as a contemplative scholar. He was an intellectual aristocrat with aristocratic tastes and sensibilities; he was not a man of action. There is little in his life or his books that betrays a need to fight in the open or to brave the risks of falling victim to passions instead of being guided by rational judgment. The task of braving the dangers of an open fight was left to others, and among these the name of Paracelsus occupies a conspicuous and memorable place.

Theophrastus Bombastus von Hohenheim (Paracelsus) was a contemporary of Vives; he was born a year later and died a year later (1493–1541). Rough, impatient, and restless in his convictions, Paracelsus had little patience with dignified niceties and refined manners of speech. In the sixth of his *Defensiones* he scornfully refutes the reproaches which the stodgy, well-mannered professors and scholars directed against him: "My style pleases me very well. In order to offer a defense for my strange fashion and how it is to be understood, know this: by nature I am not woven fine—it is not the fashion of my land that one attains anything by spinning silk. Nor are we reared on figs or mead or wheaten bread, but on cheese, milk and oaten bread. That does not make subtle fellows." Paracelsus asked and gave no quarter. When he decided to state his disregard of old authorities, he came to the bonfire which the students traditionally made on St. John's Day and, in full view of the people, threw Avicenna's *Canon* into the flames, thus disposing of this authority who was held in such high regard by the scholastic medical professor. He gave unto the Lord what belonged to the Lord, but rendered to man what belonged to man. The concept of the role and dignity of the individual—so characteristic of the time—he stated with a sharp emphasis and with unequivocal pride: "When He [the Lord] performs a miracle, He performs it humanly and through mankind; if He effects wonderful cures, He does that through men, and therefore through the physician." [16]

Paracelsus paid dearly for his impetuosity and irreconcilable temper. At the age of thirty-three, after many travels, he became professor of medicine in Basel. Less than three years later he was forced to leave the city and start a life of restless misery and bitterness, wandering from one city to another. He was treated with suspicion and contempt by the official representatives of the medical profession; he suffered poverty and dire need. The city of Innsbruck refused him permission to enter. "The burgomaster of Innsbruck," remarked Paracelsus in the preface to his *The Pestilence in the City of Stertzingen*, "has probably seen doctors in silken clothing at the courts of princes, not broiling in the sun in tattered rags." Yet Paracelsus continued his work. A John Rütiner of St. Gallen, who saw Paracelsus in 1534–1535, said about him, "Theophrastus is most laborious, sleeps little, without undressing throws himself, booted and spurred, on the bed for some three hours and ceaselessly, ceaselessly, writes." [17] Unfortunately, Paracelsus was usually unable to obtain permission to publish his writings, and the majority of them did not begin to appear until some twenty years after his death. His motto was: "Experience is science." "I pleased no one," he stated, "but the sick whom I cured." He was despised by the profession; he returned in kind and with better reason. He said about the physicians of his day: "They have gone, and still go, around the art of medicine like a cat around hot porridge." In the preface to the *Paragranum* he described himself with his characteristic scornful directness. "I am called a rejected member of the universities, a heretic of the profession, a misleader of scholars." He remained undaunted to his

---

[16] *Paramirum*, I, 21.
[17] John Maxson Stillman: *Paracelsus*. Chicago, Open Court Pub. Co., 1920, p. 164.

last day. In his will, written three days before his death, he makes the following disposition of his few earthly belongings (speaking of himself in the third person): "Fifthly, for all other of his goods and belongings he institutes and names as his heirs the poor, the wretched and the needy people who have no stipend nor other provision." Despite his toughness, his rugged cynicism and sharp fits of anger, Paracelsus, a true son of the true Renaissance, always had warm feelings toward the sick and the common cheese-eating or hungry people. He lectured only in the vernacular and he wrote in it.

The ideal which Vives formulated for the intellectual of his day Paracelsus formulated for the physician. These men of such different cast, temper, and taste both valued a self-conscious mind inspired with ardor for the public weal and for the common man. Both sought to learn from the common people and not from books and pompous dialecticians. Both were pious men and neither left the Catholic Church. Paracelsus was deeply stirred by religious feeling. Writing his will, when he was "weak in body, sitting on a couch, yet quite sound in reason, mind and spirit," he dates it "the twenty-first day of September, at midday in the seventh year of the reign of the most holy Father and Lord in God, Paul, in God's providence, the third pope of that name"; he "commits his life, death and his poor soul to the shield and protection of Almighty God, in the confident hope that the everlasting mercy of God will not suffer the bitter suffering, martyrdom and death of His only begotten Son our Saviour Jesus Christ to be unfruitful nor lost to him, miserable creature." [18] But, unlike Vives, Paracelsus, almost in the manner of a Savonarola and Luther combined, lashed out openly and freely against the excessive claims of those who were in high places. "This is certain," he cried out, "that the restoring of health is what makes a physician—their work it is that makes the Master and the Doctor,—not the Emperor, not the Pope, not the Faculty, not the *privilegia*, nor any university, for from them is hidden what makes a physician." [19]

The *archeus*, the all-pervading principle directing the individual's life, was the secret to be understood. It was a force somewhat akin to that which Hippocrates had in mind, but it was more individualized.

[18] *Ibid.*, pp. 175–177.
[19] *Paragranum*, I, 199.

Paracelsus was imbued with the neoplatonic ideas of his age. Man was to him a microcosmic edition of the great macrocosm, the universe. The sun found its parallel in the human heart; the moon, in the brain; Mercury, in the lungs; Jupiter, in the liver; Venus, in the kidneys; Mars, in the gall. But it would be a mistake to look for consistency in these views of Paracelsus. He would not lose sight of the individual in contemplation of the stars. "Therefore," he specifically states in *De Natura Rerum*, "know that the wise man can rule and master the stars, and not the stars him. The stars are subject to him and must follow him and not he them. A brutish man is ruled, mastered, compelled and necessitated by the stars, so that he has to follow them like the thief to the gallows, the murderer to the wheel." [20] Here one is inclined to believe that Paracelsus was almost ready to state that what he actually meant by the stars was the sum of the biological impulses to which man must succumb when he loses control over things as a result of a weakening of his rational life. A further, even though partial, corroboration of our assumption could be found in the distinct hint which Paracelsus gives elsewhere that man's individual endowment, his constitution as we would say today, is not subject to the mastery of the planets. "The course of Saturn disturbs no man in his life, neither lengthens nor shortens it. For if Saturn had never been in the heavens nor in the firmament, people would be born just so, and though no moon had been created still would people have just such natures. You must not believe that because Mars is cruel, therefore Nero was his child. Although they had the same nature neither obtained it from the other. You see Helen and Venus of one nature, and though Venus had never existed still would Helen have been a strumpet, and although Venus is older than Helen consider that before Helen there were also strumpets." [21]

The contribution of Paracelsus to psychological medicine cannot as yet be fully evaluated. His style is extremely confused and confusing. His chemicoastrological divagations are involved, disturbingly desultory, and seemingly arbitrary, for he was not a master of exposition and he felt more than he actually thought. He was guided more by his uncanny intuition than by rational consideration. He wrote on nu-

[20] *De natura rerum*, I, 910.
[21] *Paramirum*, I, 5.

merous subjects pertaining to medicine and some time in 1526 wrote a book on mental diseases, not published until 1567, which bore the title *Von den Krankheiten so die Vernunfft Berauben*. Like most of his writings, this book is polemical; a great many pages are devoted to querulous denials, rejections, and refutations of older views. Like Vives, he had difficulty in divorcing himself from traditional thinking, but he did not possess Vives' sensitiveness and artistic capacity for introspection. Therefore, unlike Vives, he does not seem aware—and is still less able to admit—how frequently the old mode of thinking crowded itself into his new, individual way of looking at things. His writings are ample testimony that he carried with him some of the traditions which he violently combated. His physiology and psychophysiology bear many earmarks of Galenic and Aristotelian thought although he rejected both.

A mental illness was to Paracelsus a "spiritual" disease, that is, a natural disease due to the unhealthy changes undergone at various times by the *spiritus vitae*. He rejected demonology without equivocation and enunciated a number of dogmatic assumptions and assertions as to what would cure a mental disease. Thinking in terms of heat and cold as causative agents, he advised at times that patients' toes and fingers be scarified so that fresh air might be let in to reduce the excess of heat which he thought produced a certain maniacal state.[22] On the other hand, when considering St. Vitus' dance (*chorea*), he vituperates against attaching names of saints or devils to any diseases. Without warning and by way of a startling and inexplicable intuitive insight he offers the name *chorea lasciva* and suggests the sexual nature of hysteria, a suggestion which was scientifically tested and fully corroborated by Freud almost four centuries later.

Paracelsus goes further. Discarding without any argumentation and without rational disproof everything in traditional psychology, he states that children do possess imagination, in spite of all the assertions of the scholastic professors. "Thus, the cause of the disease *chorea lasciva* is a mere opinion and idea, assumed by imagination, affecting those who believe in such a thing. This opinion and idea are the origin of the disease both in children and adults. In children the cause is also

[22] Paracelsus: *Von den Krankheiten so die Vernunfft Berauben*. Basel, 1567, chapters "Von Mania" and "De Cura Maniae."

imagination, based not on thinking but on perceiving, because they have heard or seen something. The reason is this: their sight and hearing are so strong that *unconsciously they have fantasies* [23] about what they have seen or heard." [24] As far as is known this is the first reference to the unconscious motivation of neuroses in the history of medical psychology.

While, as has been said, it is difficult to unravel and to clear up many of the obscurities which the texts of Paracelsus present, there is reason to believe that Paracelsus, again more intuitively than rationally, did conceive of man as a unitary, psychological entity, a microcosm united with the macrocosm, a well-knit organism which through the principle of life is intimately related to and connected with the universe as a whole. In other words, Paracelsus, although in a redundant and elliptical manner, definitely introduced the biological point of view, which considers the human individual as a product of total biological functions. This is a purely modern view, but in the age of Paracelsus it would have found a number of responsive and influential followers had it not been for the fact that he remained so individualistic, so unbridled and irreconcilable, that whatever theories he did wish to formulate he propounded casually, dogmatically, and obscurely, as if he were stating them for himself with little care for those who might be willing some day to ponder over them. He was a man of action. To him the treatment of the disease was more important than a true understanding of it. His was therefore chiefly a contribution of the uniquely colorful and tragic phenomenon that he was. He entered every field of medicine as if with a revolutionary cry, "Down with the past!" "Let us forget words and manners, and treat our patients." He left two or three penetrating, intuitive suggestions which proved invaluable and which, characteristic though they were of the man and the time, proved to be centuries ahead of his day—baffling in their obscurity as well as their insight.

[23] Italics ours.
[24] Paracelsus: *Von den Krankheiten, etc.*, chapter "Von Sanct Veyts Thantz."

IV

THE voice of Paracelsus was the voice of a physician. This is to be noted as an especially significant fact, because the medical profession cannot boast of many brothers who up to that time or even much later had the stamina to withstand or the courage to combat the onrush of demonology. In this connection the name of Cornelius Agrippa (1486–1535), an older contemporary of Paracelsus, cannot be forgotten. He fought valiantly and in a spirit of independence. His voice was that of Hippocrates in *The Sacred Disease;* his temper and mode of action were those of Paracelsus. The physician was beginning to come into his own again, to take his place at the vanguard of a revolution.

Agrippa's full name was Heinrich Cornelius Agrippa of Nettesheim. He was born in Cologne on September 14, 1486. The name Agrippa was of Roman origin. Aulus Gellius explains that when children are born feet- instead of headfirst, the woman experiences a great deal of difficulty in labor and that, therefore, children thus born are called "Agrippa"—an abbreviated fusion of the words *aegritudo* (pain) and *pes* (foot).[25] Cornelius Agrippa frequently reminded his readers and numerous correspondents that he was proud of his name, that it denoted the essence of his temper, for he was born feetfirst and he later entered many fights *aegris pedibus*.

Agrippa was disliked, suspected, and maligned; like Paracelsus, he died alone, without friends or relatives, in great poverty. There was no notary to help him write his last will, nor were there pennies to be distributed to the poor at his funeral. There was only his dog *Monsieur,* the black French poodle which Agrippa had acquired in Paris, to warm his cooling feet. Many, learned and vulgar, lay and cleric, were fully convinced that this dog was actually the devil with whom Agrippa was supposed always to keep company, for Agrippa must have been a wizard, a heretical magician, an evil man. "In subsequent literature, when he has been mentioned, it has been almost always with contempt or ridicule. He was scarcely in his grave when Rabelais reviled him as

[25] Henry Morley: *The life of Henry Cornelius Agrippa von Nettesheim.* London, 1856, p. 2.

Herr Trippa. Butler [who died almost one hundred and fifty years after Agrippa] jests over him in *Hudibras*, and uses the Church legend of his demon dog:

> 'Agrippa kept a stygian pug,
> I' th' garb and habit of a dog,
> That was his tutor, and the cur
> Read to th' occult philosopher,
> And taught him subtly to maintain
> All other sciences are vain.'

While . . . Southey [who died over three hundred years after Agrippa, in 1843] writes a ballad on another of the monkish tales against him. It is that about the youth who was torn to pieces by the fiends when conjuring in Agrippa's study with one of his books:

> 'The letters were written with blood therein
> And the leaves were made of dead men's skin.' " [26]

Cornelius Agrippa began his career with the study of astrology and alchemy, as did a great many scholars of his day. For a while his mystical temperament found some satisfaction in cabala and magic and other esoteric teachings. In 1525 he published a book which he had written some fifteen years earlier, *Occult Philosophy*. A man of contradictions and keen critical propensities, he published almost simultaneously a book refuting and exposing by means of "an invective declamation" the ludicrous vanity of all the occult "sciences." [27] Throughout the text of this book, while denouncing these sciences, he also attacks all the sophistries, dialectic falsehoods, and religious hypocrisies of his day. He was a doctor of both faculties (Law and Theology) and a doctor of medicine. Whatever suspicious and fanatical contemporaries may have chosen to say against Agrippa, he was a valiant man, an honest doctor, a humanitarian citizen of the world, and one of the real pioneers in combating the theory and practice of demonological philosophy. A restless personality, he was not so much a scientific leader as an irascible, stormy fighter with a predilection for bare-fisted, frontal

[26] *Ibid.*, Preface, p. viii.
[27] Heinrich Cornelius Agrippa: *De incertitudine et vanitate scientiarum et artium, atque excellentia verbi dei declamatio*. Cologne, 1532 (third edition).

attack. Conservative and peaceful by nature, a German nobleman, ambitious for court honors and positions, he cherished at the same time the modest wish to become a university professor and was an assiduous student of books. He was a good soldier; he fought in the ranks but carried books and manuscripts in his rucksack in the field of combat. He hated turmoil and always lived a restless, tumultuous existence. He hated war but invented some new machine of destruction, a sort of cannon or gun, and was eager to sell it to the emperor. He yearned to become settled yet constantly moved from place to place, and he was seldom paid for his work. He was always busy looking for, finding, or leaving a job, yet he found time to construct an optical instrument with which he apparently hoped to observe the stars and was thus at the very threshold of inventing the telescope. A man of great loyalty and devotion, he always tried to make, and not infrequently succeeded in making, a number of friends, yet he made a greater number of violent enemies among the very people whose favors he sought, on whose graces he depended, and whose powers threatened to destroy him. A devoted husband and a man of strictest matrimonial morality, a warmhearted and unusually kind father, he married three times; his first wife died of a chronic disease, his second of the plague, and the third revealed the nature of a harlot soon after marriage. Agrippa was driven hither and yon, held the position of secretary to the king, was advocate of the City of Metz, city physician in Fribourg, and historiographer in Lyons. He was twice arrested and put in prison by his creditors. He enjoyed imperial honors and suffered dire need and starvation. The books and instruments he had loved and prized more than anything else were strewn over various parts of Germany, Switzerland, France, and the Lowlands.[28]

Agrippa was a strange combination of scholar and man of action. His writings present nothing unusual or even original. They seem to have been a part of his life of action, a springboard for his combative drives. Even the simultaneous publication of his *Occult Philosophy* and of the *De Vanitate Scientiarum* which refuted it was a kind of combat rather than a considered contribution to the philosophy of nature and man. *Aegris pedibus*, Agrippa fought the world around him. Asserting his

[28] The above paragraph is a somewhat modified and re-edited quotation from *The medical man and the witch, etc.* (pp. 103–107).

aversion to the sadistic misogyny of the monks, he, like Vives, expressed particular interest in the qualities and achievements of women; he wrote a treatise *On the Nobility and Pre-eminence of the Feminine Sex*. The medical profession of his day he despised hardly less than did Paracelsus. Erasmus,[29] whom he knew and with whom he corresponded, counseled him to be more tranquil of spirit and moderate of tongue, but Agrippa could speak and feel only in a direct, sharp, and uncompromising manner: "The greatest reputation is attained by those physicians who are recommended by splendid costumes, many rings and jewels, a distant fatherland, tedious travels, a strange religion, especially the Hindu and Mohammedan, and who combine with these a monstrous shamelessness in the praising of their medicines and cures. They observe times and hours most exactly, dispense their medicines always according to the astrological calendar, and hang all kinds of amulets on the patient. Simple and native medicines are quite neglected. Costly foreign remedies are preferred, which latter are mixed in such enormous numbers that the action of one is counteracted by that of another, so that no human sagacity can foresee the effects which will arise from such an abominable mixture." [30]

In 1518 Agrippa became the advocate of the City of Metz, where he worked among those stricken with the plague and those hounded by the Inquisition in the person of the implacable Dominican, Nicolas Savin. These years were made very turbulent by the activities of Luther, particularly in Metz, since through it the reformers tried to gain a foothold in France. The atmosphere there was charged with hatred and the will to kill, and Agrippa naturally suffered in it. The first man to preach the new doctrine in Metz was one Jean Le Clerc. Agrippa, who was already known for his battles with the monks, was subjected to a new trial of nerves and soul. Nicolas Savin had Le Clerc apprehended and publicly whipped on several successive days. Savin kept the poor man in custody and in torture for about a year, and then had his nose and soon his right hand cut off; then a hot crown was put on the martyr's head, following which the man, still not dead, was burned

---

[29] Erasmus himself was harsh about the contemporary medical profession. In his *Praise of folly* he states, "The whole Art as it is now practiced is but one incorporated compound of craft and imposture."

[30] Agrippa: *op. cit.*, p. 351.

alive.[31] No wonder Agrippa wrote: "I never was in any place from which I could depart more willingly than . . . from this city of Metz, the stepmother of all good scholarship and virtue." [32] In letters, in conversations, in open court, Agrippa denounced the Inquisitor, attacking the hated Dominican as "that brotherkin (I err), that great, swollen, and fat brother, Nicolas Savin, of the Dominican Convent, Inquisitor." "The hypocrite dissembles his iniquity under the shadow of the Gospel!" When a woman was accused of being a witch, Agrippa said, "Let this brotherkin, priest, or Levite, turn his heart from her. I will be pitiful with all my power, and call myself Samaritan, that is to say not a favourer of heretics, but a disciple of him, who when it was said to him that he was a Samaritan, and had a devil, denied that he had a devil, but did not deny that he was a Samaritan." [33] Through legal and moral trickery Savin tried to hold the young woman within the clutches of his jurisdiction. The woman's mother had been burned as a witch and this fact was held against the unfortunate daughter—a sort of perverted theory of heredity. Hence, insisted Savin, this girl from the village of Vouypy had to be subjected to torture. Agrippa was furious. He wrote to the judge, "Lest you be led astray by false prophets who claim to be Christ, and are Antichrist, I pray your reverence to bear with a word of help, and only pay attention to a conversation lately held with me upon the position of this article by the before-named bloodthirsty brother. For he asserted superciliously that the fact was in the highest degree decisive, and enough to warrant torture; and not unreasonably he asserted it according to the knowledge of his sect, which he produced presently out of the depth of the *Malleus Maleficarum* and the principles of peripatetic theology. . . . Oh, egregious sophism! Is it thus that in these days we theologize? Do figments like these move us to the torturing of harmless women?" [34]

Agrippa was ultimately forced to leave Metz. The monks had their revenge. For fifteen years, until he died, Agrippa was victimized by slander and calumny. The report of his death by a priest, Thevet, ends

[31] *Histoire générale de Metz par des réligieux Bénédictins de la congrégation de St. Vannes.* Metz, 1775, vol. III, p. 8. Cited by Morley: *op. cit.,* vol. II, p. 51.
[32] Morley: *Ibid.,* pp. 55, 56.
[33] *Ibid.,* pp. 58, 59.
[34] *Ibid.,* p. 62.

as follows: "In perpetual testimony of his base and depraved life, there has been composed over his tomb this epitaph:

This tomb scarcely the graces keep, but the black daughters of hell;
Not the muses, but the furies with the snakes spread abroad.
Alecto collects the ashes, mixes them with aconite,
And gives the welcome offering to be devoured by
The Stygian dog, who now cruelly pursues through the paths of Orcus,
And snatches at that of which when alive he was the companion,
And he leaps up at him.
And he salutes the furies because he had known them all,
And he addressed each by her own name.
O wretched Arts, which afford only this convenience
That as a known guest he can approach the Stygian waters!" [85]

Agrippa's English biographer Morley concludes the story of Agrippa's life by citing this epitaph and remarks, "So like a Pagan spat the Monk upon the Christian's grave!" [36]

This was the somber tragedy of a dying civilization killing those of its best children who voiced the call for a new life.

About three years before his death Agrippa received under his roof at Bonn a seventeen-year-old student whose name was Johann Weyer. Here, turning over the pages of Trithemius' *Steganographia*, this young man got his first glimpse into theoretical occultism. Here, too, he read the writings of Agrippa and became acquainted with his master's burning protests against the world in which he lived and especially against the cities which had become "stepmothers of all good scholarship and virtue." Thus to Agrippa belongs the honor of being the first teacher of the man who made the greatest contribution to psychiatry during the Renaissance.

v

VIVES died in his forty-ninth year, as did Paracelsus. Cornelius Agrippa was forty-nine at his death. They seem to have belonged to a genera-

[85] Thevet: *Portraits et vies des hommes illustres.* Paris, 1584, vol. II, p. 543. Also, Morley: *op. cit.*, vol. II, p. 320.
[36] Morley: *op. cit.*, vol. II, p. 320.

tion which lived hard and worked and thought swiftly. Paracelsus and Agrippa were both physicians, and by temperament and manner as well as birth they were not the leisurely, scholarly noblemen but men who had to struggle hard for mere existence. All three, but particularly Paracelsus and Agrippa, knew what poverty and dire misery were.

Johann Weyer was a plebeian by birth, a quiet, slow-moving, methodically thinking man who lived to be seventy-three years old—in striking contrast to those of the older generation who were his spiritual teachers. The young Weyer studied under Agrippa for about three years before going to Paris to study medicine. He was an assiduous student, a tranquil, pensive man who watched the turbulent events of his day with compassion yet not without humor; with a certain ponderousness yet not without wit; with caution yet not without courage. He was moderate, yet he instigated a revolution in medical thought. He was pious but not bigoted, of deep convictions but without that passion which seems to have consumed both Agrippa and Paracelsus before they were fifty. There was a quality of sedateness—security and stability—in Weyer. Early in his career he became the personal physician of Duke William of Jülich, Berg, and Cleves and he held this position for thirty years. It would be impossible to imagine Vives, or especially Agrippa and Paracelsus—who so longed for a peaceful haven and security—holding one position for so many long years.

As one studies the life and peruses the writings of Weyer one gains the impression that a new man, a new type of individual has entered upon the scene of medicine and medical philosophy. Weyer was a pious, conventional man, yet he named one of his sons Galen, a truly pagan name to be borne by the Christian son of a church-going, Christian father. An archiater of a duke, always close to the court, Weyer was not pompous, as was the wont of the brothers of his profession. He had a doctor's work to do and he did it. Jean Jacques Rousseau once said, "Bring me medicine but not the doctor"; had he known Weyer, he might have been less caustic and might not have objected to the physician's representing the art of medicine.

Weyer was born in 1515 in Grave on the Meuse in what some biographers call the Dutch Brabant; some prefer to consider him a Netherlander, others a Rhenish German. He wrote in Latin and German. When he studied with Agrippa and discovered Trithemius' *Stegano-*

graphia, a book on occult knowledge, he not only read but secretly copied it. He wanted to know things and he collected data wherever he could, but he was not a bookworm. He knew how to observe and to gain ever-increasing knowledge from his empirical observations, and he knew how to apply his knowledge in practice. When in Paris, he was singled out as an able student and capable doctor. He looked after the sons and nephew of the Queen of Navarre, whom he followed to Orléans. He died suddenly but undramatically at Tecklenburg on February 24, 1588. He had lived and he died honorably and with honors.

Weyer was a serious practitioner of medicine who made a number of original observations. He made an excellent description of scurvy, of quartan fever, and of the "English sweat," or hydropsy, of occlusion of the neck of the uterus, and of retention of menstrual flow. He invented a speculum for vaginal examination. But his major interest was mental diseases; this interest was awakened early in his career and he preserved it to the last. He entered the services of the Duke in 1550, having spent five years as the city physician of Arnhem. Within twelve years he had completed his monumental work *De Praestigiis Daemonum,* a book of great scholarship containing an enormous mass of historical, theological, and medicopsychological detail. This book was published in Latin one year later, in 1563. Weyer translated it into German in 1567. In the same year appeared the *Pseudomonarchia Daemonum* and also the *De Irae Morbo,* on the "disease of wrath" and its philosophical, medical, and theological cure. Weyer took as an epigraph for this latter book the words of the Roman satirical poet Aulus Persius Flaccus: *O curas hominum, O quantum est in rebus inane!* ("O cares of man, how inane some of them are!")

Weyer was naturally unable to approach the problem of mental diseases without dealing with demonology and the Inquisition. An enlightened observer could view these only with anger and disgust. Weyer was moved by both against the judges of his day. "The judges would discharge their duties much better and more reasonably if the logs and the fagots on which innocent people are burned were put to better use and if the expenses incurred in order to maintain this carnage were considerably cut down." [37] He had nothing against the humane

---

[37] Weyer: *De praestigiis daemonum.* The French text of 1579, apparently the most complete, was used for this study. It was reprinted by the Bibliothèque Diabolique in

bishops, but he disliked the "incendiary" bishops and the hordes of "encowled" witch-hunters. The duty of a monk is to learn how to cure, not how to kill. "It is highly unpleasant to see how people in order to kill errors are busy killing human beings." [38]

Weyer's clear and composed mind is at times almost devastating in its neat irony and simplicity. When he discusses the popular belief that certain people carry a devil in the glass of a ring they are wearing, Weyer remarks with mock naïveté, "It is however a marvelous thing; how is it that this glass does not melt, since the devil must have got into it all fresh from the depth of infernal fire?" [39] To a contemporary reader this remark may appear superfluous and naïve indeed, for the preposterousness of the belief attacked is too obvious; but Weyer said this in 1562. It required courage to make such a statement; it required great intellectual penetration and daring to think of it. This manner of thinking presents a totally new note; it betrays a special pleasure in intellectual activity, a serene, unaffected reasonableness quite different from the emotional cry of an Agrippa or the caustic scorn of a Paracelsus. It was new and it led to new ways of seeking for truth and new possibilities for discovering it.

In 1573 Weyer accompanied the Duke to Königsberg. Everywhere there was talk about wonderful, miraculous happenings. One of these miracles was the subject of particularly frequent dinner-table conversations among the dukes and the counts: certain people could live without eating. As a matter of fact, they said, there was a girl in Unna who never ate and yet was perfectly well. Weyer would not believe this. He might not have known at the time of the phenomenon of psychopathological malingering but the whole story would not appeal to his realistic mind. Thus, upon his return from his trip with the Duke, he went to the town of Unna to see whether there was such a fasting maiden. There were many stories of fasting women all over the country and he did find the girl in question. Her name was Barbara Kremers.

The story as reported here is told by Weyer himself; he describes the case in detail in a booklet of fifteen pages published in 1577 under the title *De Commentitiis Jejuniis* ("On Alleged Fasting"). He re-

---

1885 in two volumes: *Histoires, disputes et discours des illusions et impostures des diables, etc.* Vol. II, p. 276.

[38] *Ibid.*, vol. II, p. 289.

[39] *Ibid.*, vol. II, p. 214.

views the various cases of fasting mentioned in the Bible and does not contradict them. He always makes use of the Bible in order to underscore, as it were, the fact that his faith in the Scriptures has never wavered, but he refuses to give credence to the allegations that unnatural phenomena occur among simple, natural people. Weyer found Barbara Kremers in the house of her mother and stepfather. She was only ten years old, but physically developed beyond her age. Her mother said that the miracle of not eating had followed a severe illness of six weeks' duration, after which she had remained mute for six months. She had come out of her stupor but since her recovery she had eaten and drunk nothing, nor did she urinate or move her bowels. The mother was very proud of her daughter. The girl was good and devout, and noblemen, city councilors, and learned men came to see her. The city council of Unna gave her a special certificate, duly signed and sealed, testifying to the truth of this wonder. There was no swindle about it. Weyer observes that the girl looked well and that as he approached to examine her she shied away, whining. He remarks that many people streamed in to see the child, as they had Diana of Ephesus, and that a great deal of money was left in her house. Although Barbara looked very well, she walked on crutches because her back was, supposedly, lame.

Weyer asked the Duke for permission to have Barbara brought to Cleves, where Weyer lived. The Duke consented. After some difficulty with her parents, Weyer was finally able to bring Barbara to his house; she had to be accompanied by her sister Elsa, who was twelve years old. The parents were given generous gifts. They were to return to take back their children within three weeks. Weyer describes how everyone in his house treated the little girl with care and kindness; his wife, Henrietta, a pious and goodhearted woman, was especially co-operative. The malingering of the little girl was exposed in every respect; her sister Elsa had been her accomplice and had secretly brought Barbara the necessary food. In commenting on the case, Weyer, who never missed a chance to make a reference to the Bible, said that Elsa was Barbara's Habakkuk—who performed similar services when he supplied food to Daniel in the lions' den. In less than a week the miraculous girl from the town of Unna came regularly to meals at Weyer's table; her appetite was excellent. Soon the crutches were given up. Weyer cured her of her lameness merely by rubbing bland oil on her back. The girl had also suffered from a twist in her arms. This, too, disappeared.

The next problem which confronted Weyer was, however, very serious. The Duke was angry. The girl was a criminal swindler. Her parents were even more guilty. It took a great deal of persuasion, but Weyer finally succeeded in convincing the Duke that the girl and her sister were not guilty and that the parents should be forgiven. The enlightened Duke relented and sent the two children back to Unna at his own expense. At the same time he wrote to the magistrate of Unna, reproaching him for having been so credulous and counseling him to be more intelligent in the future. As to the two girls, the Duke advised that they be brought up more carefully and taught to fear the Lord. As to the various certificates and testimonials about Barbara's fasting, they should be gathered carefully and burned in the market place. Supplied with the ducal letter, the two girls were sent back to Unna on May 13, 1574; Weyer concludes the story with the remark, "This was the cheerful catastrophe of this comedy."

The amusing story is of more than anecdotal interest. It reveals a wealth of telling detail which is well-nigh revolutionary. First, the calm, methodical, and systematic curiosity of Weyer should be noted. His procedure is truly scientific and his objectivity is more than unique. In that age of horror and cruelty such objectivity was a greater miracle than the alleged transvection of witches. If we recall Judge Boguet and the Inquisitor Savin, whose names were legion, and if we recall the gruesome fate of Jean Le Clerc, the tolerance and the kindness of Weyer will appear as the Christlike manifestation of a saint. It is to be noted, too, that Weyer and his whole family were working on the problem in harmonious co-operation. All were taking part in a scientific experiment—a phenomenon rare in history, exceptional or even miraculous in 1574. To us of the first half of the twentieth century this case appears rather trivial. No contemporary city council would even take notice of it and, since the story could not very well be exploited for monetary gain, some free clinic would take care of it. But in 1574 the whole machinery of the State was set in motion and the sovereign himself had to handle the administrative details of the situation and carry out the final adjudication.

The case of Barbara Kremers is significant in another respect. It reveals Weyer the clinician. His theoretical considerations are meager and traditional. He was by no means an extreme empiricist who neglected learning; he was a very learned man, but his knowledge of medical theory naturally did not go beyond the trodden path of Hippocratico-Galenic humoralism. It seems to have been his preeminent characteristic to accept respectfully the older authorities, utilizing them whenever they were helpful and, with a polite bow, proceeding in his own practical way whenever they failed to be of service. Weyer used what is commonly but mistakenly called common sense.

It is in this spirit that he approached the most acute problem of his day, the problem of witchcraft. His magnum opus, *De Praestigiis Daemonum*, betrays his unique ability to avoid disrespect for old authorities and to smother the new and erring under the weight of his scholarship and keen, direct logic. He seems even to accept the devil as inferentially described in the Bible. Weyer appears to admit that the devil does play all sorts of injurious tricks, but he denies him any power over people in the sense which the *Malleus Maleficarum* made so authoritatively popular. This somewhat oblique mode of approach, or the wry terminology, exposed Weyer to criticism. Some of those who followed him suspected him of being superstitious, and even gullible; others were merely puzzled. But as one peruses his writings, one more and more clearly gains the impression that his frequent references to the devil represent a sort of jargon of the day. The word "devil" was as much a byword in the sixteenth century as "infection," or "virus," is today; it denoted a number of obscure concepts and a still greater number of things of the nature of which men were totally ignorant.

From the first page of *De Praestigiis Daemonum* it becomes clear that Weyer is about to introduce a new concept, or at least a very important new thought. In the complete title he speaks of witches and "poisoners"; he continues this differentiation throughout the book. He attempts to establish the fact that there are evil people, men and women who secretly use a variety of poisons to cause evil to their enemies. These people are devilish criminals and they should be punished. They should not be confused with the majority of witches who are innocent and sick people; these should be turned over to a physician for treatment. This is a new and revolutionary demand and Weyer is unequivocal and uncompromising on this point. There are some priests and monks whom he would not hesitate to put on the roster of magicians and sorcerers. "These people are, as well as ignorant, both impudent and cruel in the extreme. I do not mean by these words to detract anything from those people who are good men, whom I honor and revere. [But the others] impudently boast that they know the sacred science of Medicine (although it is quite certain that they have never tasted it even with their lips) and are not ashamed of making the poor people, who come to them ill and seeking advice, believe them. (I am ashamed to name these advisers, men of learning, judgment, and authority.)" [40] Weyer accuses such priests and monks of being real sorcerers. Describing their pseudomedical abuses, he concludes, "Thus are these good pillars of the church the principal slaves of their master Beelzebub, who glories in having been well served, chiefly under the cloak of religion. For in order to attract more money, and as if to divert themselves from the boredom of being held in esteem . . . [they maintain] their opinion that natural maladies are but forms of enchantment," and by doing so "prejudice the life and safety of Medicine, the most ancient, most useful, and most necessary of all sciences. . . ." [41] "What people possess naturally should not be considered as being connected with the powers of the witches." [42] Weyer repeatedly pleads for the right and the duty of medicine to intervene and by means of rational observations and treatment relieve the poor women who are called witches. He calls them by various names connoting compassion and regret: *aniculae, mulierculae, vetulae, dementitae delusae, miseriae.*

When Weyer completed the manuscript of *De Praestigiis,* he wrote a letter to Duke William: "Of all the misfortunes which the various fanatical and corrupt opinions, through Satan's help, have brought in our time to Christendom, not the smallest is that which, under the name of witchcraft, is sown as a vicious seed. The people may be divided against themselves through their many disputes about the Scriptures and church customs, while the old snake stirs the fire; still no such great misfortune results from that as from the thereby inspired opinion that childish old hags whom one calls witches or sorcerers can do any

[40] *Ibid.,* vol. II, p. 254.
[41] *Ibid.,* vol. II, pp. 255, 256.
[42] *Ibid.,* vol. II, p. 457.

harm to men and animals. Daily experience teaches us what cursed apostasy, what friendship with the wicked one, what hatred and strife among fellow creatures, what dissension in city and in country, what numerous murders of innocent people through the devil's wretched aid, such belief in the power of witches brings forth. No one can more correctly judge about these things than we physicians whose ears and hearts are being constantly tortured by this superstition.

"I notice more from day to day that the bog of Camarina blows its plague-laden breath stronger than ever. For a time one hoped that its poison would be gradually eliminated through the healthy teaching of the word of God, but I see that in these stormy days it reaches farther and farther and wider than ever. In the same way the sly devil watchfully uses each propitious circumstance. In the meantime the priests sleepily allow him to continue. Almost all the theologians are silent regarding their godlessness, doctors tolerate it, jurists treat it while still under the influence of old prejudices; wherever I listen, there is no one, no one who out of compassion for humanity unseals the labyrinth or extends a hand to heal the deadly wound.

"Therefore I, with my limited means, have undertaken to challenge the grievous thing which disgraces our Christian faith. It is not arrogance which impels me. I know that I know nothing and that my work allows me little leisure. I know too that many others could do this work better than I. I would like to incite them to outdo me. I shall gladly listen to reason.

"My object is chiefly of a theological nature: to set forth the artfulness of Satan according to Biblical authority and to demonstrate how one can overcome it. Next, my object is philosophical, in that I fight with natural reason against the deceptions which proceed from Satan and the mad imagination of the so-called witches. My object is also medical, in that I show that those illnesses the origin of which is attributed to witches come from natural causes. And finally, my object is legal, in that I speak of the punishment, in another than the accustomed way, of sorcerers and witches.

"But in order that I shall not meet with the reproach that I have overstepped the boundaries of my intellectual power and the limits of my profession with too great a faith in my own intelligence, I have submitted my seemingly paradoxical manuscript to men of your Highness' family as well as to theologians, lawyers, and excellent physicians, that it may be read in a critical sense. The manuscript shall remain protected through their authority if it is founded on reason; it shall fall if it is judged to be in error; it shall become better if it needs supplement or revision. For there is nothing in the world which can be made immediately and at once completely perfect.

"One might rejoin here that the *Malleus Maleficarum* has already fulfilled this mission. But one has only to read in that book the silly and often godless absurdities of the theologians Heinrich Kraemer and Jacob [Johann] Sprenger and to compare these quietly with the content of my manuscript. Then it will be clearly seen that I expound and advocate a totally different, even an opposite, point of view.

"To you, Prince, I dedicate the fruit of my thought. For thirteen years your physician, I have heard expressed in your Court the most varied opinions concerning witches; but none so agrees with my own as does yours, that witches can harm no one through the most malicious will or the ugliest exorcism, that rather their imagination—inflamed by the demons in a way not understandable to us—and the torture of melancholy makes them only fancy that they have caused all sorts of evil. For when the entire manner of action is laid on the scales, and the implements therefor examined with care and scrutiny, the nonsense and falsity of the matter is soon clear to all eyes and more lucid than the day. You do not, like others, impose heavy penalties on perplexed, poor old women. You demand evidence, and only if they have actually given poison bringing about the death of men or animals do you allow the law to take its course.

"When a prince of such virtues protects me, I have faith that I can make short work of the snapping teeth of insolent quarrelers, especially since it is certain that on my side stands invincible truth. I implore God, the Highest and Best, the Father of our Lord Jesus Christ, that He may profitably extend through greater employment of the Holy Spirit what in His benevolence He has so happily begun in Your Highness, to the honor of His Name, to the glory of Your Highness and to the flourishing happiness of your country. Your Highness' most obedient servant, Johann Weyer, Physician." [43]

Weyer, no matter how proud of his calling as a physician and no

---

[43] Binz: *op. cit.*, pp. 26 *et seq.*

matter how reverent toward the science of medicine, does not mince words when discussing some of his less enlightened or more conservative colleagues. While admitting the usefulness of chemistry, which he himself employs, he cannot tolerate "one named Theophrastus Paracelsus," whom he accuses of glorifying himself arrogantly in the smoke of a chemical fire, as well as of speaking too loudly and using ugly language.[44] He decries the physicians who adhere to the demonological theories: "Ignorant physicians and surgeons cover their stupidity and errors by referring to sorcery and the virtue of saints." [45] "Ignorant physicians seek the aid of saints in cases of a bite by a mad dog." [46]

Weyer proceeds with implacable will and stubborn systemization to refute all the superstitions and practices connected with the whole problem of witchcraft. He leaves not a stone unturned. He reviews in detail all Biblical references to witches and wizards. He reviews the same problem in Greek mythology and history. He subjects to careful analysis the phenomena mentioned in the *Malleus Maleficarum:* transvection, sexual relations with the devil, sexual impotence of man, the witches' alleged ability to affect the health of man and beast, the confessions made by the witches, their propensities to elaborate on their crimes, their alleged impiety. Weyer goes over in minute detail all the practices from exorcism to the endless varieties and refinements of torture, from the days of the past to his own. He leaves no doubt that but one conclusion is warranted: the witches are mentally sick people, and the monks who torment and torture the poor creatures are the ones who should be punished.

The true physician should rid himself of the blasphemous and erroneous beliefs instilled in him by the monks. The Witch of Endor did not take Samuel out of his tomb. The devil is unable to transform blood into water or dust into lice or sweat—which is salty—into water. He cannot make water into wine, nor can he restore eyesight to the blind, make sterile women fertile, or trouble anyone's soul. All talk about the power of the devil and about certain men's communing with him is loose and foolish. Weyer takes the opportunity to defend his "host and

[44] Weyer: *Histoires, disputes, etc.* Vol. I, pp. 260 *et seq.*
[45] *Ibid.*, vol. I, p. 259.
[46] *Ibid.*, vol. I, p. 267.

preceptor," Cornelius Agrippa. Many writers insisted "that the devil kept company with Agrippa till the latter's last breath, and that after Agrippa died the devil disappeared, in I [Weyer] know not what manner. I cannot be too astonished at the fact that men of great reputation sometimes write such inept things for the vain benefit of the populace. I have seen and known that dog in question [Agrippa's] quite intimately; it was a black dog of moderate size, and its name was *Monsieur*. During my stay with Agrippa I frequently led that dog on the leash. It was a real, male dog which had a female companion, a bitch of the same size and color called *Mademoiselle*. I think the false opinion about the dog was based on the fact that Agrippa was very affectionate with it. After all, many masters have this attitude toward their dogs. He kissed it, he kept it at his side while at the table, and the dog slept on Agrippa's bed, particularly after Agrippa repudiated his wife in the year 1535. He kept this dog beside him in his study, which was full of books, and usually the dog would sit between Agrippa and myself." [47]

Having brought a mass of facts and authoritative statements from literature and the Scriptures and a good measure of cold, simple logic to bear upon his thesis, Weyer felt satisfied that he had refuted the superstitious nonsense of the time. But this he did not consider enough. To him refuting meant disproving the alleged fact and proving the opposite by means of sound, empirical data. He therefore began by proving that the words "witch" and "sorcerer" were mistranslations from the Scriptures. He points out that the Hebrew word *khasaph* does not mean sorcerer; it is nearer to the Greek *pharmakos*, a person who uses medicaments or poisons unwisely or with criminal intent. In the days of Weyer various drugs were in use which in certain doses caused stupor or delirium. Weyer wonders to what extent many of the so-called witches are women who suffer from the influence or the aftereffects of drugs. He speaks of "the herb which the Italians call *belladonna*" (atropine), of thebaic opium, of hyoscyamus (henbane), and of hashish. Weyer had apparently studied the effect of these drugs not only carefully but in a completely modern manner. He is interested to know not only how the patients feel, but what they actually think—their ideational content. He gives an excellent description of optic hallucinations, which are usually due to such drug-poisoning as hashish. "They [the women, or the

[47] *Ibid.*, vol. I, p. 191.

witches] think that they see theatres, beautiful gardens, festive dinners, beautiful decorations, dresses, handsome young men, kings, magistrates—everything which delights them and which they think would give them pleasure. They also see devils, crows, prisons, deserts, torments. All these things are causes of violent dreams." [48] In speaking of stupors as probably produced by drugs, Weyer cites a case which, incidentally, sheds a characteristic light on the times. Referring to a case of mutism, he says, "If this witch were one of those enchantresses, shouldn't one marvel at the fact that the devil did not let her speak, choked her throat to such an extent that she was unable to speak. He apparently did not want her to be able to prove her innocence. Yet her falsehood was uncovered just through this silence.

"We recently saw a similar example in the case of an executioner, a Frenchman from Antwerp. This man committed a thousand remarkable misdeeds known to everyone, yet it was impossible to force him to confess despite even the most cruel torture. For no sooner would they start torturing him than he would fall into a state of alienation and lose all his senses. The very wise Senate turned to ordinary physicians, for the Senate knew that such a stupor could not be induced by anything except dormitive medicaments, which we have described in book two, chapter seventeen of this book. One may add that the Lord allowed him to suffer torture and be cruelly dismembered in order that somehow by force he would be brought to the recognition of some of his mistakes and be reproved by means of rude torment for his misdeeds. After having been tortured by various means, he was put to death, showing no sign of repentance, so stupefied was he and so drunk with the blood of the infinite number of men and women whom he had caused to die in the name of the Lord in the course of the few preceding years." [49]

However, Weyer at times pursues his arguments without caustic scorn and rather with his usual, dry humor. There was a woman who was given to singing, to fainting spells, and other afflictions pointing to possession by the devil; persuasion and other modes of suggestions were of little avail. "No sooner did she start singing than the woman let herself fall to the floor; however, she cast a glance in advance for a

[48] *Ibid.*, vol. I, p. 379.
[49] *Ibid.*, vol. II, pp. 68, 69.

place to fall on most comfortably. Presently the wise and honest lady [in whose house the woman was staying], together with her chambermaid, a girl of gentle spirit, lifted the woman's dress and gave her a few switches quite harshly, without passing the limits of what would be reasonable, of course. This worked so well that the demoniacal woman began to pull her dress down in order to cover and protect herself as best she could. As Hippocrates said, one ought to use strong remedies against strong and pernicious maladies. Thereupon the lady persuaded the sick woman that the medicine she administered to her was a preventive of great virtue against the assault of the devil and that she had learned this from very learned men." [50]

Weyer reviews the preposterous opinions of the learned and the vulgar and the *Malleus Maleficarum* on sexual impotence, and the even more preposterous methods of dealing with this neurotic affliction. He mentions such methods as writing certain mysterious characters on virginal parchment, repeating a psalm of David over it seven times, and tying the parchment to the husband's groin. "I shall say no more and would that such remedies be dispatched to Hell. However, I shall herewith report to the reader quite confidentially, provided he promises me to keep the secret, and tell him another very humorous cure which was practiced with devotions by a woman, Catherine Loë, whose children I know personally. She discovered at the very beginning [of her marriage] that her husband did not possess the virtues of the male. After having tried various expedients to cure him of his trouble, she finally went to the church of Everfeld in the Duchy of Mont and prayed to St. Antony. With great devotion she hung at the Saint's altar a piece of wax which was fashioned to look like the male genital organ. She hoped thus to obtain a cure for her husband. The curé, who knew nothing of the woman's offering, came in and, eyes closed, pronounced the canon of the mass; then, as was his custom, he opened his eyes and raised them upward; he suddenly noticed the offering and knew what it was and cried out loudly and with great anger: Take that devil away from here!" [51]

"There was a melancholic girl in Burg who after having been conjured for a long time confessed that she was possessed by the spirit of

[50] *Ibid.,* vol. II, p. 180.
[51] *Ibid.,* vol. II, p. 184.

Virgil. People believed this with so much more readiness since she was a simple and devout girl who had always lived at home; she was a Tuscanese who tried to speak Mantuan, that is to say the language of Lombardy, and she occasionally let drop a few words in Latin. After the conjurers had wasted time on her, a physician cured her by the Grace of God: first, in accordance with the precepts of his art, he gave her some purgative medicament used in cases of melancholia, then he administered some medicines which had the virtue of fortifying her and making her more comfortable. Thus, after the girl's body was purged, the minister of the Church was able to use his means more easily to expel the evil spirit. For with the natural obstacles removed, he could easily undertake the rest of the treatment." [52]

Passages like this mislead a number of Weyer's readers, making them inclined to think that he himself believed in evil spirits. If one views them in their relationship to the total spirit of the book, one is impressed with the fact that Weyer seems to have known more than he himself suspected. To him the "evil spirit" means illness, since in speaking of the priest's efforts following successful medical intervention he uses the word "treatment" or "cure." This is one of the earliest references to purely psychological treatment, which the French psychiatrists of the nineteenth century called "moral therapy," the German psychiatrists "psychological means of help" (*Psychologische Hilfsmittel*), and which has become known in the twentieth century as "psychotherapy." This method of treating the mentally ill—first putting them in the hands of a physician and then turning them over or leaving them to the good graces of a minister of the Church—has survived till our days, as has the old and worn tradition of considering neuroses inseparably within the province of the Church and its alleged psychotherapeutic wisdom. There are many churches of various denominations which consider a part of their regular activities the treatment of neuroses and even more serious but not properly recognized mental illnesses. It would be a mistake, however, to impute to Weyer the considered approval of this type of psychotherapy. What he stresses are such innovations—almost revolutionary wisdom—as consulting a physician when an executioner is stuporous or when a girl is possessed with the spirit of Virgil. It was indicative of the coming victory of med-

[52] *Ibid.*, vol. II, p. 153.

icine over stubborn, self-satisfied ignorance that Weyer was inspired to report such cases. He knew that the answer to the problem was to be found in medicine; he knew that the doctors were woefully inadequate; he knew also that medicine itself was not yet ready to meet the problem. He felt that a psychiatry must be created, and he sensed that if it was to be created it would be brought about by medicine and not by theology, philosophy, or jurisprudence. That is why, no matter how conservative, Galenic, and seemingly unimaginative his psychophysiology was, once Weyer had become steeped in the subject he could permit his intuition to combine itself with his humanism and broad sympathies. Thus, although he left us no system, no well-rounded theory—in fact no theory at all—he actually viewed the psychopathological problems of his day with an empirical matter of factness which proved revolutionary in the history of medical psychology.

When he has to deal, for instance, with a number of mild and even with more severe epidemics of mental diseases, his approach is bafflingly simple and disarming. "If there are several bewitched or demoniacal persons in one place, as we ordinarily see it to be the case in monasteries, particularly in convents among the women . . . it is necessary first of all that they all be separated and that each of the girls be sent to her parents or relatives. In this way they could be better enlightened and cured. One must, however, consider each procedure in accordance with the needs of each girl." In other words, Weyer recognizes the element of mass contagion and, most important, the need for individual treatment of the mentally ill. Separating the girls and sending them to their respective homes meant but one thing: creating a set of conditions under which each afflicted girl could be treated as a separate person, and not as a corporeal generality in the manner of the *Malleus* or of traditional law.

Weyer refuses to be impressed by the weight of traditional authority and is also devoid of anxiety when he embarks upon a new path. Hence, he looks around quietly in what might be called unpuzzled disbelief. We remember how the *Malleus* stressed the sexual aspects of witchcraft. Sexual ignominy occupied the central place in the system of demonological psychiatry. Weyer studies all the views of the monks, lawyers, and doctors who would not abandon the errors of the community and states simply that the whole, devilish sexology is a grandiose piece of nonsense. As to the *incubus*, it is not a devil but a sickness—a very typical illness which manifests itself at night. "Those who are tormented by it think in their sleep that a heavy burden is pressing on them; this interferes with their breathing and consequently with their power to give voice and speak. They force themselves to cry out, but they cannot. They have terrifying dreams and they imagine that someone has come to do them harm. . . . Pliny occasionally calls this state 'suppression.' . . . The Arabs, according to Avicenna, called it *Albealilon* or *Alcranum*. Averrhoes called it *Elgadum;* . . . our vulgar expression for it is *Coquemare* or *Cauchemare,* and it seems to denote a sense of heaviness over the stomach. The Alemans called it *Diemarydetuns.* . . . Aristotle spoke of it in his book of sleep and waking. The Greeks named it *Ephialte*—a sort of jumper—inasmuch as it feels as if something jumps upon us. . . . Themison for the same reason calls it *Pnigalie.*" [53] All this is explained on the basis of the humoral theory and the theory of animal spirits in the manner of Galen, but these Galenic reiterations, like the repeated references to Satan, present in Weyer a sort of respectable refrain, almost a mannerism, a kind of secondary garnishing of the basic idea which is an absolute confutation of the prevailing demonology. Weyer asserts that "the man who does not want to remain a blockhead will easily judge that these things do not hold water, that they are absurd and do not deserve our credence." [54]

People who are particularly suggestible or, as Weyer puts it, "people who possess a temperament or a complection which makes them easily obey a persuasion," succumb most frequently to the prevailing mental diseases. "And it is certain that [they are sick] in their sleep as well as in their waking state; they see and hear the same things because their contemplation is arrested and because they have faith [in their illusions]. Rhazes tells us of a man who as a result of madness thought he was a rooster. For several years he would rise at a certain hour to cry in the manner of a rooster." [55]

Time and again Weyer cites his own experiences and observations, betraying a wealth of clinical experience and a great ability to bring out the chief trends in the psychological puzzle. His examples, disclosing

[53] *Ibid.,* vol. I, pp. 388 *et seq.*
[54] *Ibid.,* vol. I, p. 285.
[55] *Ibid.,* vol. II, pp. 249, 250.

the type of trends which then predominated, reveal a striking similarity of the psychoses of that time to those of our own day. The sexual trends are the same, almost without a single change due to time. The megalomanic fantasies, the depressive, self-accusatory reactions—all are clearly defined in the sixteenth century. There is little doubt that they had been as clearly apparent centuries before, but for too many centuries the physician had been interested in man in general and in illness in general rather than in the individual psychology of a personality. Therein lies Weyer's unique contribution: he collected *personal* experience, from his own practice, to explain *persons* and not principles.

"I knew once a melancholic Italian," he relates, "who thought he was the Monarch and Emperor of the whole world, and who said that these titles belonged only to him. He was eloquent, quite at ease, and showed no other signs of illness. Yet he took singular pleasure in certain Italian verses which he composed and in which he discussed the state of Christianity, the differences which occurred because of religion, the methods of quieting the troubles of France and of Flanders; he spoke of all these [problems] as if they had been revealed to him from on high. At every pretext he would announce his titles with the letters R.R. D.D. M.M.—*Rex Regum, Dominus Dominatium, Monarcha mundi.*" [56]

This is a masterpiece of clinical description, for it is succinct, direct, factual, and contains no expression of opinion. It is as a true report of an illness should be, facts leading to opinion and not vice versa. Weyer calls the Italian a "melancholic," an old term connoting depression rather than exaltation. The man he describes was rather at his ease and content with his great and lofty duties, but it is typical of Weyer that he never misses or fails to follow the old terminology, no matter how truly unusual his clinical judgment and scientific daring.

In the course of his work Weyer accumulated a number of examples and clinical illustrations which present a true and solid foundation for a new, descriptive psychopathology, but he never unified his descriptions into what might be called a textbook of mental diseases. There is no doubt that both the *Malleus* and the *De Praestigiis Daemonum* are really textbooks, but the first was intended to prove a false belief, the second to disprove it; they were both polemical torches of propaganda and contention. As Michelet said: "The witch was born out of despair"; and so were these two textbooks. They are manuals of desperate battle tactics, and the medicopsychological aspects of both books are subject to the major goal of the battle. This is true even of Weyer. In his fervent appeals that the physician be designated the guide of the witch he systematized his argument but not his medical psychology. Weyer did recognize that the basis of his medical psychology was derived from his study of the thoughts, the pathological fantasies, and the sum total of his patients' inner life, and not from the few, external abnormalities which were shocking to the journalistic, self-adulatory authorities of the time. "In order that it may not seem strange to you to hear me say, as I have before, that the agencies of the imaginative faculty are thus involved and that the eyes of these poor little women are dazzled [abnormally], I beg you to examine closely the thoughts of those melancholic people, their words, their visions and their actions, whereupon you will recognize to what extent all their senses are deprived by the melancholic humor which is spread over their brains. All this burdens their minds to such a degree that some of them imagine themselves to be animals the gestures and voices of which they try to imitate; some of them think that they are pieces of earthenware and they shy away from passers-by for fear of being broken to pieces; others are afraid of death and yet frequently take their own lives; still others imagine themselves guilty of some crime so that they tremble with horror and are frightened whenever they see someone coming toward them, always fearing that they will be grabbed by the scruff of the neck and made prisoners and put to death by the arm of the law. There was an old nobleman who used to jump out of bed very suddenly, thinking that he was being attacked by his enemies whom (so it seemed to him) he would forcibly catch and lock up in the furnace." [57]

This is a very correct description of a number of schizophrenic fantasies and delusions met with in mental institutions of today. In Weyer's day these delusions and fantasies were but signs of humoral disturbances. Their true meaning and their significance from the standpoint of the causes of mental diseases were not elucidated until almost three hundred and fifty years later, but the clinical records left by Weyer are as alive and permanent as any a modern, experienced clini-

[57] *Ibid.*, vol. I, pp. 303, 304.

cian would gather. Once they are written down, his clinical records give the impression of a very simple task easily performed; this is characteristic of all really scientific truths. Some of the truths established by Euclid and Kepler and Newton also appear simple, and they also have the quality of permanence and immutability, as every scientific truth does once the centuries-old labors of many generations have been patiently completed—at the price of endless physical and spiritual effort and even torture, and of personal life itself.

Weyer continues, "I have seen a man who stubbornly refused to eat and drink, thinking that he was condemned. There are people who are so miserably tormented by little scruples of conscience that they look for five legs in a ram when a ram has but four; they imagine mistakes where there are none and, uncertain of the divine clemency, they weep day and night thinking themselves damned. I knew a man who thought that he saw his brother (who, however, lived very far from him). I knew another sodomite who complained that he always heard passers-by come to cause noise in his ears; even his parents, he said, were doing it; he wrote to me on his own behalf, quite secretly, asking me whether I could not give him some advice since some people had told him that his trouble was in his organ of hearing." [58] Here, as far as is known, is the first clinical, descriptive suggestion that some persecutory trends and auditory hallucinations are psychologically related to homosexuality (mostly unconscious). Weyer apparently enjoyed an extraordinary reputation and not only had the opportunity to examine carefully a great number of patients but evidently corresponded with a number of mentally sick who lived too far to come to see him.

It should be noted how frequently Weyer uses the words "I saw," or "I knew a man or a woman." The advanced minds of his age stressed the importance of personal experience; the early psychological philosophers of the late Renaissance therefore emphasized the importance of self-observation, of introspection. Vives' psychological constructions were all based on courageous analytical introspection. Since Roger Bacon, experience had been the characteristic slogan of all those who had broken or had tried to break away from the deadening authoritarianism of the medieval tradition. The mathematician and the astronomer understood experience as independent observation of the phe-

[58] *Ibid.*, vol. I, p. 307.

nomena of nature, of things outside the individual. This was the direction into which the scientific efforts of Tycho Brahe, Kepler, and Galileo were turned. Throughout the ages, however, the medical psychologist found himself in a very unenviable position. For introspection, even when it is inspired with the most laudable intentions of scientific curiosity, is self-limited and too individualistic, too personal, to warrant the conviction that all other people feel and think and fantasy in the same manner. The knowledge thus obtained is too subjective and it is obviously limited by the scope of the observer's propensities and his psychological proclivities.

On the other hand, the purely objective study of man soon led the early philosophers and medical men to see little more than man's body, and at most only his external behavior. It was the achievement of the twentieth century to evolve a scientific attitude and a method of approach to man which permits us to treat his states of mind, his most intimate thoughts and fantasies as objective facts, as external phenomena characteristic of the person whom we are studying, regardless of our own prejudices and moral or social principles. To attain this achievement it was necessary first to recognize the full value of man as an individual, to rise above authoritarian generalities and treat man as a part of nature, respecting the phenomena of nature regardless of where we find them—in the sky, on the earth, in beast, in man, in slave or in king. In other words, an intimate blend of humanism and naturalism had to be achieved before a medical psychology could be born at all.

In this respect Johann Weyer stands out as the true founder of modern psychiatry and as a true revolutionary genius in the science of man. One would hardly suspect this religious man of undue conceit and frivolity. He was modest, conventional and pious. He liked the simple, homely qualities of undisturbed sedateness and respectability. He was a true forerunner of what we would call today the conservative, neighborly middle class. Yet it was Weyer who was the first physician to become imbued with humanism in matters of psychological medicine. He was the first who knew and who demonstrated to others the importance of seeing patients as they actually are, of recognizing the inner independence of their personalities, and of looking at them and into them as a naturalist, without shock at what he discovered and without flinching at the incongruities and contradictions of human psychology. To Weyer a psychological fact was a fact to be understood and not a phenomenon by which to be aroused or which should be approved or condemned. This explains how he, the bourgeois of the latter part of the sixteenth century, was able to sit down quietly at his desk and jot down for posterity the salient observations which were so foreign to his own personality: "I knew a melancholic who insisted that someone smelled of sulphur and tar. He thought that the food which was offered him smelled of pepper; it was obvious that what he said was actually not so. He also said that his private parts were tormented with so much inflammation and stench that he was painfully afraid that they would rot and die away, yet these parts were found healthy. I could cite here an infinite number of examples in which you could see the senses involved in many ways, by humors and melancholic vapors which affect the basis from which all these monstrous fantasies spring." [59]

The true power of imagination and the role of fantasies in the formation of mental diseases were not appreciated till the very opening years of the twentieth century. Weyer, in this respect too, was a forerunner of our contemporary clinical psychologists. He thinks something must have happened within the individual if his fantasies are abnormal. Neither the individual's senses nor his environment are responsible for his pathological fantasies, but certain inner processes which vitiate even the cold facts of the outside world, so that they are either disregarded or perceived as something else. Weyer, relying on certain writers of the past (Iamblicus) and on certain neoplatonic thinkers of the generation which immediately preceded him (Marsilio Ficino), stresses this point in his rather quaint manner: "But it [imagination] receives unto itself the images of all things; it fashions and represents all the activities of the mind and *adjusts outside things to those within*.[60] . . . It brings out fantasies which go much further than the senses; it goes beyond any senses. . . . It is like a proteus or a chameleon." [61] With striking perspicacity Weyer asserts, as Freud and a number of Freud's psychiatric followers were to prove so much later, that some of the severe mental diseases represent in the waking

[59] *Ibid.*, vol. I, pp. 307, 308.
[60] Italics ours.
[61] Weyer: *Histoires, disputes, etc.* Vol. I, p. 309.

state beliefs and convictions which normally occur merely in dreams and which normally are recognized as dreams.[62] He cites a "very beautiful example of a fantastic woman" and says that "witches do not at all produce the maladies to which they confess being the cause. It is proven by examples that all they tell does not merit being considered and established as truth, but merely as fables." [63] Weyer admonishes his contemporaries in a tone of ironic matter-of-factness to abandon their belief in fantasies. "If you occasionally meet the dangerous wolves which run about the region of Livonia and which are presumed to be witches, such as the Germans call *Werwolf*, realize that these are real wolves who are tormented and driven by the devils to perform tragic [devastation]; this, however, by its diverse and wandering course and action fills the organs of fantasy of those known as 'lycanthropes' . . . to such an extent that they think and confess that they are the authors of these . . . disordered actions, for their imagination is so severely corrupted." [64]

Weyer's contributions can be summarized as follows: He was the first physician whose major interest turned toward mental diseases and thereby foreshadowed the formation of psychiatry as a medical specialty. He was the first clinical and the first descriptive psychiatrist to leave to succeeding generations a heritage which was accepted, developed, and perfected into an observational branch of medicine in a process which culminated in the great descriptive system of psychiatry formulated at the end of the nineteenth century. Weyer more than anyone else completed, or at least brought closer to completion, the process of divorcing medical psychology from theology and empirical knowledge of the human mind from the faith in the perfection of the human soul. He reduced the clinical problems of psychopathology to simple terms of everyday life and of everyday, human, inner experiences without concealing the complexity of human functioning and the obscurity of human problems. He left no theory, no dogmatic philosophy of his own. His was the task of combating misguided dogma, and he studied the field of human relations through free observation and objective evaluation of man in nature, rather than through con-

[62] *Ibid.*, vol. I, pp. 312, 313.
[63] *Ibid.*, vol. I, p. 339.
[64] *Ibid.*, vol. I, p. 321.

sideration of what man might and should be and most of the time is not.

All this Weyer accomplished without developing that cold objectivity which betrays a frigid unconcern about man and which insists that the only thing which matters is the gratification of scientific curiosity. Instead, he repeatedly stressed the fact that he was a physician and that the "sacred art of medicine" must be practiced on man and *for* man. "Love man," he admonished, "kill errors, go into combat for truth without cruelty." [65] He studied theology and history and law because these had to do with man. To those who objected to his legal arguments, he merely replied that it was the duty of the doctor to look for the truth about man wherever he could find it. In this respect Weyer was also the forerunner of the great consciousness of our day that a psychiatrist must not limit himself to a knowledge of anatomy, physiology, internal medicine, surgery, and neurology, but that he must go further into those fields of human activity which reveal man in his totality, that he must acquire sound knowledge of history, sociology, and anthropology.

In the professional personality of Weyer a very old tradition found its first true synthesis. The doctor who once was a priest and later became a layman and scientist was in the course of the centuries almost isolated from the main streams of human activities. Religion, civics, law—all took over the guidance of human affairs, leaving to the doctor only the obvious frailties of the body, like the fracture of a leg, a deep wound, a fever, or a bloody cough. Medicine and surgery were permitted to continue their development and the doctor was permitted to keep his status, but at a very dear price. He had to accept this state of isolation, serve the community (but mostly the lay and ecclesiastic princes and their retinues), and be careful not to trespass beyond the confines of the field assigned to him. The doctor soon learned to be content in his psychosociological confinement and even to accept the prevailing rules of how to avoid a better understanding of the human mind. Psychiatry, almost from the moment it was delivered from the womb of medicine in the days of Hippocrates, was kidnaped and brought up in the strange home of theology and in the flowery, multicolored gardens of abstract philosophy. When the complexities of our cultural development brought forth and imposed upon those who

[65] *Ibid.*, vol. II, p. 289.

stood in a position of leadership the very psychiatric problems which grew and flourished in the soil of man's attempts at adjustment to life, the doctor either paid no attention to these problems or turned away from them as from matters which disturbed his complacent, professional narrowness. He did it naturally, as it were, for he, too, was a man and he, too, was afraid and he, too, had learned to serve the dogmatic errors of an everlastingly frightened world which always loved God but feared Satan, whatever his guises. A Cornelius Agrippa or a Paracelsus fulfilled his role as a medical rebel in the disturbed world of which he was himself a part. The world, including the medical world, treated such men with cruelty and their memories with contempt. The medical profession degenerated into a formalistic, self-satisfied pomposity which had little concern for man and less for his mind.

In the light of these considerations the fervent, revolutionary humanism of Weyer stands out as a phenomenon which must be assessed not merely as a striking episode in medical history, but as a momentous step in the whole history of man. For Weyer had to conquer the field of psychiatry and incorporate it into the field of medicine. Scientific curiosity combined with therapeutic intent and humanism formed a synthesis theretofore unknown. Unlike surgery and general medicine, to which the sick man came to ask for help, psychiatry had to come out into the open fields of human passions and penetrate the jungles of cosmological, metaphysical, and esoteric dogmas. Psychiatry had to liberate the sick from the thorns and tentacles of political prejudice, theological tradition, and legal intricacy. This process of conquest—not complete even today—is in itself a paradoxical phenomenon characteristic of no other branch of medicine. It was Weyer who started the process with relentless conviction, boundless compassion, and great effectiveness.

Wherever he saw mental patients being misused, he fought to square the accounts between persistent dogma and fear. The field of law was teeming with clinical material, and he boldly attacked the Law and lawyers. In this respect he should be considered the first truly scientific and humanistic medicolegal psychiatrist. There were others who stood up in open court accusing the accusers, as did Agrippa in Metz, for instance; but Agrippa's arguments in defense of the poor witch were technical, legal, political, emotional. Weyer's were less revolutionary in external appearance, but more rational and scientific, and more lasting. As we have seen, he disclaimed any validity for the Law's dealing with the confessions of witches and sorcerers. Those confessions themselves, he insisted, were forms of madness, forms of abnormal fantasy, an indication and a part of a severe mental disease in which the whole personality was involved. He raised his voice against the frightful punishment of witches and as always he brought forth ethical, human, and rational arguments. "But I beg of you to permit me to explain this confession in a few words. The fact to which [this witch] confessed, that she had withdrawn from God and joined the devil, is not a civil crime at all; for is there any one of us who does not do similar things? In so far as he who commits a sin is a slave of sin in accordance with the word of Jesus Christ, he who commits a sin is of the devil, since the devil sins from the very beginning. This is how the children of the Lord are distinguished from the children of the devil. Any man who fails to act justly is not a child of God, nor is he who does not love his brother. For Jesus Christ said: He who is not with me is against me." [66] Weyer points out that doing penance is the only cure in such cases, and that the law has no right to have any opinion on the subject, still less to punish the poor sinners.

Since confessions of the kind are of no legal value, Weyer, in consonance with most of the humanists of his day, protests against the misogyny of his age and by means of arguments, demonstrations, and admonitions he comes to the conclusion that in matters of punishment women should receive special consideration: "Women should be punished less than men." [67] He insists that not only the confessions but the alleged or actual deeds of the indicted witches should be viewed in a totally different light. The Law, assuming an extreme attitude on the question of free will, merely followed a cruel tradition devoid of true understanding of people, particularly of mentally sick people. "If there is anyone who wishes conscientiously to maintain that the will must be punished severely, I wish him first of all to distinguish the perfect will of a sane man from that of a man who has started to act with the sense of a troubled spirit, or, if you wish, from the corrupted

[66] *Ibid.*, vol. II, p. 251.
[67] *Ibid.*, vol. II, p. 313.

will of a person who is out of his senses and with which the devil plays his game, as if the person were in the power of someone else. Such a corruption of will could also be imputed to melancholics, to the insane, to little children, about whom one may easily make believe that they have done this or that; the children themselves imagine falsely that this is so. The Lord who knows the heart of man does not permit that all be punished in the same manner as those whose mind is free; so much less should a man permit such things to happen." [68]

Strange as it may seem, this plea of Weyer translated into modern language still stands unanswered for the most part by almost all the courts of the civilized world. The tradition fully established by the penal practices of the medieval world has remained almost unchanged. All the laws governing capital crimes and problems of so-called insanity, as we read them in contemporary penal codes, recognize the concept of so-called legal insanity as different from medical insanity, and the jurist still opposes the medical man today even as he did in the days of Agrippa and Weyer. This is one of the most patent survivals of the psychological and cultural struggle of which Weyer was such an eloquent and impassioned exponent.

As Weyer finished his monumental work, he felt that he had a concluding word to say to the imaginary reader who he hoped would listen to his pleadings without prejudice.

"Gentle reader, I have no doubt that I shall fall [as a result of this book] into the bad graces of some people; to compensate me for the pains I took in accordance with my feeble efforts, they will cover me with calumny and despise the things which they do not understand. For this is the way of the wicked. Others will attempt by any available means to defend the old opinions which have been rooted in the mind of man for many long years; they will try to corroborate them as if by right of custom. There will be still others who will take the opportunity to bite more sharply. The peripatetics, caustic in combat, will at once bring all sorts of miracles and prodigies into the consideration of natural phenomena. They will make a stubborn effort to drag in Plato or Aristotle in support of their faith in the very Holy Scriptures. . . .

"There will be frowning theologians who will cry out and say an injury was done to them by a physician who undertook to explain

[68] *Ibid.*, vol. II, p. 317.

passages from the Holy Scriptures, thus passing beyond the limits of his vocation. . . . My only answer will be that I shall say nothing else but that St. Luke the Evangelist was a physician in Antioch. . . .

"If I have not sufficiently satisfied certain learned and sensitive men of our state—which I certainly confess readily, for I know my limitations—I feel that at least within the limits of my capacity I have offered them an opportunity to weigh and to investigate the whole problem more precisely, by more learned means, in a more orderly manner, with clearer sequence, with more appropriate words, and with arguments more powerful on behalf of truth. If these men admonish and convince me of having committed some errors, I shall be very grateful to them, just as I shall be grateful to all who will do me this favor; for I shall never be ashamed to retract my mistaken views, since I am not at all such a great friend of myself. . . .

"I do not pretend to be so absolutely certain of everything which I propound in this book and I submit it in its totality to the most equitable judgment of the Catholic Church of Jesus Christ, and I stand ready to correct myself if I am convinced that in any part I have made a mistake." [69]

When a supplement to the *Index Librorum Prohibitorum* was published a few years after the above humble lines were written, Johann Weyer's name was listed as that of an *auctor primae classis:* not a line of his writings could be read by a good Catholic communicant. In 1581 his name was put among *auctores secundae classis;* only the reading of the *De Praestigiis* was forbidden. In 1590 the *Index* made Weyer again an *auctor primae classis.* His name remained in this category until it was finally removed at the beginning of this century.

Nine years after the publication of *De Praestigiis Daemonum* the criminal code of Saxony was published under the title *Consultationes Saxonicae* (1572). In it we find the statement: "In the course of the past few years many books have appeared in which sorcery is considered not a crime but a superstition and a melancholy, and these insist violently that it should not be punished by death. The *Wieri rationes* [Weyer's reasonings] *are not very important, for he is a physician and not a jurist.*" [70]

---

[69] *Ibid.*, vol. II, pp. 385–391.
[70] Binz: *op. cit.*, pp. 73, 74. Italics ours.

To be sure, there were some who congratulated Weyer on his efforts, but in many quarters he had the success a rational person would have addressing a crowd of mentally ill.[71] A certain Andreas Masius wrote to Weyer, "It is a raw piece of work put together without sense and understanding. . . . You should work it over in part, and in part destroy it." Scribonius wrote in 1588, "This Weyer insists that the judges should favor witches; because their deeds come from pathological imagination and fantasies and from dormitive drugs; in other words, he claims that the witches only imagine that they have committed crimes, that in reality they have done nothing. He bases his conclusion on nothing else but his wish to take the responsibility off the shoulders of the witches and to free them of any punishment— all this only in order to bring everywhere into play the art and friends of sorcery! Yes, I speak out freely; with Bodinus [Jean Bodin], I believe that Weyer, who defended the witches and the mixers of poisons in all circumstances, is himself a sorcerer and a mixer of poisons. Oh, if only a man like this had never been born, or at least if he had never written a word! Instead he, with his books, offers so many opportunities to people to sin and thus enhance the Empire of Satan." [72]

No wonder Weyer foresaw the possibility of such attacks and spoke in advance of "the overthrowers of Christian Faith" and the "perturbators of the Republic."

The immediate influence of Weyer was not at all great. Protected by his position as personal physician to Duke William, he was able to write and to work. But shortly before Weyer's death a great misfortune occurred: the Duke had a stroke and as a result of a cerebral hemorrhage developed certain mental symptoms which do at times appear in the wake of a stroke. Tongues began to wag: Weyer *was* a sorcerer after all, and the liberal-minded Duke but his accomplice.

Weyer died at his post. In February, 1588, he was called to Tecklenburg to attend a patient. He became ill and died. The church in which he was buried is no longer in existence, nor is his grave. In a book written by one of his opponents, Toppeus, one may find the full inscription from Weyer's grave; among the laudatory enumerations of Weyer's qualities as a physician and a public servant, one reads that he "tired of

[71] *Ibid.*, p. 67.
[72] *Ibid.*, p. 75.

the age he lived in, but with invincible faith in Christ surrendered his soul to the Maker." [73]

While almost nothing is known of Weyer's personal emotions and reactions to the animosity with which the world treated his views, one has little reason to doubt that in his indomitable courage and steadfastness he must truly have felt tired of the age in which he lived.

He did not acquire a true following until almost a century after his death. In the meantime the spirit of the *Malleus Maleficarum* was still alive and active. Scribonius, whose attitude was cited above, was a more typical representative of the time than was Weyer, and Jean Bodin—whom Scribonius mentioned—a learned lawyer and the bitter opponent of Weyer, was the most ardent and the most characteristic proponent of what the dying sixteenth century wished to preserve for history.

VI

JEAN Bodin (1530–1596) was a commoner, born in Angers. He studied law in Toulouse and was admitted to the bar, but soon proved a failure as a trial lawyer; he was not much more successful in consultative practice. He therefore turned to writing books. He was a man of encyclopedic knowledge and of some political acumen and courage. When the Duke of Alençon went to England to sue for the hand of Queen Elizabeth, Bodin accompanied him as his secretary and counselor. The Duke died prematurely. Bodin went to Laon in 1576 and, representing the third estate, served as deputy from Vermandois to the Etats Généraux. For a while he was a favorite of Henri III, but later he opposed the King in the Etats and had to seek favor elsewhere.

Bodin was one of the first to consider the problems of political economy and political sciences in general. In 1577 he published his *Republic*, which made him famous. It was a good treatise on government. Bodin was considered a liberal; he was in favor of freedom of conscience and was thought to be a friend of the Reformation. However, his liberalism concerning matters of current politics appears not to have been so much a result of any special enlightenment as it was due

<hr/>

[73] *Ibid.*, pp. 164, 165.

to the fact that the third estate, even two hundred years before the French Revolution, began to be sufficiently differentiated from the feudal system to assert itself in the political life of the country. Culturally Bodin belonged to the conservative tradition; he looked into the future very little and drew upon the past only in so far as it would help him to support the present and the prevailing views of the Law as it stood.

In 1580 he wrote a book on the *démonomanie* of the witches, adding nothing to and subtracting nothing from the traditional ideas on the subject. The book was about to go to the printer when Bodin heard that Johann Weyer had written a new book, *De Lamiis*, supplementing in some respects the *De Praestigiis Daemonum* which had appeared about ten years previously. Bodin decided to hold up the publication of his own book, for he felt that he had to refute Weyer's views. He added to his *Démonomanie* sixty-five pages dealing only with Weyer.

Bodin's book is not of great interest in itself. A number of books of the kind had been published before and were published after his. Nor does his defense of witch-hunting contain any original or otherwise valuable psychological views. Yet it occupies a conspicuous place in the history of psychological medicine. A challenging refutation of Weyer, it is the unequivocal response of the age to the first psychiatrist in the history of medicine who asserted his right to treat mentally sick people. Through the pen of Bodin theology, law, and political science fulfilled their obligation of locking psychiatry out of the major fields of human activity. The theologians for over a century to come continued to attack Weyer (Delrio, King James I); the legal profession was well represented by Jean Bodin.

Bodin states that only "a very ignorant or a wicked man" could write *De Praestigiis* and *De Lamiis*. Weyer, he admits, is not ignorant; hence, he is wicked. He is a "protector of witches." "I cannot read all this without horror," he exclaims.[74] True, Weyer frequently quotes the Scriptures, but he misrepresents and misinterprets them. The fact that he tries to appear pious and well meaning is only a sham, for if "he did sometimes speak of God and the Law, it is an old imposture that has

---

[74] Jean Bodin: *Réfutation des opinions de Jean Wier*, in *De la démonomanie des sorciers*. Antwerp, 1586, p. 375.

always been used by Satan and his subjects." [75] Weyer is one of Satan's subjects. For was he not the pupil of Cornelius Agrippa, "his master sorcerer," "the greatest sorcerer of the age"? Has not Weyer himself admitted that he led Agrippa's dog on a leash—that black dog which was a devil? [76] That Agrippa published a book refuting his own *Occult Philosophy* is of no consequence; the devil frequently pretends to espouse proper views only to conceal his satanism.

Bodin takes sharp issue with Weyer on the question of differentiating poisoners (*venefici*) from witches and sorcerers; [77] he deems the differentiation faulty. Calling upon a wealth of learning worthy of a more deserving cause, Bodin reviews everything from Greek mythology to Aristotle—the scriptural writers, the Arabs, the Christian theologians, Cicero, all the lawyers, pagan and Christian—and proves to his satisfaction that Weyer is wrong, that a witch and a poisoner are one and the same thing. Everything imputed to witches is true. Everything Weyer denies about witches is a pernicious, impious denial of the truth. Witches do not eat human (baby's) flesh? What about Solomon's allegory of the eagle who feeds his young on blood? Solomon had just this cannibalism of witches and sorcerers in mind, for by the eagle he meant Satan, of course, who feeds his subjects on human blood. Witches cannot be transvected? Was not Christ, with the Lord's permission, lifted aloft by the devil? Did not Romulus and his whole army disappear by the devil's artful arrangement? Were they not lifted into the air en masse and transported elsewhere?

Bodin uses many arguments of forced subtlety regarding physics and metaphysics, accusing Weyer of being a poor physicist and mathematician. But one of the most poignant arguments of refutation is that dealing with Weyer's feminism. "God's law wanted to prove that men are less corrupted with the affliction [witchcraft] than women." [78] There are fifty witches to one sorcerer. Quintilian said that women are worse than men. Plato himself said that woman is a transitional stage from wild beast to man. Women are liars. Women have larger intestines than men—wisdom never comes from women. How dare Weyer

[75] *Ibid.*
[76] *Ibid.*, p. 377.
[77] *Ibid.*, pp. 378 *et seq.*
[78] *Ibid.*, p. 385.

assert that witches are melancholic women? As a physician he should know that men can become melancholic but not women. Women are by nature "cold and humid" and they never suffer from gout; melancholy comes from heat and dryness. How could women develop that disease of men? Bodin is disgusted with the "fanatical errors of those who want to defend women as melancholics." [79]

Weyer also denies that there exists a pact between Satan and the witch and the sorcerer. This denial is an act of wickedness; Weyer as a physician should know better, or he ought not to trespass into domains foreign to his calling. "A simple consent suffices to make a pact. This pact can be concluded with or without stipulation, without a word, without writing, just by a wink and, according to the law, *mutu solo,* by a mere nod of the head." [80] At every point Bodin reminds us sarcastically that Weyer was a physician; as a physician he should have accepted and not denied the theory that the devil, appearing in the guise of an *incubus* or *succubus,* has sexual intercourse with human beings. Bodin refutes Weyer's theory of nightmares with one stroke of the pen. "The obstruction of the liver and the oppression of the spleen cannot affect healthy and gay women"; [81] only witches show signs of this. States of unconsciousness are but other manifestations of the devil's power over his human subjects. Ecstasy and stupor seem to interest Bodin only in so far as the soul does return to the body after consciousness is regained. This serves him as clinical proof of the immortality of the soul, for which the body serves as a prison according to Orpheus. Empedocles and Zoroaster called it a tomb; Socrates, a cavern; Plato called it *soma,* which comes from *sema,* which again means tomb.

Having thus established complete contempt for the body, Bodin seems preoccupied with the future of the law and the courts. He knows that these are powerless against Satan's widespread authority. He knows, too, that the law must be so devised that it will impede Satan's effectiveness. "The judges cannot bring Satan into court, but they can diminish the scope of his power by taking from him those witches who help him, pray to him, pay obeisance to him, and carry out his instructions." [82] This conclusion set down clearly the principle of punish-

[79] *Ibid.,* p. 390.
[80] *Ibid.,* p. 395.
[81] *Ibid.,* p. 397.
[82] *Ibid.,* p. 405.

ment. It is not a question whether this or that punishment is deserved; it is a question of the systematic elimination of the servants of Lucifer from the community. It is the duty of the community, as represented by the judicial arm, to cling to its lofty duty and to enforce with fervor and with rigor the standards of good and evil, right and wrong. Any interference with the discharge of this duty marks one not only as a bad citizen, but as a wicked man, an accomplice of the Great Doer of Evil. A physician who waves his medical flag a bit too threateningly against the judicial branch of the government is an even more dangerous defender of Satan, for the human art of medicine might serve as too attractive a screen for concealing the ill will of the true collaborators of the devil.

Thus, in the personality of Bodin the Law defied medicine with a strict and uncompromising "No Trespassing." The problem of the relationship between medicine and law is a very old one, of course, but it was Weyer who was the first in the history of medicine to present a systematic criticism of that branch of the law governing the punishment of the mentally sick, and it was Bodin's questionable honor to be the first to respond negatively to this legitimate demand of medicine. To Bodin belongs the credit for having stated the grievances—voiced today in almost the same language—which the bar and the bench had against the medical psychologist. In this lies the historical importance of Bodin's *Refutation of Johann Weyer's Opinions;* Bodin brought into sharp focus the irrational divergence of opinion between medicine and law in all criminal cases in which a death sentence is mandatory and in which a plea of insanity is interposed. In such cases the Law always disregarded the advances made by medical science, and Bodin formulated the reasons. "If Weyer's sophisms and those of his wonderful doctors held good, the thieves and robbers might always appeal for mercy by blaming the devils for their deeds; and since the officers of the law have no jurisdiction or power against the devils, one might as well cancel and erase all those divine and human laws which deal with the punishment of crimes. This type of argument [Weyer's] was used by an Academic against Posidonius the Stoic, to demonstrate the absurdity of the doctrine of fatal necessity. This principle was based on the assumption of certain jurists who variously interpreted the law of God to the effect that an offender, if he acted under compulsion, should be acquitted. This fatal necessity cannot be considered by the law. Posidonius saw the point and to avoid such absurdities he renounced his opinion. . . . Therefore, Weyer and those good doctors should not protest against the punishment of witches and sorcerers. . . . Weyer and his good doctors insist that one must not set too much store in confessions unless these deal with things that are true and possible. I agree with him. But his assumption that nothing is possible in law that is not possible in nature is not only wrong but wholly impious." [83]

Bodin, citing the Lord's "fury and vengeance" against idolatry, treats Weyer with the same words of fury and vengeance. Weyer's insistence that things which are contrary to nature cannot happen arouses him to particular anger. "Men cannot cause hail and thunderstorms or make the harvest perish by natural means; but such things *are* accepted as facts by the law, though they cannot happen naturally. Persons who avail themselves of such [unnatural] means are sentenced to death. This goes to show clearly that pagan and divine laws do accept some things as facts which, though impossible by nature, are possible in spite of the course and order of nature. Weyer and his accomplices would gladly eliminate these laws, the statutes, and the penal codes." [84]

All the claims and arguments of Weyer on this medicolegal problem Bodin considers merely "dialectic incongruities." Bodin's assertion that what may prove not true in nature may still be true in the law stood the test of centuries and with remarkable conspicuousness and tenacity, *mutatis mutandis*, it was preserved in the penal codes of Europe and America. This assertion of Bodin appears in our law books in the form of the differentiation between "medical" and "legal" insanity: a man who commits a capital crime and who interposes a plea of insanity may be adjudged "legally sane" even if he is in reality "medically insane."

A generation after Bodin, Paul Zacchias (1584–1659), the first physician who devoted himself almost exclusively to medicolegal problems, who may be considered the founder of legal medicine, deviated little from the views of Bodin on the problem with which Weyer so boldly confronted the Law. Zacchias, the personal physician of Pope Innocent X, brought about a helpful co-operation between doctor and

[83] *Ibid.*, pp. 409–411.
[84] *Ibid.*, p. 412.

jurist in many problems of civil and criminal procedure. But scientific medicine and the Law did not seem able to find a point of convergence unless the medical man in contradiction to his medical convictions accepted the psychological concepts of the statute books. Today the psychiatrist and the jurist are unable to find any point in common in any case of capital crime unless the psychiatrist subscribes to the meaningless, Bodinesque principle that what is true in psychiatry may not be true in law.

At least as far as the law in the English-speaking world is concerned, this principle stood fast, only changing in language and mode of argumentation. Lord Hale (1609–1676), following the tradition of which Bodin was such an able exponent, formulated his views in his *Pleas of the Crown*. Lord Hale himself convicted two witches to death. He was more convinced of his views than his scientific competence warranted, and his influence was greater than his knowledge. "The moon," he said, "hath a great influence on all diseases of the brain, especially in this kind of dementia: such persons, commonly in the full and change of the moon, especially about the equinoxes and summer solstice, are usually at the height of their distemper. . . . But such persons as have their lucid intervals (which ordinarily happens between the full and change of the moon) in such intervals have usually at least a competent use of reason." [85] This principle of Lord Hale's is still prevalent in present-day criminal law; it is known as "partial or temporary insanity," a concept of purely legalistic origin devoid of any medicopsychological foundation. Enlightened legal minds and medical men have combated this encroachment of the Law on medical knowledge, but with infinitesimal success. Lord Hale's insistence on total insanity as the only condition relieving a criminal from legal responsibility was but a reassertion of the Law as it governed the innumerable trials of witches and sorcerers.

It is striking and not a little discouraging to those who continue to follow the open road which was discovered by Weyer to find that as late as 1800, almost two and a half centuries after Weyer's *De Praestigiis Daemonum*, the courts of justice were still able to speak the language of Lord Hale and Bodin but unable to understand the lan-

[85] Lord Hale: *Pleas of the crown*. Quoted by Henry Weihofen: *Insanity as a defense in criminal law*. New York, The Commonwealth Fund, 1933, p. 3.

guage of Weyer. "On the trial of Hadfield, for shooting at the King [George III] in Drury Lane theatre, in 1800, there occurred for the first time, in an English criminal court, anything like a thorough and enlightened discussion of insanity as connected with crime; and the result was that a fatal blow was given to the doctrines of Lord Hale by Mr. Erskine, who brought all the energies of his great mind to bear upon the elucidation of this subject. In accordance with these doctrines, the attorney-general had told the Jury that to protect a person from criminal responsibility there must be a total deprivation of memory and understanding. To this Mr. Erskine very justly replied that if these expressions were meant to be taken in the literal sense of the words—which however he did not deny—'then no such madness ever existed in the world.' " [86]

Hadfield was a war veteran who had been discharged from the army on the ground of insanity. He suffered from what we would call today a paranoid type of schizophrenia; he felt that he should sacrifice himself in the manner of Jesus Christ in order to save the world. He therefore decided to shoot the King, to be executed as a result, and consequently to be duly sacrificed for the salvation of the world. Erskine described dramatically his conception of what mentally ill persons were and pointed out that such persons "have in general been remarkable for subtlety and acuteness. Defects in their reasonings have seldom been traceable—the disease consisting in the delusive sources of thought:—all their deductions, within the scope of their malady, being founded on the *immovable* assumptions of matters as *realities,* either without any foundation whatever, or so distorted and disfigured by fancy, as to be nearly the same thing as their creation." [87] This statement established the principle of recognizing delusions (on certain occasions only!) as a valid component of legal insanity. But even Erskine was not fully convinced of his own eloquent formulation, for in another case he stated that "his counsel could not show that any morbid delusion had overshadowed his understanding." [88]

The more enlightened opinion of Erskine did not prevail. The Law proceeded in its own way and in the criminal courts of today, almost

[86] I. Ray: *Medical jurisprudence of insanity.* Boston, 1838, pp. 27, 28.
[87] *Ibid.,* p. 28.
[88] *Ibid.,* p. 29.

four hundred years after Weyer and Bodin had their dispute before the forum of the learned world, the authority of Jean Bodin stands guard, refusing to admit the plea of Johann Weyer for the same reason given by the Saxon criminal code: he was a doctor and a psychiatrist, not a lawyer. Certain partial, very conditional exceptions do exist, of course. The State of New Hampshire, to some extent the Briggs Law of the Commonwealth of Massachusetts, and certain aspects of the criminal law recently recodified in Mexico show an enlightened deflection from Bodin and a willingness to adhere to the humanism and medicopsychological perspicacity of Weyer. But these are only exceptions. The psychological attitude toward the criminal, the hatred of the witch and the sorcerer as an emotion of "fury and vengeance" proved much stronger determinants in civilized justice than did rational science. The straight line of jurisprudence which presents the succession, idolater—heretic—witch—sorcerer—insane murderer, remains both psychologically and historically unbroken. The contempt for Weyer's "good doctors" whom Bodin accused of "apostasy of urine," if not as intense as in 1584, has percolated into modern jurisprudence in sufficient concentration to make Bodin a figure of the first magnitude in the history of the struggle on the part of psychiatry for the possession of its rightful domain.

The sixteenth century, so horrible and so glorious, was destined to point the way in two directions, toward obscurantism and enlightenment. Such progressive and humanistic concepts in modern law as that of the "irresistible impulse" were fully and clearly stated by Weyer. In the language of today this concept means that man may be considered not responsible for his crime if he acted under the influence of an uncontrollable compulsion, arising from inner, pathological, emotional reactions. As Bodin states it in the language of the sixteenth century, it was "fatal necessity"; Bodin opposed the recognition of this concept, which he considered apostatic and criminal. Only about one hundred years ago two American judges were enlightened enough to make the first serious attempt to recapture the spirit of Weyer's plea and give this concept the substance of legal precedent. Chief Justice Shaw of Massachusetts and Chief Justice Gibson of Pennsylvania began to formulate their opinions and charges to juries in terms of the concept of irresistible impulse. In the main, the objections raised by great legal authorities throughout the nineteenth century and even today against the recognition of the irresistible impulse as a valid plea of legal insanity were and are the same as those which Bodin raised against fatal necessity. The admission of this plea as a legal principle "would open the door for the escape of criminals," [89] "would be the cover for the commission of crime and its justification, rendering persecution for crime impossible," [90] or "it would mark the end of civilization." "It will be a sad day for this state," one court foreboded, "when uncontrollable impulse shall dictate a 'rule of action' to our courts." [91]

Today the principle of "fatal necessity" of the sixteenth century, the "irresistible impulse" of contemporary usage, stands adopted by only seventeen [92] states of the Union and by the United States Supreme Court (1895).[93] The accusation of "dialectic incongruity," which Bodin threw in the face of Weyer's psychiatry, has not been vindicated, although with the centuries it has lost a considerable part of its scornful sting. Medical psychology is still but a stepchild of jurisprudence, as it was a stepchild of theology in previous centuries. The road which Weyer pointed out was long and arduous and its end is apparently not yet near. But it can be said, at least, that the sixteenth century made its exit into history with the platform of medical psychology finally stated.

[89] See Weihofen: *op. cit.*, p. 61.
[90] *Idem.*
[91] *Idem.*
[92] Weihofen: *op. cit.*, p. 64 (1933).
[93] Davis *v.* U.S. 160 U.S. 469, 16 Sup. Ct. 353.

8

THE AGE OF RECONSTRUCTION

I

THE Renaissance discovered man. It was a mighty flood of light
sweeping into a bleak world. It was the revival of the classical
tradition of viewing man and nature as a unit, one and indivisible. The effort it required was both magnificent and painful; it was
heroic daring and martyrdom of body and soul combined. It created
more problems than it solved and more suffering than joy. Michelangelo Buonarroti sought to tell in stone and color what Weyer attempted by word and deed: to tell man that he is human, that the
wisdom of the Lord does not compromise the wisdom of nature or
the wisdom of human and animal organization. Both Michelangelo
and Weyer were personal failures in the very greatness of their performance. Both worked incessantly and hard; both were tormented
with the need to bring about a greater respect for the wonder that is
man; both died leaving behind them a world unsettled and fretful, a
world unwilling or unable to abandon its morose insistence that man
does not matter, that he is but a frail, sinful, corruptible, and corrupted
being, and that life is but a pious anticipation of death.

It was the lot of the sixteenth century to become the battleground
of all the conflicts which raged in man, State, and Church. The outcome
of the battle was not settled in the sixteenth century; the struggle went

on with unremitting force. It will be remembered that in the second year of the century Magnus Hundt published his *Anthropologia*. As if symbolizing the ideological status of the age, Delrio's *Disquisitionum Magicarum* appeared in the last year of the century, a short time before Giordano Bruno was burned. Delrio referred to the father of modern psychiatry as *Wierus Hereticus*.

The old world would not surrender willingly; the new world just born was too young to fight a winning battle, yet too vigorous to succumb. As a result a singular confusion reigned over the thought of man as history entered the seventeenth century. The center of interest was man and his relation to nature and nature and its relation to man. This statement of the problem may appear trite to the present-day reader, for he, born to a scientific age, lives almost from the cradle with this problem. It is to him both a preoccupation and a game. He enjoys pondering over it and he is forever thrilled or horrified by the awareness of his struggle with nature for the mastery of the world. His technological achievements leave him with little doubt of his worth to himself and others, or of his strength to assert himself and to command others. The man of the seventeenth century was not so certain of himself. He wondered. He was anxious. He was curious and he was frightened. Galileo was not a coward when he stood in agony before those who admonished him to abandon his scientific endeavors. There must have lurked in him an anxious doubt of his own views on the world. He was ready to recant what he himself found to be true, and then to reassert in a tortured whisper that "the earth does move." This was the tragedy of the man of the first half of the seventeenth century. The Copernican conclusion that the world was not the center of the universe was no mere breaking with a false, traditional dogma. The tradition which Copernicus, Kepler, and Galileo were called upon by history to break had deep roots in human emotions. Their seemingly innocent and serene scientific curiosity led them to the sudden and discomforting realization that this earth in which we live is not the center of everything, that the sun and the moon and the stars are not in the heavens merely to serve man so that he can serve the beyond and the unknown, that the earth is but one of perhaps many worlds rushing around the sun with relentless regularity and precision and unrevealed purposiveness.

The transition from the geocentric to the heliocentric theory of the universe threatened to and did put an untold burden on man's mind. The consciousness of his frailty was perhaps increased, but the awareness that he must become his own free master became rather keen. His curiosity was sharpened and his eagerness to solve the mystery of his own nature and of nature as a whole became intense. Strangely, he seemed suddenly to lose interest in that which he had become accustomed to call his soul, and in its immortality. He was ready to leave this puzzle to the theologian and thus to abandon his concern with the feeling that the soul was in good hands. But the theologian, jealous of his own conception of life, and fearful that it might be desecrated by truth not revealed but independently acquired by the sheer effort of man himself, was not yet ready to permit man to shed his age-long concern. The theologian hated Weyer and Galileo, and theology continued its efforts to turn the awakened scientific curiosity away from purely observational, empirical reasoning and bring it back into the fold of revelatory contemplations.

Thus the scientist—at the very time when vistas of unforeseen knowledge revealed themselves before his eyes—had to sacrifice his scientific interest in the human mind, so frequently confused with the soul. Consequently the seventeenth century, and for that matter the greater part of the eighteenth, presents a striking paradox: the scientist and the physician, so seriously concerned with nature and man, gave up their preoccupation with the human mind and left it partly to the theologian who had always claimed it as his own domain and partly to the enlightened layman-philosopher who began to appear in an increasing number. Knowledge as a whole became more and more secularized, more and more free from the postulatory thinking of the theologians. It would, therefore, be a mistake indeed to assume the view that it was the Church and theology which militated against the scientific development of psychology; it was man and man alone who was responsible. He was afraid of self-knowledge and whatever his social guise, ecclesiastical or secular, he seemed to prefer to consider least matters which concerned the nature of his mind. The more pervasive his curiosity, the more he became preoccupied with things outside himself. Thus the efflorescence of scientific activity marked, rather paradoxically, a partial but definite turning away from the problems of medical psychology, from the problems of mental disease, its nature, its manner of development, its rational control.

II

THE scientist was coming into his own, and he was preoccupied with the magnitude of his task: to steal as many secrets as possible from nature. He came out of his personal isolation. He no longer limited himself to working alone in his own study and occasionally supplementing his gropings by a conversation or exchange of letters with friends or colleagues, as Agrippa, Weyer, Vives, Erasmus, and Paracelsus had. He now felt the need for constant contact with his colleagues; the cumulative effect of this need was so great that shortly after the century passed its midpoint a number of associations of scientists were organized. The Accademia del Cimento was founded in Florence in 1657, with Galileo, Torricelli, and Borelli as its most illustrious members. The Royal Society of London was founded in 1662, with Newton, Boyle, Hooke, and Christopher Wren, and a number of physicians as well, among the members. The Académie des Sciences came into being in Paris in 1666. Leibnitz, the mathematician and philosopher, drew up the plan for the Berlin Akademie, founded in 1700. Eight years before, a society of German physicians had been organized under the name of Academia Naturae Curiosi; the group started a publication dealing with matters of medical research. The *Philosophical Transactions* of the Royal Society began to be published in 1664, the *Journal des Savants* the following year. These academies and their publications functioned under the patronage of the State and its princes, but the social security of the scientist was far from fully established. The Accademia del Cimento, for instance, was disbanded in 1667 and some of its members were prosecuted by the Inquisition; one of them, Antonio Oliva, was put in prison, where he committed suicide.

But the influence of the Inquisition was ebbing; the Church was no longer able to exert its all-inclusive control over scientific thought. From within the Church itself, even from among those to whom absolute obedience was the cornerstone of faith, voices began to be heard against the tradition of witch-hunting and against the cruelties of the day. The saintly Jesuit Friedrich von Spee is a case in point. He protested against the principles and the procedures which were sanctified by the *Malleus Maleficarum* and he fought violently in defense of his ideas.[1] Science was flourishing, throwing off old fetters by the sheer power of devotion to truth and by the systematic unveiling of new facts and new phenomena of nature, by a new insight, and by intellectual integrity and perspicacity.

The age of tormented restlessness of which men like Agrippa and Paracelsus and to some extent Galileo were the colorful representatives, the age of quixotic combats, was definitely receding. The new scientist was a rather conservative, placid, modest man who loved learning and shied away from fervent proselytism. Newton with his quiet, contemplative modesty and earnestness now represented the spirit of scientific endeavor. The primary interest was astronomy, optics, and physics. These disciplines served as the groundwork for the future growth of zoology, botany, and chemistry. Man's reason came into its own, so to speak, and careful, logical, systematic, orderly, and methodical reasoning became the basis of cultural life. The dictum of Descartes, *cogito ergo sum*, was the true expression of the age. It was both the point of departure and the foundation of the rationalism and enlightenment which mark the eighteenth century.

The scientist-physicist soon discovered that his experiments and observations were handicapped by lack of proper instruments, and a number of new instruments appeared. Jansen invented the compound microscope; Hooke of the Royal Society developed microscopy as a technique of research and published his *Micrographia* in 1664. Telescopes were constructed in England and in Holland. The thermometer was gradually evolved by Galileo, Santorio, and Drebbel. Torricelli invented the barometer and Guericke the air pump. The study of nature no longer meant the mere observation of it in its totality and the production of an inspired synthesis, an all-embracing philosophy. Looking into details and seeking out new facts, experimenting, collecting empirical data, and calculating became the most important and the strongest links in the chain of science. Magnetism began to be studied, and electricity was observed and included among the natural

---

[1] Von Spee's *Cautio criminalis, etc.* appeared in 1631.

phenomena by Queen Elizabeth's personal physician, Gilbert, and by Newton. Boyle founded the theory of chemical elements. The word "gas" (the *chaos* of Paracelsus) was introduced by van Helmont, who revived some of the ideas which Paracelsus had held on the *archeus*. Brand discovered the phenomenon of phosphorescence.

These scientific advances continued rapidly into the eighteenth century. The thermometer was perfected by Fahrenheit, Réaumur, and Celsius. Galvani made his preparation of the frog on which he demonstrated the passage of electric currents in muscles. The work of Stahl and particularly of Priestley, Cavendish, and Lavoisier advanced the chemistry of gases and combustion. The classificatory botanical studies of Linnaeus, who was himself a physician, made history. As if suddenly, anatomy and physiology, under the influence of physics, mathematics, and chemistry, developed to an extraordinary degree. The great work of Vesalius was a contribution to the statics of the human body. The question of muscles and bones acting as a complex system of levers began to interest the anatomist. The physics of fluids permeated gradually into the minds of those who studied the human body. In 1628 William Harvey published his discovery of the circulation of blood. Microscopy permitted the investigator to go beyond the mere observation of the gross phenomena of the cardiovascular system: Borelli discovered the minute blood vessels, the *capillaria*; Malpighi made the direct observation of the circulation of blood in capillaries; Hooke was able to describe the plant cell. The human body began to be understood as a physicomathematical apparatus. Descartes' term *l'homme machine* is a reflection of the vogue in which physics was held and of the profound impression it made on the whole course of scientific thought for the centuries to come. Glisson thought of the nerves and other organs as assemblies of minute fibers which all possessed the quality of *irritability*—automatic response to stimuli, as we would say today.

By way of emphasis of the true scientific spirit of the time, one may say that now only very rarely a voice from the past was heard, and that voice was now more a curiosity than an authority. Thus Thomas Petrucci, who published a book on adrenal glands in 1675, still deemed it necessary to support the demonstration of these organs by a reference to Leviticus in which the discovery of the glands was supposed to be prophesied.[2] The general trend of the scientific investigator was now away from theological references. To be sure, the emphasis on piety continued as a part of the decorum of respectability and reliability, but the age of authoritarian dogma was coming rapidly to an end. Empirical knowledge, wariness about too many hypotheses, an interest in and a respect for the tangible and visible and verifiable commanded the mind.

The medical man for the first time in the history of science became a conscious and deliberate beneficiary of the efforts of scientific research. No longer a medical product of dogmatic tradition, he was now an iatro- (medical) physicist, or an iatromathematician. He was equally responsive to the rising sun of chemistry, the intuitive conceptions of which he traced to Paracelsus. Van Helmont's elaborations on the subject found their sequential continuation in the works of Georg Ernst Stahl (1660–1734), particularly in his phlogiston theory, which sought to create a more specific conception of heat in the human body than the general abstractions suggested by Aristotle. Stahl's thought was in many respects a reaction against the growing influence of the mechanistic trends of the iatrophysicist. It was coincidentally an attempt to formulate a theory which would enable the physician to include mental diseases in the orbit of his investigation and control.

The iatrochemist perhaps a little more than the iatrophysicist paid attention to the problem of health and disease and life and death. Neither of them, however, no matter how scientific the new mathematicophysical and chemical terminology appeared, was as yet able, particularly when considering mental diseases, to reach out beyond speculative assumptions. There was the question of life and death, and the question of the origin or generation of life. The members of the Royal Academy regularly used to dissect the bodies of executed criminals and animals; they were particularly active in doing this under the presidency of Samuel Pepys. They were considerably puzzled by the appearance of maggots in the decaying flesh of dead human and animal bodies. Here was life come from nothing and from nowhere. The little animals had been seen before: "For if the sun breed magots in a dead dogge, being a good kissing carrion";[3] but the question of

[2] Diepgen: *Geschichte der Medizin*. Vol. III, p. 60.
[3] *Hamlet*: II, 11.

the meaning of this appearance of life—spontaneously generated—had never been raised with such acute curiosity and scientific persistence. The question was how to determine the natural, that is, biological, meaning of life and how to recognize living tissues and living things. Glisson's suggestions as to the property of irritability of organ fibers not only meant that he pointed out a phenomenon. They also meant that a new problem had arisen: the origin or nature of this irritability as a manifestation of life. Stahl and Friedrich Hoffmann (1660–1742) sought for a concept of life which would at once harmonize with the growing body of physicochemical knowledge and also permit them to avoid the pitfalls of theological preoccupations. Hoffmann reintroduced the old Hippocratic idea of a life force and was preoccupied with the differentiation of living from dead bodies; he thought of the normal tension, of the tonus of muscles and other organs as the expression and distinguishing sign of life.

This concept, however, did not at once acquire or result in any practical values, since the center of attention was the empirical study of the phenomena of life; it was physiology rather than natural philosophy which preoccupied the physician. Hoffmann investigated the chemical changes of the human body and he looked to chemistry for an answer to the treatment of diseases. Many combinations of various chemicals were introduced; they were not as complex and mysterious as the long recipes of Paracelsus, and they appeared to be both more practical and more effective. "Hoffmann drops," a mixture of approximately one part ether and two parts alcohol, are still in use today.

Toward the middle of the eighteenth century the medical man seems to have become fully convinced that the answer to his many problems was to be found only in a thorough knowledge of anatomy, physics, and chemistry, that the three combined would gain him a thorough knowledge of physiology. The greatest contribution to this field was made by the genius of Albrecht von Haller (1708–1777), who was the true founder of modern, experimental physiology. He evolved more authoritatively the concepts of the sensibility or irritability of body tissues, particularly of the nerves. Harvey proclaimed that every living being must grow out of an egg (ovum); embryology became a part both of the newly born physiology and of biology. But the riddle of the life force, its origin and manner of action, remained unsolved, of course.

The physician turned partly philosopher; on the other hand the philosopher himself, turning more and more toward rationalism, found it difficult to refer and to defer to the older theurgic views. He was profoundly influenced by the rapidly growing body of biological knowledge; consequently he offered certain abstractions as a consolation. Descartes, who described the reflex reactions to certain nerve stimuli, was satisfied to look upon man as a machine and saw in the process of reasoning a sign and proof of being, that is, living. In conformity with the age-long tradition, Descartes denied animals a soul and considered them mere machines. Yet animals were living things and not simple, mechanical toys. Leibnitz, himself a mathematician, was more interested in the problem which Descartes seems to have brushed aside. Leibnitz created his theory of monads. The monad is, strictly speaking, an irreducible entity, a force; it is neither material nor immaterial. It is a deepened and complex concept of the life force which has preoccupied the biological philosophers from ancient Greece to our own day. It is this concept of the monad which led Caspar Friedrich Wolff (1733–1794) to his ideas of *epigenesis* according to which every body and every body organ grows out of the living forces inherent in a primary substance without definite form, a substance which today we call protoplasm. The idea of life force, the *principe vital*, entered into and took a prominent place in medicopsychological thought. The University of Montpellier, through Bordeau and particularly Barthez, was the carrier of this trend, which became known as vitalism. The trend proved of immeasurable importance in the history of medical psychology. On the one hand, Philippe Pinel, colleague and to some extent follower of Barthez, proved to be the great reformer and revolutionary reorganizer of hospital psychiatry; and on the other, the same trend served as a stimulus to the development of neurology and also of the theory of instincts which Freud introduced early in the twentieth century.

As ONE reviews the great progress which observational and experimental sciences made in the seventeenth century and as one finds such names as Deleboë, Daniel Sennert, Thomas Sydenham, and Thomas Willis gracing the roster of clinical medicine, one is justified in anticipating a corresponding growth of medical psychology. And yet to the historian it is as impressive as it is disappointing to discover that Weyer is hardly, if ever, mentioned in the medical treatises by the great clinicians of the time, and that mental disease occupies but a secondary place in their systems of medicine. There has never been a dearth of psychopathological material, and the seventeenth century was rich in demonopathies, theomanias, convulsive ecstatic states and stupors. Mentally sick abounded in cities and in villages. They were in prisons and cellars; they wandered in the streets of the town and on the highways, to the amusement of the populace and occasionally to its horror. The doctor could not fail to notice them, but it does seem that he did little more than that. He seldom studied or attempted to understand them. It would seem as if medicine deliberately turned away from mental disease. This very puzzling indifference of the Hippocratic fraternity is of great historical meaning, for it not only kept psychiatry behind the general course of medical science but also reflected an unspoken fear and a frequently outspoken hatred of the mentally ill. Apparently the demonological tradition was still strong in the mind of the seventeenth century, and the conservative caution of the medical man seems to have rejoiced at the opportunity to turn attention to biological sciences and thus be well rid of the disagreeable and fear-provoking problems which Weyer so squarely laid at the door of Medicine, the Church, and the Law. The physician of the seventeenth century was not only an empirical scholar; he was a student of books. He knew well the atmosphere of the bedside and the dignified quiet of his library or study, or the thrilling moroseness of the dissecting room. But he knew nothing of the dungeons and the prisons where most of the mentally sick were kept in filth and in chains, nor was he attracted by the scaffold or the bonfire. Hence he seems to have almost completely missed the mentally sick.

The seventeenth century was the century in which Greek medicine was finally revived in all the glory of its rational, clinical, observational approach. Paracelsus' vituperations against Galen bore fruit. Galen was still studied and some of his inaccuracies were still followed, but it was the spirit of Hippocrates which asserted itself after almost twenty centuries of cultural exile. Men like Thomas Sydenham (1624–1689) were the worthy carriers of the revived tradition. Sydenham was a practicing physician. He studied the patient, his symptoms, the course of his illness, the relationship of such environmental factors as climate and weather on the course of the given illness. He was successful with his patients; he cared little about theories and less about general assumptions.

One is not able easily to rid oneself of the impression that the very progress of clinical medicine militated against the progress of psychiatry. The learned doctors knew well what Hippocrates had to say about mania and melancholia and the black bile, but this classificatory and humoral wisdom failed to fit very well into the picture of men roaming about asserting that the devil was seducing their wives, or of women swooning into frightening stupors and writhing in convulsions, constantly invoking ghosts and other weird visions. For the practical and the strictly clinical, Hippocrates no longer sufficed. The world had gone through many tragic changes since the Age of Pericles—economic, spiritual, military, racial. Christianity had established itself as a faith and an institution. Protestantism had shaken the Christian world, unleashing most unchristian animosity, venom, and bloodshed. The feudal system had developed to its peak and was beginning to show signs of disintegration; both the agrarian masses and the coming middle class began to show signs of self-assertion and restlessness. The psychology of the average man had changed considerably since Hippocrates first described his epileptics and melancholics, and the mentally ill reflected the cataclysmic cultural and social conflicts of the time. They were the true, although pathological, mirrors of the inner struggle and the inner pains with which humanity had to pay for the changes history chose to bestow upon it.

The doctor whose ethical and cultural *niveau* was so very low in the sixteenth century was apparently able to do little more than to save his own status and attempt to raise it to an acceptable level of scientific dignity. No wonder that, impressed with his own new knowledge of anatomy and physics, he looked upon the manifestations of mental disease with great scientific dignity and as great naïveté. Fr. Deleboë (Sylvius) (1614–1672), who observed the numerous convulsive neuroses prevalent in those days, thought those convulsions were due to some abnormality in the workings of the levers—the bony structures of the body.[4] Deleboë's suggested explanation was, of course, as valid as would be the explanation of sleep by an assumed periodic weakness of the eyelids. But to the doctor of the seventeenth century such a clean-cut, physical hypothesis was a source of true intellectual satisfaction; it relieved him from the discomfort of looking into the obscure recesses of psychological problems. Historically, too, this trend is of great meaning. The psychology of the Renaissance was the striving toward the discovery of the self-conscious individual, but the revival of Hippocratism, which was due to the Renaissance, and the amalgamation of formal Hippocratism with physicomathematical thought eliminated the concern for purely individual psychology. Man's behavior began to be viewed not from the standpoint of his individual, personal needs and strivings but from that of his general physical and physiological organization. Weyer's precept requiring that each person be studied carefully and that the ideational content of the illness be fully understood seems to have been abandoned at the very moment it was proclaimed and almost accepted. In other words, clinical psychiatry continued to follow the age-old principle of reducing men to a common denominator and considering all individuals alike. The new medicine, so successfully and fruitfully wedded to physics and physiology, followed the principle established by the theological demonologists who reduced all beings to a common denominator of good and evil will. By the early seventeenth century the common denominator seems to have become iatrophysical or iatromathematical postulates.

It is this feature of seventeenth-century psychiatry which marks it as transitional, for despite the burst of true scientific spirit the world, Catholic and Protestant, lay and scientific, remained confused on the subject of mental diseases. Even in England "it was the luckless advent of James [I] that fanned the expiring embers into an infuriate flame,

---

[4] Calmeil: *De la folie considérée sous le point de vue pathologique, philosophique, historique et judiciaire*, vol. I, p. 386, referring to Deleboë: *Opera medica*, 1677.

that literally sent thousands of crazy gaffers and doting beldames to torture and the stake." [5] King James published his *Daemonologie* to refute Reginald Scot's *Discoverie of Witchcraft*, which he ordered seized and burned. Scot represented what in those days were advanced views. Not a physician, he followed in the footsteps of Weyer and four years before the latter's death published a scholarly, painstaking study, the nature of which is revealed in its full title:

THE

DISCOVERY OF WITCHCRAFT:

PROVING,

That the Compacts and Contracts of Witches
with *Devils* and all *Infernal Spirits* or *Familiars,* are but
Erroneous Novelties and Imaginary Conceptions.

Also discovering, How far their Power extendeth in Killing, Tormenting, Consuming, or Curing the bodies of Men, Women, Children, or Animals, by Charms, Philtres, Periapts, Pentacles, Curses, and Conjurations.

WHEREIN LIKE WISE

The Unchristian Practices and Inhumane

Dealings of *Searchers* and *Witch-tryers* upon *Aged, Melancholly,* and *Superstitious* people, in extorting Confessions by Terrors and Tortures, and in devising false Marks and Symptoms, are notably Detected.

And the Knavery of *Juglers, Conjurers, Charmers, Soothsayers, Figure-Casters, Dreamers, Alchymists* and *Philterers;* with many other things that have long lain hidden, fully Opened and Deciphered.

ALL WHICH

Are very necessary to be known for the undeceiving of *Judges, Justices,* and *Jurors,* before they pass Sentence upon Poor, Miserable and Ignorant People; who are frequently Arraigned, Condemned, and Executed for *Witches* and *Wizzards.*

IN SIXTEEN BOOKS.

By Reginald Scot *Esquire.*

[5] Montague Summers: "Introduction" to Reginald Scot's *The discoverie of witchcraft.* 1930, p. xvii.

THE
Discovery of Witchcraft:

PROVING,

That the Compacts and Contracts of WITCHES
with *Devils* and all *Infernal Spirits* or *Familiars*, are but
Erroneous Novelties and Imaginary Conceptions.

Also discovering, How far their Power extendeth in Killing,
Tormenting, Consuming, or Curing the bodies of Men, Women, Children,
or Animals, by Charms, Philtres, Periapts, Pentacles, Curses, and Conjurations.

WHEREIN LIKE WISE

The Unchristian Practices and Inhumane
Dealings of *Searchers* and *Witch-tryers* upon *Aged, Melancholly,*
and *Superstitious* people, in extorting Confessions by Terrors and
Tortures, and in devising false Marks and Symptoms, are notably Detected.

And the Knavery of *Juglers, Conjurers, Charmers, Soothsayers,*
Figure-Casters, Dreamers, Alchymists and *Philterers*; with
many other things that have long lain hidden, fully Opened and Deciphered.

ALL WHICH

Are very necessary to be known for the undeceiving of *Judges,*
Justices, and *Jurors,* before they pass Sentence upon Poor, Miserable and
Ignorant People; who are frequently Arraigned, Condemned, and Executed
for *Witches* and *Wizzards.*

IN SIXTEEN BOOKS.

By REGINALD SCOT *Esquire.*

Title Page of Reginald Scot's Discoverie of Witchcraft

(EDITION OF 1665)

Throughout the first quarter of the seventeenth century demonological literature continued to appear, vying in popularity and authority, venom and influence, with the *Malleus Maleficarum* and Bodin's refutation of Weyer's views. In 1613 Pierre de Lancre published his *Tableau de l'inconstance des mauvais anges et démons;* in 1622, *L'incrédulité et mécréance du sortilège plainement convaincue.* In 1623 Francesco Torreblanca's *Demonologia* appeared. These demonologists, like their predecessors, were keen observers and gave excellent clinical descriptions. The descriptions leave no doubt that the number of mentally ill in those days was enormous and that the severity of mental illnesses was extreme. The hallucinatory and delusionary states which are characteristic of the most serious illness, known to us as dementia praecox or schizophrenia, were still treated in the manner of blood and fire. In Königsberg in 1636 a man thought he was God the Father; he claimed that all the angels and the devil and the Son of God recognized his power. He was convicted. His tongue was cut out, his head cut off, and his body burned.[6] At approximately the same time de Lancre was roaming through the province of Labourd in which, he says, "there were very few families who did not have some connection or other with sorcery." De Lancre disapproved of the Spanish Inquisition, which appeared to him too lenient, and reporting on a meeting of the Grand Chamber of the Parliament of Bordeaux he stated: "Of the ten of us present, eight agreed that one should put witches to death for merely having attended the Sabbath, even if they had not committed any felony."[7]

It is against this background that the physician quietly observed mental disease. The spirit of inquiry and the recognition of the fact that personal observations were of great importance led some medical men to undertake serious and even daring studies, with results typical of this period of transition. Felix Plater (1536–1614) went directly into the dungeons and dark cellars where the mentally ill were kept. He produced a carefully thought-out classification of mental diseases in which the emphasis was put on idiots, morons, cretins, and mute, depressed, so-called melancholics. Plater believed that the causes of these

---

[6] Karl Haase: *Kirchengeschichte,* vol. III. Cited by Kirchhoff, in Aschaffenburg's *Handbuch der Psychiatrie, Allgem. Teil,* 4 *Abt.,* p. 33.

[7] René Semelaigne: *Les pionniers de la psychiatrie française.* Paris, 1930, vol. I, p. 51.

conditions were in the brain, but he had only chains to offer for the very disturbed patients, and for those whose delusions and hallucinations dealt with highly erotic themes or religious trends, only the conclusion that they were possessed by the devil. Plater was unable to deny either the devil or Galen. He used purgative measures freely. He spoke of the dryness of the brain as a cause of mental diseases. The days of the months, the seasons, the summer solstice in cases of repeated attacks—all played a definite role.

On the other hand, a step forward was made by Charles Lepois (1563–1633), who insisted that the cause of hysteria is to be sought not in the uterus but in the brain; since this is the case, hysteria is a disease to which men as well as women are subject. This seemingly casual and very obvious conclusion had to wait a long time before the medical profession felt ready to accept it and safe in doing so. Lazare Rivière, who died almost a quarter of a century after Charles Lepois, wrote in the second volume of his *Praxis Medica* a chapter *De hysterica passione* [8] and a chapter *De furore uteris.*[9] Two hundred and fifty years after the death of Lepois, young Sigmund Freud, recently returned from the Charcot Clinic at Paris where he had observed a great number of cases of hysteria, found it impossible to gain a sympathetic hearing for his report on some of the cases of hysteria which he had studied in men. The presiding officer of the Viennese Society of Medicine, Dr. Bamberger, declared that what Freud reported was incredible. Meynert, the leading neurologist and psychiatrist, at one time Freud's own professor, kindly but apparently not without irony advised Freud to find a case of hysteria in a man in Vienna, and present it to the Society. "I tried to do so," stated Freud, "but the senior physicians in whose departments I found any such cases refused to allow me to observe them or to work at them. One of them, an old surgeon, actually broke out with an exclamation: 'But, my dear sir, how can you talk such nonsense? *Hysteron* [sic] means the uterus. So how can a man be hysterical?' " [10] Young Freud's statement that he had actually observed such cases appeared still too radical, despite the fact that respect for the brain as

[8] Lazare Rivière: *Praxis medica.* Lyon, 1660, vol. II, p. 294. See R. Semelaigne: *Les pionniers, etc.,* vol. I, pp. 46, 47.

[9] *Praxis medica,* p. 287. *Idem.*

[10] Sigmund Freud: *Autobiography.* Translated by James Strachey. New York, 1935, pp. 23, 24.

the "seat" of mental disease was at the time fully established in the medical profession.

The advance of science apparently did not interfere with the physician's own fear of the phenomenon of mental disease. Daniel Sennert (1572–1637), who was an excellent Hippocratic clinician, was even more puzzled and unoriginal on the subject than Plater. Cases of ecstatic mental disease he considered due to the devil and, learned though he was and possibly even acquainted with Weyer's discussion of the subject, he considered lycanthropy a real, demoniacal transformation of human beings into animals.[11] Van Helmont (1577–1644), who placed the *archeus* at the pyloric opening of the stomach, still connected disease with sin. Thomas Willis (1621–1675), one of the greatest physicians of his day and a great neuroanatomist, also believed in devils and in the efficacy of severe treatment of the mentally ill. "The primary object is, naturally, curative," says Willis. "Discipline, threats, fetters, and blows are needed as much as medical treatment. . . . Truly nothing is more necessary and more effective for the recovery of these people than forcing them to respect and fear intimidation. By this method, the mind, held back by restraint, is induced to give up its arrogance and wild ideas and it soon becomes meek and orderly. This is why maniacs often recover much sooner if they are treated with torture and torments in a hovel instead of with medicaments."[12]

It is obvious that the increased interest in mental diseases did not proportionately decrease the rather aggressive attitude toward the mentally sick, nor did it substantially change the methods of treatment. The two-thousand-year-old tradition established by Melampus was practiced with respect and fervor: faith in purgatives remained unshaken. Harvey's discovery of the circulation of blood was one of the greatest achievements of man's genius, but in psychiatry it seems to have added to the pernicious zeal for bloodletting.

Théophile Bonet, one of the great pioneers in pathological anatomy, relates the history of a young woman who was afflicted with mania. Referring to this case, a medical historian of the first half of the nineteenth century says that "this unfortunate woman, endowed with rare beauty, was bled thirty times in ten days and finally with the last drops

[11] Daniel Sennert: *Opera omnia*. Paris, 1666, vol. II, pp. 393–395.
[12] Quoted by R. Semelaigne: *Aliénistes et philanthropes*. Paris, 1912, pp. 543, 544.

of her blood surrendered the last breath of her life." [13] Bonet did the autopsy and found it instructive, but it did not reveal the secret of mania nor did it suggest to Bonet the uselessness of bloodletting. Willis thought, to use the words of Calmeil, that bloodletting, emetics, and cathartics "should be prescribed with courage bordering on audacity." Guy Patin (1601–1672), a proponent of sound medical practices and otherwise a reasonable man, swore by bloodletting. He even waxed poetic on the subject, and in a letter to a friend written the day after Christmas, 1622, he speaks of bloodletting in very enthusiastic terms and concludes, "Long live the good method of Galen and long live the beautiful verse of Joachim du Bellay: O good, O holy, O divine bloodletting." [14]

The devotion or rather the addiction to this age-honored practice persisted into the eighteenth and even the nineteenth century. There was a prominent professor in Paris, Edouard François Marie Bosquillon (1744–1816), who was famous for his knowledge of Greek but more so for his reckless use of bloodletting. His students coined a special word for this procedure, *bosquillonner*, thus honoring the name of the good professor.[15] Bosquillon's contemporary in the New World, Benjamin Rush (1745–1813), despite his great achievements in medicine, psychiatry, and hospital building, also swore by the psychiatric "trinity" of emetics, purgatives, and bloodletting. In conformity with his European colleagues, Rush also believed in intimidation of refractory patients.

Despite this continuation of blind Galenism, the medical student of the seventeenth century did make a positive contribution. To him goes the credit for exploring the human body in search of the cause of mental disease. The spleen, which was supposed to be the greatest offender, was exonerated by the careful studies of Willis, Highmore, Glisson, and Bartholinus. The terminological tradition lingered on, however, so that "to suffer from the spleen" for a long time meant to be melancholy, depressed, and spiritually discomforted. Many of the old, false beliefs in medicine show this tendency to persist in the language of common usage. Today we still ascribe a certain physical and

[13] Calmeil: *op. cit.*, vol. I, p. 411, referring to T. Bonet: *Sepulchretum,* 1790 [first edition 1679], vol. I.

[14] Quoted by R. Semelaigne: *Aliénistes et philanthropes,* p. 496.

[15] *Ibid.*, p. 417.

mental malaise to the liver, even as Hippocrates did, and people to whom the name of Hippocrates is but an unintelligible word still believe in "liver pills" and corresponding purgatives. The word "indigestion" is not a medical term at all and it denotes no known pathology, but it is used with gullible and glib persistence despite the fact that it refers to a discomfort indicative more frequently than any other of a neurotic reaction on the part of the individual. The "suffocation of the stomach" referred to by the ancients and the role ascribed to the stomach throughout the centuries, rather than rational, realistic, medical knowledge, must have been responsible for van Helmont's choice of the end of the digestive pouch as the location of the *archeus,* and for the particular attention which Pinel and later Broussais (1772–1838) paid to the stomach in the consideration of mental diseases.

The age-long persistence in seeking for a "seat" of the soul and for a "seat" of mental disease was particularly accentuated in the seventeenth century. This was due to the fact that the study of pathological anatomy soon convinced the physician that diseases are produced by diseased organs or *by consensus, by sympathy.*[16] Also, the recapture of the Hippocratic view that the seat of madness is in the brain led to a most enthusiastic and careful study of the brain and the newly discovered nerves and some of their reactions. Neurology was established, if not as a medical specialty at least as an important branch of medicine. The beginnings of neurophysiology, too, can be traced back to the seventeenth century (Glisson). In the century following, neuropathology was established (Cullen).

The most important and by far the most influential representative of the new branch of medicine was Thomas Willis, whose *Opera Omnia,* published in 1681, contains over one hundred pages on cerebral pathology, as well as chapters on melancholia, mania, idiocy, and apoplexy. Willis was a careful clinical observer but his direct observations of living patients and of the brains and nerves of many patients who had died did not always harmonize with his rather arbitrary hypotheses. Willis was the discoverer of the eleventh pair of cranial nerves, and the discovery testifies to his excellent technique of dissection and to his powers of observation. But his psychological acumen lagged behind his other scientific achievements, and he would rather beat a mentally sick man or

[16] See p. 73.

consider him possessed by the devil than attempt through compassion to gain sympathetic understanding. In striking contrast to his painstaking accuracy of observation, Willis permitted himself to wander freely in the field of speculative assertions. "Willis sins by his great love for explanations, for theories which he would be able to prove only by appealing to the testimony of the senses and of which reason would never approve. For instance: the details he gives on the alleged acidity of nervous juices and animal spirits in mania; or the effervescence of these juices which he compares to that which develops in a vessel when certain reagents are put into concentrated acids; the possibility of the rise and sudden expansion of the animal spirits which he assumes push themselves beyond their natural confines and cut through an exit across the substance of the brain and the numerous branches of the nervous paths in order ultimately to excite a sort of torment of the intellect . . . [According to Willis] if we are to believe him, the nervous system of the mentally sick resembles a laboratory in which various liquids altered by bad ferments incessantly act on the mind and trouble its equilibrium." [17]

Thus Willis combined Galenic views with Hippocratic humoralisms, with the Greek tradition of methodism which was based on the theory of expansion and contraction of substances, and with the so-called solidistic theories—also inherited from the Greeks—which made it seem important to him to pay attention to the volume and form of the brain, with the physics and chemistry and conceptions of irritability of tissues, particularly of nerve tissues, which preoccupied the biologist and physician of his day. These views of Thomas Willis, despite the fact that in the forties of the nineteenth century they already appeared dated even to such a sympathetic follower as Calmeil, represent more than a mere historical curiosity. The work of Willis, Théophile Bonet, and Baglivi (1668–1707) laid the foundation of a psychiatry without psychology which took root in medical science and which, while rendering inestimable service to neuroanatomy, neurophysiology, and neuropathology, almost totally discarded the study of the very psychological phenomena which these men seem to have set out to study.

Nearly three hundred years have elapsed since the death of Thomas Willis, yet the basic ideas which he introduced as collateral speculation

[17] Calmeil: op. cit., vol. I, p. 388.

resulting from his excellent anatomical and pathological studies of the central nervous system and the general trend of his theoretical assumptions continue to prevail in the greatest part of the field of medical psychology. The exceptional development of chemistry, physiology, and bacteriology reinforced the resources and resourcefulness of neurophysiological research and reaffirmed the nonpsychological orientation of medical psychology which was so authoritatively established by Willis. The term "neurologist" has been used for a long time—and is in some quarters even today—as the synonym for psychiatrist. The tendency apparent in the recent years of our century to speak of "neuropsychiatrist" rather than of "neurologist" is indicative of the fact that the tradition established by Thomas Willis has finally begun to give way to newer orientations. But psychology lost favor with medicine at the very moment it was presented to the medical mind. It was delivered into the hands of the purely speculative thinker. It was Francis Bacon, Descartes, Hobbes, Locke, Malebranche, Spinoza who carried the burden of wonderment about the manner in which the mind, volition, and emotions work and make man act. None of these men was a physician with the exception of John Locke. None of them, including Locke, had much to offer for the understanding of mental disease.

Despite this strict separation and even deep cleavage between practical medicine and theoretical psychology, so well defined in the seventeenth century, it would be a mistake to overlook the fact that the organicists of that century made some extraordinary and valuable observations. While strictly descriptive and empirical, they proved to be important beginnings in many fields of future research and in some aspects of future therapy. To be sure, attempts at localization of various psychological faculties in the various parts of the brain were purely speculative. Vieussens (1641–1716), for instance, thought of the corpora striata in the brain as centers of imagination, in the same manner as a great many neurologists today insist that the thalamus is the seat of emotions. Of greater medical value and of greater scientific permanence proved to be such observations of Thomas Willis as the fact that melancholia and mania may merge—one of the first suggestions that alternations of excited and depressed states may be different forms of one and the same mental disease. This became an established fact toward the close of the nineteenth century, and the illness began to be designated as manic-depressive psychosis. Too, Willis observed a case of what he called "stupidity" which was cured as a result of an illness accompanied by fever.[18] Deleboë also observed that a severe physical illness made certain mental symptoms disappear. These were clinical observations ungarnished by theories and unsupported by hypotheses, but they were correct observations which in the course of centuries were repeated frequently both observationally and experimentally, ultimately giving rise to so-called fever therapy or treatment with malarial inoculation or induced convulsions.

Another direct result of the clinical empiricism of the seventeenth century was the increased interest of the physicians in singling out certain mental conditions from the welter of the many and releasing them from the narrow confines of traditional classifications which had been taken over from the Greek texts and had outlived their practical and theoretical usefulness. Charles Lepois, for instance, noticed that certain women develop mental diseases following childbirth or that they develop delirium during the puerperium, that is, immediately after childbirth. He thought the illness was caused by special dark humors. Lepois could not at that time know that the delirium might be due to the so-called puerperal infections; the observations of Semmelweis on these infections were not made till almost two hundred and fifty years later. But Lepois did observe and did think in terms of mental disease following childbirth as a separate clinical entity and with the years he proved correct. It has been found that approximately one in four hundred women giving birth to a child develops a mental illness which for a time was called puerperal psychosis; the term "postpartum psychosis" was introduced later.

No new step is ever made and no new discovery is ever brought forth without the shadows of the past hovering over it. Therefore it is not surprising to find that the Italian anatomist and pathologist Baglivi chose to describe by way of tradition what was doubtless a nonexistent mental disease, a sort of excitement resembling a toxic state and known under the name of *tarantism,* because it was supposed to be due to the bite of a tarantula.[19] Another clinical phenomenon which had attracted

[18] Calmeil: *op. cit.,* vol. I, p. 399.
[19] *Ibid.,* vol. I, p. 415. Also, R. Semelaigne: *Aliénistes et philanthropes,* p. 404.

the attention of physicians from the time of early Greek medicine was singled out by some seventeenth-century observers: the phenomenon of depressive states in connection with being in love, the moodiness of this condition, the frequent states of emotional instability and malaise. Théophile Bonet (1620–1689) observed these reactions and thought that the animal spirits "lit by love" were responsible, but, almost three quarters of a century before Bonet, Jacques Ferrand proved less speculative and more empirical. He approached the problem in a manner reminiscent of Weyer's procedure in examining Barbara Kremers or the girl who had (supposedly) vomited a wad of cloth and other objects believed to have been deposited in her stomach by the devil. Such clinical curiosity and the tendency to differentiate a mental from another similar condition is expressive of the age and is especially characteristic of French psychiatry, which less than a century later proved to be the most creative and, through leadership initiated by Philippe Pinel, the most fruitful in Europe for several generations. Some details of Ferrand's procedure are worth citing:

"In May, 1604, Ferrand was consulted about a young man whom he had known previously as a cheerful, energetic person. He found him very sad, depressed. A change of scene made his condition only worse. Dr. Ferrand was palpating the young man's pulse when a good-looking young girl happened to enter the room, carrying with her a lamp. Ferrand noticed that the pulse of his patient at once became irregular; his face grew pale. Ferrand guessed where the trouble lay and the patient confessed. The family objected to marriage as a solution of his trouble. Ferrand took charge of the boy and obtained a successful cure. From that time on Ferrand devoted a great deal of energy to the study of similar disorders. 'Some people,' he said, 'treat melancholias and other manias caused by love in the very same way as they treat other melancholics and madmen without considering the true cause and seat of the disease.' . . . Ferrand consulted every possible book on the subject and as a result published . . . in 1612 a treatise . . . entitled *La maladie d'amour ou mélancolie érotique*." [20] Eleven years later the second edition appeared, the full title of which read as follows: *De la maladie d'amour ou mélancolie érotique. Discours curieux qui enseigne*

[20] R. Semelaigne: *Les pionniers, etc.*, vol. I, p. 47.

à connaître l'essence, les causes, les signes et les remèdes de ce mal fantastique.[21] Ferrand was thus one of those pioneers of psychiatry who combined in himself a healthy awareness of the clinical phenomena which came under his observation with a serene intuition and an earnest studiousness requiring that the experience of others as found in the relevant literature be not overlooked. Ferrand's was an almost fully modern psychiatric mind.

IV

ONE may safely conclude that the trend toward the purely scientific which had developed in the medical world of the seventeenth century had comparatively little effect in the domain of psychiatry proper. Idiocy, cretinism, apoplexy, certain aspects of epilepsy, certain consequences of obvious brain injuries, and certain paralyses—a number of conditions which were due to actual brain defects, congenital or acquired—attracted the attention of the medical man. Passing over some of his flights of theoretical imagination, we should credit him with the successful advancement of our knowledge of what we learned in later centuries to recognize as organic diseases or defects of the central nervous system, which are accompanied with more or less gross mental disturbances—disturbances characterized mostly by deviations from normal intellectual functioning. The old tendency to consider all mental diseases as diseases of intellect or reason was reaffirmed and reinforced. These allegedly purely intellectual disturbances were viewed as results of anatomical or physiological abnormalities. Even those diseases in which the symptoms were primarily emotional such as melancholy (known later as depression) and mania were viewed as conditions produced by organic causes, as indeed they are still considered in very many quarters today. The thirty well-described cases of hypochondria, a form of depression accompanied by a number of gastrointestinal complaints, which Théophile Bonet reports in his *Sepulchretum* were all demonstrations of the work of the animal spirits which in devious ways were supposed to have wrought physical and consequently mental, that is, intellectual, defects. The severe psychological condi-

[21] *Ibid.*, p. 49.

tions such as hysterical, convulsive states, or hystero-epilepsies as they were later called for a short period, the ecstasies, the hallucinatory, persecutory states—in short, the vast majority of severe neuroses, so-called borderline conditions, and psychoses—were disregarded by those who felt themselves fully wedded to physics, chemistry, and physiology.

The doctor felt hopeless in face of these diseases, for he did not know how to cure them; as a man of his age he was anxious in the presence of the incomprehensible, of which only God and the Church were supposed to know the secret. For ages the mentally sick had been considered not only hopeless but bad people who came from evil, carried evil in themselves, and brought evil on others. All this complex emotional attitude on the part of the doctor could not fail to perpetuate the demonological tradition of unequivocal hostility and cruelty toward those who rightfully belonged in the hands of the psychiatrist and whom Weyer so compassionately called *miserae*. There was a need for courageous and dispassionate understanding. This was a very difficult task for the human spirit to perform. Even Paracelsus, whose turbulent heart and soul were so eager to minister to the sick and who recognized the magnitude of the problem that mental diseases presented, became impatient with the severer mental illnesses. He called the people who were afflicted with them animals and beasts, and he advised that they be chained and fettered and thus eliminated as pariahs of the human community.

It was the task of the seventeenth century to follow the road which Weyer had pointed out. In the midst of the indifference or hostility toward the mentally ill which the outburst of science supported, maintained, and even aided and abetted, there appeared clinicians who were perhaps more humanistic than scientific. They were steeped in the rediscovered Greek empirical medical tradition and, leaving theories behind, approached the whole problem in the best Hippocratic tradition. They were inspired by a desire to be of help, by the need to cure, by the therapeutic intent. The growing respect for the human personality which was felt in the new political and social conditions and philosophies of the time added to the sense of medical responsibility and courage. A man like André du Laurens (d. 1609), a physician who knew the writings of Galen and Avicenna, was fully aware of the difficulties facing the doctor who was interested in mental diseases. Melancholics, he said, should inspire compassion and their disease, he admitted, was "the torment and the scourge of the doctor." [22] Here we have an attitude totally different from the formalistic, theoretical, and detached approach of a Sennert or a Willis, and different also from the moralistic bent of a van Helmont.

Physicians like du Laurens were naturally at once confronted with the problem of witchcraft, which continued to plague the world. Their courage was taxed to the utmost as was their sense of tactful caution and their desire to help. Jacques Ferrand, in view of his special interest in the "malady of love" and the "erotic melancholy," was brought face to face with the tormenting problem of *incubi* and *succubi*. "I can attest," he said, "that I saw in the town of Castelnaudary in Lauraguay, two young women who maintained that the devil or a magician lay in bed with them every night, while their respective husbands lay at their sides; the Lord cured them through my remedies and the women now recognize that it was all a depravity of their imagination and a madness." [23] These simple lines reveal a point which cannot be overestimated. Ferrand not only reports the cure of the mentally ill women, but he thinks it necessary to state that the patients themselves recognized what their trouble was. In other words, they developed what we call technically today "insight as to illness," one of the most important, if not *the* most important, prerequisites of mental health. The burden of cure was shifted from penance and voluntary or enforced salvation of the soul which was supposed to be desecrated by ill will to the patient's own insight as to what his emotions and illusions do to him. The human personality in its very illness was thus credited with the ability, with the Lord's help and the doctor's remedies, to overcome its trouble, to understand and to master it. To be sure, neither Ferrand nor his enlightened contemporaries formulated their attitude in these modern terms, but their intuitive insight and their psychiatric attitude present the germinal form of what was to become one day real psychiatry—psychiatry based on actual human psychology and not on physiological speculations or ethicotheological prejudices. Of these there were still very many. The following episode illustrates the state of affairs quite well.

[22] R. Semelaigne: *Les pionniers, etc.*, vol. I, p. 39.
[23] Quoted by R. Semelaigne: *ibid.*, p. 49.

François Bayle (1622–1709) was a capable physician and teacher. He was a member of a group of people who would gather after the day's work to discuss scientific problems. The nights were dark and they all used to carry lanterns; hence they were known as the *Lanternistes*; it was this group which in 1729 became the Société des Sciences. Bayle enjoyed an excellent reputation as a physician and in 1681 the Parliament of Toulouse entrusted him with the examination of a woman who was suspected of being a witch. This was an act of great enlightenment on the part of the Parliament, especially as compared with the Parliament of Bordeaux where de Lancre won his demonological victories. Bayle found out that the woman had been roaming the streets of the parish, jumping about and talking nonsense. One day a crowd had followed her. She had entered the church, undressed herself, and danced until she fell to the ground in an attack of convulsions. Other women around her had soon begun to display the same symptoms and one of them had declared that the devil spoke through her mouth. Bayle examined the sick women and reported to the Parliament that the superstitious talk about witchcraft, so widespread among the population, had propitiated the imitative tendencies of the sensitive women who thus were caught by a sort of contagion when they saw the sick woman in a convulsive attack. "It is my opinion," stated Bayle, "that none of the above accidents or affections in particular, nor all of them together, can serve as proof of sorcery, possession or obsession [by the devil]. . . . One might expect a complete cure or at least an alleviation of the symptoms of all these girls if one could send them to some place in which they could find some consolation and where they could not hear talk about sorcerers or the devil; it will be necessary to make them understand their errors and to treat them in order to prevent the appearance of the effects of the melancholy which turns them to sad thoughts." [24]

Bayle was not alone in his views and influence but the enlightenment was not widespread. In Normandy only eleven or so years before the above statement was made a mass indictment for witchcraft was returned against five hundred people, of whom seventeen were convicted and sentenced to death. The king formally opposed the carrying out of the execution; the Parliament of Normandy was so shocked by this

[24] *Idem*, pp. 50, 51.

clemency that it addressed a document remonstrating His Majesty. The physician François de Saint-André intervened. Saint-André had already been sharply criticized by many for "reducing everything to the natural." He was a man of courage and apparently of a somewhat Rabelaisian irony. His name was François André but he preferred to sign his name as Mésange de Saint-André. He read the remonstration against the king and took it upon himself to declare: "This [document] proves only that there are sorcerers in imagination, people who believe themselves real sorcerers and who are convinced that they bodily go to the sabbath, that they worship the devil there, and that they commit there all sorts of abominations, impieties, and sacrileges; they even confess to have done all this. This also proves that there are enchantresses and poisoners, people who commit felonies on man and beast, but it does not justify the assumption that the witches' sabbath is something real, that these people are transported bodily, or that they actually do the things which allegedly occur to them. Nor, furthermore, does it prove that the devil is usually the author of the poisonings and felonies which happen to be committed. Yet such was the assumption which led to imposing the death sentence on the accused." [25] In 1682 Colbert on the insistence of Louis XIV abolished capital punishment of sorcerers and witches—almost one hundred years after Weyer's death and one hundred and twenty years after the appearance of the *De Praestigiis Daemonum*.

v

THE obvious conclusion to be drawn from the above survey is that in the field of mental diseases the medicine of the seventeenth century groped between organicism and humanitarianism. The strict organicist was absorbed in his laboratory, that is to say, in the dissecting room. The humanitarian aspects of mental disease, involving constant conflict with the judicial authorities, with politicians and die-hards, were left to take care of themselves. On the other hand, the humanitarian practitioner was plunged in the midst of the social conflicts and so was deprived of the opportunity of working out in greater detail the psy-

[25] *Idem*, p. 53.

chological problems which his patients presented. The organicist isolated himself from the study of psychology because his major interest was anatomy and physiology; the humanitarian practitioner had to rely on his intuition and remained outside systematic psychology as much as the physiologist. The questions which interested Vives so much— the solution of which he considered so important for the general improvement of society, for the elimination of social ills, and for the organization and treatment of mental disease—these questions continued to ferment but mostly in a desultory, sporadic manner. The correlation of psychiatry with sociology, the necessity of which was so clear to Vives, clearer than to any other humanist, was left to the physicians of the nineteenth century to accomplish and to improve. The purely psychological questions raised by Vives were taken over by the nonphysician, by the philosopher. The reader will have to be referred to standard books on the history of philosophy and psychology for a detailed study of theoretical psychology. For our purposes it will suffice to state in a general way that the empirical, introspective, descriptive method established by Vives bore extraordinarily rich fruit in the seventeenth century. Not only did it enrich man's thought about the workings of the human mind, but it expanded the field of self-observation and increased the ramifications of man's interest in himself.

The influence of philosophy on psychiatry is indisputable and yet imperceptible, almost elusive. Francis Bacon exerted a profound influence on the orientation of psychological science. Despite the inherent propensity of man to generalize and to postulate, the scientist and the physician became aware that only factual observation and the painstaking collection of facts would lead to the solution of the riddles of nature and man. The Baconian inductive method of thinking was accepted with ease. Science welcomed it; mathematics, physics, and astronomy found in it a most powerful scientific tool. In psychology, however, the tendency to think intuitively and deductively persisted for a much longer time, and the influence of Bacon, while incontestable to our day, was only partial. Bacon's division of our psychological attributes into memory, imagination, and understanding remained fundamental and relieved one from the age-old propensity of viewing psychology as religious ethics only, and from the tendency to ask oneself the unanswerable, metaphysical questions: Whence and how memory? Whence and how imagination? To Bacon, memory was represented by human activity, knowledge by history, imagination by poetry, and understanding by philosophy. Philosophy in the Baconian sense included more than mere abstract thinking, of course, but as Bacon classified the sciences abstract philosophy and introspective psychology remained united. Consequently his contribution to psychology was more methodological than substantial.

Descartes used mathematics as his point of departure. His psychology was mechanistic; his physiology was partly Aristotelian. He still spoke of a fire burning in the heart, although he placed the seat of the soul in the pineal gland, a rather central location in the brain—a claim with which François Bayle disagreed with as much scientific validity as that of the Cartesian contention itself. But the Cartesian system, whatever the defects of its psychophysiology, left its impression on the minds of people by the special attention it paid to the sense organs and by the role it ascribed to sense organs in the whole problem of mental functioning. All the psychologies of the century, those of Hobbes, Malebranche, Locke, Condillac, Nicholas Tetens, whatever their individual variations, had this in common: the sense organs were elevated to a specially high degree of value. Nothing, it was thought, could be perceived or otherwise converted into psychological reactions without sense organs. These were considered the pathways to the brain and the brain was considered the central organ of transformation of all stimuli into thought, feeling, and behavior. This point of view harmonized very well not only with the mechanistic trends of the philosophers but also with the increasing interest in physiology and the study of sensations as the starting point of psychological activity. Spinoza's pantheistic philosophy with its emphasis on passions (emotions) and the important role they play in knowledge was overlooked by the contemporary psychologies, and some of its profound, intuitive insights did not become subjects of medicopsychological considerations until over two hundred and fifty years later when Freud's theory of instincts was formulated.

Summarizing the keen speculations of the philosophical psychologies of the seventeenth century, we may say that they did give the spontaneous, empirical orientation of the physician a certain dignity of philosophical depth. Introspection of the observer, his sensations, and empir-

ical descriptions of various details of human behavior became the substance of psychiatry. Moreover, philosophical psychology, in so far
as it was a descriptive analysis of mental functions, relieved medical
psychology from the pressure of theology. Here at last was a system of
thought, or a group of systems of thought, which dealt with the minutest details of human nature and even with the soul—without re-
course to dogma or to any definite religious faith. Human reason itself
with breadth and depth could penetrate into the obscure recesses of
man's mind, correlate man's mind with his body and central nervous
system and make a synthesis without having to consult the revealed
and the miraculous. The foundation for the rationalism of the following century was thoroughly prepared. Theological dogmatism began
to wilt; the very validity of religion began to be doubted. Voltaire's
deism and the pride in the achievement of human reason culminated
in the temporary discard of the dogmas of the Church and in the assertion of the dogma of reason, which the atheism of the French Revolution was to proclaim.

The combination of philosophical sensualism, narrowly conceived
but not a little inflated rationalism, and mechanistic, mathematical
psychophysiology brought about a certain monotony of views on mental
diseases. Mental diseases were differentiated and classified in accordance with their external manifestations, but they were all ascribed to
the faulty functioning of body juices, particularly in the blood and the
brain, or of the fluid which was supposed to flow through the nerves.
Consequently the treatment of mental diseases was characterized by
the same monotony in its methods, and the century distinguished itself
by its addiction not only to therapeutic bloodletting but also to blood
transfusions. "The transfusion of blood was used for the first time as a
treatment for mental diseases by Denis in 1667. In 1662 Moritz Hoffmann had suggested transfusion for the cure of melancholia. Denis
made the first transfusion on a thirty-four year old man who as a result
of an unhappy love had developed a mental disease. Denis was successful in his first attempt, in which he let out ten ounces of blood from a
vein of the arm and let in five or six ounces of blood obtained from a leg
artery of a calf. The next day Denis let out another two or three ounces
of the patient's blood and replaced it with at least one pound of calf's
blood. By the next day the patient had quieted down and his mind

had cleared, and soon he completely recovered; this was corroborated by all the professors of the Ecole de Chirurgie. In the same year [1667] Sir George Ent attempted to introduce blood transfusion in the treatment of mental diseases in England. . . . In Germany Klein recommended blood transfusion . . . as did Ettmüller in his 'Chirurgia Transfusoria' in 1682, particularly in cases of melancholia. The change of mood produced by the transfusion they explained easily; just as, according to Aristotle, an old man needs only the eye of a young man in order to look like a young man, so too will the blood of a young man make an old person keen and bright." [26] Little would Harvey have suspected that his great discovery would be put to such rather naïve use by the medical man whose eagerness to cure a mental disease always surpassed his understanding of the underlying psychological processes.

This episode of the seventeenth century represents something fundamental in the attitude of medicine toward mental disease. Any physiological or chemical discovery throughout the history of the past two hundred and fifty years has at once attracted the attention of the worthy descendants of the professors of the Ecole de Chirurgie and at once all mental conditions regardless of their clinical and individual variations have become equated and the remedy in vogue applied with naïve empiricism and frequently with the relentless persistence which has overshadowed scientific enlightenment and humanitarian considerations. Thus at the opening of the twentieth century the observations of Wagner-Jauregg in Vienna, which were similar in some respects to those of Thomas Willis when he noticed that a fever once cured a man of stupidity, led to the universal use of various agencies from malaria to sterile milk and other proteins in order to induce high fever in the mentally ill and thus produce the always hoped-for cure. There was also a period—originated in the United States by Cotton—of universal use of gastrointestinal and dental surgery to cure mental disease. Endless numbers of feet of intestines and thousands of teeth were removed from the young and old of all varieties of mental disease, with as inconclusive results as the blood transfusions which were initiated by Denis with the blessing of the professors of the Ecole de Chirurgie.

Of recent years another vogue has replaced the vogues of surgery

[26] S. Kornfeld: *Geschichte der Psychiatrie*, Neuburger and Pagel: *Handbuch der Geschichte der Medizin*, vol. III, p. 610.

and fevers. Chemical agents producing convulsions, such as insulin, cardiozol, and metrazol, began to be used extensively in almost all varieties of mental diseases, and even cerebral surgery came to claim its share of credit by self-assertive but unfounded empiricism. Patients are made to fall into convulsive states and patients have little holes drilled into their heads and small portions of their frontal lobes destroyed; [27] claims are brought forth that curative results are produced. Melampus claimed his cures with the same honesty; Patin was just as certain of the worth of his bloodletting. The neuroiatromechanical speculations of the seventeenth century seem to have laid the groundwork for or brought to expression the fundamental error, or need, of man of building psychiatry without psychology.

The century did not come to a close, however, without a reaction against the mechanistic theories and practices which it established. This reaction, while expressive and energetic, was not at once effective; but it represents an important milestone in the history of psychological medicine. It is exemplified by the work of Stahl.

VI

GEORG Ernst Stahl was born in Ansbach, Germany, in 1660. In his doctor's dissertation, *De Sanguificatione*, written at the age of twenty-four, he expresses his convictions against the prevalent theory of animal spirits and ascribes the process of circulation of blood to a *soul*. This soul is not conceived as a spirit but as a special force, a drive characteristic of every living organism. Thus at the very beginning of his career Stahl took an unusually revolutionary attitude. Theretofore tradition had never failed to emphasize the profound difference between animals and men. Man was supposed to have and animal not to have a soul. From the early days of medical speculations, and particularly from the time theology infiltrated medicobiological thought, it was emphasized that the brute is but a soulless, mechanical contraption. This contention survived in Thomas Willis and in Descartes. Stahl, postulating the presence of a soul, of a special vital force distinguishing living from

---

[27] Paracelsus advised drilling small holes in the patient's skull to let out mania. See ch. II on *De cura maniae* in his *Von den Krankheiten, etc.*

dead matter, definitely equated living animal with living human matter. This equation was of utmost value to biology and is fully established in present-day biology.

It is very curious to observe that the most revolutionary thought which either broke or forecast the breaking of older views rooted in religious dogma were uttered not by apostates and freethinkers but by the pious and devout. Weyer, Paracelsus, Vives were deeply religious men whose revolutionary innovations seem to have been dictated by their very piety. Stahl, too, was very devout. He was also morose, bitter, and on occasion as sharp of tongue as Paracelsus. Disregarding the tradition of his day, Stahl avoided quoting either ancient or contemporary authorities. He was convinced of being right and he stated his convictions unequivocally. There was a quality of the crusader in this little, inconspicuous, earnest-looking, somewhat depressed man. He felt called upon to refute the self-complacency and unjustified pride of the iatromathematicians and iatrophysicists, one of whom was Friedrich Hoffmann, his colleague on the medical faculty in Halle. Stahl was appointed personal physician to the Duke of Weimar in 1687; he also occupied the chair of theory of medicine in Jena. In 1694 he was called on Hoffmann's recommendation to take over the professorship of medicine in the newly founded University of Halle, where he taught for twenty-two years. He could not get along with Hoffmann and finally moved to Berlin, where he died eighteen years later in 1734.

Stahl's major work was *Theoria Medica Vera*, published in 1707, in which he discussed mental diseases. A year later he continued his discussion of the same problems in *De Animi Morbis*. He felt repelled by the increasing cleavage between body and mind. He felt that this dichotomy was unjustified and that it did harm to true understanding of disease in general and of mental disease in particular. Stahl therefore is to be considered a great pioneer in medicine in putting squarely before the doctor the task of forming a synthesis of physical and mental phenomena, of the organic and psychological as we would say today. Despite his deeply religious feelings, he approached the problem without theological preoccupations and as a true seventeenth-century empiricist. The separation of the consideration of living body from the problem of life he considered untenable. Inorganic matter and a dead body are different from living matter, the body. The fact that the body is alive is in itself proof that it is moved by a living force—a drive, an instinct which is closer to our affects, emotions, than it is to physics and chemistry. Stahl went to the extreme on this point. He even believed that a knowledge of chemistry and physics is much less useful to a physician than an understanding of how the soul, the vital force, functions.

Except for the terminology, Stahl's conception of mental diseases coincides in many points with the advanced psychodynamic views of the twentieth century. In a dissertation published in 1702 under the title *De Medicina Medicinae Necessaria,* he pointed out "the stupendous, sudden and quick effect of the so-called passions and affects on the body." He believed that certain emotions might interfere with the recovery from a physical disease. In general, the various psychological reactions which Stahl observed in physical diseases, reactions which did not attract the serious attention of the psychopathologist until the twentieth century when they appeared under the name of pathoneuroses (Ferenczi) and psychosomatic disorders, should be considered of great clinical importance, for these psychological reactions are a sign of the self-preservation drives of the individual. Stahl even made the correct observation that dreams occasionally reflect the condition of certain abnormal bodily states. This he said was due to the *anima sensitiva* —putting it into modern terminology, to unconscious perception. Stahl's views are based on the conception of *motus tonico-vitalis,* which he discussed for the first time in his dissertation *De Motu Tonico-Vitalis* in 1692. He held the life force responsible for all motions, that is, for the functions, of a living organism. Mental diseases occur when the soul is impeded in its free function. This impediment or inhibition is frequently due to a mood or, what is the same thing, to an idea which is foreign or contrary to the direction of the life force. This is a somewhat awkward formulation of a concept which Freud promulgated early in his career when he spoke of the unconscious origin of symptoms and of the repressed, instinctual drives as capable of producing neuroses and psychoses.

Stahl was the first to attempt to point out that certain deliriums or mental states are of a physical (organic) and others of an emotional (psychological, functional) origin. One should, for instance, differentiate certain erotic states which come from increased sensibility of the organs involved from those of purely psychological origin which are characterized by the predominance of erotic fantasies. This point of view proved extremely fruitful. The modern psychiatrist, totally unaware of this source of his clinical procedure, considers that one of his cardinal problems and duties is to differentiate organic from functional symptoms in every case which he is called upon to diagnose and treat. We are indebted to Stahl, more than we know, for the fact that major neuroses and psychoses, which even throughout the seventeenth century were grouped under the heading of demoniacal possessions by many great physicians, were finally captured by the student of mental diseases as belonging to him in his capacity as psychiatrist.

Stahl truly expresses the spirit of transition from the enthusiastic iatromechanistic views which prevailed among the most authoritative men of the seventeenth century to the birth of a medical psychology based on a biological synthesis of the processes of life. His immediate influence was small, particularly in Germany where he was rediscovered, so to speak, by Ideler one hundred years after his death and made to serve the establishment of true psychological psychiatry. Ideler issued Stahl's *Theoria Medica Vera* in a new German edition in 1831–1832. Stahl's influence was much greater in France, particularly in the University of Montpellier where Boissier de Sauvages, Barthez, and Philippe Pinel taught.

VII

THE eighteenth century, despite the fact that we think of it primarily as the great century of rationalism and enlightenment, was actually a multicolored century of contrasts, of turbulence, of passionate struggles and confused rearrangements of thought. It was this century which proclaimed the importance of the inalienable rights of man. It was this century which gave birth to the guillotine and watched more heads fall than at any other time in history except our own.

Mental disease, which medicine finally wrested from the clutches of superstitious sadism, began to be looked upon as the misfortunes of man as a person; the lunatic became as much an object of human concern as any sick man. Yet it would be impossible to understand the nature and the extent of this changed attitude unless we viewed it in the light of the complex spirit of the age. It would be one sided and inaccurate to consider the psychiatric achievements of the century only in the light of the abolition of the chains and fetters which held the insane to the walls of their cells. For this act of liberation, performed almost simultaneously in Italy, England, and France, cannot be looked upon merely as the expression of what the French writers called "the spirit of philanthropy." This century was hungry for experiences, intellectual, spiritual, political, and emotional, and it grasped ravenously for everything which promised new insight or new knowledge. For psychiatry it did more than merely liberalize and humanize the management of the mentally ill; it tried to learn something about the riddle of mental illness, and in doing so it reflected all the manifold trends and multicolored vagaries of the age.

In many respects it was a practical age. Technology and industry were developing; the steam engine was invented. Problems of finance and economics only sketched in the previous century and a half began to develop as practical, political instruments and empirical disciplines. A new class of semi-industrial, semimerchant commoners came rapidly into being, demanding a voice in politics, science, art, in the whole body cultural that was Europe and the New World. It was a century of scientific enlightenment, the century in which Morgagni (1682–1771), the Italian pathologist, heedful of the world's newly acquired respect for facts, reminded his medical colleagues of Homer's words: "In saying things that were probable, he uttered many falsities." Only things which actually *were* deserved scientific statements. Philippe Pinel reproached Baglivi for his "mania for hypotheses." Yet James Graham built his Aesculapian Temple in London with its queer "celestial bed" and made people pay one hundred pounds for the privilege of spending one night in it thus to be permeated with the mysterious curative "magnetism" it was supposed to contain and to convey. Emma Lyon, the future Lady Hamilton, presided over this singular establishment almost at the very time when the epoch-making *Elementa Physiologiae* of Albrecht von Haller appeared turning biology and medicine into newer and wider roads of investigation and usefulness. Mesmer was fascinating the credulous with new "curative" mass convulsions and other manifestations of "animal magnetism" and "magnetic fluids." John Hunter in London was making gigantic strides in scientific surgery, and Frederick the Great, the friend of Voltaire, decreed from Sans Souci that the Prussian executioner should supplement his work with the treatment of fractures and wounds. It was the century which gave us soda water (1772 and 1790) and castor oil (1764), the rise of Napoleon and the execution of Condorcet and Bailly, the death of Rousseau and Voltaire, and the work of Lamarck. Lavoisier enriched chemistry and Berkeley, Hartley, Hume, and Condillac made their permanent imprint on psychology and psychiatry.

Great men and great names there were, but it is no longer possible to associate the turn of thought or other cultural events with one man. That great yet intangible, eventful, and implacable process which is generically called history was on the move as one gigantic "blend of bundles of perceptions," as David Hume would have said. From this century on one can speak only of certain trends and forces of which the great men are but illustrations, rather than of men who as if from nowhere gathered new thoughts and courageously offered them to an inhospitable and refractory world.

The trends of the eighteenth century were many. The workings of the human mind continued to engage the attention of the thinker. Berkeley (1685–1753), ultimately a philosophical idealist and admitting the possibility of "imageless thought," as a psychologist insisted on the primacy of man and his consciousness. In paragraph twelve of his *New Theory of Vision* he declines to accept anyone's perception "so long as I myself am conscious of no such thing." Only that of which man is conscious is important. And he is conscious only of what he perceives through his senses. David Hume (1711–1776) —who was so unpromising as a boy that his mother described him as "a fine, good-natured crater but uncommon weak-minded," and who became Undersecretary of State—Hume, too, stressed the blending of perceptions, their coming together in "bundles" and forming *impressions* and *ideas*, the two basic forces of our mentation and activity. Hume's "bundles of perceptions" were not entirely original with him; he obtained them from Locke (d. 1704) or from William Molyneux who was Locke's source. Hartley (1705–1757), a medical man and therefore a person with a special flair for the material and tangible, wrote his *Observations on Man*, in which he remarked that "matter, if it could be endowed with the most simple kinds of sensation, might also arrive at all that intelligence of which the human mind is possessed." Condillac (1714–1780) followed Hartley for the most part. He conceived of an inanimate statue successively endowed with each of our sense organs. If the statue had the sense of smell it would, in the same manner as Hartley's matter, arrive at certain reactions which are no different from those of humans. Diderot (1713–1784), whose life span was almost fully coincident with that of Condillac, discussed deaf-mutes from the same point of view as Hartley and to some extent in the manner of Berkeley, who "vindicated," that is, verified, his theory of vision through some subsequent observations of the blind.

This extreme sensualism and materialism was a highly simplified application of physics to psychology. It carried with it a simplification of the concept of the human personality and an inner contradiction in relation to the philosophy of man. In scientific psychology man was conceived as a mere machine, a piece of stone enlivened by sense organs, a statue living by the grace of the senses of touch, smell, taste, vision, and hearing. In philosophy and sociology he was a greatness, a miracle, a part of immortality endowed with inherent rights and inherent duties. This double attitude toward man was expressed in the whole system of Berkeley's thought and was less articulately present in the views of even the most inveterate rationalists and materialists, who fought and killed and died for ideals of human rights and universal justice and who yet thought of man as but a physicochemical apparatus.

This inner contradiction did not at once become obvious to those who were working out their systems of thought, but very early there appeared signs that some synthesis was required, that something was lacking in the whole scheme of the sensualistic-materialistic psychology of the age. Cabanis (1757–1808), not a physician, was very much interested in physiology and medicine. He was the brother-in-law of Condorcet, friend and to a certain extent patron of Philippe Pinel, a habitué of the *salon* of Madame Helvétius which was also assiduously frequented by Benjamin Franklin. He was professor in the Ecole de Santé; he was a representative of the people in the Council of Five Hundred and later a member of the more conservative Senate. He thus was close to man as a physiological apparatus and not at all unaware of man's political passions. Cabanis believed in every man's right to have work and was therefore opposed to the mere almsgiving type of charity. He was one of the first and most passionate opponents of capital punishment, of those "juridical assassinations with which the decemviral tyranny covered France." He wrote a *Note sur le supplice de la guillotine* (1795), and the *Rapports du physique et du moral de l'homme* (1796–1802). He observed the movements of decapitated bodies and inferred a partial reflex reaction of the nervous system which had been severed at the neck. It was a function on a level without consciousness, a lower level. One may not, insisted Cabanis, study an individual in his various parts without considering him as a whole. Consciousness depends upon the wholeness of man. Cabanis had a pretty clear idea of what we call today the total personality, and he spoke of certain states of consciousness of our life processes of which we are not aware. He did not use the word "unconscious," a term introduced by Pierre Janet almost three quarters of a century later. Cabanis had considerable insight into the phenomenon of hallucinations. He had sensed the importance of the organic predisposition which we call instincts, the prime mover of the personality as a whole.

The influence of Cabanis was only personal and local. He did not create a "school" nor did he have any followers. His views are cited merely as an illustration of the fact that even in the midst of materialism and rationalism trends were appearing which tended toward a more unified psychology, normal and abnormal. On the other hand, Cabanis undoubtedly influenced the general orientation of Pinel, although Pinel himself always cited Locke and Condillac as his sources of psychobiological orientation.

VIII

EVEN in Cabanis, who always built on a strictly physiological foundation, one may notice a tendency to consider an understanding of the pure mechanics of the body insufficient for explaining the psychology of man as a whole. The problem of the relationship of sensation and consciousness, of body and mind, imposed itself with all its implacable obscurity on anyone who approached a psychological, or particularly a psychopathological, problem. The physician especially felt baffled, and he sought some kind of body-mind synthesis. But his efforts were not crowned with success. As a matter of fact they seemed not even to hold out much promise. The potentially fruitful ideas of Georg Ernst Stahl did not take hold. His conception of the vital force was a good working idea but it also led the medical inquirer imperceptibly but inevitably into philosophical speculations devoid of any practical clinical value.

Ernst Platner (1744–1818) taught that each separate organ had its own vital force ("soul"). Gaubius (1705–1780), one of Hermann Boerhaave's followers, insisted that psychological influences, the vital force, determine even the act of breathing. Frank Nicholls (1699–1778) watched the state of mind of patients with fever and concluded that psychological forces are at play in our reactions to high temperatures. Boissier de Sauvages (1706–1767) considered the motive power of the life force as expressing itself independently in the form of consciousness and in connection with sensory organs in the form of movements.

It may easily be seen that these abstract considerations led to but little fruitful research. They satisfied the intellectual propensities of the doctor; they offered him a few concepts which he felt made disease appear more understandable; they even stimulated him here and there to suggest a new principle for managing patients. Stahl, for instance, felt that one should make no effort to suppress fever, since through fever the "soul" attempts to mobilize the curative forces of man's nature. This view is absolutely modern but as redundantly and obscurely expressed as any of the abstract conceptions of Paracelsus. Richard Mead (1673–1754) followed Stahl in his considerations on the problem of managing fevers. But on the whole practical results were rather meager. The inner principles underlying the vitalist theory were soon forgotten; the interest in the emotional aspects of physical or mental disease, however, could not disappear, for the role of emotions in the course of disease became more and more evident. Clément Joseph Tissot (1750–1826), for instance, in response to an inquiry by the Académie de Chirurgie of Paris, wrote De l'influence des passions de l'âme dans les maladies, et des moyens d'en corriger les mauvais effets (Paris, 1798). Needless to say, these purely practical questions resulted in almost naïvely empirical conclusions of great simplicity and of an optimism which, to say the least, was as premature as it was full of faith. Tissot believed that tickling to evoke the "emotion" of cheerfulness and laughter in children suffering from rickets had a curative effect. He also thought that the playing of music would produce curative emotions in patients discouraged and therefore impeded by low spirits in the process of recovery.

It took a long time before the relationship of mind and body was understood a little better and approached a little more scientifically. The term "psychosomatic medicine," introduced in the third and fourth decades of our century, reflects that the problem is still as poignant and as unresolved as it was two hundred years ago. However, no century before the eighteenth had become so aware of the problem. Joseph Lieutaud (1703–1780) remarked that "the mind and the body exercise on one another a reciprocal power, the extent of which we do not know." [28]

The question continued to be agitated throughout this century and the nineteenth, but in the meantime other theories were put forward which seem to conform more to the iatrophysical tradition established in the seventeenth century. The influence of Haller's *Elementa Physiologiae* (1757) on medical thought was both instantaneous and lasting and overtly or covertly has been reflected in psychiatric theories ever since. The theory of the excitability of tissues seemed to fit into the scheme of psychiatric predilections since so many of the mental diseases so conspicuously displayed states of excitement and states of depression—which William Cullen designated as states of *collapse*. [29] John Brown (1735–1788) was destined to become the most influential exponent of the theory of irritability and exhaustion of the nervous system leading to asthenic states. His *Elementa Medicinae* (Edinburgh, 1780) was widely read not only in England; he had a number of followers in France and Germany. Brown's theory seemed so plausible to contemporaries and to future generations that such terms as "neurasthenia" (Baird) and "psychasthenia" (Pierre Janet) introduced in the nineteenth century reflected the theoretical premises of a century before.

Yet the clinical approach, the treatment of the mentally sick, remained the same. Celsus, almost two thousand years before, had recom-

[28] R. Semelaigne: *Les pionniers, etc.*, vol. I, p. 57.
[29] William Cullen: *First lines of the practice of physic.* London, 1777.

mended chains as a useful form of restraint. Jacques-René Tenon (1724–1816), who investigated the need for mental hospitals and wrote in 1788 a speech *Mélanges sur les hôpitaux de Paris*, recommended better hospitals but still advised chains. John Brown recommended intimidation and frightening of patients to the point of arousing in them a state of desperation. Theories were being created, modified, abandoned, revived, and refined, but the fundamental attitude toward the handling of the mentally sick persisted. It continued to be a mixture of psychophysiological studiousness and studied cruelty. Even some of those who were true geniuses of science and who had an excellent flair for psychiatric phenomena were lost between the Scylla of anatomy, or what the Greeks used to call solidism, and the Charybdis of semimoralistic cruelty toward mental patients.

Johann Christian Reil (1759–1813), who literally became rhapsodic about psychological treatment of the mentally ill, advised what he called "noninjurious torture." In 1803 appeared his *Rhapsodieen über die Anwendung der psychischen Curmethode auf Geisteszerrüttungen*. The fourth volume of his study of fever is also devoted to mental diseases. Despite the many enlightened views which Reil held, he considered throwing patients into water and firing cannons in order to bring them to their senses rational and legitimate "psychological" methods of treatment. He believed it was useful to arouse anger and disgust and pain in certain cases. Invoking the rationale of calming or arousing the overexcited or too dormant senses of the patients, he would place some of them in an absolutely dark and "dead quiet" cell and let them talk. He wanted to have a special theater in a mental hospital in which employees would play the roles of "judges, prosecutors, angels coming from Heaven, dead coming out of their graves which in accordance with the needs of various patients should be played to produce the illusion of utmost verisimilitude." [30] Whenever necessary, prisons, lions' dens, places of execution, and operating rooms should be presented on the boards of this psychotherapeutic theater. This was Reil's conception of "noninjurious torture."

It would be a mistake, however, if on the basis of these ethicosadistic fantasies we were to adjudge Reil an unctious and pious nonentity of the pseudohumanistic brand of the late sixteenth or seven-

[30] J. C. Reil: *Rhapsodieen, etc.* Halle, 1803, pp. 237 *et seq.*

teenth century. He was a gifted and enlightened representative of a certain trend which was typical of a part of the eighteenth-century medical world. One cannot easily agree with Kirchhoff when he honors Reil with the title of founder of rational psychology. One would rather judge some parts of Reil's psychiatry in the same manner as Voltaire did the writing of Antoine Le Camus (1722–1772). Le Camus published in 1753 a handsome volume of three hundred and ninety-three pages. Its motto was from Cicero's *Tusculanes*. It was dedicated to the Marquis de Paulney and was entitled *Médecine de l'esprit: Où l'on traite des dispositions & des causes physiques qui, en conséquence de l'union de l'âme avec le corps, influent sur les opérations de l'esprit: & des moyens de maintenir ces opérations dans un bon état, ou de les corriger lorsqu'elles sont viciées.* Voltaire read the book and commented on it in the *Dictionnaire Philosophique:* "Ah, monsieur Camus! vous n'avez pas fait avec esprit la Médecine de l'Esprit." [31] Voltaire had been dead for twenty-five years when the *Rhapsodieen* appeared and in Germany there was no contemporary Voltaire to judge Reil in the light of consistency. What should be carefully noted is that Reil's psychotherapeutic methods and the rationale which he offered for them were conceived in the light of an excellent clinical knowledge of medicine and clinical psychiatry. Reil was the son of a pastor and himself a religious man. It was to a preacher that he dedicated his psychotherapeutic rhapsodies. In 1796 he published *De Structura Nervorum*, which established him as one of the great men in the history of neurology. His greatest contribution was to our knowledge of the cerebellum; an area in the brain bears his name, "the island of Reil." He founded, in 1796, the *Archiv für die Physiologie* which he opened with an article on the *Lebenskraft* (life force). He described the conditions which we would call today psychoneuroses. He observed cases of depersonalization and of double personality. He was interested in the patients' introspective self-observations, that is, in the ideational content and what we call *trends*. He gave a detailed and truly enlightened description of what a mental hospital should be. He objected to the name "asylum" and preferred the name "pension" or hospital for nervous diseases. He described in detail how such a hospital should be organized, how the grounds should be landscaped, and how the spirit

---

[31] Quoted by R. Semelaigne: *Les pionniers, etc.*, vol. I, p. 65.

of communal contact or, as we say today, the spirit of socialization, should pervade the organization of the institution and the management of the patient.

It will easily be seen from the previously mentioned idea of a hospital theater that Reil had a high conception of law and justice and of divine and worldly order and orderliness. Apparently there lurked somewhere in his mind remnants of the centuries past, some already inarticulate conviction that mental disease is a sin, or that it comes from sin, from a faulty sense of justice, from something unsocial, something which deviates man from the principle of abiding by the law. There is another aspect of Reil's medical personality which should be noted. He was close to Wagnitz, the Lutheran preacher to whom *Rhapsodieen* was dedicated, and it was apparently Wagnitz's nonmedical influence which inspired Reil's psychotherapeutic ideas. That this rather unofficial collaboration was not fortuitous nor based merely on personal friendship is proven by the fact that in 1805 Reil founded, with the philosopher Kayssler, the *Magazin für psychische Heilkunde*, in which he published an article on "Medicine and Education." In 1808 he joined with another philosopher, Hoffbauer, to publish *Beiträge zur Beförderung einer Kurmethode auf psychischem Wege.*

It would seem as if Reil bowed to the old tradition which was being revived and was becoming more self-assertive at the time, particularly in Germany. As we have seen, psychology was already definitely in the hands of the philosopher. Toward the end of the eighteenth century the philosopher claimed the fields of psychopathology as well, and psychotherapy and even forensic psychiatry. When Hufeland (1762–1836), one of the pioneers in public health—which began to arouse the interest of the medical profession at that time—published a book on the subject, he included in it considerations of mental health, or what is known today as mental hygiene. Hufeland sent the book to Immanuel Kant, asking Kant's opinion of his views on mental hygiene. Kant replied with a booklet, *Von der Macht des Gemüths durch den blossen Vorsatz seiner Krankhaften Gefühle Meister zu seyn.* It was Kant who insisted that expert psychiatric witnesses in criminal cases in which the question of insanity arises should be invited not from among the members of the medical faculty but from among those of the faculty of philosophy.

Reil, too, sought the help of philosophers; he apparently had little self-reliance in psychotherapeutic matters despite his enormous knowledge of medicine, neurology, and clinical psychiatry. He felt the need of the psychiatric wisdom with which the philosopher was supposed to be endowed by virtue of his vocation. Even the psychiatrist (and there is no doubt that we should consider Reil as one of the founders of psychiatry as a specialty), while he sensed keenly the inadequacy of purgatives, emetics, and bloodletting and while he felt the imperative need for psychotherapy, tended to consider it something beyond his ken. In a circuitous and veiled manner the priest, who was supposed to be the only one possessing psychic healing powers, came back for a moment under the guise of the philosopher. This officially unacknowledged but potent tradition has survived in the form of faith-healing, or "re-education" by self-made and self-appointed "psychologists" or Doctors of Philosophy in psychology, and in the attitude of viewing the psychotherapeutic work of the psychiatrist and medical psychoanalysts as something mysterious, esoteric, nonmedical. Mental disease and its treatment have not yet been fully divested by our present-day civilization of theurgic colorings and mystical implication, and Reil and a number of his contemporaries of the eighteenth century merely reflected the perennial frailty of man's own attitude toward his own mind, and the tenuous threads which hold him attached to the scientific investigation of mental processes, particularly abnormal ones. The psychiatrist seemed at times either to be ready to cede his position as healer to the philosopher or to become a philosopher himself. He sensed and even observed the importance of emotions and the presence of co-ordinating forces other than the physiological responses of the body, but he could gain no insight into the nature of emotions and he stood askance at once before philosophy and physiology. Questions continued to be asked. The answers continued to be confused and unoriginal. The important thing to be noted is that the discussions of the relationship of mind and body and passions, discussions which started with such definiteness in the eighteenth century, were never abandoned despite the fact that other developments in psychiatric history seemed at times to overshadow the problem.

The German physicians were more actively interested in this aspect of psychopathology than the French or English. Johann Christian

Bolten stated that psychological measures such as persuasion and consolation are of curative value not only in mental but also in physical diseases.[32] Ludwig thought that fantasy may cause mania or melancholia.[33] Zückert wrote *Von den Leidenschaften* ("On passions") in 1774, and Scheidemantel *Von den Leidenschaften als Heilmittel betrachtet* ("Passions considered as means of cure") in 1787. These were remnants, vague and uncertain, rather than continuations, clear and definite, of the ideas suggested by Stahl. Characteristically for the age, the physician who felt impressed with the ideas of Stahl either branched out into studies of the anatomy and physiology of the central nervous system (Unzer), or acquired a greater interest in the classification of mental diseases (de Sauvages), or in hospital organization and administration (Langermann). Johann Unzer (1727–1799), the first German physician to use the term *Lebenskraft,* at first followed Stahl. He apparently possessed a profound and lucid mind; Goethe admired him a great deal. Unzer was soon attracted by the ideas of Haller, whose adherent he became, and devoted himself to the study of reflexes.[34] Boissier de Sauvages belongs to the group of systematizers of diseases, the so-called nosographers or nosologists.

Johann Gottfried Langermann (1768–1832), the plain son of a plain peasant, stands chronologically and ideologically on the dividing line between the eighteenth and the nineteenth centuries, even as Stahl whom he followed stood on the line between the seventeenth and the eighteenth. Langermann was thirty-two years old at the opening of the nineteenth century and he died thirty-two years later. He wrote but one work on mental diseases—his doctor's dissertation which was published in 1797 under the title *De methodo cognoscendi curandique animi morbos stabilienda* ("On the method of recognizing and curing lasting mental diseases"). He follows Stahl in dividing mental diseases into functional and organic. He rejected the ever-growing insistence, which became almost a postulate, that the seat of mental diseases was in the brain. He even insisted that many physical diseases are of a psychological origin, and he therefore stressed the need of a systematic, well-rounded psychotherapy. According to Kirchhoff, this

---

[32] J. Ch. Bolten: *Gedanken von psychologischen Kuren.* Halle, 1751.
[33] Ch. G. Ludwig: *Institutiones medicinae clinicae.* Leipzig, 1758.
[34] T. Kirchhoff: *Deutsche Irrenärzte.* Berlin, 1921, vol. I, pp. 13–15.

one work of Langermann's on mental diseases was the first dissertation on psychiatry to be submitted in Germany for a doctorate.

Langermann was close to some of the great minds of his time—the philosopher Fichte, Goethe, and Schiller. His professional activity was in harmony with the spirit of his time. He was the founder of the first mental hospital in Germany—that of St. Georg in Bayreuth—of which he was director from 1805 to 1810. His was the mission of a psychiatric humanist and he opposed cruelty toward mental patients in any form. He was against all restraint and abolished the strait jacket. He saw mental patients in a hospital as people to be treated and not to be controlled and held in check. Langermann's personality was that of a humane and warmhearted, enthusiastic teacher, and one of his greatest services to psychiatry was his informal teaching of medical psychology in a comparatively small circle of young men whose interest and enthusiasm for psychological medicine he maintained and nurtured. One of these young men was among the leading psychiatrists of the next century, Karl Wilhelm Ideler.

Gradually, but with more and more clarity and steadiness, the major interests of psychiatry became hospital organization, hospital reform, and the teaching of psychiatry. That this spirit should appear so definitely in Germany is particularly significant, for Germany lagged behind in the general development of psychiatry until almost the very close of the eighteenth century. As cultural conditions in England and France fully matured toward the close of the century and produced such efficient and scientific reformers as William Tuke and Philippe Pinel, Germany, which seems to have awakened to the problems much later, did catch up with the times. Perhaps it was not entirely fortuitous that from Germany had come the first voice of scientific and humanistic psychiatry in Johann Weyer—a French doctor of medicine.

Despite the increasing national consciousness all over Europe, social consciousness and the consciousness of cultural unity which came to such cataclysmic expression in the French Revolution and the Napoleonic Wars proved the stronger and more creative forces, for a while at least. Medicine became gradually imbued with these ideological strains, and as a result problems of reform, public health, and proper care of the mentally ill came to the fore. Hufeland's pioneering work in public health has been mentioned. The name of Peter Frank

(1745–1821) deserves notice; one of the founders of the pathology of the spinal cord, Frank was a true reformer. He originated the idea of *Medizinische Polizei*—a community-wide organization of medical supervision. Frank was the first in Germany to repeat the substance of Cicero's eloquent appeal in the *Tusculanes*.[35] Frank said that a doctor should study mental diseases as much as he studies pharmacology. This statement was unquestionably original with him; it is doubtful whether he was aware of Cicero's interest in psychiatry. It was also Frank who was the first to suggest that certain psychological causes might produce skin rashes. In this suggestion he anticipated psychiatric history by more than a hundred years; not until the twentieth century did skin reactions to psychological conflicts, known as trophoneuroses, become well-established, clinical facts.

IX

THE discussion of the relationship between body and mind and the philosophical speculations on the nature of the mind, while strongly influencing certain small groups of physicians, had to recede before other more pressing problems. But such discussions and speculations should not be dismissed as insignificant phenomena in psychiatric history; the animistic and vitalistic trends which appeared sporadically throughout the century were not limited to medicine. Natural philosophy (the older term for biology) also began to show signs of not being fully satisfied with the purely mechanistic views which dominated the field. It was Lamarck (1744–1829) who broke the seemingly unbreakable ranks of mechanistic rationalism, but the welter of socioeconomic problems which swarmed over the century, the technological advances, the steady growth of the number of discoveries in physics and chemistry—to which the seventeenth century gave such great impetus—made the first appearance of vitalistic biology and psychology look insignificant and actually stunted the proper development of their theoretical and practical implications.

It is so much more significant, therefore, that despite the very fleeting and none too articulate impression of Stahl's consideration of medi-

35 See p. 65.

cal psychology his ideas did make some valuable contributions to clinical psychopathology. The differentiation between organic and functional mental diseases, for instance, is fundamental and is a direct result of the ideas which were fermenting throughout the century lying between Stahl and Langermann. This differentiation became the cornerstone of modern psychiatry, for the question of how to treat a patient cannot be answered unless the problem of whether a given mental disease is organic or functional is definitely and scientifically solved. Also, it is impossible to overestimate the importance of the very formulation of the problem as Stahl and his few followers set it forth. Here for the first time in almost eighteen hundred years, if not for the first time in the whole history of medical thought, an attempt was made to establish the principle, if not yet the fact, that psychological, that is, biological forces—not physical, mechanical, or metaphysical, spiritualistic forces—might produce a mental disease. It was an unequivocal assertion that mental disease may be considered *mental* without being related to theological dogma or metaphysical principles of freedom of the will. It was the first assertion that the human mind, despite the obscurity of its origin and the impossibility of observing it directly, may be studied and treated with nonphysical or nonchemical means which are at the same time not means of exorcism, fire, absorption in the unknown, or ceremonial mysticism.

It is true that the theological tradition in relation to mental diseases, in itself a derivative of the magicoanimistic tradition the roots of which are deeply imbedded in the remotest past of man's history, could not easily be discarded by the scholar, who ever was but a man. Therefore it was not at once possible to gain a secure, scientific footing for the psychobiological orientation which was inconspicuously born and at first so ineffectively stated. This is reflected in the evidence of doubt which was forever present in the minds of those who felt inclined toward the psychological approach to mental diseases. Langermann, for instance, was on one hand inclined to go to the extreme of considering even physical diseases of a psychological nature, even as a few extremists of twentieth-century psychiatry or the nonmedical theorists of the revived magicoanimism represented by Christian Science, New Thought, and other magic philosophies steeped in metaphysics but speaking the vernacular of modern science. On the other hand, the same Langermann, considering the problem of suicide, showed considerable uncertainty about his own psychological views, and not a little inclination to accept the traditional view that certain psychopathological reactions may be considered due to the ill will of man, and that therefore man should shoulder the responsibility for his illness and be duly penalized. It is this trend which made Langermann think that not every case of suicide should be viewed as caused by mental illness and that some of those who took their own lives should, therefore, be denied religious burial.

Language difficulties, to which Vives called attention early in the sixteenth century, also stood in the way of the new psychobiological orientation. Language, the most powerful expression of the human mind, is at the same time its weakest tool; words are steeped in the traditions of man's psychological development. New concepts and new knowledge are not infrequently ahead of the word. While given a new meaning, the old word still carries with it old connotations to the scientific as well as the popular mind: such a word as *mind* still carries with it a confusing series of metaphysical connotations, no matter how great our propensities to view it biologically. Therefore, when the medical man turned his attention to psychological phenomena and began to use the word "mind" in the medicopsychological sense, he failed to convey a clear-cut scientific meaning. The Germans still use the word *Geisteskrankheiten*, which through its etymological construction still connotes the meaning of diseases of the spirit, the soul. The French speak of *maladie d'esprit* or more recently of *maladies mentales*, still connoting the concept of spirit, or mind—intellect. The English-speaking people use "mental diseases," a term which carries the connotation of intellect or reason. The German psychiatrist uses the words *Geist* (spirit) and *Seele* (soul) interchangeably. The French speak of *esprit*, which now means intellect and then spirit, psyche, or the word *âme* (soul) which among the eighteenth-century writers was used interchangeably with *esprit*. The words "spirit" or "mind" became the standard terms of English-speaking psychiatrists. We may observe in this usage of words a series of attempts to divorce ourselves from the theological tradition, attempts which were never fully successful and which almost always failed to rid our thinking of the very concepts which we wanted to abandon. The words *Geist, esprit,* "spirit," when they were not used to carry the meaning of "soul," would connote a physiological, that is, physiochemical, substance—a concept inherited from the Hippocratic and particularly Galenic physiology, which was based on the concept of the so-called animal spirits.

This conceptual confusion definitely stood in the way of a clearer understanding of the ideas which the Stahl-Langermann orientation attempted to introduce into psychiatry. Psychologically speaking, it stood in the way of Stahl and Langermann and their followers. But it must be carefully noted that despite these difficulties, and despite the lack of initial scientific success, these eighteenth-century ideas presented the continuation of the great effort which the sixteenth century had made to separate the forthcoming science of psychology from theology. It must be constantly borne in mind that this effort of the eighteenth century was made by physicians, as it had been made primarily by physicians and not philosophers in the sixteenth. It cannot be repeated too often that it was medicine which tried to capture the field of mental diseases. The struggle, while seemingly not as intense and not as difficult in the eighteenth century, required nevertheless an immense effort. The effort split into two definite directions, which frequently converged, however, throughout the course of psychiatric history. One was the development of empirical clinical observations and of their systematization. The other was the reform of the care of the mentally sick, which led to the formation of hospitals for mental diseases.

x

GREATER and greater numbers of mentally ill had come to the attention of the physician, who found himself confronted with the age-long problem of jealously protecting his field of observation and operation from metaphysical intrusions. The intense, bloody, and fiery struggle of the preceding demonological centuries only accentuated the physician's human propensities to shun his own psychology and to revert to a purely physical, corporeal, organic point of view. The recapture of the spirit of Hippocratic medicine so obvious in the seventeenth century became an established principle in the eighteenth. The physician accustomed to dealing with physical diseases as special, well-defined entities transferred the same habit of thought into his consideration of mental diseases. An abscess certainly looks quite different from a headache. These are two different pathological conditions. True, Roman medicine had introduced the concept of symptoms *by consensus* or *by sympathy*,[36] thus making it possible to understand that one may have an illness in the stomach and have a headache "by sympathy." Yet the principle that each disease has its own way of starting, its own set of symptoms, its own course, and its own typical outcome was preserved and yielded inestimable values to the art of diagnosis, prognosis, and healing. That the physician should approach mental diseases with the same preconception which had proved so realistic and useful in the treatment of physical diseases was but natural, particularly since the influence of Hippocrates was so thoroughly re-established and since science and technology offered so many more means for the differentiation of masses of symptoms and other manifestations of disease.

One is not surprised to find that the physician of the eighteenth century devoted a great deal, if not most, of his attention to the differentiation and classification of mental diseases, in the same manner as he proceeded with physical diseases. As a matter of fact, whatever psychological labels he attached to mental diseases, he considered them physical; they belonged to the general scheme of classification of diseases. Nosology became the order of the day. The Hippocratic classification of all diseases into febrile and afebrile was found convenient and was readopted almost without amendment. Hippocrates' division of mental diseases into mania and melancholia was also accepted almost without question.

Hermann Boerhaave (1668–1738), the great medical teacher of Leyden, defined melancholy textually in almost the same way as had Hippocrates: "Physicians call that disease a Melancholy, in which the patient is long and obstinately delirious without a fever, and always intent upon one and the same thought." [37] The point of view on the diseases does not seem to have changed: "This disease arises from that Malignancy of the Blood and Humors, which the Antients have called *Black Choler:* and again, though this Disease doth begin in what is

[36] See p. 73.

[37] Hermann Boerhaave: *Aphorisms: concerning the knowledge and cure of diseases.* Translated from the last edition printed in Latin at Leyden, 1728. London, 1735. Aph. 1089.

called the Mind, it yet doth render the Choler black in the Body very soon. It will be therefore needful to draw a small sketch of this wonderful Disease, whose Doctrine is supposed commonly to be so dark, that Antiquity is unjustly blamed for it." [38] Boerhaave, it must be admitted, was in need of the same tolerance on the part of history which he invoked toward antiquity.

He added a consideration of the blood to his considerations of the black choler, thus making us aware that Harvey's discovery of a century before had not been overlooked. But in the very next aphorism Boerhaave speaks of *Atrabiliar Humor,* or *Melancholy Juice,* and a little further of the evil "already advanced to a great Acrimony with the Bowels much corrupted." Aphorism 1109 reads: "If this Disease doth continue long, it occasions Foolishness, Epilepsies, Apoplexies, furious Madness, Convulsions, Blindness, wonderful Fancies, Laughters, Cryings, Singings, Sighings, Belchings, Anguishes; great Evacuations of Urine. . . ." The simplicity and grossly empirical nature of the psychological approach is thrown into relief by this listing of symptoms in which belching and wonderful fancies are given equal scientific attention. The difference between one state or another is almost a matter of nomenclature only: "If Melancholy increases so far, that from the great Motion of the Liquid of the Brain, the Patient be thrown into a wild Fury, it is call'd *Madness."* [39] Boerhaave differentiated this *Madness* from *Dog-Madness* "because of its [the latter's] desperate ill nature." He observed that melancholia and mania might be different phases of the same disease. As to treatment, he again repeated some of the observations which are found among the Greco-Roman writers: "When all Remedies have been tried in vain, it has sometimes happen'd that varicous Tumours, Piles, Dysenteries, Dropsies, great Haemorrhagies come of themselves, and Tertian or Quartan Agues have cured this Disease." [40]

Being, however, a great clinician in his own right and abreast of the development of physics, Boerhaave adapted a little too ingeniously some of his therapeutic ideas to the old theories: "The greatest Remedy for it is to throw the Patient unwarily into the Sea, and to keep him under

[38] *Ibid.,* Aph. 1090, 1091.
[39] *Ibid.,* Aph. 1118.
[40] *Ibid.,* Aph. 1124.

Water as long as he can possibly bear without being quite stifled." [41] This method of "ducking" was even used nearly one hundred years later by Benjamin Rush in Philadelphia. In the time of Boerhaave the building of various instruments for experimentation appealed to the therapeutically inclined psychiatric observer. A special twirling stool was invented to spin the patient until he became unconscious. The spinning was supposed to rearrange the brain and thus bring it and the patient to normalcy.

The first half of the eighteenth century seems to have been unable to reach out beyond the established Hippocratic dogma. In re-establishing Hippocrates it brought demonology to its ultimate demise; but its service to medical psychology presented primarily an achievement of a negative nature. As an illustration of this aspect of psychiatry we may consider a book published in London in 1733: *The English Malady: or, a treatise of nervous diseases of all kinds, as spleen, vapours, lowness of spirits, hypochondriacal, and hysterical distempers,* "written by George Cheyne, M. D., Fellow of the College of Physicians at Edinburgh and Fellow of the Royal Society." The truly distinguishing feature of this book is that it is supplemented "with the author's own case at large." This fact is far more important than any theories or remedies reported by Cheyne or by dozens of his more distinguished colleagues. A neurosis or a more serious mental illness had begun to be looked upon more soberly, as a disease in fact not merely in name. Cheyne relates his own case as a clinical illustration, without false shame or that mysterious self-consciousness which is characteristic of our attitude toward psychological troubles even today. Rational self-observation and a frank medical attitude toward psychopathological phenomena were and are the prerequisites of a scientific medical psychology. Vives was an excellent example of this method of approach, and for the same reason the otherwise traditional contribution of Cheyne cannot be given too honorable a place in the psychiatric literature.

"What I pretend to have done in some Degree in the following Treatise," says Cheyne, "is That I hope I have explain'd the Nature and Causes of Nervous Distempers (which have hitherto been reckon'd Witchcraft, Enchantment, Sorcery and Possession, and have been the constant Resource of Ignorance) from Principles easy, natural and

[41] *Ibid.,* Aph. 1123.

intelligible, deduc'd from the best and soundest Natural Philosophy; and have by the plainest Reasoning, drawn from these Causes, and this Philosophy, a Method of Cure and a Course of Medicines specifically obviating these Causes, confirm'd by long Experience and repeated Observations, and conformable to the Practice of the ablest and best writers on these Diseases." [42] The naïve dietetic physiology and the conviction, ever increasing despite constant citations of successfully curative remedies, that mental diseases are actually incurable are further reflected in another paragraph: "After all, I would not have it thought, that I am of Opinion that none ever fail'd or died, who enter'd on a Milk, Seed, and Vegetable diet under these mention'd Distempers. The noble Organs may be spoilt or irretrievably obstructed, which the wisest Physician alive cannot absolutely foreknow; the Time remaining and necessary for a total Cure of such tedious Diseases, may not be sufficient in the common Duration of Life. All I affirm therefore, is, that such a Diet in the mention'd Distempers, with the usual proper Medicines, duly persisted in, will do the Whole that Art can possibly do, or Mortality will admit; and infinitely more than the same Medicines under a full and free Diet of Animal Foods and Spirituous Liquors; and at the very least, will make their Pains and Sufferings less both in Life and Death." [43]

If the insight into mental diseases developed with extreme slowness in the course of the eighteenth century, the literature on the subject showed an almost luxuriant growth. It was in this respect more productive than any previous century—a definite demonstration that psychiatry as a specialty had been born. The psychiatrist at that time was not, of course, the well-defined, circumscribed specialist we know today. He was always a practitioner of general medicine; his specialization was more a matter of emphasis of interest than an abandonment of practice in other diseases, and his psychiatric interest was definitely more neurological than psychiatric.

The brain, its structure and role continued to preoccupy the psychiatrist. Gall (1758–1828) attempted to reduce the whole field of psychology to cerebral localization, even as is being done with a different methodology today. Gall's approach was purely anatomical and he

[42] Cheyne: *The English Malady, etc.,* "Preface," p. x.
[43] *Ibid.,* pp. ix–x.

sought to justify his conviction that each part of or spot on the brain had a special (rather complex) psychological function to perform, and that each of the most important parts or formations of the cerebrum was imprinted in the configurations of the skull. J. K. Lavater, whose *Physiognomische Fragmente* were published in 1775, looked to the foundation of an empirical classification of character on the basis of facial expressions ("physiognomy").

It would be difficult and perhaps of no particular consequence to review in detail the whole mass of the psychiatric literature of the eighteenth century. A great deal of it is repetitious and diffuse. From the few examples already cited it will have become sufficiently clear that the various authors dealing with the subject, rejecting any psychology as speculative and unscientific, fell themselves into the pit of speculation, naïve theorizing, and fanciful hypotheses. These speculations, theories, and hypotheses appealed to the writers and apparently to the enlightened public as more plausible and more acceptable than any psychology because they represented an anatomic, physical, chemical, organic orientation. It was in the eighteenth century, it would appear, that in matters psychiatric the word "scientific" became equated with "organic," "corporeal," "physiological." The word "scientific" was not in use then to the extent or with the same glibness as it is used today, but its meaning was conveyed by such terms as "of the Art" or "artificial" (used by Francis Bacon) and "belonging to or in accordance with Natural Philosophy."

It is this steadfast adherence to what appeared to be scientific, Hippocratic psychophysiology, and the monotonous references to "Black Choler," "Nervous Fluid," and other juices which made the literature for the most part devoid of originality and rather stagnant as to psychological insight. The original and refreshing parts of the literary contribution to medical psychology are to be found in the ever-increasing number of case reports, in the observations of certain psychological details which even though not a little desultory represented an important contribution and a remarkable step forward. Among these empirical observations one may mention John Ferriar's *Medical Histories and Reflections* (1792), W. Perfect's *Select Cases in the Different Species of Insanity or Madness* (1787), William Battie's *A Treatise on Madness* (1758), which dealt primarily with the brain, or Benjamin

Fawcett's *Observations on the nature, causes and cure of melancholy, especially of that, which is commonly known as religious melancholy* (1780). It is noteworthy that while in the seventeenth century Thomas Willis still relegated to the devil the mental diseases which were of an ecstatic nature and which showed prominence of religious trends, in the eighteenth Benjamin Fawcett reflects the enormous changes which the century had wrought in the medical mind when he considers religious melancholy but a subdivision of general melancholy and believes it to be as much a physical disease as other mental diseases. Medical thought was swinging fully to the other extreme.

Out of the mass of observations there began to be delineated certain particular aspects of individual diseases. Anne Charles Lorry (1726–1783) found it necessary to differentiate a *Melancholia Nervosa* from a *Melancholia Humoralis*.[44] Thomas Arnold (1742–1816), in his two volumes of *Observations on the Nature, Kinds, Causes, and Prevention of Insanity* (1782, 1786), made a further step in differentiating certain details of mental disease. He considered the characteristics of what he called "ideal and notional insanity," by which he meant the type of illness in which the ideas and the concepts ("notions") are abnormal. His was an attempt to take stock, or at least to consider in greater detail, one of the forms of what we know now as schizophrenia, in which the outstanding symptoms are presented by illusionary and delusionary thinking. J. Haslam (1764–1844), pursuing more carefully than any of his predecessors the investigation of the relationship of mental disease to certain forms of paralysis, gave us what appears to be the first clinical description of what is known as paresis, or general paralysis.[45] That this disease was due to syphilis contracted years previously Haslam did not know, of course. The exact relationship of syphilis to mental disease remained unknown for a long time, and was not definitely proven till one hundred and fifteen years after Haslam's description appeared. Scientific knowledge moves with an exasperating slowness for which it compensates with certainty. Syphilis had attracted the attention of the doctor toward the close of the fifteenth century. Medicine had watched it and studied it ever since. Psychiatry was impressed

[44] A. Lorry: *De melancholia et morbis melancholicis.* Paris, 1765.

[45] J. Haslam: *Observations on insanity with particular remarks on the disease and an account of the morbid appearance on dissections.* London, 1798.

with the mental manifestation of its consequences. The task of correlating cause and effect and the nature of each took almost exactly four hundred years; not until Noguchi and Moore demonstrated in 1913 the presence of syphilitic spirocheta in the parenchyma of the brain could the problem be considered solved. The great value of Haslam's contribution lies in the fact that his clinical description was made not as a result of preconceived theory or even of a working hypothesis, but through the sheer effort of keen observation of minute, seemingly unrelated details, through dogged tabulation and orderly arrangements of these details until finally a coherent clinical picture of a disease came to the fore.

Such was the task which the eighteenth-century physician was facing and meeting with considerable success. This, too, was the task the psychiatrist had to face, a task much more difficult than the one faced by Haslam, who thought primarily in terms of neuropathology. Haslam found his answer in the dissecting room. The psychiatrist who dealt with purely psychological phenomena had no established methods of observation, no special tools to "dissect" the mind except his own intuition and not many ways and methods for the verification of his conclusions. Therefore, the achievements of those who succeeded in discovering or in describing a new psychological detail, a new aspect of a psychological symptom, in bringing some order to the confused mass of impressions—those achievements cannot be overestimated. They not only filled an important need of the time; they placed psychiatry on a scientific basis and made it a true and autonomous branch of medicine.

Haslam was able to remark in the eighteenth century that states of excitements and depressions alternate in the same individual, and that if these states continue to alternate the ultimate outcome is grave. This method of viewing a mental disease from the standpoint of its prognosis was destined to become an important aspect of psychiatry toward the end of the nineteenth century.

It will be recalled that love used to be considered one of the causes of mental disease. This problem of love and its relationship to mental illness continued to interest psychiatric observers but it remained unsolved; mental illnesses in which erotic motives dominated or neuroses in which sexual trends were the point of preoccupation were supposed to be caused by an especially morbid erotism, just as neuroses in which gastric complaints were prominent were thought to be caused by a disease of the stomach. Women were still considered more predisposed to psychopathies connected with erotic trends, and even in the third quarter of the century the ideas of the past were still held by many. Bienville published *La Nymphomanie ou Traité de la Fureur Utérine* in 1771; the theory of "uterine furor" died hard. On the other hand, there were such names as A. R. Vetter (1765–1806), who saw more clearly that the sexual trend does not by itself constitute a sign of a separate disease. In his *Dissertatio de Morbis Amatoris* Vetter considers this disease a form of melancholia.

Whatever the individual studies and biases, enough single psychiatric observations were accumulated so that there was not a system of medicine nor a general classification of diseases which did not take into account mental diseases. This was the age of systems and psychiatry became a part of the general trend. Natural as this consequence may appear and obvious as its need may seem to be, it must be noted that any classification of diseases presupposes some basic principle of differentiation. We might classify physical diseases on the principle of the parts affected and speak of diseases of the bones, diseases of the liver and intestines, diseases of the blood vessels. We might use the principles of causation and speak of infectious diseases, diseases of metabolism, diseases due to certain tissue alterations such as arteriosclerosis. We might be guided by any principle of differentiation, provided this principle had a basis in the actual facts of the disease. But at no time, even today and particularly in the eighteenth century, has psychiatry enjoyed the advantage of having the causes of mental diseases actually known. At the time under consideration the physician still remembered that, historically speaking, only yesterday the devil was the one and only true causative agent. The new and varied theories as to what caused mental diseases were all speculative, and no proponent of any of them was able to demonstrate the validity of his views but only his sincere convictions. As to the help theoretical psychology had to offer, it was a no less speculative help based on postulates about certain faculties of man's mind. Psychiatry had to limit itself to descriptions of rather general observations which were based more on clinical impressions than on sound scientific criteria. The physician had to assume that the various conditions he observed were separate diseases, and on the basis of this assumption he proceeded to give each disease a name. The usefulness of such nosological systems is definitely doubtful, but their historical significance cannot be overlooked. These systems tell us more eloquently than any other single aspect of psychiatric history how medicine in its conquest of the field of psychopathology attempted from the very outset to fit psychopathology into a preconceived place and to view it from a preconceived, traditional standpoint.

XI

ONE of the leading nosographers of the period was François Boissier de Sauvages (1706–1767), who was dubbed by his colleagues and students *médecin de l'amour*. This nickname was more in the nature of a friendly joke than the expression of a critical attitude; de Sauvages was a serious student and a good and conscientious clinician. The nickname was suggested by the topic he chose for his doctor's dissertation, which he defended before the medical faculty of Montpellier in 1726 at the age of twenty. The dissertation bore the title *Si l'amour peut être guéri par des remèdes tirés des plantes*. De Sauvages was of a conservative bent of mind but by nature far removed from the demonological prejudices which were still in evidence in certain academic circles. He expressed himself definitely against Bodin, who was apparently not fully forgotten in those days. Yet, despite the fact that he thought all mental diseases were caused by anatomical lesions, he thought the will had something to do with mental aberrations. He was reluctant to absolve the will of any responsibility in the matter because he was afraid that if everyone were to do so there would be no justice. Patients, he felt, ought to be approached with friendliness so that their confidence might be gained, confidence being considered one of the major prerequisites for good curative results.

Discussing the diseases accompanied by convulsions, de Sauvages recognized a type of epilepsy which he thought was of syphilitic origin, curable by the "methodic administration of mercury." It is obvious that de Sauvages dealt here with paretics. He thought that epileptic attacks might be simulated, apparently failing to recognize the difference between attacks of *grande hystérie* and those of true epilepsy. The physiçian of the next century continued for a time to consider these two conditions related and the term "hystero-epilepsy" was frequently used. De Sauvages reports: "A seven-year-old girl feigned attacks of epilepsy so well that no one in the general hospital suspected her deception; I asked her whether she did not feel a wind passing through from her hand to the shoulder and from there to the back and leg and she said yes, she did. I prescribed the use of switches and as soon as she heard about it, she was cured." [46] De Sauvages and the majority of his colleagues were frequently naïve in their therapy and credulous about their cures, yet keen in their clinical observations and meticulously accurate in their classification—a combination of contradictory intellectual propensities frequent at the time.

De Sauvages' *Nosologie Méthodique* comprises three volumes. The first appeared three years after his death, and the last two one year later, in 1771. This careful classification had as its source of inspiration the orderly system of Sydenham and the classificatory arrangement of plants by Linnaeus.[47] For a considerable period Linnaeus' classification served as a model and principle for the majority of medical systems. In his theory of diseases de Sauvages was influenced by Stahl, but his major interest was orderly classification. His *Nosologie Méthodique* describes ten classes of diseases of which the eighth is called *Folies*. This class is subdivided into four orders: errors of reason, bizarreries, deliria, and anomalia. The "vaporous affections" are placed under order five of the sixth class.

It is at once evident that the classification, despite its orderliness, lacks inner unity. For such terms as "errors of reason," or "deliria," refer to abnormal behavior of the patient, while the term "vaporous affections" refers to the alleged cause of the disease rather than to its external manifestation. Each order has a number of subdivisions. Hypochondrias are counted among the deviations of reason. Fourteen varieties of melancholy are noted. De Sauvages denotes as "paraphrosynias" the majority of mental disorders which are ecstatic in nature. He puts into a separate group those mental diseases which are due to alcoholism, or opium, or other poisons such as belladonna or datura stramonium. How the interest in mental diseases had grown and how great the number of observations had become may be judged from the fact that in his *Nosologie* de Sauvages devotes to mental diseases a total of three hundred and twenty-six pages.

The classifications of mental diseases grew in number. They soon became but ponderous and unwieldy collections of new terms so that their very purpose—the clarification of clinical pictures—threatened to be defeated by terminological confusion. The classifiers revealed a great deal of ingenuity and inventiveness as well as a none too healthy tendency to become medical bookkeepers, rather than investigators in harmony with an orderly plan. De Valenzi (1728–1813) enriched medical psychology with a number of new terms: dysmnesia and amnesia, apanthropia and agriothymia. William Cullen (1710–1790) under class two, Neuroses, established four orders: comata, adynamias, spasms, and vesanias. "Vesania," a term known from the days of Cicero, was frequently used by nosologists to denote generally what is called in English "insanity." Erasmus Darwin (1731–1802), the grandfather of Charles, offered a classification which was perhaps the most typical for the physiological orientation which prevailed at the time and the most telling from the point of view of the determined effort to produce a psychiatry without psychology. Darwin, who studied medicine in Cambridge and Edinburgh, was a physiologist and a poet —a combination both useful and dangerous in a nosologist. His *Zoonomia, or the Laws of Organic Life* bespeaks his chief interest. He classifies diseases into maladies of irritation, of sensation, of volition, and of association. By "association" he means the association of movements, not of ideas. The maladies of volition he divides merely into those of augmented and those of retarded volition.

The professional philosopher was not able to escape the temptation to introduce his views on systematization into psychiatry. True, the philosopher did not have at his disposal any direct clinical observations but, since the emphasis in any proper classification is more on formal logic than on empirical correlations, it must be said that the psychiatric nosologies of the philosophers compared favorably with those of many physicians. Their orderliness was undeniable, their theoretical value doubtful, their clinical usefulness a matter of personal taste, their helpfulness to the individual patient not a matter of particular concern.

J. B. Erhard, for instance, offers a classification of mental diseases in M. Wagner's *Beiträge zur philosophischen Anthropologie*.[48] He divides the vesanias into three groups. He speaks of false perceptions, of paraphrosynias, deliria, and amentias. Two years after the publication of this article he separated melancholia from the paraphrosynias and designated certain melancholias as *melancholia hypochondriaca, melancholia thanatophobia,* and *melancholia demonomania.* We see here a trend which later proved to be one of the most troublesome difficulties in psychiatry; the zest and assiduity with which classifications were prepared and respected finally led the psychiatrist to consider almost every symptom as indicative of a separate disease. If the patient was depressed and complained of gastrointestinal trouble, he had a separate *hypochondriacal* disease, inferentially brought about by a definite cause different from those which produce a depression during which the patient is afraid of death, or one in which he is preoccupied with fantasies about the devil; such depressions are, then, *thanatophobic* and *demonomanic,* respectively.

The greatest philosopher of the century, Immanuel Kant, whose influence extended for generations to come, was not only directly interested in mental diseases but was not reluctant to set down his views with unquestionable intellectual authority and keen speculative insight. For a period of years he was apparently interested in a proper classification of mental disturbances. In 1764 he published a five-page article on the subject [49] and again in 1798 in his *Anthropologie* he resumed the classification of mental diseases. "The primitive man," says Kant, "is subject to very little insanity or stupidity. His needs are always closely connected with experience and they offer his healthy judgment such a light task that he hardly notices that his activities require understanding." The primitive man "will of course, when he is ill in the head, become insane or idiotic, but this must occur most rarely, for he is healthy most of the time because he is free in his movements." [50]

The course of Kant's thought is highly interesting. First, while he

[48] J. B. Erhard: *Über die Melancholie.* In Wagner's *Beitr. zur phil. Anthro.* Vienna, 1794–1796.
[49] In *Königsbergische gelehrte und politische Zeitungen. Cf.* Neuburger and Pagel: *op. cit.,* vol. III, p. 651.
[50] *Ibid.,* p. 652.

admits and accepts the fact that mental diseases are due to organic brain disease, he nevertheless introduces a point of view and a methodological suggestion which at the time was highly original and which was to prove extremely fruitful. He calls our attention to the primitive man; he imagines this primitive man healthy "because he is free in his movements." In other words, Kant suggests that mental disease has something to do with the interaction of man's needs and the demands his environment makes upon him, or the frustration to which it subjects him. This, like many other thoughts expressed casually and in passing by great minds, was slow and imperceptible in its passage through generations of thought. It did not become articulate and primitive man did not become a subject of particular attention on the part of the psychiatrist until the twentieth century, when studies in genetic psychology threw valuable light on all mental diseases from milder neuroses to deteriorating schizophrenias. Kant imagined the primitive man mentally healthy, that is, fully adapted to his environment, and thought that the faulty development of judgment and understanding was the chief cause of mental disease—of maladaptation as he would say if speaking today. The point of view is purely intellectual; although Kant spoke in some detail about the disturbances of emotions, he seems to have laid much more stress on the intellectual than on the emotional aspects of mental disease. In this he may be considered one of the authoritative originators of the purely formalistic, intellectual point of view which characterized German psychiatry and which influenced more than it would appear on the surface English and American and to a great extent French psychiatry throughout the nineteenth century.

By way of purely formal description, man was considered to possess the powers of perception, understanding, and feeling; by way of the same descriptive formalism, it was considered that he might be mentally ill because something was wrong with his powers of perception, or understanding, or feeling. This point of view offered the opportunity for endless combinations of mental troubles which, when formulated, were at times one in spirit and in substance with the best scholastic subtleties of the previous centuries. Kant, for instance, was in agreement with the Abbé Terrasson that a person may suffer from false notions on the basis of which he thinks quite correctly but naturally arrives at false conclusions, or that his notions may be correct but his thinking incorrect and the conclusions arrived at will consequently again be false.[51]

The idea of the wholeness of man, which was sensed by Stahl and Cabanis, seems to have been lost to the great conceptual thinkers. Therefore their classifications, while all-embracing and all-inclusive, remained not a little stilted. They were correct; they covered everything about the man they were describing. Yet the man himself as an individual was lost in the orderly accumulation of detail. Kant considered that every insanity presented a loss of the *sensus communis* and the establishment of a *sensus privatus*. The formula was clear but it offered no added insight into man himself.

Kant fortunately made no new contribution to psychiatric terminology; he used the terms hypochondria, mania, raptus, melancholia, amentia, dementia, vesania. In addition to introducing the consideration of primitive people as a methodological approach to the study of mental diseases, Kant made a suggestion which, while not properly noticed at first, proved in the light of later nosological studies to be of inestimable value. In his *Anthropologie* he expressed the belief that the germ of insanity develops simultaneously with the germs of procreation, for he knew of no child who developed a mental sickness. Kant was factually wrong about children, for it was found that they do develop all forms of mental illness from milder neuroses—studies of which were made by Freud, who thereby opened a new field of child psychiatry and child guidance—to severest psychoses, some of which were described by de Sanctis at the beginning of the twentieth century, under the name of dementia praecocissima. But Kant's observation about the critical significance of the period of puberty proved correct. The term "dementia praecox" originally meant mental deterioration which sets in at puberty. The whole structure of psychoanalysis as it was developed by Freud brought ample proof of how crucial the period of puberty is in the development of mental diseases.

One is then justified in concluding that even toward the close of the eighteenth century, by way of direct observations and careful, even though confusing, systematization and classification of symptoms and diseases, medical psychology was brought face to face with the aware-

[51] *Ibid.*, p. 652.

ness that a new psychology was needed—a psychology which would be both genetic and sociological, a psychology which would enable the psychopathologist not only to observe more intelligently but to *understand* mental disease as a developmental process. This awareness, however, was only partial. In the meantime the value of the individual, the discovery of whom had been responsible for the birth of psychiatry as a medical discipline, began to be disregarded and man was almost fully lost in the forest of formal arrangements of psychophysiological classificatory concepts. Just as in the past man's mind was left to the theologian and later to the philosopher, so man as an individual was now being left to the philanthropist, the public-minded citizen. This neglect of man by the scientific psychiatrist was at first more apparent than real. As time went on it became, particularly in the nineteenth century, more real than apparent.

In the meantime the march of history was pressing forward with new problems and new ideas which were concrete and not abstract, political and social and not purely philosophical. The best medical minds could not help but sense the changing of the tide.

XII

WHENEVER the general problems of psychopathology are discussed we naturally think, as we have in these pages, of the great physicians of the past, of the theories they offered to explain the riddle of mental illness, of the manifold suggestions as to the treatment of the so-called insane, of the ingenuous ways which doctors and philosophers found to prove in what respects the mentally ill are different from what man should be. There are literally myriads of examples from the remote past till our own day which could demonstrate that wittingly or unwittingly the most scientific mind or the most favorably disposed person always considers himself in some unknown respect superior to the person who is mentally ill. At times the sense of superiority appears in the crude, sadistic form exemplified in the attitudes of a Nider, or a Bodin, or a Delrio; at times it remains concealed under the respectable and neat self-complacency of a classification.

We may take as an example the apparently most innocuous statement of Erasmus Darwin that diseases of volition are divided into those of augmented and those of retarded volition. Here quite obviously a most important and telling assumption is silently made and used as the very foundation of a classification—the assumption that there is such a thing as normal volition which is neither augmented nor retarded, that everyone knows what it is, that both the doctor who classifies the diseases of volition and the reader who studies the classification know well and are possessed of this normal volition. An undefined, undescribed, and even unspoken assumption is taken by general and silent consent as a standard of comparison. This weakness in the chain of scientific thinking is of more than philosophical import; the general problem as to what is normal, particularly mentally normal, is an abstract question, and its solution may be of no more than abstract value. The psychological aspects of this weakness, however, are of great importance; it signifies a definite trend on the part of the lay and medical world to consider themselves as separate from and superior to the mentally sick, superior by virtue of this assumed, unproven, but generally accepted state of being normal. Consequently, the so-called insane, regardless of our scientific theories, are at a disadvantage in relation to the very world upon which they have become so dependent as a result of their illness. Psychologically the world considers them stepchildren of life. Perhaps it is this psychological factor which has been more responsible than any other for the sad lot of the mentally ill throughout the ages. Perhaps it is this factor, rather than the philosophical and theological errors of the Sprengers and the Kraemers, which throughout the demonological centuries brought down upon the mentally sick the full weight of human cruelty. Perhaps this psychological factor has survived in the human community as an atavistic but potent inheritance from those remote days when primitive peoples summarily killed the sick and the aged merely because they had become burdens to a community which refused to be discommoded by the dead weight of the inept.

It is impossible otherwise to explain the really striking fact that until the very end of the eighteenth century there were no real hospitals for the mentally sick. Places where they were *kept* there were, of course; hospitals in which some few "maniacs" and "melancholics" were *kept* can also be found in the records of the past. But there were no hospitals which were properly organized for the purpose of *taking care* of and treating the mentally sick. From the formal, historical point of view we may state that Bethlehem was founded in 1247 and became known as Bedlam. We may also say there was a hospital in Paris originally known as Grange aux Gueux; the property on which it stood belonged originally to the Cardinal of Winchester and the corrupted pronunciation of his name produced the word Bicêtre. This hospital served as a retreat for mutilated officers and men. In 1660 it became a part of the General Hospital of Paris. These statements are historically correct and formally accurate, but, from the standpoint of the care and treatment of the mentally ill, Bedlam and Bicêtre were no more hospitals than a trench on a battlefield is a retreat and shelter of safety. What is true of Bedlam or the Bicêtre is equally and in some respects even more true of the *Narrentürme* in Germany or of any of their equivalents in the Old and later on also in the New World. The insane were pariahs who wandered over the countryside in the manner of werewolves, seeking shelter in stables and pigsties. We shall recall that people mocked at them, beat, tortured, and burned them for sadistic pleasure or for delusionary salvation. If apprehended and interned, the mentally sick were placed side by side with murderers and other criminals in chains and in fetters, without hope of redemption. The criminal would serve his term and sooner or later leave or be liberated by execution, but the insane who were so unfortunate as to be adjudged afflicted with a *natural* illness could not obtain liberation even by fire at the stake. Without sufficient nourishment and covered by their own excreta, they would literally rot in flesh and in spirit. The community thought of them as little as of refuse once it is taken care of by the organization for sewage disposal, unless it was occasionally to come and look at them for a small admission fee and enjoy seeing them rave and perform their "antics," thus contributing to the salary of the keepers who were usually ignorant, sadistic jailers.

Until the close of the eighteenth century this was the status of the majority if not of all of the places where the mentally sick were kept. There were a very few places, like those in Paris called *maisons de santé*, in which the insane were given some humanlike care, but these were extremely expensive and were naturally outside the reach of the great majority of patients. The poor and indigent—the great bulk of the insane—remained outside the pale of human consideration, even as the witches and sorcerers had. If we recall that many hundreds of thousands of men and women were brought to their deaths as witches and sorcerers during the sixteenth century alone, we shall be able to conceive of the staggering number of the mentally sick who now needed attention and failed to obtain it. The enlightenment of the age saved their lives but it failed to save them from slow torture. The well to do, even in the days of witch-hunting, might have found ways of at least dying more comfortably, but not the hordes of the other mentally sick. If we recall the preferred methods of treatment—the number of medical concoctions, bloodletting, clysters—all requiring personal medical attention and complicated medical paraphernalia and involving considerable expense, it will become even more clear that the preponderant majority of the insane and their families had to carry their burdens unrelieved.

The perusal of the contemporary medical literature impresses one with how indifferent the medical man of the sixteenth and seventeenth centuries, engrossed in his traditional ceremoniousness, was to the problem which could not have escaped his observation. The bitter and impetuous criticism of the medical profession which made Paracelsus so thoroughly hated by his colleagues was fully merited by the doctor of the time. And even in the eighteenth century the doctor had not fully awakened to social consciousness and public responsibility. Felix Plater, who was physically in closer contact with the mentally sick than was any other of his colleagues for a generation before or after him, had little to say about the miserable common lot of the insane. The heartrending appeals of Weyer two hundred and twenty-five years before Philippe Pinel's appearance on the psychiatric scene seem to have been totally forgotten.

Reference has been made to the fact that the progress of science is very slow; for instance, it took over four hundred years to trace the syphilitic infections through their development into a brain disease and insanity. Certain human emotions which seem to us so spontaneous and inherent, as if they are and have always been a part of our endowment since the birth of the race—these emotions, too, require time to develop and to become an integral part of man's daily ethicosociological existence. For reasons that are both complex and almost untraceable, homo sapiens with all or because of all his pride in himself develops with exasperating slowness, particularly in matters of corporate and co-operative responsibility for his fellow men. The automobile and the airplane have made more progress in forty-odd years of the twentieth century than did the social consciousness of the physician between 1563, when Weyer published his *De Praestigiis Daemonum*, and 1792, when William Tuke started his plans for the foundation of a humane hospital for the mentally ill and Philippe Pinel, appointed physician in charge of the Bicêtre, started removing the chains from the mentally ill.

The rumblings of the social conflicts which were soon to become the conflagration of the French Revolution, the effects of which spread and struck deeply all over Europe, awakened everywhere not only the sense of the individual's social responsibility but particularly the sense of the community's responsibility toward its members. The appeal of Vives,[52] insisting that the city (the State) has as great a responsibility toward its indigent and sick as a father has toward his children, was only now beginning to take practical root and bear fruit. It was over two hundred and fifty years after Vives' *De Subventione Pauperum* that Necker's report on the reform of hospitals was filed (1781) and that Colombier's report on the same subject (1785) and Bailly's (1786) were also duly filed with the chancelleries of the proper ministries in the proper offices, to await the day when the patient, bureaucratic mind of the State would awaken from the slumber of its misplaced tolerance and proceed to take some action.

While the philosophic and general cultural leadership of France at the time is incontestable, the general awakening was not, of course, limited to France. Protestant or Catholic, Europe was rapidly becoming a unitary economic and cultural organism functioning as a whole. The old Greek ideal stressing the responsibility of the individual citizen to the State was being gradually replaced by the revolutionary ideal of the duty and the responsibility of the State toward its citizens. It took over two thousand years of social growth before this psychosocial trans-formation became deep enough and strong enough to affect the structure and the functions of society, and even this slow and gradual process could not be completed without the sharp struggle and spilling of blood

[52] See p. 187.

and social upheaval which were the American Revolution of 1776 and the French of 1789.

It is in the light of these historical changes that one understands the pleading of Jean Colombier (1736–1789) who observed: "It is to the weakest and most unfortunate that society owes most diligent protection and care." [53] Colombier was a physician in charge of the Hôtel-Dieu. He was disturbed by the lax and irresponsible behavior of the community toward the indigent mentally ill. "The communities who are charged with paying the expenses of the capture and board of the insane do not bestir themselves to do their public duty; they even avoid doing it." [54] The insane wander about because there is no place to put them. And those who are behind walls are not treated well. "The bad treatment and particularly the beating should be considered crimes deserving of exemplary punishment." [55] "Thousands of deranged are locked up in prisons without anyone's thinking of administering the slightest remedy; the half-deranged are mixed with the completely insane, the furious with the quiet; some are in chains, others are free in the prison; finally, unless nature comes to their rescue and cures them, the term of their misery is that of their mortal days, and unfortunately in the meantime the illness but increases instead of diminishing." [56]

Colombier made these remarks four years before his death on August 4, 1789—the day on which the feudal privileges were abolished. The Revolution was already on the march. Voices similar to, if not as articulate as, the French were heard elsewhere. Anton Müller (1755–1827) in Germany, working in a hospital for mental diseases, preached humane treatment of the insane and protested against brutal restraint of patients. Vincenzo Chiarugi (1759–1820) in Italy published his hundred observations on the mentally ill and demanded the humanization of treatment of the deranged. [57] In England W. Perfect (1740–1789) and A. Harper spoke in the same vein. [58] The layman William

---

[53] R. Semelaigne: *Les pionniers, etc.*, vol. I, p. 87.

[54] *Ibid.*, p. 85.

[55] *Idem.*

[56] *Idem.*

[57] V. Chiarugi: *Della pazzia in genere e in specie trattato medico analitico con una centuria di observazioni.* Florence, 1793–1794.

[58] W. Perfect: *Select cases in the different species of insanity, or madness; with the diet and medicines used in the cure.* London, 1791. A. Harper: *A treatise on the real*

Tuke, aroused at the age of sixty by the abominable conditions in which the mentally ill lived and died, devoted the remainder of his days to reform. He founded York Retreat, which became an example to a number of hospitals established in the United States, of which Bloomingdale Hospital was one of the first. Tuke, whom René Semelaigne, the grandnephew of Philippe Pinel, calls a true apostle, inspired his family for generations to come with the same proselytic spirit of helping the mentally sick. His son Henry continued the work with great courage and self-sacrifice in the face of snarly opposition; Samuel, Henry's son, carried on the same work with the same devotion. They were all laymen. Finally Daniel Hack Tuke (1827–1895), Samuel's son, William's great-grandson, studied medicine, became a psychiatrist, and contributed a number of writings on mental diseases. His major work naturally was done at the York Retreat.

Just as the French Revolution was the vanguard of the new order to which Europe was maturing, so the French doctor was the most representative worker for the new psychiatric order. The contemporary and to some extent the precursor of Philippe Pinel was Joseph Daquin (1733–1815), whose voice was the true voice of a new era. Daquin was fifty-four years old when he took over the direction of the institution at Chambéry. "I had little experience with the treatment of the disease," admitted Daquin. "I applied more or less the same method which was practiced by the doctors and which I observed in the Hôtel-Dieu in Paris. There is no doubt that it is my fault, if I have not achieved great success with this method. . . . *I understood, however, that the course of treatment of insanity should be highly analogous to the methods used in the study of natural history, and that only in hospitals could one observe the various guises in which the malady appears, describe its history, regulate the therapeutic methods which cannot be always the same in all varieties of mental derangements, rid one's self of all the prejudices one has about the various types of insanity, and apply moral treatment in all cases.*" [59]

Daquin introduced a new and truly revolutionary note: here, for the first time since Weyer, the psychiatrist approaches the problem of men-

---

cause and cure of insanity; in which the nature and distinction of this disease are fully explained, and the treatment established on new principles. London, 1789.

[59] Quoted by R. Semelaigne: *Les pionniers, etc.,* vol. I, pp. 77–79. Italics ours.

tal disease with humility and with a curiosity without preconceptions. He wants to learn and he states a truth heretofore totally overlooked: that a hospital for mental diseases is primarily an institution for treatment and, equally important, a place of research; only in a hospital does one have enough clinical material to learn psychiatry and to make new investigations. General medicine established the value of hospital training in the thirteenth century in the days of Frederick II, the Hohenstaufen. Psychiatry as a medical discipline and psychiatric education along medical lines were almost five hundred and fifty years behind the times. In 1791 Daquin published his *Philosophie de la Folie,* which he dedicated to humanity, defining humanity as "enlightened philosophy, the reunion of all virtues." The second edition Daquin the pioneer dedicated humbly to his younger, great contemporary, Philippe Pinel, "to a friend of mankind, a man of virtue and enlightenment, an able physician in all departments of the art of healing, particularly in the one which is most thorny." [60] The fact that some of the theoretical preconceptions of Daquin were a little dated—he still believed that the lunar phases affect the mind—is of no more importance than the fact that Pinel continued to be inclined to believe that the seasons of the year have something to do with mania; such leftovers of the past are found even among psychiatrists of the twentieth century. What matters is that Daquin and Pinel were men of enlightened action of which psychiatry was in great need, that they were organizers and medical teachers and research workers, humanitarian doctors in psychiatry and not merely medical keepers of the insane or theorizing masters in the dissection of cadavers of the insane. "He who sees a madman," appealed Daquin, "without being touched by his state, and who looks at him only to be amused, is a moral monster." It was not mere sentimentality but true humility and consciousness of great responsibility toward the mentally sick which made Daquin say, "At least, what calms me is that my errors do not have their source in my heart, but rather in my intelligence." In the meantime, in Paris, Philippe Pinel made Daquin's principles and dreams, and his own, realities which not only survived historically as great achievements but became a permanent part of scientific and humanitarian psychiatry for generations to come.

[60] *Ibid.,* vol. I, p. 79.

XIII

To UNDERSTAND both the personality and the accomplishments of Philippe Pinel one must take into account the period in which he lived. Pinel was born in 1745 and died in his eighty-first year, in 1826. He arrived in Paris as a young doctor, eleven years before the French Revolution. Under the influence of Benjamin Franklin he almost went to live in the United States. In line of duty he had to be present at the execution of Louis XVI; he served as physician-in-chief of the Bicêtre and the Salpêtrière under the Revolution and the Terror. He served in the same capacity under Napoleon; he was almost appointed personal physician to the Emperor, but was too modest and disinterested and was therefore pleased when Corvisart was appointed to the position and he himself was made only consultant physician to the Emperor. Pinel saw Napoleon come and go and served assiduously under the restored Bourbons. He bore the decorations and honors of all these conflicting regimes, yet remained true to himself—a consistent and devout hospital worker to whom the care of the mentally ill was a task beyond and above the historical agitation which he witnessed and which actually knocked at his door, daily and sharply. Pinel was no recluse, and in view of the importance of his position he had to be in frequent if not constant contact with the highest state authorities. To live in Paris during those eventful forty-eight years from the year in which Rousseau and Voltaire died to within four years of the 1830 Revolution meant to live in the very center of the historical caldron of the age.

Pinel died at his post in his living quarters at the Salpêtrière. He was a conservative man, warmhearted yet detached, elastic, adaptable, but courageous. Despite the fact that he lived under and co-operated with so many self-contradictory political regimes, he was not a politician or a schemer; his job and his achievements survived solely by virtue of the single-mindedness of the man, of his simple sincerity and his intellectual honesty. He was not afraid to help Condorcet to go into hiding when the young philosopher's head was sought by the Revolution. He was frank and outspoken whenever he was deeply concerned; in a letter to his brother written on January 21, 1793, he said, "It is with great regret that I was obliged to attend the military execution [of Louis XVI] with the other citizens of my section; I write you, my heart pervaded with pain and in a stupor of profound consternation." [61] Pinel looked upon the political conflagrations from a height, as it were, commenting that he fully understood "the total value of so many pygmies who are making so much noise."

Intellectually and morally Pinel represented the very best of the French *tiers état* before it degenerated into the bourgeoisie of the Third Republic. He was serene, moral, moderately pious, and conservative in an enlightened way even at the height of the Revolution, even in his own sympathetic response to the revolutionary ideals of equality and freedom. He was a studious and a learned man. From his adolescence on he was much interested in Greek, Latin, and the sciences. Like many of the best minds of the century he considered classical knowledge and the classical attitude toward science and public problems ideal. It was the rational and the scientific, the orderly, the clear-cut and the logical which appealed to him most. He was at once the typical Frenchman and the rational humanitarian of a classical age. Almost imperturbable yet sensitive, he was polite, composed, matter of fact yet quick witted.

Pinel obtained his Master of Arts from the University of Toulouse. His thesis betrayed little of his future interest: *De la certitude que l'étude des mathématiques imprime au jugement dans son application aux sciences.* He received his medical degree in 1773. The theme of his doctor's dissertation is unknown; there is no university record of it. The bent of mind which he showed during the following five years, spent at the University of Montpellier, is interesting. He befriended a gifted young student, Chaptal, who, overwhelmed with what he had to study and what he was able to achieve, was somewhat discouraged and restless. Chaptal confided in Pinel, who did not fail to recognize that his friend suffered from a mild depression. "My young friend," said Pinel, "it is urgent that I ask you a slight favor. Please come to see me every day and let us read together a few pages of Montaigne, Plutarch, and Hippocrates." [62]

In 1778 Pinel came to Paris. It is rather characteristic of him that he

[61] R. Semelaigne: *Les grands aliénistes français,* vol. I, p. 112.
[62] *Ibid.,* vol. I, p. 21.

did not start to practice medicine. He found for himself a modest place in the Latin Quarter and obtained a position tutoring in mathematics. For a few years he occupied himself with medical, literary work, always jealous of the leisure which he used only for further studies. He abstracted and edited the first three volumes of the *Philosophical Transactions* of the Royal Society, noting especially the curious case of one Samuel Clinton who suffered from pathological sleeping. Pinel's great interest in William Cullen led him to translate the *Institutions of Medicine* into French and to publish it in 1785. Three years later his translation of Baglivi's *Opera Omnia* was published. Pinel was impressed with Baglivi's dictum that the patient is the best medical textbook. He made frequent visits to a *maison de santé* of a Dr. Belhomme where private mental patients were treated. He read with interest Colombier's *Instructions sur la manière de gouverner les insensés et de travailler à leur guérison dans les asiles qui leur sont destinés* (1785). It was in this report that Colombier insisted on the obvious necessity for each patient to have his own bed; Colombier had found that more frequently than not there was but one bed for every four patients. Pinel contributed a few articles in the *Journal de Physique* and in 1784 he was invited to edit the *Gazette de Santé*. The direction of this magazine he held until 1789. He contributed to Fourcroy's periodical *La Médecine Eclairée par les Sciences Physiques*. He worked hard on a book to be called *Hygiène*, parts of which he published in the *Gazette de Santé*. The book was never published separately. Pinel assured his friends and readers that they need not be afraid that he might "revive the abuses of that which is known as mechanism in medicine" and although prejudiced in favor of mathematics he enjoyed quoting the words of the encyclopedist d'Alembert: "People wished to reduce to calculus even the art of healing; the human body, this so complicated machine, was treated by our medical algebraists as if it were the simplest machine and the easiest to analyze." In 1787 Pinel began to publish articles dealing mostly with mental diseases; one of these was on suicide.[63]

The decree appointing Pinel to the Bicêtre was published on August 25, 1793. He assumed his duties on September 11th. What he found

---

[63] P. Pinel: *Observations sur une espèce particulière de melancolie qui conduit au suicide, La médecine éclairée par les sciences physiques.* Paris, 1791, vol. I, p. 154.

in this "vast pandemonium" is easy to imagine. He decided at once to remove the chains and fetters. Paris was in the midst of a revolutionary convulsion that shook the world and nothing, it would seem, would have been easier in this atmosphere of breaking down the Bastille and of the proclamation of ideals of liberty, equality, and fraternity. Revolutionary Paris knew no more of psychiatry than did the Paris of Marie Antoinette but certainly it should have appreciated the dramatic act of restoring corporal liberty to those who were eaten to the bone by iron chains. Yet Pinel was informed that he could not carry out his plan without the permission of the Bureau Central and the authorization of the Commune.

Pinel waited a few days and then decided to plead personally before the Commune itself. The spirit of Marat pervaded that august body. Everyone was suspicious. Everyone was afraid that a lurking enemy was ready to kill him and everyone was ready to return in kind. The president of the Commune was Couthon, a cripple who was paralyzed and unable to walk but a man with a passionate soul, imbued with the spirit of strife and aflame with the idea of defending the Revolution against any danger. He turned on Dr. Pinel: "Woe to you, if you deceive me and if you hide enemies of the people among your insane!" Pinel quietly explained that what he was presenting to the Commune was the truth. "We shall see," threatened Couthon. The following day, Couthon, before whom everyone trembled, had himself carried directly into the Bicêtre. He wanted personally to question the insane. "He received in answer for the most part only curses and vulgar apostrophies." Couthon turned to Pinel: "Well, citizen, are you mad yourself that you want to unchain these animals?" Pinel's reply was simple: "Citizen, it is my conviction that these mentally ill are intractable only because they are deprived of fresh air and of their liberty." Couthon retorted, "You may do what you please, but I am afraid that you are the victim of your own presumptions." [64] It is noteworthy that the spontaneous attitude toward the mentally ill is always that of suspicion and disgust, whether it comes from the reactionary Bodin, who considered the mentally ill enemies of the Church and justice, or from the revolutionary libertarian Couthon, who either suspected them of being enemies of the people or considered them merely ani-

[64] R. Semelaigne: *Les grands aliénistes français*, vol. I, pp. 41, 42.

mals. Couthon left the Bicêtre, however, without forbidding Pinel to go on with his plan. Pinel first ordered the chains removed from a small number of patients. "People awaited impatiently the result of the experiment. One of the patients who was led outdoors and saw the sun exclaimed, 'Oh, how beautiful!' He was an English officer who had been incarcerated for a period of forty years; no one had dared to come close to him after the day when, in an attack of fury, he had killed a guard. After two years of remaining calm, following his liberation from the chains, the officer was allowed to leave the hospital."

René Semelaigne tells of several of those whose chains were removed. "A man of letters who as a result of a number of misfortunes had lost his reason repulsed Pinel with horror. Delivered from his chains, he started running. He finally collapsed, breathless and exhausted. He recovered within a few weeks. He left the Bicêtre, but he perished on the scaffold in the month of Thermidor.

"Another man, of athletic build, had been locked up in the Bicêtre for ten years as a result of some accidents resulting from drinking. He was a soldier of the French Guard; dismissed from his regiment, he had been arrested in a brawl during which he had insisted on passing for a general. 'Give me your hand,' said Pinel to him, 'you are a reasonable man, and if you behave well I shall take you in my employment.' The man, whose name was Chevigné, at once became calm and docile.

"A fourth man, crouching down, had been in chains for thirty-six years; he had killed his son in order, as he said, to spare him the torments in Hell. The man's limbs were deformed by contractions and he was dying. He did not notice that his chains had been removed; he died shortly afterwards.

"A little farther on was a priest who was convinced that he was Christ and who had endured his martyrdom for twelve years with an unalterable patience. 'If thou art God,' other patients shouted at him incessantly, 'then break thy fetters.' To which he responded without fail, 'Thou temptest thy Lord in vain.' This priest recovered ten or eleven months after [he was freed from his chains]." [65]

"The mentally sick," observed Pinel, "far from being guilty people

[65] *Ibid.,* vol. I, p. 43.

deserving of punishment are sick people whose miserable state deserves all the consideration that is due to suffering humanity. One should try with the most simple methods to restore their reason." The almost trite simplicity of these words is reminiscent of the quiet and artless serenity of Johann Weyer. Thus, two hundred and thirty years after the doctor of Duke William of Jülich, Berg, and Cleves raised his voice of commiseration to demand medical interference in the crimes against the mentally ill, his plea was translated into deed by a doctor of the French Revolution. The world had distrusted Weyer almost as much as the Revolution at first distrusted Pinel. Pinel, unlike Weyer, did not have the protection of a sovereign. Moderate and conservative, he was fighting for the very ideals which the French Revolution proclaimed, but the Revolution itself was not aware of his struggle; it suspected his every step along the road of humane liberation of sick men and women. Revolutionary France thought of him as of a man unworthy of the greatness which history was creating in the city of Paris. They thought of him as Bodin and Delrio had thought of Weyer. To Bodin and Delrio, Weyer was a heretic; to the Revolutionary combatants Pinel was an aristocrat and a madman engaged in the liberation of animals. The psychology of the opposition remained the same, regardless of the change in historical setting or political vernacular.

Pinel was suspected of harboring in his hospital priests and émigrés who had returned secretly after their flight from France. One day an angry crowd surrounded Pinel in the street and seized him, shouting, "To the lamp-post!" He would have been lynched had it not been for the athletic Chevigné, the drunkard who, discharged from his regiment, had been in chains for ten years in the Bicêtre. Chevigné, having become Pinel's bodyguard since his deliverance from fetters, fought off the crowd, which soon dispersed to let Pinel pass. This incident may be viewed as a symbol of the historical vicissitudes of psychiatry. It was the doctor who had to annex psychiatry to medicine—almost forcibly. It was the patient who protected the new domain. It was society, or at least the populace, which still threatened to conquer the doctor and to recapture the territory on which it had no moral and less scientific right.

In the midst of these tumultuous days and this immense activity Pinel continued to study and to write. He reorganized the whole administrative apparatus of the Bicêtre. He studied his patients methodically, carefully; he talked to them frequently; he made daily rounds among them and made careful notes of what he saw in the patients and of what they said. Thus it was Pinel who actually introduced the taking of psychiatric case histories and the keeping of case records. At first the majority of these records were Pinel's personal notes made for his own use, but the principle was established and it proved the cornerstone of a psychiatric research which would have been totally impossible without the permanent, systematic case records which are now the measure and the identifying sign of a good mental hospital. This principle, it must be said, took less root in Pinel's own country and in Germany than it did later in the United States, where the art of making case histories as Pinel construed them has developed to a considerable degree, particularly since the early part of the current century, under the leadership of Adolf Meyer, August Hoch, and George H. Kirby in the New York Psychiatric Institute. The Institute was founded as a part of the New York State hospital system for the sole purpose of psychiatric research on the basis of the clinical material obtained from State mental hospitals.

Daquin's dictum that only in hospitals could one adequately study mental disease took practical root throughout the world, thanks especially to the reform and influence of Pinel. Pinel himself was the first to demonstrate by personal example the value of hospital research. For some time he had been working on a system of medicine, and he continued to write it while in the Bicêtre. Within a short time he had collected a sufficient amount of material to write a book dealing exclusively with psychiatry proper.

His work at the Bicêtre only begun, he was called upon to take over the administration of the Salpêtrière. Today a large hospital, almost a true city of six thousand inhabitants, it was originally called the Petit-Arsenal, or Salpêtrière, because saltpeter for the Royal Army's gunpowder was manufactured there. By an edict of Louis XIV a hospital was built in 1656 "to lock up there the poor indigents of the city and suburbs of Paris." In 1660 an act of Parliament provided that it should also serve as a place "to lock up mad men and women." Pinel started to abolish the old order at Salpêtrière. Here, too, he first ordered the chains removed. He had to reorganize, or rather, train the personnel, for there were no trained nurses or hospital guards, no trained medical personnel. Moreover, the times had not become less turbulent. Insurrections, executions, the rise of the Convention, its fall, the rise of the Directory, and finally the rise of Napoleon to the Imperial throne— all these events were accomplished by endless disturbances, bloodshed, and social and personal uncertainty.

Pinel continued at his task. Far from detached, he was keenly aware of world events. "What time could be more favorable [for the study of the different forms of mental alienation]," he wrote, "than the stormy years of a revolution, which always is apt to arouse human passions to the highest degree?" And study Pinel did. The three monumental volumes of his *Nosographie Philosophique* were published in 1798. At the same time he prepared the first edition of his *Traité Médico-philosophique sur la Manie* which appeared in 1801. He wrote this treatise on the basis of his experience in the Bicêtre but he did not consider it sufficient. He revised and supplemented the book in the light of new observations at the Salpêtrière and issued a second edition in 1809.[66]

Pinel's medical theories and classifications are of no special interest to us here. They are very methodical and clear and they contain some original ideas, but their importance pales in comparison with his work of hospital reform and reorganization by which a new tradition was established and a new perspective opened for practical and research psychiatry; it is this achievement which always comes to mind when the name of Philippe Pinel is mentioned. An endless variety of momentous issues, the existence of which does not seem to have been suspected theretofore, arose before the careful observer. Pinel faced them squarely. Each time he sketched the answer to a problem or the solution of a hospital question he established a valuable precedent and a tradition. The various purely administrative issues, such as arrangement of rooms and general supervision of the staff and patients, are important, but it is Pinel's contribution to the ideas on medical and psychiatric education which seems to have been most effective. Upon his entrance into the Salpêtrière, he wrote, "Is it possible to pass over in silence that which they called the cell service, where six hundred mentally sick were

[66] The title of the second edition reads *"sur l'aliénation mentale"* instead of *"sur la manie."*

massed together without order and left to the rapacity and ineptness of subalterns? It was a picture of disorder and confusion." After the reorganization he remarked, "It is now for medicine to complete the work and to collect not only most accurate information on the various types of mental disease but also to explore the whole scope and limits of the reciprocal effect of moral and physical treatment." One may say without risk of exaggeration that it is the organization of proper mental hospitals which made "moral treatment," that is to say, psychotherapy, possible. Without proper hospitals there was no possibility of making tests, or of following up the results for a certain length of time, or of comparing and verifying the tests on a sufficient number of patients or variety of mental illnesses.

Pinel, the author of a great nosography, did not look with favor on pure classification of mental diseases. "I do not believe," he said, "that medical science is sufficiently advanced to allow of any change in the classification I introduced." His divisions were simple: mania, melancholia, dementia, and idiocy. Yet he was more sympathetic to nosology than it would appear. Psychiatry was as yet on too uncertain a terrain to abandon its nosological propensities.

Pinel was violently opposed to bloodletting. He was just as violently opposed to the practice of "ducking" patients. "One blushes," says Pinel, "when one thinks of this medical delirium; it is a delirium worse than the one of which the mentally sick, whose reason we want to reestablish, suffer." Pinel "belonged to that school of which a master once said: It is better to stop and wait than forge ahead in the dark." [67] Consequently he objected to the indiscriminate use of drugs, the bane of psychiatry not only then but in many hospitals even today. René Semelaigne rightly points out that in this objection Pinel was influenced by Stahl.

Pinel lived until after the conclusion of the first quarter of the nineteenth century; the influence of his manner of thinking, his enlightenment, his classical objectivity—which even the cataclysm of the French Revolution could not shake—extended into, and was felt primarily in, the nineteenth century, and he may therefore rightly be placed at the head of nineteenth-century psychiatry. Moreover, Pinel was also a founder of a psychiatric dynasty, so to speak, a dynasty both benevolent

[67] *Ibid.*, p. 82.

and enlightened. His son Scipion followed in the footsteps of his father and was a prominent psychiatrist in his own right. A nephew of Philippe, Casimir Pinel, was a leading psychiatrist in the middle of the nineteenth century. Through the marriage of Armand Semelaigne to a daughter of Casimir, the psychiatric tradition of the family continued through the Revolution of 1870, and to our own day through Armand's son, René, who died in 1934. Armand Semelaigne was the first true psychiatric historian, and René devoted almost thirty-five years to research in the history of psychiatry. The Pinels and the Semelaignes may be considered the last in the long line of erudite medical men whose medical thought and practice were deeply rooted in the studies of classical medicine, in classical and contemporary philosophy, and in an intimate knowledge of the history of sciences. They represent a strong vein of the enlightened, encyclopedic age which marked primarily the birth of a new industrial world.

XIV

PSYCHIATRY entered the nineteenth century with the ground more firm under its feet than it had been at any previous century since the Age of Pericles. No one could describe this ground better than Philippe Pinel, who had so much to do with its preparation. His preface to the first edition of his *Traité Médico-philosophique*, written in the opening year of the new century, is both a postscript to the eighteenth and a preface to the nineteenth century.

In the preface to the second edition of the *Traité*, Pinel reminds his readers of the great difficulties one encounters in observing medico-psychological phenomena as compared with other medical conditions. He continues: "If one wants to try to understand the reasons underlying the phenomena observed, one must be careful about another stumbling block, that of confusing the science of facts with metaphysical discussions and certain ideological divagations." The concluding words of this preface are a rhetorical question: "Does not the deranged need to breathe pure and healthy air?" Pinel was far from satisfied with the practical work done, or with the old-fashioned and irrational architecture of the mental hospitals, or with the general scientific status of psychiatry. What he had to say in introducing the first edition of his *Traité* he felt it necessary to repeat in full in the second edition; he could still have said it on the day of his death a quarter of a century later. It is one of the most valuable texts in the history of psychiatry and is here given in full.

Introduction to the First Edition.[68]

"As one takes up mental alienation as a separate object of investigation, it would be making a bad choice indeed to start a vague discussion on the seat of reason and on the nature of its diverse aberrations; nothing is more obscure and impenetrable. But if one wisely confines one's self to the study of the distinctive characteristics which manifest themselves by outward signs and if one adopts as a principle only a consideration of the results of enlightened experience, only then does one enter a path which is generally followed by natural history; moreover, if in doubtful cases one proceeds with reserve, one should have no fear of going astray.

"Mental disease appears greatly to tax the attention of good observers because it presents itself to us as a mixture of incoherence and confusion. In a very great number of public and private establishments for the mentally ill we find empirical methods based on contradictory opinions, or a blind routine respected as law. There are other institutions in England and in France in which one must admire the happy results of legitimate methods of approach, the value of which has been confirmed by numerous experiences. One must admire as well the light which has been shed on certain facts reported to illustrious scientific societies, and the general agreement of the most enlightened physicians of the past and those of today on certain fundamental principles.[a] Especially in certain hospitals for the insane one can convince one's self that supervision, a well-run service, a sort of harmony among

---

[68] The footnotes which follow are Pinel's.

[a] Celsus insists chiefly on a moral regime and he warns that one must be guided by the particular type of mania one is called upon to treat. Caelius Aurelianus is not less definite, and he advises that the patient's furor should not be augmented either by too much indulgence or by misplaced contradictions. This writer felt the necessity of having the patients directed by a physician capable of inspiring them with feelings which would be a mixture of respect and fear.

all the elements serving the re-establishment of health, and a happy choice of moral remedies constitute real understanding more truly than the refined art of elegant formulas.

"But one's difficulties do appear increased as soon as one embarks upon a medicopsychological career, because it becomes necessary to acquire such a variety and such a great amount of additional knowledge. Can the physician really forego the study of the history of the strongest passions of man? These passions are the most frequent causes of mental aberrations. And is it not necessary to study the lives of men famous for their strivings for glory, for their discoveries in the sciences, for their enthusiasm in fine arts, for the austerity of their solitary life, or for the deviations caused by unhappy love? Is it possible for a man to trace all the perversities of the functions of judgment, if he has not meditated deeply upon the writings of Locke and Condillac and familiarized himself with their theories? Is it possible to take strict account of the innumerable facts which pass before his eyes if he drags along the beaten path and if he is deprived equally of sound judgment and an ardent desire to learn? Rousseau, in a moment of caustic humor, invokes medicine and asks it to come without the doctor. He would have rendered humanity better service, if he had raised his eloquent voice against presumptions and ignorance and urged true talent to study the sciences, the profound knowledge of which is most essential.

"From the very beginning, a narrow-minded empiricism has led man to adopt so-called specifics. Their virtue has been exaggerated and their application has been modified innumerable times in an attempt to assure their success or to forestall their drawbacks. In ancient Greece the prescription of hellebore to cure mania or other chronic diseases, and the knowledge of how to choose, prepare and apply it, comprised a kind of mysterious secret which seemed to be known by only a small number of initiated. Some of these rules seemed reasonable and accurate, others unsound; they depended on popular prejudices or superstitious ideas. They were subjects of serious discussion. Which hellebore was preferable, that from Mount Oeta, from Galathy or from Sicily? What about the food which should be taken the night before the hellebore was administered? Should the stomach be full or empty? What potions might enhance its emetic action? The embarrassment caused by the patients' fierce stubbornness was often extreme, and many innocent ruses and great cunning were necessary to disguise the medicine by combining it with food. The art of correcting or modifying the too strong or shall I say pernicious action of this plant, and the precautions to be taken in each individual case in accordance with the temper of the patient or of his disease were critical problems even for the most ingenuous person.[b] But what a triumph it was for the ingenuity and sagacity of the physicians of the time when they finally discovered certain procedures which would assure the success of the remedy: repeated washings of the mouth, strong scents, changing the position of the body, frictions of the extremities. If there was danger of suffocation, of a spasm of the throat, of violent hiccoughs, of faintings, of delirium, all the subtleties of helleborism were displayed: balancing in suspended beds, fomentations, sneezing stimuli, innumerable expedients to help the stomach and to get rid of the symptoms.

"The tremendous field which opened before Hippocrates was so vast that he was unable to develop any particular views on mania. But he has given us an example of how to proceed with the most correct descriptive method. And men who appreciate this method adopt it as a model in their first essays on the history and treatment of mental disease. Nothing is more sensible than the descriptions Aretaeus has left us of the distinctive manifestations of mental disease, and his views on the probability of remissions and the degree of physical and mental excitement the disease produces—despite the fact that Aretaeus dwells too long on his own influence and on his own supposed knowledge of science and the fine arts.

"The theories of Celsus are even more useful for the cure of mental patients and show that he was accustomed to observe their deviations; there are rules for directing them, for correcting false ideas in certain cases, indications of the means of restraint which must sometimes be used and of the methods of warmheartedness and kindness which are often apt to disarm them, express rules for sustained physical exercise and hard work. Such are the views of Celsus; the experience of later centuries has always confirmed their wholesome effect. Why should his name be used as authority for various modes of treatment and acts of violence which he considered necessary in only certain cases?

[b] For details consult the articles on *Hellebore, helleborism,* which I have published in *L'Encyclopédie Méthodique,* arranged according to subject matter.

"Caelius Aurelianus, so inferior to Celsus in elegance and purity of style, seems to have striven for another kind of glory in his article on mania. The accidental causes of this disease, its precursory signs, its distinctive symptoms are noted with care. He recommends that mental patients avoid impressions which might be too vivid for their sensory organs. He passes on to the methods of supervision which seem suitable for the correction of their deviations, and he indicates two danger spots which those who direct mental patients should avoid: an unlimited indulgence and a forbidding harshness. Caelius Aurelianus suggests a happy medium between the two extremes: the faculty of being able to assume either an appearance of impressive dignity or the simple manner of true feeling, each in the proper time; the faculty of gaining their respect and esteem by a frank and open attitude; the faculty of making one's self loved and feared at the same time. This last ability has been attributed to some present-day physicians and I shall indicate the source of it.

"One wonders why such clear and fruitful principles did not develop further in the long succession of centuries, particularly in Greece and Italy where mental disease is so frequent and where it appears in such varied forms. But Galen, anxious to become famous by new systems and by the application of Aristotelian doctrine to medicine, gave a new direction to minds and in so doing set up one of the greatest obstacles still in the way of the development of that branch of medicine which deals with mental alienation.[c] The continuous struggle which Galen

[c] The following story makes us regret that Galen is not used solely for the study of mental alienation, for the story bears the mark of rare wisdom in bringing to light the hidden moral affection.

He was called to see a lady who during the night suffered from insomnia and continuous agitation. He asked various questions searching for the origin of the trouble and, far from answering, the lady turned her back on him and covered herself with a veil, pretending to sleep. Galen retired and concluded that this despondency tended toward melancholia or some grief of which the lady was making a secret. He tried to make another examination the next day, but at his second visit the slave in attendance declared that his mistress was not to be seen. Galen withdrew again, and came back a third time; the slave, dismissing him again, asked him to torment his mistress no longer, as after the second visit she had got out of bed to wash and take some food. The physician refrained from insisting but he came again on the following day and from conversation with the slave he learned that the lady's affection came from a deep grief. At the same time he saw her and observed that the name of the actor Pylades spoken by a person who had come from the theatre caused a change in her color and in the expression of her face. Her pulse rate seemed increased, which was not the case then or later when the name of some other dancer was mentioned. The object of the lady's passion was no longer uncertain. (Galen: *Book of prognosis*)

had to maintain against the different sects of dogmatists, methodists, empiricists, and eclectics, his ambition to become a rival of Hippocrates and to rule the schools, his talent for diagnosis bordering on the miraculous, and his careful study of anatomy left him no time or will power to devote himself exclusively to one special doctrine. The influence which he later exerted on others has led them astray because they have been devoted to him as to a kind of superstitious cult—this includes almost all who, in the course of more than sixteen centuries, have studied medicine in Europe, Asia, and Africa.

"The disputes which have arisen between Galenism and a false chemistry applied to medicine have caused much bitterness without furthering the wiser and more certain progress of the human mind. The study of mental alienation has given rise only to weak compilations which were, so to speak, lost in the general systems of medicine, crowded with words devoid of sense, and voiced in the sterile language of that school. Sennert, Rivière, Plater, Heurnius, Horstius, etc., all thought they had said everything and made everything more profound by repeating at will such words, sanctified by use, as *intemperateness of the brain, diagnosis, prognosis, symptoms to be followed,* etc. They took advantage of their academic titles to propagate their doctrines in this and other respects and to make themselves admired by their numerous disciples who were always eager to extol their praises and to share in their fame. According to their fine and learned explanations, nothing seemed easier than the cure of mental illness. Its cause was doubtless 'a malign and igneous indisposition of the spirits,' or a humor which to be expelled had to be treated first by prescriptions. Others thought the cause was an injurious matter which must be extracted from the brain and heart, that, being superfluous and pernicious, it should be made to undergo a change and then should be eliminated at once.

"The entire realm of nature seemed to contribute to these clever operations by giving birth to innumerable natural remedies: there were some herbs endowed *with cold and moistening qualities to dilute the black bile;* others were designed to follow them as more or less active purgatives. It is easy to imagine that hellebore was not forgotten. The internal application of certain substances suitable for the strengthening of the heart and brain was accepted as a secondary method of healing, as was the use of narcotic powders. External applications were made to the head, the heart, or the liver, as Heurnius says, 'to rebuild that entrail.' I shall not mention the mysterious specifics sanctified by blind credulity and so entirely worthy to stand side by side with the complicated formulas of Arabian medicine.

"Each of the three famous schools which appeared in Germany in the first half of the eighteenth century limited itself to the individual formulation of general systems of medical knowledge in its relation to instruction. But mental alienation, like every other malady, was treated as of only secondary importance, as something which was merely a part of a great whole—which amounts to saying that it made no marked progress. Hoffmann merely introduces vague theories and the verbose and redundant language of the universities. Stahl contributes the glimmering light of his profound and puzzling theory. Boerhaave, endowed with a more subtle spirit, seems to go in an opposite direction and characterizes mania in a precise and laconical style which he seems to have borrowed from Tacitus: 'Most of them [the "maniacs"] have an unbelievable perspicacity and a tremendous muscular strength, enabling them to endure fasting and cold and horrible fantasies.' Yet how could Boerhaave recommend as a fundamental remedy, *princeps remedium,* a sudden immersion in water, which is nothing more than one of van Helmont's dreams turned into a rule? In the time of Boerhaave people limited themselves to writing case histories of mania which appeared in academic papers and in the journals. The results of research on organic lesions of the brain were sometimes added to these case histories to attract the scientists' interest by some stimulating peculiarity, to contribute by some novelty to the progress of medicine.

"The monographs and special treatises which were dedicated to mental alienation in England [d] during the second half of the eighteenth century seem to give promise of more real progress, due to the care with which their authors concentrated their attention on one particular subject. But a careful, impartial examination discloses nothing but vague dissertations, repetitions, compilations, scholastic formality, and some scattered facts which from time to time serve as rallying-

[d] Battie's *Treatise on madness.* London, 1758.—Th. Arnold's *Observations on the nature etc. of insanity,* 1783.—Harper's *Treatise on the real cause of insanity,* 1789.— Pargeter's *Observations on maniac disorders,* 1792.—Ferriar's *Medical histories and reflections,* 1792.

points but which offer no real body of doctrine based on a sufficient number of observations. The same is even more true of the writings which have been published on the same subject in Germany,[e] where the art of skillful compilation is so developed. One must, however, exclude Dr. Greding from this group; he did most careful anatomic research on the most frequent manifestations of insanity and on the structural lesions or defects of formation which seem to be peculiar to them. He has published his notes on the varieties of the size of the head in mental disease, on the degrees of strength and weakness of the skull, on the meninges, on the brain in general, its cavities, the pineal gland, the cerebellum, the pituitary gland, the irregularities of the base of the skull. But although we should praise his attempts to shed new light on the organic affections of the insane, are we able to establish any connection between the physical appearances manifested after death and the lesions of the intellectual functions which we have observed during life? How many analogous diversities may we find in the skull and the brain of people who have never shown any sign of impaired reason? And how dare we fix the limits which divide what is normal from what borders on a state of illness?

"The number of types of mental disease is limited, but their varieties can multiply indefinitely. It therefore seems only natural that attempts have been made to give a clear concept of several of these varieties by publishing a long series of detailed observations gathered in some mental asylum directed according to fixed rules and known principles. This has been done in England by Dr. Perfect.[f] He has explained the causes and the particular progress of several cases of melancholia, some of which were combined with an irresistible impulse to suicide. He has also described plethoric hypochondria, giving specific cases, as well as a mania which arrogance had made incurable, mania which was complicated by apoplexy, mania which follows childbirth or appears after the menopause, mania due to excessive fanaticism, mania which comes as a reaction to skin eruptions, mania resulting from continual intoxication, and mania which is hereditary. This careful work

---

[e] Faucett: Über Melancholie. Leipzig, 1785.—Auenbrugger: Von der stillen, etc., 1783.—Greding: Vermischte, etc. 1781.—Von D. Zimmermann: Erfahs. 1763.—Weickart: Philos. Arzt. Leipzig, 1775.

[f] Annals of insanity comprising a variety of select cases in the different species of insanity, lunacy, or madness, etc. The second edition, London, 1801.

contains one hundred and eight observations and is more deserving of mention than many others, as much for its tone of moderation and frankness as for the variety and simplicity of the methods the author has used—which seem to have been justified by the success obtained in a great number of the cases. In this work there is certainly a great deal of material appropriate for use in correlation with other known facts. But how far this collection is from a regular body of doctrine, from a general and thorough treatise on mental disease!

"I leave it to others to decide whether the analysis of the functions of human understanding has added much to our knowledge of mental disturbances. But another analysis which is even more closely related to the study of human understanding is that of the passions, of their undertones, their varying degrees, their violent outbreak, their varied combinations; we must set aside all morality and consider them simply as plain phenomena of human life. Crichton has tried to explain the signs and early effects of these moral causes of mental disease and as examples he gives grief, fright, anger and, above all, love carried to delirium by the vicissitudes through which it sometimes has to go.[5] The same holds true in his opinion of the feeling of joy, which is susceptible to great diversities. Pleasure, which is one of its first stages, can come directly from the possession of the desired object, or even from a simple recollection which makes the object seem present to us, for we remember with interest the scenes of our childhood, the follies of our youth, the emotions formerly felt through kindness, friendship, love, admiration, esteem. We may attribute to this same principle the pleasures which we obtain from works of art, from reading good books or from the discoveries made in science, since these produce a mixed feeling: admiration for the superiority of the author and an inner satisfaction related to the needs which our education or our mode of living has created. Can we put among the feelings of joy those sudden outbursts of good humor, those thrills which make us laugh, sing, and dance and which are provoked by puns, by quick and unexpected repartee, by grotesque imitations, by satirical touches, as if by a sort of reaction of the brain on the diaphragm and the respiratory organs? What a great difference between these foolish outbursts of convulsive

[5] *An inquiry into the nature and origin of mental derangement, etc.* London, 1798.

gaiety and the deep, calm feelings which have their origin in the practice of the domestic virtues, in the cultivation of talents and the application of them to some great cause in the public interest, in the impressive and majestic spectacle of the beauties of nature!

"In medicine there are few topics as fruitful as insanity, because of its many points of contact and because of the necessary relation of this science to moral philosophy and to the history of human understanding. But there are even fewer topics against which there are as many prejudices to be rectified and errors to be destroyed. Derangement of the understanding is generally regarded as the result of an organic lesion of the brain and therefore as incurable—which in many cases is contrary to anatomic observations. Public mental asylums have been considered places of confinement and isolation for dangerous patients and pariahs. Therefore their custodians, who in most cases are inhuman and unenlightened, have taken the liberty of treating these mentally sick in a most despotic, cruel, and violent manner, though experience continually shows the happy results of a conciliating attitude, of a kind and compassionate firmness.

"Empiricism has often profited from this realization due to the establishing of asylums suitable for mental patients; numerous cures were discovered, but no substantial literary contributions to the progress of science were made. On the other hand, the blind routine of a great number of medical men has moved always within the narrow circle of numerous bloodlettings, cold baths, and violent and repeated showers, with almost no attention paid to the *moral side of the treatment*. Thus in all aspects of the subject man has neglected the purely philosophical viewpoint of the derangement of understanding, the knowledge about the physical or moral causes likely to produce it, the distinction between the various kinds of mental derangement, the exact history of the precursory symptoms, the course and end of the attack if it is an intermittent one, the rules of interior policy in the hospitals, the careful definition of those circumstances which make certain remedies necessary and of those which make them superfluous. For in this illness as in many others the skill of the physician consists less in the repeated use of remedies than in the careful art of using them or avoiding them at the right moment.

"Ferriar, an English author whom I have mentioned, has concerned himself with another object in his works on mania. One after another he has tried out various *internally applied medicines,* which he has used with a kind of empiricism, without distinguishing, however, the various kinds of mania and the circumstances which vary the choice and application of the medicines. He has followed a course analogous to that of the German physician Locher. The only difference is in the choice, nature, and order of the application of the medicines.

"It was Chiarugi's [h] lot to follow the beaten track, to speak of madness in general in a dogmatic tone, then to consider madness in particular, and to return again to the old scholastic order of *causes, diagnosis, prognosis* and *symptoms* to be followed. The spirit of research hardly shows in his work; it is more evident in the one hundred observations which he published, although even these offer little material for conclusive implications. The facts scattered throughout the academic collections [1] and the collections of specific case histories will be cited later, not as appropriate for extending the limits of medical science, but only as a type of material which should be welded by a skillful hand to form a unified whole.

"In Germany, England, and France men have arisen who, although unacquainted with the principles of medicine and guided only by their sound judgment or by some obscure tradition, have devoted their lives to the treatment of the insane and have cured a great number by temporizing, by putting them to regular work, and by adopting methods of kindness or energetic repression at the right moment. Among others we might mention Willis in England,[j] Fowlen in Scotland,[k] the superintendent of the hospital for the insane at Amsterdam,[l] Poution, director of the hospital of Manosque,[m] Haslam, head of the dispensary

[h] V. Chiarugi, D. M. Professor of Med. and Surgery: *Della pazzia en generale ed in spezie, trattato medico-analitico: con una centuria di osservazioni.* Florence, 1794.

[1] Acad. des Scienc., 1705. Acad. des Sciences de Berlin, 1764, 1766. *Transact. Philos. Trad. franc.* Paris, 1791. *Act. hafniensia,* vols. I, II. *Disput. ad morb. hist.,* by Haller, vol. I. *Med. essays,* vol. IV, *Lond. Med. Journ.,* 1785. Gerard van Swieten: *Const. epid.,* edited by Stoll, 1783, etc.

[j] *Détails sur l'établissement du docteur Willis pour la guérison des aliénés.* Bibl. Brit.

[k] *Lettre du docteur Larive aux Rédact. de la Bibl. Britann. sur un nouvel établissement pour la guérison des aliénés.* Bibl. Brit., vol. VIII.

[l] *Description de la maison des fous d'Amsterdam,* par M. Thouin, Décad. Philosoph. An 4.

[m] *Observations sur les insensés,* par M. Mourre, administrateur du département du Var. Booklet of 22 pages.

at the Bethlehem hospital in London,[n] and finally M. Pussin, former supervisor at the Bicêtre and now holding the same office at the Salpêtrière,[o] who in enthusiasm and skill is superior to all those whom I have just mentioned. The habit of living constantly in the midst of the insane, of studying their habits, their different personalities, the objects of their pleasures or their dislikes, the advantage of following the course of their alienation day and night during the various seasons of the year, the art of directing them without effort and sparing them excitement and grumbling, the gift of being able to assume at the right time a tone of kindness or of authority, of being able to subdue them by force if methods of kindness fail, the constant picture of all the phenomena of mental alienation, and finally the functions of supervision itself—the combination of all these must give an intelligent and zealous man an immense number of facts and minute details usually lacking in the narrow-minded physician unless he has taken a special interest during fleeting visits to asylums. Can such men—otherwise unacquainted with the study of medicine, and without preliminary knowledge of the history of the human understanding—bring order and precision into their observation, or even rise to a language appropriate for the rendering of their ideas? Can they distinguish one kind of alienation from another and then describe it and correlate several observed facts? Will they ever be able to link the experience of past centuries to the phenomena they see, or hold themselves within the boundaries of philosophic doubt in uncertain cases, or adopt a firm and sure course to direct their research, or last but not least, arrange a series of objects in systematic order?

"It is as important in medicine as in other sciences to value sound judgment, a natural shrewdness, and an inventive mind unspoiled by any prejudice. It is hardly necessary to determine whether a man with such a mind has made certain routine studies or complied with certain formalities; it is only necessary to determine whether he has really contributed to some branch of medical science or discovered some useful truth. During almost two years of practicing medicine at the Bicêtre I have become acutely aware that these ideas must be realized for the

[n] *Observations on insanity, with practical remarks on the disease, and an account of the morbid appearances on dissection,* by John Haslam. London, 1794.

[o] *Observations faites par M. Pussin sur les fous de Bicêtre.* An 4. (A manuscript of nine pages which has been entrusted to me.)

sake of further progress of the doctrine of mental alienation. The writings of ancient and modern authors correlated with my own observations on the subject have not enabled me to escape a certain circumscribed circle. And should I have neglected what the observation of mental patients through many years and the habit of reflecting and observing had taught a man (M. Pussin) endowed with profound intellect and thoroughly devoted to his duties, a man in charge of the supervision of the mentally sick of a hospital? I abandoned the dogmatic tone of the physician; frequent visits, sometimes lasting several hours a day, helped me to familiarize myself with the deviations, shouting, and madness of the most violent maniacs. I held repeated conversations with whatever men knew best their former condition and their delirious ideas. Extreme care is necessary to avoid all pretensions of self-esteem and many questions on the same subject if the answers are obscure. I never object if patients make equivocal or improbable remarks but postpone my questions to a later examination, for the purpose of enlightenment and correction. I take careful notes on the facts observed with the sole object of having as many accurate data as possible.

"Such is the course I have followed for almost two years, trying to contribute to the medical theory of mental disease by all the insight acquired through a kind of empiricism, or perhaps I should say, trying to perfect the theory and bring to it general principles which it has always lacked. An isolated infirmary reserved for the care of a certain number of mental and epileptic cases helped me in my research on the effects of medicaments and on the benefits to be derived from a regimen varied to comply with the disposition and particular disease of each case.

"Thus, the Bicêtre Hospital, of which I have been in charge as physician-in-chief during the years 2 and 3 of the Republic, opened up for me a wide field for the research on mania which I had begun in Paris some years before. And what time could be more favorable for such a study than the stormy years of a revolution, which always is apt to arouse human passions to the highest degree, or I should say, to produce all kinds of mania! The supervision and intramural organization of the mental hospitals were consistently regulated and directed with as much zeal as intelligence by those men who seemed most capable of assisting me. But several circumstances combined to make the medical treatment itself very incomplete. The mental patients had previously been treated with traditional methods one or many times at the Hôtel-Dieu, and they were afterwards brought to the Bicêtre so that the complete, permanent re-establishment of their reason might be achieved—a fact which could not fail to impair my results. The use of chains to restrain a great number of mental patients was still widely accepted—they were not removed until three years later. How were we to distinguish between the exasperation caused by the chains and the symptoms peculiar to the illness? The drawbacks of the premises, the absence of any division of patients according to the degree of their excitation or calm, the continuous shifting of administrations, and the lack of baths and several other necessities presented new obstacles. The chief object of my research in the Bicêtre has been the history of the individual phenomena of mental alienation, and I have tried to determine the various kinds of distinctive symptoms, the differences between continuous and intermittent mania, the rules to follow in the moral treatment of mental disease, the supervision and intramural regulations in similar hospitals, and finally certain fundamentals for a medical treatment based only on observation and experience. A medical work published in France at the end of the eighteenth century should have a character different from that of a work produced at any other time; it should be distinguished by a certain free play of ideas, by a tempered frankness, and above all by the orderly spirit of research which rules in all parts of natural history. It should be dictated neither by individual prejudices nor by the flights of keen imagination, but by a truly sincere love of mankind, or rather by the honest desire to contribute to the general welfare. I shall leave it to the enlightened reader to decide whether I have achieved this aim."

9

✳ ✳ ✳ ✳ ✳ ✳ ✳ ✳ ✳ ✳ ✳ ✳ ✳ ✳ ✳ ✳ ✳ ✳ ✳ ✳ ✳ ✳

THE DISCOVERY OF NEUROSES

I

IN 1778, in the same year in which the thirty-three-year-old Philippe Pinel came to Paris, Anton Mesmer arrived in the same city; older than Pinel by eleven years, he was less mature, much less composed, more turbulent, aggressive, volatile, and quixotic. The death of Voltaire in the same year seems to have been a symbolic coincidence; down into the grave with Voltaire seem to have gone the keen rationalism and enlightened skepticism of the Paris of his day. The city was at that time entering a period in which rationalistic, political ideals were being realized into emotional, hectic deeds. In the words of a contemporary, Paris represented a "singular spectacle of a people whose political state of mind was calm, but whose soul was agitated." [1] The rationalistic *Encyclopédie*, the *Mémoires* of Beaumarchais, and the American War of Independence engaged equally the attention of those responsive to the pulse of history.

Mesmer (1734–1815) took Paris by storm. He came to it not quite willingly. He had discovered "animal magnetism" in Vienna, and at the very outset had got into a squabble with an earnest physicist, the Jesuit Father Hell, over the priority of the discovery. Mesmer felt injured. Whenever Mesmer felt injured he attacked, and whenever he

[1] *Biographie Universelle.* Paris, 1821, vol. XXVIII, pp. 409–417.

attacked he was neither fair, nor kind, nor reasonable, nor truthful. He did everything with éclat and with rather offensive impetuosity. He found a girl, a Miss Paradis, who apparently suffered from severe hysteria and possibly neurotic blindness. He "magnetized" her and claimed she was regaining her sight. She was a very gifted musician, a protégée of the Empress herself, who paid for her musical education. The court physician Stoerk and the great ophthalmologist Wenzel considered Mesmer's claims a hoax. Mesmer fought back, as was his custom, vociferously and abusively. He had to leave Vienna.

He went to Paris, which had been the hospitable, cultural hub of Europe since the thirteenth century. Mesmer's temperament and temper were always in the way of his ambitions, and his ambitions were great and unscrupulous. "His chief and invariable desire was to make a reputation and a fortune, and he frequently succeeded in obtaining both through profiting by man's love for the miraculous." [2] He wanted to conquer all and everyone and at once. He got in touch with princes, courtiers, and medical and scientific societies, with individual physicians and with the common people, and he wanted them all convinced that his discovery was great and true, that his theory was unassailable, that his power to cure people dramatically and thoroughly was unquestionable. He had little to offer by way of scientific writings but a great deal to catch the eye; he magnetized people in private and in public, singly and en masse, bringing them into what was called a *crisis*, that is to say, a variety of singular attacks, of laughing, crying, convulsive contortions, unconsciousness, and clairvoyance. The public responded, as it usually does to a novelty which borders on the miraculous. People flocked to Mesmer and his assistants, one of whom was Dr. Deslon, a convert to mesmerism, an earnest and honest and loyal man whom Mesmer ultimately repaid with peevish denunciation and calumny.

The scientific world was more conservative and reserved than the public. It was willing to listen and to see and to verify; it was unwilling to take anything on faith. Mesmer felt insulted. All he had to offer was his claim that he was right and a booklet, *De Planetarum Influxu*—"a bizarre combination of Newtonian discoveries and astrological reveries"—which he had published in 1766, some fifteen years previously. In this booklet Mesmer claimed that all human beings are

[2] *Ibid.*

under the influence of the stars, that this influence is exercised by means of the constant flow of a magnetic fluid which fills the universe, that a certain harmony or balance of this fluid within us always protects us from various ills. A disequilibrium of fluid causes a variety of illnesses. The magnetizer was a person who could re-establish the necessary balance by initiating a greater flow of the magnetic fluid into or from the patient through contact with him or even at a distance.

Mesmer built a contraption called the *baquet,* a sort of troughlike arrangement of mirrors and iron rods which could be placed in various directions by manipulation. People would surround the *baquet,* forming a closed chain by holding hands; Mesmer would appear, magnetic wand in hand, and the treatment would be carried out under his direction, the patients being touched, stroked, closely apposed to the magnetizer in the initial stages of the séance.

On the 12th of March, 1784, the Académie des Sciences appointed a committee led by Jean Sylvain Bailly, consisting of de Bory, Benjamin Franklin, Lavoisier, and Le Roi. These five were to act jointly with a committee, appointed by the Faculty of Medicine, consisting of Borie, Darcet, Guillotin, and Sallin. These gentlemen were to examine the practice and the curative effects of magnetism as it was practiced by Dr. Deslon. Mesmer refused to be so blatantly investigated. He wished his claims to be discussed and approved but he brooked no intrusion on the part of scientists whom he considered uninitiated.

The roster of these committees will bear close attention. Bailly was a serious scientist and passionate revolutionary. He was at the head of the commission which in 1785 surveyed the project of a new hospital building, Hôtel-Dieu. It was Bailly who wrote the report submitted in 1786. In this "Bailly described the lamentable conditions in the old hospital, in which recently operated patients and those suffering from fevers were in a ward adjacent to the one in which the insane were kept; the shouting of the latter disturbed the very sick patients. There were only twenty-eight beds for the insane of both sexes, and some beds had to accommodate as many as three patients. Complete reform was badly needed." [3] Bailly presided over the session

---

[3] R. Semelaigne: *Aliénistes et philanthropes,* p. 407. See p. 321 of this text for similar observations by Colombier.

of *Jeu de paume*. He was the Revolutionary mayor of Paris in 1791. He finally abandoned politics, but one day when visiting his friend the astronomer Laplace he was apprehended, brought before the Revolutionary Tribunal, and executed on November 12, 1793. His head was cut off by the guillotine, the contraption invented by one of his colleagues who had served with him nine years previously on the committee to examine the mesmeric practices of Dr. Deslon. Benjamin Franklin, the then aging ambassador of the United States, was still sound of mind and limb and active. His appointment to the committee was not a perfunctory honor; Franklin's services were valuable to the Académie des Sciences. Lavoisier was the great chemist. Guillotin was a medical man who knew how to utilize scientifically and practically the Newtonian laws of the accelerated motion of a falling mass of steel in the art of "humanizing" judicial assassination.

The joint committees went and saw the work of Dr. Deslon and on August 11, 1784, submitted their report written by Bailly. The report concludes, "The committees, aware that the magnetic fluid could not be noticed by any of our senses, that it had no effect on the members of the committees, nor on the patients who were submitted to it; having assured themselves that the touchings and the pressures [applied by the magnetizers] cause changes rarely favorable to the animal economy and disturbances always harmful to the imagination; having finally demonstrated by decisive experience that imagination without magnetism produces convulsions and that magnetism without imagination produces nothing, [the members of the committees] have unanimously concluded in regard to the question of the existence and usefulness of animal magnetic fluid that such fluid does not exist and therefore cannot be useful, that the violent effects seen in public treatments result from the touching [of the patients], from the imagination which is set into action, and from the machine of incitement, which we must admit against our own desire is the only thing which impressed us. At the same time [your committees] feel obliged to add the following observation which they deem important: the touching of patients and the repeated excitement of the imagination to produce crises may prove harmful; the spectacle of the crises is equally dangerous because of that imitation of which nature, it seems to us, made a law; consequently, any public magnetic treatment cannot but have at length very harmful results." [4]

This judicious report might be supplemented by Philippe Pinel's personal impressions found in a letter made public by his grandnephew René Semelaigne.[5] Pinel wrote to Desfontaines on November 27, 1784:

"I must tell you a word about magnetism, although it is already on the decline especially among sensible people since the report which was made by the committees of the Académie and the Faculty. Public replies have been made, a number of brochures have been issued; but, unfortunately for the authors, the majority of these books are not read. For a long time the Government has desired that the public be enlightened on this type of mania, which came into vogue only through the efforts of partisans. I believe that it has just been given the final blow by having been brought onto the boards of the stage. A play has just appeared in the [Théâtre des] Italiens entitled *The Modern Doctors*, in which Mesmer and De[s]lon, the two chiefs of the sect, are played with charming gaiety and pleasantry. People watching this play burst with laughter, and if you were here you would find it an excellent antidote for melancholy. Nothing seems to have brought so much consternation to Mesmerians as this last blow. But be it as it may, the ladies here harbor a great zeal for this new medicine; and as certain contacts are required and the development of a certain industry on the part of the doctor who magnetizes, the ladies find it all very sweet. I too wanted to be instructed in the secret, to know for myself what it is all about, and I frequented the *baquet* and even magnetized at Dr. De[s]lon's for about two months. This resulted in a certain galant little adventure; when my reason falls into a slumber, I am a little inclined to prescribe to the ladies the charming maneuver of magnetism. As to men, I repulse them harshly and send them to a drug store."

Good humor somewhat distorted Pinel's perspective. A quarter of a century after his death, more than forty years after his letter to Desfontaines, Europe was still preoccupied with animal magnetism and the Paris Académie had a record of several committees appointed successively to investigate the nature and the results of mesmeric practices.

Mesmer died eleven years before Pinel, but in the same Salpêtrière which Pinel reorganized and humanized, and of which he remained head until his death, Jean Martin Charcot started his studies of hypnotism—a direct outgrowth of mesmerism—ninety-four years after Pinel's epistolar pleasantries and humorous stage burial of Drs. Mesmer and Deslon. Under various guises and purposes mesmerism retained its hold on many individuals, lay and medical. As late as 1837 Baron du Potet found a hospitable reception in the house of John Elliotson, who was professor of medicine in the University of London and who was so impressed with the performances of magnetism as demonstrated by du Potet that he resigned the chair of medicine, gave up his position at St. Thomas' Hospital, and devoted himself to magnetizing. Elliotson helped to organize the Mesmeric Infirmary and with friends started a journal, *The Zoist,* in which reports were published on surgical operations performed under anesthesia induced by mesmerism. One of his most loyal supporters at the time was James Esdaile, who published in 1846 *Mesmerism in India, and its practical application in surgery and medicine.*

Mesmerism reached the shores of the United States. A French magnetizer, Charles Poyen, came to give public séances of magnetism. It was at these séances that P. P. Quimby, the watchmaker and genius of intuition, obtained his first conceptions of faith healing. He tried it successfully on Mary Baker (Eddy) in 1861, curing her of her hysterical paralysis. The direct historical and inner psychological continuity from Mesmer to Christian Science is both telling and striking.

The scientific understanding of mesmerism and the proper evaluation of the clinical facts which mesmerism brought to the attention of the world proceeded rather slowly. This was due partly to what is commonly called the natural conservatism of science, but one may not overlook the fact that under the guise of this natural conservatism a host of inveterate prejudices and standpat self-complacencies made a bid for respectability and set a claim for survival to which they were not entitled either morally or historically. It was this euphemistic conservatism that made both Sennert and Willis consider that true psychoses were of demonological origin, and that made the Paris Académie scoff at Pasteur when he came to report his history-making discoveries which led to the recognition of infectious diseases. It was the same fear of and hostility toward the new and at first incomprehensible that made Weyer a suspicious character, Galileo a criminal heretic, and Lister a fancier of allegedly useless innovations in surgery. Lister was not recognized for his introduction of antiseptic methods into the operating room until he successfully overcame the conservatism of his world.

What was overlooked by the rationalistic, scientific humanitarian and good medical scientist of the end of the eighteenth and the beginning of the nineteenth century was the simple fact that by liberating the witches, sorcerers, lycanthropes, and somnambulists from theologico-juridical sadism they accomplished a historical fact or fulfilled a historical mission which was only a beginning and not an end. As the fires of the Inquisition stopped burning so did the fires of compassionate medical curiosity. The medical literature of the period is full of valuable data on lesions of the brain as found in the dead, on vapor and distempers, on manias, idiocy, imbecility, and melancholy. But one is hard put to find in this literature anything enlightening about the immense masses of those mentally ill who as if only yesterday had populated the cities, towns, villages, and hamlets. There certainly were not enough hospitals to house them, nor did they all suddenly go into hiding, nor were they automatically cured merely because the Bodins and Delrios stopped vituperating and the fagots stopped burning.

It was apparent that medicine concentrated primarily on those who were flagrantly insane, those whom we call today psychotics. But the greatest mass of the bewitched and the possessed were not psychotic. These were neglected and left to their own resources; they represented the masses of those whom we today call neurotics. Philippe Pinel may have been justified in speaking twittingly of the ladies who flocked to the mesmeric séances for "maneuvers of magnetism" which they found "very sweet." But it is hardly probable that Pinel was fully right. The attitude of the great psychiatric pioneer is only too familiar and is reminiscent of the popular attitude toward neuroses found even now as we approach the middle of the twentieth century. Usually only a woman is thought of as neurotic. A neurosis is usually shamefacedly concealed by the patient and treated derisively by those who consider themselves normal. A neurotic is still not fully recognized as a sick person, and despite our modern enlightenment a neurosis is still viewed as a weakness and judged with amused, condescending contempt or benevolent disapproval. This negative attitude represents the attenuated form of the harsh condemnation with which the possessed and the bewitched were viewed in the sixteenth and seventeenth centuries. Toward the end of the eighteenth and throughout the greater part of the nineteenth century these large masses of neurotics were overlooked. There was a service in the Salpêtrière in which the "non-insane" were kept, but these were severe epileptics and just as severe hysterics who were more or less incapacitated. There was still an immeasurable though unrecognized number of neurotic people who had no contact with medicine and with whom medicine either did not seek contact or established it but reluctantly. It was from this great mass of unknown neurotics that people flocked to Mesmer and Deslon and their followers all over Europe. There was no doubt that a number of the "mesmerians" capitalized on the susceptibility of the public, even as a number of "psychologists," particularly those who without right assume the appellation "psychoanalyst," capitalize on the responsiveness of the public in the twentieth century.

Mesmerism became a growing concern and a large literature on the subject grew up. Not all of it was mere propaganda or plain advertising. Deleuze's *Histoire Critique du Magnétisme Animal,* the *Mémoires* of the Marquis de Puységur on the subject, and a number of other books reported certain clinical facts which one could not neglect. The theoretical concepts of the magnetizers were not many and were of no consequence, for mesmerism was a grossly empirical procedure with its sole accent on therapy. It was a new phenomenon; somnambulism, anesthetic states, certain forms of convulsions were induced at will and would disappear under the very eyes of the observer. This was something unexplained and heretofore unknown. The mass convulsions which came into prominence among those who sought cures at the Cemetery of Saint-Médard were known to many, to be sure, but these were now induced at will by the magic of the human touch and what Mesmer called *rapport.* One could not dispose of these phenomena by mentioning mesmerism in the great *Dictionnaire des Sciences Médicales* [6] under *Libertinage,* nor could one consider valid such a suggestion as that propounded by Desgenettes, who at the meeting of the

[6] The *Dictionnaire,* written by a group of doctors and surgeons including Bayle, Esquirol, and Pinel, comprises sixty volumes completed between 1812 and 1820.

Académie des Sciences on February 20, 1826, demanded that one should not even consider looking into the question of magnetism, "because it came from Germany." The clear and pure and curious minds were very few. It required courage and a profound sense of scientific detachment for Georget, the pupil of Pinel and Esquirol, only thirty-one years old at the time, to stand up and say at the April 26th meeting of the Académie:

"For forty years magnetism has been studied, practiced, and propagated in France and in a greater part of Europe by a multitude of educated men who are disinterested and who claim that it is a real thing—this despite the ridicule with which people try to suppress them. All this is very surprising. Magnetism is not known even by name among the ignorant masses of people; it is supported only by the enlightened. People who have received some education have taken up its cause; among these are scientists, naturalists, physicians, and philosophers, who have composed numerous volumes in which numerous facts are accumulated and cited in its favor. Yet people represent the magnetizers as ignorant imbeciles whose testimony merits no consideration. How is it that these ignorant men produce daily more converts among distinguished men, who once having seen the facts become the zealous partisans of such contemptible opinions? We must admit that an error which spreads itself in this manner, in direct opposition to the ordinary course of events, represents a new species of hallucinations, the cause of which it would be very important to examine, to say the least.

"One hears cries of charlatanism . . . but does the behavior of the magnetizer really deserve this reproach? A charlatan always hides himself and makes a mystery of the means he uses; the magnetizers, on the contrary, call for us to examine their work; they constantly repeat: Do as we do and you will obtain the same results. Among those who believe in magnetism one finds only men who have seen, examined, and experimented; among their adversaries one finds only those who deny what they have not seen or did not want to see."

The classical tolerance of young Georget was that of a scientist, but it was certainly not representative of the medical profession as a whole. The struggle for recognition of a science free from the encumbrance of self-satisfied conceit continued in the middle of the nineteenth century, at times with even greater bitterness than in the sixteenth. We shall recall that Jacques Dubois, the teacher of Vesalius, thought his pupil was mad and that his anatomy, since it did not agree with that of Galen, could not be true.[7] The world had changed since 1543. The great value of man as an individual had been recognized and had become an integral part of man's daily life and of the scientist's constant awareness. This great cultural step forward rendered valuable services to society through the development of humanism and truly humanitarian medicine and psychiatry. But it also elevated the individual medical man to a level of self-conscious authority beyond and above what an average mortal deserves. Instead of the one and indivisible dictatorial authority of Galen each doctor, particularly if invested with honors and position, was, in his own eyes at least, an authority in himself, and he felt the right to impose this authority once he knew he had the power. The current psychophysics and psychophysiology which made Pinel swear by the names of Locke and Condillac undoubtedly contributed to this sense of self-satisfied power. The doctor cherished and nurtured it; he always jealously defended it.

We shall remember the reference to our senses in Bailly's report on mesmerism to the Académie des Sciences in 1784. What our senses cannot perceive, the medical world claimed, just is not there. The multitude of history's stark examples of times when emotional prejudice has prevented the proper functioning of our senses seems to have been chronically forgotten, even by the scientist. That the whole field of demonology was such a perversion of our senses, due to a severe emotional predilection, was for a moment almost understood but as soon almost forgotten. As a result, the appearance of any innovation or discovery in medicine—organic and particularly psychological—was more or less hissed down as a matter of emotional tradition. An innovator was never welcome and hardly ever treated politely. When Elliotson, working at St. Thomas' Hospital, began to show signs of responsiveness to things which were new, he was treated as an intruder and a disturber of the routine peace. This was true not only when he expressed his interest in mesmerism but also when he wished to perfect the methods of examining and diagnosing the physically sick. Elliotson was the first in England to use a stethoscope. "The stethoscope, as well as the facts of percussion and auscultation as described by Auenbrugger, were con-

[7] See p. 166.

demned as fallacies by the foremost teachers of medicine in London, while, even at a much later date, they were treated at St. Thomas' with indignation or silent contempt. At the College of Physicians a senior fellow, in a Croonian lecture, denounced the folly of carrying a piece of wood into a sick room.[8] Another condemned the stethoscope as worse than nonsense and said, 'Oh! It's just the thing for Elliotson to rave about.' While a third, on seeing one on Elliotson's table, said: 'Ah! Do you use that hocus pocus?' On Elliotson replying that it was highly important, he added: 'You will learn nothing by it, and, if you do, you cannot treat disease the better.' " [9]

In 1837 the Council of University College ruled "That the Hospital Committee be instructed to take such steps as they shall deem most advisable to prevent the practice of mesmerism or animal magnetism in future within the Hospital." [10] Elliotson was trying at that time to obtain some data for the use of mesmerism as an anesthetic in surgical operations. "In 1846, Elliotson's turn came to deliver the Harveian Oration, but, as soon as it was known that he had accepted the office, he was attacked in the most savage manner, in order to prevent his appearing. For example, the *Lancet* called him a professional pariah, stated that his oration would strike a vital blow at legitimate medicine and would be a black infamy degrading the arms of the College." [11] Twenty years after Georget's appeal to reason in the Académie des Sciences the profession was still engaged in denying what they had not seen or had not wanted to see. And if they did happen to see they denied just the same.

In 1842 a surgeon, Dr. Ward, performed an amputation at the thigh while the patient was in a mesmeric trance. Dr. Ward reported the case to the Royal Medical and Chirurgical Society. No one believed the truth of the report. Dr. Marshall Hall suggested the ingenious explanation: the patient was an impostor! Dr. Hall, leaning heavily on his neurology, suggested that if the patient were really insensitive he would have shown reflex movements in the good leg while the bad one was being cut. Dr. Copland was even more definite and self-righteous in his

---

[8] The early stethoscopes were tubes made of wood.

[9] J. Milne Bramwell: *Hypnotism, its history, practice and theory.* Philadelphia, J. B. Lippincott Company, 1930, p. 5.

[10] *Ibid.*, p. 7.

[11] *Idem.*

incredulity. He suggested that the fact that this case report was ever presented to the Society should not be recorded in the minutes. His intuitive sense of history apparently made him feel the need of denying that such a case had ever existed, as if by the act of secretarial omission medical facts could be truly eradicated. Dr. Copland even resorted to teleological morality in support of his attitude: "If the history of the man experiencing no agony during the operation were true," he averred, "still the fact is unworthy of consideration, because pain is a wise provision of nature, and patients ought to suffer pain while their surgeons are operating; they are all the better for it and recover better." [12]

That we deal here not with a simple error of judgment but with a deeply seated emotional prejudice is seen from the fact that these honest and earnest doctors were not satisfied merely by the expression of their disagreement and with letting the future judge as to who was right; they even resorted to flagrant falsehood. Eight years after the reported mesmeric trance during operation, Dr. Marshall Hall, who had suspected the patient of being a liar, stood up at a meeting of the Society and announced that the patient had finally confessed that he did suffer pain during the operation. There was purported to be a signed confession from the patient himself, but the Society would not allow this to be read or recorded in the minutes. There was obviously doubt as to whether Dr. Hall had ever actually seen the patient.

Surgery was soon to be rid of the mesmeric controversy. The anesthetic properties of "laughing gas" and ether had been discovered (1800, 1818) and anesthesia soon was established on a nonpsychological basis. It might be mentioned incidentally that the same "ladies" of whom Pinel spoke so chivalrously when they flocked to Deslon's *baquet* proved as responsive to the discovery of ether as they had been to the introduction of animal magnetism; "ether parties" were common in Boston, where sniffing of handkerchiefs on which some ether had been dropped was indulged in, and for a while the well-known ether jag constituted a pleasant and acceptable parlor game.

Psychiatry, however, could not dispose so easily of mesmerism. The therapeutic intent and the dramatic results inherent in the procedure were too impressive. For the first time a really new therapeutic agent

[12] Quoted by Bramwell: *op. cit.*, p. 10.

had appeared, something different and something much more effective than the blistering, purgation, bleeding, and drugs which continued to be used with continued lack of efficacy, particularly in cases of neuroses. "Elliotson asserted that mesmerism was especially useful in hysteria and other functional nervous disorders [that is, neuroses]. These diseases, he said, were generally misunderstood, and treated in a worse than useless manner. . . . Marriage, with disastrous results, was sometimes suggested as a remedy for hysterical women, on the supposition that the disease was essentially of a sexual character. It was not, however, necessarily connected with the uterus, nor confined to the female sex, but occurred frequently both in boys and men. Mesmerism, not medicine [that is, drugs], was the appropriate treatment for hysteria." [13]

Elliotson's is one of the earliest articulate statements of the newly born therapeutic intent. By the forties of the century the direct consequences of mesmerism and its place in the history of medical psychology had acquired more or less clear delineations: attention had been sharply drawn to neuroses, which had nearly been lost sight of in the dust raised by the rapid march of anatomy, physiology, neurology, and the reorganization of the prison-hospitals for mental diseases; therapy by agents other than drugs had intruded into the peaceful routine of medical practice; the medical profession with few exceptions, having at first rejected any claims of the new therapy and having refused it admission into their sacred precincts, had gradually turned toward a more serious consideration of the matter.

This last point is of some historicopsychological import. As has been repeatedly stated in these pages, it was medicine which rose to conquer the field of psychiatry. But, curiously enough, medicine was quite unwilling to accept, was even harshly opposed to, psychotherapy; it was the sphere of diseases which it was anxious to capture, but it seemed unable to abandon the tradition of the dissecting room, the apothecary, or the kitchen and insisted on anatomy, drugs, and diet. Medicine captured psychiatry, brought it into its scientific empire, and offered it rights of citizenship only on the condition that it learn the language and submit to the administration. Medicine refused to have psychology

[13] Bramwell: *op. cit.*, p. 9.

admitted; any appearance of psychology was considered an intrusion or an illegal importation. As a result of this paradoxical attitude, the introduction of psychological therapeutic agents was naturally left in nonscrupulous medical, or nonmedical, hands.

It is not because Mesmer was an unpleasant person, a psychological sans-culotte, a charlatanic contribution of Imperial Vienna to France on the eve of the Revolution, that mesmerism fared so poorly with the medical profession. Mesmerism encountered trouble because psychology (particularly abnormal psychology), neuroses (particularly convulsive neuroses), and psychological medicine (that is to say, psychotherapy) were traditionally associated either with the soul or with the devil. And whether it was with heaven or hell that it was considered in association, mesmerism was not of this earth with its earthly diseases and earthly remedies. The terms "natural philosopher" and "nature" seem to have acquired an unconscious meaning of *this earth;* the word "natural" seemed to have only the meaning of *corporeal* existence on this earth, in so far as this existence is accessible to our limited physiological senses. In other words, despite Copernicus, Kepler, and Galileo, the heliocentric theory did not fully prevail. Psychology seemed to have no history, no genesis, no biological meaning; it was an empirical comfort in so far as it made it possible for us to be thinking beings, but it was an empirical encumbrance, an embarrassment, and a true enemy of our emotional though unconscious egocentric tradition. Consequently, it was kept at a distance; it was left to the adventurous spirit or to the charlatan and impostor. And as soon as psychology was grasped by these eager hands medicine could redouble its opposition on the ground that it was all an imposture, that it was not what it was claimed to be, that it was of the charlatan—the devil in modern dress. Georget's admonition was unheeded, as was the earnest pleading of Elliotson. That the problem was a medical one in spite of all the protestations of the medical academies and societies is easily seen by the fact that the leaders of mesmerism, and later of hypnotism, were mostly physicians. The admixture of varying numbers of laymen seems due more to the inhospitable and refractory attitude of official science and medicine than to the charlatanism of those who became interested in the problem or to any inherent impurity of the problem itself.

II

MESMERISM was unable to offer any plausible theory in explanation of the phenomena with which it had to deal. From the standpoint of theory it was an atavistic splinter of the astrological tradition and of the imaginative contentions of Paracelsus. Mesmerism never was a system of thought and therefore never had a real intellectual hold on the scientific thinker. In the absence of a well-defined, working hypothesis, the enormous mass of clinical data became confusing.

The necessity of bringing order into such confusion and scientific poise into an atmosphere so charged with partisan ceremonialism became more and more apparent. That the somnambulistic, mesmeric trances which were induced at will had more to do with psychological factors ("with imagination," in the language of the day) was suspected from the very beginning, but that the various "stages" of being mesmerized were but incidental results of the procedure was not fully clear at first. In the course of time, a number of magnetizers noticed that curative results were obtained regardless of the type of reaction or stage of mesmerization of the patient. The deep trance was required only for surgical operations. Even in 1820 Bertrand, the mesmerist, observed the state of what later became known as "hypnotic sleep." Bertrand "was the first to say plainly that artificial somnambulism could be explained simply on the basis of the laws of the imagination. The subject falls asleep merely because he thinks of falling asleep and he wakes up because he has the thought of waking. The works of Abbé Faria, of General Noizet in France, of Braid in England only contributed a clearer statement of this conception and developed this psychological interpretation more precisely." [14] Historically, Bertrand's observation may be considered the transition point in the development of mesmerism into hypnotism.

The English surgeon James Braid (1795–1860), like Elliotson, studied mesmerism. He soon became impressed with the subjective factors in the whole phenomenon of response to the magnetizer; although old-fashioned and a believer in phrenology, and although a surgeon and therefore not in close touch with psychological problems,

[14] Pierre Janet: *La médecine psychologique.* Paris, 1924, p. 22.

Braid fully grasped what Bertrand had felt some twenty years before—that the whole mass of mesmeric phenomena had nothing to do with magnetic fluid or the magic of the ceremony. Neither Braid nor any of his contemporaries was able to understand the phenomena from the standpoint of the psychological processes involved. These processes were, and in many respects still are, obscure, but there is no doubt now in anyone's mind that the influence and effect of the magnetizer or hypnotizer are based primarily, if not solely, on the deep unconscious reactions of the subject. The concept of the unconscious was not in existence in the time of Braid, and his task was that of formulating in a purely descriptive manner what he sensed intuitively. In 1842 he published a paper, *Satanic agency and mesmerism reviewed, in a letter to the Rev. H. McNeile, A. M., of Liverpool, in reply to a sermon preached by him at St. Jude's Church, Liverpool, on Sunday, April 10th, 1842.* In his *Neurypnology, or the rationale of nervous sleep* (1843) Braid introduced the new terms: hypnotism, hypnotize, hypnotic.

The mesmeric terminology thus disappeared after a little over sixty years of vicissitudes in which scandal, honest research, therapeutic intent, and unscrupulous ambition were intertwined. But the impulse which mesmerism released continued unimpeded in the direction of new knowledge and new achievement. Dr. Azam discussed Braid's views in the *Archives de Médecine* in 1859, and Dr. Broca spoke on Braid to the Académie des Sciences a year later.

In the same year (1860) a quiet, pleasant, benevolent, and hard-working French country doctor, A. A. Liébeault (1823–1904), began to study mesmerism, of which he had had some acquaintance while he was still a medical student, but to which he did not return until after many years of general medical practice. He settled in Nancy in 1864. He spent two years collecting clinical data and working on his book *Du Sommeil et des états analogues, considérés surtout au point de vue de l'action de la morale sur le physique.* According to Bramwell, only one copy of this book was sold. Liébeault was beloved by the poor, who called him *le bon père Liébeault;* they trusted him and he understood them well. He discovered hypnotic sleep and used it for treatment and research. He knew how to make the simple peasants co-operate with him. He would tell them: "If you wish me to treat you with drugs, I will do so, but you will have to pay me as before. But if you will allow me to hypnotize you, I will do it for nothing."

It is significant that the introduction of hypnotism into the practice of medicine was performed by single individuals more or less widely scattered over the Continent and England. It was introduced without benefit of fanfare or scientific upheavals or the solid support of what is generally called the profession, that is to say, the official medical organizations. It is also significant that at no time did there appear to be any dearth of clinical material. The poor people of Nancy, whom Georget would have called the "ignorant," certainly did not flock to Liébault's clinic out of idle curiosity or in order to add to their armamentarium of parlor tricks. They were sick people and they wanted to be cured. Medicine theretofore had had little to offer them; it was still reluctant to understand the new principle of *l'action de la morale sur le physique*. That medicine might accept this principle in anything but general philosophical discussion was literally unthinkable. The whole orientation of medicine throughout its history had been based on a reverse conception.

J. Milne Bramwell, M. B., who practiced hypnotism in England, went to see Liébault. "In the summer of 1889, I spent a fortnight at Nancy in order to see Liébault's hypnotic work. His *clinique*, invariably thronged, was held in two rooms situated in a corner of his garden. The interior of these presented nothing likely to attract attention; and, indeed, anyone coming with preconceived ideas of the wonders of hypnotism would be greatly disappointed. For, putting aside the methods of treatment and some slight differences probably due to race-characteristics, one could easily have imagined oneself in the outpatient department of a general hospital. The patients perhaps chatted more freely amongst themselves, and questioned the doctor in a more familiar way than one is accustomed to see in England. They were taken in turn, and the clinical case-book referred to. Hypnosis was then rapidly induced . . . suggestions given and notes taken, the doctor maintaining the while a running commentary for my benefit. Nearly all the patients I saw were easily and rapidly hypnotised, but Liébault informed me that the nervous and hysterical were his most refractory subjects." [15]

[15] J. Bramwell: *op. cit.*, p. 31.

The unassuming and unpretentious, almost casual, workmanlike atmosphere of Liébeault's establishment at once suggests that we have reached a new era, a new phase in this aspect of medicine. The doctor does his job. He seems very different from those of his colleagues of a generation or two before, when contentiousness, passion, philosophies, and sentiments prevailed. There is little upon which one theorizes. The fact that the psychological has an influence on the physical is taken at the empirical value. A technique is tested, evolved through practice and checked by results—an important aspect of the new orientation. That the phenomenon is puzzling is recognized; that it may be understood some day is hoped; but no speculation is permitted to becloud the work. The method is practical, the approach purely descriptive. It is very striking, indeed, that the first contact with purely psychological phenomena aroused less speculation—excluding Mesmer's fancies, of course—and less philosophic flight than did medicine when it began to utilize physics and chemistry.

True and scientific psychological methods of treatment started modestly, quietly, and with an earnest sense of responsibility. Liébeault was a poor man; he earned very little; he refused to accept money from the patients whom he treated with hypnotism. He did not want, he said, to appear to capitalize on a new method which had not been sufficiently tried. His own work he characterized merely as one brick added to the construction of a new building.

That hypnotism still has the reputation of something mysterious with not a little tinge of charlatanism and malevolence is but a reflection of the popular fantasy of still seeing the devil behind purely psychological phenomena. The birth of psychotherapy through Braid and Liébeault was a unique event in medical history. As we shall see later, it was much more than the discovery of a new technique of treating certain ailments. It failed, of course, as so many other things had failed, to uproot the age-long prejudices of the average man about neuroses. But it opened a new road of investigation and brought neuroses more definitely into the sphere of psychiatry. It prepared the ground for a broader conception of mental disease than science had theretofore known.

It is characteristic of the progressive spirit of England of the time that, despite the refractoriness of such men as Marshall Hall and Copland and of the British Medical Association, the idea that psychological influences may and do play an important role in mental disease took root more quickly there than in France or, especially, Germany. As late as 1891 the British Medical Association in meeting assembled heard the report of their own committee on hypnotism—a report rather moderate in tone and conclusions. The Association would not reject a report of their own colleagues; but neither would they accept even a mild endorsement of hypnotism. The suggestion was made that the report be tabled and someone seconded the motion. But another member had a much happier thought: the Association, it was moved, should *receive* the report. It was voted "received" with the scientific position of the British Medical Association on this important issue thus officially well defined as indefinite. Yet as early as July, 1866, Daniel Hack Tuke took cognizance of the phenomenon in the *Journal of Mental Science* with an article on "Artificial Insanity or Braidism." D. H. Tuke, the first physician in the Tuke family, was the great-grandson of William Tuke, the founder of the York Retreat. He was a man of exceptional culture and kindness and of a scientific earnestness and responsiveness which are very rare. His general views on mental diseases appear rather sedate and conservative, yet he was more keenly responsive to new ideas than anyone of his generation at home and than all but a few abroad. In his *Dictionary of Psychological Medicine* published in 1892 he still defined insanity formally as a brain disease, "idiopathic or sympathetic"; but he was quick to recognize the value of psychological factors. His article *Hypnosis Redivivus* [16] revealed a serious, scientific interest in this new therapeutic measure and a hope that the subject would be studied. The whole problem was of vital interest to Tuke. In 1872 he published his *Illustrations of the influence of the mind upon the body in health and disease*.

Germany showed no special interest in hypnotism. Forel's *Der Hypnotismus* was published in Stuttgart in 1889, and by 1923 it had gone through twelve editions; but Forel was of German schooling and he worked mostly in his land of origin, Switzerland. In Russia Bechterev, one of the first psychiatrists of a broad European viewpoint, began to use hypnotism in the eighties. In Paris in 1878 Charcot (1825–1893) started what has become known as the Salpêtrière school of hypnosis, as differentiated from the Nancy school founded by Liébeault, although strictly speaking there was no "school" of Nancy. Liébeault continued his quiet but efficient work. Bernheim (1837–1919) visited Liébeault in 1882 to learn how he had cured a refractory case of sciatica with which Bernheim had failed after six months. Bernheim became a friend and pupil of Liébeault. In 1890 Dr. Felkin published *Hypnotism, or Psychotherapeutics*—one of the earliest uses of this term. Two years later Dr. George Robertson, Superintendent of the Murthly Asylum in Perth, published an article in the *Journal of Mental Science* on "The Use of Hypnotism among the Insane."

Hospitals for the mentally sick began to favor the application of psychotherapeutic methods discovered and developed outside the hospital itself—a point of no small historical importance. One should not, of course, fail to observe that the hospitals—dealing mostly with psychotics—were not infrequently rather inept and crude in the efficiency of their approach. Bramwell relates an example: "In certain cases of insanity, the late Dr. Auguste Voisin, of Paris, attempted to induce hypnosis by force. The patient, either held by assistants or placed in a strait-jacket, had his eyes kept open, and was compelled to look at the light of a magnesium lamp or at Voisin's fingers. If necessary, the process was continued for three hours; suggestions meanwhile being made. The patients, who at first usually struggled, raved and spat in the operator's face, eventually became exhausted and, in successful cases, passed into a condition of deep sleep." [17] The results of these "successful cases" are unknown. Quite obviously in "Voisin's Method" we are dealing with an absence of the little that was understood at the time of the nature of hypnotism.

III

HYPNOTISM as a going concern was fully established by the eighties. It was both a method of treatment and a method of research. Further, it was itself a subject of research. While it was being used it was also being probed. Attempts to understand the phenomenon were not successful. It was dramatic, baffling; it would not yield its secret. This

[17] Bramwell: *op. cit.*, p. 43.

was natural, for the study of the deeper psychological aspects of suggestibility was impossible with the methods then available. Charcot and his assistants who created the school of so-called *grand hypnotisme* were limited to purely descriptive studies of what they observed when a patient was hypnotized. Patients succumbing to hypnotic sleep passed regularly through three successive stages: lethargy, catalepsy, and somnambulism. A criterion had to be established for recognizing and differentiating these three stages.

Charcot, a thoroughly schooled neurologist and an extremely keen medical investigator, thought only in terms of the nervous system. He considered thorough and refined neurological examinations the safest and most accurate approach. Moreover, bent on being extremely scientific—which consciously or unconsciously still meant to base everything only on the functions of the brain and nerves—Charcot felt that the possibility of simulation would be thoroughly eliminated if the neurological signs of paralyses and anesthesias were carefully checked. That the fact that a patient would be willing systematically to simulate all these singular states and to go through the variety of such complex deviations with such skill would in itself constitute a neurotic phenomenon apparently did not occur to Charcot or his assistants. "For a neurologist accustomed to examining the symptoms of tabes and lateral sclerosis, the only clear-cut signs which could not be simulated were the modifications in the state of the musculature, the reflex movements, and the characteristics of various sensory responses." [18] These signs were carefully noted and tabulated in corresponding order. In other words, it was a method which tended to establish what changes occur in the brain and nerves during hypnotic states. Painstaking work was done; an immense amount of material was accumulated; the conclusion was reached that all these characteristic states could be induced and observed only in those people who suffered from hysteria. In other words, the phenomena of hypnotism were considered as being themselves manifestations of abnormality. This was the point of view which differentiated the Salpêtrière school from that of Nancy.

"These were the ideas which Charcot presented to the Académie des Sciences on February 13, 1882, in a paper on the diverse nervous states determined by the hypnotization of hysterics. One must not forget that

[18] Janet: *op. cit.*, p. 24.

the Académie had already condemned all research on animal magnetism three times and that it was a veritable *tour de force* to make the Académie accept a long description of absolutely analogous phenomena. They believed, and Charcot himself believed, that this study was far removed from animal magnetism and was a definite condemnation of it. That is why the Académie did not revolt and why they accepted with interest a study which brought to a conclusion the interminable controversy over magnetism, about which the members of the Académie could not fail to have some remorse." [19] And remorse they well might have, for, from the standpoint of the actual facts observed, Charcot did nothing more than what Georget had asked the Académie to do fifty-six years previously. Whether one called the phenomenon animal magnetism, mesmerism, or hypnotism, it stood the test of time. The scientific integrity of the Académie did not. Like a government reluctant, indecisive, and uncertain of itself, it did nothing whenever it was safe to do nothing and yielded only when the pressure of events forced it to act and the change of formulatory cloak secured its face-saving complacency. Pierre Janet emphasized the enormous historical importance of Charcot's success with the Académie, for "it broke a dam and let in a torrent which was ready to rush" into the field. "It would be necessary to cite the names of all the neurologists of that time in and outside of France" who responded to this success, "for at the time the majority of them turned to the Salpêtrière for their studies."

Among this majority we find in 1885 a young neuropathologist who came there on a traveling fellowship. The neuropathologist was Sigmund Freud, who less than fifteen years later revolutionized our views on hysteria and on psychopathology in general. In the meantime he applied himself with full faith and industry to learn what Charcot had to teach. The general spirit of the clinic and its chief scientific orientation are well illustrated by a passage in a letter Freud wrote to Charcot soon after he first met the master. "I can still remember a phrase in the letter," recalls Freud forty years later, "to the effect that I suffered only from *'l'aphasie motrice'* and not from *'l'aphasie sensorielle du français.'*" [20] Freud, facetiously to be sure, adopted the jargon of Charcot's circle, the jargon which reflected the one-sidedness

[19] *Ibid.*, p. 25.
[20] Freud: *Autobiography*, p. 18.

and the prejudices which reigned in the minds of that active and industrious scientific group. If a man had a good sense of the language but was not able to speak and write it well, it was supposed to mean that the various fiber connections in his brain were so arranged that he was able to feel but not to act or move or speak out what he sensed. In other words, even one's normal psychological reactions were viewed from the standpoint of brain defects or pathology.

Charcot's psychological intuition was always greater and truer than his official views on psychological reactions. He used the term "hystero-epilepsy," while admitting that the condition had nothing to do with epilepsy. He admitted the importance of autosuggestion in hysteria but did not utilize it in his scientific evaluations. Toward the end of his career he perceived the effect of faith-healing, but, although he gave evidence that he was fully aware of deeply seated psychological currents and countercurrents in hysteria, he seems nevertheless to have been fully convinced that these were by-products of a physical, organic, morbid cause combined with heredity. Solid, conclusive proof of this organic origin of hysteria was conspicuously lacking, but the anatomico-physiological foundation of the psychopathological theories built in the eighteenth century remained the only one on which the Charcot school felt able to rely. From this point of view, no progress seems to have been made in the direction of a better understanding of hysterias or neuroses in general.

Due to its great popularity and authority, the Charcot school exerted a strong influence, however, and it stimulated further study of neuroses more than did any other center in the world at the time. It made one more step in the direction of unmasking that which still appeared mysterious and spiritualistic. In 1887 Charcot, in collaboration with Paul Richer, published a study of *Les Démoniaques dans l'Art*. This study was a great step in the history of medical psychology, for it demonstrated that psychopathology might gain considerable insight into the problems which preoccupied it not only from the study of the mentally ill but from the study of artistic self-expression as well. In the course of the nineteenth century, and particularly the twentieth, this sphere of investigation extended to anthropology, sociology, literature, art, and music. There was another aspect to Charcot and Richer's study: it unmasked further the puzzle of many centuries regarding demoniacal possessions, which still lingered on at that late date. The study demonstrated conclusively that demoniacal possessions as reflected in art were typical of hysterical individuals, and Charcot called the ecstatic individuals suffering from demoniacal preoccupations the "aristocrats of the possessed."

The fundamental contribution of the school of the Salpêtrière and its essential historical value lie in the fact that it was the first to capture for psychiatry the very last part of demonological territory, which up to the middle of the eighteenth century had belonged to the clerical and juridical marshals of theology and from the middle of the eighteenth century to the last quarter of the nineteenth had remained for the most part a no man's land. Charcot and his assistants took the territory by storm. But no sooner did they come into possession of the field than a new battle broke out. This battle was not a new war for possession; it was a war among those who, once in full control of the field, had to find ways and means to bring order into it, reconstruct it, make it more livable. The finer subtleties of the theories of hysteria are of some psychological and historical interest and would present valuable material for a special history of this aspect of medicopsychological evolution. From the standpoint of a general history of medical psychology they naturally appear to be but incidental in the general process.

The name "hysteria" was preserved, although it gradually lost its etymological meaning. Because this psychological reaction was at times accompanied by convulsions, and because epilepsy was also accompanied by convulsions, it was still called hystero-epilepsy. Names and labels do not matter as a rule, but the terminology of the time is highly instructive. The term "hystero-epilepsy" reveals, first, that the physician, even as the layman, for want of better understanding paid attention to the purely external. In this case it was the convulsive attack, that is, the symptom, which was the external sign and determining factor. Man's judgment gravitates to the obvious even if it misleads him. Neither Charcot nor the host of his great predecessors in the history of psychiatry were exceptions to this propensity. The existence of the term "hysteria" misled generations of doctors to believe that such a thing really existed. Hence they all worked on the assumption that the existence of the disease is not to be questioned and that the sole task of the physician is to study its nature, its course, and its stages. It did not occur to them, for instance, that among the great numbers of *convulsionnaires* and stupors there were real psychoses—not neuroses at all—perhaps some of the severe psychoses which later, or even at the very time they were studying them, were named catatonias (Kahlbaum in 1874). To what extent the power of the word made itself felt may be judged from the fact that the sexual aspects of hysteria, which had made physicians for centuries think in terms of uterine "suffocation" or "furor," still drew the attention of Charcot to the female genital apparatus; he thought the ovaries had something to do with the convulsive crisis. "It is to the ovary and the ovary alone," he said, "that one has to look for the source of the fixed iliac pain of hysterics. . . . The compression of the painful ovary frequently has a decisive effect on the convulsive attack, the intensity of which may thus be diminished; at times it may even stop the attack." [21] Such names as ovarian mania and hysterical mania were still coined.

Surgery, never reluctant to adhere to the gross anatomical conceptions of some psychiatrists, was equally responsive to surgical interference in mental disease. On March 28, 1882, Péan performed an operation removing an ovary to cure hysteria.[22] We might note that at that early date there were physicians in the United States, like Spencer Wells and Emmet in New York, whose medicopsychological enlightenment outweighed their surgical predilections to a greater extent than it did those of their colleagues of the twentieth century. Spencer Wells was definite on the subject: "The operation [ovariotomy]," he said, "is inadmissible in any case of nervous disturbance." [23] Bytord, on the other hand, performed castrations on cases of hystero-epilepsy, "Baker-Brown of London and Brawn of Vienna tried the surgical removal of the clitoris, Friedreich of Heidelberg practiced the cauterization of the clitoris." [24] Charcot at no time approved this medical sadism, but there is no doubt that the tradition of which he, the great authority of the time, was not entirely free made him contribute, no matter how in-

[21] J. M. Charcot: *Leçons sur les maladies sur le système nerveux.* Paris, 1887–1888, vol. I, p. 339.
[22] Cesbron: *Histoire critique de l'hystérie,* p. 171.
[23] Spencer Wells, in *American Journal of Medical Sciences* for October, 1886. (*Cf.* Cesbron: *op. cit.,* p. 172.)
[24] Cesbron: *op. cit.,* p. 172.

directly, to what is euphemistically known in scientific medical circles as "mistakes."

Charcot, as has been said, was not unaware of the psychological aspects of hysteria. In his famous and monumental *Leçons* he admits that autosuggestion and imagination of the hysterical individual may lead to "realizations," that is, to formation of the physical hysterical symptoms. He was definitely aware that certain hysterias are without convulsions and he called these cases of *minor hysteria,* leaving to the convulsive manifestation the name of *major hysteria.* Here again the terminology itself suggests how difficult it was to be rid of the preconception that one was dealing with a single definite disease; the names of the supposedly various forms of the disease merely reflect the doctor's own subjective attitude: a convulsion was a dramatic, conspicuous, *major* affair; other manifestations were consequently *minor.*

In the meantime the school of Nancy under Hippolyte Bernheim worked along the lines of Liébeault. Like Liébeault, the beginning and the end of Bernheim's interest was the cure of the patient; theories were of comparatively little interest. He was a careful, judicious observer and an attentive doctor; he accumulated an immense mass of empirical material. In 1886 he published *De la suggestion et de ses applications à la thérapeutique,* consisting of four hundred and twenty pages. Two years later a second edition of five hundred and ninety-six pages appeared. Bernheim was assisted by Professor Beaunis, a physiologist, and Professor Liégeois, a legal authority. In the first four years of work they collected data on five thousand hypnotized cases and in a few more years had data on ten thousand. Certainly Charcot's clinic could not boast of such an impressive accumulation of clinical material. Bernheim raised many and legitimate objections to Charcot's method of investigation and to his views. The school of Salpêtrière, Bernheim insisted, was not careful enough in hypnotizing; they overlooked the fact that an endless variety of the manifestations they observed were the result of the hypnotizer's inadvertent suggestions and not of the nature of the disease. "The observers of Nancy, on the basis of their experience, conclude that all the phenomena established at the Salpêtrière—such as the three phases, the neuromuscular hyperexcitation during the period of lethargy, the special contractions provoked during the period of somnambulism, the transference by magnets—do not exist at all under conditions in which suggestion is not set into play. . . . The hypnotism of the Salpêtrière is a cultured hypnotism," [25] that is to say, not natural but like a cultured pearl.

At length Bernheim won the battle. Charcot was unable to disprove Bernheim's contentions, which were based on much more knowledge and understanding of the problem involved. Bernheim stressed that we should study the process of suggestion and the characteristics of suggestibility; he rightly claimed that the latter were not limited to hysterical individuals alone. To Bernheim all people, with rare exceptions if any, were suggestible; he believed that an endless variety of normal and abnormal social and antisocial reactions are due to suggestions and autosuggestions which are not always evident at once. He would reserve the appellation "hysteria" for the convulsive crises only. He thought of "hysterogenous" tendencies in man. In brief, he extended and expanded the whole field of psychoneuroses and through the study of suggestibility attempted to gain insight into human behavior in general. Historically this conception of Bernheim's, no matter how tentative, should be considered the first (known) attempt to evolve a general understanding of human behavior and its motivation on the basis of the study of psychopathology rather than on the basis of philosophical systems.

This trend in Bernheim led him to introduce the problem of the legal responsibility of criminals. In 1897 before the International Congress of Medicine in Moscow he read a communication entitled *L'Hypnotisme et la suggestion dans leurs rapports avec la médecine légale et les maladies mentales*. Using as a point of departure his views on suggestion and autosuggestion, Bernheim was the very first to absolve the will, the allegedly great free agent and author of all evil, from the tarnished, old-fashioned stigma of being the origin of mental disease and crime. His was a momentous attempt to destroy the tradition responsible for the mistakes, the cruelty, the complacent sadism, and the just as complacent ignorance which had reigned in theology, law, and medicine for almost two thousand years. Bernheim recognized the existence of involuntary "psychisms," of psychological "automatisms," that is, acts devoid of conscious intent or even conscious origin which

[25] Quoted by Janet: *op. cit.*, p. 28.

impose themselves upon us and through us upon the world through the multiplicity of obvious and obscure ways in which our imitativeness and suggestibility, or as Bernheim said, our *crédivité naturelle*, works and manifests itself. "In truth," he insisted, "we are all potentially or actually hallucinating people during the greatest part of our lives." He thought that suggestion to be effective does not need the induction of hypnotic sleep. Even in the waking state suggestion works. Persuasion is a form of suggestion: "Suggestion, that is the idea, no matter where it comes from, imposes itself on our brain and plays a role in almost all crimes." The criminal therefore is no more responsible, legally, than "a weak tree." [26]

Bernheim was thus the first scientific psychologist to advocate the principle of the "irresistible impulse," a principle disregarded even now by the majority of the penal codes of the world. No matter how convincing Bernheim's clinical demonstration, the Law, paraphrasing the thrust against Johann Weyer, persisted for the most part in the attitude that "Bernheim was just a doctor and not a lawyer."

IV

WHATEVER the differences between the school of Salpêtrière—an investigative, systematizing school—and that of Nancy—empirical, therapeutic, more humanitarian, less socially detached—they both released a new impetus in psychiatry. We might say that from these two sources sprang a new orientation in medical psychology, which became much more aware of *real life*, of the social setting of our civilized existence, and of our problems as human beings rather than as walking textbooks of physiology. It is true that we shall search in vain for any articulate reflections of this attitude in the Salpêtrière, for there they were still preoccupied with the anatomy and physiology at hand.

Charcot was born in 1825. His father must still have had vivid memories of the Revolution and of Napoleon's rise and fall; Charcot himself was five years old when the Revolution of 1830 took place. He became an *interne des hôpitaux* in 1848, the year of another revolutionary upheaval which this time engulfed most of continental West-

[26] Quoted by R. Semelaigne: *Les pionniers, etc.*, vol. II, p. 232.

ern Europe. He became a professor of pathological anatomy in 1872, shortly after France's tragic defeat and after the Commune which brought down the monarchical Empire and established the Third Republic.

Charcot was still one of those rationalistic, post-Revolutionary scientists of France to whom history was like the weather: noticed only casually, observed but incidentally, interfering not at all with one's daily tasks. Bernheim stood closer to the people and their problems and he was aware of the needs of man as a man rather than as an anatomy. This explains the fact that his conceptions were broader than Charcot's and led him to considerations of such sociological problems as criminality. But what is most telling as far as consequences are concerned is the fact that both schools brought medicine in close contact with neuroses, with that mass of "noninsane" and nonhospitalized men, women, and children and their psychologies. Psychiatry was brought into direct contact with living, functioning individuals and not only with the "deranged," the mentally deteriorated. The Plater of the nineteenth century no longer had to descend into the dungeons, caves, and abandoned cellars to study abnormal psychology. Nor did he even have to confine himself to the hospital. The streets, the offices, the parlors, the kitchens, the factories, and the highways—all equally offered him "material." The reader will recall the appeal which Vives made to the scholar of his day, enjoining him to go to the workshop and artisans to learn about life, living, and nature. This ideal was at last having an opportunity to be put into practical use, or at least circumstances became more favorable for the realization of Vives' sociological ideas and ideals of scientific work. However, the century was closing its calendar. It was the task of the twentieth century to take up the admonitions of a humanist of the sixteenth—four hundred years after his death.

It is difficult to overestimate the aspects of this historical role of the schools of Salpêtrière and Nancy, as it would be impossible to overlook the fact that theretofore a well-trained physician with an excellent knowledge of anatomy, physiology, and pharmacology, when confronted with a number of neuroses of which he knew nothing, had only his benevolent or not so benevolent ignorance upon which to rely. He was equipped only with all the drugs available, with his knife, and with the protective shield of a medical doctor's degree covering his mistakes, his prejudices, and his ignorance. Perhaps this circumstance, born out of necessity, is responsible for the tradition that the internist even today dabbles in psychopathology which he has never learned and "treats" neuroses which he does not understand. Charcot's and Bernheim's work, particularly Charcot's, acquires therefore particular value, because both men were teachers. Physicians of all ages from all over Europe flocked to the Salpêtrière. It was the first center of postgraduate psychiatric education, particularly important since the graduate work done by the doctor included no psychiatry. Psychiatric education was thus established under the authoritative wing of a hospital and a medical school, of which Charcot was a professor.

One cannot easily exhaust the multiple consequences of the Nancy-Salpêtrière influence on medical psychology. Here was a group of doctors who were keen, hard-working, excellent clinicians. None quoted the philosophers Locke and Condillac and all practiced the dictum of Baglivi which Pinel admired so much: the patient is the doctor's best textbook. The work of this group also marked the origin of a totally new methodological approach to medicopsychological problems. Heretofore the "insane," the madman, was the first source of knowledge for the doctor interested in mental disease; with the insane as a point of departure, the doctor tried to understand the possessed—the neurotics. A start was made, particularly by Bernheim, toward reversing this process. The noninsane were now studied first. Through the knowledge thus acquired greater insight was gained in both directions. Normal people were understood better and the insane were to become more intelligible on the same basis. It was more than a bon mot on the part of Bernheim when he said that we were all "hallucinables or hallucinés." He meant it and he could mean it because he had learned it from his clinical observation of neuroses. The old aphorism of Pascal, *Les hommes sont si nécessairement fous, que ce serait être fou par un autre tour de folie de n'être pas fou,*[27] thus acquired substantial corroboration and value.

The historical value of this new approach to mental disease stands out in particular relief not only because Charcot and Bernheim uncovered so many new facts about hysteria. A great deal that was new they undoubtedly observed, but it is more important that they brought a

[27] Pascal: *Pensées*, VI, 414.

new scientific and clear understanding to old facts which had been known for centuries—facts which had plagued the curious, frightened the unquestioning faithful, and prompted the zealous to greater punitive expeditions.

The "stigmata" of the hysterics, the insensitive, anesthetic areas on their bodies had been known to every witch-hunter, for they were the conclusive marks of the devil and one had to know them to do a good and honest job. The demonologist de Lancre, and he was not the only one, even stated that "the witches are completely unaware that they are marked, until they have been examined." [28] "The judges noticed that these symptoms shift from place to place and from this they concluded that Satan wished to outwit the judge's sagacity." [29] It was Bernheim's observation on suggestibility—a word so readily understood today, so taken for granted, but denoting so new and revolutionary a concept some fifteen years before the close of the nineteenth century—it was Bernheim's convincing description of the suggestibility of the patient—producing additional symptoms not there originally—which lifted the lid from the puzzle of the satanic "fugacity" of the symptoms in question. "When the judges found those insensible spots," said Bernheim, "and when the accused were made aware of them, the patients would give free play to their imagination and the *anesthesia became complete;* there were witches who, convinced of their relations with the devil, succeeded in creating at will an almost complete analgesia." [30]

Singular as it may sound, it took over three and a quarter centuries from the time of Weyer's assertions that witches were sick women to the time when conclusive scientific proof of what the witches' symptoms meant was given by another member of the medical profession. How the witches of yesterday and the patients of today "create their symptoms at will" to their own incapacity and misery Bernheim was unable to explain. This was another problem which was left to the twentieth century to ponder over and to solve, in part at least. The nineteenth century was as yet unable to step out of the confines of pure description of the phenomena observed. The approach was empirical in the best sense of the word but it naturally was unable to accelerate

[28] Quoted by Cesbron: *op. cit.,* p. 124.
[29] *Idem.*
[30] *Idem.*

the march of history, which never moves quickly. History is spectacular at times. It opens new pathways with a dramatic conspicuousness which may appear sudden to the contemporary observer, but it is never sudden and it is always slow. To the contemporary this lack of suddenness is at times agonizing; to the historian it presents itself as a morose and fatal, on occasions benevolent, on occasions cruel majesty of restraint, at once as a fundamental weakness of generations of men and as their interminable great patience. The performance of the Charcot and Bernheim schools might appear spectacular and sudden, like a meteoric flare from the dark, spontaneously self-generated out of the mesmeric earthquake. But this is only the way in which a man is inclined to view the performance by the two or three generations which precede him and to whose industry he owes his own performance. The work of Charcot and Bernheim was imperceptibly prepared; there was a time about a half century before them when men spoke almost the language they used. Though the ideas of these forerunners seem to have passed unnoticed, their work and observations could not help but present a steppingstone in the general progress of medical psychology.

Boissier de Sauvages looked upon hysteria as *passion hystérique* and expressed the thought that it was different from hypochondria; he observed the convulsions which appeared "without any evident cause." But de Sauvages' intuition, like the intuition of most of his contemporaries, was always tempered or hampered by the desire to classify. His nosology contained seven types of hysteria: hysteria verminosa, hysteria chlorotica, hysteria a menorrhagia, hysteria a leucorrhoea, hysteria emphractica (with obstruction of the viscera, of the liver and spleen), hysteria libidinosa, hysteria febricosa. The fundamental point to bear in mind is that Boissier de Sauvages, like most of his predecessors in the history of medical psychology before the closing quarter of the nineteenth century, observed in order to recognize and to classify. The question of therapy would arise afterwards; it was considered important, of course, but it was always last in the succession of investigative procedures. Therapy was not used as an instrument for the discovery of new facts, nor was there a suspicion that it could serve such a purpose. Only the manifestation of the disease was observed. In an autopsy one is able to find a number of diseased organs which would throw light both on the cause of the disease and on the signs and symptoms which had been manifest during the lifetime of the diseased and deceased. But hysterics, neurotics, and for that matter psychotics never die from their mental illnesses and when they do die from natural causes it is, to say the least, impossible to determine whether the diseased organ of the cadaver had anything to do with the mind or with the so-called natural cause. Under these circumstances one must marvel at the tenacity and the sagacity of the observers of the past who trained themselves to see the manifestations of a disease they could not understand, were unable to manipulate or control, and yet were able to see and to see so well.

One is therefore particularly impressed to find that thirty-five years before Bernheim, Sandras,[31] like Bernheim, observed that anesthesias and many other symptoms which Charcot considered permanent characteristics of hysteria are not always present and are not necessary attributes of the disease. And one year before Charcot started his studies of hysteria at the Salpêtrière Lasègue and Falret considered the phenomenon of psychological contagion and described the mutually induced neurotic conditions to which they gave the name *folie à deux*,[32] a term still widely used today and a neurosis which plays a particularly great role in so-called suicide pacts and in certain criminal acts performed by two or more people together.

The work of Brodie is most striking. He observed a girl with unspecified pains in her knee. The pains finally disappeared but the patient had hysterical attacks. Brodie came to the conclusion that the pains in the knee were also of hysterical origin and that in the upper classes four fifths of the women who complained of pains in the joints were merely hysterical women.[33] Brodie was certain that the hysterical paralyses were not due to any direct pathology of the brain or spinal cord. He considered the gastrointestinal symptoms of the hysterics and came to the then striking conclusion that "fear, suggestion and *unconscious simulation* [34] are the primary factors"—a thought even more advanced than those of Bernheim.

In other words, in so far as the two schools of Salpêtrière and Nancy

[31] C. M. S. Sandras: *Traité pratique des maladies nerveuses.* Paris, 1850.
[32] Falret and Lasègue: *Folie à deux ou folie communiquée.* 1877.
[33] Benjamin C. Brodie: *Lectures illustrative of certain nervous affections.* London, 1837, No. 2.
[34] Italics ours.

remained purely descriptive they represent but a natural continuation and extension of the persistent work done for over a century by the number of physicians who were interested in neuroses. Also, in so far as the purely descriptive tradition continued, the whole concept of hysteria threatened to deteriorate into a formalistic, diagnostic procedure with occasional refinement of true insight. This concept, despite the real perspicacity of the observers, remained almost as sterile as Gall's assertion that the seat of hysteria was in the cerebellum because the latter was the seat of carnal love. P. J. Moebius (1853–1907),[35] for instance, thought that hysteria was a mental disease in which representations (*Vorstellungen*) produce physical symptoms; Adolf Strümpell (1853–1925) was of the same opinion.[36] Babinski, who had few points on which he disagreed with most of the leading views of his time on hysteria, observed that hysteria could be cured by persuasion, that deep hypnotism is not required. It is this characteristic of hysteria that Babinski chose to consider most important, and he created a new term, *pithiatisme*, a word derived from two Greek words meaning *persuasion* and *curable*. When a medical problem becomes a question of terminology or of quickly recognizable signs for purposes of labeling a disease, it is definitely suggestive of a deterioration of scientific solidity.

That same trend is to be observed, paradoxically as it may seem, in the very brilliant work of Pierre Janet (b. 1859). Janet truly deepened the knowledge of hysteria by the extraordinary mass of psychological data which he assembled during a period of many years of clinical studies.[37] He is frequently classed among the adherents to the school of Salpêtrière, but in actuality he was far removed from it and did not belong to the Charcot group. Better than anyone before him, he recognized the importance of the "automatic" psychology of the neurotics. These automatisms he described with an excellent sense for psychological detail. He studied the mental state of hysterics with a great deal of acumen and differentiated the *idées fixes* of the neurotics and their inner conflict with actuality—reality in present-day termi-

---

[35] Moebius: *Ueber den Begriff der Hysterie.* In *Centralblatt für Nervenheilkunde,* 1888, No. 3.

[36] Strümpell: *Ueber die Entstehung und die Heilung von Krankheiten durch Vorstellungen,* 1892.

[37] Pierre Janet: *L'état mental des hystériques.* Paris, 1911. Also, *Névroses et idées fixes.* Paris, 1924, 1925.

nology. He recognized the importance of unconscious factors in the formation and manifestations of hysteria. Janet actually used the word "unconscious," seemingly ascribing to it the value of a truly dynamic psychological factor, but he stood before his own excellent description and failed to draw the consequences.

Janet's attitude toward his psychological findings was almost the same as Charcot's toward his clinical observations. Freud neatly summarizes the substance of Charcot's attitude in the following words: "No doubt the whole of what Charcot taught us at that time does not hold good today: some of it has become doubtful, some has definitely failed to withstand the test of time. But enough is left over and has found a permanent place in the storehouse of science. Before leaving Paris I discussed with the great man a plan for a comparative study of hysterical and organic paralyses. I wished to establish the thesis that in hysteria paralyses and anaesthesias of the various parts of the body are demarcated according to the popular idea of their limits and not according to anatomical facts. He agreed with this view, but it was easy to see that in reality he took no special interest in penetrating more deeply into the psychology of the neuroses. When all is said and done, [he entered this field through] pathological anatomy." [38]

As to Janet, he was unable to rid himself of the feeling that hysteria was the result of a constitutional weakness of the mind and nervous system. He still used the word *dégénérescence*, which was in vogue in French psychiatry after the middle of the nineteenth century. Whatever Janet's psychological insight, he looked upon hysteria as an inevitable manifestation and result of heredity and "degeneracy." Yet he was actually on the verge of gaining the same insight as Breuer did at the close of the century in Vienna. It is difficult to rise above the age to which one has pledged one's uncompromising loyalty.

The following incident as related by Freud is a characteristic summary: "I always treated Janet himself with respect, since his discoveries coincided to a considerable extent with those of Breuer, which had been made earlier but were published later than his. But when in the course of time psychoanalysis became a subject of discussion in France, Janet behaved ill, showed ignorance of the facts and used ugly arguments. And finally he revealed himself to my eyes and destroyed the value

[38] Freud: *op. cit.*, pp. 20, 21.

of his own work by declaring that when he had spoken of 'unconscious' mental acts he had meant nothing by the phrase—it had been no more than a *façon de parler*." [39] Freud is not entirely fair to Janet. Janet was right and entirely candid when he admitted that his use of the word "unconscious" was but a *façon de parler*, for, following strictly the tradition of purely neurological-physiological views, he used the word only as a literary, parabolic expression of "automatic."

Despite Janet's adherence to what he called psychological methods of treatment, his psychotherapy was mostly environmental and persuasive. His premise exercised a deadening effect on the therapeutic intent of his psychopathology, since its cornerstone was degeneration and the neurosis almost a natural consequence of this fatal biological handicap. A true psychopathology of neuroses was and is impossible without a rational, investigative therapy. The great success of the school of Charcot and particularly of that of Bernheim was due primarily to the fact that their methods had their origin in therapeutic efforts. The further these efforts went, the clearer it became that while alleviating the condition of the patients they revealed a great deal that we did not know and never suspected about the patient's inner life. Psychiatrists learned more about the patient and were able to direct their therapy deeper and more effectively, thus gaining more knowledge and more understanding of the nature of the neurosis. This is shown by an expression of Bernheim which is both succinct and revealing: "The therapy of hysteria is not suggestion but de-suggestion." [40] In other words, the therapy is directed against what the patient "unconsciously simulates," as Brodie said; it reveals, brings forward, analyzes if you wish, that part of the patient's ideational content which underlies the illness, and then "de-suggests" the patient to remove the nocuous ideas and the symptoms for which they are responsible. This is the essential intuitive content of Bernheim's statement, and in this respect he was the true forerunner of Freud, whose older contemporary he was.

Psychotherapy had thus become a tool of research and the source of all that we have learned about the true nature of hysteria and later of all other neuroses. While this is probably the greatest achievement

---

[39] *Ibid.*, pp. 57, 58.
[40] Quoted by Cesbron: *op. cit.*, p. 267.

in the whole history of medical psychology, and beyond doubt the most fruitful achievement of the nineteenth century, it is not remiss to recall that the field of psychopathology had its direct origin in the appearance of Mesmer with his quixotic therapeutic performances. The perspective of history smooths many roughnesses and rounds off many sharp angles. It is impressive that Mesmer became the originator and the bearer of a totally new orientation in psychological medicine, an orientation which brought psychotherapy to the forefront and with it, ultimately, the deepest insight yet attained by man into the inner workings of the human mind. It also led to the most decisive and most effective step in the history of the medical conquest of demonology. Psychiatry's road had been hard and long—over two thousand years—and as the figure of Mesmer emerges through a past made dim by the dust and fog of scandal, rasping egotism, and harsh disloyalties, his services appear greater than his sins, and history reminds us of the injunction: "Thou shalt not judge."

10

THE ERA OF SYSTEMS

I

THE work of Charcot and Bernheim belongs to the last two decades of the nineteenth century. Those who followed and developed it, or those who used it as a point of departure and modified and advanced it, closed the century and opened the twentieth. But important as Charcot and Bernheim's contribution to psychological medicine was, it presents but one page in a heavy volume of the psychiatric history of the century. The growing interest in the mentally ill, the study of mental illness, the building of hospitals and clinics, the foundation of psychiatric societies and psychiatric periodicals, the publication of many and voluminous books on medicopsychological subjects make the psychiatry of the nineteenth century a confusing and complex structure of manifold aspects. It was a century teeming with activity, controversy, and enthusiasm. The outlines of theories and practice coupled with the hospital reform and administration which took shape toward the end of the eighteenth century released an impetus long overdue, and in the course of the nineteenth psychiatry became not only a separate branch of medicine but a potent force in the cultural development of Europe and the United States.

The French Revolution and the Napoleonic Wars awakened widespread national feeling all over Europe. The vernacular was established as a legitimate, even inevitable, form of literary and scientific expression. When Paracelsus started to give his lectures in the vernacular the faculty at Basel was shocked to the point of derisive animosity. In the course of the eighteenth century it was still more the rule than the exception for a physician to write and publish his medical works in Latin. In the nineteenth it became the rule to write in one's native tongue, and it was Latin which became the exception. John Revere, the son of Paul, traveled from America to study medicine in Edinburgh. His doctor's dissertation (1811) appeared in Latin and was entitled *Insania*, reflecting the increased interest in mental disorders. Johannes Friedreich published in 1830 a booklet of eighty-four pages entitled *Synopsis Librorum de Pathologia et Therapia Morborum Psychicorum*. But Latin was becoming a curiosity in medical literature. The national spirit of the age made one's national language not only a more convenient mode of expression, but psychologically imperative; it was a manifestation of the democratic ideals which the French Revolution had proclaimed and baptized in a sea of human·blood. The medical writer, too, though a little later than the poet and the novelist, had to abandon his exclusivistic dais of pomposity and descend to the vulgar. He had to become a part of life and could no longer stand above the people and orate in the manner and language of a dead past and of esoteric books of antiquity. The psychiatrist, at least in the language he used, came down to earth.

Valuable as this closer and more direct congress with people was, the use of the national language had a partially disrupting effect on the unity which psychiatry had presented until almost the end of the eighteenth century. With Latin no longer the international language, the psychiatrist of Germany was isolated from his colleague in England or France. In order to keep in touch, he had to become a polyglot. Pinel felt and more than adequately met this new necessity, as evidenced by his preface to the *Traité Médico-philosophique*, in which he quotes English and German writers whom he read in the original.

The need for continued unity was great despite the growth of national feeling, and those who studied foreign languages began to translate the important contributions of their colleagues of foreign lands. Heinroth translated Georget's *De la Folie* into German within a year after its publication in Paris in 1820. Esquirol's contributions to the

Dictionnaire des Sciences Médicales were worked over in 1827 by Hille under the general title *Allgemeine und spezielle Pathologie und Therapie der Seelenstörungen.* Benjamin Rush's first American textbook on psychiatry, *Medical Inquiries and Observations upon the Diseases of the Mind* (Philadelphia, 1812), appeared in König's German translation in 1825. Germany, having entered the field later than France and England, showed a uniquely energetic responsiveness and before the century was half over developed an independent psychiatry which was soon to take the lead over both France and England.

But quite naturally even frequent translations from and into foreign tongues did not close the gap along national lines; this was the reverse side of the scientific medal which had been so laboriously struck by the preceding generations of scholars. Within borders of given national units the language in which the psychiatrist spoke underwent certain refinements and polish. This process is strikingly evident in the writings of all—German, French, and English—psychiatrists. There is a conspicuous difference between the spelling and style of the first edition of Pinel's *Traité* published in 1801 and the second which appeared in 1809. Books on psychiatry became accessible to a larger mass of readers. The psychiatric literature grew to immense dimensions, and an interest in the history of psychiatry came into evidence—a sign of a certain maturity in a science. In 1830 Friedreich published his *Versuch einer Literaturgeschichte der Pathologie und Therapie der psychischen Krankheiten;* in 1833, *Systematische Literatur der ärztlichen und gerichtlichen Psychologie;* in 1836, *Historisch-kritische Darstellung der Theorien über das Wesen und den Sitz der psychischen Krankheiten;* and in 1842, *Zur Psychiatrischen Literatur des Neunzehnten Jahrhunderts: (1801–1836).* The opening thirty-five years of the century offered so many writings on psychiatry that this last book of Friedreich's grew into a rather imposing volume. Ulysse Trélat published in 1827 his *Aliénation Mentale: Recherches Historiques,* which reappeared twelve years later as *Recherches Historiques sur la Folie.* Lélut in 1846 published *L'Amulette de Pascal, pour servir à l'histoire des hallucinations.* D. H. Tuke published his imposing *Chapters in the History of the Insane in the British Isles* (1882).

In short, the development of psychiatry reached a point where it not only made history; it had its history and was taking full cognizance of it. Kurt Sprengel's history of medicine devotes a considerable number of pages to the history of psychiatry.[1] Medical psychology became crystallized as a unit, coherent in its present and correlated with its past—a living discipline.

For the record of hospitals opened during this century the reader is referred to the corresponding chapter of this volume; the number of hospitals was great. The work of Dorothea Lynde Dix in the United States during and after the Civil War stands out as one of the most heroic and most efficient and beneficial revolutions in the care of the mentally sick in history. It was performed by one person—a woman, a retired schoolteacher whose name in the beginning carried no authority whatsoever, whose influence at the start was nil, and whose immense energy, staggering grit, combative determination, and single-minded enthusiasm were unknown to herself when she first embarked upon her mission to have hospitals built for the pariahs which the mentally ill were considered at the time. Dorothea Dix traversed the whole country. Bad roads, unseasonable weather, poor means of transportation, inhospitable politicians, parsimonious rich, the self-complacency of bureaucrats—all this formidable mass of obstacles seemed to her but so many small pebbles on the road which she swept aside with her energetic broom of conviction and faith, to march on without respite. She reached, she broke into state legislatures, the United States Congress, the English Parliament. While she knew disappointments, anguish, anger, even despair, she never gave up and she always conquered.[2]

It is perhaps not entirely a mere accident but a symbolic act of history that it was a woman of the New World—coming from New England at the time when the spirit of freedom was demanding the liberation of the Negro—who should have done so much for the humanization of the care of the insane. In the history of psychiatry from the *Malleus Maleficarum* to Mesmer it was woman who paid more dearly than man for the ignorance about mental diseases. The *miseriae* of Johann Weyer might well look through the mist of

[1] K. Sprengel: *Histoire de la médecine, depuis son origine jusqu'au dix-neuvième siècle.* (1815, 9 vols.)

[2] For a biography see Francis Tiffany: *Life of Dorothea Lynde Dix,* Boston, 1891; and for a detailed description and moving report of her achievements see Albert Deutsch: *The mentally ill in America.* Garden City, 1937. Ch. IX.

three centuries and offer thanksgiving to one of their own sex. The performance and achievements of Dorothea Dix were a true historical vindication and a deathblow to the misogynous trends which had dominated the field of mental diseases for so many centuries. Her work was a vindication of Cornelius Agrippa's proclamation *On the Nobility and Pre-eminence of the Female Sex* and of Vives' admiration of the cultural achievements of great women. The achievement of Dorothea Dix came after psychiatry itself had become fully aware of its needs, after it had begun to organize itself as an administrative and scientific unit.

A number of psychiatric societies and periodicals began to appear, reflecting a lively and uninterrupted discussion of clinical, theoretical, and administrative problems. The publications which Reil started in the beginning of the century were at the time more or less isolated phenomena; moreover, as has been mentioned, psychiatry when it first embarked on the creation of its own scientific press did not feel entirely secure as an independent discipline. Reil sought the collaboration of laymen such as the philosophers Kayssler and Hoffbauer. Toward the close of the third decade and the beginning of the fourth the needs and security of medical psychology became crystallized and psychiatry entered the field as a self-conscious, energetic branch of scientific medical discipline. From 1818 to 1893 almost fifty journals, monthly, quarterly, and yearly, appeared in France, England, Germany, the United States, Spain, Portugal, Italy, the Netherlands, Belgium, Scandinavia, and Russia. Over fifteen national and international psychiatric societies were organized on the European continent and in the New World. Not all of the publications survived but many did and many new ones took the place of the old.[3]

[3] *Zeitschrift für psychische Ärzte, mit besonderen Berüsichtigung des Magnetismus,* edited by Nasse, 1818. It became the *Zeitschrift für Anthropologie* in 1823. Ceased in 1826. *Magazin für die philosophische, medicinische und gerichtliche Seelenkunde,* Friedreich, 1829; from 1833 on, *Archiv für Psychologie für Ärzte und Juristen. Blätter für Psychiatrie,* Friedreich and Blumroeder, 1837. *Zeitschrift für die Beurteilung und Heilung krankhafter Seelenzustände,* Jacobi and Nasse, 1838. *Annales Médicolégales,* Crommelinck and Dejaeghère (Belgium), 1842. *Annales Médico-psychologiques,* Baillarger, Cerise, and Longet, 1843. *Allgemeine Zeitschrift für Psychiatrie,* Damerow, 1844. *American Journal of Insanity,* Brigham, 1844. *The Journal of Psychological Medicine and Mental Pathology,* Forbes Winslow (England), 1848. *Nederlandsch Tydschrift voor Gerechtelyke Geneeskunde en voor Psychiatrie,* Ramaer, 1853. *American Psychological Journal,* Mead, 1853. *Correspondenzblatt der deutschen Ge-*

II

IT would be impossible to review in detail the activities of all the psychiatric organizations and even more difficult to analyze the contributions of all the individuals involved. Only typical trends and their representatives can be singled out. Perhaps the most characteristic aspects of the psychiatrist of the first half of the nineteenth century can be seen in Guillaume Ferrus (1784–1861), who worked in the Salpêtrière under Pinel. Ferrus' father was active in the Revolution and was seldom at home; young Ferrus was entrusted to an uncle who was a physician. He was initiated into the study of anatomy at

sellschaft für Psychiatrie und gerichtliche Psychologie, Erlenmeyer, 1854. Annali frenopatici, Miraglia, Cirillo, and Cera, 1860. Journal de Médecine Mentale, Delasiauve, 1861. Archivo Italiano, Verga, Castiglione, and Biffi, 1864. Quarterly Journal of Psychological Medicine and Medical Jurisprudence, Hammond, 1867. Archiv für Psychiatrie und Nervenkrankheiten, Griesinger, Meyer, and Westphal, 1868. Psychiatrisches Centralblatt, Beer, Leidesdorf, and Meynert, 1872. The Journal of Nervous and Mental Disease, Sachs (America), 1874. The Chicago Journal of Nervous and Mental Disease, Jewell and Bannister, 1874. Rivista sperimentale di freniatria e di medicina legale, Livi, 1874. Quarterly Journal of Inebriety, Crothers and Binghamton (America), 1876. Mind, Robertson (England), 1876. Centralblatt für Nervenheilkunde, Erlenmeyer, 1877. Archivie di psichiatria, Lombrosi, Ferri, Garofalo, and Marselli, 1879. The Alienist and Neurologist, Hughes (America), 1880. Jahrbücher für Psychiatrie, Fritsch, 1880. American Journal of Neurology and Psychiatry, McBride, 1880. L'encéphale, Ball and Luys, 1881. Rivista frenopatica Barcelonesa, Partagus, 1881. Psychiatrische Bladen, Donkersblood, 1883. Medico-legal Journal, Bell (America), 1883. American Psychological Journal, Parrish, 1883. Archives of Psychoneurology and Legal Medicine, Kovalevsky (Russia, in Russian), 1885. The Psychiatric Messenger, Merjeyevski (Russia, in Russian), 1885. Il manicomio, giornale di psichiatrica, Ricco and Venturi, 1885. Rivista de neurologia e psychiatria, Bettencourt (Portugal), 1888. L'anomalo, Zuccarelli, 1889. Deutsche Zeitschrift für Nervenheilkunde, Strümpell, 1891. The Neurological Messenger, Bechterev (Russia, in Russian), 1893.

As to psychiatric associations: Medico-psychological Association (England), 1841. Association of medical superintendents of American institutions for the insane, originally twelve members, 1844; after 1892, Medico-psychological Association; now American Psychiatric Association. Section of anthropology and psychiatry of the Deutsche Naturforscher, originally thirteen members, 1847. Société médico-psychologique, Ferrus presiding, 1852. Psychiatric Association at St. Petersburg, 1861. Berliner medizinische psychologische Gesellschaft, Griesinger presiding, 1867; after 1885, Gesellschaft für Psychiatrie und Nervenkrankheiten. Société phréniatrique belge, 1869. Netherlands Association of Psychiatrists, originally ten members, 1871. Società freniatrica Italiana, 1873. Congrès international de médecine mentale, Baillarger presiding 1878. Société de psychologie de Paris, Charcot presiding, 1885. Congress of Russian psychiatrists, in Moscow, eighty members attending, Merjeyevski presiding, 1887. Society of Neuropathology and Psychiatry, in Kasan (Russia), Bechterev presiding, 1892.

the age of fourteen, at which time he helped his uncle in the dissecting amphitheater; very early he had to overcome his fear of cadavers and death. He became a doctor of medicine in 1804, at the age of twenty; his doctor's thesis was on sutures.

Like his father, Ferrus was responsive to the political events of his day, and he was loyal to Napoleon. He became a surgeon in Napoleon's armies and took part in the Battle of Austerlitz, his first active war experience. At Eylau he barely escaped being crushed by enemy cavalry when he noticed the wounded General Dahlman on the battlefield. Ferrus took out his white handkerchief and, waving it before the enemy, rushed toward the stricken commander. He was allowed to attend the wounded man and carry him back to the French lines. Ferrus resigned from the army when Napoleon abdicated, rejoined it when Napoleon returned from Elba, and abandoned it completely after Waterloo. He joined Pinel's staff in 1818, only after a thorough investigation of his liberal opinions had been made.

In 1826 Ferrus became physician-in-chief at the Bicêtre. Before assuming his duties he made a tour of inspection of the mental hospitals in France and England. This was almost thirty years after Pinel removed the chains from the mentally ill. It is therefore of particular interest to hear Ferrus tell of the lamentably few hospitals for the mentally ill, and of the very poor living conditions which he found to be the rule. "The insane are kept almost always in humid cells, dark and revoltingly dirty. The doors and windows are bolted with iron bars and offer a terrifying spectacle. The beds are usually built into the walls and are absolutely unfit for quieting the disturbed insane; when it is necessary to fix a patient to his bed, they use enormous iron rings which are attached to the wall for this purpose. In some localities, these unfortunates are tied to the wall . . . in a standing position. Thus segregated as a simple measure of policy and in the interests of public security, the patients remain deprived of the treatment which is essential for their recovery." [4]

When Ferrus assumed his duties at the Bicêtre in which Pinel had started his reforms, the insane and the criminals had not yet been separated. This separation Ferrus considered urgent. He thought the criminal insane needed particular attention; these "should be distrib-

[4] Quoted by R. Semelaigne: *Les pionniers, etc.*, vol. I, pp. 153, 154.

uted in such a manner that escape would be impossible; yet mental and physical treatment should not cease." [5] Ferrus found a number of cells in the Bicêtre totally unsuitable and introduced a revolutionary measure. He chose from among the patients those capable of working, and with their assistance ninety-six unhealthy cells formerly built for criminals were demolished. Ferrus was thus the first to inaugurate what later became known as occupational therapy. To this end, after a long, successful struggle against deadening tradition and bureaucracy, he had a large farm built in the place where the Hospital St. Anne stands today in Paris. There was a dairy; there were pigs; there were workshops. This type of therapy later took firm hold in the United States and developed into an integral part of the treatment in almost every hospital for mental diseases, state or private. But in France it soon fell into desuetude. As soon as Ferrus left the Bicêtre, the farm was forgotten. Even the little drugstore was closed, so that medicaments had to be brought from the Bicêtre. There was no resident physician and patients wandered about without care or supervision. At length the whole project was abandoned.

Ferrus introduced clinical teaching in the Bicêtre; it had existed in the Salpêtrière since Esquirol inaugurated it in 1817. Ferrus was fastidious in selecting his students and extremely considerate of the patients. He questioned the patients himself, permitting his assistants only to take notes; he was careful that the patients did not become fatigued or otherwise annoyed; he held gatherings of the students where they would analyze and discuss what they had observed and heard.

Ferrus was one of the founders of the Société Médico-psychologique (December, 1847). He was its first president and a most assiduous attendant of its meetings. Through his good offices the Société was permitted to meet in the Faculté. From 1835 he held the position of inspector general of insane asylums, and he was very active in the improvement of the conditions of the mentally ill. René Semelaigne says that Ferrus was the soul of all the preparatory work done for the law of June 30, 1838, which protected the insane and humanized their care. Criminals and prison reform preoccupied Ferrus, and he worked to improve prison conditions and wrote a great deal on the subject.

[5] *Idem*, vol. I, p. 154.

In 1850 he published a serious and enlightened treatise: *Des Prisonniers, de l'Emprisonnement et des Prisons*. He carried on the tradition of humaneness and kindness to patients, but he was practical and outspoken about the purely idealistic conceptions of *nonrestraint*. This term was introduced by John Conolly (1794–1866), the English contemporary of Ferrus. Conolly had been interested in mental diseases from his student days. In 1821 he submitted his doctor's dissertation on *De Statu Mentis in Insania et Melancholia*. Six years later he was appointed professor of practical medicine at University College in London. He tried hard to introduce the teaching of psychiatry into the curriculum. Apparently the time was not yet ripe; Conolly failed. In 1830 he became inspector of the asylums of Warwick County, and in 1839 physician-in-chief of the Hanwell asylum. Upon arrival in Hanwell, Conolly removed all forms of mechanical restraint from the patients. As early as 1830 he had published *An inquiry concerning the indications of insanity; with suggestions for the better protection and cure of the insane*. He originated the nonrestraint movement which spread to all Europe and to America. His follower, Robert Gardiner Hill (1811–1878), chief surgeon of Lincoln Asylum and later head of a private mental hospital, Eastgate House, wrote a great deal against any form of restraint.

The question was heatedly debated everywhere. Humanitarian and practical considerations clashed sharply. In the United States a discussion of nonrestraint was so stormy that at one of the meetings of the Association of Medical Superintendents Isaac Ray arose to express the opinion that nonrestraint might work with Europeans, who sane or insane are accustomed to obey orders, but not with Americans, who believe in liberty and who unless restrained would assert themselves even in a state of insanity.[6] The discussion of nonrestraint was heated in France, as well. Ferrus reported that he "saw at Conolly's own hospital, in a well-padded cell, a furious epileptic submitted to nonrestraint. Four powerful guards held the arms and limbs of the unfortunate patient." Ferrus was an outspoken person; he told the Belgian king in plain language that the Gheel colony for the mentally sick, of which Belgium was so proud, offered very little of which to be proud. Upon his return to France he described the cruelty which prevailed in

[6] Deutsch: *op. cit.*, pp. 216, 217.

the colony and remarked that "the treatment there was nil and the only thing the insane had was detrimental liberty." Ferrus had great clinical experience and he was deeply interested in the management of the mentally ill, which at that time meant in their treatment; aside from purgatives and the occasional use of drugs, treatment meant making the patient comfortable and treating him like a human being. Ferrus in this respect followed the French tradition brilliantly, with devotion, insight, and energy.

His theoretical views conformed to the established pattern. He believed that a mental disease was a brain disease; he believed in brain localization. When Jolly presented his findings to the Académie de Médecine in March and April, 1845, demonstrating on pathological material that mental diseases are not caused by inflammatory processes in the brain, Ferrus arose in favor of the organic point of view: "An alteration, or at least a powerful organic modification [in the brain], is the only thing which can explain the perseverance and the long duration of the malady. Moreover, one must admit the presence of an individual predisposition, because all people are subjected in the course of their lives to vivid and sudden moral shocks, but fortunately only a small number of them fall victim to insanity." [7]

Though Ferrus considered constitutional predispositions the fundamental causes of mental disease, he kept an open mind on many subjects. In 1857, at one of the meetings of the Société Médico-psychologique in which magnetism was discussed, Ferrus remarked, "Magnetism as it is presented by its adepts is an extravagant, foolish thing; I combated it for twenty years. Yet I have recognized since that it does present facts which deserve the attention of science. . . . There is in these mystical phenomena perhaps nothing which is completely mysterious, nothing which in a final analysis one cannot penetrate." [8]

Ferrus' classification of diseases is of no historical moment; he was inclined to use the criterion of intellectual defects. He observed what he called "temporary idiotism," Esquirol "acute dementia," and Georget "stupidity."

[7] R. Semelaigne: Les pionniers, etc., vol. I, p. 159.
[8] Ibid., vol. I, p. 160.

THE story of the work of Ferrus is typical for the psychiatric orientation of the first half of the nineteenth century. The psychiatrist was the head of a hospital. His major preoccupations were hospital administration, careful recording of clinical material, humanization of the care of the patients. He was constantly concerned with legislative improvements and with the promotion of professional organizations and professional publications. He was seriously interested in criminology and medicolegal problems involving the care and the future of the so-called criminal insane. He was oriented by a scientific eclecticism with the accent on cerebral pathology. This description would correspond in many respects to a typical psychiatrist of today.

The life and work of Ferrus demonstrate the enormous extension of the scope of psychiatry. Its influence was felt in many channels of public life: hospital administration, civil and criminal law, education. Depending upon his acumen and erudition, the institutional psychiatrist would extend his knowledge by way of more profound or more superficial description of the clinical material which was always at his disposal. The nineteenth century was the golden age of descriptive psychiatry, for at no previous time had the psychiatrist had at his disposal such a great number and variety of mental diseases. To bring some order into the mass of facts observed there was naturally the need to classify the data. The French and for that matter the English were not addicted to classification, nor were the classifications of any great originality when they did undertake them. The French seem to have centered their attention more on separating every now and then one set of symptoms or one group of symptoms, which seemed likely to turn out to be an independent clinical entity, a separate "disease." The French brought forward no new theories and no complex nosological systems. Officially their orientation was always neuroanatomical, cerebrospinal, neurophysiological. Exceptions there were, but they exerted no influence on the general development of the specialty. François Broussais, for instance, the sharp, acrimonious critic of Pinel, created few if any adepts for his physiological theory of irritation. His was a belated edition of Haller's and Brown's conceptions transformed into a systematic theory in which the stomach appeared as a sort of Aristotelian *sensorium commune.*[9] The clinical and therapeutic results of this short-lived theory were negligible. The tradition of French psychiatry remained the one established by Philippe Pinel and has been maintained through our own day. It is a tradition of keen description and brilliant separation and analysis of the various nuances of consciousness and its aberrations.

J. E. D. Esquirol (1772–1840), the pupil of Pinel, was one of the ablest in this tradition and one of the greatest. The two volumes *Des maladies mentales considérées sous les rapports médical, hygiénique et médico-légal,* published in 1838, two years before his death, comprise more than just another book on mental diseases. The book is a summary of the years of clinical teaching which he began in 1817; it is an excellent synthesis of a man's great and fruitful intellectual effort. Esquirol was one of the first, if not the first, to apply statistical methods to his clinical studies. He tabulated what were then called psychological causes, that is to say, disappointment in love, financial worries, and similar factors which we know now are but precipitating factors and not true psychological causes of mental disease. Esquirol's figures are in themselves imposing and speak for the enormous mass of material the psychiatrist of the time had at his disposal. Esquirol pointed out that in the Bicêtre four hundred and nine out of fifteen hundred and seventy-eight men and in the Salpêtrière five hundred and eighty out of nineteen hundred and forty women became mentally ill as a result of psychological factors. As early as 1805 Esquirol respected the emotions as a source of psychological illness; the title of his doctor's thesis reads: *Les passions considérées comme causes, symptômes, et moyens curatifs de l'aliénation mentale.*

His theoretical views contributed little that was new but his keen analytical approach made more than one dent in tradition. While not fully appreciated at the time, his contention that disturbances of intelligence might not be primary but only a result of disturbed attention was of great importance. Imperceptibly it diverted the student from considering every defect in judgment as a result of a special brain lesion. Esquirol taught with enthusiasm and conveyed to his students his own analytical observational keenness. He established a

[9] François Broussais: *De l'irritation et de la folie.* Paris, 1828.

prize for the best essay on mental diseases.[10] The prize was two hundred francs and a copy of Pinel's *Traité Médico-philosophique*, which was still considered the psychiatrist's Bible.

Esquirol differentiated certain depressive states from the other psychoses and called them *lypemanias*—a forerunner of the modern concept of depressions. He introduced the term *hallucinations*, giving it the clear-cut definition of today, that is, limiting it only to hearing or seeing things which are not there and underscoring that these are not false perceptions (illusions) but actual pseudosensory products of the mental disturbance itself. He defined his concept of monomania by separating from other psychoses those which showed a predominance of one idea or one set of ideas which was in the center of the patient's attention and the chief source of his behavior. Monomania was the forerunner of one of the schizophrenias of our day; Esquirol based most of his medicolegal views on this concept. He was active in the amelioration of conditions in prisons; his *Mémoire* to the minister of the interior on conditions in hospitals and prisons is one of the ablest and most influential documents in the history of administrative psychiatry. Esquirol traveled to Italy, where the king showed him a hospital just completed for the mentally sick. Esquirol was apparently as candid with the king of Italy as Ferrus was with the king of the Belgians. The king was impressed. He gave orders that the hospital be used only as an armory, and a new hospital was built in accordance with Esquirol's ideas.

Esquirol was as prodigious a writer as he was a hard worker. In addition to a great number of contributions on clinical and medicolegal psychiatric problems, he contributed thirteen articles to the monumental sixty-volume *Dictionnaire des Sciences Médicales*, including articles on monomania, suicide, mental hospitals, demonomania, and erotomania.

He was unequivocal in his defense of criminals who were mentally ill; this theme continues to sound with increasing power and passion in the writings of French psychiatrists. Esquirol was attacked for his views on monomania in connection with criminology. He replied, "These conclusions may appear strange today; some day, we hope,

[10] Georget was the first to receive this prize with his work on autopsies: *Ouvertures du corps des aliénés.*

they will become popular truths. Where is the judge today who would condemn to the bonfire a deranged man or a gypsy accused of magic or sorcery? It has been a long time now that the magistrates have sent the sorcerer to an insane asylum; they no longer cause them to be punished as swindlers." [11]

The same tradition and the same excellence of clinical judgment are to be found in E. J. Georget (1795–1828), who died so young but who in his very short life proved to be a prodigal worker and an ardent scholar. In quality and quantity his contributions compare favorably with the work of Esquirol, who died at the age of sixty-eight, and with that of Ferrus, who died at the age of seventy-seven. Georget submitted his doctor's thesis, *Dissertation sur les Causes de la Folie*, in 1820. How mature his thought was at the age of twenty-five one may judge from the fact that he published his masterwork *De la Folie* in the same year. He was dead eight years later. His orientation was organic but his clinical descriptions were masterpieces.

The writers and the clinicians of the time seem monotonously alike in the theme they treat and even in the titles of their works. Fodéré (1764–1835), for instance, wrote a two-volume treatise, *Traité du délire appliqué à la médecine, à la morale et à la législation* (1817). The title points to the same sphere of interest as that designated by Esquirol or Ferrus, but despite this apparent sameness all three introduced additional medicopsychological ideas which were both original and penetrating. Thus we find in Fodéré the perspicacious remark that a mental disease is *un sommeil des sens externes et une veille des senses internes*, a purely modern and extremely valid thought in medical psychology, one which in present-day language could be stated: a mental disease is a loss of the sense of reality and a free play of one's fantasies.

Fodéré's observations are typical of the whole trend of French psychiatry. "When one has seen many insane people," he said, "one can recognize that there are as many [individual] differences among them as there are personalities among individuals whose minds are healthy. . . . It is therefore really difficult to make up classes of diseases which would not prove fictitious." [12] It is this keen sense of psychological discernment of individual trends that made the French

---

[11] R. Semelaigne: *Les pionniers, etc.*, vol. I, p. 133.
[12] Fodéré: *Traité du délire*. Paris, 1817, p. 333.

psychiatrists capable of differentiating certain complex mental pictures on the basis of their psychological manifestations as well as their organic reactions. It is this characteristic that made Philippe Pinel and Esquirol so influential at home, in England, and all over Europe. *Maladies Mentales*, for instance, not only stands out historically as a basic text, but for over two decades after its appearance it was considered a fundamental guide.

Perhaps just because of this authority and profound influence of Pinel and Esquirol the general principles of medical psychology in France have undergone little fundamental change. The cardinal lines of French psychiatry were drawn by Pinel and Esquirol with bold security and sharp definition; generations of their pupils and successors followed these lines with little deviation from the chief topics Pinel and Esquirol assigned to them. In the years which followed more details were added to the treasury of descriptive psychological observations, more neuroanatomic data were permitted to evolve into a clearer conception of certain organic diseases; but from the array of illustrious, enthusiastic, and creative workers it is not possible to select one whose contributions stand out of the general, although brilliant, picture of the French psychiatric effort—with perhaps the exception of Morel and Magnan, who closed the nineteenth century honorably and impressively in the best tradition established by Pinel and Esquirol.

IV

THE general inclination to single out typical groups of psychological symptoms was particularly fruitful. There were some, like Fodéré, who saw in the mass of the mentally sick too great a variety of individual reactions to warrant an attempt to delineate specific diseases. Georget also was reluctant to lose himself in classificatory outlines. He was more inclined to speculate along broad psychological perspectives and therefore could even dare to reproach the master, Philippe Pinel, for "collecting facts and daring little." To Georget mental illness was apparently one idiopathic brain disease with a great variety of manifestations which were, however, not separate diseases. In this formulation he was one of the earliest psychiatrists to believe in the unity of all mental diseases as representing different stages of one process. This problem did not particularly preoccupy the French psychiatrists, but in Germany almost throughout the century a lively discussion was maintained on whether mental illness is one process (*Krankheitsprozess*) or a series of strictly separate diseases (*Krankheitsbegriff*). Georget remarked: "One can see a mass of intermediary types [of illness], which fact warrants [the assumption] that there is an imperceptible transition between one form of mental illness and another." [13] But one form seemed to impress itself particularly upon the French observers: the states of depression which were related to or which alternated with states of excitation or elation. Such observations had been made many times by many people through many centuries. From the time of Hippocrates physicians had suggested that mania and melancholia are related or are forms of the same disease, or merge one into the other. These suggestions, however, were more or less speculative ideas, based on fleeting impressions or intuition rather than on true experience.

The development of mental hospitals, because it offered the opportunity to observe a great number of patients and to observe each individual patient for a prolonged period of time, put at the disposal of the discerning observer the material he needed. With this opportunity was coupled a new attitude which was the direct result of the re-established Hippocratic tradition in medicine. One of the outstanding characteristics of Hippocratism which returned to medicine with particular clarity early in the eighteenth century, especially under the influence of Sydenham, was the systematic approach to each and every disease. The disease had to have a characteristic beginning, a typical course, and a typical outcome. This Hippocratic principle was not fully applied to mental cases until late in the nineteenth century, but even in the eighteen twenties, under the influence of Pinel and Esquirol, attempts at this approach were being cautiously made. Some convulsive and paralytic states associated with mental symptoms lent themselves particularly to consideration from this point of view, but those diseases which showed no dramatic involvement of the central nervous system—diseases with purely psychological manifestations—were more difficult to fit into the Hippocratic scheme. Moreover, psychological manifestations are multifarious and protean; there was no

[13] R. Semelaigne: *Les grands aliénistes français*, vol. I, p. 382.

established technique for psychological examination, and the finer points of psychological deviation proved too elusive and perhaps too vague to the observer of those days. On the other hand, the common emotional states, such as sadness and gaiety, were conspicuous in their manifestations and easy to notice. A man with sufficient clinical experience and with a flair for swings of emotion had his attention naturally attracted to this aspect of mental diseases and was able to sort out certain typical manifestations from the mass of clinical material.

Jean Pierre Falret (1794–1870) was such a clinician. A pupil of Esquirol, he very early became interested in those abnormal reactions which are accompanied by suicidal drives or which terminate in suicide.[14] He studied especially a morbid state to which seafarers were subject—the Spanish called it *calentura*—in which men impulsively jump into the sea and drown.[15] He evolved a method of careful interrogation of patients and taught it to his students. To him a patient was a complex living psychology, and when a new law governing the insane was projected in 1837 it was Falret who prevailed on the authorities to eliminate from the statute books such age-long monstrosities of the juridical jargon as "imbecility," "dementias," "furor," and substitute for them the words "mental alienation" (*aliénation mentale*).

Falret was continually active in many fields which now claimed the psychiatrist's attention: hospital reorganization, legislation, general medicine, problems of public health. Public health problems became particularly acute when an epidemic of cholera broke out in Paris in 1832 and engaged the energies of Esquirol, then a member of the council of public health, and of many of his assistants. Falret was living at Vanves at the time and was not as close to the public health problem as were so many of his colleagues. While studying such organic conditions as apoplexy and general paralysis, he had become more attuned to purely psychological symptoms. He traveled to see the mental hospitals in England, Scotland, and Ireland, and he came back with a keener awareness of the *lésions psychiques*, that is, of the abnormal psychological reactions. "We endeavored," he said, "to penetrate into their doctrines and we created a psychology which we could

---

[14] His major work is a volume of 519 pages, entitled *De l'hypochondrie et du suicide*. Paris, 1822.

[15] J. Falret: *Délire*. In the *Dictionnaire des études médicales pratiques*. Paris, 1839.

use, and which could shed light on our understanding of the psychic lesions found in the diverse forms of mental alienation." [16]

Falret, according to Lasègue, was possessed of "earnest, convinced and convincing faith in the future of psychological medicine," but the latter was also "the part of his life that disappointed him." For thirty-two years Falret studied the abnormal depressions which were accompanied by suicidal impulses; he noticed that some of them wear off by turning into a state of abnormal elation and that some of the elations, after running a certain course, turn into profound depression. It was a sort of closed emotional circle. He recognized in this cycle a separate type of mental disease and in 1854 he published his communication *De la folie circulaire*.[17] This type was later called by Baillarger (1851) *folie à double forme*, a concept which was finally established in psychiatry under the name of manic-depressive psychosis in the last years of the nineteenth century by Kraepelin.

Baillarger (1809–1890) followed up Esquirol's studies of hallucinations, and despite his many activities, including the editing of the *Annales Medico-psychologiques*, he found time to make valuable contributions to the problems of hallucinations and general paralysis. Baillarger's was not a formalistic mind, and his psychological insight was unusual. He was the first to sense that hallucinations are what we would call today spontaneous results of a psychological reaction; he called them "involuntary." He also studied the role of the state which is intermediary between that of being asleep and that of being awake, at which time normal people have hallucinatory experiences, now called hypnagogic.[18] He also differentiated alcoholic hallucinations. Studying the varieties of *folie à double forme*, Baillarger did not fail to notice that certain depressions (melancholias) merge with states of stupor—an observation of more than passing importance. Stupors had always been considered a sign of hopelessness and incurability. In the seventies of the nineteenth century this attitude became established as a rule; a stupor was taken for a sign of catatonia—a form of dementia praecox which was then considered definitely incurable. It

[16] R. Semelaigne: *Les pionniers, etc.*, vol. I, p. 175.
[17] Jean Falret: *De la folie circulaire, Bulletin de l'Académie Médicale.* Paris, 1854. Vol. 19, p. 382.
[18] J. Baillarger: *De la mélancholie avec stupeur, Annales Médico-Psychologiques,* 1853, vol. 5, p. 251.

is possible that some of the stupors observed by Baillarger were catatonias, but the fact that he associated them with melancholia, that is
to say, with depressions, suggests that he also dealt with a form of
stupor which many years later proved not as hopeless prognostically
as it had been thought previously. Over half a century after Baillarger,
August Hoch (1868–1919) in the United States described the "benign
stupors" as a form of manic-depressive psychosis. This diagnostic designation, although of questionable validity in many cases, acquired rights
of citizenship in American clinical psychiatry and stimulated deeper
psychological studies of depressions.

Whatever the diagnostic labels and whatever the new appellations,
the French psychiatrist continued to single out neatly circumscribed
groups of psychological symptoms, thus broadening and deepening his
psychological vision. He now embarked upon working out a body of
facts and creating an independent clinical and virtually general descriptive psychology without having to rely on the theoretical, nonmedical psychologist. By the middle of the century psychiatry, particularly that of the French, seems to have abandoned its official
dependence on Hartley, Hume, Berkeley, Condillac, and Locke. The
hospital, the clinic, established itself as the only reliable source and
as the natural laboratory of human psychology.

There was in this natural laboratory a certain type of patient which
presented a particularly difficult and intriguing problem. The number
of patients suffering from partial or general paralysis combined with a
mental disease ("delirium") and, not infrequently, convulsions seemed
to be increasing. Anything that was connected with physical weakness
and convulsions attracted great attention not only because the symptoms
were so conspicuous but also because the convulsive disorders other
than epilepsy had for centuries been a part of the psychopathological
plague of Europe. The general propensity of man to believe in the
obvious, physical defects as the causes of mental illness was here propitiated by the great amount of convulsive and paralytic material.

The French psychiatrists for the most part never abandoned their
neuroanatomical and neurophysiological views. Even those who, like
Falret, were attracted primarily to psychological phenomena stressed
the importance of the cerebrospinal system in mental disease. The psychological life of man was still called *soul*, and this soul was considered

a sort of flexible, submissive tool in the hands of fate, which inflicts damage on the brain and spinal cord; it was, in the words of an Italian psychiatrist who like all his colleagues was under the influence of the French views, an *anima impassible*.[19] Falret remarked in 1822, "I believe firmly that in all cases, without exception, one could find in the mentally sick appreciable lesions in the brain or its membranes; these lesions are sufficiently marked and sufficiently constant to account satisfactorily for all the various intellectual and affective disturbances in insanity."[20] And Parchappe (1800–1866) is, characteristically, even more outspoken; as Delasiauve puts it, Parchappe was a man whom people esteemed but feared. Parchappe seems to have rejected psychology almost as much as Griesinger did. Speaking for himself and for the great majority of his contemporaries, Parchappe insisted that only lesions in the brain could serve as a basis for a classification of diseases. "A psychological classification could be based only on psychological systems, that is, on the most secondary and collateral manifestations."[21]

The orientation insisting on a psychiatry without psychology achieved here its full expression; it served an excellent purpose despite its narrow and one-sided viewpoint, for attention was concentrated on the very symptoms which gradually came to be recognized as those of general paralysis—a chronic disease, of slow development, due to the invasion of the brain by the syphilitic spirochete. Haslam had already given a creditable description of the disease, the cause of which was unknown then, as it remained unknown till the beginning of the twentieth century. The bulk of the recognizing, describing, and differentiating of general paralysis was done, however, by the Frenchmen A. L. J. Bayle (1799–1858) and J. L. Calmeil (1798–1895). Baillarger made important contributions, and, finally, Delasiauve (1804–1893) and Falret established definite diagnostic criteria (in 1851 and 1859 respectively) which, in conjunction with the later-discovered Wassermann and other serological tests, are still used today.[22] Of major work in general paralysis there remained only the

[19] G. Fantonetti: *Della pazzia teoretico-practico*, 1830.
[20] Quoted by R. Semelaigne: *Les pionniers, etc.*, vol. I, p. 174.
[21] *Ibid.*, vol. I, p. 269.
[22] For details see Dr. Henry's chapter on Organic Mental Diseases. Neuburger and Pagel: *Handbuch*, vol. II, part II, p. 665, states that the first to describe general pa-

perspicacious clinical experiments of Krafft-Ebing (1840–1903) who, before the Wassermann reaction was discovered, definitely established the relationship of general paralysis to syphilis.

The successful differentiation of general paralysis was not only a momentous step in the history of medicine. Not only did it seem to solve a puzzle which taxed one's curiosity and observational ingenuity or challenged one's steadfast faith in scientific research, but, rather dramatically, it added weight to the prevailing theories that mental diseases are physical diseases of the central nervous system. It strengthened the general tendency which had prevailed in psychiatry for centuries to consider psychology a branch of philosophy; it increased the enthusiastic hope that someday a scientific psychiatry would be built independent of and without the benefit of psychology. The early suggestion of G. E. Stahl that organic mental diseases should be differentiated from functional seems to have been forgotten almost at the moment it was made. Adolph Wachsmuth, who in 1859, over one hundred years after Stahl, made the first attempt at an outline of general psychopathology, recaptured Stahl's thought and stated the truth, so well known today, that not all diseases of the brain produce mental symptoms and that not all mental symptoms are due to brain lesions.[23] Wachsmuth's thought was not heeded.

The stupendous step forward which the clinical delineation of general paralysis was proved a step backward for the general psychopathology of the severe neuroses and psychoses, that is to say, of mental diseases proper. It proved a blessing for hundreds of thousands of unfortunates suffering from a syphilitic infection which had not been properly cured and which had become invisible for a period of years, only to reappear in the form of a devastating disease of the brain and spinal cord—a disease which was destructive to the whole personality of the individual and was invariably fatal. Studies in serology and empirical therapeutic efforts, stimulated and made possible by the discovery of the nature of general paralysis and its cause, had finally reduced substantially the number of fatal outcomes, increased the

---

ralysis as a disease *sui generis* was Légal-Lasalle in *De quelques points de l'histoire de la paralysie des aliénes*, 1843. I failed to locate this work, in spite of a careful search. G. Z.

[23] Hans W. Gruhle: *Geschichtliches*, Bumke's *Handbuch der Geisteskrankheiten*, vol. IX, part v, p. 18.

number of recoveries, and, what is most important, led to rational-preventive measures which at least in some countries (Scandinavia) almost entirely eliminated general paralysis as a disease.

However, this blessing turned a number of psychiatrists away from the psychoses. The great ambition cherished by all from Daquin and Boissier de Sauvages, Boerhaave, Pinel and his pupils, the ambition not only to capture psychiatry but to make it a legitimate branch of general medicine or neurology seems finally to have entered the phase of actual fulfillment. Virchow (1821–1902) was bringing medicine out of its rut by his epoch-making clinical and pathological work. The not less great Claude Bernard, the first indisputable genius in the field since Albrecht Haller, was doing for experimental physiology what Virchow did for pathology and clinical medicine, and by his lucid and ingenious experimentation he ensured the further growth of the scientific heritage that was Virchow's. The experimental laboratory entered the field of medicine. It soon became the adjunct, the integral part of medicine—the very legs of the patient's bed, the doctor's right hand at the bedside.

Everywhere this great change was felt; everywhere this revolution, bloodless but majestic in its very peacefulness, was taking hold, gaining adherents, and establishing its empire with armies of peaceful men whose combat was work, whose power was scientific research, and whose law was treatment of disease. France, which had been the psychiatric leader of Europe since Pinel, reflected the effects of this revolution and began to show signs of definitely turning away from purely psychological interests. The leadership of France is clearly demonstrated by the fact that when a Bavarian count was tried for murder it was the French physician Benedict Augustin Morel who was invited to Munich to give his expert psychiatric opinion on the defendant. He was so convincing in his testimony to the effect that the count was mentally sick that the jury relented and the count was sentenced merely to twenty years of imprisonment, only to be sent a few weeks later to a mental institution because he had developed acute attacks of excitement and grandiose ideas. Morel was received by King Ludwig I who showed the crown prince to the French psychiatrist and exclaimed: "Are not these eyes the passionate eyes of

Adonis?" Morel replied, "These are eyes that forbode the coming of madness." Morel, as is known, proved right.

The evolution of Morel (1809–1873) as a psychiatrist is typical and illustrative of the developmental process just sketched. In his first published work on mental diseases [24] he, like Falret at the beginning of his career, pointed out that psychological studies were much neglected in favor of the anatomical and pathological. Two years later he embarked, at first in collaboration with Lasègue, upon a historical study of mental diseases,[25] in which he earnestly evaluated the psychological schools of Germany and particularly the theories of Stahl. The six years which followed (1844–1850) Morel devoted to more historical studies, to a review of psychiatry in Belgium, Holland, Germany, Italy, Switzerland, Great Britain, and the United States, and to an inclusive study of the psychiatric and medical literature of these countries.[26] Medicolegal problems, the point of particular interest to every French psychiatrist of the day, preoccupied Morel and gained him a well-deserved reputation.

During these years he established a warm friendship with Claude Bernard, with whom he conducted endless and enthusiastic discussions on physiology and psychology. The influence of Claude Bernard on Morel was deep. Morel's was a sensitive, perspicacious intellect, and the achievement and the yet unfulfilled potentialities of physiological research appealed to him. He was interested in goiter and cretinism at the time, and around 1850 he began to ponder over the problems of degeneration. While working in the asylum of Maréville he studied for a long while with Renaudin, but his mind seems to have become diverted from his original thesis that psychology was being neglected in favor of anatomy.

Renaudin (1808–1865), only a year older than Morel, was, like Morel, typical of the French tradition and of the spirit of his psychiatric generation. Both men were constantly preoccupied with problems of

[24] B. A. Morel: *Mémoire sur la manie des femmes en couches, Bulletin de la Société de Médecine*, Paris, 1842.

[25] Morel and Lasègue: *Etudes historiques sur l'aliénation mentale, Annales Médico-Psychologique*, 1844, vol. II, p. 40.

[26] These were all published as articles in the *Annales Médico-Psychologique*, 1844–1850.

hospital administration and improvement; both were vitally concerned with medicolegal problems. But Renaudin, although originally interested in physiological problems,[27] paid more attention to the psychology of the psychoses. His *Etudes Médico-psychologiques sur l'Aliénation Mentale*, published in 1854, is an imposing volume of over eight hundred pages. In this work he insisted on the "psychosomatic duality" of man and saw in mental disease "an automatism which takes the place of spontaneity." He made some keen observations on hallucinations and was on the verge of formulating the concept of the total personality. According to Renaudin the three basic forms of psychological expression were feeling, understanding, and acting (behaving). Consequently: "Impressionability, intelligence, will, these are, if we may express ourselves this way, three distinct psychological entities, yet they always act in concert so that it is impossible in most cases to distinguish in every fact which of these elements is more prominent." They all act as "a unitary bundle." A mental disease is characterized by the breakdown of this unitary functioning.

The scientific evolution of Morel followed its own course, and in 1856 Morel and Renaudin parted. In 1853 Morel had attempted to subject mental patients to the effects of ether. Outside purely medicolegal problems Morel's attention was absorbed by the problem of degeneration. In 1857 his magnum opus appeared, a volume of seven hundred pages entitled *Traité des dégénérescences physiques, intellectuelles et morales de l'espèce humaine*. He viewed mental disease primarily as a "result of hereditary weaknesses." Degeneration was a hereditary phenomenon, of course, and Morel developed a detailed method for discovering the great variety of "stigmata of degeneration" to be found among the mentally sick. These were mostly physical signs—various malformations—but also various intellectual and moral deviations from the normal. His *Traité des Maladies Mentales* (866 pages) which appeared in 1860 was written with his theory of degeneration as the foundation of his psychiatry. The accent was on heredity, toxins (such as alcohol, narcotics, metal poisoning, pellagra, goiter) and "sympathies," that is, mental diseases due to primary brain disease. Hysteria, hypochondria, and epilepsy are grouped together,

---

[27] His doctor's thesis (1832) dealt with "medicochemical properties of hydrocyanic acid."

and what appear to be psychoses proper are put in the next-to-last (fifth) group as "idiopathic"—a term, frequently used even today and not only in psychiatry, having no meaning but that of a verbal label.

Morel saw the French Empire destroyed and the German Empire founded. He died three years after the Third Republic was established, and with him, strictly speaking, passed the leadership of French psychiatry in Europe. The center of psychiatric thought shifted to Germany. This shift was not sudden; it was not due to Moltke's victory over Napoleon III at Sedan. For more than two generations Germany had been building up a psychiatric tradition which had its roots in France; now she came into her own. The shift cannot be considered a decline, or one of Morel's forms of degeneration. We must not forget that nine years after Morel's death the illustrious work of Charcot began at the Salpêtrière and that at the same time the star of Magnan was already high in the French psychiatric skies. Morel appears to be the last of the French psychiatrists in the sense of originality of approach and true interest in psychopathology. He started in the best French tradition, but he finished with a detailed classification in which the so-called functional psychoses, the major subject matter of psychiatry, were relegated to a more or less shadowy place in the scheme of things psychiatric. The element of fatalism which lurks in all such concepts as heredity and degeneration was more prominent than the element of psychological inquiry. This orientation is, in the last analysis, impersonal, and it treats the mentally ill more or less impersonally. When one looks, as Morel looked, even for geological influences on mental diseases (discussed in Morel's correspondence with the Archbishop of Chambéry, Monsignor Billiet), one is bound to relegate the psychotic to a well-organized hospital where he is kept awaiting a dubitable better day or the indubitable end. This orientation has and has always had a rather deadening effect on the therapeutic intent, on the effort to cure. For, unless one luckily finds substantial, obvious causes of a physical nature, there is little left but with the aid of humanistic disposition to bow to fate, which the scientific psychiatrist became accustomed to call euphemistically heredity or degeneration.

Morel's humanistic drives found expression in medicolegal work, with which his fatalistic theory failed to interfere. But the general course of psychiatry was definitely chartered in the direction of organic, physiological interests. In the last analysis this was the orientation of Charcot, and more specifically that of Magnan who, unlike Charcot, dealt with psychoses. This orientation coincided with that of the rapidly maturing German psychiatry. In the meantime Magnan closed the century for psychiatry in France not so much as a French but already as a European psychiatrist.

When Magnan (1835–1916) started his medical career he worked at the Bicêtre under Marcé (1828–1864) and later under Baillarger and Jean Falret. His work was inaugurated by studies of general paralysis, especially of the anatomical findings in the brain affected by this disease. His first lecture as a teacher at St. Anne was on general paralysis. His first scientific publication (1864) was on the toxic effects of absinthe. To absinthe he ascribed an especially morbid effect. He organized a laboratory in which he began to study the effects of absinthe, alcohol, morphine, and cocaine. Together with some of his colleagues Magnan organized a course of lectures and clinical demonstrations. There were to be twelve of these; four of them, Magnan's third of the course, were devoted to the following: (1) acute alcoholism, delirium tremens with fever, treatment; (2) chronic alcoholism, semianesthetic form; (3) the parallel between chronic alcoholism and general paralysis, from the point of view of diagnosis and anatomical lesions; and (4) puerperal insanity.

It is apparent, first, that Magnan had unusually rich clinical material for the study of alcoholism. The days following the debacle at Sedan and the Commune were troubled, and many a person sought solace in drinking. But it is also obvious that Magnan's major interest lay in this type of illness. What he studied was not alcoholism, of course, but the mental and neurological results of alcoholism.

An interesting incident in connection with the above-mentioned course took place. The course was extremely well attended, even overcrowded. The press took cognizance of the fact, and newspapers began to attack the professors for demonstrating patients to students: the insane should not be exhibited; professional secrets should not be divulged. Complaints were lodged with the administration. After some hesitation, permission to resume the course the following year was withdrawn, and for two years it was not renewed. While the teaching of psychiatry had been going on for years, ever since the days of Philippe Pinel, there was no official professor of psychiatry until later. Royer-Collard taught officially for a while in 1816 in the medical school of St. Anne; Esquirol's clinical courses at the Charenton were very popular. But the first professor of psychiatry in the medical school of St. Anne, Benjamin Ball, was not appointed until 1877. His title was professor of mental and cerebral diseases.

After two years Magnan resumed his teaching. In 1874 he published his monograph on *Alcoholism*. He treated the problem from the standpoint of public health and advocated special hospitals for alcoholics. Magnan's studies of the subject were very stimulating. In Russia, where alcoholism was widespread, Korsakov described in 1889 the whole mental and neurological picture of the chronic alcoholic psychosis, today known officially as Korsakov's psychosis.

Magnan was strictly speaking a neuropathologist and hospital administrator. To him goes the credit for abolishing the camisole and other forms of restraint at St. Anne. His general psychiatric theories were not distinguished by any originality. He considered mental disease mostly hereditary. At a session of the Société Médico-psychologique in 1886 he remarked, "All the numerous conditions which are confused with consciousness under the name of insanity—*folie raisonnante*, mania without delirium, pseudo-monomania, etc.—are merely psychological stigmata of hereditary insanity."

Magnan's terms began to be used with increasing frequency. The differentiation of general paralysis and the toxic states such as alcoholism and drug addiction left a conspicuous number of diseases which did not correspond to the older ideas that each serious mental disease, being a severe affection of the brain, direct or indirect, must show a *delirium*, a disoriented state with loss of memory and loss of the sense of time or place. These are the usual characteristics of an organic disease. Most of the organic mental diseases having been separated from the rest of the psychoses, the psychiatrist became more definitely aware that there *are* mental diseases in which there are no deliriums, in which reasoning does not seem impaired, in which something is wrong—but not those things which were supposed to be wrong. The psychiatrist then became aware that a man might appear fully normal in all respects and yet have impulses, compulsions, uncontrollable drives which affect his total behavior. In so far as those people remained quiescent they may have never, or have seldom, reached a mental hospital, but in so far as their personality disorganization brought them into conflict with the law as a result of stealing, arson, assault, or murder, the psychiatrist was called upon to see them, study them, and render his opinion. Magnan, like Morel, was greatly interested in this aspect of psychiatry and, with Morel, accepted Prichard's view on so-called "moral insanity."

We may note in concluding these pages of French psychiatry that the general, but far from vague, outlines of the psychosis with persecutory trends usually ending in complete mental deterioration—a phenomenon later on covered by the term "schizophrenia"—were well observed and described by the French. Lasègue published a study on *délire des persecutions;* [28] Morel published one on *manie avec conscience.* [29] The general approach toward this psychosis was becoming Hippocratic: the questions of form, course, and outcome were in the foreground. Magnan spoke of the periods of incubation, persecution, ambition, and dementia.

By a striking coincidence a number of the greatest psychiatrists of France did their best work in times of severe crises. None of them seems to have been deterred by the social tragedies of his time from remaining at his professional and scientific post until death overtook him. Pinel's work proceeded within the shadow of the guillotine. Ferrus' career was bound up with the fate of Napoleon. Jean Falret died in Vanves during the siege of Paris, unable to communicate with his son, a psychiatrist in his own right, living in Paris. Morel did a good part of the writing of his medicolegal material during the Franco-Prussian War and the Commune, and he was scientifically most active during the Revolution of 1848. Magnan died in the midst of the first World War, hoping for a French victory in the dark days of 1916.

v

FRENCH medical psychology was at once humanistic, rational, practical, and experimental. It did not shrink from speculation, but at all times

[28] E. Lasègue (with Legrand du Saulle): *Sur un cas supposé de délire des persecutions, Annales d'Hygiène et de Médecine Légale,* 1871.
[29] B. Morel: *Les aliénés avec conscience, Annales Médico-Psychologiques,* 1870, vol. III, p. 110.

it remained on the chosen foundation of neurological studies; whatever psychological interests there were, they did not entice the clinician into theoretical, speculative flights. The humanism of the French clinicians was not sentimental, but rather was tempered by a constructive rationalism which sought practical expression in the deepening of medicolegal studies, the extension of medicolegal practice, and the refinement of hospital medicopsychological care. The French school was free from the romanticism which swept over German psychiatry toward the first half of the century; from Pinel to Magnan the clinicians were careful to describe the psychological manifestations of mental disease rather than to seek for their ultimate psychological origin. They were the first classical phenomenologists in modern psychiatry. Characteristically enough, the Gallic spirit which is both lucid and sequential, logical and skeptical, made the psychiatrists of France almost distrustful of their own psychological propensities.

This attitude is rather well expressed in the work of J. B. M. Parchappe, who was opposed to any classificatory attempts. Classifications, he believed, should be based on sound findings—and psychology was not sound enough for a basis. Such enlightened conservatism combined with humanism appealed to the measured, liberal mind of the Anglo-Saxon and is perhaps one of the most potent forces leading to French psychiatry's influence on the psychiatry of England and America. The intellectual bond between England and France which existed throughout most of the century was eminently visible in medical psychology; the admiration of Montesquieu and Voltaire for the English and the growth of liberal thought in England brought the British Isles and France to an affinity which even Burke's vituperations against the French Revolution, even Lord Wellington's co-operation with Blücher in the defeat of Napoleon, did not affect. There was a singular quality of poise and true concern about man in the mind of the French and English psychiatrist.

Both England and France began their reform of mental hospitals simultaneously. William Tuke and Philippe Pinel were contemporaries both chronologically and psychologically. The foundation of the York Retreat and the reform at the Bicêtre created a community of interest and a mutual admiration which lasted through the century. It was as a matter of course that leading French psychiatrists traveled to

England to view the asylums of the United Kingdom and Ireland, especially the York Retreat. The writings of the French were studied with responsive interest by the English. Of course, there were always old-fashioned representatives of self-sufficiency who grumbled against the French influence and particularly that of Philippe Pinel. The *Edinburgh Review* of April, 1803, published a review of the *Traité Médico-philosophique* in which Pinel was treated with caustic superiority. Of his work the *Review* said: "It may be considered as a sketch of what has already been done, with some notices of what the author intends to do; though he seems frequently to wonder, with a smile of self-approbation, at what he thinks his own discoveries. . . . Dr. Pinel is desirous that France should have some claim to a judicious treatment of the disease of the mind, the honour of which has hitherto been exclusively confined to England." The *Review* concludes with patronizing acidity: "We are therefore inclined to make an indulgent allowance for the imperfect execution of many parts of Dr. Pinel's essay, and to entertain hopes of further information from his diligence and discernment."

"Insular conceit could surely scarcely go further," commented Dr. Daniel Hack Tuke almost eighty years later, and he added, "However, the Edinburgh reviewer is forgotten and his name unknown, Pinel's name covered with glory, although not a popular hero." Tuke proceeds to relate that, when on a visit to Paris in 1878, "I made a pilgrimage to his grave in the great Paris cemetery *Père la Chaise*. . . . I am glad to see it announced that the *Société Médico-psychologique* of Paris is about to erect—not too soon—a statue in his memory." [30]

The memory of Pinel must have been deep in the heart of British psychiatry if a hundred years after Pinel's appearance in Paris the most eminent British psychiatrist could utter such sharp reproof to an anonymous Scotsman of the beginning of the century who was too conceited to be understanding. Tuke was in Paris in 1878 acting as one of the vice-presidents of the International Congress of Mental Medicine, but at the time of the unveiling of the statue of Pinel at the Salpêtrière, in 1885, he was unable to leave England to attend the ceremony. He sent a letter which was read at the ceremony; it is one of Tuke's best

[30] The quotation from the *Edinburgh Review* and Tuke's words are from D. H. Tuke: *Chapters in the history of the insane in the British Isles.* London, 1882, pp. 142–145.

pieces of writing, a document of warmth and admiration, of piety and profound, humble respect. In it he stated that Pinel was truly a messenger of the Lord to the insane: *Homo homini Deus, si officium sciat*. He reminded those gathered around the statue of the pioneer and master of the humanistic and intellectual bond between the French and English psychiatrists by recalling that from Delarive in 1798 to Ferrus and Parchappe the French had come to pay their respects to the York Retreat.

Tuke was typical of English psychiatry; his personal and professional life represents the very substance of its strivings and accomplishments in the nineteenth century. His life represents too, in many of its aspects, the spirit and substance of American psychiatry of the same period. Daniel Hack Tuke occupies a unique place in the history of the medical psychology of the English-speaking world, and he deserves particular mention and appreciation. This in no way infers that other personalities in England and particularly in America are of secondary importance. The number of great men who devoted their lives to psychiatry and who made creative contributions to the welfare of the mentally sick was truly imposing, and no one paid them a greater tribute and evaluated them and their work in more appropriate terms than did Tuke himself in one of his addresses to the Medico-psychological Association in England.

The English-speaking people devoted their energies more to the care of the mentally ill than to theories of psychopathology. The nineteenth century seems to have assigned to them the task of building mental hospitals, of improving the lot of the tens and even hundreds of thousands of "insane," and of organizing their aftercare. In the United States the physician interested in the mentally ill devoted himself almost exclusively to hospital administration, to an almost devotional training and organization of appropriate staffs of attendants, and to the creation of a unique type of mental hospital medical superintendent—a man humane and learned who was to be physician and guide, master and assiduous pupil. In the course of the century the theory and practice of American psychiatry was the theory and practice of institutional psychiatry, which culminated in a unique achievement. Starting later than their European colleagues, handicapped by the youth of the country and by the national crisis of the

Civil War, the United States not only caught up with Europe, but following the conclusion of the first World War a number of young physicians from England and the Continent began to come to the United States to study the methods used in the care and treatment of the mentally ill in hospitals, in the keeping of psychiatric case records, and in clinical research. Some members of the staff of Maudsley Hospital in London took part of their training in American hospitals. Gillespie, an English professor of psychiatry, was trained primarily in the Phipps Clinic of Johns Hopkins University under Adolf Meyer. The young psychiatrist Manfred Bleuler, the son of the great Swiss professor Eugen Bleuler, came to gain experience in Bloomingdale Hospital in New York.

From the end of the century the United States began to reap a rich scientific harvest from its industry; it created a psychiatric apparatus which surpassed in professional excellence and progressive responsiveness the hospitals and the clinics of continental Europe and England. It devoted almost all the energies of its genius to the mental hospital and to the organization of teaching, and it is but natural to discover that the contributions of American psychiatrists to the medicopsychological theories and to a deeper understanding of psychopathology were left to the generation of the twentieth century. From the standpoint of the needs of the time the nineteenth had another and perhaps more important task to perform.

The history of medical psychology in America during the nineteenth century is the history of the American Psychiatric Association and the life of Dorothea Dix. Until the forties of the century no one reached the stature of Benjamin Rush, and even he, though a pioneer and innovator of his day, brought little originality into the field of psychiatry in the United States. The field was still virginal and to Rush goes the historical credit of an energetic, articulate beginner. His viewpoint was in conformity with the European tradition, and, although a revolutionary and one of the signers of the Declaration of Independence, he was conservative in his psychiatry.

Toward the middle of the century what is now known as the American Psychiatric Association was formed (1844). Thirteen superintendents of hospitals for the insane met to discuss their problems; they founded the *Journal of Insanity* (also in 1844). From that time on the true active history of American psychiatry began. The Association first met every two years, but from its third meeting on it convened once a year, omitting only the year 1861 because of the "disturbed condition of the country." The story of American psychiatry still awaits its historian. Samuel B. Woodward (1787–1850), Luther V. Bell (1806–1862), Isaac Ray (1807–1881), Thomas Kirkbride (1809–1883), Pliny Earle (1809–1892), Amariah Brigham (1798–1849), John P. Gray (1825–1886), John M. Galt (1819–1862) are important names in American psychiatry. They were earnest students and humanists, most of them learned men whose contribution to medicolegal studies and reforms and to hospital improvements and teaching was substantial and in some cases truly great. But in the general course of psychiatric thought the leadership still belonged to England and continental Europe. Some of the outstanding traits of their work will be left to D. H. Tuke to note and evaluate, for Tuke followed the growth of America with the understanding, discerning, sympathetic eye of a practical psychiatrist, scholar, and historian.

With few exceptions England occupied itself very little with the investigation of the nature of mental disease, or with medicopsychological theories. The foundation of the York Retreat by William Tuke in 1792 opened an era of hospital reform, legislative reform, and organization to which most of the nineteenth century was devoted. Those who were interested in clinical investigations followed the tradition established by Thomas Willis and John Haslam and concentrated on the study of the brain and the blood vessels which fed it. The titles of their works at once indicate both their interests and prejudices. Mason Cox (1762–1822) in his *Practical Observations on Insanity* (1804) states that too much blood in the brain is the cause of all mental disease and that purgation is the cure. Bryan Crowther (1765–1840) published his *Practical remarks on insanity; to which is added a commentary on the dissection of the brains of maniacs; with some account of diseases incident to the insane* (1807). Andrew Marshall (1742–1813) wrote on *The morbid anatomy of the brain in mania and hydrophobia* (1815). Andrew Combe (1792–1847) produced in 1831 *Observations on mental derangement: being an application of the principles of phrenology to the elucidation of the causes, symptoms, nature and treatment of insanity,* and, in 1838, *Outlines of phrenology.*

It is difficult to miss the tone of certainty and the note of expansiveness which animated these writers. The authors' convictions were too well established and too deeply rooted in fundamental tradition and in the soil of intellectual authority to be shaken. The clinical facts at their disposal were flagrant and clear enough. Of brain lesions they found a great number. To correlate these pathological findings with the psychological symptoms was impossible and at times, as if by silent agreement, was considered unnecessary. Symptoms, like delusions, hallucinations, persecutory trends, and depressions, were looked upon as but incidental, almost fortuitous results of a brain lesion, unless, of course, one espoused the ideas of Gall and thought it was possible to "localize," that is, find a "seat" for, each deviation in the brain. Barring this faith, which Gall was unable to prove and his pupil Spurzheim unable to demonstrate either in Europe or in America, the symptoms of mental disease were considered but one mass of curious phenomena, important only because they were signs of a brain disease. This anatomicopathological orientation led at times to great therapeutic optimism which reality failed to justify. G. M. Burrows (1771–1846) claimed that nine out of ten insane could be cured, yet his methods of therapy remained traditional.[31]

However, this orientation was not the most characteristic of English psychiatry. Like the French, the English medical psychologists pursued their studies of those mental conditions which brought the individual in conflict with the law and they persisted in extending their humanitarian theories and practices in mental hospitals. The efforts in these two directions sprang from the same ideological sources. The right to live and to be treated as a human being—which the psychiatrist demanded for the insane—and the duty to let live and to serve man instead of ruling him were inherent in the psychological revolution of the Renaissance. The recognition of this right and the acceptance of this duty was not and still is not easy. Neither the American nor the French Revolution, neither the consequent growth of British liberalism nor the democratization of the electoral system in England (1832), was sufficient to make these ethicosociological principles any-

---

[31] G. M. Burrows: *An inquiry into certain errors relative to insanity and their consequences physical, moral and civil.* London, 1820. Also, *Commentaries on the causes, forms, symptoms, and treatment, moral and medical, of insanity.* London, 1828.

thing more than a creed of social idealism, a motto powerful and im pressive yet feeble as compared with the inherent inflexibility of man when certain of his age-old habits of mind are touched. These habits were too deeply rooted in man's nature to bow even to the ever-grow ing consciousness of man's communal needs, ethical principles of reci procity, and social interdependence. Neither the Calvary, nor the Augsburg confession of faith, nor the birth of Republican democracy, nor the growth of parliamentary economic liberalism, nor the almost prayerful humanity of the medical men from Johann Weyer to Isaac Ray and D. H. Tuke was able to extinguish man's lifelong fear and dislike of the lunatic and the criminal. Despite the leadership and many victorious steps of the Tukes and the Pinels the State—or, to use the later more democratic terms, society, the community, public opinion— was unable to rid itself of that anxiety, that sense of insecurity, that naïve impulse of instinctive but impractical self-defense which makes man seek more methods for getting rid of the criminal and the insane than ways and means for the rehabilitation of the criminal or the restoration of the insane to sanity. The struggle which had started centuries before continued, is continuing, and will be continuing for a long time to come. It is fundamentally not so much the struggle for the humane recognition of the criminal's psychopathological shortcomings and the insane individual's human needs as it is a struggle for that enlightenment without which the average man is unable to cease being afraid of the lawbreaker and the lunatic. As long as this deep-seated fear persists, the criminal and the insane are bound to be treated with that harshness and neglect which does not permit public opinion to comprehend that those anti- and unsocial manifestations are accidents of life that are painful and at times horrible but never disgusting, reprehensible, or punishable.

As England approached the middle of the nineteenth century, it made its original contribution to medical psychology in voicing the growing consciousness of the value of and respect for the individual. This consciousness was expressed in three specific ways.

It demanded from the community that it concern itself with its duties toward the mentally ill and advocated as in France that the law of the land protect and take seriously its responsibility toward the mentally sick and not merely call them such names as "lunatic," "imbecile," "insane." It demanded that the law abandon its opprobrious superiority and formalistic self-righteousness. The psychiatrist sought to remove the shadow of Bodin which still hovered in the statute books, in the law courts, and in the now almost inarticulate but potent anxiety of the community.

The new current of democratic respect for man—good or bad, mentally ill or sane—expressed itself secondly in the striving to make people treat the mental patient with the same consideration and sense of responsibility with which we treat our so-called normal equals. The abolition of chains was but a beginning, and the English medical psychologist went further than the French: he insisted on the abolition of all forms of mechanical restraint. Conolly's *An inquiry concerning the indications of insanity; with suggestions for the better protection and cure of the insane* (1830) was more than the expression of a personal opinion, and his nonrestraint reforms at Hanwell were more than the personal experiment of an enthusiastic reformer. They were illustrative of the humanistic ambition which made itself felt with increasing power in the national evolution of England and which at once captivated the English mind.

Not only the removal of mechanical restraint but further steps in the same psychological direction imposed themselves on those who guided the destinies of British mental hospitals. In some hospitals the system of "open door" was tried; patients' rooms and the general wards were not locked and patients were permitted to feel free to move about as much as they wished. Whether this system proved successful or not and whether it complicated the task of supervising the patient is of no great import. It is not the administrative problem itself that matters but the ideas of the medical psychology of the time, a psychology which made the psychiatrist assert that the mental patient is a person like the psychiatrist himself. Emphasis was laid on how much we have in common with the mentally ill instead of how different we are from them. The past centuries had stressed the differences between the man in the street and the lunatic; the new age strove to assert the similarities between the two. This in itself was a sign of an immense psychological revolution, for if the medical psychologist was ever to understand the mentally ill it was incumbent upon him to identify himself with the insane. It is this feature of medical psychology that came out of England as a true sign of an inner evolution, the course of which has not yet been fully completed, if it ever will be, in our civilized world.

This nonrestraint campaign had another consequence of no small significance: since it enhanced the need for greater ingenuity in supervising and managing the mental patients, it naturally imposed the need for better training of the supervising personnel—the attendants and the orderlies. This was the added circumstance which later created special training schools for psychiatric nurses. It was America which refused to accept the radical abolition of nonrestraint that ultimately overtook both England and France in the field of education and training of psychiatric nurses, yet today there is hardly a mental hospital of good standing in the United States which does not have its own nurses' training school, official or unofficial, and the number of people without special training who take care of mental patients is now almost negligible.

Nonrestraint, as has been indicated before, created both a mild revolution and a minor war in the psychiatric world. The French were skeptical of its efficacy. The Americans were almost violently opposed to it. Even Isaac Ray, one of the greatest and most humane personalities in psychiatry, disagreed with Conolly's premises and practices. In England, too, despite the more or less general acceptance of Conolly's ideas, the problems involved continued to be debated for almost half a century. W. L. Lindsay (1829–1880), of the Murray Hospital, Perth, published a book on *The theory and practice of non-restraint in the treatment of the insane* as late as 1878, and even in the twentieth century there were English psychiatrists who reproached their American colleagues for the use of wet packs, which the English considered a form of restraint and the Americans a form of calmative therapeutic measure.

The third potent expression of the general humanization of medical psychology was the development of psychiatric medicolegal theories. It will be remembered that from Esquirol, Pinel's first pupil, to Magnan French psychiatry was constantly busy studying the problem of the legal responsibility of the mentally ill and demanding from the courts a greater enlightenment than that of which this arm of justice was capable then or now. French psychiatry evolved a number of ingenious and subtle arguments to prove the existence of madness in a variety of criminal acts and to insist that the Law should not continue to presume to punish a mentally sick individual.

The age-long arguments about the free will and the clear reason of the transgressor were always brought forth by the Law, and it always threw these survivals of theological and metaphysical ages directly into the lap of the psychiatrist. The psychiatrist, confronted with this unrelenting adherence to criteria which had lost their meaning one hundred years before and even earlier, felt stimulated by this struggle, not discouraged. He was convinced that he was right and pursued his studies and arguments deeper and further. Pinel had called attention to that form of madness which even in his day was called *la folie raison-nante*, a mental illness in which one's reason seems not appreciably affected, in which the intellect is unimpaired. This is a term and a conception not easily accepted by either the scientist or the layman.

It seems to be one of man's greatest intellectual weaknesses not to be able to understand that intellect alone is not the decisive factor in his behavior, that comprehension is not the one and only source of man's carrying on, that one may be an intellectual genius and yet do things which even the average pedestrian of life, the simple, "reasonable" person, would not do. To admit that one may be psychologically quite abnormal and yet intellectually so very normal has always seemed to man to admit a paradox against which he must revolt with all his instincts, seducing his reason to argue much and well. Reason does respond to this seduction and does argue well in favor of its own omniscience and omnipotence. Long before we were able to perceive the importance of the mostly unconscious emotions in our daily life and their frequent although insidious and invisible mastery over man as a whole—including his reason—Cicero called attention to the fact that the Law should ask not *si insanus sed si furiosus est*. The question of what might be called intellectual sanity was considered not an appropriate judicial question even in the days of Cicero. Through almost eighteen centuries this weakness of man was expressed in the Law, in its adamant and refractory insistence that mental disease is a disease of the mind and that mind is reason and that only the disintegration of consciousness, reason, intellect, is insanity. Such a term as *folie raison-nante* seemed to the legal mind but a self-contradictory psychiatric

of natural feelings" meant then what we would designate today by the word "antisocial." The doctrine of "natural rights" in the eighteenth century proclaimed the responsibility of government, of the organized community in relation to its individual members. The "natural feelings" of the individual members meant now, in addition to the feeling of traditional morality, the feeling of social responsibility.

The world had undergone profound changes since 1776 and 1789. Prichard died in 1848, another year in which the revolutionary forces of society were speaking not only in terms of natural rights but of democratic, economic self-assertion and of industrial conflicts. The years 1776 and 1789 carried the slogan "Reason and Enlightenment"; 1848 had as its slogan "History." Thomas Paine, Thomas Jefferson, Benjamin Franklin, Robespierre, Saint-Just, or Danton saw man in all the glory of his accomplishment living in a just, reasonable community. The year 1848 tried to visualize a new society born out of the great march of history. Jefferson had striven toward an individualistic society; Marx strove toward a socialized individual. The whole tone of history changed, even as had the economic structure of the world. Feudalism was either gone or had lost its former power over the functioning of the human community. Prichard's "moral insanity" was already more a sociological than a purely ethical concept. Perhaps this accounts for the fact that it was considered a somewhat unfortunate term. It was not positive, not dynamic enough, despite the accepted fact that it designated a substantially correct concept. That is why D. H. Tuke with his characteristic intuitive sagacity was a generation ahead of his time when he suggested the term "inhibitory insanity." The term is not wholly a happy one, since it might suggest that the cause of the trouble lies in the increase of certain inhibitions, whereas Tuke's thought ran in another direction. To him man functioned by virtue of certain inhibitions (social and moral) and it was improper functioning of these inhibitions that Tuke designated as "inhibitory insanity"—a trend of thought and a concept fully in harmony with our present-day views on psychopathological reactions, particularly those involving criminal behavior.

Whatever the advantages or the defects of the various terms, the amount of intellectual energy and hard work devoted to the problem of criminal behavior made English and American psychiatry distinc-

subtlety. Still more self-contradictory appeared the term *man.
delirio,* which Esquirol (as *manie sans délire*) considered an imp
psychopathological entity. Even many psychiatrists of the time re
it; how could one be maniacal, insane, without any apparent conf
of mind, that is, without a *delirium?* The term *manie avec consc*
(Morel) was still another attempt to express the same thought—
one might be abnormal, mentally ill, and yet preserve his intellec
faculties. Clinical observations more convincing than statutory pa
graphs of the past did impress the psychiatrist that such a phenomen
exists, that the psychological earth *was* moving despite the insistence
the Law that it stood still with the sun of abstract justice revolvin
around it and bathing it in the warmth and light of juridical rightnes
Esquirol's monomania, a state of mind which is characterized by th
predominance of one "insane" idea while the rest of the mind remains
normal, also contained in part the same implications as the other terms
mentioned. This made it possible for Trélat to speak of an "arson insanity" (*monomanie incendiaire*) and *folie lucide* and defend them
against the punitive expeditions of the Law.

English medical psychology was deeply preoccupied with the same
problems, and it made its own original contribution to the discussion
and to medicolegal practice. J. C. Prichard (1786–1848) [32] introduced
the term "moral insanity" as designating a special type of illness. It was,
according to Prichard, "madness consisting in a morbid perversion of
the natural feelings, affections, inclinations, temper, habits, moral dispositions and natural impulses without any remarkable disorder or
defect in the intellect or knowing and reasoning faculties and particularly without any insane illusion or hallucination." This definition is
sufficiently inclusive to need no further elucidation. It will be observed,
however, that it is more a negative definition than a positive delineation. It is obviously based on the assumption that what Prichard called
"natural feelings" are well known and need no definition. What "natural" meant in the English language at that time and in this context
was partly the spontaneous sense of right and good and partly the extended sociological connotation which it had begun to acquire. "Natural" conveyed the meaning of moral in the social sense; "a perversion

[32] J. C. Prichard: *A treatise on insanity and other disorders affecting the mind.*
London, 1835.

tive in its original endeavors and in its contribution to this branch of medical psychology. The American efforts in this field did not lag behind those of the English. Isaac Ray can be singled out as one of the most thoughtful and scholarly contributors in the field.[33] If not many problems were actually solved and if no great improvement was introduced into the system of adjudication of criminal cases, enough was done to prepare the administrative, ideological, and scientific foundation for the more concrete work of the twentieth century. Criminology today, like demonology of yesterday, is a battlefield for the rightful possession of which the psychiatrist is still fighting.

VI

FROM the middle of the century English psychiatry, like the French, began to show signs of becoming more generally European than English. The point of convergence of interests proved to be the problem of the systematic arrangement of clinical facts. The mass of clinical material clamored for some sort of order. The question of how to tabulate the clinical conditions observed was not merely a question of the need to be orderly and to give names to various illnesses; it was not a matter of merely satisfying one's bookkeeping propensities. The nosographers of the previous century who had just begun to come in close clinical contact with mental diseases felt baffled, and they were occupied merely with the problem of finding for mental diseases a convenient place in the long list of all physical diseases then known to medicine. For Boissier de Sauvages or Erasmus Darwin, who as if only yesterday had seen all mental diseases brought into the field of medicine, the problem was how to place them in such a way that they would fit into the general medical scheme. Few clinical details and even less fundamental knowledge of mental disease were at their disposal to allow of a truly scientific, empirical classification. When Pinel devoted himself exclusively to mental diseases, he had at once stated that the existent knowledge was scant and vague, and his classificatory suggestions were deliberately few and simplified.

In less than three quarters of a century, however, a great number of

[33] Isaac Ray: *A treatise on the medical jurisprudence of insanity.* Boston, 1838.

men appeared who devoted their lifetime to mental disease alone. True, they traditionally and rightly kept in close touch with all branches of medicine. There were, for instance, a great many psychiatrists in Paris in 1832 who worked hard as general medical men during the epidemic of cholera, but even then most of their attention was concentrated on psychopathology. Esquirol converted his experiences during the epidemic into a study of the influence of cholera on mental disease. As to the ever-growing number of purely institutional physicians, theirs was a twenty-four-hour-a-day job, and they accumulated a real treasury of data which required some systematic understanding. The search for a proper classification of mental diseases became a search for an understanding of a rich experience requiring synthesis.

The question of the causes of mental diseases plagued the curious observer; even if he were inclined to substitute speculation for knowledge, he still was curious enough to remain unsatisfied and to hope for a reasonably specific and substantial answer to his query. A classification became therefore a partial proclamation of one's views on the causes of the various mental diseases. The number of these diseases appeared almost larger than the combined number of all known diseases in other fields. An independent psychiatric classification was now sought instead of a corner in the orderly structure of general medical classification. There was an initial confusion. A classification, it was hoped, would lead one out of this confusion. Strangely enough, however, the first attempts to classify led directly into a new confusion.

One group argued that observers could speculate on causes but not on facts. The symptoms observed are facts. The assumed causes of these symptoms are not yet facts. Hence mental diseases could be arranged in proper order only in accordance with symptoms—the only aspect of mental diseases which was well understood. This was the premise of David Skae (1814–1873) and his followers.[34] Skae then proceeded to place idiocy, including "moral idiocy," in the first group of his classification. It is remarkable how idiocy from time immemorial has always been put in the fore part of all psychiatric classifications. This condition aroused no doubt in the observer's mind no matter how

[34] David Skae: *The classification of the various forms of insanity on a rational and practical basis.* 1863.

little it was understood. Yet idiocy as it had been understood in the past was not infrequently the end result of a psychosis of long standing ending in mental deterioration (idiocy), rather than a primary defect. With the exception of the traditional mention of epilepsy, the purely symptomatic approach of Skae starts and ends with idiocy. His next group was that of chronic masturbators. It was to masturbation that Skae ascribed, as a great many of his contemporaries mistakenly did, a number of neurotic and psychotic conditions and even suicidal drives. In other words, Skae began to classify in accordance with an assumed cause. Other points in his classification followed the same confusing principle of unknown causes with corresponding confusion of terminological trends: "sthenic," "asthenic," "idiopathic." No wonder D. H. Tuke said that Greek etymology never helped us to understand the nature and causes of mental illness. The tendency to overclassify was well established at the time, particularly in Germany; it is natural, for instance, to find that G. F. Blandford, who established twenty groups of mental diseases,[35] was translated into German in 1878.

On the other hand, there were those to whom a good classification of mental diseases was based on etiology alone. H. Maudsley (1835–1918) was the classical representative in England of this method of viewing mental diseases. Maudsley's system was typical of the time and appealed to the Germans even more than Skae's. His textbook [36] was translated into German within three years after its appearance in England. Maudsley was purely materialistic and purely descriptive. To him mental diseases were brain diseases. It is remarkable how trends of thought and even the terminology of the descriptive psychiatrist of the time still showed signs of Hippocratico-Aristotelian influence. Maudsley postulated the existence of an *intellectorium commune*. He thought of brain disturbances "by sympathy." He paid particular attention to the shape and size of the skull. He brought together all the theories of the past which in his day had become crystallized almost as postulates. Anemia, toxic states of the blood, other circulatory defects, infections, poison—all were considered causative agents of mental illness. The only psychological causes which Maudsley was willing to recognize were overwork or overexertion of some of our

[35] G. Fielding Blandford: *Insanity and its treatment*. Edinburgh, 1871.
[36] Maudsley: *The physiology and pathology of the mind*. London, 1867.

functions, which in itself is a physiological rather than a psychological point of view. Psychiatry had become a purely descriptive discipline. Maudsley's classification follows the traditional division into the disturbances of emotions (depressions), affective or pathetic insanity, and disturbances of imagination.

The classificatory effort of Maudsley appears unenlightened; were it not for his insistence on careful historical studies of each individual patient, one could not easily discern the human being behind the classificatory frame. Much simpler and much clearer was the classification of Tuke and Bucknill,[37] based on recognition of the most outstanding symptom which presents itself, but here again no new viewpoint was offered. D. H. Tuke presented a classification of his own.[38] He described three classes with twenty-two groups. These betrayed a great deal of clinical acumen, but like all psychiatric classifications they underscored the symptoms, they threw little light on etiology, and they were confusing because each name was supposed to designate a special mental condition, that is, disease. Yet the psychiatrists who worked out such classifications could not prove that they dealt really with separate diseases, and many of them did not even attempt to prove it. Consequently, the classificatory endeavors were frequently but a list of the outstanding symptoms which people were unable to understand. It would appear justifiable to state that with rare exceptions the tendency to develop classifications grew in inverse proportion to the psychiatrist's clinical interest in the patient as an individual. Maudsley, despite his insistence on detailed individual studies, undoubtedly had less feeling for the individual than Tuke. Maudsley produced a comprehensive classification; Tuke limited himself to simpler divisions.

The history of Tuke's professional life is in more than one respect the history of English-speaking psychiatry. Daniel H. Tuke was born on April 19, 1827, in York, where the York Retreat had been founded by his great-grandfather William Tuke thirty-five years before. Hack Tuke was a sickly child and grew up to be a young man of rather delicate health. He was not physically fit to become a businessman and join the family business. He was interested in poetry and loved to

---

[37] Bucknill and Tuke: *A manual of psychological medicine.* London, 1858.
[38] In *A dictionary of psychological medicine. London,* 1892, vol. I, p. 330.

read Pope and Young. He tried for a while to work as a clerk in a solicitor's office, but neither his state of health nor his intellectual interests permitted him to continue. He was in need of a rest and went to stay for a while at the York Retreat which he had known since childhood. He loved to lie under the majestic elms which his great-grandfather had planted on the hospital property. The young Tuke watched the patients of the Retreat and mingled with them; he grew to know many of them well.

The question of a definite career was still held in abeyance. At the age of twenty-one Tuke worked for a while in the Retreat, as steward of the hospital under Dr. Thurnam, who was chief physician. Tuke's interest in mental patients was apparently more than casual; he seems to have been absorbed in this experience of living with the mentally ill. He became interested in sick people in general and throughout the year (1848) frequented the hospital at York. Two years later he was working at St. Bartholomew's Hospital in London, and two years after that at the Royal College of Surgeons. In 1853 he was in Germany, where he received his doctor's degree from the University of Heidelberg.

Tuke's was a studious, methodical mind, but never dry and formal. He was curious, eager to know, careful not to miss a fact or a detail. He always made careful notes of what he saw or heard. Upon hearing something in a conversation which particularly struck him, he would take out his notebook, ask that the remark or statement be repeated, and write it down with an air of utmost seriousness. René Semelaigne (1855–1934), the great-grandnephew of Philippe Pinel, and Daniel Hack Tuke, the great-grandson of William Tuke, were lifelong friends, carrying on the tradition of spiritual psychiatric intimacy between these two families. "I had the opportunity," relates René Semelaigne, "as all those who knew Hack Tuke had, to observe his habit [of making notes in the notebook]. It was in Hanwell, in the last days of 1888. He was asking me about the genealogy of the Pinel family. He asked me to repeat certain things and wrote down the names I dictated. A few years later, in June, 1894, after the Dublin Congress, we were walking one evening in his garden and he asked me to give him the French names of certain plants; he wrote down those he had not known before." The Frenchman Semelaigne continues: "All his life he betrayed a total indifference to the pleasures of the table. He ate little and drank hardly anything; when he was working, he frequently forgot the time to eat." [39]

Tuke's great curiosity was combined with phenomenal industry. Immediately after his return from Germany he wrote on his impressions of Holland, where he visited the mental institutions. These were published in 1854.[40] Certain conclusions which he draws in this article shed a good light on the mind and interest of the very young physician —Hack Tuke had just become a doctor and was only twenty-six years old. He criticized the institutions in Holland: they had no resident physician, the superintendent was not a physician, the hospitals were situated in the center of the city instead of in the country, there was too much mechanical restraint, the classification and distribution of the patients was poor, there were not enough attendants to care for the patients. These views showed great maturity and knowledge of the field.

Tuke became the physician at York Retreat and within four years published jointly with Bucknill the excellent *Manual of Psychological Medicine*. The uncertain young man of delicate health and with a predilection for reading poetry under the elms of the Retreat proved capable of prodigious literary and administrative effort. To his many duties and interests was soon added teaching in the medical school.

Hack Tuke was the first physician in the Tuke family. That he became a psychiatrist is not surprising considering the family tradition due to its relationship to York Retreat, but it is of special interest that Tuke turned to medicine and to psychiatry after he had not only seen a mental hospital, but had worked in it and actually lived with patients for almost two years. Tuke chose his career after he had gained intimate knowledge of the patients and their problems and after he had been imbued with the knowledge that a mental patient was a human being, natural and simple, not a difficult person with whom to live. Before Tuke started his medical career he was already free of the traditional fear of the man who is called a lunatic.

He was fully aware of his own feelings and inspirations, yet took full cognizance of the achievements of his predecessors. As early as 1854

[39] Semelaigne: *Aliénistes, etc.*, p. 362.
[40] In the *Medical Critic and Psychological Journal*, 1854, vol. VII, p. 441.

he won a prize for an essay on the changes in the treatment of the mentally ill after Pinel. He was free of what he himself called insular conceit and traveled on the Continent frequently, meeting his European colleagues, studying, and reporting his observations and experiences. He took care to be acquainted with the various trends of his day and studied what he called Braidism, or "artificial insanity" (hypnotism). His *Hypnotism Redivivus* has been referred to before. A trip to the Pyrenees aroused his interest in anthropology. In 1880 he and George Savage took over the editorship of the *Journal of Mental Science*, which Tuke edited till he died.

Tuke hoped that his son William Samuel would follow in his footsteps as a doctor, but it was the lot of the Tukes who had done so much for mental diseases to give us but one psychiatrist, and it was the sad lot of Hack Tuke as a father and as a doctor to have to bury William Samuel in 1883, when the young man was but twenty-six.

In 1884, two years after the appearance of Hack Tuke's *Chapters in the History of the Insane in the British Isles*—an imposing book full of detail, historical perspective, and humanistic inspiration—he visited the United States and Canada; he published excellent studies on the status of psychiatry in both countries. In 1892 the *Dictionary of Medical Psychology* appeared, in which one finds sixty-seven contributions from the pen of Hack Tuke. He was professor of mental diseases at Charing Cross Hospital. In 1879 the After Care Association was formed. D. H. Tuke was one of its founders and a most active participant in its work.

The winter of 1894–1895 was his last, and it was the most difficult. Tuke, who was not given to complaints and who took life as a steady task, now felt the burden of ill health. In February, 1895, he wrote to Semelaigne, who was twenty-eight years younger, that the winter in England was severe, that probably it was just as bad in France, but for a young man in the prime of life it was only a salutary stimulant. The last words of the letter were "It is terrible!" Tuke was dead in less than three weeks. His influence on English psychiatry was inestimable and it is sad to relate that no one of equal stature arose in England to replace him. His professional authority was immense, and the combination of scholarship and leadership which he presented was rare.

As an illustration of Tuke's extraordinary thirst for knowledge and of his ability to learn one may cite the following amusing incident. Sometime in 1869 he was struck by a newspaper account of a man who fell ill with an acute attack of rheumatism. The man was in Manchester at the time of the attack and decided to return at once to his home in London, for he did not want to remain ill in a hotel room. He lay in a compartment of his train in severe pain; apparently he had a chill and his teeth were chattering. There was a sudden jolt —a train wreck. The sick man struggled out of the debris, extremely tense, but suddenly cured of his illness. Tuke conceived of an idea. In 1870–1872 he published a series of articles in the *Journal of Mental Science* under the title *Illustrations of the influence of the mind upon the body in health and disease.* In 1884 the second edition of this series presented two volumes.

Tuke never left a subject until he had become thoroughly conversant with it. Despite or perhaps because of his steadfast and unceasing intellectual activities, and despite or perhaps because of the immense scope of knowledge which he embraced, absorbed, and assimilated, he left no solid synthesis of his psychiatric experience. There is a quality of enlightened eclecticism in his psychiatric views, not the superficial eclecticism of a psychiatric administrator but eclecticism nevertheless. His typical English tolerance made it impossible for him to takes sides, particularly in matters of scientific controversy. But it was not only tolerance that prevented him from evolving a more definite theory of his own; it was also his major practical interest in mental patients which diverted him from becoming a partisan. What was uppermost in his mind was the organization of the care for hospitalized patients and the aftercare of those who became well enough to leave the hospital. This concentration on therapeutic management dims the significance of theoretical divergences and makes one ready to accept help from whatever partisan quarter it may come. The accent, the center of interest, is always empirical. The enormous gain which this historical tradition and temperamental disposition of Hack Tuke brought to psychiatry is incontestable and is of permanent value.

On the other hand, even enlightened eclecticism inevitably diverts one's attention from the highly individualized problems one meets with in dealing with patients as persons rather than as members of a group which is the hospital. The classification of patients is apt to be made from the standpoint of management, that is, administrative convenience, rather than from the standpoint of the deeper meaning of the patient's own problems. The result is a certain lack of individualized therapeutic effort, a certain and definite loss of creative understanding of the deeper psychology of mental disease. Hack Tuke was typical of this aspect of psychiatry. His genius saved him, as it saved a number of his gifted American colleagues, from becoming settled in a rather stultified, managerial eclecticism, but it also prevented him from utilizing more creatively the great knowledge and experience which he accumulated.

In 1881 the Medico-Psychological Association met at University College in London. It was the occasion of its fortieth anniversary and Daniel Hack Tuke was its president. The presidential address [41] delivered on August 2 is a perfect rendition of the historical psychiatric status of England toward the close of the century, as well as the best delineation of Tuke's own position and of his masterful intellectual authority. At the very outset he reminded his hearers of Arnold of Rugby, who said that but for the fact that the English were a very active people "our disunion from the Continent would make us nearly as bad as the Chinese." As Tuke proceeds to refute the suspicion that any disunion from the Continent or from the New World ever existed in psychiatric England, he demonstrates the vastness of his horizon and the scope of his learning. He reviews briefly but respectfully and knowingly the contributions of France, Germany, Belgium, Holland, and Italy. With simplicity and almost pride for the profession as a whole, he states, "Abroad, psychological journalism has been in advance of ours."

He pays respect to the pioneers in American psychiatry—Rush, Woodward, Bell, Brigham and Howe—and then says, "I have to include among the dead an honoured name, over whom the grave has recently closed.[42] Saintship is not the exclusive property of the Church. Medicine has also her calendar. Not a few physicians of the mind have deserved to be canonized; and to our psychological Hagiology, I would now add the name of Isaac Ray." Recalling later on that Isaac Ray

---

[41] D. H. Tuke: *Chapters in the history of the insane in the British Isles*, pp. 443–501.

[42] Isaac Ray died on March 31 of that year (1881) in Philadelphia. He was buried at Butler Hospital, Providence, Rhode Island.

did not accept the doctrine of nonrestraint, Tuke reminds his listeners of Ray's own words: "Here, as well as everywhere else, the privilege of free and independent inquiry cannot be invaded without ultimate injury to the cause." [43] Tuke pays a warm "tribute of respect to that remarkable woman, Miss Dix, who has a claim to the gratitude of mankind for having consecrated the best years of her varied life to the fearless advocacy of the cause of the insane, and to whose exertions not a few of the institutions for their care and treatment in the States owe their origin." This tribute to Dorothea Dix, who was still living at the time, was paid by Tuke in the very London where some years previously the American woman had arrived to the great disquietude of British bureaucracy. Her energetic advocacy of reform provoked Home Secretary Sir George Gray, in approving one of the bills for which Dorothea Dix was responsible, to regret that the reform was achieved by "a foreigner, and that foreigner a woman, and that woman a dissenter." [44] Tuke was both more democratic and more cosmopolitan than the Home Secretary, whose "disunion from the Continent" was as pronounced as Tuke's universality.

Tuke returns to Isaac Ray when he speaks of hospitals: "But what, gentlemen, would be the best-contrived separation of cases, what would the best-constructed asylum avail, unless the presiding authority were equal to his responsible duties? . . . One Sunday afternoon, some years ago, Dr. Ray fell asleep in his chair while reading old Fuller's portraits of the Good Merchant, the Good Judge, the Good Soldier, etc., in his own work entitled 'The Holy and Profane State,' and, so sleeping, dreamed he read a manuscript, the first chapter of which was headed, 'The Good Superintendent.' Awakening from his nap by the tongs falling on the hearth, the doctor determined to reproduce from memory as much of his dream as possible for the benefit of his brethren. One of these recovered fragments runs thus [Tuke then quotes directly from Ray]: 'The Good Superintendent hath considered well his qualifications for the office he hath assumed, and been governed not more by a regard for his fortunes than by a hearty desire to benefit his fellow-men. . . . To fix his hold on the confidence and goodwill of his patients he spareth no effort, though it may consume his time

[43] *American Journal of Insanity*, April, 1855.
[44] Francis Tiffany: *Life of Dorothea Lynde Dix*, p. 239.

and tax his patience, or encroach seemingly on the dignity of his office. A formal walk through the wards, and the ordering of a few drugs, compriseth but a small part of his means for restoring the troubled mind. To prepare for his work, and to make other means effectual, he carefully studieth the mental movements of his patients. He never grudges the moments spent in quiet, familiar intercourse with them, for thereby he gaineth many glimpses of their inner life that may help him in their treatment. . . . He maketh himself the centre of their system around which they all revolve, being held in their places by the attraction of respect and confidence.' " [45] Tuke agrees with "another Transatlantic worthy," John Gray, Superintendent of Utica State Hospital, who epigrammatically wrote in response to Ray:

> " 'The Good Superintendent!' Who is he?
> The master asked again and again;
> But answered himself, unconsciously,
> And wrote his own life without a stain."

"In what a strange land of shadows the superintendent lives!" exclaims Tuke. "But for his familiarity with it, its strangeness would oftener strike him." Tuke sketches the variety of contacts which the superintendent can have with the complexity of the human mind, and he cheerfully enjoins him to form more and more of these contacts. "I have heard it suggested that superintendents should have six weeks' extra holiday every third year, five of them to be spent in visiting asylums. . . . It may be said, indeed, that the appropriate motto of the medical superintendent is—'*Insanitas insanitatum, omnia insanitas.*' "

Tuke considers the problem of hospitals. To him they are not merely bricks and mortar. He outlines his ideas on the proper construction, arrangement, and atmosphere of hospitals. He recalls Dr. Kirkbride of Philadelphia, who insisted that "asylums can never be dispensed with—no matter how persistently ignorance, prejudice, or sophistry may declare to the contrary—without retrograding to a greater or less extent to the conditions of a past period with all the inhumanity and barbarity connected with it. To understand what would be the situa-

[45] Isaac Ray: *Ideal characters of the officers of a hospital for the insane.* Philadelphia, 1873.

tion of a people without hospitals for their insane, it is only necessary to learn what their condition was when there were none." [46] To Tuke an asylum is a sanctum; the sooner and "the more this [proper hospital organization] is carried out, the easier, it is to be hoped, will it be to induce the friends of patients to allow them to go in the earliest stage of the disorder to an asylum, as readily as they would to a hydropathic establishment or an ordinary hospital, to which end medical men may do much by ignoring the stupid stigma still attaching to having been in an asylum. The treatment of the insane ought to be such that we should be able to regard the asylums of the land as one vast Temple of Health, in which the priests of Esculapius, rivaling the Egyptians and Greeks of old, are constantly ministering, and are sacrificing their time and talents on the altar of Psyche."

Tuke reviews with great succinctness and always with sympathetic understanding the various psychological and neurological theories prevalent during the last quarter of the century. He seems to be inclined to credit the psychological trends with considerable validity; he recalls the controversy over mesmerism and its evolution into hypnotism. He pleads for the tolerant and objective evaluation of facts: "It is no reason because we have re-christened mesmerism that we should ignore the merit of those who, as to matters of fact, were in the right, however mistaken their interpretation may have been." To Tuke respect for fact, caution as to opinion, are axiomatic. "We must not confound clearly ascertained facts in biology and mental evolution with the theories which are elaborated from them. The former will remain; the latter may prove perishable hay and stubble, and when we overlook or ignore this distinction, it must be admitted that we expose ourselves to the just rebuke of the celebrated Professor of Berlin when he protests against 'the attempts that are made to proclaim the problems of research as actual facts, the opinion of scientists as established science, and thereby to put a false light before the eyes of the less informed masses, not merely the methods of science, but also its whole position in regard to the intellectual life of men and nations.' "

The words Tuke quotes are those of Rudolf Virchow, who had an

[46] Thomas S. Kirkbride: *On the construction, organization, etc., of hospitals for the insane.* Philadelphia, 1880, p. 300.

enormous influence in raising the scientific method in medicine to a level of solidity and accuracy never before attained in clinical investigation. Tuke, like all the great physicians of the time, was under the influence of the great Virchow. But, impressed by the great strides which clinical medicine was making, physicians tended to forget the special difficulties which psychological medicine has to meet and the essential differences between psychological and organic medicine. Consequently, there was a tendency to draw parallels which were not valid and which violated the very principles which Virchow proclaimed as inalienable. Tuke could not help warning against false hopes and, not without benevolent dryness, he remarked, "It must be frankly granted that Psychological Medicine can boast, as yet, of no specifics, nor is it likely, perhaps, that such a boast will ever be made. It may be difficult to suppress the hope, but we cannot entertain the expectation that some future Sydenham will discover an *anti-psychosis* which will as safely and speedily cut short an attack of mania or melancholia as bark an attack of ague."

VII

FROM the beginning to the middle of the nineteenth century medical psychology was under strong Franco-English or, if one takes cognizance of "insular dissolution," Anglo-French leadership. There followed a brief period of pellucid thinking suggestive of a reorientation. Morel was concluding his work in France, and Maudsley's materialistic psychiatry came to the fore. The originality of the French and English psychiatrists—so energetic and creative up to the middle of the nineteenth century—began, however, to wane. The enlightened eclecticism of Daniel Hack Tuke in England and Isaac Ray in America, a trend apart, was an outgrowth of institutional psychiatry and therefore was not an active agent in the development of medical psychology; it was, rather, a receptive apparatus which welcomed every new contribution to medical psychology and tried to put it to practical use in the management and care of the mentally ill. Not until the twentieth century—when the American mental institutions became centers of research—did true contributions to medical psychology begin to come from the institutional psychiatry of the New World and, to a lesser extent, from that of England. Too, the scientific unity of Europe and its cultural interdependence became fully established toward the middle of the century and the purely national divisions of medical psychology began to fade.

The Industrial Revolution, the Napoleonic Wars, and the full development of capitalism brought to an end the last remnants of feudal exclusivism. A paradoxical phenomenon came into evidence. Politically and socially Europe was divided into separate units, each keenly conscious of its national life. The feeling of nationalism which was dramatically released by the French Revolution was in the ascendancy, and in this respect European culture was divided into separate cells, each presenting its own exclusivism in mode of living and views on life. On the other hand, the increasing industrialization of Europe and the rapid development of commerce on an international scale engendered a spirit of international or cosmopolitan interdependence which knew no national boundaries and less national prejudices. Science, and with it medical psychology, was involved in this process of internationalization. The responsive co-operation of men of science and the organization of international scientific congresses were both expressions of and contributing factors to the further internationalization.

Every now and then, it must be conceded, a scientist or otherwise sober philosopher would assume a narrow, nationalistic attitude as did, for instance, Carl Starch, to whom Magnan felt constrained to reply with an article entitled *La dégénérescence du peuple français, ses symptômes et ses causes. Contribution de médecine mentale à l'histoire médicale des peuples.*[47] This acrimonious interchange of views was a direct result of the Prussian victory over France. Instances of the kind are results not of the nationalist spirit of a given scientific discipline, but rather of the fact that a given scientific thinker under the stress of the times sheds his scientific attitude and acts as a citizen, a member of a nationally conscious community. Under these circumstances he may and he usually does use the scientific vocabulary, with which he is more familiar than any other, but he expresses neither the substance nor the science which he represents.

Despite deviations of an ideological, nationalistic nature, European

[47] *Annales Médico-Psychologiques*, 1871, vol. VI, p. 291.

science was fully cosmopolitan toward the middle of the century. For the first time since the French Revolution Europe achieved an intellectual unity equal to that of the middle of the sixteenth century, when books by Paracelsus, Vives, Bodin, Erasmus, and Weyer were read with equal interest in Basel, Paris, Valencia, London, Bruges, and Nuremberg. Esquirol was equally respected by the Germans and the English, Tuke by the French and the Germans, Virchow by the English and the French. This cultural unification of Europe presented great advantages; it was not completed without certain national sacrifices.

As has been said, French and English medical psychology soon began to lose some of its creative initiative and to receive more than it gave. In one branch of medical psychology France and England continued to be in the lead—the branch which grew out of mesmerism. The work of Braid, Elliotson, Charcot, and Bernheim represents an immense contribution and made France, especially, the center of attraction. Toward the middle of the century Maximilian Jacobi, who had visited the York Retreat, was still under English influence; Griesinger traveled to Paris to become acquainted with mental hospitals; Freud came to Charcot in the early eighties of the century. But soon the center of gravity shifted. When Tuke quoted Virchow in the presidential address on the fortieth anniversary of the Medico-Psychological Association, it was not fortuitously that he did so, nor was it merely an individual expression of individual scholarship. Virchow, Johannes Müller, Schoenlein were representative of a new, scientifically vigorous and creative Germany, which seems to have been more or less dormant for a time following the Napoleonic Wars. Before the fifties were far advanced Germany joined the concert of medicopsychological workers and asserted its entry into the field of clinical psychiatry with an authority and with a richness of thought which before long imposed its leadership on Europe and the New World. It was not entirely an accident that Daniel Hack Tuke received a doctor's degree from the University of Heidelberg in 1853.

Germany came into the field rather late. It had to build hospitals and medicopsychological theories at the same time. Its approach to mental diseases was uneven and it had little time to establish a medicopsychological tradition. Its universities were established much later than those of Italy, France, or England, and its teachers were few. Weyer was not a real German and his influence was greater abroad than at home. Felix Plater was more the exception than the rule. Georg Ernst Stahl appeared too philosophical for practical psychiatric beginnings. The Reformation with its intense sense of personal piety retarded rather than accelerated the separation of medical psychology from theology.

It will be recalled that Reil, the excellent clinician, at the beginning of the nineteenth century was more mystical than psychological in his first approach to mental diseases. His attitude toward mental patients was still undefined and self-contradictory. On one hand he wished to awaken them to reason by means of fear, by firing cannon shots; on the other he wrote, "At all events the strait jacket, confinement, and hunger, or a few blows with a cowhide—of which a third person is to be notified by a duly made written decision—will suffice to check the patient in a short time." [48] Not many years after these lines were written, Nasse remarked, "Those who talk to us about lunacy, insanity, and diseases of the mind should first be asked what they mean by these expressions; it is only luck if a mutual understanding can be reached. . . . Recently there have been as many writers dealing with these diseases as there are classifications." [49]

Here we have the best expression of the two problems which both inspired and disturbed German psychiatry: hospital organization and the establishment of proper care of patients, and the search for a system, for a means of sorting the mass of psychological phenomena into an orderly arrangement. The history of German psychiatry of the nineteenth century is the history of psychiatric systematization. The beginning of the century was characterized by romantic thinking in all fields, and psychiatry reflected this influence. The proponents of anatomical and physiological points of view did not take kindly to the psychological theories which grew out of this romanticism, and a great struggle ensued in German psychiatry—the struggle between the somatologist and the psychologist. This strife, while belonging chronologically to the first half of the century, represents a separate page in psychiatric history and is psychologically more related to this later

[48] Reil: *Rhapsodien,* p. 387.
[49] Friedrich Nasse: in *Zeitschrift für psychische Ärzte,* 1818, vol. I, pp. 17 *et seq.*

period of medicopsychological history. The somatologist won the battle, and in the middle of the century German psychiatry asserted the supremacy of the brain over any other structure and proceeded systematically to produce a psychiatry without a psychology. Of course, psychology could not be dispensed with easily, and it was used in accordance with the individual observer's intuition and psychological ingenuity but only for the purpose of pure description.

The outstanding and most influential leader in this process was Wilhelm Griesinger (1817–1868). Until Griesinger entered the field of psychiatry, the somatologist lacked security of method as well as scientific poise. When Jacobi (1775–1858) proclaimed his respect for the brain by asserting that one needed no psychology to understand and treat mental diseases, Leupoldt [50] exclaimed in 1833 that Jacobi was committing infanticide by killing Heinroth's psychiatry. Johannes Friedreich (1796–1862), the materialist, exclaimed with idealistic fervor that Heinroth's theories were false, immoral, and wrong. The method of the materialist singularly enough was faith. Thus, when an insane patient died and on autopsy Friedreich found three hardened glands in the abdomen, he recalled that the patient during his psychosis had insisted that he had three frogs in his stomach; the explanation was clear to Friedreich and he considered his finding sufficient proof that all mental conditions are due to physical causes.[51] Greding considered the odor of the brain indicative of mental disease. Friedreich thought that since the brain has two halves a half-sided insanity was possible,[52] and that if one fails to find a physical proof of a mental disease it is the fault of the observer.[53] To Blumroeder the brain (*Grosshirn*) was the "God-brain" (*Gotthirn*).[54]

Griesinger, a man of enormous energy and will power, was of a different temperamental and intellectual caliber. He was only seventeen years old when he started studying medicine. An independent, self-willed spirit, he did not attend his classes with much assiduity: "I'd rather read Müller's physiology," he would explain, "than be

---

[50] J. M. Leupoldt: *Über den Entwicklungsgang der Psychiatrie.* Erlangen, 1833, p. 29.

[51] Johannes Friedreich: *Historisch-kritische Darstellung der Theorien über das Wesen und den Sitz der psychischen Krankheiten.* Leipzig, 1836, p. 146.

[52] *Ibid.*, p. 174.

[53] *Ibid.*, p. 127.

[54] Kirchhoff: *Deutsche Irrenärzte.* Berlin, 1921, vol. I, p. 203.

dictated to by old theories." [55] Griesinger received his doctor's degree at the age of twenty-one, went to France, came back the next year. He spent two years studying in a mental hospital and then devoted himself to medical practice and to the study of physiology. He was an excellent writer and soon began to edit the *Archiv für physiologische Heilkunde*. He was twenty-eight years old when his textbook, *Pathologie und Therapie der psychischen Krankheiten*, a volume of three hundred and ninety-six pages, was published (1845). Griesinger did not resume his contact with clinical psychiatry until 1866 when he became chief of the division of mental diseases at the Charité in Berlin. He died two years later at the age of fifty-one.

Griesinger's was a busy life. Within its short span he crowded a great deal of learning, teaching, and administrative activity. He edited a journal of physiology; he introduced nonrestraint in mental hospitals; he founded a new periodical, *Archiv für Psychiatrie und Nervenkrankheiten;* he did an enormous amount of work on the pathology of the brain. His impression on German psychiatry is still evident.

By sheer grit and force of leadership Griesinger settled the sharp controversy between the psychologists and the somatologists. Mental diseases were somatic diseases, he proclaimed—specifically, diseases of the brain. Although in his textbook he demonstrates a unique intuitive insight into the psychological reactions of patients, he seems unaware that it was intuitively that he worked. Diagnoses were to be made only on the basis of causes, and the causes were always physiological. He saw no difference between organic and functional disorders. Many of the psychological reactions were due to *reflex* actions of the brain; psychology might be nothing more than reflex action. In this thought he was the forerunner of Bechterev's and Pavlov's reflexological ideas and also of the more mechanistic American behaviorism of the twentieth century.

Shortly before his death Griesinger wrote, "Psychiatry and neuropathology are not merely two closely related fields; they are but one field in which only one language is spoken and the same laws rule." By this statement he shook to some extent the very doctrine he preached, for neither within his lifetime nor afterward was it pos-

[55] *Ibid.*, vol. II, p. 1.

sible to prove this absolute identity of neuropathology and psychiatry. To him it was a deeply felt conviction and it is the strength of his conviction that made him overlook the fact that he lacked the needed facts to prove his contention. Griesinger "knew no dividing line between psychological and somatic, subjective and objective, phenomenological and theoretical; all these fuse into one vague whole. It is difficult today to understand how it happened that Griesinger's textbook went through so many editions." [56] This surprise at the success of Griesinger's textbook, which Gruhle expresses not without a tinge of pathos, is not difficult to understand. Griesinger admitted that he knew no psychology; in his foreword to the textbook he definitely stated that he followed the psychological principles of the philosopher Herbart. In standing firmly for a psychiatry without psychology Griesinger fulfilled a historical need of German psychiatry—that of removing from psychiatry the heavy semitheological incrustations from which it had suffered ever since the Reformation. While he insisted on a genetic viewpoint, Griesinger understood by this a viewpoint which requires the understanding not of the psychological origin of our psychological attributes but only of their anatomical and physiological origin.

Man feels. Griesinger looked at the fact and considered that this attribute might show deviations from the normal; hence the affect might be abnormal. What normal affect is was never stated but always silently assumed. Man imagines. Griesinger watched the vicissitudes of imagination and tried to describe its abnormal deviations. The normal was here again silently assumed. Man wills. Griesinger observed man's actions and described the disturbances of will. The existence and nature of a normal will were assumed to be known.

Griesinger was strictly descriptive and seemed to abandon completely the idea that in mental diseases we deal really with a variety of diseases. To him they were no more diseases than was a headache. Just as a headache may be a sign of a brain tumor, so a mental disease whatever its apparent character is but a manifestation of a brain disease. This sharp insistence appeared to be a retrogression to the solidism of the end of the seventeenth and early eighteenth centuries, but it was

[56] Hans W. Gruhle: *Geschichtliches* in Bumke's *Handbuch der Geisteskrankheiten*. Berlin, 1932, vol. IX, part 5, p. 18.

at the same time a sharp order to abandon the speculative tradition of considering every mental symptom a new disease.

Psychiatry before Griesinger had been saturated with nomenclature and that Latin and Greek etymology which Tuke said was never of much help. Heinroth's forty-eight diseases were offered in place of Plater's twenty-three. There was a host of melancholias—*furens, misanthropica, erotica, attonita, errabunda, simplex, religiosa, catacriseophobia, oneirodynia*—and manias—*chimero-erotica, saeviens, ecstatica, per metaschematismum acuta epileptica ex iracundia.*

No wonder a contemporary of Griesinger, Heinrich Neumann (1814–1884), bemoaned the mediocrity of the times and insisted that "we shall never be able to believe that psychiatry will make a step forward until we decide to throw overboard the whole business of classifications. . . . There is but one type of mental disturbance and we call it insanity." [57] This was the only point of convergence of Griesinger's and Neumann's views. Neumann insisted on strict empirical and critical observations; he was almost sarcastic about the descriptions of patients in which each trend was put down in the light of the observer's personal predilections. Those were not histories but novels, he exclaimed.[58] He viewed the human personality as a functional whole; the personality functions are normal as long as all the individual functions and reactions act as a whole. This oneness of functioning is built up gradually as the individual grows and develops. Any loosening of the normal wholeness between the functions produces a mental illness. Neumann incidentally was the one who introduced the term "recovery with defect." As we can see, the point of view that mental disease is but one illness regardless of the various forms it may acquire could serve as a point of departure both for an extremely materialistic, organic point of view (Griesinger) or for a point of view more definitely psychological (Neumann).

VIII

GRIESINGER's authoritative influence turned German psychiatry definitely toward the body, living or dead. It was the body which was

[57] Heinrich Neumann: *Lehrbuch der Psychiatrie.* Erlangen, 1859, p. 167.
[58] Neumann: *Blödsinnigkeitserklärung.* Erlangen, 1860, p. 87.

charged with the duty of answering what mental disease is, or rather, it was assumed that psychopathological reactions, once men chose to call them diseases, were diseases in the traditional medical sense, and that it was the physician's duty to look into the body for the source of the illness. This conception, while it inevitably narrowed the general psychological perspective, at the same time emphasized that medicine once in possession of the field of psychopathology was not going to surrender it to theology. Psychological theories, no matter how empirical, unless they were purely descriptive of the obvious were considered as belonging to philosophy, and philosophy was perceived by the medical man as an extension and secular transformation of theology. Thus the nearly three-hundred-year-old struggle of medicine for the possession of psychopathology was culminating in an irreconcilable attitude based on anatomicophysiological postulates. Of treatment— outside the humanization of hospitals and the use of drugs, baths, and electricity—there was little discussion. Since the decline of mesmerism the subject of treatment had aroused little controversy, and therapy showed little progress. Psychological medicine still cooled its heels at the door of physics and chemistry, awaiting their pleasure and ready to use anything new in the hope that it might prove, in the words of D. H. Tuke, an antipsychosis.

The controversy raged around beliefs. The psychologically-minded psychiatrist had as little to offer in a truly practical way as the somatologically-minded, but the material of the somatologist was more tangible: actual brain tissue, visible nerve ganglia, actually diseased body organs. If these did not speak and tell the secret of mental disease in any articulate way, one could well recall Pinel's contemporary Broussais who said, "If the cadavers do appear to us occasionally mute, it is because we do not know how to question them." If on the other hand psychological speculations were offered, one could recall Friedreich's remark about "the mystical ethereal devil regions of Heinroth," and his statement: "Voltaire said, 'I advise the devil to address himself always to the faculties of theology and never to the faculties of medicine.' Well, Heinroth put this true statement to shame." [59]

The somatologist withdrew to the dissecting room and the laboratory. The mental life which he saw on the wards was to him "brain-

[59] J. Friedreich: *op. cit.*, pp. 21, 25.

life" (*Hirnleben*), as Leidesdorf (1818–1889) expressed it; he was able to make truly great contributions to the problem of the structure and function of the brain and spinal cord and the sympathetic nervous system. Strikingly enough, however, he had to resort to skillful speculative constructions as soon as he attempted to correlate his anatomical findings with the psychoses, that is, with the "deliria," of persecution, with profound suicidal depressions, obsessive thinking, compulsive behavior, psychopathological fears.

In this respect the brain psychiatry which was officially inaugurated by Griesinger differed little in content from the psychiatry of the past, even if it did acquire a marvelous laboratory technique and an excellent scientific armamentarium. Some forty years before Griesinger, Reil, despite his philosophical inclinations, felt he was correct when he repeated the hoary contention of Aristotle that insanity is due to temperature changes in the brain. Ernst Bartels (1778–1838) persisted in his adherence to the principles of cerebral localization.[60] G. H. Bergmann (1781–1861), an older contemporary of Griesinger, recalled, perhaps without knowing it, the days of Erasistratus and Herophilus and attached great importance to the ventricles of the brain; at the same time he considered the sideric influences on the brain. It must be admitted that there was considerable confusion in the minds of the medical psychologists before Griesinger made his position, and with him the position of German psychiatry, clear and unequivocal. There still reigned the tendency, partly neoplatonic, partly Paracelsian, to combine physiological speculations with metaphorical psychological vulgarity. Ten years after Griesinger's textbook was published, D. G. Kieser (1779–1862) published a book in which he paid his respects to the brain and the ganglia and considered the first the carrier of day and light and the second of night and darkness.[61]

There were soberer empirical minds which studied seriously the various psychological phenomena and not infrequently stood askance before the puzzle, hesitating not a little to espouse a purely anatomicophysiological point of view yet unable to explain the phenomena at hand. It would seem that any time a psychiatrist of those days turned toward a psychological analysis of mental diseases he fell into the

---

[60] E. Bartels: *Pathogenetische Physiologie*. Cassel, 1829.
[61] D. G. Kieser: *Elemente der Psychiatrik*. Breslau and Bonn, 1855.

pit of a singular neoplatonic, anthroposophic mood and would either abandon the secure precincts of medical empiricism or re-enter the field of solidism. Friedrich Nasse (1778–1851) was typical of this state of mind. He failed to solve the problem of psychosomatic relationship. He sought a clearer point of view; he founded a journal for this purpose.[62] His was no mere speculative mind; he was an earnest student, a learned physiologist and good clinician. He finally turned to the purely organic orientation; even somnambulism, clairvoyance, and character defects he considered caused by neurological changes.

This undertow toward extreme somatology culminated toward the end of the century in the accumulation of a body of theoretical constructions which obscured the very object which the somatologist set out to study; the mental patient seems to have been forgotten because the somatologist found himself too busy with the visualization of the patient's brain and spinal cord to understand the man who was mentally sick. Theodor Meynert (1833–1892), Freud's professor in the Medical School in Vienna, typifies this extreme. He even objected to the term "psychiatry"; he formulated an elaborate and complex theory according to which psychoses are due to a variety of changes in the circulatory system. This vasomotor theory, combined with a systematized outline of what each part of the central nervous system does or fails to do in mental diseases, permitted Meynert to offer a classification of mental diseases on a purely anatomical basis. The forebrain, he thought, was in constant physiological antagonism with the brain stem. Delusions and hallucinations, he thought, were due to subcortical irritation of the brain, melancholia and mania to changes in the cortical blood vessels or cortical cells. The conviction derived from this viewpoint on mental diseases was great, almost as great as that derived from Boerhaave's statements on black choler; the viewpoint seemed to need as little factual confirmation, since it was a matter of unshakable belief. This trend was evident throughout the century and was not confined to the German-speaking world. It was deservedly called by Gruhle the school of "brain mythology."

It would be a mistake, of course, to consider this "cerebromythological" trend nothing more than a rejection of psychology. It was a direct

[62] *Zeitschrift für die Beurteilung und Heilung der Seelenzustände.* With Jacobi. 1838. (See p. 383.)

outgrowth of a narrowly conceived opposition to speculative psychology; it was a narrowly conceived attitude toward disease. But it was also a stimulus to further study of such organic diseases as general paralysis and to the deepening of the studies of various febrile exhaustive states, alcoholic mental disorders, and senile psychoses due to severe vascular changes in the brain. The great contributions of Nissl (1860–1919) and Alzheimer (1864–1915) were a direct result of this somatological philosophy.

Alcoholism, to which the French contributed a great deal of attention (Magnan, his pupil Legrain), was studied carefully both as a clinical phenomenon and as a problem of public health. Hufeland introduced the term "dipsomania" at the beginning of the century. Magnus Huss (1807–1890) spoke of *alcoholismus chronicus* (1849) and Wernicke described alcoholic hallucinosis. Korsakov (1854–1900) described the alcoholic psychosis and neuritis; alcoholism was more prevalent in Russia than anywhere else in Europe—the government controlled the sale and consumption of alcohol. The effects of morphine and morphine addiction were also subjects of attention. The first case of morphinism was reported by Heinrich Laehr (1820–1905) in 1872 in the *Allgemeine Zeitschrift für Psychiatrie*. The term "morphinism" was introduced a year later by Fiedler (1835–1921). These studies led to more comprehensive investigation of the mental illnesses due to poisons or infections, that is to say, the exogenous psychoses. These were best systematized at the beginning of the twentieth century by Karl Bonhoeffer of Berlin who was born in the year of Griesinger's death and who later occupied Griesinger's post at Berlin University. Moebius (1853–1907) was able to divide mental diseases into two large classes of exogenous and endogenous diseases, and Kraepelin accepted the division as a basis for his classification.

The field of psychoses and neuroses remained of necessity more or less neglected by the somatologist. He did not neglect them as far as his attempts to help them were concerned, but his means of help were limited, since the assumption that there was a true cortical irritation meant that there was no way of curing it, and the assumption of a fatal antagonism between the forebrain and the brain stem meant that there was no practical way of reconciling this antagonism. This point of view enhanced the traditional feeling that mental diseases as a whole were incurable. Outside of hospital management and drug therapy there was little to do. To the spirit of therapeutic nihilism, so prevalent in the nineteenth century, the extreme somatological philosopher contributed a great deal. The therapeutic efforts which did appear were a result of certain variations of the somatological theories, particularly those derived from the views of Brown in the previous century. It will be recalled that according to Brown the nervous system was subject to sthenic and asthenic states; the tonus of the nervous system was supposed to vary. Hence the views of George Miller Beard (1839–1883) who introduced the term "neurasthenia." Beard wrote on *Electricity as a Tonic* (1866) and on *Stimulants and Narcotics* (1871). His *American Nervousness, with Its Causes and Consequences* (1880) was translated into German by Neisser almost immediately after its appearance in America. Hence, too, Silas Weir Mitchell's (1829–1914) "rest treatment," which required temporary complete isolation and silence on the part of the patient. The pure somatologist, however, had narrowed his own field of vision, and his field of effective influence, clinical or therapeutic, was correspondingly limited.

The somatically oriented psychiatrist who by temperament was more interested in clinical work than in laboratory preoccupations was not long in discovering that another approach, a different methodology, was needed. The extreme somatic viewpoint was fundamentally not only an outgrowth of the success of physiology and of Virchow's creative leadership in clinical medicine and pathology. Historically somatology in psychiatry springs from Hippocrates, and his influence, revived with such enthusiasm in the previous century, undoubtedly had a great deal to do with a phenomenon like Griesinger. But all this was Hippocratism too narrowly conceived; as a matter of fact, it was more Galenism, which was followed traditionally although it had been verbally rejected by so many from Paracelsus to Pinel. There was another side to Hippocratism which seems to have faded since the days of Sydenham and which never seems to have taken proper hold in psychiatry—the enlightened medical empiricism which demands that the physician desist from speculations and limit himself to strict observations of the patient and follow each stage of the disease carefully until the very end, whether this end lead to recovery or death. In this side of Hippocratism all signs of disease are important, as well as their succession and the time of their appearance and disappearance. A good understanding of the course of the disease is sometimes more important than the knowledge of its cause; it certainly is most important when the cause is unknown.

This Hippocratism had already borne fruit in psychiatry. General paralysis, for instance, would never have been understood had it not been for the careful observation of the course this disease took in an individual. The time of its appearance was carefully noted, or carefully reconstructed, and the development and the end were well observed and correspondingly noted. French psychiatry already showed the way of this methodology in medical psychology, not only in that it succeeded in discovering general paralysis—an organic disease—but also in that it described the *folie circulaire* or *folie à double forme,* a functional disorder. These discoveries were made by means of purely psychological observation, not organic findings.

German psychiatry followed the lead given it by the French and it did so with singular success. As the establishment of mental hospitals starting in the beginning of the century brought together under the same medical roof a great number of mental patients, it became possible to verify a number of observations already made and also to make new observations. K. F. Flemming (1799–1880) studied the manifestations of anxiety and introduced the term "precordial anxiety." [63] K. G. Neumann (1774–1850) already had enough experience with patients whom he had observed over a considerable period of time to note that certain of them after their recovery were not fully as well as they had been before their mental illness, that a certain change in their personality had occurred which failed fully to disappear after their recovery. He introduced the term "recovery with defect" and was apparently one of the first to call attention to what we would call today gradual mental deterioration. The total psychological picture of a psychosis impressed F. W. Hagen (1814–1888) and he formulated an observation that fully stood the test of time and proved, as a matter of fact, a true discovery in medical psychology. As frequently happens, it passed unnoticed at the time and had to be rediscovered later. Hagen said that the psychotic delirium was a form of dreaming while one is awake; it was an expression of

[63] K. F. Flemming: *Pathologie und Therapie der Psychosen.* Berlin, 1859.

one's dream life—dreamed not as a result of sleep but as a result of illness.[64] Equally important from the therapeutic rather than the theoretical point of view was R. Leubusher's (1821–1861) observation that it is very important that the patient understand that he is mentally ill; this remark was one of the first clear statements of how important it is for the patient to have "insight as to illness." Carl Westphal (1833–1890) was one of the very first to describe obsessional mental states in which the patient is constantly preoccupied with one and the same thought or set of thoughts which seemingly bear no direct relation to his life as a whole—thoughts out of the context of life, so to speak.[65] Westphal also made some observations on homosexuality and on the pathological fear of open spaces—agoraphobia. The topic of neuroses thus began to be discussed more distinctly in German psychiatry. Westphal still considered obsessional thoughts (*Zwangsvorstellungen*) as "abortive insanity," but the observations made were a great step toward a detailed study of neurotic, alias psychoneurotic, reactions, which Krafft-Ebing described more fully and which in France found their most gifted exponent, Janet.[66]

The old ideas did not entirely disappear, of course: August Cramer, for instance, reminds one of Deleboë, who ascribed convulsions to the disturbances in the lever actions of the limbs, in that he ascribed compulsive neurotic acts and compulsive talking to disturbances of the muscle sense of the limbs or of the vocal apparatus; he called it a muscle-sense hallucination of the locomotor apparatus.[67] However, despite certain "mythological" interpretations which appeared every now and then, the acuity of psychological vision increased. Details of momentous importance began to be differentiated, as, for instance, Carl Wernicke's (1848–1905) observations on aphasias, which led him to the observation that loss of memory for recent events may be combined with a perfect memory of events long past—a distinctive manifestation of organic brain disease which differentiates it from certain psychotic states of functional origin.

[64] Cf. Neuburger and Pagel: *op. cit.*, vol. III, pp. 684, 685.

[65] Carl Westphal: *Über Zwangsvorstellungen, Berliner klinische Wochenschrift,* 1877.

[66] Pierre Janet: *Les obsessions et la psychasthénie.* Paris, 1903. Janet here introduced the term "psychasthenia."

[67] A. Cramer: *Die Halluzinationen im Muskelsinn bei Geisteskranken und ihre klinische Bedeutung,* 1889.

From this very brief sketch of various clinical observations it is easy to see how far advanced the German clinician was in the nineteenth century and how deeply he was able to pursue his observational methods and his individual sagacity. It would be remiss, therefore, not to mention that at the very time of these studies the immense work of building up a system of psychiatric institutions and of centers of psychiatric education was being accomplished, and that the German professor of psychiatry from the very beginning had to be administrative chief of a hospital or clinic as well as teacher, research worker, and doctor to his patients. The job was enormous in scope and particularly taxing, and it was not easy to discharge all of these duties effectively when the process of organization had not been fully completed. It was necessary to build and to organize while the scientific work was being carried on.

The creative genius of the German psychiatrist seems to have risen to the needs of his day with more than creditable efficiency and dispatch. The work of nonrestraint alone—a matter of struggle, contention and bureaucratic obstacles in many parts of France and England—was carried out in the greater part of Germany almost without difficulty. Griesinger and particularly C. M. Brosius (1825–1910) were successful in introducing the principles of Conolly, Edward Charlesworth (1783–1853), and Robert Gardiner Hill (1811–1878). The German hospital became an institution for treatment and research work almost within one generation. Nowhere in the world during the middle part of the century was so much research work done in psychiatry as in Germany.

It is impossible to relate in detail the activities of even the most important of the medical psychologists of Germany. Their number increased more rapidly than in France or England. The whole system of life in Germany reflected the tempo of rapid industrialization and the ever-increasing sense of communal relationship, and these were in turn reflected in the psychiatric profession. The individual worker, no matter how gifted, became a part of a whole; the total accomplishment began to count more than the performance of any individual. As a result a certain uniformity spread itself over German psychiatry. There was little strife. The rift between the somatologists and the psychologists was well-nigh forgotten. German psychiatrists were almost without exception good neurologists and good neuroanatomists who in fact if not in spirit followed Griesinger's postulate and equated mental and nervous disease.

This orientation, coupled with the ever-increasing influence of biological sciences and their methods, generated two characteristic trends which become typical of German psychiatry: the differentiation of certain diseases on the basis of their origin, course, and outcome, and the classification of diseases on the basis of the above principle.

The first clinical picture to stand out with great clarity in the German psychiatric literature is that of paranoia. In France Lasègue described in 1852 the persecutory delirium. The *folie raisonnante, folie lucide,* had been mentioned before. Esquirol had described as "monomania" the strange condition in which the individual seems to preserve all his mental faculties as well as systematized persecutory ideas. But the working out of the detailed phenomenology of paranoia was accomplished by German psychiatry.

Wilhelm Sander (1838–1922) described it in 1868.[68] Griesinger put it among his "primary deliria." Meynert's assistant Fritsch studied the paranoid states carefully. Meynert himself described the disease under the name of "amentia." Heinrich Cramer (1831–1893) tried to establish the method of diagnosing paranoia.[69] The German clinicians from the middle of the century to Ernst Kretschmer (b. 1888) [70] developed the detailed characteriology of the individuals who suffer from paranoia. They considered it a separate disease and it always occupied a separate place in their psychiatric classifications. However, the true psychological meaning of the disease was not understood and no light was shed on it until greater familiarity with the psychology of the unconscious permitted the investigator to understand its intimate relation to homosexual trends. This understanding was not gained until the first years of the twentieth century.

The need for purely clinical methods of study impressed itself upon the nineteenth-century psychiatrist with particular intensity. There was no other way of bringing order into the welter of clinical material which accumulated with such suddenness. Clinicians appeared who,

---

[68] Wilhelm Sander: *Originäre paranoia, Archiv für Psychiatrie,* 1868.
[69] Heinrich Cramer: in *Allgemeine Zeitschrift für Psychiatrie,* vol. LI, 1895.
[70] Kretschmer: *Der sensitive Beziehungswahn.* Berlin, 1918.

unable to determine and perhaps despairing of finding a physical, cerebrospinal cause for the diseases they observed, began to watch the course of the diseases with greater attention. These men were gifted clinical phenomenologists. Among them Karl Ludwig Kahlbaum (1828–1899) and his pupil and lifelong friend Ewald Hecker (1843–1909) deserve particular mention.

Kahlbaum was inspired with the thought of applying the principles of natural science to clinical psychiatry. He took as his motto the words of Karl Ernst von Baer, who once said, "If an investigator of nature were to say: 'I wish to beware of natural philosophy,' then it would mean, 'I wish to observe nature, but I shall be careful not to think.'" [71] Kahlbaum abandoned consideration of imaginary causes and proceeded to watch the beginning of certain illnesses, their course, and their usual outcome. He did not speak of diseases, but rather of forms or types of abnormal behavior (*Krankheitsformen*). Like many others before him, he described a disease which begins rather slowly and after having run its course ends in mental deterioration. His attention was then turned to a type of reaction which is in some respects similar to the above but which is characterized by singular muscular spasms, peculiar attitudes and postures, and stuporous states. In 1874 Kahlbaum published a monograph describing the condition under the name "catatonia." [72] In this monograph he introduced the term "verbigeration." Three years before Hecker had described hebephrenia,[73] a puberty psychosis ending in rather rapid deterioration.

Kahlbaum, to use the words of Neisser, gave a *monograph* of each disease form, a "symptom complex" (a term also introduced by Kahlbaum) which follows a definite course. Later on, writing on "cyclic insanity," [74] he introduced the term "cyclothymia," which is still used today to designate the predisposition to have definitely alternating moods of cheerfulness and mild depressive periods.

After Kahlbaum's and Hecker's descriptions, a period of quiescence of creative ideas seems to have set in in German psychiatry; it lasted for about twenty years and culminated in the appearance of the monu-

---

[71] Quoted by Clemens Neisser, in Kirchhoff: *Deutsche Irrenärzte*, vol. II, p. 92.

[72] Kahlbaum: *Die Katatonie oder das Spannungsirresein*. Berlin, 1874.

[73] Ewald Hecker: *Die Hebephrenie, Archive für pathologische Anatomie und Physiologie*, vol. LII, 1871.

[74] Kahlbaum: *Über zyklisches Irresein, Irrenfreund*, no. 10, 1882.

mental work of Kraepelin. In the meantime the psychiatrists in their search for order attempted to classify the clinical data and a number of classifications appeared. These classifications temporarily added to the vastness of psychiatric terminology, but they were mostly short lived. As long as there was no unitary principle for classifications there could be nothing but terminological attempts at improvement. The German psychiatrists were in this respect following a tradition of their own. They followed it so efficiently that Neumann's rebellion against classification was more than justified. The general grouping of the diseases was such that the label stood out more definitely than the condition it was supposed to designate. This is true even of Kahlbaum's grouping, despite his brilliant clinical descriptions.

The predilection for classifications had showed itself early in the century. Heinroth's forty-eight diagnoses have been mentioned. All these separate diseases Heinroth put into three classes: hypersthenias, asthenias, and hyposthenias. Karl Wilhelm Stark (1787–1845) made an even more ingenious arrangement. He divided all mental diseases into dysthenias, dysbulias, and dysnocsias. Each of these had a hyper-form, an a-form, and a para-form. If dysbulia meant disturbance of mood, then a hyperbulia meant elation, abulia depression, etc., along the line of all possible combinations. The patient behind the illness seems to have disappeared as fully as the illness behind the word. Kahlbaum in the same vein spoke of neophrenias, paraphrenias, enphrenias, and dysphrenias.[75] Heinrich Schüle (1840–1916) offered fewer new terms in his classification of "cerebro-psychoses,"[76] but hardly a smaller number of illnesses. Schüle conceived of allo- and deutero-pathic conditions, of cerebropsychopathies and cerebropsychoses, and of hereditary neuroses. He included melancholia among psychoneuroses and general paralysis among the "pernicious exhaustion states of the brain" in the same class as "hallucinatory stupor." Carl Wernicke spoke of allo-, somato-, and autopsychosis, also of akinetic, hyperkinetic, and parakinetic motility. Krafft-Ebing was simpler in his approach but hardly more enlightening as far as scientific classification of diseases is concerned. His textbook[77] underwent only few and insignificant

[75] Kahlbaum: *Die Gruppierungen der psychischen Krankheiten und die Einteilung der Seelenstörungen.* Danzig, 1863.
[76] H. Schüle: *Handbuch der Geisteskrankheiten.* Leipzig, 1878.
[77] R. Krafft-Ebing: *Lehrbuch der Psychiatrie,* 1879.

changes during the seven editions which appeared between 1880 and 1903. It is to be noted that even in the late seventies, before Kraepelin published the first edition of his text on psychiatry, there began to appear in the psychiatric classifications a criterion which was destined to play a great, if not very salutary, part in clinical psychiatry. Curability and incurability seem to have been considered in themselves symptoms of different diseases.

The number of classifications grew. The number of criteria increased with the number of individual predilections which might vary from time to time as the scientific development of the classifier underwent changes. To give a comprehensive nosology, to classify carefully, to produce a well-ordered classification almost seems to have become the unspoken ambition of every psychiatrist of industry and promise, as it is the ambition of a good tenor to strike a high C. This classificatory ambition was so conspicuous that the composer Berlioz was prompted to remark that after their studies have been completed a rhetorician writes a tragedy and a psychiatrist a classification.

IX

THE latter part of the nineteenth century presents a rather confusing psychiatric picture. "Classifications had accumulated since the beginning of the century, but with the help of neurology and other branches of medicine psychiatry succeeded in differentiating groups of conditions the etiology of which became known and the nosological entities of which were established. As to the rest of the psychoses in which the etiology remained unclear—there reigned the same state of confusion that had existed for one hundred years." [78] Classifications were of little or no help. As the century was entering its last quarter a young student appeared who was destined to leave a permanent imprint on the history of psychiatry.

Emil Kraepelin (1855–1926) entered the field of psychiatry when he was still a medical student. He submitted a competitive essay to the medical faculty at Würzburg entitled *On the influence of acute diseases on the origin of mental diseases*. His medical interests were

[78] Gruhle: *op. cit.*, p. 22.

thus defined early in his career. In 1878 he became Gudden's assistant at Munich—the same year in which Charcot started his studies of hysteria at the Salpêtrière. This year serves as a line of demarcation between the major interests of Germany's and France's medical psychologies. Germany took over the trends of Morel and Magnan and centered its attention on psychoses, on the severe mental diseases which in the past were called madness, insanity; France concentrated more on the neuroses, the "noninsane alienations of the mind."

Kraepelin's student essay reflected the primary trend of German psychiatry, the major efforts of which were directed to anything physical which resulted in any form of mental disturbance: fevers, head injuries, poisons. Today we do not consider a patient who is delirious because of high fever a mentally sick patient. The psychiatrists of those days were more correct; they considered any delirium a mental illness, which it certainly is, no matter how transitory or how dependent upon the rise and fall of the patient's temperature. It is a psychological reaction of the given patient's personality. Kraepelin, as well as his teachers and older colleagues, did not, of course, use the concept of personality, which was not developed until later. They were interested not so much in the patient's character as in the clinical phenomenon itself. Maximilian Jacobi's assertion that there was no need for psychology to understand mental diseases and Meynert's later objections to the term "psychiatry" were not merely expressions of a whim but the reflection of a true orientation.

Kraepelin was born to this orientation. That he was seriously influenced by it is clearly seen in the early course of his professional life. He left Heidelberg in 1882 to become an associate of Flechsig in the psychiatric hospital at Leipzig known as the Flechsig Clinic, but almost immediately after his arrival he left the hospital to work with Erb and Wundt. Flechsig's clinic was at the time, as it is now, a small hospital for the mentally ill, and then as now it contained not a few cases of organic diseases of the central nervous system. Erb and Wundt did experimental work. Wundt's fame was already great as a teacher and keen psychological experimenter. His chief interest was the phenomenon of psychological associations. He was what we know today as a physiological psychologist.

Those who knew Kraepelin personally—and there are many contemporaries who did, for Kraepelin died only in 1926—tell of his rather pleasant, responsive personality, of his tactful ability in bringing people together to work as an organized group, and of his great gifts as a teacher; yet it is curious that his scientific personality was so very detached, almost distant from the inner life of the patient. To Kraepelin a mentally sick person seems to have been a collection of symptoms. He was a true son of the great, energetic, and creative age that was interested greatly in humanity but comparatively little in man. Perhaps this trait in Kraepelin as a psychiatrist, which today would be considered a defect, was the very characteristic which helped rather than hindered him in the creation of his great system and school. He was able to collect and to study thousands of case histories, covering not only the story of each illness, but the history of each patient's life before the illness and a follow-up history of his life after he left the hospital. Dealing with such large masses of data, Kraepelin was able to sort out everything these many individuals had in common, leaving out of consideration the purely individual data. He thus arrived at an excellent general picture, at a unique perspective of a mental illness as a whole. But he seems to have been almost unaware that in his careful study he lost the individual.

It is doubtful whether he would have much regretted this loss had he been aware of it, for he was the convinced proponent of the biological method in the study of psychiatry. Biology does not easily tolerate the individual; the purely biological method, seeking to discover the laws governing natural phenomena, cannot apprehend these laws unless all individual variations are fully discounted so that it becomes possible to make a proper generalization. Kraepelin, a proponent of the methods of natural sciences, was careful that he should not be confused with the "natural philosopher" of the previous century. He cited Daquin's *La philosophie de la folie* and Pinel's *Traité Médico-philosophique* as examples of *philosophic* tendencies in the past in contradistinction to his own attitude which followed the principles of the *natural sciences*.[19] This contention is very revealing; it sheds a definite light on the changes which history had wrought in Europe in the course of the hundred years between Pinel and Kraepelin. Kraepelin failed to understand the age of Pinel in that he overlooked the meaning which

[19] Emil Krapelin: *Hundert Jahre Psychiatrie*. Berlin, 1918.

the word "philosophy" had at the close of the eighteenth century. Kraepelin thought of Fichte, Schelling, Kant, and Nietzsche when he reproached the psychiatrist of the eighteenth century for leaning toward philosophy; the great speculative German philosophers of the nineteenth century would certainly have disavowed Daquin and Pinel as philosophers. Kraepelin's confusion came from the fact that he apparently was not aware that the term *natural philosophy* had in Pinel's day meant biology equally as much as the term *natural sciences* in his own day came to mean the same thing. Kahlbaum, while following essentially Kraepelin's method, refused to abandon his right to be a "natural philosopher," but to Kraepelin the word *Wissenschaft*—science—already had that magic appeal which made one contemptuous of the term "philosophy." To him *Wissenschaft* meant more than philosophy, although it was no more than an etymological improvement on the older concept.

This improvement had its singular appeal not because of the word itself, of course, but because Fechner, Wundt, Helmholtz, and, most of all, Darwin produced a scientific atmosphere which was diametrically opposed to the romanticism which had set in in Europe after the Napoleonic Wars. The extraordinary development of technology and industry, particularly in Germany after the Franco-Prussian War, produced a spirit of socialized strivings, an atmosphere of almost disindividualized and united national effort for the unity and stability of the social structure. In other words, the individual again began to be a servant of the State. Even public health measures, so progressive in Germany, protected the individual only for the ultimate protection of the community.

In short, the scientific spirit of the last quarter of the nineteenth century was the spirit of a highly socialized community in which the individual was but a statistical element to be viewed only as such. The Nietzschean flights into the beyond, seemingly so adventurous and so romantic, and the measured, methodical procedure of Kraepelin have in common that fundamental disregard, even contempt, for man as a person. Nietzsche spoke of the weak and the slaves; Kraepelin was interested in the *form*, the *types*, of mental illness, rather than in their ideational content. Kraepelin did not want to know *what* the patient thought when he was ill, but *how* he thought. It was the general and not the particular, the social and not the personal that inspired the Kraepelin school, which was the loyal psychiatric testimonial to an industrial, technological age disquieted by the too personal, the "romantic," the "philosophical."

This attitude is reflected in the whole trend of Kraepelin's scientific career. The first edition of his textbook of psychiatry, published in 1883, was called a *compendium*, that is, but a brief outline. In the second edition four years later Kraepelin, following Kahlbaum in part, divides mental diseases into those caused by external conditions, which are *curable*, and those caused by inherent constitutional factors, which are *incurable*. This is the first indication of Kraepelin's principle of prediction as the basis for the diagnosis of mental diseases. There is an element of fatalism in this attitude. It is not the philosophic fatalism of the contemplative yet restless romantic but the serene, calculated, and calculating fatalism of the astronomer and the physicist and the chemist, who take the phenomena or the elements as they are since one does not quarrel with natural phenomena. One cannot reject them; one accepts them because there is no doubt as to their acceptability.

Kraepelin never suspected that despite his convictions he was closer to the natural philosophy of the eighteenth century, which was based on physics, chemistry, optics, and mathematics, than to biology in the contemporary sense, which deals with the phenomena of life in a more comprehensive and much less impersonal fashion than it might at first appear. Claude Bernard, who was more intimate with biology than the psychiatrists of the school of Kraepelin, dared to state that there is no essential difference between health and disease, but the Kraepelinian approach seems to have been based on a deep misapprehension of Samuel Butler's saying that "we cannot reason with our cells, for they know so much more than we do that they cannot understand us." Since we cannot reason with living cells, it was mistakenly assumed, we need not learn their language; rather, we ought to limit ourselves to the mere observation of external phenomena. Only these deserve the designation of "facts." We must assume that mental disease exists as a separate entity and that this disease is different and is predetermined. We ought to look for the diseased, the abnormal; what health is is so fully self-evident that it is not subject to doubt, still less to discussion.

This was Kraepelin's fundamental assumption: mental disease was predetermined. Even the words "curable" and "incurable" were misnomers, for the actual attitude was that some patients *naturally* recover, others *naturally* fail to recover and instead deteriorate. Not only the outcome of a mental disease is predetermined but its course as well, even as is the course of a planet or a chemical reaction. There is a natural law governing mental disease and it is this law which is to be the subject of psychiatric curiosity. The purely personal side of the patient's illness is but incidental or accidental.

This way of thinking is logical, consistent, and seemingly irrefutable. It dominated the psychiatric orientation of Kraepelin. In the fourth edition of his *Lehrbuch* (1893), no longer a compendium but a handsome volume, Kraepelin accepts the Kahlbaum-Hecker methods and conclusions regarding catatonia and hebephrenia. With the fifth edition (1896) the Kraepelinian system came to its full expression.

Kraepelin spent a few years in Munich after his stay in Leipzig with Wundt. From 1890 he worked in Heidelberg, which soon became a psychiatric center of world-wide renown. After 1904 he returned to Munich, heading the Forschungsanstalt which became world famous under his leadership; this institute was financially supported to some extent by resources coming from the United States. But psychiatry was developing with such energy and rapidity that even despite the immense activity of the Forschungsanstalt—with its numerous and original contributions in the field of physiology, pathological anatomy (particularly cerebral anatomy), and heredity in mental diseases—the system of Kraepelin appears to have become a thing of the past as soon as it announced its own birth in 1896.

Clear detail, well-ordered groups of observations, well-plotted curves, and fully documented statistical tables led to the conclusion that there were two major mental diseases or two large groups of diseases: dementia praecox and manic-depressive psychoses. The detailed clinical descriptions of these psychoses are easily found in any textbook of psychiatry. The actual details of these descriptions are really of no great importance. It is important to note the establishment of certain facts. Manic-depressive psychoses, first mentioned as such in the sixth edition of Kraepelin's *Lehrbuch* (1899), run a cyclic course as a series of attacks of elations and depressions, the patient usually "recovering" between the attacks and going through a "normal" interval.

Dementia praecox is characterized by the symptoms found in catatonia and hebephrenia and also in Kahlbaum's *vesania typica*, auditory hallucinations and perhaps persecutory trends. Paranoia is still classified as a separate disease. Manic-depressive psychoses are *recoverable* psychoses, while dementia praecox invariably leads to mental deterioration, to dementia proper.

The most distinguishing point of the Kraepelinian system was the prognostic attitude, closely connected with diagnosis. The Hippocratic principles of prognosis thus entered into psychiatry under a very singular guise. One diagnosed by prognosis, as it were, and if the prognosis proved ultimately correct, the diagnosis was considered correct. This was a departure from a vital and sound principle of general medicine. One cannot say that because a disease ends in a certain definite way it is a certain definite disease. Kraepelin himself was apparently unaware of this singular deviation from medical principles and did not foresee that the fatalism with which it was imbued weakened even further the rather unstable and never too strong rational therapeutic interest with regard to mental diseases. There is no doubt that it was not Kraepelin's intention to diminish the therapeutic efforts or to keep them only within the limits of the aging tradition of hospital management and humanitarian tolerance. But the therapeutic efforts were to become based on the complacent, expectant attitude that if the disease is a manic-depressive psychosis the patient will get well, and if it is a dementia praecox the patient will deteriorate—or, in the more turgid language of psychiatric formalism, if it is a manic-depressive psychosis "the prognosis is good for the attack," and if it is a dementia praecox the prognosis is unfavorable.

Kraepelin covered the whole field of psychiatry. He continued constantly to work out new details and to work over old ones. From the one volume of 825 pages (the fifth edition of 1896) his textbook became an imposing two-volume work (2425 pages) in the ninth edition of 1927, which was issued in co-operation with Lange one year after Kraepelin's death. The contribution of Kraepelin which left the most distinct imprint on posterity is not, however, the detail of his clinical investigations of general paralysis or of exhaustive states, but his prognostic, phenomenological, descriptive delineation of the two major psychoses. There is perhaps a certain justice in a partial misjudgment on the part of posterity, for while Kraepelin did change some of his views with the years, he changed them slowly and little. For instance, not until 1912 did his classificatory outline include *paraphrenia*, a term suggested by Kahlbaum many years previously. The immense success of the Kraepelinian system made those who came after him overlook certain facts. First, he was far from having been accepted at once; as a matter of fact, he appeared too radical to be adopted by the more conservative psychiatrists until Bleuler's influence began to make itself felt. Second, the historical origin of Kraepelin's clinical viewpoint was not clearly seen. It is not taking away from Kraepelin's originality to state that the whole concept of dementia praecox had been gradually developing for almost forty years before he finally synthesized and described it.

Following Moebius, Kraepelin divided the psychoses into those which were endogenous and those which were exogenous. Dementia praecox was an endogenous illness—that is, one not caused by external causes. It was assumed to be caused by some organic brain changes. Kraepelin was later inclined to the view that dementia praecox was of metabolic origin. On November 27, 1898, he presented to the Twenty-ninth Congress of Southwestern German Psychiatry a paper entitled "The Diagnosis and Prognosis of Dementia Praecox." Of those present only Aschaffenburg approved of the contents of the paper.

Objections to Kraepelin's diagnosis of dementia praecox were raised at home and abroad. Pappenheim (b. 1881) disagreed with it. Ernst Meyer (1871–1931) was opposed to it. Korsakov (1854–1900) disagreed and so did Korsakov's compatriot Serbski, who called attention to the fact that even Kraepelin admitted that about 13 per cent of dementia praecox patients apparently recover without defect. If then, argued Serbski, dementia praecox is to be diagnosed as such because it ends in deterioration, what about those who recover? Should we consider those recovered cases cases of deterioration without deterioration, of dementia without dementia? Robert Sommer (b. 1864) and Leonardo Bianchi (1848–1927) joined in these objections.

Nor was the diagnosis of manic-depressive psychosis accepted wholeheartedly. Mendel (1839–1907) objected to the establishment of this nosological group and pointed out that paranoias, too, show periodic swings of mood. Similar swings were observed by Kahlbaum in catatonia. Kraepelin designated a form of melancholia (involution melancholia) as a separate form of disease. Jolly (1844–1904) objected to this separation and in 1907 Dreyfus suggested that the disease belonged to the manic-depressive group.[80] Kraepelin was only reluctantly ready to agree.

Despite these numerous objections the Kraepelinian division of the major psychoses into two groups remained a classical division in all subsequent psychiatric nosologies. The reason for the stability of the Kraepelinian diagnostic views is mainly the fact that they rested on a historical foundation. Kraepelin's dementia praecox was related to the crucial age of puberty. So were hebephrenia and catatonia. The term "dementia praecox" was used as early as 1860 (*démence précoce*) by Morel. Morel's description is close to Hecker's of hebephrenia. Morel even followed the descriptive methodology of considering course and outcome. B. Rousseau spoke of a puberty disease in 1857, and so did Moreau in 1859. Gautier wrote his doctor's thesis in 1883 on *démence précoce*. Magnan's pupils Saury and Legrain used the term *démence précoce*, and at the first congress of French psychiatrists in Rouen in 1890 Charpentier read a paper *Démence précoce simple des enfants normaux*. As to manic-depressive psychoses, the studies of Falret the older, of Baillarger, and of Kahlbaum in 1882 have been mentioned, as has been the fact that Kahlbaum introduced the term "cyclothymia."

In other words, both from the standpoint of terminology and clinical descriptions Kraepelin's nosological innovations were but the natural culmination of a generation of efforts in both France and Germany. It is of more than passing interest to note that the influence of French psychiatry on the Germans can be traced to the very end of the nineteenth century and directly into the Kraepelinian system itself, despite its originality. The most outstanding feature of this originality, the prognostic approach, proved a double-edged sword. It threatened for a while to retard the whole course of psychiatric progress and perhaps would have had it not been for the later work of Kraepelin's contemporary Eugen Bleuler (1857–1939), who revised the whole concept

[80] G. Dreyfus: *Die Melancholie, ein Zustandsbild des manisch-depressiven Irreseins.* Jena, 1907. Kraepelin wrote a foreword to this monograph.

of dementia praecox, even to the point of renaming the disease, and who led descriptive psychiatry out of an apparently blind alley.

The reasons for Kraepelin's sudden success and for his partial failure lie in the powerful currents of psychiatry which made themselves felt at the very beginning of the twentieth century and which therefore belong to another era, although originating at the very time when Kraepelin's conceptions were being formulated. This era presents the concluding steps of psychiatric history and merges into the medical psychology of the first quarter of the present century.

x

THE work of Kraepelin is sometimes considered as having established a new era in psychiatry. As one continues a historical appraisal of the period, it becomes clear that neither chronologically nor scientifically is it possible to delimit such a Kraepelinian era. The system of Kraepelin emerged from a definite past and it did so not suddenly but very gradually, methodically, certain of its ground and of its attitude. There was an age-long scientific attitude which assumed as an established fact that mental disease is a physical disease. There was also an assumption, which was perhaps less overtly expressed, that everyone knows what a mental disease is and that it is something definite. This certainty about a matter so uncertain is in itself a uniquely puzzling phenomenon in science.

It seems that the madman, the insane, the town fool, known to all from time immemorial, had never really puzzled anyone as a psychological problem. When people thought that the madman was possessed by spirits they were just as convinced of the validity of their thought as they were when they decided that his bile was poisoning his animal spirits; they were equally convinced with equal lack of evidence when they claimed that he had a diseased brain, or that he was a degenerate, or that his metabolism was all wrong, or that he was "constitutionally inferior." Morel never doubted that he knew what a "taint of degeneration" was, nor Kraepelin that dementia praecox was a disease entity. For each period of history the question of mental disease seems to have been settled in a manner corresponding to the spirit of the age. The nineteenth century took it for granted that it *was* a disease like any physical disease and it was the express belief of the clinician that his only duty was to proceed in an attempt to prove as comprehensively as possible that the assumption of the age was correct. The nineteenth century learned more than all previous centuries about physical illness; the method of clinical medicine reached a high degree of precision; more and more diseases became well defined. Medical psychology, borrowing the pattern of clinical medicine and resting on its assumptions, had to prove that at least some of these assumptions were correct. Consequently, psychiatric nosology flourished.

The Kraepelinian system was a true triumph of a settled question. Historically and psychologically the triumph was very great because it brought about, in textbooks at least, the fulfillment of the age-long ambition of bringing mental disease into medicine, carrying it in through the front door, so to speak, bringing about a complete union of psychiatry and medicine. Griesinger had attempted to do it, but what Griesinger demanded was a fusion of psychiatry with neuroanatomy. His voice was decisive but not original, since Thomas Willis had tried to do the same thing in the seventeenth century with almost as great, if not greater, authority. Friedreich knew this well enough to state a few years before Griesinger's textbook appeared that the organic point of view had actually been introduced by the English. Kraepelin, on the other hand, came half a century after Griesinger. Chemistry and physiology had made immense strides during these fifty years. The foundation for the understanding of infectious diseases had been laid by Pasteur and Koch. Virchow and Claude Bernard dominated medical methodology; the ancient cell of the alchemist had grown into the fascinating complexity and precision of the experimental laboratory. Medicine was rapidly becoming as dependent on the laboratory as man has always been on air. Kraepelin established the fact that mental disease, like any other disease, like quartan or tertian fever, is a disease running a regular course. He also took it for granted that, like any other disease, it is due either to a defective organ, or to heredity, or to improper body economy, or to metabolic changes, or to internal secretion—endocrine conditions. He thus brought the physiological laboratory into psychiatry and psychiatry into the laboratory.

The final fusion of medicine and psychiatry seemed completed at last. From the day Hippocrates raised his protest against calling epilepsy sacred, through centuries of puzzled uncertainty and later centuries of fire and blood, the protest of Hippocrates was somehow kept alive. It finally spoke through Weyer and through an ever-increasing number of ardent and convinced spokesmen, and Hippocrates seemed to have won his final and most decisive victory with the inauguration of the system of Kraepelin. The warning that Schüle issued some years previously admonishing the psychiatrist not to forget that he was treating sick individuals, not merely sick brains, was destined to remain unheeded for a while because it clashed too much with the newly established harmonious relationship between medicine and psychiatry.

There was potentially a great danger in this harmony, in the assertion that a mentally sick individual is a personality and not a person with a sick body organ. There was the danger that an attempt to emphasize *personality* might introduce philosophy into psychiatry and undermine the recently erected stately nosological structure. That Emanuel Mendel spoke of a periodic paranoia almost a decade before the fifth edition of Kraepelin's *Lehrbuch* appeared, and that Sollier spoke even three years previously of a circular form of neurasthenia, and that Kahlbaum himself observed cycles in catatonia—these facts had to be overlooked in order to preserve the sense of solidity and correctness which made such a great appeal in the nosological comprehensiveness of Kraepelin. There was not a little truth in Serbski's remark that Kraepelin's outline on manic-depressive psychoses presented "a comfortable point of view."

Thus, the Kraepelinian system from the time of its emergence showed certain characteristics of artificiality; it seems to have been forced to sacrifice too much to maintain its systematized integrity. It reduced man to a system of organs, and mental disease to a process of predestined course. It was the great synthesis of those half-fatalistic, half-static views to which the geniuses of Morel and Magnan, Kahlbaum and Hecker had arrived after so many brilliant observations and not less brilliant clinical efforts. The birth of the Kraepelinian system was the ultimate achievement of an attitude which expected little from man once he was mentally ill; it stood ready to take him into the kindly custody of a well-organized and well-conducted hospital where he could await his fate with the maximum comfort his psychological condition, social position, and financial ability would allow. The very definiteness and clarity of the Kraepelinian system seem to have become the source of its own weakness, for they excluded so thoroughly any consideration of the human personality.

Yet it was in order to save the human personality which was being hunted and haunted by misunderstanding, superstition, and cruelty that medicine had arisen to include mental disease in its own domain. This is one of the most astounding paradoxes in the history of psychiatry. It explains why even at the peak of psychiatric development as it was exemplified by what Kraepelin and his school achieved psychiatry still lagged behind, still lacked a true medical psychology, and still seemed to shy away from one. It was not easy to be optimistic under these circumstances, and one's optimism ran the risk of bordering on the naïve, as did Krafft-Ebing's when he said at the turn of the century that we know more about the etiology of mental diseases than of others.

Krafft-Ebing's optimism is easy to understand, for his brilliant experimental attempts to inoculate general paralytics with syphilis had yielded very satisfying results. When the paralytics did not respond to the inoculation, he had conclusive proof that general paralysis was due to syphilis, since only those who have once had syphilis cannot contract it. Only the serological proof of this observation remained for future discovery. Krafft-Ebing did not even suspect the possibility of such a proof, but his findings were the most conclusive yet brought forward. It was in the communication of this experiment at the International Congress in Moscow in 1897, five years before his death, that Krafft-Ebing coined the epigrammatic expression "civilization and syphilization." He spoke also of "our nervous age." These remarks were clear indications that even the traditional, organically-minded, and purely descriptive medical psychologist already felt that a relationship between mental disease and cultural functioning exists, that the study of mental disease cannot be limited to laboratory work, and that the whole of community life is interrelated with psychopathology.

Krafft-Ebing's contemporary Moebius (1853–1907) was even more aware of the need of correlating these two manifestations of man's creativeness: psychology (and therefore psychopathology) and artistic, literary, and general cultural activity. Moebius translated Magnan into German and wrote a number of pathographies. There is not a little irony and not a little criticism against his and his colleague's organicism in Moebius' remark about himself that he was a *dégénéré supérieur*—a true contradiction in itself. The remark sounded like an intuitive premonition that psychopathology might some day become the best source and foundation for the formulations of a general psychology of man, that mental disease might prove not a pernicious deathblow and might even become the source of the very creative powers of cultural growth. The genius may be insane and yet be a genius, a valuable, if not at times the most valuable, asset to civilization.

Thus, at the very moment when the Kraepelinian system was established questions began to be asked within the most conservative circles of German psychiatry itself which the Kraepelinian orientation was unable to answer. However, these questions were not entirely new; they had been imposing themselves for many years on those who dealt with mental diseases. Fodéré, it will be recalled, was almost inclined not to draw any sharp line between the insane and the sane. Even Reil, whose views were frequently self-contradictory and whose concepts were vague, sensed that there must be an inner relationship between our insanities and our civilized functioning. At the opening of the century he wrote: "We draw step by step closer to the insane asylums, so as to be able to go forward on the road of our *physical* and intellectual culture. The physical man must first become [mentally] ill in order that the birth of the intellectual forces can begin." [81] The deep relationship between social creative forces and psychopathology seems to have been first sensed by the Frenchman J. J. Moreau (1804–1884), who wrote as early as 1859 on the relationship of morbid psychology to philosophy of history.[82] Charles Darwin was interested, although in a rather general way, in the problem of the relationship of genius to insanity. This problem was also linked to problems of criminology. Lombroso's (1836–1909) work on the criminal appeared in 1876.[83]

---

[81] Reil: *Rhapsodien*, p. 12.

[82] Jacques Joseph Moreau: *La psychologie morbide dans ses rapports avec la philosophie de l'histoire, ou de l'influence des neuropathies sur le dynamisme intellectual.* Paris, 1859.

[83] Cesare Lombroso: *L'uomo delinquente in rapporto alla antropologia, alla giurisprudenza ed alle discipline carcerarie.* Milan, 1876.

It was obvious that psychiatry was seeking a new field of investigation because life was asking it questions it was unable to answer. The very contemporaries of Kraepelin seemed to be presenting the problems about genius and insanity in concrete, practical, not purely philosophical aspects. Friedrich Nietzsche (1844–1900) was mentally ill; so was Guy de Maupassant (1850–1893). Dostoevski was a tortured person and an epileptic; most of his heroes were criminals, epileptics, psychopaths. The whole question—what mental disease is, how it works in man, and how it makes man work—was knocking at the door of psychiatry.

XI

In order to gain a proper perspective on how medical psychology met the demands of the time toward the close of the nineteenth century, we shall have to retrace our steps in some respects. It will have been noted that our review of German psychiatry began with Griesinger, almost at the very middle of the century. The gap of the first forty-odd years can now be properly filled. It is to the credit of the German romanticists that from the very beginning they approached medico-psychological problems from a broader and more inclusive point of view than did their successors of the second half of the century. They seem to have been able to realize better than the generation which followed them that a psychological phenomenon is more complex than a physical one. They asked themselves what mental disease was and they wished to find an answer to the question before proceeding with any further assumptions or with practical steps. Unfortunately, they had much less clinical experience than those who followed them. There were fewer hospitals, their organization was not as developed, the methods of investigation were not seasoned, and the general scientific heritage was not as great or as solid. Yet the few men before 1845 seem to have worked harder on and produced more in the field of the psychology of mental disease than the imposing army of great psychiatric workers of the latter half of the century, who had at their disposal so many more patients, so much better an organization, and such delicate methods of investigation.

The men of the first half of the century were rich in ideas but they were still steeped in the past; their terminology was religious, sentimental, metaphysical. They were called philosophers by their somatological colleagues. The somatologists expressed their unequivocal contempt for these "philosophers" and "theologians" and "psychologists." The psychologists retreated to leave the field of battle. They left not because of their inherent weakness, but rather because the "spirit of the times," the industrialization and socialization of German culture, left behind it the romantic trends of thought and with them the problems of more serious and deeper preoccupation with the individual and the individual's mind. A few of the romanticists' preoccupations continued to ferment under the surface, and toward the close of the century these seem to have reacquired a certain value denied them by the practical generations which had supervised them with so much energy and so little spiritual generosity.

The trait common to all the representatives of the "psychological" group is their interest in the subjective state of the mentally ill, in the actual feelings and thoughts of the patients. These were their points of departure, the source from which they hoped to acquire true knowledge about mental disease. The second characteristic common to all of this group is that they looked upon the mental illness as capable of giving them a clue to what mental health is. In other words, they had no preconceived notion or silent assumption of what health is, and they looked upon a mental disease as a result of the individual's psychological development.

The individual stood in the very center of their field of observation. The terminology of the time was not very helpful; it was too diffuse and the writer in his romantic contemplation frequently used one and the same word to cover a multitude of psychological phenomena. The French *passion*, the English *passions*, the German *Leidenschaft* meant passions, strong feelings, emotions, spontaneous drives, affects, what we would call today instincts, automatisms, the emotional coloring of reflex reactions, etc. That romanticism should have had its strongest influence on psychiatry in Germany rather than in France, England, or America is striking, and this curious and very instructive phenomenon would require, and it well deserves, a special historical study. That this romantic, cultural-philosophical trend, brief as its official life may appear, made a lasting contribution to psychiatry, particularly to the psychiatry of the twentieth century, there is no doubt. Georg Ernst Stahl's teachings, Langermann's early theories, the psychological speculations of the romanticists in psychiatry from Friedrich Groos to Ideler present a continuous stream of creative thought which was only temporarily halted at the materialistic dam erected by Griesinger, and which continued to work its way into clinical psychiatry. Ideler, the last of the great romanticists, died while chief of the Charité in Berlin in 1860, fifteen years after Griesinger's textbook appeared and only eight years before Griesinger died, at the head of the same Charité. The theoretical trends thus overlapped chronologically as they did clinically. It would be a mistake indeed to assume that the romanticists were only philosophers. They were clinicians and they worked with patients steadily; it is on the basis of their clinical and not purely intellectual experiences that they tried to formulate their theories.

That these theories had the force of clinical truth behind them and that they did not spend themselves with the general romantic impetus of the first half of the century is, it would appear, amply proven by the brilliant contemporary contributions made to clinical psychiatry by men like Gaupp, Gruhle, and Kretschmer, whose place in modern psychiatry is honorable and permanent. These, like their early predecessors in the first half of the nineteenth century, looked upon man in his totality; if one does look upon the individual in his totality, one must take into consideration the whole structure and content of our civilization, its past as well as its present, the cultural anthropological history of man, the psychobiological unity of man's personality.

The mistake made by the somatologists was that they grasped the opportunity to learn more about one organ of the human body, the brain, and inadvertently reduced the human personality to the functions of that organ. They were thus driven by the necessity of their self-imposed limitations to discount the whole history of man, except his organic history, which after all is but a hypothesis, a theoretical presupposition which became particularly reinforced after Darwin. This hypothesis, surprising as it may appear at first in so far as it affected medical psychology, was based on a very old, idealistic, almost theological faith which the somatologists appear to have combated vehemently. Friedreich, it will be remembered, had criticized Heinroth on the grounds of morality. To Friedreich it appeared a sacrilege to deal with the soul in a scientific, analytical manner; everything psychological was of the soul, and the soul being immortal and perfect could not be considered subject to illness. Here we have the reverberation, the almost unconscious but deliberate re-establishment of the old medieval point of view which on purely theological grounds insisted that all illnesses, including mental illnesses, must be physical.

Thus the most scientific and most rationalistic system of psychiatric thought, which reached its peak at the close of the nineteenth century, unawares reasserted a principle which had been combated by medicine for several centuries. This historical paradox reveals that the handicap from which medical psychology had been suffering from the beginning of time was not overcome by scientific psychiatry; in fact, psychiatry ultimately almost succumbed to this handicap in the very substance of the Kraepelinian system. Scientific medicine merely achieved a more or less clear delimitation of zones of action. The heart, lungs, stomach, intestines, liver, and a few other "minor" organs were permanently assigned to general medicine; the bones and muscles and on special occasions the viscera were assigned to surgery; the brain, ganglia, and spinal cord and the nerves derived from them were assigned to psychiatry, or to what is sometimes called today neuropsychiatry. The mind in its purely formal aspects was left partly to experimental physiological psychology, which in the last analysis deals only with physical equivalents of the mind and not with the mind itself or with its psychological manifestations.

Having accepted rather than overcome this old handicap, the classical nosologist officially abandoned his interest in the individual and in his psychology, which imposed itself, however, no matter how unwanted, with all the dynamic power inherent in the age-old problem of mental disease. Consequently, at the turn of the century descriptive psychiatry found itself at the crossroads; it had become a fully recognized medical specialty, a legitimate branch of medical and biological sciences, but it offered no new light on the very problems of human personality which it made the subject matter of its specialty. It stood at the crossroads even as it had at the close of the eighteenth century, but its task was more difficult and imposed a greater responsibility. The nineteenth century had found a partial answer to the puzzle in hospital reform, organization, training of supervising staffs, teaching of psychiatry to medical students, classification of mental diseases, organization of psychiatric societies, foundation of psychiatric journals, preparation of textbooks of psychiatry, organization of the aftercare of mental patients, and the introduction of psychiatry into the courtroom, making the psychiatric branch of medicolegal problems an integral part of the process of justice. Of this Herculean task the nineteenth century acquitted itself with a brilliance, industry, and devotion unique in the whole history of medicine. But having solved the many practical problems of organization, description, and classification, the same century discovered that in matters of actual treatment and direct influence of mental disease it had made staggeringly little progress.

The rise of chemistry at the expense of physics proved of little help to psychiatry. To be sure, organic mental disorders ultimately benefited by this rise, for the treatment of general paralysis with drugs injurious to the syphilitic treponema was directly due to the development of physiological chemistry. But the use of drugs was often but "chemical restraint," supplanting the older forms of mechanical restraint. The psychoses "of a fully developed brain" remained outside the psychiatrist's power as much as they had been in the previous century; the neuroses fared no better. These were the real problems; these represented the real field of psychiatry; and these could neither be understood nor helped by means of better classifications or by assertions of constitutional, hereditary, or degenerative characteristics. The question of what mental disease is, which the eighteenth century had avoided of necessity and skillfully, was raised again at the very close of the nineteenth century. The French frequently spoke of psychological causes of mental disease, but they never really investigated the problem more carefully. Guislain, the reformer and pioneer psychiatrist of Belgium, was perhaps more psychologically inclined than the majority of his French-speaking colleagues, but he followed the positivistic, purely external psychology which was characteristic of Esquirol and Georget. What Guislain understood as psychological factors were actually environmental factors such as loss of work, family problems, theft, political troubles, onset of old age.[84] The French were under the in-

[84] Guislain: *Traité sur l'aliénation mentale.* Amsterdam, 1826. *Traité sur les phrénopathies.* Brussels, 1833.

fluence of formal rationalism, and the great success of the Revolution of 1789 marked a turning away from what the average practical man vaguely calls "spiritual problems." Napoleon, in making his peace with the Pope, reflected no turn toward religious views; the rationalistic, positivistic trends persisted throughout the eighteenth century. To Napoleon or to the Bourbons who succeeded him official religion was but a good trading point of practical political and social value. The turning away from religion meant automatically a turning away from those problems which involved the soul; only reason could and should be considered.

The situation was quite different in Germany. Luther's Protestantism made a great part of Germany conscious of its religious independence and piety, and this sense of spiritual independence and responsibility was a source of inner craving for learning and improvements in practical living. As the nineteenth century began, and with it the Napoleonic invasions, the national spirit arose and became coupled with a number of religious emotions. Consequently, German romanticism as it was reflected in the German psychiatry early in the century represented a variation of the *pietas literata* of Thomas More and Vives. It was piety that provided a sense of oneness with the world, a protestant piety that deepened the sense of personal responsibility toward the community and the world. It was a need to find some lines of integration which would make the personal, the public, and the universal properly correlated. The German philosophers of the time (Fichte, Schelling) were deeply preoccupied with this orientation; the German psychiatrists felt the need of correlating mental disease with these general trends. This partially explains the fact that the earliest representative psychiatric minds of the century still spoke almost like theologians (Heinroth), and that some of the psychiatrists were physician-poets (Justinus Kerner [1786–1862]) or physician-philosophers (August Eschenmayer [1768–1852], Friedrich Groos [1768–1852]). But one should not be deterred by their recondite, semitheological, semi-philosophical terminology any more than by the confusing avalanche of words and fantasies which was offered us by Paracelsus. If one is armed with patience and tolerance and the desire to learn, one can perceive through the mist and thunder of what Paracelsus had to say a number of extremely valuable new thoughts, and one can perceive the true meaning of the great medical revolution of which Paracelsus was one of the leaders.

The same can be said with even greater reason of the medical psychologists of the early part of the nineteenth century. Johann Christian Heinroth [85] (1773–1843), whom Friedreich berated with such raspy intolerance, was not less pointed in his opposition to the increasing spirit of narrow somatology. In conformity with the spirit of the time, Heinroth was declamatory and pungent: "Soul!" he exclaimed, "the great, most meaningful word! The only treasure of man, the very being of the self. How they drag you down by making you the slave of the body! Yes, they drag you down when they look upon you as a cadaver which one could cut to pieces with a knife, or as a chemical compound which could be broken down into elements, or as a mechanical contraption the workings of which one could calculate with the help of mathematics." [86]

Heinroth is usually unclear and very emphatic. In his textbook he devotes one hundred and forty-three pages to the consideration of God and finally concludes that mental illnesses are derived from "unfree" states of the soul and that all unfree states of the soul are due to sin. There is no doubt that Heinroth's purely theological terminology is sufficiently confusing, but there is also little doubt that he misrepresents himself, for his conclusions on mental diseases were not theological. He translated Georget into German. He classified mental diseases on a purely clinical basis. He used the word "soul" merely because there was no other word in the German language of the time to denote that complex phenomenon called "human mind" or our present-day "sense of guilt." This was a definite step toward a general psychopathology, because it went beyond the purely formal considerations of the patient's mode of reasoning or of his manner of registering sensations—the chief points of interest to the traditional somatologist.

Heinroth was a good clinical psychologist who was eager to establish the unity of mental phenomena and who wished to delineate mental reactions in terms which would describe the dynamic processes of human psychology. He described with great insight the psychologi-

[85] Heinroth's chief work is *Lehrbuch der Störungen des Seelenlebens.* Leipzig, 1818.
[86] Quoted by Gruhle: *op. cit.*, p. 6, from Heinroth's *Psychologie.*

cal struggle which culminates in a sense of guilt.[87] He denoted melancholia as *Insichversunkenmachen*. This is a typical German word compound serving as the substitute for a whole sentence and carrying the meaning that melancholia is the result of a psychological process during which the individual sinks into himself—a somewhat redundant, but very articulate, way to describe the withdrawal of the depressed individual's interest from the outside world and an absorption into himself with correspondingly extreme egocentricity, which is so very characteristic of depressions.

Heinroth was probably the first clinical psychiatrist to sense the need of a unitary concept in psychology—like that of the total personality today. He was probably the first to whom the ideational content of the mentally sick presented not merely a set of aberrations but a psychological process full of meaning. His whole attitude was that of a man who intuitively sensed but was unable clearly to formulate the principle that there is no sharp dividing line between mental health and mental disease, that psychology and psychopathology are not two different fields, and that psychopathology may serve as a basis for the foundation of a general psychology of man. In other words, in Heinroth's confusing references to the freedom and unfreedom of the soul, to the clash (we would say today conflict) between the tendency to freedom and the obstacles which make the soul unfree, to sin and guilt, we find a more than vague reference to a concept of a psychological set of forces which function as a series of biological, dynamic forces.

In the first quarter of the nineteenth century there were many attempts to formulate a unitary biological point of view on psychology from which one could study the psychological phenomena themselves as natural phenomena subject to certain although as yet unknown laws.

Alexander Haindorf (1782–1862), the author of the first German textbook of mental diseases,[88] like Heinroth, also spoke of free will, but, unlike Heinroth, he seems to have excluded the problem of the soul from psychiatry. To him the "unfree spirit" is almost equated with emotion (*Gemüth*). Man, according to Haindorf, possesses a consid-

[87] Bertram D. Lewin: *Zur Geschichte der Gewissenspsychologie, Imago*, 1928, vol. XIV, pp. 441–446.
[88] Alexander Haindorf: *Versuch einer Pathologie und Therapie der Gemüths- und Geisteskrankheiten*. Heidelberg, 1811.

erable amount of animal egoism which he expresses through the spinal cord and the bones—through his reflexes and automatisms, as we would say. Man keeps in touch with the objective world through the sensory organs. Man has wishes and drives and these he expresses through the motor system. His "self-feeling" is regulated through the cerebellum. Inner sensations—what we would call today "consciousness"—are lodged in the brain.

This whole series of characteristics is enumerated by Haindorf in the order of a psychological hierarchy. The lowest are located lowest and the highest (the inner sensations) in the highest organ, the brain. Haindorf's outline presents a very interesting and refined version of the Hippocratico-Galenic psychophysiology, but unlike the latter it is fully modern in that Haindorf derived from it the concept that ideas, ideals, and imaginations enter into reasoning; he thought the drives might flow from below upward or from above downward and produce a variety of mental diseases. He made an attempt to establish a characteriology.

In other words, Haindorf made a step further in the direction of a unitary psychobiological point of view and sought to understand mental disease psychologically, not only anatomically or physiologically. He sought to produce a psychological working hypothesis of mental disease and in seeking came rather close to establishing the concept of the psychophysical unity of man, as he came close to the concept of a psychological conflict as one of the causes of mental diseases. The idea that such a conflict might be one of the causes of mental diseases hovered in the minds of the early years of the nineteenth century, but these minds seemed unable to formulate the idea clearly. The same thought is found in its germinal form in D. G. Kieser's conceptions of polarity and oscillations of psychological forces. It is apparent even earlier in Reil's conception of psychological disharmony. Reil was rich in purely psychological speculations which he almost always tempered with naïve rationalistic materialism. He considered stupor from a psychological point of view and suggested that it be treated by infecting the patient with "the itch" (scabies) so as to awaken him to life.

By the middle of the century these early strivings toward a general psychopathology had almost matured, as exemplified in the work of Adolf Wachsmuth, who went a long way toward differentiating organic from functional mental disorders, as Stahl had suggested over a century before him. Wachsmuth pointed out that not all lesions of the brain produce psychoses and that not all psychoses are caused by organic brain lesions.[89] He insisted on the need for a proper clinical psychology. Such a psychology was not forthcoming for almost another half century. No one made as serious an attempt to formulate one as Friedrich Groos, a pupil of Nasse.

Groos was a psychiatrist in Heidelberg, where by contrast the Kraepelinian system was ultimately born about seventy-five years later. Groos first studied philosophy and then medicine. He was a cultured and very intuitive person. One is tempted to say that it was unfortunate that he came into psychiatric history so early. He is fully forgotten now by both clinician and theorist and yet he does not deserve this oblivion. His ideas did not really die in psychiatry; they only appear to have because one no longer hears his name. He wrote a considerable amount and did a great deal of clinical work, but he was not voluble. His views are concisely and succinctly expressed in a number of articles, but particularly well condensed in a small booklet of no more than ninety-six pages.[90]

The old problem of free will—a problem no psychiatrist of past or future generations was permitted to pass over without comment—Groos approaches as a psychologist rather than as a philosopher. He recalls Fichte's saying that only after man sees his own actions does he become conscious of them, but that the driving force behind his actions remains concealed from him. Groos thinks of the natural forces which are operative in man as a living whole and concludes that will is an expression of these natural forces which operate in man without man's being aware of them. Man feels free because he can wish only that which nature demands from him. In other words, man's behavior is psychobiologically determined and man feels free in automatically following these determinants. Health (mental health) is therefore a state of integrity between the natural forces of the individual and his actions. Whenever a natural force is impeded (we would say inhibited or frustrated) and is therefore unable to come to expression in a natural way, illness

---

[89] Wachsmuth: *Allgemeine Pathologie der Seele.* Frankfurt, 1859.
[90] Friedrich Groos: *Entwurf einer philosophischen Grundlage für die Lehre von den Geisteskrankheiten.* Heidelberg, 1828.

ensues. Mental illness is therefore nothing positive; it is something negative, a negation of life and of good; it is a negation of the full development of man's nature. Man's life is governed by a drive which Groos calls the drive of freedom (*Freiheitstrieb*). This drive exists in man even in the foetus. The foetus appears to be passive, but it contains an active drive which Groos considers the major aspect of mental life.

Groos therefore was singularly modern in that he looked upon our psychological life as a biological continuum which at times may not be manifest and which is yet fully active; psychology is a developmental phenomenon and has its own history. Groos was predicting the development of genetic psychology. He warns against concentrating one's attention only on that which appears on the surface—a warning which was never fully heeded by the descriptive nosological psychiatrist. Groos claims that since mental disease is a negation, a reaction to an obstacle, the obstacle may be psychological as well as physical or somatic. Groos has in mind not the external environmental obstacles which man knows how to combat, but the inner obstacles, psychological or organic.

Groos' views, in the main, are fully shared by a great number of clinical psychiatrists of the twentieth century. But these psychiatrists arrived at their views not by way of the increasing influence and testing of Groos' ideas but rather by the circuitous road of new discoveries of old things under different names and different guises, discoveries which another age, in many respects akin to the age in which Groos had lived and worked, felt historically compelled to make. What is emphatically salient in Groos' thought is the attempt to make psychology a biological science without losing the substance of psychology in purely anatomical and physiological speculations. Groos was the true forerunner of a scientific psychology which takes into consideration not only the increased blood pressure in certain states of anxiety but also the states of anxiety which underlie the increase. His was a point of view striving to bring about a biological psychology, a psychology in full harmony with "natural sciences." Groos used this term more accurately and much more inclusively than did Kraepelin, to whom a psychiatry based on natural science was a psychophysiology without psychology. To Kraepelin a neurotic sense of guilt, if he would consider it at all, was but a deviation from the normal. To Groos this sense of guilt was a real expression of a certain arrangement of natural forces which prevents their proper expression and which consequently produces a mental illness.

It is important in this respect to point out the progressive regularity and increasing articulateness with which this scientific psychobiological trend continued to develop throughout this period. Friedrich Eduard Beneke (1798–1854), for instance, was sufficiently sure of his ground to speak of the "abnormal building up of mental life." He expressed the belief that there is a symbolic relationship between our psychological states and our bodily processes, a thought both revolutionary and totally abstract at the time but having quite a familiar and empirical ring to a psychologist of the twentieth century. The very titles of Beneke's writings constantly emphasize his pragmatic and biological point of view.[91] This point of view reached such a degree of development that attempts to present a systematized theory appeared. As one peruses the literature of the period one truly wonders why this trend seems suddenly to have come to a halt in the middle of the century; it disappeared as if by the touch of a magic wand. The ideas of Carl Wilhelm Ideler (1795–1860) and E. Feuchtersleben (1806–1849), particularly those of the latter, certainly signalized a new era in psychopathology and a new approach to the study and treatment of mental diseases; yet these ideas were buried and almost forgotten by the medical psychology of the second half of the century.

Ideler was chief of the Berlin Charité for twenty-eight years. He considered that a psychological theory of mental disease was fully possible. He was one of the very few who respected the memory of Georg Stahl, from whom he derived his inspiration. Langermann, it will be recalled, was in many respects a follower of Stahl; he was Ideler's teacher. The first article of the first volume of Ideler's *Fundamentals of Psychiatry* is devoted to Langermann and Stahl as the founders of psychiatry.[92] The details of Ideler's theories, his views on "religious insanity," his considerations of "hypertrophied passions" are of some

---

[91] F. E. Beneke: *Beiträge zu einer rein seelenwissenschaftlichen Bearbeitung der Seelenkrankheitskunde.* Leipzig, 1824. *Lehrbuch der Psychologie als Naturwissenschaft.* Berlin, 1845. *Pragmatische Psychologie.* Berlin, 1850.

[92] C. W. Ideler: *Langermann und Stahl als Begründer der Seelenheilkunde, Grundriss der Seelenheilkunde,* 1835.

historical interest even if they are not entirely pertinent from the standpoint of the general history of psychopathology. Ideler, like many of his younger contemporaries, covered a great variety of phenomena by the word *passion;* but it is quite evident that in the forties the clinical psychologists mentioned above, including Ideler, denoted by passions what we call today instinctual life or the sum total of biological strivings of man. When Ideler spoke of the passions acting as "usurers" he obviously had in mind the immense toll the instinctual drives exact from man if these drives are impeded in their full expression. Ideler in the language of his day called these drives "strivings to infinity." When he wanted to say that our instinctual impulses if too intense and ungratified produce a mental illness, he spoke of "the action of the unsatisfied, over-excessive longings." [93] Yet Ideler was not given to purely theoretical considerations. He published a series of clinical histories which are full of psychological details and which reveal that he was an excellent psychological observer.[94] We owe to Ideler the exceptionally accurate observation that too strong aggressive drives in certain people before they become mentally ill produce persecutory delusions when these people develop a psychosis. Hence Ideler concludes: "When an idea breaks through the actual life circumstances, insanity ensues." [95]

Apparently Ideler, despite his extraordinary endowment for psychological penetration, was a very unpractical man, and to be unpractical while at the head of a mental hospital, particularly in those days of enthusiastic hospital building and management, was a great defect which German psychiatry never forgave. There was hardly a trace of his influence after his death in 1860. His colleagues of later years considered him merely an idealist, and Kraepelin, with his characteristic contempt for the psychological, spoke of Ideler's writing as "pure play of thoughts." Whatever criticisms one may level against Ideler—and some of them are undoubtedly justified—the fact remains that his general psychopathology sought and almost stumbled upon a true understanding of mental disease in terms of the individual's psychological growth and his relationship to life as a whole. His was another

[93] Ideler: *Der religiöse Wahnsinn.* Halle, 1847, p. 25.
[94] Ideler: *Biographien Geisteskranker.* Berlin, 1841.
[95] Ideler: *Der Wahnsinn.* Bremen, 1848.

attempt to assert that mental disease, unlike physical disease, ought to be measured not by structural, physical changes, assumed or established, but by criteria, psychobiological, sociological, and anthropological.

Ideler was fighting definitely a losing battle; even at the time he died he was an anachronism in psychiatry everywhere in the world, as well as in Germany, a sort of leftover of a romantic age which the world seemed either to have outgrown or failed to live up to. What is true of Ideler is also true of Feuchtersleben, although Feuchtersleben was more systematic and undoubtedly more practical than Ideler. Feuchtersleben, like Groos, attempted to synthesize physiological and psychological phenomena, to consider them a unitary biological whole. "The living physical being," he said, "is the spiritualized body and the soul [mind] is embodied spirit; both are a single phenomenon, invariably one and indivisible." [96] Consequently, "Wherever psychological abnormalities appear we are dealing with a mental disease; the cause of it is the soul [mind] in so far as it expresses itself through the medium of a perceptive organ, and it is in the body in so far as the organ is the mediator for the soul [mind]." "Every psychosis is at the same time a neurosis, because without the nerves as an intermediary no psychological change can come to expression; but not every neurosis is a psychosis."

Feuchtersleben had a clear conception of a total personality and considered mental diseases—diseases of personality—in the same manner as does the psychiatry of the twentieth century for the most part. He also looked upon mental disease as a developmental result of a series of normal and not fully normal mental states, such as sleep, dream, the state of being inebriated, or the state of vertigo. Feuchtersleben offered a classification which was of no consequence, but he stressed more than anyone else the importance of psychotherapy for mental disease. He thought it the most logical method of treatment, one which would reconstruct some of the mental deviations. He spoke of it as a "second education"; the term used today is "re-education." Feuchtersleben came closer than any one of the "pure psychologists" of the first half of the century to the solution of the problem of how

---

[96] This as well as the following quotations are from Feuchtersleben's *Lehrbuch der ärztlichen Seelenkunde*, Vienna, 1845, as given in Neuburger and Pagel: *op. cit.*, vol. III, pp. 687–688.

mental disease develops and affects the personality, and to the conclusion of the great importance of psychotherapy. He died in 1849,
and both the theoretical orientation he represented and the practical
suggestions he made were soon submerged by the activities of the
nosological age which followed him.

❁ ❁ ❁ ❁ ❁ ❁ ❁ ❁ ❁ ❁ ❁ 11 ❁ ❁ ❁ ❁ ❁ ❁ ❁ ❁ ❁ ❁ ❁

THE SECOND PSYCHIATRIC
REVOLUTION

I

AS ONE arrives at the outskirts of the twentieth century and begins to distinguish the familiar contemporary trends in the rising sun of a day which is no more a past, one feels the need of a double armor of caution. The very familiarity which the present offers is an impediment to a proper historical appraisal. While it is true that the present is best understood in the light of the past, the present is never really understood until it becomes itself a past. History is the past and cannot be contemporary. If a trend or a thought or an influence becomes a past in the very midst of its activity, it usually loses its historical importance. That which is still potent, dynamic, and influential is not yet subject to historical appraisal.

The true history of medical psychology really stops with the inauguration of the descriptive nosological psychiatry which has become known as Kraepelinian psychiatry. What follows must of necessity be considered but a brief survey of the battlefield of thought while the battle is still on, an attempt as humble as it should be brief to take stock of what is happening, of how it came about, of how medical psychology entered the contemporary scene, and of how it is behaving in the traditional parlor of scientific endeavor. It is an attempt to understand how the old meets the new and how their manners clash or harmonize, how dignified is the old as it prepares itself to face its makers, and how well the new is preparing itself to shoulder its historical task. The task of an even cursory appraisal is further impeded by the circumstance that such terms as "old" and "new" are merely conventional. The border between the two is but an imaginary one. The old and the new are always intimately merged together at every given point of history and the border becomes but a figure of speech enabling the contemporary to enhance his self-esteem at the expense of what he considers to be passing.

We could take as an illustration the two generations between Reil and Feuchtersleben, representing a period of about one hundred years ago. These generations spoke the very language which the majority of the medical psychologists of the fifth decade of the twentieth century speak. Is the language, the thought, old or new? Should one survey that part of our century which has just elapsed in a spirit of welcoming the new or in one of honoring the old which came back almost unexpectedly, with rejuvenated energy? Consider as an example the question of the role of the puberty period in the causation of neuroses and psychoses. Every medical psychologist and almost every cultured layman of the twentieth century has at least a speaking acquaintance with this problem. The physiological sexual, the psychological sexual, the cultural and therefore intellectual revolution which takes place in the human personality at the time of puberty is almost universally accepted as a fact established by the psychopathologists of the twentieth century. The understanding of the meaning of these complex psychological changes at puberty is usually credited to Freud and to psychoanalysis. Yet in a psychiatric treatise written in 1826 one can read: "Mental diseases begin to make their appearance at puberty; it is during this period, as is known, that man seems suddenly to come out from a long sleep, to open his soul to multiple impressions, and to gain gratification of the feelings and inclinations which nature bestowed upon him. But quite often these [feelings and inclinations] by virtue of their violence make him lose the very tranquillity which he has heretofore possessed. These [mental] diseases increase with oncoming age, because man's psychological existence becomes extended to the greatest possible degree and, as an active member of the body social, he brings into play all his intellectual potentialities. These diseases diminish [in number] as man, having reached the height of his vigor, is brought back by the circle of life to the weakness of childhood. He falls back gradually and imperceptibly into the physical and mental nothingness which characterizes childhood." [1] These lines are, of course, in many respects dated, but in many other respects they so clearly express a present-day point of view that our close relationship to those of one hundred years ago becomes almost uncomfortably evident. This relationship can never be overlooked without completely warping the picture of the present, which is warped at any rate by the fact of our active participation in it.

As the nineteenth century completed its term, it found that it had lived for almost a generation in complete international peace. The memories of the wars and of the fall of both Napoleons were almost completely dimmed. It had been a generation of peaceful development, of progressive comfort and almost contentment. The world seems to have settled down in an atmosphere of increasing cultural steadiness, and the ideas of individual growth and individual freedom established themselves as an integral part of living. Medical psychology, too, seems to have settled in the comfortable seat of nosological law and order, and it was accomplishing its work with the steadiness of method and uniformity of system so characteristic of a highly industrialized culture. Medicopsychological theories appear to have become more an intellectual pastime than a search for the practical solution of a problem.

The theories did not affect the methods of treatment. Despite his purely psychological theories, Ideler still used emetics and salves to cure the mentally ill. The somatologist, the descriptive nosologist still treated his patients with a little static electricity and comfortable hospital environment, as if a few months of proper surroundings would be able to effect a change in those cells of the brain which were supposed to be responsible for the disease. Therapy in psychiatry was not even empirical; still less was it causal. In this respect psychiatry was in a rut of the past and lagged far behind general medicine, which was learning more and more about the causes of disease and which was

[1] Felix Voisin: *Des causes morales et physiques des maladies mentales*. Paris, 1826, p. 88.

adopting a more and more scientific method for their removal. Psychiatry had a philosophy of causes but no demonstrative, empirical proof; it was aware of the problem, but it was also enjoying the comfort of a well-ordered fatalism which lurked behind the emphasis on prognosis. Hypnotism was used occasionally but rather sparingly. Forel and Krafft-Ebing practiced it to some extent. They wrote on it, but as a curative method it did not impress itself upon the profession except in the Nancy school.

In short, in psychiatry as in the rest of European culture there reigned an atmosphere of spiritual contentment and relative inactivity. Yet currents of discontent were being felt. Man seemed to be free. Everyone asserted the existence of that freedom. Yet it was so well organized, so well regulated, so neatly settled that actually man was far from free. The Victorian era had its full equivalent in Germany as well as in Republican France. Man who was discovered with such fervor and éclat by the Renaissance seems to have been lost in this regulated life. The Soames Forsyte, the man of property of the last days of Queen Victoria, was not inwardly free and despite himself he sometimes felt that he was unfree, that his self-expression was squeezed in the vise of an overorganized and overregularized community. At times he behaved as if he had forgotten how to wish for his freedom. Even as this process of general, almost scientific standardization of man was going on, protest from within the community began to come to the surface. Man was sought again.

Naturalism in art and literature, which came to demand the right of citizenship, not only brought to focus the saga of the Forsytes or Madame Bovary; it also wished to draw attention to the *bête humaine*, to the assertion of human instincts lower as well as higher which clamored for self-assertion. The interest in human instincts, in their constant demands, and in the conflicts they generated was not accidental; it was a form of the awakening of protest which like all protests expressed itself first through that which was usually most repressed. This is probably the meaning of the increased frankness about sexual matters, as reflected in Zola and Guy de Maupassant and a little later in Marcel Proust, and as seen in some of the scientific literature: Krafft-Ebing's *Psychopathia Sexualis*, Näcke's studies of homosexuality, Forel's *The Sexual Problem*, Weininger's *Sex and Character*, Havelock Ellis' monumental sexological studies—which were published first on the Continent. Freud arrived at his discovery that unconscious sexual conflicts underlie the formation of the majority of neuroses. The Expressionist School in painting appeared at the end of the century. *Die Brücke* or the so-called Ethnographers worked under the direction of Emil Nolde at the Dresden Museum. The similar Trocadero, known as *les fauves*, developed in France; this group included Rouault, Matisse, and Dérain. Both the Ethnographers and the Trocadero were inspired with the more spontaneous, primitive rendition of the most fundamental instinctual drives.

These were phenomena of a cultural process which demanded some sort of recognition of man as he is. They were forms of individualistic self-assertion. The need for freedom of expression, the protest against a culture which seemed to be forgetting the human personality, was reflected with equal force in Shaw's *Candida* and in Ibsen's *Nora*, as it was in Nietzsche's rebellion against Christianity and in Dostoevski's mystic struggle with God. It therefore does not seem accidental that this particularly restless period should have concentrated its attention on the inner life of man and his primordial drives, the *élan vital* which was threatening to disappear from the field of society's vision. Bergson's *Essai sur les données immédiates de la conscience* and his *L'évolution créatrice* are the expression of the same trend.

This neoromanticism could not but enter the field of medical psychology. Moebius, as a person rather than as a psychiatrist, was typical of his age; when he dubbed himself a *dégénéré supérieur* he admitted more than he knew that the formalistic, disindividualized psychiatry of his day would not suffice. His interest in the great men whose pathographies he wrote was a practical recognition and expression of the neoromantic trend of the time. The same may be said of Schopenhauer, who considered the great role our emotional life plays in human existence and activity and foresaw the importance of repetitiveness of emotional patterns. Nietzsche's *Genealogy of Morals* betrays a profound intuitive knowledge of the instinctual life of man; it was Nietzsche who before Freud gave a sort of history of human instinctual development. Freud never read Nietzsche until much of his own scientific work had been done. This only emphasizes to what extent the problem was in the wind and to what extent it imposed itself upon the philosopher, writer, artist, and psychiatrist. As the nineteenth century was about to enter its last decade it was fully ready to recapture the study of man as man and not as a nameless pawn in a sociological process. It was against this background that Sigmund Freud entered the field of medical psychology.

II

It was natural that Freud should enter medical psychology through the front door of therapy. He knew well the laboratory which for a time threatened to become the only authorized source of knowledge about the mind of man. His first work was in neuroanatomy and in his early writing he called himself a neuropathologist. The history of his scientific development is extremely instructive and demonstrates the transition to a new age more clearly than the life history of any scientist of our times. No one could tell it better than Freud himself.[2] No attempt to retell it will be made.

Freud was born on May 6, 1856, at Freiberg, a small town in Moravia, then a part of Austria-Hungary. He lived most of his life in Vienna. He died in London, having been expelled from Vienna by the Nazi Government. He wrote almost to his last day, concluding a period of over fifty years of active scientific work.

Freud began as a research worker; he later received a teaching appointment as lecturer on nervous diseases in the University of Vienna. He was a gifted neurologist: "The fame of my diagnoses and of their *post mortem* confirmation brought me an influx of American physicians, to whom I lectured upon the patients in my department in a sort of pidgin-English. I understood nothing about the neuroses. On one occasion I introduced to my audience a neurotic suffering from a persistent headache as a case of chronic localized meningitis; they quite rightly rose in revolt against me, and my premature activities as a teacher came to an end. By way of excuse I may add that this happened at a time when greater authorities than myself in Vienna were in the habit of diagnosing neurasthenia as cerebral tumor." [3]

[2] Freud's *Autobiography* was written some fifteen years before his death. The American edition was published in 1935, in James Strachey's translation.

[3] *Autobiography*, p. 17.

In 1884 Freud came close to proving the anesthetic properties of cocaine. In 1885 he was in Paris with Charcot. In 1886 he was back in Vienna, where he started in private practice. He tried to learn something about electrotherapy from Erb's textbook, since Erb was one of the best authorities of the time. "Unluckily I was soon driven to see that following these instructions was of no help whatever and that what I had taken for an epitome of exact observations was merely the construction of phantasy. The realization that the work of the greatest name in German neuropathology had no more relation to reality than some 'Egyptian' dream-book, such as is sold in cheap bookshops, was painful, but it helped to rid me of another shred of the innocent faith in authority from which I was not yet free. So I put my electrical apparatus aside, even before Moebius had solved the problem by explaining that the successes of electric treatment in nervous disorders (in so far as there were any) were the effect of suggestion on the part of the physician." [4] Freud turned to hypnotism. He saw it used at the Salpêtrière and he heard of the work done in Nancy. In 1889 "I witnessed the moving spectacle of old Liéb[e]ault working among the poor women and children of the laboring classes; I was a spectator of Bernheim's astonishing experiments upon his hospital patients; and I received the profoundest impression of the possibility that there could be powerful mental processes which nevertheless remained hidden from the consciousness of men." [5]

A link in a chain was thus closed and a new era of psychology began. The chain read Mesmer-Charcot-Liébeault-Bernheim-Freud. The new psychology had as little in common with hypnotism as Mesmer with actual magnetism. Yet the chain was not fortuitous; it was made up of therapeutic links. The chief problem was rational treatment.

Another chain was also completed, that which led always to the plaguing question: What is mental disease? This chain ran from Stahl and Langermann to Ideler and was then interrupted by chronic systematizations. Freud returned to the original principles of Baglivi, who had insisted that the best textbook was the patient himself. Unfortunately, the psychiatrists of descriptive, nosological propensities more frequently than not read into the patient their own preconceived

[4] *Ibid.*, pp. 25, 26.
[5] *Ibid.*, pp. 28, 29.

views on supposed neuroanatomic changes. It was one of the momentous turns in the history of medical psychology when Freud, having decided to use hypnotism, stood before his patient ready to read out of him that which the patient knew but of which he was unaware.

Freud associated himself in this task with Josef Breuer, a general practitioner in Vienna who had been using hypnosis on his neurotic patients. Breuer had been working with a hysterical patient for some time between 1880 and 1882, before Freud went to study with Charcot. Breuer introduced the following innovation: he let the patient under hypnosis talk and tell him what it was that oppressed her mind. The patient as a rule talked freely under these circumstances, and while doing so she displayed a great deal of emotion. Upon awakening from the hypnotic state she was relieved. Freud was impressed with Breuer's method and findings. He communicated them to Charcot, who appeared rather indifferent. Upon his return to Vienna Freud resumed his friendly contact with Breuer. After his trip to Nancy, Freud used only Breuer's method. No suggestions were made to the patient. Hypnosis was used only in order to permit the patient to speak spontaneously and to discharge a considerable amount of the emotions connected with the fantasies or the memories which the patient was relating while in the hypnotic state. Because of the regular discharge of emotions the method was called the "cathartic method." In 1893 the joint paper by Breuer and Freud appeared,[6] and in 1895 their book.[7]

This was the discovery of the unconscious. It will be noted that the discovery by Breuer and Freud was made three years before the fifth edition of Kraepelin's *Lehrbuch* appeared with the formulation of the concept of dementia praecox. The discovery was made on a neurotic patient, not a psychotic; it was made by means of a successful therapeutic test. This was the first time in the history of medical psychology that a therapeutic agent had led to the discovery of the cause of the illness while attacking or attempting to remove this cause. It was the first time in the history of psychopathology that the cause of illness, the symptoms generated by the cause, and the therapeutic agent revealing and removing the cause were combined in one succession of factors.

[6] Freud and Breuer: *On the psychical mechanisms of hysterical phenomena.* Vienna, 1893.
[7] Freud and Breuer: *Studien über Hysterie.* Vienna, 1895.

It is doubtful whether the full meaning of this historical fact has as yet been properly appreciated. It was this combination that made clinical psychopathology a true medical discipline for the first time in the history of medicine's struggle for the incorporation of neuroses and psychoses into its field of scientific investigation and treatment.

Freud very soon discovered that he could dispense with the hypnotic state as easily as he had with suggestion. By letting the patient talk at random he found that the patient after a while would overcome the inner obstacles which stood in the way of remembering, and the therapeutic results of this modification were found to be more efficient than those obtained by the earlier methods. This new method was called that of free associations. The method of analyzing and interpreting what the patient said and did was called psychoanalysis.

For obvious reasons it would be impossible to tell the history of psychoanalysis without writing both a textbook and a complete review of the whole literature on the subject, which has become truly enormous. The bibliography from 1893 to 1926 compiled by John Rickman contains almost five thousand titles,[8] and probably as many contributions have appeared since. Moreover, from the standpoint of a general history of medical psychology the contribution of Freud at this early date stands out not by virtue of its details but by virtue of its principles and methodology. Fifty-odd years is a very short time for a scientific discovery to take root, particularly a discovery relating to that field of human functioning which for centuries has been a battlefield of prejudice, passions, rancor, piety, and sacrilege.

Man could not accept gracefully the now seemingly trite assertion that there is an unconscious. To admit that he might act without knowing why and yet be in full possession of his senses meant to admit the existence within himself of something normally inaccessible to his mind. This neither the philosopher, nor the scientist, nor the man on the street had ever been able to admit. When D. H. Tuke referred to Isaac Ray's dream about the Good Superintendent as a bit of "unconscious cerebration," it sounded like a good figure of speech both to him and to his audience. But when one is called upon to admit that there are energies within us which accumulate, and that these accumulations of energy produce impulses, and that these impulses seek an

[8] John Rickman: *Index psychoanalyticus*. London, 1928.

outlet, and that in order to obtain an outlet these impulses invade the body innervations, and that this invasion of body innervations produces a symptom called a "conversion symptom," and that these accumulations of energy if they come to expression in words appear in the form of fantasies charged with emotion, and that these emotions when discharged release the tension both in the innervations and in one's feelings—when one is called upon to admit all this, one is obviously puzzled. Admission means acknowledgment of an enormous, rich, complex, and unknown life within us of which we are seldom or never aware. So strong is our fear of surrendering our belief in the omniscience of our own minds that we overlook the simple fact that from the very outset Freud expressed his hypothesis in terms of physiology, of energy, and of the constant interrelation of our energies with our body functions. Freud at no time departed from the scientific point of view and at no time spoke of the soul as a special philosophical or theological concept. From the very beginning his was a concept of a total personality. His method was clinical, empirical, descriptive, phenomenological. What he described was not the external form of the disease but its inner ideational content. The major contribution of Freud was his introduction of the descriptive method of subjective psychological states. This he did not by means of questioning the patients and thus smuggling in his own subjective conceptions but by letting the patients reveal their own subjective states. Freud introduced the objective method of study of the subjective conscious and unconscious states of the patients.

He made an attempt to subdivide the unconscious. "The subdivision of the unconscious is part of an attempt to picture the apparatus of the mind as being built up of a number of *instances* or systems whose interrelations may be expressed in spatial terms, without reference, of course, to the actual anatomy of the brain. (I have described this as the *topographical* method of approach.) *Such ideas as these are part of a speculative superstructure of psychoanalysis, any portion of which can be abandoned or changed without loss or regret the moment its inadequacy has been proved. But there is still plenty to be described that lies closer to actual experience.*" [9]

The fundamental characteristics of the unconscious are that it is

[9] *Autobiography*, p. 61. Italics ours.

dynamic and that it determines our behavior. Only when the unconscious is made conscious in an integrated manner—not in the manner of an obsessional neurosis—can it become subject to the conscious control of volition. The whole mass of the unconscious is no more subject to logic than chemical reactions or other biological processes. It knows no time, no space, no contradictions; it is primitive, spontaneous, shifty, dynamic, yet unorganized. It is subject to what Freud called the *primary process*. Only when its energies begin to percolate into integrated behavior does it meet with an inner psychic organization called the "psychic apparatus." Freud never considered the soul any more than had Pietro Pomponazzi or Vives. He limited himself to its manifestations, to the psychic apparatus, in accordance with the strictest principles of scientific empiricism.

Very early in his work Freud found that his patients revealed a great deal of preoccupation with sexual matters. This he described. It is very illuminating to note that his observation was at once mistaken for an assertion and proselytic attitude with regard to sexual behavior. But one need only peruse the *Malleus Maleficarum* or Bodin or Delrio to become convinced that the demonologists had discovered the role of sexual impulses in the formation of neuroses four centuries before Freud. Freud merely completed Weyer's work of subjecting these impulses and trends and fantasies to a scientific, observational analysis. Freud's observation led him to another discovery: that the patient's unconscious fantasies, charged with masses of energy, at times have such power that psychological reality appears to have more meaning to the patient than material reality. When unconscious psychological reality dominates the real world instead of the (normal) reverse mental disease occurs. The answer as to what constitutes mental disease was thus perceived for the first time. A new theory of man's development had to be conceived, a new working hypothesis on the embryology of human instinctual development and of sexuality as it is represented psychologically.

In 1905 appeared Freud's *Three Contributions to the Theory of Sex*, which incidentally gave origin to a new approach to children's psychology and to a revision of this subject in a totally new light. Five years previously *The Interpretation of Dreams* had appeared, a report on the immense material Freud had accumulated over a period of

years from his observations on patients and on himself. "When it [psychoanalysis] came to dreams it was no longer dealing with a pathological symptom, but with a phenomenon of normal mental life which might occur in any healthy person." [10]
Freud thus invaded the field of normal psychology. In 1904 the *Psychopathology of Everyday Life* was published. Psychoanalysis was obviously extending its findings and the borderline between normal and abnormal psychology began to disappear. Claude Bernard's dictum that there is no essential difference between health and disease—a sound biological principle—was proving valid in the field of psychology. Just as there is no borderline between normal and abnormal physiological chemistry, there is no borderline between normal and abnormal psychology. The chemical laws, the valences of chemical elements, and their respective properties are never altered by a disease; nor are the laws (mechanisms) of repression, displacements, condensations, projections, and introjections altered by a neurosis or a psychosis.

In addition to a number of purely clinical papers, Freud continued to publish studies of literary productions, such as of Jensen's *Gradiva* and a brief study of Leonardo da Vinci. He introduced the study of anthropology [11] into psychoanalysis and in the last two decades of his life began to work with increased interest on general cultural problems such as religion.[12] Some of these were but collateral studies while others, such as his anthropological hypotheses, proved the beginning of a new methodology in the study of anthropology as well as the introduction of an ethnological analysis of the psychic apparatus. Under certain outer and inner pressure the psychic apparatus reacts in a certain manner, which is called "regressive"; a clear understanding of these regressive phenomena seems to be gained if one studies the evolution of primitive people, their customs, institutions, and civilization as a whole. The psychic apparatus and the mechanisms in accordance with which it operates were thus made a subject of biological, sociological, and ethnological studies. Mental disease became the source of new knowledge about man and of a new understanding of causal therapy of psychopathological reactions.

[10] *Ibid.*, p. 93.
[11] *Totem and Taboo.* Vienna, 1912–1913.
[12] *The future of an illusion.* Vienna, 1927. *Civilization and its discontents.* Vienna, 1930.

It is unnecessary to retell the history of the opposition to Freud, or of the cleavages within the psychoanalytic movement. Opposition and cleavages are constant historical phenomena in relation to anything new. Despite the severe opposition, which has far from subsided, Freud's contribution to medical psychology made itself felt more strongly than any other discovery in the whole history of mental science.

As early as 1906 E. Bleuler (1857–1939) and his assistant C. G. Jung (b. 1875), working at the psychiatric hospital at Burghölzli near Zürich, became interested in the work of the Viennese innovator. In 1908 Freud, Bleuler, Jung, and a few others held a scientific meeting in Salzburg; in 1910 a second meeting was held in Nuremberg, at which the International Psychoanalytic Association was formed. A yearbook [13] began to be published under the editorship of Freud, Bleuler, and Jung; six volumes appeared before the War of 1914 brought publication to an end. Two more journals were soon founded; [14] their publication was terminated by the Nazis after the occupation of Vienna.

In 1909 Freud visited the United States on the invitation of Stanley Hall, then president of Clark University. It was the occasion of the twentieth anniversary of the University. Freud delivered the *Introductory Lectures on Psychoanalysis*. The lectures remain a classic of psychoanalysis. It is worth while to note that although delivered in German they were formulated in the United States.

Two years later, in 1911, Jung and Adler left psychoanalysis. Jung, the more brilliant and more profound of the two, branched out into more impersonal considerations of psychology. He was apparently unable to follow the purely biological views of Freud and the examination of the sexual phenomena involved. His valuable contributions on associations and on psychological typology are permanent, but his metaphysical, anthropological speculations suffered from the same defect as all theoretical constructions which consider man in general and no individual in particular. The same psychological difficulty stood in the way of Alfred Adler, who wished to reduce all phenomena of

[13] *Jahrbuch für psychoanalytische und psychopathologische Forschungen*. First volume appeared in 1909.
[14] *Imago*. First volume appeared in 1912. *Internationale Zeitschrift für ärztliche psychoanalyse*. First volume appeared in 1913.

mental life to man's striving for power. Although Adler wished to call his school the school of Individual Psychology, his psychology was fully disindividualized; it attempted to erect one sociological criterion for all men of all times.

Freud's libido theory, his theory of instincts, and his views on anxiety remained rather elastic and, as Freud himself repeatedly insisted, subject to revision in the light of new facts. This very elasticity of Freud's theoretical premises was an object of reproach on the part of many of his opponents. To these reproaches Freud answered: "Clear fundamental concepts and sharply-drawn definitions are only possible in the mental sciences in so far as the latter seek to fit a department of facts into the frame of a logical system. In the natural sciences, of which psychology is one, such clear-cut general concepts are superfluous and indeed impossible. Zoölogy and botany did not start from correct and adequate definitions of an animal and a plant; to this very day biology has been unable to give any certain meaning to the concept of life. Physics itself, indeed, would never have made any advance if it had had to wait until its concepts of matter, force, gravitation, and so on, had reached the desirable degree of clarity and precision. The fundamental concepts . . . [of] any of the [scientific] disciplines . . . are always left indeterminate at first and are only explained to begin with by reference to the realm of phenomena from which they were derived; it is only by means of a progressive analysis of the material of observation that they can be made clear and can find a significant and consistent meaning. I have always felt it as a gross injustice that people always refused to treat psycho-analysis like any other science." [15]

Had Freud glanced back at history he would have quickly perceived that this "gross injustice" had been meted out to every innovator, particularly in the field of medical psychology. In this respect one is even inclined to be a little complimentary to this century, for it treated Freud with responsive understanding. True, Freud, a Jew and a dissenter in a world of standardized psychiatric phenomenologists, did not achieve the personal honors a man of smaller caliber might have won. Only two official honors were bestowed upon him in the lands of his own language. The first was the Goethe prize for literature, which he received in 1930; he was then seventy-five years old. His

15 *Autobiography*, pp. 117, 118.

daughter Anna received it for him, for he was already very ill. The second official recognition accorded him was the burning of his books in Berlin upon the advent of Hitler and his expulsion from his home when Hitler took Austria. Yet the actual recognition of Freud was so great that even Hitler in his speech before marching on Poland in 1939 used quasi-Freudian terminology to describe his contempt for the Poles.[16] The English-speaking world did not take official cognizance of Freud until he was close to death. He was elected honorary member of the American Psychiatric Association on his eightieth birthday in 1936, and in 1939, during his last illness, he was waited upon by a representative of the Royal Society who came to apprise him of his election as a Foreign Fellow of this scientific body.

Freud's influence in the field which was closest to him—psychopathology—was greater than he himself realized. Many of his pupils not only learned from him and learned well but soon, under the direct influence of his discoveries, made great contributions to the field of medical psychology. Carl Jung published his monograph on dementia praecox in 1907, bringing into the consideration of this psychosis a point of view radically different from the formal attitude of academic psychiatry which only a few years previously had been given so much prestige by Kraepelin and which already appeared so dated. Karl Abraham (1877–1925), who died so very young, made original and inclusive studies on the dynamics of depressions. Ferenczi and Simmel made valuable contributions in their studies on war neuroses.

The whole field of psychopathology was revolutionized within Freud's lifetime, for psychiatry, whether officially opposed to or officially approving psychoanalysis, had to take cognizance of the new facts and the new orientation. The witch was not fully freed from contempt and suspicion until the revolution wrought by psychoanalysis set her free. Even Janet, who came almost to the same conclusions as Breuer, shied away from the facts before his eyes and rested his case with reference to the "fundamental weaknesses" of the neurotic—an appellation of attenuated contempt, which was the hereditary feature of European psychopathology. Freud gave the neurotic and the human

---

[16] In his Danzig speech of September 19th Hitler said: "These inferior people [the Poles] because of their inferiority complexes display all manner of barbaric treatment of others."

being behind the neurosis the status of an individual in full possession of all the creative forces which life chooses to bestow on man, the status of a person who lives and functions and whose relation to reality has been disturbed in the course of his biological development to psychological and cultural maturity.

Whatever theoretical objections or prejudices one may have against Freud's libido theory and his theory of instincts, one must admit that he brought the instinctual drives to the surface, laid them out on the psychological dissecting table, and carefully studied them both in their gross appearance and under the psychological microscope. He refused to consider the psychic apparatus as a subject unfit for scientific investigation and he elevated it in all its crassness and sublimeness to the status of scientific and human dignity. He not only believed in but he proved that there is scientific substance to the dictum that man is man and that nothing human is alien to him.

In this respect Freud would appear almost strikingly a kindly shadow of the past, the last representative of the Renaissance and the humanism which wanted man free, which studied man and his humanness, which wished him well in his frailty and admired him in his greatness. Freud achieved great success during his lifetime; there were many more who accepted him unwillingly and unwittingly than those who rejected him arbitrarily and consciously. "The contributions of my pupils and collaborators have been growing more and more in importance, so that today, when a grave illness warns me of the approaching end, I can think with a quiet mind of the cessation of my own labors." [17] It is perhaps not without symbolic import that fifteen years after these lines were written Freud—burdened with years, driven from his home in Vienna—walked in a Paris railroad station flanked by an American ambassador and Princess Marie Bonaparte—his pupil and friend—to entrain for London where he went to finish his book *Moses* and to die on September 23, 1939.

III

No ADEQUATE and equitable appraisal of Freud's contribution is possible unless one takes cognizance of the fact that formal descriptive psy-

[17] *Ibid.*, p. 111.

chiatry, having reached its peak in the closing years of the past century, stood rather puzzled at the end of the blind alley it had reached. After the century of effort—inaugurated by Pinel—spent in studying the forms of mental illness, after fifty years of persistent attempts to exact from the anatomy of the central nervous system and from general physiology an answer to the question of what mental disease was, medical psychology could not help but sense and admit that it did not know the answer. Dubois-Reymond's famous *Ignorabimus* was a solemn and authoritative admission on the part of biology that one cannot obtain any light on the deeper functions of the mind by the formal means at the disposal of narrowly conceived biological science. Moebius' assertion of the "hopelessness of all psychology" was a no less authoritative voice coming from psychiatry itself. As contemptuous and skeptical as formal psychiatry was of the romantic "toying with thoughts," it was itself frequently forced to indulge in almost as romantic speculations in order to formulate its observations.

In most of the classical works of the period from Griesinger to Meynert, even in Maudsley, one can find a number of purely psychological speculations which were at times keen and perspicacious. But since they were so formulated as to protect and defend at all times their "brain mythology," these observations remained but sparkles of casual brilliance and of fortuitous psychological insight. Such psychological speculations could not be either systematized or scientifically tested; they remained the private property of each individual observer. Scientific truths differ from intuitive truths in that they are always public property and are always ready to be used, tested, questioned, probed, and experimented with by anyone who is interested in science and who respects its at once dignified reticence and rational hospitality.

The psychology offered by descriptive psychiatry was not science and it could not be until those who studied the mentally ill were ready to admit that the human personality contained much more than, and much that was different from, the data which formal descriptions of physiological reactions and conscious mentation, normal and abnormal, could offer. It was necessary to bring the whole province of unconscious processes within the orbit of a scientific medical psychology. It was necessary to gain insight into the origin, structure, and manifestation of human emotions in order to make a scientific psychology possible.

What formal psychiatry chose to consider as emotions were not emotions at all but their verbal and muscular manifestations. Emotions were considered a separate functional department of man's body structure; they were considered subject independently to abnormal variations and were therefore thought to cause "affective psychoses"—disturbances of the so-called "affective field" or of "the emotional level," which could be considered apart from other faculties such as thinking and imagination. Such a departmentalization of the human personality made it easy to give one's methods of psychological investigation the appearance of scientific work. Each part could be studied separately and "objectively," that is to say, only from the standpoint of what it looks like from the outside and not how it works from within. The "work from within" was concealed from the observer and readily left to the philosopher and theologian whose intuition was frequently misguided merely because they had only their penetrating fantasies to fall back on and no scientific clinical methods of investigation to verify their assumptions.

It is singular and quite baffling to observe how strikingly prejudiced the formal scientific psychiatrist actually was against scientific psychology. He readily admitted the validity of animal experimentation. It was easy for him to see that a rat, a cat, a rabbit, a guinea pig, a dog, and an ape could have their stomachs, intestines, and even brains experimented upon, and that on the basis of the experimental findings thus obtained conclusions could be drawn about human health and illness. The laboratory, experimental descent to lower forms of living beings was not considered injurious to the dignity of man. To experiment on the brain and spinal cord reflexes of cats and dogs and on the basis of these experiments to draw conclusions as to man's reflex reactions, simple and conditioned, was not considered lowering the dignity of man. To produce an experimental, reflexological "neurosis" in a dog (Pavlov, who never was a clinical psychiatrist, and his school) and to compare it with a neurosis in man was in no way considered an infringement on the dignity of man. To consider a *succus melancholicus*, a *black choler*, or any other body juice or plain "indigestion" a cause of depression, pessimism, and suicidal thoughts was not considered offensive to the dignity of man. But to consider that mental disease was caused by primitive, infantile drives, which are operative in us as constantly as the physiological activity of elimination, was considered a kind of humiliation of man, a sign of "psychopathy" or "inferiority" or "degeneracy." Such terms as will power, strong or good psychological constitution were used as designations of simple, irreducible elements subject to no analysis or doubt.

The strictly scientific formal psychiatrist seems to have accepted, covertly to be sure, a mystical concept of a psyche which was untouchable. Such a concept made one feel irreverent if one tried to reduce the psyche to its humble and primitive elements. Hence the tendency to reject all psychology. In order to be able to approach the human personality as a psychobiological unit and in order to be able to leave the soul in the hands of religion, ethics, and philosophy but preserve the psychic apparatus as an object of dispassionate study, it was necessary to divorce one's self from the prejudices of an age which demanded that man's mind be left alone and that only his body be studied. It was necessary to make one's self able to accept man as he is and not as one thinks he ought to be. It was necessary to give up the megalomanic idea that physiology and reflexes, euphemistically called habits, could be so controlled that man could be ultimately remade very scientifically into a very scientific automaton doing automatically whatever society and science might require of him.

No matter how well concealed under the masses of laboratory instruments and syllogistic construction, a strong megalomanic trend lurked behind this seemingly strict scientific attitude. Behaviorism and reflexology (Bechterev, Pavlov) brought this trend conspicuously to the surface: man was conceived as even more a machine than Descartes' *l'homme machine*. Man could be manipulated, rearranged, "reconditioned." The manipulator and reconditioner was man himself. In other words, man can and should be able to create the human personality. Man is more or less a *tabula rasa*, even as he was conceived by medieval tradition, and he can inscribe this tablet in accordance with his own liking or with the needs and dictates of others. This not readily visible but very definite reversal to the past was, of course, the last thing that formal psychiatry expected to achieve by its strict adherence to a method which excluded any other method except that dealing with forms and not contents of psychological activity.

From the cultural, psychological point of view this was exactly the position of the science of man toward the close of the fifteenth century. At that time the problem had been partially solved by the birth of humanism, which was but a sixteenth century name for what in later centuries became romanticism. The humanists demanded that man should be considered as he really is—not before sin, not during sin, not after sin,[18] nor, we might add, with all the sin he contains. To assume this attitude one should not disregard the personality nor should one consider it something constitutionally established. In short, man should be treated with the same tolerance and respect accorded any other natural phenomenon. Such tolerance and respect is fundamentally a form of love, a mode of identifying one's self with others. This was the foundation of the psychology, ethics, and sociology of Vives and Thomas More. This is the fundamental meaning of Freud's libido theory, of his conception of the psychic apparatus, of his tolerant and enlightened acceptance of man as he is in all the complexity of his psychological adaptation, in all his psychosocial and psychobiological development from primitive impulses and archaic forms of thought. Only this approach would make possible scientific, detached, and objective studies of those highly subjective states, the intensity of which produces emotions, fantasy, and thought—not as separate departments of specialized endowments but as a psychobiological unit of interrelated forces. In such a consideration both fantasy and thought would appear as but different forms of adaptation, and should the energy charges (emotions) be more connected with fantasy, we might have—depending upon the degree and intensity of the charges—anything from a poet to a criminal, from a philosopher to a paranoia. Should these charges be more attached to outside reality instead of psychological reality, we might have anything from a politician to an honest carpenter, from a good family man to a big game hunter.

The borderline between disease and health thus fades. One imperceptibly merges into the other and both are constantly interacting. An extreme turn of the libido on one's own self will produce a catatonic stupor; an extreme turn of the libido onto the outside world makes possible very hard work and a high degree of social awareness and a sense of social responsibility. Freud's libido theory was thus from

[18] See p. 130.

the historical point of view a reassertion of Eros as the prime moving force and the ultimate ideal of life—which is the quintessence of humanism despite the fact, or perhaps even because of the fact, that humanistic philosophy was couched in traditional Aristotelian terms. The *pietas literata* of Vives appeared in the twentieth century as the scientific respect for man's psychobiological destiny. Perhaps the most concise and the most succinct appraisal ever made of Freud in this light is that of one of his oldest and most philosophic pupils, Ludwig Jekels, who on the occasion of Freud's death spoke at a special meeting of the New York Psychoanalytic Society.

"You may think me mystic when I contend that it is altogether fitting that this man should have left the world at this very time. I say it not because Freud had reached an advanced age and had suffered from a severe illness . . . for a period of almost twenty years. What I wish to say is that it seems wholly natural that this man whose entire being was devoted to the noblest principles of humanism should abandon this world at a time when the crassest contradictions to these principles prevail.

"Thirst for truth and love are the fundamentals of humanism. They pave the way to that broader understanding of fellow men which is the mainstay of humanism. Freud's immense drive to learn the truth reveals itself in the story of his research and in his uncompromising battle for the verification and assertion of the truth as he saw it. This was acknowledged by an honored although immutable opponent of Freud's teaching when Dr. Beep, professor of theology at the Catholic University of Freiburg, stated: 'Freud is a fanatical searcher for the truth and I believe he would not hesitate to unveil it even though it should cost him his life.'

"As to love, did not Freud's work reclaim for mankind the right to love? Did he not elevate love to the level of a legitimate, vital and natural factor of life? This he saw fit to do at a time when love was given recognition only by poets and was more generally regarded as a play of the imagination, a whim, or a mood. . . . Let us not overlook the fact that for a long time psychoanalysis was closely identified with the libido theory and no man could have constructed such a scientific gospel of love if he himself, to use the words of the evangelist, 'had not love.' Perhaps indeed his great need to love was an obstacle to

Freud in his work because he discovered so late that in the development of man hate is the forerunner of love. He wrote in his The Predisposition to Obsessional Neurosis: 'It may be that this is the meaning of W. Steckel's contention that hate and not love is the primary emotional relationship between men. At the time Steckel wrote this, it seemed to me inconceivable.' " [19]

Perhaps the true secret of Freud's immense influence all over the world is to be found in the fact that he was the first humanist in clinical psychology, which although it followed a humanitarian tradition had become rather static and indifferent toward the deeper psychology of man. The fact that Freud's system grew out of therapeutic effort and continued to remain wholly dependent on therapeutic work for its scientific research was another potent factor which in itself is a derivative of humanism.

IV

Nowhere in the world did Freud's influence on medical psychology express itself so dynamically and so fruitfully as in America. Psychoanalytic societies and publications in Germany, Austria, Hungary, England, and later in France were very active in psychoanalytic education and research, but in Europe psychoanalysis on the whole remained isolated, for academic and hospital psychiatry failed to establish contact with it. In France there was partial co-operation with psychoanalysis through the sympathetic attitude of Professor Henri Claude and the hospital of St. Anne in the late twenties, but elsewhere psychiatry remained officially and actually out of touch with psychoanalysis.

Individual psychiatrists, or for that matter the great majority of psychiatrists, despite their academic separatism did not escape entirely the influence of Freud. "The unconscious," "repression," "displacement," "mental mechanism" became household terms of a great many if not the majority of medical psychologists. In Vienna one member of the academic fraternity, Paul Schilder (1886–1940), who later settled in New York, was close to psychoanalysis; he was a member of the

Viennese Psychoanalytic Society. Schilder was the first to attempt to formulate more or less systematically a psychoanalytic psychiatry. In Switzerland, after a brief period of co-operation, Bleuler and Jung broke off their official contact with psychoanalysis, but Bleuler remained under its partial influence throughout his scientific career. There is no doubt that it was due to the impetus provided by Freud that Bleuler, like some of his younger colleagues in Germany (Gruhle, Kretschmer), conducted his psychiatric studies with less formalism and with a greater sense for a more detailed, deeper consideration of the ideational content of the mentally ill. Certain theories of psychological symbolism propounded by psychoanalysis were freely utilized by many, and the insight into the primitive, archaic modes of feeling and thinking of certain psychotics was directly due to psychoanalysis.[20]

The most important contribution to psychiatry made by the twentieth century was in part the outgrowth of Freud's influence: Bleuler's epoch-making monograph on dementia praecox [21]—a product of many years of careful research—utilized in part both the psychoanalytic orientation in regard to emotions and the concept of psychological associations. Bleuler introduced the term "schizophrenia," by which he denoted a group of psychotic reactions rather than one formal disease. He disproved the absence of affect in schizophrenias as well as the theory of their incurability, and he established the specific psychological loosening of associations as the typical aspect of the disease. All the manifestations of this loosening of associations he described as the group of basic symptoms. Bleuler demonstrated that the whole clinical picture of dementia praecox as given by Kraepelin was secondary in nature and not specific. Bleuler's description of autistic, or dereistic, thinking—a typical form of fantasy-thinking which is determined more by emotions from within than by outside realities—was a fundamental contribution coinciding with some of Freud's descriptions of narcissistic reactions.[22] Bleuler thought schizophrenias were pre-eminently characterized by autistic thinking. His theory of the special disturbance of normal associations could be in part traced to Wernicke's *Sejunktions-*

[20] A. Storch: *The primitive, archaic forms of inner experiences and thought in schizophrenia*. Washington. Original German edition in 1922.
[21] Eugen Bleuler: *Dementia Praecox oder die Gruppe der Schizophrenien*. Leipzig, 1911. In vol. II of Aschaffenburg's *Handbuch der Psychiatrie*.
[22] E. Bleuler: *Das autistische Denken, Jahrbuch*, 1912, vol. IV, pp. 1–39.

begriff (the concept of severance), but there is no doubt as to Bleuler's originality and comprehensive revision of Kraepelin's purely formal views. His description was made under the direct influence of the psychoanalytic method of approach.

Thus within about thirty years after catatonia was first described by Kahlbaum and within fifteen years after Kraepelin stated that there was a definite disease "dementia praecox," the whole concept was changed. Kahlbaum still believed that one might die of catatonia; Kraepelin believed in the inevitability of mental deterioration as a result of dementia praecox; Bleuler's schizophrenia became a group of reactions which are curable. Freud's views on schizophrenia, particularly on its paranoid form, were based not on the direct study of a case observed but on the detailed diary of a psychotic who at one time had been a prominent judge. This study, commonly known as the Schreber case,[23] was more or less speculative, but later clinical studies corroborated Freud's views that certain aspects of unconscious homosexuality are the determining factor in the development of schizophrenia. The work of Tausk [24] and Nunberg [25] and a number of others clarified many of the unconscious determinants of schizophrenia.

Bleuler's views on schizophrenia were generally accepted in America and Freud's studies of the unconscious mechanisms of schizophrenia also took deep root in the United States. Psychiatric America at the beginning of the century proved the most hospitable and most responsive of all countries. It was not only Bleuler and Freud who were given the place of honor in American psychiatry. European psychiatry as a whole found itself at home in America, and here it was that it was subjected to reappraisal, clinical verification, readaptation, and resynthesis.

The best tradition of European psychiatry was introduced in the United States by Adolf Meyer, who for almost fifty years has been and is at the time of this writing the dominant figure in American psychi-

---

[23] Freud: "Psycho-analytic notes upon an autobiographical account of a case of paranoia (dementia praecox)," *Collected papers*. London, 1925, vol. III, pp. 387–470. First published in German in 1911.

[24] Victor Tausk: *Über die Entstehung des "Beeinflussungsapparates" in der Schizophrenie, Internationale Zeitschrift für ärztliche Psychoanalyse*, vol. V, 1919, pp. 1–33.

[25] Hermann Nunberg: *Über den katatonischen Anfall, Int. Zeits.*, vol. VI, 1920, pp. 25–49. *Der Verlauf des Libidokonfliktes in einem Falle von Schizophrenie, Int. Zeits.*, vol. VII, 1921, pp. 301–345.

atry. Born in Zürich, he came to this country in 1892, soon to become pathologist in the Illinois Eastern Hospital for the Insane at Kankakee. From 1895 to 1902 Meyer was pathologist at the Worcester (Mass.) Insane Hospital, and from 1902 to 1910 pathologist and director of the New York State Psychiatric Institute. In 1910 he became professor of psychiatry at Johns Hopkins, from which position he retired in 1941.

Adolf Meyer introduced the spirit of erudition and broad biological concepts into American psychiatry; he is rightfully its dean. His influence on psychiatric education in the United States, on hospital organization, on the mental hygiene movement has surpassed that of any other living psychiatrist. Meyer has written surprisingly little, but his personal leadership and personal teaching gradually brought about a well-systematized psychiatric point of view to which he gave the name of "psychobiology." His psychiatric classification is elaborate and complete, and yet it is not a classification of diseases but of various psychopathological reactions. Meyer very early abandoned the concept of individual diseases which dominated the Kahlbaum-Hecker-Kraepelin tradition. He prefers to speak of reaction types, and to him the total personality reaction in all its aspects is the only basis for a proper understanding of the patient.

Meyer did not accept psychoanalysis and remained aloof from Bleuler's views. This aloofness is in complete harmony with his scientific personality, which does not tolerate well-defined, no matter how ample, borders for the delineation of mental disease. Strictly speaking, Meyer's theory is nonadherence to any theory in particular, and yet he is not eclectic. Rather, he would incorporate all available data into the picture of the phenomena of pathological mental reactions. To him the total picture is first the summation, then a possible synthesis of all the forms and aspects of the life of the individual—organic, sociological, general cultural, and purely psychological. Meyer's chief contribution to psychiatry, as well as the chief aspect of his system, is his enlightenment and great learning. In this respect he is one of the very last representatives of a great age which required that a psychiatrist be acquainted not only with the routine of managing mental patients but with the history of medicine and science, with the theories one accepts and opposes, with the sum total of the cultural heritage which a current civilization represents. It is within this current civilization that man stays healthy or becomes ill, depending upon the interaction of his total personality with the world he is called upon to meet.

Meyer was one of the founders of the American Psychoanalytic Association. Although no longer identified with psychoanalysis, he is a perfect example of a scientist who studies carefully that which he opposes. Despite his inestimably great influence, he is a phenomenon apart in American psychiatry. For a generation he has been the strongest and most effective link between European and American medical psychologies.

The second link between the psychiatries of Europe and the United States is Smith Ely Jelliffe (b. 1866), whose name is more closely identified with psychoanalysis. A truly encyclopedic and proselytic mind, Jelliffe was intimately associated with another great American figure, William Alanson White (1870–1937). Jelliffe, for many years editor of the *Journal of Nervous and Mental Diseases* and of the *Psychoanalytic Review* (founded in 1913), and White, his coeditor and for thirty-four years superintendent of St. Elizabeths Hospital, were both active and dynamic proponents of those trends in medical psychology which developed directly under the influence of Freud.

This influence in so far as it reached the shores of the United States cannot be properly assessed without considering one of Freud's first pupils, who was more responsible than anyone else for the introduction of psychoanalysis in this country and for the extension of its influence into American psychiatry—A. A. Brill. Freud, it will be remembered, came to the United States in 1909 for a very brief stay. Stanley Hall and James J. Putnam of Harvard were already familiar with Freud. But there were few if any others in the United States at the time who really sensed, still less understood, the historical and scientific importance of the new arrival in the field of psychopathology. Even at that time Brill, with his characteristic intuition and indefatigable enterprise, proceeded to translate Freud's writings. In 1909 Freud's *Psychic Mechanisms of Hysterical Phenomena* appeared in Brill's translation. This was Freud's original communication, written jointly with Breuer. It was one of several which appeared in Brill's translation in monograph form under the title *Selected Papers on Hysteria and Other Psychoneuroses.*

In this manner Brill began the history of psychoanalysis in the United States. He studied for a time at Burghölzli under Bleuler and was thus exposed at once both to the psychoanalytical influence and to that of the newer orientation in psychiatry. Brill not only translated most of Freud's work but published a number of original contributions to psychoanalysis. In 1911 he founded the New York Psychoanalytical Society.

There are few people whose intuition is keen enough at once to appreciate a new phenomenon in history or a new discovery in science, particularly in psychology. There are fewer who even when they grasp the full meaning of a new idea are courageous and strong enough to become its open and active proponents. Brill was one of these proponents. The history of medical psychology knows many examples of how inhospitable and hostile it can be to everything new at the time of its appearance. Freud and psychoanalysis could not be exceptions and they were not. Those who felt the importance of the new and who were ready to give battle rather than retreat occupy a special place in the history of psychiatry. Writing on *Twentieth Century Psychiatry* in 1936, William A. White reminds us of the following words of Whitehead: "It is a well-founded historical generalization, that the last thing to be discovered in any science is what the science is really about. Men go on groping for centuries, guided merely by a dim instinct and a puzzled curiosity, till at last 'some great truth is loosened.'" With these words White introduces the story of psychoanalysis in the United States. "And so in [those] early days there was a great deal of groping and puzzling curiosity, which was compensated for by youth and enthusiasm and which was based upon an intuitive feeling of certainty that we were on the right track." [26]

Brill's youth and enthusiasm supported his psychoanalytic curiosity, which was apparently free from puzzlement from the very outset. Jelliffe—with his immense erudition and his editorial talents—and William A. White—a pensive and deeply human personality, whose knowledge of men and books made him truly great—at once became the chief spiritual and actual assistants in Brill's pioneer work.

The true historical import of Brill's contribution has become sufficiently crystallized. It is through him that the English-speaking world

[26] William A. White: *Twentieth century psychiatry*. New York, 1936, pp. 29, 30.

first became acquainted with Freud's work; it was not until 1920 that England began to publish the *International Journal of Psychoanalysis* under the leadership of Ernest Jones. Added to the accomplishment of offering Freud's text to the English-speaking world was the introduction of the actual practice of psychoanalysis. It was through Brill's untiring efforts and through his firm conviction and will to conquer that two of the most important events in the medicopsychological history of our century took place: the introduction of the rational treatment of neuroses in the United States, and the introduction of the psychoanalytic point of view in psychiatry. The combination of these two was more responsible than anything else for the fact that America in the first decades of the century imperceptibly but firmly assumed the leadership in medical psychology.

Before the advent of psychoanalysis, neuroses were neglected in America as much as in Europe. The struggle for the recognition of psychoanalysis as the therapy of choice in neuroses continued with sufficient sharpness both in Europe and America, but America proved much more responsive. The response was so energetic that Freud even expressed concern for fear America would take psychoanalysis too uncritically. In America it was at once utilized both for the treatment of neuroses and for the study of psychoses. As the first quarter of the century came to a close, a solid body of psychoanalytic observations was accumulated from studies of neurotics, psychotics, and criminals. August Hoch made some observations on psychotics. John T. Mac Curdy's "dynamic psychology" was based almost exclusively on clinical material obtained from study of psychotics. William A. White as president of the American Psychiatric Association (1924–1925) spoke out boldly and with erudite conviction in favor of the newer conceptions of mental diseases in the light of psychoanalysis. In another five years schizophrenias and deeply depressed hospitalized patients were being analyzed within the walls of certain mental hospitals by psychiatrists who had received special psychoanalytic training.

v

Despite the general tendency to consider psychoanalysis as separate from psychiatry, it is not separate; psychoanalysis requires separate training only as a highly specialized technique of treatment. As a method of investigation, as an interpretative science, as an integral part of general psychology, it cannot, of course, be separated from medical psychology any more than optics can be separated from astronomy or quantitative chemical analysis from general chemistry. What the future of psychoanalysis will be, what its significance and role in the formation of a general scientific psychology normal or abnormal will be, is impossible to say. The judgment of the contemporary is apt to be wrong whether he be an opponent or proponent of psychoanalysis.

The value of psychoanalysis has already proved an established fact. It is a fact that the medical man throughout the course of medical history stood before the growing edifice of science always ready to borrow from its store every new discovery and every new device, to convert either for purposes of treatment or for purposes of speculating about the nature of disease. From time immemorial the medical man had borrowed whatever he could from other sciences. Physics, chemistry, optics—all contributed to newer interpretations and newer methods of treatment. When mental diseases began to attract his attention, the doctor was more concerned with the fact that it was a disease than with what kind of disease it was, and he used the chemical and physical remedies at his disposal. For many the actual curative treatment, excluding the protective hospital management of patients, had remained unaltered for generations. Whether it was venesection or emetics, the twirling stool or ducking, the explanation of the disease was always couched in the terms most popular at the given time. Even the *Malleus Maleficarum* reluctantly agreed that certain physical measures relieve some of the witches, but the explanation was given in terms of magic. Venesection was explained as valuable because it released the vapors which were supposed to be in the blood and later because it relieved the pressure from the brain.

In the mind of the medical man mental disease became a purely physical disease long before he had the slightest conception of the anatomy of the brain or of the physiology of the glands of internal secretion. The scientific trends of all ages were brought to bear in order to justify the conviction rather than to explain the disease. This conviction has always been the most potent factor in the formation of purely somatological theories. When Georg Stahl introduced more coherently than anyone before him the concept of the vital force and wished to derive from the concept a theory of disease, particularly mental disease, he was not merely introducing a concept; he was suggesting a revolution. For the first time in the history of medicine a medical man who was unwilling to leave mental disease in the hands of theology was suggesting a new source of information, a new biological factor—for biological it was despite the fact that it could not be measured or taken by mouth. The concept of energy had not been developed in the days of Stahl and the medical man had to wait until science progressed sufficiently.

When Ideler suggested that insanity was "the fairytale-like poetry of a boundless craving of the heart," [27] when Neumann suggested that it was a "loosening of the togetherness," each was expressing the same thought in the language of his time. They were not implying a return to abstractions or an absorption in fantasy. They were merely suggesting that the answer to the question of what mental disease was was not in the better dissection of bodily organs but in the empirical understanding of personality functions regardless of whether or not we are able to define what mind is. We may never know what mind is. We still do not know what electricity is, but we know a great deal about its behavior and we know that it works only when it is not short-circuited. The physicist would never mistake the spark for the electricity itself, nor would he try to understand the nature of electricity by the color of the spark or by the noise it makes. The same is true of the mind. What it is we may never know, but we may learn a great deal about it without knowing. We must study the mind directly instead of its "spark-equivalents."

This was Freud's method when, under the general influence of Darwin, Goethe, and Fechner, and face to face with his patients' own psychological productions, he discovered the dynamic power of the unconscious and those accumulations of energy and its tensions which now appeared as fantasies, then as symptoms, and then again as inarticulate emotions. These discoveries proved a shock to man, who had always preferred to believe that he understood himself when he used the means of metaphysics and theurgic fantasies. The civilized European of the closing years of the nineteenth century followed in the path

[27] Ideler: *Der Wahnsinn.*

of his ancestors. He continued to rely on the same ways and means which gave him the *feeling* of understanding himself. He used brain mythology and general body mythology as his most convenient fantasies for intellectual constructions.

Freud's discovery suddenly offered this civilized man a real, pragmatic opportunity to observe himself, and man was truly frightened. He found that in order to take this opportunity he had to sacrifice one of his most cherished possessions—his perennial fantasy that his own thought was omnipotent and that if permitted free reign it would conquer his ignorance of himself. He was invited to give up his sense of omnipotence and he shrank away from the frightening truth that his own mind is but a plaything in the hand of nature, that more implacable biological laws than mere principles of formal logic stand in mastery over his mind. He had always been willing to admit that his liver or heart or lungs were playthings in the hands of natural laws which he had to obey or suffer disease; he knew that an external accident or an internal chemical mishap was sufficient to injure or to destroy the given organ. These were accidents of fate and he was willing to admit his own organic limitations in the face of fate. But to admit that his own mind was subject to similar vicissitudes of natural laws meant to him to admit that mind in general is neither omnipotent nor free; thought is not free; will is not free. Man, then, had never been what he had fantasied himself in his own eyes.

This—the principle of psychological determinism—was what made Freud's discovery so difficult, so frightening, so fantastic, so inacceptable. That this empirical determinism really has nothing to do with the philosophical problems of free will was and still is overlooked. We refused to apply the principle of Averrhoes and particularly that of St. Thomas—that what is true in philosophy may not be true in theology and vice versa—the principle which once, centuries ago, had saved science from total disappearance. We have learned to accept the fact that everything in the body is determined by the sum total of physiochemical forces; we readily admit this biological determinism. But, tormented by an invisible anxiety, we seem to be unwilling and unable to admit to ourselves that our thoughts, our fantasies, our mental pains, and our joys are also subject to determining biological forces, that they are not merely results of our willful making or of our fainthearted lack of courage. It would seem that we prefer to believe in personal miracles as far as our minds are concerned; we believe in a sort of psychological spontaneous generation and in the magic of conscious, rational wishing.

Should we find ourselves able to accept psychological determinism, a true revolution would ensue. We shall then abandon our megalomanic, inflationary self-appraisal. We shall become more humble and shall acquire a greater understanding and a greater tolerance of others. We shall have to go to many strange fields never used by medicine to learn how our minds work. We shall have to turn to history, sociology, and anthropology and combine them with the medicine we have learned. Only then shall we be able to gain some knowledge about how our fantasies work in relation to things and people, how they develop genetically, and how our whole past is an integral part of our present. We shall have to learn a great deal more.

We shall then have performed a revolution, in that we shall understand actually, not merely intellectually, that that of which we seem to be aware is but the smallest part of us. We shall learn that our instincts and unconscious emotions are as effective in making us act when they are left outside the field of awareness. We shall be able to acknowledge that we do leave them out of the field of awareness even as we are unaware of our brain when we think or of the contraction of our muscle fibers when we use our hands.

We shall then have greater knowledge about mental disease, for we shall have learned that it is a function of everything that is in us —our remotest past, our life experience, our loves, our hatreds. Only when these become available to our awareness can reason in the light of reality guide us to act accordingly. To expect reason always to act wisely while remaining ignorant is a contradiction in terms. To admit that our reason does not know much means to undergo a revolution and to teach reason to learn. It is this revolution that Freud performed, and like all revolutions it became a battle, a bitter struggle. Its outcome cannot be predicted.

12

EPILOGUE

WRITING of "Locke and the frontiers of common sense," George Santayana states, "Locke, who was himself a medical man, knew what a black cloak for ignorance and villainy Scholastic verbiage might be in that profession." One readily agrees with this appraisal of the medical profession of the latter part of the seventeenth century. One would find it difficult to agree with such an appraisal if one thought of the early eighteenth century. One would be hardly able to accept it if one had in mind the middle and inclined to reject it if pondering over the latter part of the nineteenth century. One would spurn it completely when watching the twentieth.

The closer we come to our own time, the less displeased we are with the history of a science and the more proud we feel of its achievements, in which we enjoy a vicarious participation. With a respectful bow we turn our back on the past, glance hurriedly at the present with self-contentment and pride, and fix our cheerful gaze on the future. It has been customary to use history almost exclusively for this purpose of looking into the future, of trying to establish a perspective—which is but another way of saying that we are admittedly counting the mistakes of the past only in order to reinforce our propensity to fantasy about the future in terms of traditional optimism and cheerful faith in the ultimate infallibility of man. This custom will not be honored here, lest we forget that despite our conviction of being right a future

Galileo or Newton of psychiatry will find it necessary to judge us in the same terms as Locke judged the generation which preceded him, or as we ourselves judge the prejudices of Ambroise Paré or Jean Fernel.

How truly simple is the course of Locke's own logic when "he seriously invoked the Scholastic maxim that nothing can produce that which it does not contain. For this reason the unconscious, after all, could never have given rise to consciousness." [1] When looking back at Locke we may choose to pride ourselves on our progressive resilience and point out that we did overcome the obscurity of Locke's mistake and that those who will follow us will improve on our own performance. Such a choice would be natural. It would be in keeping with the tradition of indulging ourselves in the pleasure of writing in advance the history of the future. The only thing that is really at hand, the present, will then be thoroughly overlooked with a complimentary smile. However, if we wish to take stock of the past and consider it not as a springboard for our fantasies about the future but as a solid foundation for our present, we shall become humble and a bit diffident. We shall leave the future to take care of itself as it always does, and amidst the cheerful confusion of the present we shall seek to sort out and to formulate the tasks which we have inherited from the past and the burdens which it threw upon our shoulders. We shall wonder whether and how the task can now be accomplished and the burden lightened.

To espouse this point of view is not easy, because it is so very difficult to restrain ourselves with a humility which tells us that "error is not an exception but the rule of history," and which demands that we abandon our addiction to gazing into and reading the future as if we were inveterate James Boswells of history. We must guard ourselves against the fate of the prodigal Boswell whose "efforts at amendment never ceased . . . [who] took a vow of sobriety under 'a venerable yew,' . . . swore a solemn oath that he would give up drinking altogether —that he would limit himself to four glasses of wine at dinner and a pint afterwards; but it was all in vain." [2] Our efforts at amendment would also be in vain, for the knowledge of our past inspires us with

---

[1] George Santayana: "Locke and the frontiers of common sense." *Some turns of thought in modern philosophy*. New York, 1934, p. 15.

[2] Lytton Strachey: *Portraits in miniature*. New York, 1931, p. 93.

such a deep sense of solemnity and respectful ministry to the future. This is the spirit of almost all historians and particularly of those of psychiatry. The history of this branch of medicine has so many black and bloodstained pages that—for one who has vicariously wandered among the bonfires of the fifteenth and the sixteenth centuries, for one who has been sick at heart and nauseated walking along the stony passages of the Bicêtres and the Salpêtrières of Europe and America, peering into ill-smelling cells and listening to the cold and soul-wearing clang of the chains of the mentally sick, for one who has made a weird tour of this world with Heinrich Kraemer and Jacob Sprenger and Nider and Bodin and Delrio serving as expert guides—it is impossible to restrain the exuberant feeling of relief and joy in breathing the fresh air of a century which has forgotten Sprenger and Kraemer and which worships the Pinels and the Tukes as its saints. There is charm and exhilaration in this consciousness of our age of human excellence. One wonders whether it is our right to be proud of our day on this score, or our duty to be grateful to that generation whose daring and performance corrected the sins of our history and thus afforded us the opportunity of easing our conscience.

Such a question brings to mind the last psychiatric descendant of the great line of Pinels, Dr. René Semelaigne, who through careful study of psychiatric history and through family tradition still saw in the Pinels and the Tukes the greatest and almost the only reform psychiatry needed to become worthy of its mission. Surrounded with old books, with a few scorched pages of the second volume of his father's history of psychiatry—saved from the printing shop in which it was being set up when the shop was burned during the revolution of 1870 in Paris—and with a few pages written in the hand of his great-uncle Philippe Pinel, René Semelaigne was one day good enough to receive the writer. Vivacious and wiry, although then almost eighty years old, he was reliving the past of psychiatry with enthusiasm, fervor, and gratified faith. He read a few chapters of this volume and wrote the following lines to serve as an introduction or a postscript: [3]

"The writers of this book desire to fill a gap, to educate a special public, and to facilitate the task of the research men. It takes a great deal of precious time to go over a number of works written in different

---

[3] Written by René Semelaigne in 1931, three years before his death.

Les auteurs de ce livre ont voulu combler une lacune, indiquer au public spécial et faciliter la tâche des chercheurs. Parcourir, pour obtenir quelques renseignements, de nombreux ouvrages, écrits dans des langues différentes, fait perdre un temps précieux, et plus d'un recule devant l'effort. N'est-on pas en droit d'espérer que l'apparition de ce travail stimulera l'ardeur des jeunes, secouera les indifférents, et empêchera certains auteurs de s'attarder sur des problèmes résolus, de considérer comme une découverte des faits antérieurement notés et de publier sous un nom nouveau des symptômes que d'autres ont décrits? Comme les peuples, les sciences ont leur histoire, et nul, parmi leurs adeptes, ne devrait l'ignorer. Malgré l'évolution des idées et la continuité du progrès, la tradition, s'épurant d'âge en âge, se maintient vivace, et le présent est plein du passé. La sagesse conseille de jeter parfois un regard en arrière, d'étudier les écrits de nos pères, de scruter leur pensée, et de se souvenir qu'à côté de la mauvaise il y a une bonne hérédité.

Les observations concernant les affections mentales, dans les vieux livres de médecine, sont celles de malades aisés, tandis que les indigents n'étaient l'objet d'aucuns soins. On a beaucoup parlé d'établissements charitables, créés de bonne heure dans les pays musulmans, mais nous manquons à cet égard de renseignements précis. Un conte arabe parle d'un homme qui, se prenant pour le calife Haroun-Al-Raschid, avait été conduit à l'hôpital des fous; le concierge lui administrait quotidiennement sur les épaules des coups de nerf de bœuf et lui disait tranquillement, l'opération terminée: "es-tu toujours commandeur des croyants?" Ce n'est qu'un conte, mais souvent les contes renferment une part de vérité, et cette thérapeutique attribuée au concierge de l'hôpital de Bagdad ne diffère guère, en ses intentions du moins, du traitement moral de Leuret qui prétendait, au siècle dernier, contraindre certains aliénés, par des douches froides répétées sur la tête, à abandonner leurs conceptions délirantes. Les premiers qui, en Europe, paraissent s'être occupés du sort de ces infortunés sont les frères de la Merci, ordre fondé au XIIIᵉ siècle pour le rachat des chrétiens

Facsimile of René Semelaigne's Comments Cited in Translation on pages 513–519.

languages in order to obtain even a few bits of information; many hesitate before such an effort. Does not one have a right to hope that the appearance of this work will stimulate the ardor of the youthful, shake the indifferent from their lethargy, and prevent certain workers from losing time on problems which have already been solved by others, or from thinking they have made a discovery when the facts have been observed before, or from publishing under a new name symptoms which have already been described? Sciences, like nations, have their history, and no one belonging to a branch of science may ignore its history. Despite the evolution of ideas and the continuity of progress, tradition, becoming more and more refined, is kept alive, and the present is full of the past. Wisdom counsels us occasionally to glance backward, to study the writings of our fathers, to scrutinize their thoughts, and to recall that side by side with bad heredity there is good heredity as well.

"The observations of mental diseases which are found in old books of medicine were made on the rich; the poor were not the object of any care. People spoke a great deal of charitable institutions founded early in the Mohammedan countries, but we have no accurate data on the subject. An Arabian story tells of a man who thought that he was the caliph Harun-al-Rashid and who was taken to a hospital for the insane. The keeper of this hospital daily administered a few blows on the patient's back with a whip and the daily operation duly completed, he would quietly ask: 'Well, are you still the chief of the faithful?' This is just a story, of course, but such stories contain a grain of truth and the therapy attributed to the hospital-keeper of Bagdad does not differ, in spirit at least, from the treatment of Leuret, who in the last century contended that by means of cold showers he was able to compel certain mental patients to abandon their delirious ideas. The first in Europe who seem to have occupied themselves with the lot of these unfortunates are the Brothers of Mercy, an order founded in the thirteenth century in order to ransom the Christians who fell into the hands of the infidels. Each member of the order said the following prayer morning and evening: *Ut catenas et gravia eorum vincula dirumpere digneris, ut captivos omni solatio et medicina destitutos sanare digneris, te rogamus.* [We implore Thee to deign to shatter their fetters and heavy chains, to deign to cure those captives who are deprived of all solace and medicine.]

captifs des infidèles. Chaque membre de l'ordre récitait matin et soir cette prière: « ut catenas et gravia eorum vincula dirumpere digneris, ut captivos omni solatio et medicinâ destitutos sanare digneris, te rogamus? » Des êtres privés de la raison, sans abri, sans ressources, sans consolation, ne devaient-ils pas attirer la pitié de ces religieux? Grâce aux ardentes démarches ~~religieuses~~ du frère Juan Gilberto Jofré, la construction à Valence d'un asile était décidée en 1409, et peu d'années après d'autres établissements s'ouvraient à Saragosse, Séville, Valladolid et Tolède. C'est dans une maison du même ordre, à Grenade, que Jean de Dieu fut enfermé au siècle suivant et soumis à une sévère fustigation jugée propre à faire cesser son exaltation; après cette épreuve il prit la décision de se consacrer désormais au service des pauvres. On pourrait sans doute s'étonner du traitement infligé au fondateur de l'ordre des frères de la Charité, mais il nous est difficile de juger les hommes d'autrefois avec nos idées actuelles. Ceux qui maîtrisaient par le fer et les coups les malades violents et dangereux n'étaient pas inhumains; la plupart étaient animés d'intention bienveillante et avaient pour but la guérison. Les mœurs de nos aïeux étaient autrement rudes que les nôtres, et à une époque où les châtiments corporels étaient d'usage courant, où l'on éduquait les écoliers à coups de verges, il n'est pas étonnant que des aliénés, assimilés à des enfants indociles, aient été soumis au même régime. D'ailleurs Celse conseille en principe les procédés affectueux, réservant les peines aux récalcitrants, et ces préceptes étaient plus conformes aux coutumes anciennes que ceux de Caelius Aurelianus qui préconisait uniquement la douceur, et dont seuls, au cours des siècles, quelques précurseurs à l'âme tendre ont suivi l'exemple. Et ces magistrats qui, pourchassant les sorciers et les démoniaques, allumèrent tant de bûchers, doivent-ils, comme on l'a fait souvent, être accusés de cruauté? Eux aussi étaient des hommes de leur temps; ils en avaient les préjugés, les croyances, les convictions, et ils estimaient, dans leur âme et conscience, frapper justement des coupables,

Continuation of René Semelaigne's Comments

"Human beings deprived of their reason, without shelter, without means for livelihood, without consolation, should indeed have attracted the pity of these monks. Thanks to the ardent steps undertaken by Brother Juan Gilberto Joffre it was decided in 1409 that an asylum should be built in Valencia; a few years later other institutions were opened at Saragossa, Seville, Valladolid, and Toledo. It is in one of the establishments of the same order in Granada that Jean de Dieu was locked up in the next century; he was subjected to a severe beating, which was considered permissible to put a stop to his exaltation. After this trial Jean de Dieu made up his mind to dedicate his life to the service of the poor. One might be surprised at the treatment which was inflicted on the founder of the order of the Brothers of Charity, but it is difficult to judge people of past ages by the ideas of today. Those who tried to master the violent and dangerous patients with irons and blows were not inhuman people; the majority of them were inspired with benevolent intentions and by their goal of bringing those people to health. The manners of our ancestors were rude in a way different from ours. It was a time when corporeal torture was of current usage. Schoolboys were being educated with switches, and it is not surprising that the mentally ill, likened to disobedient children, were subjected to the same treatment. Moreover, Celsus counsels gentle procedures as a matter of principle, reserving pain for the recalcitrant; his precepts were more in conformity with ancient customs than those of Caelius Aurelianus, who preached only gentleness and whose example was followed in the course of centuries by but a few forerunners with gentle souls. Those magistrates who persecuted witches and demoniacs and who lit so many bonfires—should they be accused of cruelty, as they frequently are? They too were people of their time and thus had their prejudices, beliefs, and convictions; they thought in their souls and conscience that they were just when they struck the guilty in accordance with the law. We cannot judge them equitably; we do not understand them, for our ideas and principles are different.

"When Pinel was appointed physician of the Bicêtre, the hour seemed propitious for effective action, and yet he had to fight then, as he had had to at the Salpêtrière. He fought for nine years before he triumphed over routine and resistance, and only as late as 1802 was he able to devote himself completely to the treatment of patients. At that

conformément aux lois. Aujourd'hui nos idées et nos mœurs sont à l'opposite
des leurs, et nous ne pouvons les juger avec équité, car nous ne les comprenons
pas.

Quand Pinel, en 1793, fut nommé médecin de Bicêtre, l'heure semblait
propice pour une action efficace, et pourtant il lui fallut, tant à cet hospice
qu'à la Salpêtrière, neuf années de luttes et d'efforts avant de triompher de la
routine et des résistances, et c'est seulement en 1802 qu'il put, sans arrière
pensée, se consacrer au traitement des malades; il avait alors cinquante-sept
ans. Dans l'œuvre de bonté qu'il sut mener à bien, beaucoup d'autres
l'avaient précédé; il n'en reste pas moins le grand initiateur des temps
modernes, et il a tracé une voie féconde ouverte à toutes les bonnes volontés.
Depuis quelques années l'hygiène mentale a fait des progrès rapides, et
parmi ceux que passionne cet apostolat, il est un nom que nous ne saurions
oublier; c'est celui de Mr. Clifford Beers. Ayant éprouvé personnellement,
à une sombre époque de son existence, l'amertume de la tristesse et de la
douleur, il s'est voué, avec l'ardeur d'un néophyte, à une tentative de
rénovation mentale. Dans son autobiographie "A mind that found itself,"
il nous cite cette pensée d'un psychiatre: "what the insane most need is a
friend." N'est-ce pas la doctrine même de Pinel! Il faut, déclare-t-il, que
le malade soit dirigé par des principes d'humanité, et que le médecin devienne
le confident de ses peines et de ses sollicitudes."

En toutes choses, pour réussir, la conviction, la patience et la ténacité
sont nécessaires. Si la tâche semble lourde et le but éloigné, ceux qui
gardent la foi dans une cause juste, loin de perdre courage, poursuivent
vaillamment leur route, confiant en cette parole de l'Évangile:
"la nuit est avancée et le jour va bientôt paraître."

René Semelaigne

Conclusion of René Semelaigne's Comments

time he was fifty-seven years old. In his noble work, which he carried on so happily, he had been preceded by many others; nevertheless, he remains the great innovator of modern times, and he has traced a fertile path that is open to all men of good will.

"For several years mental hygiene has been making rapid progress, and among those impassioned by this apostolate there is one name that we shall never forget: that of Mr. Clifford Beers. Having himself experienced the bitterness of sadness and of pain during a somber period of his life, he has devoted himself with the ardor of a neophyte to efforts at mental rehabilitation. In his autobiography 'A Mind That Found Itself,' he quotes this thought of a psychiatrist: 'What the insane most need is a friend.' Is this not the very doctrine of Pinel? The patient, he declares, must be guided by principles of humaneness and the physician 'should become the confidant of his pains and solicitudes.' In all matters, conviction, patience, and tenacity are prerequisites of success. If the task seems difficult and the goal distant, those who keep faith in a just cause, far from losing courage, will valiantly pursue their path, putting their trust in the words of the Gospel: 'the night is far spent and the day is at hand.'"

But after all is said and done, after our respects to Pinel and Tuke and Conolly and Weyer and Vives have been reverently paid, one wonders whether the bright light of the accomplishments of these men does not dazzle us too much and make us overlook the heritage with which we have been charged. One should not be misled by the gratifying fact that the dungeons and asylums are now hospitals, that the insane are now patients, that psychiatry is now a legitimate branch of medicine. The formal inclusion of psychiatry into medicine does not fully discharge psychiatry of its responsibility nor medicine of its duties. On the contrary, it makes one more keenly aware of the confusion not yet dispelled and of the problems not yet solved.

One of the most conspicuous features of psychiatric history is that it is totally different from medical history. Psychiatry still lags behind medicine as to the certainty of its task, the sphere of its activity, and the methods to be pursued. General medicine, in the narrow sense of the word, never had to ask itself what disease is. It always knew what it meant to be ill, for both the patient and the doctor knew what pain and other forms of physical suffering were. Psychiatry never had such a clear criterion of illness. Only a very small proportion of the mentally ill show any suffering: very few if any are aware that their suffering is caused by a mental illness. The greatest majority either consciously wish to suffer death or are totally unaware of any discomfort. They are either sullen or indifferent or exhilarated, happy or angry or aggressive.

The concept of "psychic pain" caused by unconscious conflicts is very new; it was introduced by Freud as a working hypothesis. It is helpful to the physician, but for the most part it is foreign to the patient. It is extremely impressive as well as baffling to find that both mental patient and general medical man still understand the term "illness" only in the narrow medical sense and do not always understand the psychiatrist when he speaks of sickness. "He is all right and perfectly well, but . . ." is a common statement about a neurotic or a psychotic. After more than two thousand years of medical history, neither psychiatry nor the public has yet reached any understanding of what mental illness is. It is still recognized only after it is so fully developed that comparatively little can be done for the rescue of the patient.

In methods of treatment medicine has also always acquitted itself with honor. If it knew the cause of illness and also the remedy, treatment was rationally applied; if it did not possess the knowledge of the cause, it still was and is able to relieve pain with a palliative drug— relief of pain being a major duty of medicine and the chief desire of the patient. On the other hand, psychiatry until very recently knew nothing about the causes of nonorganic, functional psychoses. Only recently, as a result of the discoveries of Freud, a glimmer as to the possible cause was gained. Our ignorance still outweighs however much we may appear to know. The use of drugs to quiet an abnormal excitement is of greater help to the doctor and attendant than to the patient, because the drug acts merely as a chemical restraint, making it easier to manage the patient but producing neither a cure nor even temporary relief of the fundamental psychological condition, which reappears as soon as the effects of the drug wear off. There is still confusion as to what a psychological reaction is, and medicine and psychiatry and various schools of psychiatry still do not see eye to eye on this subject.

As one looks over the turbulent history of medical psychology, one is impressed with the fact that after almost twenty-four centuries of earnest effort it has not yet answered clearly and unequivocally the fundamental question, a question which has never disturbed the course of general medical history. General medicine established an exact and specific experimental methodology of research which it borrowed almost without any need for modification from physics, chemistry, and physiology; psychiatric research needs its own methodology and it has not yet succeeded in clearly developing the fundamental prerequisites for one. When general medicine joins biology in a general discussion of the meaning of disease, it is engaged in a fascinating pastime, in a bit of luxury provided by natural philosophy; medicine does not need to solve this problem in order to do its job and do it rationally and well. But when psychiatry raises the question as to what mental disease is, it is raising a question which is vital, one without which it cannot proceed causally or even empirically. When medicine wishes to protect the community against scarlet fever or measles it has no difficulty in securing the co-operation of the community and the law; cases of contagious disease are promptly reported and properly quarantined. But only after a schizophrenic commits murder is psychiatry able at times to plead with the Law and demonstrate that the defendant is a mentally sick man and that the murder might have been prevented if the condition had been recognized before the misfortune occurred and if the patient had been hospitalized.

These are vital differences between medicine and psychiatry; these are the most instructive lessons which the history of medical psychology can teach us. It teaches us also the melancholy truth that, although officially a branch of medicine, psychiatry was accepted into the brotherhood of medical efforts only on sufferance, only on the condition that it accept in advance the tenets of medicine and consider that disease means physical disease and that mental disease be included in the organic scheme of things. Medicine had less differences with the medieval barbers who practiced surgery than it has today with psychiatry. The history of twenty-four centuries of medicine shows clearly that there has always been a strong and deep-seated antagonism between medicine and psychiatry. Thomas Willis and Daniel Sennert still considered psychoses the handiwork of the devil, and they would leave them in the hands of those who knew how to combat Lucifer. The history of the somatological contempt for psychology, which for the occasion is dubbed philosophy, betrays fundamentally the old antagonism which centuries of effort have failed as yet fully to solve.

The philanthropic, humanitarian period of psychiatric history was a great creative period, but its task is well-nigh accomplished. What it taught is generally accepted now; what it fought for it conquered to a great extent. There are still too few physicians in proportion to the number of patients. In some state institutions in America and Europe the ratio is as low as one physician to two hundred, three hundred, even five hundred patients, and in some of the best private institutions the ratio is at times not more than one physician to twenty-five or thirty patients. Such ratios do not allow of much individual treatment; yet psychiatric treatment unless highly individualized is almost totally ineffective. The only definite accomplishment of psychiatric history which became recognized by all—medicine, the Law, and the community—is the proper organization of hospitals; even this accomplishment is not yet fully completed and hospital organization is still handicapped by sociological and political factors, since both the community and the judicial system are responsible for the system of mental hospitals.

It is impressive, awe inspiring, and not a little discouraging to watch the course of psychiatric history and to observe that only now, in the closing years of the first half of the twentieth century, is psychiatry able to reach the point of raising the question upon the solution of which depends its own efficacy and creative vitality. From the day Hippocrates wrote his protesting treatise on epilepsy to the very opening of the twentieth century psychiatry has labored to sort out the definitely organic disorders from the functional psychoses and from neuroses. This task was accomplished with the thoroughness and with the genius which medicine put at the disposal of the psychiatrist. This century stands askance before the functional psychoses and neuroses and it has only now discovered that, in order to understand them, newer psychobiological methods foreign to medical tradition must be employed.

This century presents only the beginning. It seems certain now that the twenty-five hundred years of psychiatric history which are behind us have been but preliminary centuries which cleared the field of operation and prepared the ground for a true psychiatry. The Freudian revolution—with the antagonisms, misunderstandings, apparent disruption of law and order which it caused—does seem to owe its violence as well as its influence to the fact that it was the first practical empirical step in the history of medical psychology toward the foundation of a psychiatry which would be a medical discipline.

This revolution, as it subsides in violence, as its contribution to the knowledge of mental disease becomes an integral part of medical science, will yet have to be considered for a period as having created more medical problems than it solved. For, having brought the field of the neuroses within the orbit of medical sciences more definitely than even the work of Charcot and Bernheim, it also made clear that the medical psychologist who must be a physician must also include as the indispensable prerequisites for his rational, scientific, medical functioning such large territories of knowledge as sociology and anthropology. In this era of specialization the very history of medical psychology demands an almost encyclopedic training of the psychiatrist. Of all the branches of medicine, psychiatry—by the very nature of the diseases with which it deals—requires both the highest degree of specialization and the broadest medical and cultural education. Mental diseases are apparently the only diseases which deserve the appellation of social diseases, not because they are caused by social factors alone but because a mentally sick individual functions with the totality of his endowments. A psychological conflict leading to disease cannot but use as its vehicle the sum total of the cultural problems which are characteristic of the individual's age. One cannot understand the disease without understanding its language, and its language is always the language of the primitive cultural past intimately interwoven with the cultural present.

Perhaps it is this feature of mental illness that is responsible more than any other for the essential antagonism between medicine and psychiatry. The language of a physical disease is universally appealing; pain, fever, a bleeding wound are understood by all. It is never difficult for the doctor to put himself in the patient's place, since he can remember his own pains and fevers and cuts. He can identify himself with the patient, feel with and for him, and therefore understand him. In order to identify one's self with a mentally sick patient a totally different set of psychological reactions is required of the doctor. Every mental patient presents some form of unwillingness or inability to accept life as it is. Every mental patient either aggressively rejects life as we like it—and he therefore was thought of as heretic, witch, or sorcerer—or passively succumbs to his inability to accept life as we see it—and he therefore was called bewitched. In the mind of the mentally healthy man, including the medical man, a mentally ill person still appears as an adamant rebel against our cultural common sense or as a weakling who gives in to forces other than our cultural common sense. Mental illness requires a singularly humanistic tolerance on the part of the doctor, without which a proper identification with the patient is impossible.

This need for tolerance explains the fact that Weyer, Pinel, and Freud stand out so poignantly in the history of medical psychology. Weyer would not punish the girl who was simulating supposedly eternal fasting and limping. He saw in her behavior a form of reasonableness which was abnormal reasonableness; he was not shocked by the paradoxical combination of apparently rational motivation for irrational behavior. He was interested in the humanness of it all. Consequently, he was able not only to understand but to produce a cure. Pinel was not shocked by the apparent inhumanness of the patients he faced. He thought of them as human beings similar to himself, despite their abnormalities. This was not merely a sentimental, philanthropic attitude. It was the ability to understand the language of the mentally ill, which made Pinel so human and so capable of carrying out his reform. What Pinel was capable of understanding intuitively, Freud was able to do consciously and rationally. Freud, like Weyer and Pinel, was not shocked by what he saw in his patients: aggressions, sexual drives, hates, irrational fantasies—all these he had to understand before he could exert any curative influence. Even the term "psychological reality," which he introduced, reveals the process of identification. The most irrational fantasies which he discovered in his patients failed to shock him; he saw in them realities—the patients' realities—and he could therefore understand them.

The whole course of the history of medical psychology is punctuated by the medical man's struggle to rise above the prejudices of all ages in order to identify himself with the psychological realities of his patients. Every time such an identification was achieved the medical man became a psychiatrist. The history of psychiatry is essentially the history of humanism. Every time humanism has diminished or degenerated into mere philanthropic sentimentality, psychiatry has entered a new ebb. Every time the spirit of humanism has arisen, a new contribution to psychiatry has been made.

INDEX

Index

Index

Index

choler, 297, 301, 496
cholera, 420
choleric temperament, 74
chorea lasciva, 199
Christ, 94, 100, 231, 237
Christian Science, 294
Christian sects, 99
Cibo (Innocent VIII), 164
Cicero, 61, 64, 65, 66, 68, n. 106, 293, 416
clairvoyance, 106, 441
classification, 47, 297, 305-11, 327, 398, 420-2, 438, 449-50; *see also* nosology
Claude, 500
Claudius, 102
Clement of Alexandria, 98
Cleomenes, 38

clysters, 71, 314
Cnidus, 42, 44
cocaine, 404
Cockayne, n. 139
Codex Theodosianus, 103, 146
Colbert, 272
collapse, 286
Colombier, 316, 321
Combe, 411
compilers, 105
Conde, n. 120
condensations, 490
Condillac, 274, 282, 283, 284, 330, 397
Condorcet, 319
Conolly, 387, 414, 415, 446
conscientia, 177
consensus, 73, 88, 91, 92, 263
Constantine, 103
Constantinus Africanus, 128, 138
"conversion symptom," 488
convulsionnaires, 366
convulsions, 397
Copeland, 353
Copernicus, 33, 164, 246
Copho, 134
Coquemare, 222
cortical irritation, 442
Cos, 42, 44

Cotton, 276
Council of Nicaea, 112
Counter Reformation, 171
Couthon, 322, 323
Cox, 411
Cramer, 445, 447

"creationists," 111
crédivité naturelle, 369
Crichton, 336
criminal insanity; *see* forensic psychiatry
Crowther, 411
Cullen, 263, 286, 307
Cumston, 73
curability, 450, 454, 455
Cusanus, 165
cyclothymia, 448
Cynic school, 59
Cynosarges, 59
Cyprian, St., 99, 107, 109
Cyrenaic school, 59

Daemonologie, 257
Dahlman, 385
Daniel, 210
Dante, 176
Danton, 418
Daquin, 317-8, 325, 400, 452,
Daremberg, 86, 87, 105, 113, 163
Dark Ages, 92, 93, 104
Darwin, Charles, 453, 463, 466, 508
Darwin, Erasmus, 307, 312, 419
Daul-Kulb, 124
David, 29, 157
"degeneracy," 497
degeneration, 402, 403; *dégénérescence,* 376
Delarive, 409
Delasiauve, 398

Deleboë (Sylvius), 254, 256, 266, 445
Deleuze, 349
Del Greco, 5, n. 73
delirium, 53, 123, 397, 405, 406, 451; delirium tremens, 404
Delphian oracle, 38
Delrio, 236, 246, 513
delusions, 63, 224, 441
démence précoce, 458
dementia, 91
dementia praecox, 173, 259, 396, 455-9, 486, 493, 501, 502
Democritus, 45, 46, 59, 62
demon(s), 86, 99
demonology, 25, 108, 116, 140-99, 208, 280, 299, 351, 365, 382, 419; *see also* demon, devil, *incubi, succubi,* witch, witchcraft
Demonology, 145
démonomanie, 236
demonopathies, 254

Index

Index

Index

Index

Index

Index

Index

Index

Index

Index

self-preservation, 279
Semelaigne, A., 12, n. 44, 328
Semelaigne, R., 12, 259, 261, 317, 323, 328, 423, 513-9
Semmelweis, 226
Seneca, 96

Sennert, 254, 261, 270, 333, 521
sensation, 178
sense of reality, 392
sensorium commune, 40, 55, 57, 192, 390
sensualist, 89
sensus communis, 310; *-privatus*, 310
septimana medicalis, 137
Serbski, 457, 461
Servetus, 165, 166
Seville, 517
sex, theory of, 85, 158, 160, 161, 178, 221, 270, 489, 490
shaman, 21, 28
Shaw, 243, 483

Siberia, 28
Sigerist, n. 130

Silimachus, 106
silvani, 106
Simeon Seth, 116
Simmel, 493
sin, 144 ff.
Skae, 420, 421
sleep, hypnotic, 356, 357
smallpox, 121
Société Médico-psychologique, n. 384, 386
Société des Sciences, 271
societies, 383, n. 384
sociology, 186 ff., 510
Socrates, 41, 43, 45, 46, 101, 238
soda water, 282
solidism, 287; solidists, 61
Sollier, 461
Solomon, 237
sóma, 238
somatological, 521, 522; somatologist, 434, 435, 436, 437, 439-42, 465, 466, 481
Sommers, 457
somnambulism, 362, 368, 441
somniferous chemicals, 71
Sophocles, 41
Soranus, 72, 78-84
sorcerers, 237
Souda a Tabee, 123

soul, 52, 53, 56, 90, 91, 112, 277, 285, 296, 397; irascible, 92; seat of, 40; sensual, 92; transmigration of, 33, 34
Soury, n. 49, n. 89
Southard, 13
Southey, 202

Spee, von, 249
spells, 101
Spinoza, 265, 274
spirit, 22, 29, 295
spirits, animal, 90; natural, 90
spiritus, 179; *-vitae*, 199
spleen, 125, 262
Sprengel, n. 62, n. 125, 382
Sprenger, 147, 148, 150, 215, 513
Spurzheim, 412
Stahl, 250, 251, 252, 277-80, 285, 291, 294, 327, 334, 399, 401, 434, 466, 473, 475, 485, 507, 508
Starch, 432
Stark, 449
stars, influence of, 198

states, ecstatic, 29; emotional, 44, 46
statistical methods, 390
Steckel, 500
Steganographia, 206
Stella, Abbot of (Isaac), 129
stethoscope, 351
stigmata, 110, 372; "of degeneration," 402; *diaboli*, 110
Stillman, n. 196
Stoerk, 343
Stoics, Stoicism, 59, 60, 96, 106
stomach, 125, 263
Stone Age, 27
Storch, n. 501
Strachey, 18, n. 512
Strato, 57
strictum et laxum, 62
Strümpell, 375
stultitia, 91
stupors, 45, 79, 238, 254, 396, 397, 449
subacti, 106
"subcortical irritation," 441
subjectivism, 112
Subventione Pauperum, De, 187
succubi, 145, 171, 173, 238, 270
succus melancholicus, 92, 496
Sudhoff, n. 27
suffocation, 92
suggestibility, suggestion, 368, 369, 372, 374, 486; "de-suggestion," 377

Index

Index

Norton Paperbacks on Psychiatry and Psychology

Piaget, Jean. *Play, Dreams and Imitation in Childhood.*

Piaget, Jean and Bärbel Inhelder. *The Child's Conception of Space.*

Piers, Gerhart and Milton B. Singer. *Shame and Guilt.*

Ruesch, Jurgen. *Disturbed Communication.*

Ruesch, Jurgen. *Therapeutic Communication.*

Ruesch, Jurgen and Gregory Bateson. *Communication: The Social Matrix of Psychiatry.*

Schein, Edgar et al. *Coercive Persuasion.*

Sullivan, Harry Stack. *Clinical Studies in Psychiatry.*

Sullivan, Harry Stack. *Conceptions of Modern Psychiatry.*

Sullivan, Harry Stack. *The Fusion of Psychiatry and Social Science.*

Sullivan, Harry Stack. *The Interpersonal Theory of Psychiatry.*

Sullivan, Harry Stack. *The Psychiatric Interview.*

Walter, W. Grey. *The Living Brain.*

Watson, John B. *Behaviorism.*

Wheelis, Allen. *The Quest for Identity.*

Zilboorg, Gregory. *A History of Medical Psychology.*